D1192798

Quantitative Analysis

Prentice-Hall Chemistry Series

QUANTITATIVE

R. A. DAY, JR.

Professor of Chemistry
Chairman, Department of Chemistry
Emory University

A. L. UNDERWOOD

Professor of Chemistry
Emory University

ANALYSIS

Second Edition

Prentice-Hall, Inc., Englewood Cliffs, New Jersey

Quantitative Analysis, *Second Edition*
R. A. DAY, JR.
A. L. UNDERWOOD

© 1967 by Prentice-Hall, Inc.,
Englewood Cliffs, N.J.

All rights reserved. No part of this book
may be reproduced in any form
or by any means without permission
in writing from the publisher.

Current printing (last digit): 10   9   8   7   6   5   4

Library of Congress Catalog Card Number 67-12998

Printed in the United States of America

PRENTICE-HALL INTERNATIONAL, INC., *London*
PRENTICE-HALL OF AUSTRALIA, PTY. LTD., *Sydney*
PRENTICE-HALL OF CANADA, LTD., *Toronto*
PRENTICE-HALL OF INDIA PRIVATE LTD., *New Delhi*
PRENTICE-HALL OF JAPAN, INC., *Tokyo*

Preface

In the first edition of this text we stated that "analytical chemistry has experienced a remarkable development in recent years." Since that writing, developments have continued at an unprecedented rate, not only in analytical, but in all areas of chemistry and other scientific disciplines as well. The content of many of the traditional college chemistry courses has changed drastically, with a blurring of boundaries between subdisciplines and the shifting of large areas of subject matter from one subdiscipline to another.

Perhaps the greatest change in the curriculum has occurred in the traditional sophomore course in quantitative analysis, for which the first edition was written. No single format is evident, but a general pattern has emerged, as evidenced by the recommendations of the Committee on Professional Training of the American Chemical Society. A somewhat oversimplified statement of the change is as follows: The more advanced topics of the sophomore course are upgraded and given concurrently with, or following, the junior-year course in physical chemistry. The simpler, or more classical, material, which still seems to be needed by many students in spite of coverage in the general chemistry course, is either still taught at the sophomore level or is included in the freshman course.

In revising this text, we have tried to keep these changes in mind. We have not, however, attempted to write a text for any specific course. Rather, we have tried to update both classical and modern topics, presenting them in a somewhat more advanced and sophisticated manner than has been customary in earlier texts. It is believed that the present-day college student, with his better background, will find the material more interesting and challenging.

Specifically, we have collected all stoichiometry in the second chapter, where it can be reviewed quickly or omitted, depending upon the background of the student. The chapter on errors and the treatment of analytical data has been expanded to give considerably more depth to a subject that we feel is important in all areas of chemistry. The usual chapters treating equilibria related to titrimetric procedures then follow. Each of these has been treated in greater depth by giving a complete analysis of all equilibria involved in a particular situation. The student is thus provided a better insight into the "hidden assumptions" of the usual simple formulas. Potentiometric titrations are treated early in the text (Chapter 8). A fairly thorough treatment of the problems involved in the measurement of pH has been added to this chapter.

Topics in electrical methods of analysis, such as electrogravimetry, coulometry, polarography, and amperometry, are treated in greater depth than previously. We have added a short, general chapter on electrical methods in an attempt to give the student some awareness of the wide variety of modern electrochemical measurements used by research analytical chemists. The chapter on spectrophotometry has been drastically revised to remove older material and introduce modern instrumentation and practices.

The last five chapters are concerned with methods of separation: precipitation, solvent extraction, and chromatography. The last two topics have been greatly expanded to include gas chromatography, countercurrent distribution, and other important subjects. The chapters on precipitation have been modified slightly, particularly the equilibrium aspects of precipitation.

At Emory University, we use the text at two levels. We cover essentially the first eight chapters in the third quarter of the freshman year, following a two-quarter course in general chemistry. We usually present an abbreviated treatment of Chapter 3 (Errors) at this time. We introduce some of Chapter 12 (Spectrophotometry) at this level since we perform a few simple spectrophotometric measurements in the laboratory. The remainder of the text is covered in a sophomore-level course primarily for premedical students. This material also serves as a starting point for chemistry majors in the junior-year course, which is concurrent with physical chemistry. At this level, the text must be supplemented with more advanced treatments of the same material, as well as by the introduction of additional topics.

We have made no attempt to organize material into the once widely used categories of volumetric, gravimetric, and instrumental methods. Actually, much of the traditional gravimetric material has been eliminated. Also deemphasized is the detailed "descriptive" chemistry of oxidation-reduction reagents, but much of this material has been retained in the companion *Laboratory Manual* designed to accompany this text. It seems to us that material of this type will be better appreciated by the student in connection with his work in the laboratory. As before, we have included a large number of problems, some to provide drill and some to challenge the comprehension of the material; a *Teacher's Manual* with worked-out solutions is available.

We wish to express our appreciation to Dorothy Bernard, Henry Freiser, G. M. Schmid, and Walter Wagner, who have read the manuscript and made numerous helpful suggestions. Many suggestions were received from users of the first edition, for which we are grateful. Several of our colleagues, particularly Prof. Ronald C. Johnson, have been most helpful in discussing various aspects of the topics we have included in the text. Finally, we are especially grateful to Mrs. Nancy Gibson and Mrs. Lee Thorn for typing the manuscript.

R. A. Day, Jr.
A. L. Underwood

Contents

17

413 CHROMATOGRAPHY

APPENDIXES

470 ANSWERS TO ODD-NUMBERED PROBLEMS

475 INDEX

Introduction

ANALYTICAL CHEMISTRY

It used to be possible to subdivide chemistry into several clear and well-defined branches—analytical, inorganic, organic, physical, and biological. Although there was always a certain overlap among these simple categories, it was not difficult to define the branches in terms that were acceptable to most chemists. It was generally fairly clear into which category any particular chemist fitted, and a label such as "organic chemist" usually implied a reasonably clear picture of the sorts of things such a chemist did.

One of the most prominent trends in chemistry over the past ten or twenty years has been a general blurring of the borders of its branches; actually, the boundaries between chemistry itself and other major sciences such as physics and biology are considerably less clear than they used to be. Fields such as chemical physics, biophysical chemistry, physical organic chemistry, geochemistry, and chemical oceanography have achieved recognition in at least

1

a vague way, although precise definitions of these fields are exceedingly difficult to formulate.

During all of this change, chemistry courses in the undergraduate curriculum have largely retained their traditional titles, but they have undergone major changes in content. For example, it is not at all unusual to find such topics as molecular spectroscopy and chemical kinetics in organic chemistry courses. Solution thermodynamics, kinetics of electrode processes, and electronics appear in analytical courses at some schools. In most cases, the college freshman course has undergone drastic change, and interesting changes at the high school level have been initiated.

Analytical chemistry is as old, and as new, as the science of chemistry itself. It may be fairly said that analytical research, as opposed broadly to synthetic, ushered in the change from magic and alchemy to quantitative, scientific chemistry. Analytical work led directly to the revolution that over-threw the phlogiston theory, and rational experiments that would place chemistry on a sound basis of fact and theory became possible with the increasing use of the analytical balance. Careful analyses led to the laws of definite and multiple proportions, and made possible Dalton's great achievement—an atomic hypothesis grounded in fact rather than mystical speculation.

The late nineteenth and early twentieth centuries saw developments in organic and physical chemistry and in physics that were bound to dwarf other fields. The custodians of analytical chemistry for many years were a small number of giants who kept it alive as a science and an army of plodders who took refuge in the repetition of routine laboratory manipulations and measurements. The typical analytical chemist concerned himself with the chemical composition of various materials which were important in the commerce of a relatively simple industrial society. Ores and minerals, a few ferrous and nonferrous alloys, certain foodstuffs, and hard water samples are representative of the sort of analytical problems that were encountered. Many universities unthinkingly accepted the image of analytical chemistry created by the routine analyst, and took little interest in cultivating creative work in the field.

Roughly since World War II, an increasing sophistication of research in all areas of chemistry, physics, and biology and an explosive technological development have combined to create problems which may be classed as analytical but which cannot be solved by unimaginative people using stagnant techniques. Typical examples of such problems are determining traces of impurities at the part per billion level in ultra-pure semiconductor materials, deducing the sequence of some twenty different amino acids in a giant protein molecule, detecting traces of unusual molecules in the polluted atmosphere of a smog-bound city, determining pesticide residues at the part per million (or even billion) level on food products, and determining the nature and concentration of complex organic compounds in, say, the nucleus or perhaps in the mitochondria of a single cell.

The solutions to a host of problems such as these have been developed by research workers of the most diverse backgrounds. For example, a biochemist received the Nobel Prize for working out the amino acid sequence in the protein insulin, and physicists were actively involved in the first semiconductor analyses by mass spectrometry. Research workers in many fields are constantly confronted by analytical problems, and in many cases they work out their own solutions. It is interesting to note that in a recent year, nearly 60% of the papers in the journal *Analytical Chemistry* were authored by people who did not consider themselves to be analytical chemists. The papers originated in a wide variety of laboratories associated with medical schools, hospitals, oceanographic institutes, agricultural experiment stations, physics departments, and many more.

The trends of recent years have drawn analytical chemistry into the forefront of research in many exciting areas, but this very intimacy has blurred the borders of the discipline and made it nearly impossible in many cases to decide what an analytical chemist is. In this connection we may quote from the Fisher Award Address of Prof. David N. Hume[1]:

"One of the most difficult problems facing the analytical chemist today is explaining to others just what analytical chemistry is. Much of the difficulty derives from the changes in the nature of the profession and the fact that a given word may have a whole spectrum of meanings . . . . The increasing complexity of modern chemistry is to some extent the cause of this confusion, as is the fact that a chemist seldom works in only one branch of the subject, more often combining the techniques and approaches of several."

Hume views the practice of chemistry as attacking problems that are either preparative in nature or involve the determination of the properties of some chemical system. It is in the latter area that the modern professional analytical chemist works. He is a specialist in the methodology of solving problems having to do with the properties of chemical systems. He does not perform routine, repetitive chemical analyses, which instead are done by trained technicians.

One way to get a feeling for the nature of the field is to define analytical chemistry as "what analytical chemists do," and then to examine the work of some of the more outstanding people who consider themselves to be analytical chemists. In proceeding this way, one encounters research activity in such fields as kinetics of electrode reactions and other aspects of electrochemistry, the many varieties of spectroscopy, coordination chemistry including both kinetic and equilibrium measurements, practical and theoretical studies of chromatographic separation techniques, automation of analytical procedures, application of computers to analysis, studies of instrumentation per se, and electrochemical and magnetic resonance studies of compounds of biological importance.

[1] D. N. Hume, *Anal. Chem.*, **35,** 29A (1963).

With this extensive overlap into a variety of fields, what distinguishes the analytical chemist from all of the others working in these areas? It is largely the point of view. The analytical chemist has, usually, more interest in the methods and techniques in their own right. Physical, organic, and biochemists often need to develop new analytical methods for their own purposes, but they consider such work as a necessary evil. The challenge for them comes later in handling the results obtained by the methods. To the analytical chemist, developing the methods is the challenging part of the research, and grinding out results after the methods have been developed is boring. Fortunately, chemistry not only can accommodate these varying viewpoints, but indeed is enriched by them. Because of his interest in the method per se, the analytical chemist is likely to be skeptical of data presented without a full disclosure of experimental details, and retains a critical attitude toward results which some workers would perhaps like to accept so as to get on with other things. Many chemists like to deal with models and other sorts of abstractions—ideal gases, infinitely dilute solutions, orbitals, frictionless and weightless pistons, etc. The analytical chemist is more likely to be interested in real systems—nasty mixtures, concentrated solutions, and the like—and much of his effort may be expended in modifying simple models in an attempt to apply sound theory to actual chemical situations.

QUANTITATIVE ANALYSIS

We have tried to explain what analytical chemistry is like and what research analytical chemists do. With this in mind, what topics are to be considered in an introductory textbook? Obviously the beginning student cannot engage immediately in such activities as those described above for the research worker. It is reasonable to introduce him first to somewhat traditional topics which are still important, although frequently not of current research interest. The freshman chemistry course prepares him for these in a fairly adequate way, because they are based largely on simple stoichiometry and equilibrium considerations. In addition, today's student can expect an earlier introduction to modern topics and a more sophisticated approach to many traditional subjects than was common a few years ago. Nevertheless, principles are basically unchanged and as such must be mastered before a full appreciation of current problems can be gained.

Quantitative analysis is concerned with the determination of the quantity of a particular substance present in a sample. Qualitative analysis deals with the identification of substances. Although the beginning student seldom performs a complete quantitative analysis of a sample, it is important that he understand what a complete analysis entails. A chemical analysis actually consists of four steps: (1) sampling, that is, selecting a representative sample of the material to be analyzed; (2) conversion of the desired constituent into a form suitable for measurement; (3) measurement; and (4) calculation and interpretation of the measurements. Often the beginner carries out only steps three and four since these are usually the easiest ones.

The laboratory method employed in the measurement step of an analysis has led to further subdivisions in quantitative analysis: *volumetric (titrimetric)*, *gravimetric*, and *instrumental*. A *volumetric* analysis involves the measurement of the volume of a solution of known concentration which is required to react with the substance determined. Since the process of determining this volume is known as a *titration*, many writers now use the term *titrimetric* rather than volumetric. The former term is preferable since certain analyses involve measuring the volume of a gas. In a *gravimetric* analysis, the measurement is one of weight; for example, the chloride in a sample may be determined by the precipitation of silver chloride, which is then dried and weighed. The term *instrumental* analysis is used rather loosely, originally referring to the use of some instrument in the measurement step. Actually, instruments may be used in any or all steps of the analysis, and, strictly speaking, burets and analytical balances are instruments. The widespread use of instrumentation in all phases of analysis has all but erased the traditional boundaries around what was known as instrumental analysis.

Another classification of analytical chemistry may be based upon the size of the sample which is available for analysis. The subdivisions are not clear-cut, but merge imperceptibly into one another, and are roughly as follows: when a sample weighing more than 0.1 g is available, the analysis is spoken of as *macro; semimicro* analyses are performed on samples of perhaps 10 to 100 mg; *micro* analyses deal with samples weighing from 1 to 10 mg; and *ultra-micro* analyses involve samples of the order of a microgram ($1 \mu g = 10^{-6}$ g). A more or less parallel classification considers the relative amount of the *desired constituent* in the sample rather than the size of the sample itself. Constituents are considered *major* if they amount to more than about 1% of the sample, and *minor* from 0.01 to 1%. Finally, a constituent present to the extent of less than about 0.01% is considered a *trace* constituent. Instrumental measurements achieve their greatest significance in analyses for minor and trace constituents. In his early work with gravimetric and volumetric methods, the beginning student will deal mainly with major constituents of macro samples, although extensions of the classical techniques have led to the impossibility of clearly delimiting their usefulness in a brief discussion.

The beginning student should profit from the introductory course in quantitative analysis. In the laboratory, he will become familiar with the tools and instruments of the analytical chemist which will be of service to him in all other areas of chemistry. He will see the point of view of the analyst and will be exposed to the rigors of exacting quantitative work. This will generate, it is hoped, an understanding of the utility and limitations of many of the tools used by all chemists. From his study of theoretical topics, the student should gain an understanding of the principles underlying laboratory procedures and instruments. Since principles are principles, regardless of the course in which they are taught, the material learned here will broaden the student's knowledge of chemistry as a whole. Once the student has learned this introductory material and has increased his background in mathematics, physics, and physical chemistry, he will be able to appreciate more fully the work which modern analytical chemists are doing today.

Review of Stoichiometry

Calculations based upon the weight and volume relationships in chemical reactions are called *stoichiometric* calculations. Such calculations are emphasized thoroughly in general chemistry courses. Here we shall review this topic briefly, emphasizing examples commonly encountered in analytical chemistry.

CONCENTRATIONS OF SOLUTIONS

Since solutions are frequently employed in performing analyses, it is necessary to express concentrations in such a manner that the amounts of solutes can be determined conveniently. In quantitative analysis the systems of *molarity* and *normality* are most frequently employed. The *formality* system is finding increasing use. The *per cent by weight* system is commonly employed to express approximate concentrations of laboratory reagents.

Weight per cent

This system specifies the number of grams of solute per 100 g of solution. Mathematically this is expressed as follows:

$$P = \frac{w}{w + w_0} \times 100$$

where P = per cent by weight, w = number of grams of solute, and w_0 = number of grams of solvent.

PROBLEM 1. 15 g of NaOH is dissolved in 150 g of water. Calculate the per cent by weight NaOH.

$$P = \frac{15}{15 + 150} \times 100$$

$$P = 9.1\%$$

PROBLEM 2. Concentrated HCl has a density of 1.19 g/ml and is 37% by weight HCl. How many ml of the solution should be taken to obtain 5.0 g of HCl?

$$1.19 \text{ g/ml} \times 0.37 = 0.44 \text{ g of HCl/ml}$$

$$\frac{5.0 \text{ g}}{0.44 \text{ g/ml}} = 11.4 \text{ ml}$$

Molecules, moles, and equivalents

Chemical reactions take place between atoms, molecules, or ions. Since such particles are extremely small and weigh such small amounts (one H^+ ion, for example, weighs only 1.6×10^{-24} g), it is convenient to use a different unit which will have a weight of the order of a few to several hundred grams. This unit is, of course, Avogadro's number, 6.023×10^{23}.

6.023×10^{23} molecules is *one mole*

6.023×10^{23} atoms is *one gram-atom*

6.023×10^{23} ions is *one gram-ion*

Often the term *mole* is used to indicate Avogadro's number of particles regardless of whether these particles are molecules, atoms, or ions, and we shall use the term in this manner.

It should also be recalled that the weight in grams of a mole of a compound is numerically equal to the *molecular weight;* hence this unit is sometimes termed *gram-molecular weight.* Thus, the molecular weight of sodium hydroxide is 40.00, meaning that one mole or one gram-molecular weight is 40.00 g and contains 6.023×10^{23} molecules.

Chemical reactions take place, of course, between *integral* numbers of atoms, but only occasionally does one molecule (ion, etc.) of substance A react with one molecule (or ion) of substance B. For this reason the term *equivalent* was introduced many years ago.[1] In terms of the electron, an equivalent is simply Avogadro's number:

$$1 \text{ eq} \equiv 6.023 \times 10^{23} \text{ electrons}$$

In a chemical reaction one mole of hydrogen ions requires 6.023×10^{23} electrons for reduction to hydrogen atoms

$$H^+ + e \longrightarrow H$$

Hence

$$1.008 \text{ g } H^+ \equiv 1 \text{ eq} \equiv 6.023 \times 10^{23} \text{ electrons}$$

The scheme of chemical equivalence can be extended as far as one desires, as, for example:

$$1 \text{ H}^+ \equiv 1 \text{ OH}^- \equiv 1 \text{ Na}^+ \equiv \tfrac{1}{2} \text{ Cu}^{++} \equiv \tfrac{1}{2} \text{ SO}_4^=, \text{ etc.}$$

There are two important points worth noting in connection with the use of the concept of the equivalent. First, the equivalent weight depends upon the chemical reaction with which one is dealing. Since many compounds can undergo more than a single reaction with other substances, a compound may have more than one equivalent weight. For example, the permanganate ion can undergo the following reactions:

(1) $MnO_4^- + 1 e \rightleftarrows MnO_4^=$
(2) $MnO_4^- + 4 H^+ + 3 e \rightleftarrows MnO_2 + 2 H_2O$
(3) $MnO_4^- + 8 H^+ + 4 e \rightleftarrows Mn^{3+} + 4 H_2O$
(4) $MnO_4^- + 8 H^+ + 5 e \rightleftarrows Mn^{++} + 4 H_2O$

The equivalent weight of a permanganate salt would be its molecular weight divided by one, three, four, or five, depending upon which of the above reactions took place. A similar situation can arise with acids and bases. For example, the neutralization of phosphoric acid can be stopped when the following reaction has occurred:

$$H_3PO_4 + OH^- \rightleftarrows H_2O + H_2PO_4^-$$

The equivalent weight in this case is the same as the molecular weight. The reaction can be carried on further:

$$H_3PO_4 + 2 OH^- \rightleftarrows 2 H_2O + HPO_4^=$$

Here the equivalent weight is one-half the molecular weight. (It is not feasible to titrate the third hydrogen in aqueous solutions.)

[1] The term equivalent is not necessary and many chemists object, with justification, to its use. Since it is a multiple or fraction of a mole, any calculation can be done in terms of moles without introducing the equivalent. The term is so widely used, however, that it is unwise to ignore it.

The second point is that, although the equivalent weight is normally equal to or less than the molecular weight, there are instances in which it is greater than the molecular weight. For example, MnO on ignition in air is converted to Mn_3O_4, which, in turn, can be determined by oxidizing a reducing agent, such as sodium oxalate. The equation involved is

$$6 \, MnO + O_2 = 2 \, Mn_3O_4$$

Using the concept of oxidation numbers (page 24) it is seen that manganese changes from $+2$ in MnO to $+2\frac{2}{3}$ in Mn_3O_4. Hence, each Mn loses on the average $\frac{2}{3}$ of an electron and the equivalent weight of MnO, calculated in the usual manner, is

$$\frac{70.93}{2/3} = 106.4$$

Of course, no individual manganese atom actually loses $\frac{2}{3}$ of an electron. Mn_3O_4 is $MnO_2 \cdot 2 \, MnO$ and thus one of the three manganese atoms loses two electrons, thereby making an average of $\frac{2}{3}$ of an electron per manganese atom.

In precipitation and complex formation reactions the situation frequently arises in which the equivalent weight of the compound containing the anion is greater than the molecular weight, if we use the definition of an equivalent given above. For example, silver ion reacts with cyanide ion as follows:

$$Ag^+ + 2 \, CN^- \rightleftharpoons Ag(CN)_2^-$$

If we take the equivalent weight of silver ion to be the same as the atomic weight, since one electron has been lost, then

$$1 \text{ eq } Ag^+ \equiv 1 \text{ mole } Ag^+ \equiv 2 \text{ mole } KCN$$

but since

$$1 \text{ eq } Ag^+ \equiv 1 \text{ eq } KCN$$

then

$$1 \text{ eq } KCN \equiv 2 \text{ mole } KCN$$

and the equivalent weight of KCN is twice its molecular weight. Some chemists, noting that the coordination number of silver ion is two in this reaction, prefer to say that

$$1 \text{ mole } Ag^+ \equiv 2 \text{ eq } Ag^+ \equiv 2 \text{ eq } KCN$$

Since

$$1 \text{ mole } Ag^+ \equiv 2 \text{ mole } KCN$$

then

$$1 \text{ eq } KCN \equiv 1 \text{ mole } KCN$$

This approach makes the equivalent weight of silver ion half its atomic weight rather than making the equivalent weight of KCN twice its molecular weight. Actually, either approach, consistently applied, gives correct results. Because of the possibility of confusion, however, we shall normally use moles in calculations involving precipitation and complex formation reactions.

The following are some problems illustrating the calculation of equivalent weights:

PROBLEM 1. What is the equivalent weight of SO_3, used as an acid in water solution?

SO_3 does not directly furnish hydrogen ions, but it does so indirectly through the reaction with water:

$$SO_3 + H_2O \rightleftarrows H_2SO_4 \rightleftarrows 2\ H^+ + SO_4^=$$

Hence 1 molecule of SO_3 is responsible for 2 H^+, and

$$E.W. = \frac{M.W.}{2} = \frac{80.07}{2}$$

$$E.W. = 40.04\ g/eq$$

PROBLEM 2. Calculate the equivalent weight of KHC_2O_4 both as an acid and as a reducing agent. As an acid the reaction is

$$HC_2O_4^- \rightleftarrows H^+ + C_2O_4^=$$

and as a reducing agent (unbalanced)

$$C_2O_4^= \rightleftarrows 2\ CO_2$$

The equivalent weight as an acid is the same as the molecular weight, since only one H^+ is furnished per molecule,

$$Acid: E.W. = \frac{M.W.}{1} = 128.13$$

The oxidation number of carbon changes from $+3$ to $+4$ in the redox reaction. Hence each carbon loses 1 electron and KHC_2O_4 loses 2 electrons.

$$Reducing\ Agent: E.W. = \frac{M.W.}{2} = \frac{128.13}{2} = 64.07$$

PROBLEM 3. 8-Hydroxyquinoline (abbreviated HQ) can be used to precipitate various metals, such as Al^{3+}.

$$Al^{3+} + 3\ HQ \rightleftarrows AlQ_3 + 3\ H^+$$

The precipitate is filtered, washed, and redissolved in acid:

$$AlQ_3 + 3\ H^+ \rightleftarrows Al^{3+} + 3\ HQ$$

The 8-hydroxyquinoline is brominated with a mixture of KBr and $KBrO_3$ (known amount):

What is the equivalent weight of aluminum?

The aluminum ion does not lose or gain electrons, of course. Nevertheless each Al^{3+} is responsible for furnishing 3 molecules of 8-hydroxyquinoline which react with 6 molecules of Br_2 which are equivalent to 12 electrons:

$$1\ Al^{3+} \equiv 3\ HQ \equiv 6\ Br_2 \equiv 12\ e$$

Hence, the equivalent weight of aluminum is

$$E.W. = \frac{26.98}{12} = 2.248 \text{ g/eq}$$

Molarity, normality, and formality

In quantitative analysis the concentration of a solution is usually expressed as molarity, normality, or formality. All of these systems are based on the *volume of solution* and hence are convenient for our purposes. The definitions of the three systems are

Molarity = number of moles of solute per liter of solution
Normality = number of equivalents of solute per liter of solution
Formality = number of formula weights of solute per liter of solution

The formality system has become somewhat more widely used in recent years. There is a certain illogic in the molar system as it is commonly used. We speak of dissolving a mole of NaCl (58.44 g) in a liter of solution, which becomes 1.000-M. But *mole* relates to the word *molecule* (cf. gram-molecular weight). Yet there are no molecules of NaCl, either initially or in the solution, only the ions Na^+ and Cl^-. Thus some writers have urged that 58.44 g of NaCl be called one *formula weight* rather than one mole. The above solution is then called 1.000-F (formal). The solution would be 1.000-M in Na^+ and 1.000-M in Cl^-. Similarly, a solution which is 0.10-F in $FeCl_3$ would have various molar concentrations of such ions as Fe^{3+}, $FeCl^{++}$, and $FeCl_2^+$. In this book, we shall use molar in the wider sense, as do most chemists.

Mathematically, we express molarity and normality as

$$M = \frac{\text{moles}}{V}$$

$$N = \frac{\text{eq}}{V}$$

where M = molarity, N = normality, and V = volume of solution in liters. Since

$$\text{moles} = \frac{g}{M.W.}$$

and

$$\text{eq} = \frac{g}{E.W.}$$

where g = grams of solute, M.W. = molecular weight, and E.W. = equivalent weight, it follows that

$$M = \frac{g}{M.W. \times V}$$

and

$$N = \frac{g}{\text{E.W.} \times V}$$

These equations may be solved for grams of solute, giving

$$g = M \times V \times \text{M.W.}$$

and

$$g = N \times V \times \text{E.W.}$$

We have seen that the equivalent and molecular weights are usually related by a simple whole number relationship. We can write

$$\text{E.W.} = \frac{\text{M.W.}}{n}$$

where n = number of hydrogen ions furnished or taken up in the case of acids and bases, or the number of electrons gained or lost in the case of redox reagents, etc. Hence, the relation between molarity and normality is

$$N = \frac{n \times g}{\text{M.W.} \times V}$$

or

$$N = n \times M$$

If n is one or greater, as is usually the case, the normality is equal to or greater than the molarity.

In practical quantitative measurements the volumes of solutions are normally of the order of a few thousandths of a liter. The number of equivalents or moles involved is small, frequently of the order of a few thousandths of an equivalent or mole. Hence, it is convenient to adopt a smaller unit, both for the quantity of solute and for the volume of solution. The unit *milliliter*, one-thousandth of a liter is a familiar one. Similarly the terms *milliequivalent* and *millimole* mean simply one-thousandth of an equivalent or of a mole, respectively. That is,

> 1000 milliequivalents (abbr. meq) = 1 equivalent
>
> 1000 millimoles (abbr. mmol) = 1 mole

Note that normality and molarity can be expressed in either the larger or smaller units, the numerical value is unchanged. Thus, a solution containing 0.00200 equivalents in 0.00500 liters also contains 2.00 meq in 5.00 ml and the normality is

$$N = \frac{0.00200 \text{ eq}}{0.00500 \text{ l}} = \frac{2.00 \text{ meq}}{5.00 \text{ ml}} = 0.400$$

It should be noted also that the equivalent weight can be expressed with either the large or small units. The equivalent weight of NaOH is 40.00 g/eq and 40.00 mg/meq. It should be evident that

$$N = \frac{\text{mg}}{\text{E.W.} \times \text{ml}}$$

Consider the following typical calculations.

PROBLEM 1. A sample of pure As_2O_3 weighing 3.2462 g is dissolved in 600.0 ml of solution.

(a) Calculate the molarity.

(b) Calculate the normality, assuming that the arsenic will undergo a reaction in which the oxidation number changes from $+3$ to $+5$.

(a)
$$M = \frac{3246.2 \text{ mg}}{197.82 \text{ mg/mmol} \times 600.0 \text{ ml}}$$

$$M = 0.0273 \text{ mmol/ml}$$

(b) Since each arsenic atom loses 2 electrons, a molecule of As_2O_3 loses 4 electrons. Hence, the equivalent weight is $\frac{1}{4}$ the molecular weight. Then

$$N = 4M$$

or

$$N = 0.1092$$

PROBLEM 2. Calculate the number of grams of Na_2CO_3 in 4.7 l of a 0.201-N solution. The reaction referred to is

$$2 H^+ + CO_3^= \rightleftarrows H_2CO_3$$

The equivalent weight of Na_2CO_3 is one-half the molecular weight or $105.99/2 = 53.0$ g/eq. Hence

$$g = 4.7 \text{ l} \times 0.201 \text{ eq/l} \times 53.0 \text{ g/eq}$$

$$g = 50$$

PROBLEM 3. Concentrated HCl has a density of 1.19 g/ml and contains 37% by weight HCl. Calculate the number of milliliters of the concentrated acid required to prepare 2.00 l of 0.150-N solution.

In 2 liters, or 2000 ml of 0.150-N solution there are

$$2000 \text{ ml} \times 0.150 \text{ meq/ml} = 300 \text{ meq}$$

In each milliliter of concentrated HCl there are

$$\frac{1190 \text{ mg/ml} \times 0.37}{36.5 \text{ mg/meq}} = 11.8 \text{ meq/ml}$$

Hence

$$\frac{300 \text{ meq}}{11.8 \text{ meq/ml}} = 25 \text{ ml}$$

PROBLEM 4. In what volume of solution should 20.00 g of pure KCN be dissolved to prepare a 0.3000-M solution?

Since

$$M = \frac{g}{\text{M.W.} \times V}$$

$$V = \frac{g}{\text{M.W.} \times M}$$

Thus

$$V = \frac{20.00 \text{ g}}{65.11 \text{ g/mole} \times 0.3000 \text{ moles/l}}$$

$$V = 1.024 \text{ l}$$

PROBLEM 5. Concentrations of solutions are often adjusted by dilution. In such cases, there must be the same quantity of solute (mmol or meq) in the final solution as in the original solution. In other words

$$V_2 \times N_2 = V_1 \times N_1$$

where the subscript 1 refers to the original solution, 2 to the final solution. Molarity could be substituted for normality.

500 ml of a 1.250-N solution is diluted to 2500 ml with water. What is the normality of the final solution?

$$2500 \times N_2 = 500 \times 1.250$$

$$N_2 = 0.250 \text{ meq/ml}$$

PROBLEM 6. How many grams of solid $Na_2C_2O_4$ should be added to 250 ml of a 0.200-M solution of $KHC_2O_4 \cdot H_2C_2O_4$ in order that the normality of the solution as a reducing agent be four times that as an acid?

The $C_2O_4^-$ ion is oxidized to CO_2, the oxidation number of carbon changing from $+3$ to $+4$. Hence, the equivalent weight of $Na_2C_2O_4$ is one-half the molecular weight.

The equivalent weight of $KHC_2O_4 \cdot H_2C_2O_4$ as an acid is one-third the molecular weight since three hydrogens are furnished by each molecule. As a reducing agent the equivalent weight is one-fourth the molecular weight since two $C_2O_4^-$ ions are furnished, each of which loses 2 electrons.

Let w = mg $Na_2C_2O_4$ needed

Total meq as reducing agent = $\dfrac{w}{67.0}$ + (250 × 0.200 × 4)

Total meq as acid = 250 × 0.200 × 3

Therefore (note that the volume cancels),

$$\frac{w}{67.0} + (250 \times 0.200 \times 4) = 4(250 \times 0.200 \times 3)$$

$$\frac{w}{67.0} + 200 = 600$$

$$w = 26,800 \text{ mg or } 26.8 \text{ g}$$

Titer

Still another method of expressing concentration that is frequently used in analytical chemistry is the *titer*. The units of titer are weight per volume, but the weight is usually that of some reagent with which the solution will react rather than that of the solute itself. For example, if 1.00 ml of a hydrochloric acid solution will exactly neutralize 4.00 mg of sodium hydroxide, the concentration of the acid solution can be expressed as a sodium hydroxide titer of 4.00 mg/ml. Titer (T) can be easily converted to normality, as seen from the following relations:

$$T = \frac{\text{mg}}{\text{ml}}, \qquad N = \frac{\text{mg}}{\text{ml} \times \text{E.W.}}$$

Thus

$$T = N \times \text{E.W.}$$

The equivalent weight employed in the transformation is that of the substance with which the solution reacts, not the solute. In the example above, if the titer of the hydrochloric acid solution is 4.000 mg/ml of sodium hydroxide, the normality is obtained upon dividing by 40.00 mg/meq, the equivalent weight of sodium hydroxide, giving a normality of 0.1000 meq/ml.

PROBLEM 1. What is (a) the NH_3 titer of a 0.120-N solution of HCl; (b) the BaO titer of the same solution?

(a) $$T = 0.120 \, \frac{\text{meq}}{\text{ml}} \times 17.0 \, \frac{\text{mg}}{\text{meq}} \; (NH_3)$$

$$T = 2.04 \, \frac{\text{mg}}{\text{ml}} \; (NH_3)$$

(b) $$T = 0.120 \, \frac{\text{meq}}{\text{ml}} \times \frac{153.4}{2} \, \frac{\text{mg}}{\text{meq}} \; (BaO)$$

$$T = 9.2 \, \frac{\text{mg}}{\text{ml}} \; (BaO)$$

This means that 1 ml of the HCl solution will neutralize 2.04 mg of NH_3 or 9.2 mg of BaO.

PROBLEM 2. A solution of NaOH has an oxalic acid (M.W. 126.0) titer of 9.45 mg/ml. Calculate the normality of the NaOH solution. (Oxalic acid furnishes two hydrogen ions.)

$$N = \frac{9.45 \text{ mg/ml}}{63.0 \text{ mg/meq}}$$

$$N = 0.1500 \text{ meq/ml}$$

VOLUMETRIC AND GRAVIMETRIC METHODS

In quantitative analysis the principal application of stoichiometry is in calculating the percentage purity of a sample. We shall consider here examples from classical volumetric and gravimetric methods. The following is a brief review of terminology from these areas.

In a *volumetric* analysis we measure the volume of a solution of known concentration required to react with the desired constituent. The solution of known concentration is termed a *standard solution*. The process of determining the volume is known as a *titration*, and some writers speak of a *titrimetric* rather than volumetric analysis. From a rigorous standpoint the less widely-used term *titrimetric* is probably preferable, because volume measurements need not be confined to titrations. In certain analyses, for example, one might measure the volume of a gas. The standard solution used in a titration is called the *titrant*.

The chemical reactions which may serve as the basis for volumetric determinations are conveniently grouped into four types, as follows:

1. Acid-base, or neutralization

$$H_3O^+ + OH^- \rightleftharpoons 2\ H_2O$$

2. Oxidation-reduction (redox)

$$Fe^{++} + Ce^{4+} \rightleftharpoons Fe^{3+} + Ce^{3+}$$

3. Precipitation

$$Ag^+ + Cl^- \rightleftharpoons AgCl \downarrow$$

4. Complex formation

$$Ag^+ + 2\ CN^- \rightleftharpoons Ag(CN)_2^-$$

Of the host of known chemical reactions, relatively few can be used as the basis for titrations. Normally a reaction should satisfy certain requirements before it can be employed. First, it must proceed according to a definite chemical equation, with no side reactions. Second, it should proceed essentially to completion when equivalent amounts of reactants are mixed. If this requirement is met, there will be a large, abrupt change in the concentration of the substance titrated when an equivalent amount of titrant is added. Third, there must be a way of converting this sudden change into a signal which the analyst can detect. For many titrations, chemical substances called *indicators* are available which respond to the appearance of excess titrant by changing color. Fourth, it is desirable that the reaction be rapid, so that the titration can be completed in a few minutes.

In a titration involving, say, the reaction of A with titrant B, the point at which an equivalent amount of B has been added is termed the *equivalence* or *stoichiometric point*. In contrast, the point in the titration where the indicator changes color is termed the *end point*. It is desirable, of course, that the end point be as close as possible to the equivalence point. Choosing indicators to make these two points coincide (or correcting for the difference between the two) is one of the important aspects of volumetric analysis.

If the measurement step in an analysis involves a determination of weight, the analysis is termed *gravimetric*. Classically, precipitation has been the principal method used to separate the desired constituent before the final measurement of weight. A separation of some kind inevitably attends every gravimetric determination, and the following requirements should be met in order that a gravimetric method be successful.

1. The separation process should be sufficiently complete so that the quantity of desired constituent left behind is analytically undetectable (usually 0.1 mg or less in determining a major constituent of a macro sample).

2. The substance weighed should have a definite composition and should

be pure, or very nearly so. Otherwise erroneous results may be obtained.

Electrolysis is another important method of separating and determining substances gravimetrically. The technique can also be employed as a "titrimetric" technique. The stoichiometry is discussed in the next section.

ILLUSTRATIVE PROBLEMS

It is important to keep in mind the units of concentration systems we will employ. These are:

Normality: meq/ml or eq/l

Molarity: mmol/ml or moles/l

Titer: mg/ml or g/l

Per cent by weight: dimensionless

It should also be recalled that at the equivalence point of a titration the equivalents (or milliequivalents) of, say, substance A equal the equivalents (or milliequivalents) of substance B.

1. Standardization of solutions

The process by which the concentration of a solution is accurately ascertained is known as standardization. A standard solution can sometimes be prepared by dissolving a known weight of the desired solute in a definite volume of solution. This method is not generally applicable, however, since relatively few chemical reagents can be obtained in sufficiently pure form to meet the analyst's demand for accuracy. Those few substances which *are* adequate in this regard are called *primary standards*. More commonly, a solution is standardized by titrating it against a weighed portion of a primary standard.

PROBLEM 1. A sample of pure Na_2CO_3 weighing 0.3542 g is dissolved in water and titrated with a solution of hydrochloric acid. A volume of 30.23 ml is required to reach the methyl orange end point, the reaction being

$$Na_2CO_3 + 2\,HCl \rightleftarrows 2\,NaCl + H_2O + CO_2$$

Calculate the normality of the acid.

We know that

$$\text{meq HCl} = \text{meq Na}_2\text{CO}_3$$

The equivalent weight of Na_2CO_3 is one-half the molecular weight, or 105.99/2 = 53.00. Hence

$$V_{\text{HCl}} \times N_{\text{HCl}} = \frac{\text{mg Na}_2\text{CO}_3}{\text{E.W. Na}_2\text{CO}_3}$$

$$30.23 \times N_{\text{HCl}} = \frac{354.2}{53.0}$$

$$N_{\text{HCl}} = 0.2211 \text{ meq/ml}$$

PROBLEM 2. A sample of pure sodium oxalate, $Na_2C_2O_4$, weighing 0.2734 g is dissolved in water, sulfuric acid is added, and the solution is titrated at 70°, requiring 42.68 ml of a $KMnO_4$ solution. The end point is overrun and back-titration is carried out with 1.46 ml of a 0.1024-N solution of oxalic acid. Calculate the normality of the $KMnO_4$ solution.

The ionic reaction is

$$5 C_2O_4^= + 2 MnO_4^- + 16 H^+ \rightleftarrows 2 Mn^{++} + 10 CO_2 + 8 H_2O$$

We know that meq permanganate = meq oxalate, or

$$\text{meq permanganate} = \text{meq } Na_2C_2O_4 + \text{meq } H_2C_2O_4$$

$$V_{\text{KMnO}_4} \times N_{\text{KMnO}_4} = \frac{\text{mg } Na_2C_2O_4}{\text{E.W. } Na_2C_2O_4} + V_{\text{H}_2\text{C}_2\text{O}_4} \times N_{\text{H}_2\text{C}_2\text{O}_4}$$

Since the oxalate ion loses 2 electrons in the above reaction, the equivalent weight of $Na_2C_2O_4$ is one-half its molecular weight, or $134.00/2 = 67.00$. Hence

$$42.68 \times N_{\text{KMnO}_4} = \frac{273.4}{67.00} + 1.46 \times 0.1024$$

$$N_{\text{KMnO}_4} = 0.0991 \text{ meq/ml}$$

Note: Suppose that the normality of the oxalic acid solution were unknown, but that it was known that

$$1.000 \text{ ml } H_2C_2O_4 = 1.033 \text{ ml } KMnO_4$$

One could convert the volume of oxalic acid to its equivalent volume of potassium permanganate, and then subtract. The $H_2C_2O_4$ would react with

$$1.45 \times 1.033 = 1.51 \text{ ml } KMnO_4$$

Hence, the volume of $KMnO_4$ used by the $Na_2C_2O_4$ would be

$$42.68 - 1.51 = 41.17 \text{ ml}$$

and the normality would be obtained as follows:

$$41.17 \times N_{\text{KMnO}_4} = \frac{273.4}{67.00}$$

$$N_{\text{KMnO}_4} = 0.0991 \text{ meq/ml}$$

In this case, the normality of the $H_2C_2O_4$ could be calculated from the volume ratio above and the normality of the $KMnO_4$:

$$1.000 \times N_{\text{H}_2\text{C}_2\text{O}_4} = 1.033 \times 0.0991$$

$$N_{\text{H}_2\text{C}_2\text{O}_4} = 0.1024 \text{ meq/ml}$$

PROBLEM 3. It is found that 30.00 ml of $AgNO_3$ solution is required to titrate 0.2000 g of pure KCN (M.W. = 65.12). The reaction is

$$Ag^+ + 2 CN^- \rightleftarrows Ag(CN)_2^-$$

Calculate the molarity of the AgNO$_3$ solution.

At the equivalence point

$$2 \times \text{mmol Ag}^+ = \text{mmol KCN}$$

$$2 \times 30.00 \times M = \frac{200.0}{65.12}$$

$$M = 0.0512 \text{ mmol/ml}$$

2. Volumetric analysis of samples

To analyze a sample of unknown purity, the analyst weighs accurately a portion of the sample, dissolves it appropriately, and titrates with a standard solution. He then knows that

$$\text{meq titrant} = \text{meq desired constituent}$$

From the normality and volume of titrant, the milliequivalents of the desired constituent are obtained. To express the result as a percentage, the milliequivalents of desired constituent are converted to weight and divided by the weight of the sample:

$$\% = \frac{\text{mg of desired constituent}}{\text{mg of sample}} \times 100$$

or

$$\% = \frac{V \text{ (ml)} \times N \text{ (meq/ml)} \times \text{E.W. (mg/meq)}}{\text{weight of sample (mg)}} \times 100$$

Note the cancellation of units to give percentage, which is dimensionless.

PROBLEM 1. A sample of iron ore, weighing 0.6038 g is dissolved in acid. The iron is reduced to the ferrous state and then titrated with 38.42 ml of 0.1073-N potassium dichromate solution. (a) Calculate the percentage of iron (Fe) in the sample. (b) Express the percentage as FeO, Fe$_2$O$_3$, and also Fe$_3$O$_4$.

(a) Iron is oxidized from Fe^{++} to Fe^{3+}, losing one electron. Hence the equivalent weight of Fe is 55.847 g/eq or 55.847 mg/meq.

$$\% \text{ Fe} = \frac{38.42 \text{ ml} \times 0.1073 \text{ meq/ml} \times 55.847 \text{ mg/meq}}{603.8 \text{ mg}} \times 100$$

$$\% \text{ Fe} = 38.13$$

(b) To express the percentage in terms of the oxides, the equivalent weight of an oxide is substituted for that of iron in the foregoing expression. Since each iron atom loses one electron, the equivalent weights of the oxides are as follows:

$$\text{FeO:} \quad 71.85/1 = 71.85$$

$$\text{Fe}_2\text{O}_3: \quad 159.69/2 = 79.85$$

$$\text{Fe}_3\text{O}_4: \quad 231.54/3 = 77.18$$

Alternatively, the percentage of FeO can be calculated directly from the percentage of Fe:

$$\% \text{ FeO} = \% \text{ Fe} \times \frac{\text{E.W. FeO}}{\text{E.W. Fe}}$$

The student should confirm that $\% \text{ FeO} = 49.05$, $\% \text{ Fe}_2\text{O}_3 = 54.51$, and $\% \text{ Fe}_3\text{O}_4 = 52.69$.

PROBLEM 2. It is found that 25.42 ml of 0.0450-M AgNO$_3$ solution is required to titrate a sample of impure KCN weighing 0.3123 g. The reaction is

$$\text{Ag}^+ + 2 \text{ CN}^- \rightleftharpoons \text{Ag(CN)}_2^-$$

Calculate the percentage of KCN in the sample.

At the equivalence point

$$\text{mmol KCN} = 2 \times \text{mmol Ag}^+$$

$$\text{mmol KCN} = 2 \times 25.42 \text{ ml} \times 0.0450 \text{ mmol/ml}$$

$$\text{mmol KCN} = 2.248$$

$$\% \text{ KCN} = \frac{2.228 \text{ mmol} \times 65.12 \text{ mg/mmol}}{312.3 \text{ mg}} \times 100$$

$$\% \text{ KCN} = 47.7$$

3. Gravimetric analysis of samples

In the usual gravimetric analysis, a precipitate is weighed, and from this the weight of the desired constituent in the sample is computed. The term *gravimetric factor* is frequently employed, this factor being the number of grams of the desired constituent in 1 g (or equivalent of 1 g) of the substance weighed. Multiplication of the weight of the precipitate by the gravimetric factor gives the number of grams of the desired constituent in the sample. Division by the weight of sample and multiplication by 100 gives the percentage of the desired constituent:

$$\frac{\text{Weight precipitate} \times \text{gravimetric factor}}{\text{Weight sample}} \times 100 = \%$$

The following problem gives some examples of calculating gravimetric factors.

PROBLEM 1. Calculate the following gravimetric factors. (a) Cl in AgCl. (b) FeO in Fe$_2$O$_3$. (c) CaO from KHC$_2$O$_4 \cdot$ H$_2$C$_2$O$_4$.

(a) One mole of AgCl, 143.32 g, contains 35.453 g of Cl. Hence, one gram of AgCl contains

$$\frac{35.453}{143.23} = 0.24736 \text{ g Cl}$$

Letting the chemical symbol represent the atomic or molecular weights, this is usually written

$$\frac{Cl}{AgCl}$$

(b) One mole of Fe_2O_3, 159.691 g, contains or is chemically equivalent to two moles of FeO. Hence

$$\text{Gravimetric factor} = \frac{2FeO}{Fe_2O_3} = \frac{2(71.846)}{159.691} = 0.89983$$

Two things should be apparent in setting up a gravimetric factor: (1) the molecular weight of the desired constituent appears in the numerator, that of the substance weighed in the denominator; (2) the number of molecules or atoms appearing in the numerator and denominator must be chemically equivalent.

(c) Here we must know what chemical reactions are involved. The salt potassium tetraoxalate, $KHC_2O_4 \cdot H_2C_2O_4$, can be determined by precipitating the oxalate as calcium oxalate and then igniting the precipitate to calcium oxide. The abbreviated reactions are:

$$KHC_2O_4 \cdot H_2C_2O_4 + 2\,Ca^{++} \rightleftarrows 2\,CaC_2O_4 = 2\,CaO$$

Hence, two molecules of calcium oxide are produced from one molecule of the tetraoxalate, and the factor needed to calculate the weight of tetraoxalate from the weight of calcium oxide is

$$\frac{KHC_2O_4 \cdot H_2C_2O_4}{2\,CaO} = \frac{218.17}{2(56.08)} = 1.9452$$

PROBLEM 2. A 0.5012-g sample containing CaC_2O_4 is heated to constant weight at 500°, cooled to room temperature and found to weigh 0.4523 g. Assuming that the only loss in weight is from the reaction

$$CaC_2O_4 \rightleftarrows CaCO_3 + CO \uparrow$$

calculate the percentage CaC_2O_4 in the sample.

Loss in weight = 0.5012 − 0.4523 = 0.0489 g.

$$\%\,CaC_2O_4 = \frac{0.0489 \times CaC_2O_4/CO}{0.5012} \times 100 = 44.6$$

Note that the number of carbon atoms is not the same in the numerator and denominator of the gravimetric factor. This is as it should be, however, since 1 mole of CO results from 1 mole of CaC_2O_4.

PROBLEM 3. *Indirect Analysis.* Two components in a mixture can be determined if one has two sets of independent analytical data. Two equations containing the two unknowns can be set up and the equations solved simultaneously. The following is an illustration:

A 0.7500-g sample containing both NaCl and NaBr is titrated with 0.1043-M $AgNO_3$, using 42.23 ml. A second sample of the same weight is treated with excess silver nitrate, and the mixture of AgCl and AgBr is filtered, dried, and found to weigh 0.8042 g. Calculate the percentages of NaCl and NaBr in the sample.

Let x = mmol of NaCl and y = mmol of NaBr. Then

$$x + y = \text{total mmol} = 42.23 \text{ ml} \times 0.1043 \text{ mmol/ml}$$

$$x + y = 4.405$$

Also x = mmol AgCl and y = mmol AgBr produced. Hence

$$\text{AgCl } x + \text{AgBr } y = 804.2$$

$$143.32\, x + 187.78\, y = 804.2$$

Solving gives

$$x = 0.517 \text{ and } y = 3.888$$

Then

$$\% \text{ NaCl} = \frac{0.517 \text{ mmol} \times 58.443 \text{ mg/mmol}}{750.0 \text{ mg}} \times 100 = 4.03$$

$$\% \text{ NaBr} = \frac{3.888 \text{ mmol} \times 102.90 \text{ mg/mmol}}{750.0 \text{ mg}} \times 100 = 53.34$$

It should be noted that in solving this expression for y, it is necessary to divide by the difference in the molecular weights of AgCl and AgBr. The closer these two weights are to each other, the greater effect an error in the experimental data (say in the weight of the combined precipitates) will have on the value of y, and correspondingly on the value of x. In other words, the reliability of such a procedure will be greatly reduced if the two molecular weights are very close to the same value. (See problems 57 and 58.)

When a sample is a mixture of *only* two substances, such as NaCl and NaBr, only one measurement need be made in order to calculate the percentage of both constituents. The sum of the percentages of the two components must total 100.

4. Factor weight solutions

It is possible to adjust the normality of a standard solution and the weight of sample taken for analysis so that the number of milliliters used in a titration equals the percentage of desired constituent (or a fraction thereof). This is of particular advantage in laboratories where many determinations of the same constituent are made. For a similar gravimetric calculation see problem 42.

PROBLEM 2. What weight of sample should be taken for analysis so that the volume of 0.1042-N HCl used for titration equals the percentage of Na_2CO_3 in the sample. The carbonate is completely neutralized to H_2CO_3.

$$\% \text{ Na}_2\text{CO}_3 = \frac{\text{ml HCl} \times 0.1042 \text{ meq/ml} \times 53.00 \text{ mg/meq}}{\text{mg sample}} \times 100$$

Since $\% \text{ Na}_2\text{CO}_3$ = ml HCl, these two terms cancel,

$$\text{mg sample} = 0.1042 \times 53.00 \times 100 = 552.3$$

PROBLEM 3. Samples of iron ore weighing 0.4000 g are titrated with $KMnO_4$. What should be the normality of the $KMnO_4$ in order that each milliliter of

KMnO$_4$ represent 2.000% Fe$_2$O$_3$ in the sample? Iron is oxidized from Fe^{++} to Fe^{3+}.

Since iron loses one electron on being oxidized from the ferrous to ferric state, the equivalent weight of Fe$_2$O$_3$ is $159.69/2 = 79.85$. Thus

$$\frac{\text{ml} \times N \text{ meq/ml} \times 79.85 \text{ mg/meq}}{400.0 \text{ mg}} \times 100 = \%$$

Since 1.000 ml = 2.000%,

$$\frac{1.000 \times N \times 79.85}{400.0} \times 100 = 2.000$$

$$N = 0.1002$$

5. Balancing oxidation-reduction equations

We shall describe first the so-called "oxidation number" method. The first step of any method, of course, is to write down the reactants and products. Then this method calls for assigning oxidation numbers to the atoms in the reactants and products, and any changes in these numbers can be attributed to a loss or gain of electrons. The number of electrons gained by the oxidizing agent is then made equal to the number lost by the reducing agent by selecting appropriate coefficients for these two reactants.

Although the assignment of oxidation numbers can be made on an arbitrary basis, so long as one is consistent, it is convenient to select numbers that correspond to the actual oxidation states of the atoms. For example, the Zn^{++} ion is assigned a number of $+2$, and the Cl$^-$ ion a number of -1, corresponding to the number of electrons lost or gained in the formation of these ions from the corresponding elements. These same assignments would be made if zinc chloride were written as ZnCl$_2$ instead of as separate ions. Thus the algebraic sum of the oxidation numbers of the atoms in a neutral molecule equals zero. The oxidation number of an atom of an elementary substance, such as Zn, is zero.

In covalent compounds of known structure, where electrons are shared by two atoms, the oxidation number of an atom is conveniently taken as the charge which that atom would have if each shared electron pair were assigned to the more electronegative of the two atoms. For example, in the carbon tetrachloride molecule, CCl$_4$, each chlorine atom is assigned the number -1, and the carbon atom the number $+4$, making the sum of the oxidation numbers in the molecule equal to zero. In the methane molecule, CH$_4$, however, since carbon is more electronegative than hydrogen, the carbon atom is given a value of -4, each hydrogen being $+1$. When a pair of electrons is shared by two atoms of the same element, one electron is assigned to each atom. For example, in the chlorine molecule, Cl$_2$, each atom has an oxidation number of zero.

In a complex ion the algebraic sum of the oxidation numbers of the atoms must equal the charge on the ion. For example, the ferrocyanide ion, $Fe(CN)_6^{4-}$, has a charge of -4. Since the oxidation state of ferrous ion is $+2$, it is convenient to assign an oxidation number of $+2$ to iron, and -1 to each cyanide radical, the algebraic sum being -4. If it is desired to assign numbers to the carbon and nitrogen atoms within the cyanide radical, carbon can be taken as $+4$, nitrogen as -5, consistent with the assignment of -1 to the radical.

Compounds containing hydrogen and oxygen atoms are frequently encountered. The oxidation number of hydrogen is always taken as $+1$, except when hydrogen is combined with a metal, as in sodium hydride, NaH. In such a case, it is taken as -1. The oxidation number of oxygen is always taken as -2, except in peroxides, such as H_2O_2. Here hydrogen is assigned a number of $+1$, and oxygen must be -1 to make the algebraic sum equal zero.

It should be realized that the oxidation number of an atom is not necessarily the same as its valence. We frequently assign an oxidation number to an atom to correspond to the valence that we know the atom shows, and this procedure is convenient. However, in many cases the oxidation numbers turn out to be entirely different from known valences, and frequently are fractional. For example, we know that in the oxalic acid molecule, $H_2C_2O_4$, the valence of hydrogen is 1, of carbon 4, and of oxygen 2, since the structure is

$$\text{HO—C—C—OH}$$
$$\overset{\|}{O} \quad \overset{\|}{O}$$

If we assign an oxidation number of $+1$ to hydrogen, and -2 to oxygen, the oxidation number of carbon must be $+3$. The missing number results, of course, from the bond between the two carbon atoms. We assign one electron to each atom, thus eliminating this bond in our counting procedure. In a molecule such as propane, C_3H_8, if hydrogen is taken as $+1$, carbon must be $-2\frac{2}{3}$. In the molecule Fe_3O_4, the oxidation number of iron is $+2\frac{2}{3}$. Since this molecule may be thought of as comprising one molecule of FeO and one of Fe_2O_3, the oxidation number represents the average of the valences of the three iron atoms. This lack of identity of oxidation number and valence does not complicate, but actually simplifies, the process of balancing equations.

As previously mentioned, after oxidation numbers have been assigned to atoms in molecules on both sides of the equation, any changes are attributed to a loss or gain of electrons. For example, an increase of two units in an oxidation number means a loss of two electrons, or a decrease of three means a gain of three electrons. Then coefficients are inserted in the equation in order to make the number of electrons gained by the oxidizing agent equal to the number lost by the reducing agent. Once these "key numbers" are determined, the equation is balanced in the usual manner. It should be kept in mind that if the reaction is written in ionic form, the sum of the charges of ions on the left side of the equation should equal the sum of the charges on the right side.

The following are a few examples, illustrating the balancing of equations by this method.

EXAMPLE 1. Balance the following equation, determining the values of the coefficients a, b, c, d, e, f, and g.

$$a \text{ KMnO}_4 + b \text{ H}_2\text{C}_2\text{O}_4 + c \text{ H}_2\text{SO}_4 \rightleftarrows d \text{ K}_2\text{SO}_4 + e \text{ MnSO}_4 + f \text{ CO}_2 + g \text{ H}_2\text{O}$$

In KMnO_4, $O = -2$, and $4 \times -2 = -8$; $K = +1$. Thus, $-8 + 1 = -7$, and Mn must be $+7$ to make the net charge zero.

In $\text{H}_2\text{C}_2\text{O}_4$, $O = -2$, and $4 \times -2 = -8$; $H = +1$, and $2 \times +1 = +2$. Thus $-8 + 2 = -6$, and $2 \times C$ must be $+6$, or each $C = +3$.

None of the atoms in H_2SO_4, K_2SO_4, and H_2O undergoes changes in oxidation number.

In MnSO_4, $\text{SO}_4 = -2$, and $Mn = +2$.

In CO_2, $O = -2$, and $2 \times -2 = -4$. Thus $C = +4$.

Hence, the oxidation number of manganese changes from $+7$ to $+2$, a gain of five electrons. Since potassium permanganate contains one manganese atom, the potassium permanganate molecule gains five electrons. The oxidation number of carbon changes from $+3$ to $+4$, a loss of one electron. Since oxalic acid contains two carbon atoms, the oxalic acid molecule loses two electrons.

The key numbers are 2 and 5. Two molecules of potassium permanganate will gain ten electrons, and five molecules of oxalic acid will lose ten electrons. Hence, $a = 2$, $b = 5$. The other coefficients are easily found to be: $c = 3$, $d = 1$, $e = 2$, $f = 10$, and $g = 8$, making the balanced equation:

$$2 \text{ KMnO}_4 + 5 \text{ H}_2\text{C}_2\text{O}_4 + 3 \text{ H}_2\text{SO}_4 \rightleftarrows \text{K}_2\text{SO}_4 + 2 \text{ MnSO}_4 + 10 \text{ CO}_2 + 8 \text{ H}_2\text{O}$$

Had the equation been written in the ionic form, the same two key numbers would have been found. The balanced equation would then be

$$2 \text{ MnO}_4^- + 5 \text{ C}_2\text{O}_4^= + 16 \text{ H}^+ \rightleftarrows 2 \text{ Mn}^{++} + 10 \text{ CO}_2 + 8 \text{ H}_2\text{O}$$

Note that the net charge on each side of the equation is $+4$.

EXAMPLE 2. Balance the following equation, where M is some metal, and X some nonmetal:

$$a \text{ M}_3\text{X} + b \text{ HNO}_3 \rightleftarrows c \text{ M(NO}_3)_3 + d \text{ H}_3\text{XO}_4 + e \text{ NO} + f \text{ H}_2\text{O}$$

Since we do not know the identity of M or X, we cannot assign oxidation numbers to correspond to the valences of these atoms. This does not matter, however, so long as we make the net charge of M_3X equal to zero. Let us assign M a value of $+1$, and X a value of -3. On the right-hand side of the equation, $M = +3$ and $X = +5$. Hence, each M atom loses two electrons and each X atom loses 8. The M_3X molecule loses fourteen electrons, $(3 \times 2) + 8$. If we assigned both M and X values of zero, M would lose three electrons, X would lose five, and M_3X would again lose fourteen electrons, $(3 \times 3) + 5$.

There is one other point of interest in this equation. Note that nitrogen changes from $+5$ in nitric acid to $+2$ in nitric oxide, a gain of three electrons. The key numbers should then be $a = 3$, and $b = 14$. However, as soon as 3 is placed in front of M_3X, c must equal 9, thereby making 27 nitrate radicals where we have only 14 nitrogen atoms on the left side of the equation. These 27 nitrate radicals, in which the oxidation number of nitrogen did not change, must be added to the 14, in which the oxidation number did change, to make $b = 41$. The other numbers are then found to be: $c = 9$, $d = 3$, $e = 14$, and $f = 16$. Thus

$$3\ M_3X + 41\ HNO_3 \rightleftarrows 9\ M(NO_3)_3 + 3\ H_3XO_4 + 14\ NO + 16\ H_2O$$

Note that the problem of the extra nitrate radicals would not have arisen had the equation been written in partial ionic form:

$$3\ M_3X + 14\ NO_3^- + 41\ H^+ \rightleftarrows 9\ M^{3+} + 3\ H_3XO_4 + 14\ NO + 16\ H_2O$$

EXAMPLE 3. Balance the following equation for the disproportionation of manganate ion:

$$a\ MnO_4^- + b\ H_2O \rightleftarrows c\ MnO_2 + d\ MnO_4^- + e\ OH^-$$

In this reaction part of the manganese is oxidized to permanganate, and part is reduced to manganese dioxide. The oxidation numbers of manganese are as follows: In MnO_4^-, Mn $= +6$; in MnO_2, Mn $= +4$; in MnO_4^-, Mn $= +7$. Hence, manganese gains two electrons on being reduced to MnO_2, and loses one electron on being oxidized to MnO_4^-. Hence, if $a = 3$, $c = 1$, and $d = 2$, there will be two electrons gained and two electrons lost. The balanced equation is

$$3\ MnO_4^- + 2\ H_2O \rightleftarrows MnO_2 + 2\ MnO_4^- + 4\ OH^-$$

The net charge on each side of the equation is then -6.

Some chemists prefer to break a redox reaction into two "half-reactions," one for the oxidizing agent and one for the reducing agent. The number of electrons gained by the oxidizing agent is made the same as that lost by the reducing agent, and then the half-reactions are added. The following is an illustration.

EXAMPLE 4. Balance the equation

$$MnO_4^- + C_2O_4^- \rightleftarrows Mn^{++} + CO_2$$

adding water and hydrogen ion as needed. The reaction occurs in acid medium.
First treat the oxidizing agent:

$$MnO_4^- \rightleftarrows Mn^{++}$$

Water is added to the right to account for the oxygen:

$$MnO_4^- \rightleftarrows Mn^{++} + 4\ H_2O$$

H^+ is added to the left to balance the hydrogen:

$$MnO_4^- + 8\ H^+ \longrightarrow Mn^{++} + 4\ H_2O$$

The charge is balanced by placing 5 electrons on the left.

$$MnO_4^- + 8\ H^+ + 5\ e \longrightarrow Mn^{++} + 4\ H_2O \tag{1}$$

Second, treat the reducing agent:

$$C_2O_4^- \longrightarrow 2\ CO_2$$

This is now balanced except for charge. Add 2 electrons to the right:

$$C_2O_4^- \longrightarrow 2\ CO_2 + 2\ e \tag{2}$$

Multiply equation (1) by two and equation (2) by five, and add the two equations to give the final balanced equation:

$$2\ MnO_4^- + 5\ C_2O_4^= + 16\ H^+ \rightleftharpoons 2\ Mn^{++} + 10\ CO_2 + 8\ H_2O$$

Sometimes it is desired to show hydroxyl ions rather than hydrogen ions in the final equation. One simple way to do this is to proceed as above for acid media, then add sufficient hydroxyl ions to each side of the equation to completely combine with hydrogen ions. In the example above, 16 OH^- can be added to each side:

$$2\ MnO_4^- + 5\ C_2O_4^= + 16\ H^+ + 16\ OH^-$$
$$= 2\ Mn^{++} + 10\ CO_2 + 8\ H_2O + 16\ OH^-$$

On the left, hydrogen and hydroxyl ions form 16 molecules of H_2O and 8 of these cancel the 8 water molecules on the right-hand side. The final equation is then

$$2\ MnO_4^- + 5\ C_2O_4^= + 8\ H_2O = 2\ Mn^{++} + 10\ CO_2 + 16\ OH^-$$

6. Electrolysis

As previously mentioned, a substance may be determined by using the techniques of electrolysis to perform a separation or to cause some chemical change to take place. A classical example, which would be termed gravimetric, is the determination of copper, carried out by depositing the metal electrolytically on a previously weighed electrode. The increase in weight of the electrode gives the quantity of copper in the sample. The amount of a substance in solution may also be determined by measuring the quantity of electricity required to react with it completely. This method, usually classified as volumetric (or titrimetric), is called *coulometry*, since the number of coulombs is measured experimentally.

The quantity of electricity required to oxidize or reduce a given amount of substance electrolytically is given by Faraday's laws. Faraday's first law states that the weight of a substance produced at an electrode is directly proportional to the quantity of electricity passed through the cell. The second law states that the weights of different substances produced by the same quantity of electricity are proportional to the equivalent weights of the substances. The quantity of electricity that liberates one equivalent of any substance is called the *faraday*. One faraday is 96,500 *coulombs*. It will be recalled that one coulomb is obtained when a current of one ampere flows for one second. One faraday deposits one equivalent of silver (107.88 g), of copper (63.54/2 g), or of aluminum (26.97/3 g). It may be recalled that the faraday is the quantity of electricity in Avogadro's number of electrons; that is, 1.602×10^{-19} coul/electron $\times 6.023 \times 10^{23}$ electrons = 96,500 coul.

The following problems illustrate calculations involving these quantities:

PROBLEM 1. A 1.200-g sample containing lead was dissolved and the lead oxidized electrolytically, depositing it on the anode as PbO_2.

$$Pb^{++} + 2\,H_2O \rightleftharpoons PbO_2 + 4\,H^+ + 2\,e$$

A constant current of 0.500 amp was employed and the PbO_2 weighed 0.2309 g.

(a) Calculate the percentage of lead in the sample.

$$\frac{0.2309 \times Pb/PbO_2}{1.200} \times 100 = 16.67\% \ Pb$$

(b) How many minutes were required to deposit the PbO_2?

Since 2 electrons are required to produce 1 PbO_2, the equivalent weight of PbO_2 is one-half the molecular weight. Hence,

$$meq\ PbO_2 = \frac{230.9\ mg}{(239.2/2)\ mg/meq} = 1.931$$

Since 1 eq = 96,500 coul, 1 meq = 96.5 coul. And

$$96.5\ \frac{coul}{meq} \times 1.931\ meq = 186.3\ coul\ required$$

Hence,

$$\frac{186.3\ coul}{0.500\ coul/sec} = 372.6\ sec,\ or\ 6.21\ min$$

PROBLEM 2. If a time of 16.1 min is required to deposit the copper electrolytically from 100 ml of solution using a constant current of 2.00 amp, what is the molarity of the copper solution? The reaction is

$$Cu^{++} + 2\,e \rightleftharpoons Cu$$

The meq of copper can be calculated as follows:

$$\frac{16.1\ min \times 60\ sec/min \times 2.00\ coul/sec}{96.5\ coul/meq} = 20.0\ meq$$

Since 1 mmol Cu = 2 meq, there must be 10.0 mmol of copper. Hence the concentration is

$$\frac{10.0\ mmol}{100\ ml} = 0.100\text{-}M$$

REFERENCES

1. M. J. Sienko, *Stoichiometry and Structure*, W. A. Benjamin, Inc., New York, 1964.
2. S. W. Benson, *Chemical Calculations*, 2nd Ed., John Wiley & Sons, Inc., New York, 1963.
3. C. Pierce and R. N. Smith, *General Chemistry Workbook*, 3rd Ed., W. H. Freeman and Co., San Francisco, 1965.
4. C. B. Kremer and J. S. Arents, *Theory and Problems of Modern General Chemistry*, Thomas Y. Crowell Co., New York, 1965.

5. C. J. Nyman and G. B. King, *Problems for General Chemistry and Qualitative Analysis*, John Wiley & Sons, Inc., New York, 1966.

QUESTIONS

1. Explain the advantages of molar and equivalent methods of expressing concentration over physical methods, such as weight per cent.

2. What are the equivalent weights of the following anhydrides? N_2O_5, CaO, Cl_2O, and K_2O.

3. Explain the effect that the following errors would have on the standardization of a sodium hydroxide solution with pure potassium acid phthalate (KHP). Would the error cause the normality to be high or low, or would it have no effect?

    (a) The base buret is read too quickly, not allowing time for drainage.

    (b) The initial reading on the base buret is recorded as 2.10 ml when it is actually 1.90 ml.

    (c) The weight of KHP is recorded as 0.6324 g when it is actually 0.6234 g.

    (d) The sample is dissolved in 100 ml of water although the directions call for only 50 ml.

4. Repeat question 3 for the case of the analysis of an impure sample of KHP by titration with standard base. Explain the effects of the errors on the percentage purity obtained.

5. Balance the following equations, adding H_2O and/or H^+ where needed. Where basic medium is indicated, show OH^- ions rather than H^+ ions.

$$MnO_4^- + H_2S \rightleftarrows Mn^{++} + S$$
$$H_2O_2 + MnO_4^- + H^+ \rightleftarrows Mn^{++} + O_2 + H_2O$$
$$SO_3^= + Br_2 \rightleftarrows SO_4^= + Br^-$$
$$I_2 + OH^- \rightleftarrows IO_3^- + I^- + H_2O$$
$$Al + NO_3^- \rightleftarrows AlO_2^- + NH_3 \text{ (basic medium)}$$
$$Mn^{++} + BiO_3^- \rightleftarrows MnO_4^- + Bi^{3+}$$
$$MnO_4^- + Sn^{++} \rightleftarrows MnO_2 + SnO_3^= \text{ (basic medium)}$$
$$VO^{++} + MnO_4^- \rightleftarrows VO_3^- + Mn^{++}$$
$$HO_2^- + CrO_2^- \rightleftarrows CrO_4^= \text{ (basic medium)}$$
$$FeAsS + ClO_2 \rightleftarrows Fe^{3+} + AsO_4^{3-} + SO_4^= + Cl^-$$
$$NH_4OH + I_2 \rightleftarrows NI_3 + NH_4I + H_2O$$
$$SbH_3 + Cl_2O + H_2O \rightleftarrows H_4Sb_2O_7 + HCl$$
$$C_7H_8O + Cr_2O_7^= \rightleftarrows C_7H_8O_2 + Cr^{3+}$$
$$Mn^{++} + MnO_4^- + F^- \rightleftarrows MnF_5^=$$
$$FeS + NO_3^- \rightleftarrows Fe^{3+} + NO_2 + S$$
$$UO_5^= + H^+ \rightleftarrows UO_2^{++} + O_2 + H_2O$$
$$Ag_3AsO_4 + Zn + H^+ \rightleftarrows AsH_3 + Zn^{++} + Ag + H_2O$$
$$K_2NaCo(NO_2)_6 + MnO_4^- + H^+ \rightleftarrows$$
$$K^+ + Na^+ + Co^{++} + NO_3^- + Mn^{++} + H_2O$$
$$CrO_2Cl_2 + H_2O \rightleftarrows CrO_4^= + H^+ + Cl^-$$
$$(NH_4)_3P(Mo_3O_{10})_4 + Zn + H^+ \rightleftarrows Mo^{3+} + NH_4^+ + H_3PO_4 + Zn^{++} + H_2O$$

PROBLEMS

(*Note:* For redox agents the oxidized and reduced form are given at the end of the problem. For example, MnO_4^- — Mn^{++} means that permanganate was reduced to manganous ion in the reaction about which the calculation is to be made.)

1. (a) Calculate the molarity of each of the following solutions:
   (1) 8.00 g NaOH in 0.125 l of solution.
   (2) 0.630 g $H_2C_2O_4 \cdot 2\ H_2O$ in 400 ml solution.
   (3) 14.02 g of CaO in 2.00 l solution.
   (4) 24.5 mg H_2SO_4 in 20.0 ml solution.
   (5) 34.06 g NH_3 in 500 ml solution.
   (b) Calculate the normality of each of the above solutions assuming:
   $H_2C_2O_4 \cdot 2\ H_2O = 2\ H^+$; $CaO = 2\ H^+$; $H_2SO_4 = 2\ H^+$; NH_3 and $NaOH = 1\ H^+$.

2. (a) Calculate the molarity of each of the following solutions:
   (1) 7.40 g $KMnO_4$ in 4.00 l solution.
   (2) 147.1 mg $K_2Cr_2O_7$ in 10.00 ml solution.
   (3) 6.512 g KCN in 2.000 l solution.
   (4) 0.8277 g $Na_2S_2O_3 \cdot 5\ H_2O$ in 20.00 ml solution.
   (b) Calculate the normality of each of the above solutions if the reactants and products are as follows: MnO_4^- — Mn^{++}; $Cr_2O_7^=$ — Cr^{3+}; $S_2O_3^=$ — $S_4O_6^=$; CN^- — $Ag(CN)_2^-$.

3. Calculate the molarity of each of the following solutions:
   (a) HCl, density 1.098 g/ml, containing 20.0% HCl by weight.
   (b) NH_4OH, density 0.952 g/ml, containing 12.1% NH_3 by weight.
   (c) $HClO_4$, density 1.68, containing 71% $HClO_4$ by weight.
   (d) H_2SO_4, density 1.28, containing 30.2% SO_3 by weight.

4. Express the titer of the following solutions in mg/ml:
   (a) 0.120-N HCl in terms of BaO, Na_2O, $Ba(OH)_2$, and NH_3.
   (b) 0.0850-N NaOH in terms of HCl, H_2SO_4, $HClO_4$, $KH(IO_3)_2$, and acetic acid ($HC_2H_3O_2$).
   (c) 0.100-M $KMnO_4$ in terms of FeO, Fe_2O_3, and As_2O_3. Reactions: MnO_4^- — Mn^{++}; Fe^{++} — Fe^{3+}; AsO_3^{3-} — AsO_4^{3-}.
   (d) 0.150-M $Na_2C_2O_4$ in terms of $KMnO_4$ and $K_2Cr_2O_7$. Reactions: MnO_4^- — Mn^{++}; $C_2O_4^=$ — CO_2; $Cr_2O_7^=$ — Cr^{3+}.

5. The KCN titer of a silver nitrate solution is 19.54 mg/ml [for formation of $Ag(CN)_2^-$]. Calculate (a) the $BaCl_2 \cdot 2\ H_2O$ titer of the silver nitrate, and (b) the weight of sample that should be taken for analysis so that the volume of silver nitrate used equals the percentage of chloride in the sample.

6. (a) 125.0 ml of a solution is diluted to 200.0 ml and the normality of the latter solution is found to be 0.2500. What is the normality of the original solution?
   (b) What volume of water should be added to 600 ml of a 0.150-N solution to make the normality 0.100?
   (c) What volume of 0.7000-N HCl should be added to 200 ml of 0.400-N HCl to make the resulting solution 0.500-N?

(d) 60.0 ml of 0.120-N HCl is mixed with 40.0 ml of 0.300-N NaOH. Is the resulting solution acidic or basic? Calculate the normality.

7. From the following data calculate the normalities of the acid and base solutions:

Weight of potassium acid phthalate (99.9% pure)	0.7246 g
Volume of base used	40.23 ml
Volume of acid (back-titration)	1.38 ml
1.000 ml acid = 0.962 ml base	

8. A sample of pure iron wire weighing 0.2453 g is dissolved in hydrochloric acid. The iron is reduced to the ferrous state and titrated with potassium dichromate in acid medium, 41.34 ml of dichromate being required. Calculate the normality of the dichromate solution. The reaction (unbalanced) is

$$Fe^{++} + Cr_2O_7^= + H^+ \rightleftharpoons Fe^{3+} + Cr^{3+} + H_2O$$

9. It is found that 25.00 ml of a solution containing Ni^{++} is required to react with 0.5210 g of pure KCN, according to the equation

$$Ni^{++} + 4\ CN^- \rightleftharpoons Ni(CN)_4^=$$

Calculate the molarity of the nickel solution.

10. A 2.035-g sample of an impure acid required 39.43 ml of 0.0992-N base for titration. In back-titration, 1.34 ml of acid was used. 1.000 ml base = 1.018 ml acid. Calculate the percentage purity as (a) KHP, (b) $H_2C_2O_4$, (c) $H_2C_2O_4 \cdot 2\ H_2O$. Oxalic acid furnished two hydrogen ions.

11. In a Kjeldahl analysis for nitrogen the element is converted into NH_3 which is then distilled into a measured volume of standard acid. Excess acid is titrated with standard base. If a 1.325-g sample of a fertilizer containing 5.20% nitrogen was analyzed and the NH_3 distilled into 50.00 ml of 0.2015-N H_2SO_4, what volume of 0.1985-N NaOH was required for back-titration?

12. A 2.250-g sample of an acid having an equivalent weight of 75.00 was titrated with standard base. It was found that the percentage purity was exactly 100 times the normality of the base. What volume of base was used in the titration?

13. If 10.00 ml of vinegar of density 1.055 g/ml requires 39.82 ml of 0.2550-N base for titration, calculate the percentage by weight of acetic acid in the sample.

14. A sample of KHP which is about 62% pure is analyzed by adding 50 ml of 0.110-N NaOH and back-titrating with 0.125-N HCl. What is the largest weight of sample that can be taken for analysis so that no more than 10.0 ml of acid is used in back-titration?

15. About what size sample of the following should be taken for analysis in order that about 40 ml of a 0.10-N reagent is required for titration?
   (a) Pure KHP.
   (b) Pure Na_2CO_3.
   (c) 25% pure KHP.
   (d) 40% $Na_2C_2O_4$.
   (e) Arsenic ore containing 25% As_2O_3.
Reactions: $CO_3^= - H_2CO_3$; $C_2O_4^= - CO_2$; $AsO_3^{3-} - AsO_4^{3-}$.

16. (a) If 1.0-N base solution were employed for titration, what size sample containing about 25% KHP should be taken for analysis in order to use about 30 ml of titrant?

(b) Repeat the calculation for 0.010-N titrant. Suggest why titrants are usually about 0.1 to 0.2-N.

17. An instructor is preparing some unknowns for titration with standard base. He has 100 g of inert material and wishes to add a sufficient quantity of sulfamic acid so that when the samples are analyzed and the percentage calculated as potassium acid phthalate, the students will find about 30% KHP. How many grams of sulfamic acid should be added to the 100 g of inert material? Sulfamic acid is HSO_3NH_2, with one replaceable hydrogen.

18. A sample contains about 25% of 2 $Fe_2O_3 \cdot 3\ H_2O$ and about 15% of Fe_3O_4. What is the largest weight of sample that can be taken for analysis for iron without having to refill a 50 ml buret with 0.12-N oxidizing agent? The sample is dissolved in acid, all iron reduced to Fe^{++} which is then oxidized to Fe^{3+} during the titration.

19. Complete the following blanks so that the quantities of the two substances in each case are chemically equivalent.

(a) 98.92 mg As_2O_3 = _____ ml of 0.0500-N I_2.

(b) 327 mg $KHC_2O_4 \cdot H_2C_2O_4$ = _____ ml 0.150-N $KMnO_4$.

(c) 50.0 ml of 0.0200-M $K_2Cr_2O_7$ = _____ mg $Na_2C_2O_4$.

(d) 30.0 ml of 0.100-M $C_2O_4^=$ = _____ ml of 0.100-M MnO_4^-.

Reactants and products are listed below:

$$AsO_3^{3-} - AsO_4^{3-};\ I_2 - I^-;\ C_2O_4^= - CO_2;\ MnO_4^- - Mn^{++};\ Cr_2O_7^= - Cr^{3+}.$$

20. A student reported that a sample contained 10.00% NaOH. Actually the sample contained 30.00% of another base, B. What is the equivalent weight of B?

21. If a 9.432-g sample of pure $K_2Cr_2O_7$ is dissolved in exactly 1.000 l of solution, how many milliliters of this solution are required to titrate a sample of iron ore weighing 0.9634 g and containing 44.32% Fe_2O_3? Reactions: $Cr_2O_7^= - Cr^{3+}$; $Fe^{++} - Fe^{3+}$.

22. A sample of the ore pyrolusite (MnO_2) is reported to contain 6.00% oxygen. Calculate the percentage as (a) manganese, (b) manganese dioxide. Reactions: $O_2 - O^=$; $MnO_2 - Mn^{++}$.

23. Calculate the volume of 0.10-M stannous chloride required to reduce the iron in a 0.60-g sample of an ore that contains 25% goethite, $Fe_2O_3 \cdot H_2O$. Reactions: $Sn^{++} - Sn^{4+}$; $Fe^{++} - Fe^{3+}$.

24. To a sample of pyrolusite weighing 0.4800 g and containing 12.00% oxygen was added 1.000 g of pure $Na_2C_2O_4$. After digestion of the sample in acid solution, the excess oxalate was titrated with 0.1150-N $KMnO_4$. What volume was required? Reactions: $O_2 - O^=$; $C_2O_4^= - CO_2$; $MnO_4^- - Mn^{++}$.

25. A sample of iron ore weighing 0.720 g and containing 30.0% Fe_2O_3 is dissolved and the iron is reduced by the addition of 30.00 ml of 0.0500-M $SnCl_2$. The excess $SnCl_2$ is oxidized with 0.0500-M $HgCl_2$. How many milliliters of the latter solution are required? Reactions: $Fe^{++} - Fe^{3+}$; $Sn^{++} - Sn^{4+}$; $HgCl_2 - Hg_2Cl_2$.

26. What volume of 0.120-N $KMnO_4$ is required to react in acid media with 3.00 ml of H_2O_2 that has a density of 1.01 g/ml and contains 3.00% H_2O_2. Reactions: $MnO_4^- - Mn^{++}$; $H_2O_2 - O_2$.

27. If the reaction in the preceding problem is carried out and the liberated oxygen collected, what volume would it occupy at standard temperature and pressure?

28. What should be the normality of the permanganate in the previous two problems if one desired that the volume of oxygen collected (STP) be exactly twice the volume of permanganate used in the reaction?

29. A 0.5000-g sample containing MnO_2 is treated with concentrated HCl liberating Cl_2. The chlorine is passed into a solution of KI and 28.64 ml of 0.1038-N $Na_2S_2O_3$ solution are required to titrate the liberated I_2. Calculate (a) the percentage of MnO_2 in the sample, and (b) the volume occupied by the chlorine had it been collected at STP. Reactions: $MnO_2 - Mn^{++}$; $Cl^- - Cl_2$; $I^- - I_2$; $Na_2S_2O_3 - Na_2S_4O_6$.

30. A 1.000-g sample of a substance containing 20.00% PbO was dissolved and the lead precipitated as $PbCrO_4$. The $PbCrO_4$ was filtered and dissolved in acid. Excess KI was added and the chromate oxidized the iodide to iodine. How many milliliters of 0.0930-N $Na_2S_2O_3$ solution were required to titrate the I_2? Reactions: $CrO_4^= - Cr^{3+}$; $I^- - I_2$; $Na_2S_2O_3 - Na_2S_4O_6$.

31. A student analyzed an arsenic sample by titration with standard I_2 solution (iodimetry). He obtained a value of 24.55% As_2O_3, the correct answer being 24.74%. Assuming that the only error made was that the student used the wrong atomic weight for arsenic when he computed the equivalent weight of As_2O_3, what value did he use for the atomic weight of arsenic? Reactions: $AsO_3^{3-} - AsO_4^{3-}$; $I_2 - I^-$.

32. The aluminum in a 0.2000-g sample was precipitated with 8-hydroxyquinoline and the precipitate was filtered and dissolved in acid. To this solution was added 25.00 ml of 0.0500-M $KBrO_3$ and 2 g of KBr. After reaction of bromine with 8-hydroxyquinoline, 2 g of KI were added and the liberated I_2 titrated with 25.00 ml of 0.1000-N $Na_2S_2O_3$. (See page 11 for reactions.) Calculate the percentage of Al_2O_3 in the sample.

33. A permanganate solution was standardized against $Na_2C_2O_4$ and found to have a normality N. (Reactions: $MnO_4^- - Mn^{++}$; $C_2O_4^= - CO_2$.) A volume, X ml, of this permanganate was added to an excess of manganous sulfate, the following reaction occurring (unbalanced):

$$MnO_4^- + Mn^{++} + H_2O \rightleftharpoons MnO_2 + H^+$$

Set up an expression for calculating the volume, V ml, of NaOH of normality B required to neutralize the acid produced by the reaction.

34. The hydrogen sulfide in a gas sample is absorbed in water and titrated with 25.00 ml of 0.1200-N I_2 solution. What volume did the H_2S occupy as a gas at STP? Reactions: $H_2S - S$; $I_2 - I^-$.

35. A sample consisting of only $Na_2C_2O_4$ and KHC_2O_4 required three times the volume of 0.1000-N oxidizing agent for titration as of 0.1000-N base (same size sample in each case). Calculate the percentage of each salt in the mixture. Reaction: $C_2O_4^= - CO_2$.

36. Iodate ion reacts with iodide ion in acid solution as given below; iodine can be titrated with thiosulfate as indicated. Balance the equations.

$$IO_3^- + I^- + H^+ \rightleftharpoons I_2 + H_2O$$

$$I_2 + S_2O_3^= \rightleftharpoons I^- + S_4O_6^=$$

Exactly 50.00 ml of a solution of KIO_3 was acidified and excess KI added. The liberated iodine required 25.00 ml of a 0.3000-N solution of the thiosulfate for titration. What was the molarity of the iodate solution?

37. A sample of impure KI was analyzed using the reactions in the previous problem. The sample weighing 0.5810 g was dissolved in water, the solution acidified, and then 15.00 ml of 0.0500-M KIO_3 was added. The iodine liberated was boiled off and the solution cooled. An excess of pure KI was added to react with the unused KIO_3. The iodine liberated this time was titrated using 24.00 ml of 0.1000-N thiosulfate. Calculate the percentage of KI in the sample.

38. In the previous problem how many milliliters of the same thiosulfate solution would have been required to titrate the iodine that was boiled off?

39. A sample was made by mixing 0.2500 g of pure KCl and 0.4500 g of a salt assumed to be pure $BaCl_2 \cdot 2\ H_2O$. The mixture was dissolved in water and titrated with 0.1000-M $AgNO_3$, 72.30 ml being required instead of the anticipated volume.

(a) Calculate the volume that should have been required.

(b) Assuming the discrepancy was caused by partial dehydration to $BaCl_2$, what percentage by weight of the salt was $BaCl_2$?

40. Silver ion reacts with cyanide ion as follows:

$$Ag^+ + 2\ CN^- \rightleftharpoons Ag(CN)_2^-$$

The KCN titer of a silver nitrate solution is 12.50 mg/ml. Calculate (a) the $BaCl_2$ titer and (b) the weight of sample which should be taken for analysis so that the volume of silver nitrate equals the percentage of chloride in the sample.

41. In a gravimetric determination of chloride in a sample the chloride is precipitated as AgCl. The precipitate of AgCl weighed exactly twice as much as the sample itself. Another portion of the same sample weighing 0.5000 g is titrated with 0.2100-M $AgNO_3$. How many milliliters are required?

42. The chloride in a sample is to be determined gravimetrically by precipitation and weighing AgCl. What weight in grams of sample should be taken so that the percentage of chloride is obtained by simply multiplying the weight of AgCl precipitate by 10?

43. Potassium acid phthalate is to be determined in a sample by titration with standard base. What size sample should be taken so that the volume of 0.1104-N NaOH used equals the percentage of KHP in the sample?

44. Sodium hydroxide is to be determined by titration with standard acid. What should be the normality of the acid in order that twice the volume used for titration of a 0.500-g sample equals the percentage NaOH in the sample?

45. The KHP titer of an NaOH solution is T, mg/ml. Show that if a sample containing KHP weighing $100\,T$ is titrated with the NaOH, the volume of titrant equals the percentage KHP in the sample.

46. Iron is determined by titration with standard $KMnO_4$ solution. What should be the normality of the permanganate so that the volume of titrant divided by two gives the percentage of FeO in a 1.000-g sample? Reactions: $MnO_4^- - Mn^{++}$; $Fe^{++} - Fe^{3+}$.

47. The calcium in a 0.8532-g sample is precipitated as CaC_2O_4 and then ignited to $CaCO_3$. If the ignited carbonate weighs 0.3484 g, calculate the percentage of CaO in the sample.

48. A certain sample containing lead is dissolved and the lead precipitated as $PbSO_4$. The original sample weighed 0.5524 g and the dry $PbSO_4$ weighed 0.4425 g. Calculate the percentage of lead as Pb_3O_4 in the sample.

49. An iron ore sample weighing 0.5038 g is dissolved, the iron oxidized to Fe^{3+} and then precipitated as $Fe(OH)_3$. The hydroxide is ignited to Fe_2O_3 which weighs 0.2372 g. Calculate the percentage of iron in the ore as (a) Fe, (b) FeO, (c) Fe_2O_3, and (d) Fe_3O_4.

50. Iron is determined in a sample by precipitation of $Fe(OH)_3$ and ignition to Fe_2O_3. What weight of sample should be taken for analysis so that each 10.0 mg of Fe_2O_3 represents 1.00% Fe in the sample?

51. Tin is determined in a sample by precipitation of the hydrated oxide and ignition to SnO_2. What weight of sample should be taken for analysis so that one-half the weight in milligrams of SnO_2 obtained shall equal twice the percentage of Sn in the sample?

52. The sodium and potassium in a sample weighing 0.9250 g are converted into NaCl and KCl salts. The chloride mixture weighs 0.6065 g. The chlorides are then converted into Na_2SO_4 and K_2SO_4, this mixture weighing 0.7190 g. Calculate the percentages of Na_2O and K_2O in the original sample.

53. A sample containing only $CaCO_3$ and $MgCO_3$ is ignited to CaO and MgO. The ignited sample weighs exactly half as much as the original. Calculate the percentages of $CaCO_3$, and $MgCO_3$ in the sample.

54. A student determined calcium in a limestone sample by precipitating CaC_2O_4 and igniting it to CaO. He reported 40.00% was CaO where the actual value was 39.12. If the error was caused by insufficient ignition, leaving some $CaCO_3$ in the final precipitate, what percentage of this final precipitate was $CaCO_3$?

55. A sample containing only $CaSO_4$ and $BaSO_4$ contains three times the weight of the element calcium as of the element barium. Calculate the percentage of $CaSO_4$ in the sample.

56. A sample containing only $CaCO_3$ and $BaCO_3$ is heated and converted into the oxides and CO_2. The CO_2 is collected and it is noted that the volume in milliliters (STP) is exactly one-fifth the number of milligrams of sample. What percentage of the sample is $BaCO_3$?

57. A 0.500-g sample that contains both KCl and KBr gives a precipitate of AgCl and AgBr that weighs 0.4747 g. Another sample (same size) is titrated and requires 29.46 ml of 0.1014-N $AgNO_3$ for titration.

(a) Calculate the percentages of KBr and KCl in the sample.

(b) If an error was made in weighing the precipitate of AgCl and AgBr and this was recorded as 0.4774 g, what percentages would be obtained?

58. Repeat the preceding problem for the same data except that the sample contains KCl and KI. Compare the effects of the weighing error in the two cases. Can you relate it to the difference in molecular weights of the two precipitates?

59. Calculate the time (minutes) required, assuming 100% current efficiency, to deposit the following by electrolysis:

(a) Silver from 200 ml of 0.060-M Ag^+, current of 0.40 amp.

(b) Aluminum from 80 ml of 0.25-M Al^{3+}, current of 2.0 amp.

(c) Lead from 100 ml of 0.12-M Pb^{++}, current of 0.50 amp, lead being deposited on the anode as PbO_2.

60. Calculate the time required, assuming 100% current efficiency, to liberate (a) 336 ml H_2 (STP), current 3.0 amp, (b) 28 liters of O_2 (STP), current of 8.0 amp.

61. Calculate the number of electrons required (a) to deposit 1.00 mg of Ag from a $AgNO_3$ solution, (b) to liberate 1.00 ml of Cl_2 (STP) from a solution containing Cl^-.

62. A solution of copper sulfate is electrolyzed, liberating copper at the cathode and oxygen at the anode; 40 ml of 0.12-N NaOH was required to neutralize the acid produced during the electrolysis.

(a) What weight of copper was deposited on the cathode?

(b) If 10 min were required for the electrolysis, what was the average current used?

chapter 3

Errors and the Treatment of Analytical Data

INTRODUCTION

In an experimental science such as chemistry, much effort is expended in gathering data, and as chemistry has developed into a modern science, most of the data have become quantitative, i.e., they derive from measurements. When any scientific measurement is performed, it is necessary to consider the fact that an error has been made, and it is important to develop the ability to evaluate data, learning to draw justified conclusions while rejecting interpretations that are unwarranted because of limitations in the measurements. Although analytical chemists in particular like to emphasize the techniques by which data may be evaluated, it is clear that any chemist may enhance his competence by learning methods which are more reliable than intuition alone in assessing the significance of experimental results. The methods which are most suitable for the treatment of analytical data are powerful, general tools which may be used in many other scientific situations.

Most of the techniques which we shall consider are based upon statistical concepts. There is increasing awareness that statistical methods are efficient in planning experiments that will yield the most information from the fewest measurements and in "boiling down" data so that their significance is concisely presented. Statistics, on the other hand, should not be expected to lessen the necessity of obtaining good measurements, and statistical methods are most powerful when applied to good data.

Statistics and the theory of probability represent an important branch of mathematics which possesses a logical and rigorous structure. Although chemists may profit from study in this field, it is impossible in this textbook to examine the foundations of probability theory and to derive their consequences. We must here accept the conclusions of the mathematicians largely on faith, and then attempt to see how they may be useful to chemists. We may hope to learn how our intuitive judgments of data may be validated by quantitative expressions of their probable reliability, and even what the term "reliability" means in connection with measurements of quantities that are actually unknown. We shall see how sets of data may be compared to learn whether they are *really* different or whether an apparent difference could be attributable, not to an assignable cause, but to chance alone. A convenient technique will be described for "keeping track" of repetitive measurements so that correctives can be applied if they begin to wander beyond acceptable deviations. We shall see how errors are propagated through a series of experimental steps and calculations. The student should emerge from this study with a heightened skepticism of data which is moderated by an increased confidence in his ability to draw justified conclusions.

ERRORS

The term *error* as used here refers to the numerical difference between a measured value and the true value. The *true value* of any quantity is really a philosophical abstraction, something that man is not destined to know, although scientists generally feel that there is such a thing and believe that they may approach it more and more closely as their measurements become increasingly refined. In analytical chemistry, it is customary to act as though the true value of a quantity were known when it is believed that the uncertainty in the value is less than the uncertainty in something else with which it is being compared. For example, the percentage composition of a standard sample certified by the National Bureau of Standards may be treated as correct in evaluating a new analytical method; differences between the standard values and the results obtained by the new method are then treated as errors in the latter. Values which we are willing to treat as *true* are generally arrived at by a variety of methods whose limitations and pitfalls are sufficiently different that agreement among them cannot reasonably be ascribed to coincidence. Even so, it is well to remain skeptical about standard, accepted, or certified values, because they stem from experimental measurements performed by human, albeit expert, hands.

Determinate errors

Errors which can, at least in principle, be ascribed to definite causes are termed *determinate* or *systematic* errors. A given determinate error is generally unidirectional with respect to the true value, in contrast to indeterminate errors, discussed below, which lead to both high and low results with equal probability. Determinate errors are often reproducible, and in many cases they can be predicted by a person who thoroughly understands all the aspects of the measurement. Examples of sources of determinate errors are: a corroded weight, a poorly calibrated buret, an impurity in a reagent, an appreciable solubility of a precipitate, a side reaction in a titration, and heating a sample at too high a temperature

Determinate errors have been classified as *methodic, operative,* and *instrumental* in accordance with their origin in (a) the method of analysis as it reflects the properties of the chemical systems involved, (b) ineptitude of the experimenter, and (c) failure of measuring devices to perform in accordance with required standards.[1] Frequently the source of an error may lie in more than one of these categories. For example, some error may always be expected in weighing a hygroscopic substance, but it may be increased if the analyst has poor balance technique; the environment outside the system may influence the error, as, for example, in the effect of humidity upon the error in weighing a hygroscopic substance.

Constant errors. Sometimes the magnitude of a determinate error is nearly constant in a series of analyses, regardless of the size of the sample. This may be the case, for example, with an indicator blank that is not corrected for in a series of titrations. Some writers have used the term *additive* for this type of error. The significance of a constant error generally decreases as the size of the sample increases, since usually we are not so interested in the absolute value of an error as in its value relative to the magnitude of the measured quantity. For example, a constant end point error of 0.1 ml in a series of titrations represents a relative error of 10% for a sample requiring 1 ml of titrant, but only 0.2% if 50 ml of titrant is used.

Proportional errors. The absolute value of this type of error varies with sample size in such a way that the relative error remains constant. A sub-

[1] E. B. Sandell, "Errors in Chemical Analysis," Chapter 2 in I. M. Kolthoff and P. J. Elving, Eds., *Treatise on Analytical Chemistry*, Part I, Vol. 1, Interscience Publishers, Inc., New York, 1959.

stance that interferes in an analytical method may lead to such an error if present in the sample. For example, in the iodometric determination of an oxidant like chlorate, another oxidizing agent such as iodate or bromate would cause high results if its presence were unsuspected and not corrected for. Taking a larger sample would increase the absolute error, but the relative error would remain constant provided the sample were homogeneous. Errors may be encountered which vary with the size of the sample but not in a strictly linear fashion. Many writers use the term "proportional" for these also, although of course it is not strictly correct for such cases.

Data obtained a number of years ago by Benedetti-Pichler[2] are often quoted to illustrate the interplay of constant and proportional errors and to suggest how they may be distinguished. The ideas apply as well to modern measurements of a much more sophisticated type. The data are given in Table 3.1. Samples of potassium alum were dissolved and acidified with

		DETERMINATION OF ALUMINUM (as Al_2O_3) IN POTASSIUM ALUM†				Table 3.1
$KAl(SO_4)_2$ $\cdot 12\ H_2O$ taken, g	Al_2O_3 taken, g	Al_2O_3 found using stock NH_3, g	Differ- ence, g	Al_2O_3 found using distilled NH_3, g	Differ- ence, g	
1.0000	0.1077	0.1288	0.0211	0.1087	0.0010	
2.0000	0.2154	0.2384	0.0230	0.2178	0.0024	
3.0000	0.3231	0.3489	0.0258	0.3258	0.0027	
4.0000	0.4308	0.4588	0.0280	0.4352	0.0044	

† See reference 2.

proper amounts of hydrochloric acid so that the quantity of ammonia required to precipitate hydrous aluminum oxide was nearly constant. In one set of experiments, ammonia from a stock bottle was used; in the other set, freshly distilled ammonia. In the former case, it is seen that the errors were nearly constant; this was attributed to the fact that coprecipitation of silicic acid, originating from the attack of the old ammonia solution on the glass bottle, was constant because the same volume of ammonia solution was used in each case. In the latter experiments, silicic acid was absent, and the errors, now much smaller, were much more nearly proportional to sample size. These errors were attributed to the presence of water in the ignited precipitate, the quantity of water retained depending upon the quantity of alumina and hence upon sample size. In evaluating a new analytical method, information about the type of errors present and sometimes clues pointing toward their minimization may be obtained simply by varying the size of the sample.

[2] A. A. Benedetti-Pichler, *Ind. Eng. Chem.*, Anal. Ed., **8**, 373 (1936).

Indeterminate errors

If a measurement is sufficiently coarse, repetition will yield exactly the same result each time. For example, in weighing a 50-g object to the nearest gram with a good balance, only by extreme negligence could a person obtain different values or a group of people fail to agree. The only reasonable errors in such a measurement would be determinate ones, such as a seriously defective weight. On the other hand, any measurement can be refined to the point where it is mere coincidence if replicates agree to the last recorded digit. Sooner or later, the point is approached where unpredictable and imperceptible factors introduce what appear to be random fluctuations in the measured quantity. In some cases, it may be possible to specify definite variables that are beyond control near the performance limit of an instrument: noise and drift in an electronic circuit, vibrations in a building caused by passing traffic, temperature variations, and the like. Often the inability of the eye to detect slight changes in a read-out device may be invoked as a source of error. To be sure, variations which a slipshod person considers random may appear obvious and controllable to a careful onlooker, but nevertheless the point must be reached where anyone, however meticulous, will encounter random errors which he cannot further reduce. These errors are classified as *indeterminate*.

It is tempting at first glance to retreat from indeterminate errors simply by performing coarser measurements. After backing off to the point where scatter in the data ceases to exist, an observer will obtain exactly the same result each time, and superficially this seems as good as recording an additional digit which varies from one time to the next. But this withdrawal from the challenge to push measurements as far as possible is unacceptable to most scientists. More cogent, however, is the fact that the average of a number of fine observations with random scatter is more precise than coarser data which agree perfectly. Data that exhibit random scatter may be subjected to an analysis that does attach significance to the last recorded digit, as we shall see below.

Accuracy and precision

The terms *accuracy* and *precision*, often used synonymously in ordinary discourse, should be carefully distinguished in connection with scientific data. An accurate result is one that agrees closely with the true value of a measured quantity. The comparison is usually made on the basis of an inverse measure of the accuracy, viz., the error (the smaller the error, the greater the accuracy). The error is most frequently expressed relative to the size of the measured quantity, for example, in per cent or in parts per thousand. In view of the nebulous nature of true values, it is clear that accuracy cannot often be ascertained. Precision, on the other hand, refers to the agreement among a group of experimental results, and implies nothing about their relation to the true value. Precise values may well be inaccurate, since an error causing deviation from the true value may affect all of the measurements equally and hence not impair their precision. A determinate error which leads to inaccuracy may or may not affect precision, depending upon how nearly constant it remains throughout a series of measurements.

DISTRIBUTION OF RANDOM ERRORS

After the search for determinate errors has been carried as far as possible and all precautions taken and corrections applied, the remaining fluctuations in the data are found to be random in nature. Results that scatter in a random fashion are best treated by the powerful techniques of statistics; it will now be our goal to show how these techniques are applied and what information they furnish beyond what may be seen by simply inspecting the data.

Frequency distributions

Table 3.2 contains some actual data obtained by a person who prepared sixty replicate colored solutions and measured their absorbance values with

INDIVIDUAL VALUES, UNORGANIZED

Table 3.2

1	0.458	21	0.462	41	0.450
2	0.450	22	0.450	42	0.455
3	0.465	23	0.454	43	0.456
4	0.452	24	0.446	44	0.456
5	0.452	25	0.464	45	0.459
6	0.447	26	0.461	46	0.454
7	0.459	27	0.463	47	0.455
8	0.451	28	0.457	48	0.458
9	0.446	29	0.460	49	0.457
10	0.467	30	0.451	50	0.456
11	0.452	31	0.456	51	0.455
12	0.463	32	0.455	52	0.460
13	0.456	33	0.451	53	0.456
14	0.456	34	0.462	54	0.463
15	0.449	35	0.451	55	0.457
16	0.454	36	0.469	56	0.456
17	0.456	37	0.458	57	0.457
18	0.441	38	0.458	58	0.453
19	0.457	39	0.456	59	0.455
20	0.459	40	0.454	60	0.453

a spectrophotometer. (Absorbance is discussed in a later chapter, but the nature of the measured quantity need not concern us here.) The data in Table 3.2 have not been treated in any way, but are simply listed in the order in which they were obtained. We are here concerned, not with any "correct" result, but only with the relationships of the measured values among themselves. It is apparent that the values in Table 3.2 must be treated in some manner before they can be discussed intelligently. A reader with an exceptionally quick eye may notice that the lowest value is 0.441 and the highest 0.469, and perhaps it is apparent that many values are between 0.45 and 0.46, but on the whole the table is relatively uninstructive. Let us now enumerate some steps that will enable us to interpret the data more fully.

First, we arrange the results in order from lowest to highest. This has been done in Table 3.3. This simple operation discloses information not so

Table 3.3

INDIVIDUAL VALUES ARRANGED IN ORDER

1	0.441	21	0.454	41	0.457
2	0.446	22	0.455	42	0.458
3	0.446	23	0.455	43	0.458
4	0.447	24	0.455	44	0.458
5	0.449	25	0.455	45	0.458
6	0.450	26	0.455	46	0.459
7	0.450	27	0.456	47	0.459
8	0.450	28	0.456	48	0.459
9	0.451	29	0.456	49	0.460
10	0.451	30	0.456	50	0.460
11	0.451	31	0.456	51	0.461
12	0.451	32	0.456	52	0.462
13	0.452	33	0.456	53	0.462
14	0.452	34	0.456	54	0.463
15	0.452	35	0.456	55	0.463
16	0.453	36	0.456	56	0.463
17	0.453	37	0.457	57	0.464
18	0.454	38	0.457	58	0.465
19	0.454	39	0.457	59	0.467
20	0.454	40	0.457	60	0.469

readily apparent in the raw data, namely the maximum and minimum values, and, by simple counting, the middle or median value. This is still an inadequate presentation of the data, however; the mind does not grasp the meaning of sixty numbers on a piece of paper, regardless of how they are arranged. We need more compactness in order to make practical use of the data.

The second step involves condensing the data by grouping them into cells. We divide the range from the lowest to the highest value into a convenient number of intervals or *cells* and then count the number of values falling within each cell. Strictly, this process involves some loss of information, but this is more than compensated by the increased efficiency with which the significance of the condensed data may be perceived. In order to proceed, we must first decide upon the number of cells to be used and choose their boundaries. Usually the range is divided into equal intervals, and sometimes confusion is avoided by choosing cell boundaries halfway between possible observed values. In the present case, the absorbance was recorded to three decimal places, and we choose cell boundaries such as 0.4605 so that none of the values coincides with a boundary. Judgment is required in selecting the number of cells: 13 to 20 are sometimes recommended, but 10 or even fewer may be preferable if the number of values to be grouped is small, say, less than 250. A fairly satisfactory grouping of our data into eight cells is shown in Table 3.4.

	GROUPING OF INDIVIDUAL VALUES INTO CELLS		Table 3.4
Cell mid-point	**Cell boundaries**	**Number of values**	
	0.4405		
0.4425		1	
	0.4445		
0.4465		3	
	0.4485		
0.4505		11	
	0.4525		
0.4545		21	
	0.4565		
0.4585		14	
	0.4605		
0.4625		7	
	0.4645		
0.4665		2	
	0.4685		
0.4705		1	
	0.4725		

A glance at Table 3.4 shows that information buried in Tables 3.2 and 3.3 is now obvious. Thus, although the values range from 0.441 to 0.469, we see immediately that very few results are below 0.448 or above 0.464.

Next, we may devise a pictorial representation of the frequency distribution. This step is actually unnecessary, and it is rarely performed except for teaching purposes or for popular presentation of what might otherwise be "dry" data to laymen. Two types of graphs are shown in Figure 3.1 : The *histogram* consists of contiguous columns of heights proportional to the frequencies, erected upon the full widths of the cells; the *frequency polygon* is constructed by plotting frequencies at cell mid-points and connecting the points with straight lines.

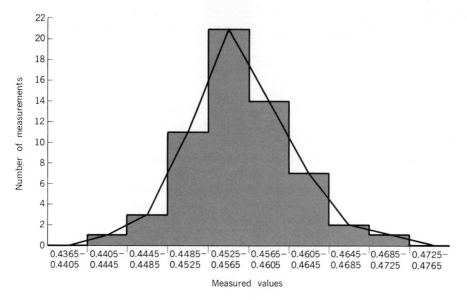

Fig. 3.1. Histogram and frequency polygon for absorbance measurements of 60 replicate solutions.

The normal error curve

The limiting case approached by the frequency polygon as more and more replicate measurements are performed is the *normal* or *Gaussian* distribution curve, shown in Figure 3.2. This curve is the locus of a mathematical function which is well-known, and it is more easily handled than the less ideal and more irregular curves that are often obtained with a smaller number of observations. Data are often treated as though they were normally distributed in order to simplify their analysis, and we may look upon the normal error curve as a model which is approximated more or less closely by real data. It is supposed that there exists a "universe" of data made up of an infinite number of individual measurements, and it is actually this "infinite population" to which the normal error function pertains. A finite number of replicate measurements is considered by statisticians to be a sample drawn in a random fashion from a hypothetical infinite population; thus the sample is at least hopefully a representative one, and fluctuations in its individual values may be considered to be normally distributed, so that the terminology and techniques associated with the normal error function may be employed in their analysis.

The equation of the normal error curve may be written for our purposes as follows:

$$y = \frac{1}{\sigma \sqrt{2\pi}} e^{-(x-\mu)^2/2\sigma^2}$$

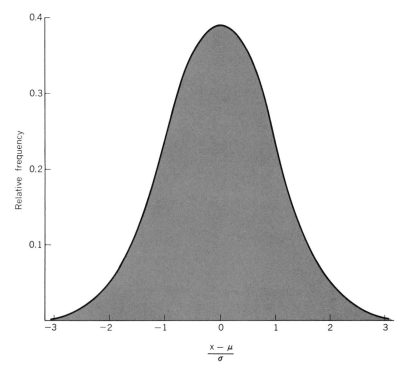

Fig. 3.2. Normal distribution curve; relative frequencies of deviations from the mean for a normally-distributed infinite population; deviations $(x - \mu)$ are in units of σ.

Here y represents the relative frequency with which random sampling of the infinite population will bring to hand a particular value x. The quantities μ and σ, called the population parameters, specify the distribution. μ is the *mean* of the infinite population, and since we are not here concerned with determinate errors, we may consider that μ gives the correct magnitude of the measured quantity. It is clearly impractical to determine μ by actually averaging an infinite number of measured values, but we shall see below that a statement can be made from a finite series of measurements regarding the probability that μ lies within a certain interval. To the extent of our confidence in having eliminated determinate errors, such a statement approaches an assessment of the true value of the measured quantity. σ, which is called the *standard deviation*, is the distance from the mean to either of the two inflection points of the distribution curve, and may be thought of as a measure of the spread or scatter of the values making up the population; σ thus relates to precision. π has its usual significance and e is the base of the natural logarithm system. The term $(x - \mu)$ represents simply the extent to which an individual value x deviates from the mean.

The distribution function may be normalized by setting the area under the curve equal to unity, representing a total probability of one for the whole population. Since the curve approaches the abscissa asymptotically on either side of the mean, there is a small but finite probability of encountering enormous deviations from the mean. A person who happened to encounter one of these in performing a series of laboratory observations would be unfortunate indeed; some of us who have faith in never obtaining such a "wild" result in our own work are inclined to the view that the normal distribution as a model for real data breaks down, and that only the central region of the distribution curve is pertinent when applied to scientific measurements by competent workers. The area under the curve between any two values of $(x - \mu)$ gives the fraction of the total population having magnitudes between these two values. It may be shown that about two-thirds (actually 68.26%) of all the values in an infinite population fall within the limits $\mu \pm \sigma$, while $\mu \pm 2\sigma$ includes about 95% and $\mu \pm 3\sigma$ practically all (99.74%) of the values. Happily, then, small errors are more probable than large ones. Since the normal curve is symmetrical, high and low results are equally probable once determinate errors have been dismissed.

When a worker goes into the laboratory and measures something, we suppose that his result is one of an infinite population of such values that he might obtain in an eternity of such activity; then the chances are roughly 2 to 1 that his measured values will be no further than σ from the mean of the infinite population, and about 20 to 1 that his result will lie in the range $\mu \pm 2\sigma$. In practice, of course, we can never find σ for an infinite population, but the standard deviation of a finite number of observations may be taken as an estimate of σ, and we may thus predict something about the likelihood of occurrence of an error of a certain magnitude in the work of a particular individual once he has performed enough measurements to permit estimation of the characteristics of his particular infinite population.

STATISTICAL TREATMENT OF FINITE SAMPLES

Although there is no doubt as to its mathematical meaning, the normal distribution of an infinite population is a fiction so far as real laboratory work is concerned. We must now turn our attention to techniques for handling scientific data as we obtain them in practice.

Measures of central tendency and variability

The *central tendency* of a group of results is simply that value about which the individual results tend to "cluster." For an infinite population, it is μ, the mean of such a sample. The *mean* of a finite number of measurements, $x_1, x_2, x_3, \ldots, x_n$, is often designated $\bar{x}$ to distinguish it from μ. Of course $\bar{x}$

approaches μ as a limit when n, the number of measured values, approaches infinity. Calculation of the **mean** involves simply averaging the individual results:

$$\bar{x} = \frac{x_1 + x_2 + x_3 \cdots + x_n}{n} = \frac{\sum\limits_{i=1}^{i=n} x_i}{n}$$

The mean is generally the most useful measure of central tendency. It may be shown that the mean of n results is $\sqrt{n}$ times as reliable as any one of the individual results. Thus there is a diminishing return from accumulating more and more replicate measurements: The mean of four results is twice as reliable as one result in measuring central tendency; the mean of nine results is three times as reliable, the mean of 25 results five times as reliable, etc. Thus, generally speaking, it is inefficient for a careful worker who gets good precision to repeat a measurement more than a few times. Of course the need for increased reliability, and the price to be paid for it, must be decided on the basis of the importance of the results and the use to which they are to be put.

The *median* of an odd number of results is simply the middle value when the results are listed in order; for an even number of results, the median is the average of the two middle ones. In a truly symmetrical distribution, the mean and the median are identical. Generally speaking, the median is a less efficient measure of central tendency than is the mean, but in certain instances it may be useful, particularly in dealing with very small samples.

Since two parameters, μ and σ, are required to specify a frequency distribution, it is clear that two populations may have the same central tendency but differ in "spread" or *variability* (or, as some say, *dispersion*), as suggested in Figure 3.3. For a finite number of values, the simplest measure of variability is the *range*, which is the difference between the largest and smallest values. Like the median, the range is sometimes useful in small sample statistics, but generally speaking it is an inefficient measure of variability; note, for example, that one "wild" result exerts its full impact upon the range, whereas its effect is diluted by all of the other results in the better measures of variability noted below.

The *average deviation* from the mean is often given in scientific papers as a measure of variability, although strictly it is not very significant from a statistical point of view, particularly for a small number of observations. For a large group of data which are normally distributed, the average deviation approaches 0.8σ. To calculate the average or mean deviation, one simply finds the differences between individual results and the mean, regardless of sign, adds these individual deviations up, and divides by the number of results:

$$\text{Average deviation} = \bar{d} = \frac{\sum\limits_{i=1}^{i=n} |x_i - \bar{x}|}{n}$$

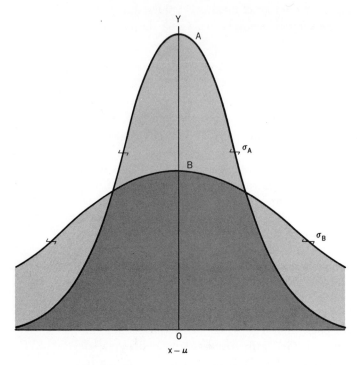

Fig. 3.3. Two populations with the same central tendency, μ, but different variability.

Often the average deviation is expressed relative to the magnitude of the measured quantity, for example as a percentage:

$$\text{Relative average deviation (\%)} = \frac{\bar{d}}{\bar{x}} \times 100 = \frac{\sum\limits_{i=1}^{i=n} |x_i - \bar{x}|/n}{\bar{x}} \times 100$$

Because analytical results are often expressed as percentages (e.g., per cent iron in an iron ore sample), it may be confusing to report relative deviations on a percentage basis, and it is preferable to use parts per thousand instead of per cent (parts per hundred):

$$\text{Relative average deviation (ppt)} = \frac{\sum\limits_{i=1}^{i=n} |x_i - \bar{x}|/n}{\bar{x}} \times 1000$$

The *standard deviation* is much more meaningful statistically than is the average deviation. The symbol s is used for the standard deviation of a finite number of values; σ is reserved for the population parameter. The standard deviation, which may be thought of as a root mean square deviation of values from their average, is calculated using the formula:

$$s = \sqrt{\frac{\sum\limits_{i=1}^{i=n} |x_i - \bar{x}|^2}{n - 1}}$$

If n is large (say 50 or more), then, of course, it is immaterial whether the term in the denominator is $n - 1$ (which is strictly correct) or n. When the standard deviation is expressed as a percentage of the mean, it is called the *coefficient of variation*, v:

$$v = \frac{s}{\bar{x}} \times 100$$

The *variance*, which is s^2, is fundamentally more important in statistics than is s itself, but the latter is much more commonly used in treating chemical data.

For the data in Tables 3.2, 3.3, and 3.4 the following measures of central tendency and variability were calculated:

Mean: $\bar{x} = 0.456$

Median: $M = 0.456$

Range: $R = 0.028$

Average deviation: $\bar{d} = 0.0038$

Relative average deviation: $\dfrac{\bar{d}}{\bar{x}} \times 1000 = 8.3$ ppt

Standard deviation: $s = 0.0052$

Coefficient of variation: $v = \dfrac{s}{\bar{x}} \times 100 = 1.1\%$

The following example illustrates the calculation of the above terms in the case of a determination of the normality of a solution.

PROBLEM. The normality of a solution is determined by four separate titrations, the results being 0.2041, 0.2049, 0.2039, and 0.2043. Calculate the mean, median, range, average deviation, relative average deviation, standard deviation and the coefficient of variation.

Mean: $\bar{x} = \dfrac{0.2041 + 0.2049 + 0.2039 + 0.2043}{4}$

$\bar{x} = 0.2043$

Median: $M = \dfrac{0.2041 + 0.2043}{2}$

$M = 0.2042$

Range: $R = 0.2049 - 0.2039$

$R = 0.0010$

$$\text{Average deviation: } \bar{d} = \frac{(0.0002) + (0.0006) + (0.0004) + (0.0000)}{4}$$

$$\bar{d} = 0.0003$$

$$\text{Relative average deviation: } \frac{\bar{d}}{\bar{x}} \times 1000 = \frac{0.0003}{0.2043} \times 1000$$

$$= 1.5 \text{ ppt}$$

$$\text{Standard deviation: } s = \sqrt{\frac{(0.0002)^2 + (0.0006)^2 + (0.0004)^2 + (0.0000)^2}{4 - 1}}$$

$$s = 0.0004$$

$$\text{Coefficient of variation: } v = \frac{0.0004}{0.2043} \times 100$$

$$v = 0.2\%$$

Student's *t*

We have seen that, given μ and σ for the normal distribution of an infinite population, a precise statement can be made regarding the odds of drawing from the population an observation lying outside certain limits. But in practical work, we deal with finite numbers of observations, and we know, not μ and σ, but rather $\bar{x}$ and s, which are only estimates of μ and σ. Since these estimates are subject to uncertainty, what we really have is a sort of blurred distribution curve on which to base any predictions we wish to make. This naturally widens the limits corresponding to any given odds that an individual observation will fall outside such limits. An English chemist, W. S. Gosset, writing under the pen name of Student, studied the problem of making predictions based upon a finite sample drawn from an unknown population and published a solution in 1908.[3] The theory of Student's work is beyond the scope of this book, but we may accept it as soundly-based and see how it may be used in chemistry. The quantity *t* (often called Student's *t*) is defined by the expression

$$\pm t = (\bar{x} - \mu) \frac{\sqrt{n}}{s}$$

Tables of *t* values relating to various odds or probability levels and for varying degrees of freedom may be found in statistical compilations; a portion of such a table is reproduced here in Table 3.5. *Degrees of freedom in the present connection are one less than n*, the number of observations.[4]

---

[3] *Biometrika*, **6**, 1 (1908).

[4] Degrees of freedom may be defined as the number of individual observations that could be allowed to vary under the condition that $\bar{x}$ and s, once determined, be held constant. For example, once the mean is obtained and we decide to keep it constant, all but

**Table
3.5**

SOME VALUES OF STUDENT'S *t*

Degrees of freedom	Probability levels	
	95%	**99%**
2	4.303	9.925
3	3.182	5.841
4	2.776	4.604
5	2.571	4.032
6	2.447	3.707
7	2.365	3.500
8	2.306	3.355
9	2.262	3.250
10	2.228	3.169
20	2.086	2.845
30	2.042	2.750

The *t* values are calculated to take into account the fact that $\bar{x}$ will not in general be the same as μ and to compensate the uncertainty in using *s* as an estimate of σ. Values of *t* such as those in Table 3.5 are used in several statistical methods, some of which are outlined below.

Confidence interval of the mean

By rearranging the equation above which defines *t*, we obtain the so-called confidence interval of the mean, or confidence limits:

$$\mu = \bar{x} \pm \frac{ts}{\sqrt{n}}$$

We might use this to estimate the probability that the population mean, μ, lies within a certain region centered at $\bar{x}$, the experimental mean of our measurements. It is more usual in treating analytical data, however, to adopt an acceptable probability and then find the limits on either side of $\bar{x}$ to which we must go in order to be assured that we have embraced μ. It may be seen in Table 3.5 that *t* values increase as *n*, the number of observations, decreases. This is reasonable, since the smaller *n* becomes, the less information is available for estimating the population parameters. Increases in *t* exactly compensate for the lessening information.

Great care must be taken to avoid confusion about the meaning of confidence limits; for beginners, there is a tricky point involved, and it is easy to draw unwarranted conclusions. Suppose a series of eight measure-

---

one observation can be varied; the last one is fixed by $\bar{x}$ and all of the other x_i values, and the degrees of freedom then equal $n - 1$. In general, if *s* is calculated from the same number of observations as were used to calculate $\bar{x}$ (which would normally be the case in treating analytical data), then the degrsee of freedom equal $n - 1$.

ments were performed, leading to mean and standard deviation values of $\bar{x}_1$ and s_1. Then, for 95% probability, the confidence limits would be

$$\bar{x}_1 \pm 2.365 \frac{s_1}{\sqrt{8}}$$

The correct interpretation of these limits is as follows: If many such sets of eight measurements were performed and confidence limits calculated for each,

$$\bar{x}_2 \pm 2.365 \frac{s_2}{\sqrt{8}}$$

$$\bar{x}_3 \pm 2.365 \frac{s_3}{\sqrt{8}}$$

etc.

then 95% of these sets of confidence limits would embrace the population mean μ. It is a common misconception that 95% of the experimental means ($\bar{x}_2$, $\bar{x}_3$, $\bar{x}_4$, etc.) would lie within $\bar{x}_1 \pm 2.365(s_1/\sqrt{8})$. Predicting the interval within which future $\bar{x}$ values will lie is a different statistical problem which can be treated only with another sort of limits which are much wider than the confidence limits discussed here.

It is possible to calculate a confidence interval from the range, R, of a series of measurements, using the relationship

$$\mu = \bar{x} \pm c_n R$$

Values of c_n for various numbers of observations and probability levels have been tabulated; some of these are given in Table 3.6. The values of c_n are

Table 3.6   SOME VALUES OF c_n FOR CALCULATING CONFIDENCE INTERVALS FROM THE RANGE

Number of observations	Probability level	
	95%	99%
2	6.353	31.828
3	1.304	3.008
4	0.717	1.316
5	0.507	0.843
6	0.399	0.628

based upon estimates of s obtained from the range. It should be emphasized that, while it is easy to calculate a confidence interval from the range, an occasional large error will have an undue impact upon the result. The range is normally used in this way only when dealing with a very small number of observations, say, 10 or less.

Testing for significance

Suppose that a sample is analyzed by two different methods, each repeated several times, and that the mean values obtained are different. Statistics, of course, cannot say which value is "right," but there is a prior question in any case, namely, is the difference between the two values significant? It is possible simply by the influence of random fluctuations to get two different values using two methods; but it is likewise possible that one (or even both) of the methods is subject to a determinate error. There is a test, using Student's t, that will tell (with a given probability) whether it is worthwhile to seek an assignable cause for the difference between the two means. It is clear that the greater the scatter in the two sets of data the less likely it is that differences between the two means are real.

The statistical approach to this problem is to set up the so-called *null hypothesis*. This hypothesis states, in the present example, that the two means are identical. The t-test gives a *yes* or *no* answer to the correctness of the null hypothesis with a certain confidence such as 95 or 99%. The procedure is as follows: Suppose a sample has been analyzed by two different methods, yielding means $\bar{x}_1$ and $\bar{x}_2$ and standard deviations s_1 and s_2; n_1 and n_2 are the numbers of individual results obtained by the two methods. The first step is to calculate a t value using the formula

$$t = \frac{|\bar{x}_1 - \bar{x}_2|}{s} \sqrt{\frac{n_1 n_2}{n_1 + n_2}}$$

(This procedure presupposes that s_1 and s_2 are the same; there is a test for this, noted below.) Second, enter a t table such as Table 3.5 at a degree of freedom given by $(n_1 + n_2 - 2)$ and at the desired probability level. If the value in the table is greater than the t calculated from the data, the null hypothesis is substantiated, i.e., $\bar{x}_1$ and $\bar{x}_2$ are the same with a certain probability. If the t value in the table is less than the calculated t, then by this test the null hypothesis is incorrect and it might be profitable to look for a reason to explain the difference between $\bar{x}_1$ and $\bar{x}_2$.

If s_1 and s_2 are really different, a much more complicated procedure, which is not discussed here, must be used. Usually in analytical work involving methods that would by ordinary common sense be considered comparable, s_1 and s_2 are about the same. A test is available for deciding whether a difference between s_1 and s_2 is significant: This is the *variance-ratio* or *F-test*. The procedure is simple: Find the ratio $F = s_1^2/s_2^2$, placing the larger s value in the numerator so that $F > 1$; then go to a table of F values. If the F value in the table is less than the calculated F value, then the two standard deviations are significantly different, otherwise they are not. Some sample F values are given in Table 3.7 for a probability level of 95%. The F-test may be used to determine the validity of the simple t-test described

**Table
3.7**   *F* VALUES AT THE 95% PROBABILITY LEVEL

$n-1$ for smaller s^2	$n-1$ for larger s^2					
	3	4	5	6	10	20
3	9.28	9.12	9.01	8.94	8.79	8.66
4	6.59	6.39	6.26	6.16	5.96	5.80
5	5.41	5.19	5.05	4.95	4.74	4.56
6	4.76	4.53	4.39	4.28	4.06	3.87
10	3.71	3.48	3.33	3.22	2.98	2.77
20	3.10	2.87	2.71	2.60	2.35	2.12

here, but it may also be of interest in its own right to determine whether two analytical procedures yield significantly different precision.

Sometimes it may be of interest to compare two results, one of which is considered a priori to be highly reliable. An example of this might be comparison of the mean $\bar{x}$ of several analyses of an NBS sample with the value certified by the National Bureau of Standards. The goal would be, not to pass judgment upon the Bureau, but to decide whether the method employed gave results that agreed with the Bureau's. In this case, the Bureau's value is taken as μ in the equation defining Student's t, and a t value is calculated using $\bar{x}$, n, and s for the analytical results at hand. If the calculated t value is greater than that in the t table for $n-1$ degrees of freedom and the desired probability, then the analytical method in question gave a mean value significantly different from the NBS value; otherwise, differences in the two values would be attributable to chance alone.

The following example illustrates the above points.

PROBLEM. Two sets of results for the percentage purity of a substance are obtained:

Method 1	Method 2
$\bar{x}_1 = 10.52\%$	$\bar{x}_2 = 10.72\%$
$s_1 = 0.05$	$s_2 = 0.06$
$n_1 = 6$	$n_2 = 5$

(a) Are s_1 and s_2 significantly different? Apply the variance-ratio, or *F*-test:

$$F = \frac{s_2^2}{s_1^2} = 1.44$$

Consult Table 3.7 under column $n-1 = 4$ (since $s_2 > s_1$) and row $n-1 = 5$, finding a value of $F = 5.19$. Since $5.19 > 1.44$, the standard deviations are not significantly different.

(b) Are the two means significantly different? Calculate a t value (either s_1 or s_2 may be used):

$$t = \frac{(10.72 - 10.52)}{0.05} \sqrt{\frac{6 \times 5}{6 + 5}}$$

$$t = 5.60$$

Consult Table 3.5 at degrees of freedom $n_1 + n_2 - 2 = 9$, finding t for 95% probability level = 2.262. Since $2.262 < 5.60$, the null hypothesis is incorrect and the difference is significant.

(c) Suppose the results of Method 1 are from the Bureau of Standards. Is the result of Method 2 significantly different from that obtained by the Bureau?

From the equation

$$\mu = \bar{x} \pm \frac{ts}{\sqrt{n}}$$

t is evaluated:

$$10.52 = 10.72 \pm \frac{t \times 0.06}{\sqrt{5}}$$

$$t = 7.5$$

In Table 3.5, at degrees of freedom = 4 and 95% probability level $t = 2.776$. Hence $7.5 > 2.776$ and the result is significantly different from that obtained by the Bureau.

Criteria for rejection of an observation

Sometimes a person performing measurements is faced with one result in a set of replicates which seems to be out of line with the others, and he then must decide whether to exclude this result from further consideration. This problem is encountered in beginning analytical chemistry courses, later in physical chemistry laboratory work, and even in advanced research, although hopefully with lessening frequency as the student progresses. It is a generally-accepted rule in scientific work that a measurement is to be automatically rejected when it is known that an error was made; this is a determinate situation with which we are not concerned here. It should be noted that it is incorrect (but all-too-human) to reject results which were subject to known errors only when they appear to be discordant; the only way to avoid an unconscious introduction of bias into the measurements is to reject every result where an error was known to be made regardless of its agreement with the others. The problem to which we address ourselves here is a different one: How do we decide whether to throw out a result which appears discordant when there is no known reason to suspect it?

If the number of replicate values is large, the question of rejecting one value is not an important one; first, a single value will have only a small effect upon the mean, and second, statistical considerations give a clear answer regarding the probability that the suspected result is a member of the same population as the others. On the other hand, a real dilemma arises when the number of replicates is small: The divergent result exerts a significant effect upon the mean while at the same time there are insufficient data to permit a real statistical analysis of the status of the suspected result.

The many different recommendations that have been promulgated by various writers attest to the conclusion that the question of rejecting or retaining one divergent value from a small sample really cannot satisfactorily be answered. Some of the more widely recommended criteria for rejection are considered below, and the student is referred to the excellent discussion by Blaedel, *et al.*,[5] and interesting briefer commentaries by Laitinen[6] and Wilson.[7]

In the first place, it is necessary to decide how large the difference between the suspected result and the other data must be before the result is to be discarded. If the minimum difference is made too small, valid data may be rejected too frequently; this is said to be an "error of the first kind." On the other hand, setting the minimum difference too high leads to "errors of the second kind," viz., too frequent retention of highly erroneous values. The various recommendations for criteria of rejection steer one course or another between the Scylla and Charybdis of these two types of errors, some closer to one and some closer to the other.

The *2.5 d rule* is applied as follows:

1. Compute the mean and the average deviation of the "good" results.

2. Find the deviation of the suspected result from the mean of the "good" ones.

3. If the deviation of the suspected result from the mean of the "good" ones is at least 2.5 times the average deviation of the "good" results, then reject the suspected result. Otherwise retain it.

Strictly, the limit for rejection is too low with the 2.5 d rule: Valid data are rejected too often (errors of the first kind). The degree of confidence often quoted for the rule is based upon large sample statistics extended to small samples without proper compensation.

The *4 d rule* is used in the same manner as the 2.5 d rule above. This rule likewise leads to errors of the first kind, although obviously not so frequently. There is no statistical justification for using either the 2.5 d or the 4 d rule, although both are widely recommended. It should be noted that these rules are meant to apply to the rejection of only one result from a group of four to eight, not to one out of three, two out of five, etc.

The *Q-test*, described by Dean and Dixon,[8] is statistically correct, and it is very easy to apply. When the *Q*-test calls for rejection, confidence is high (90%) that the suspected result was indeed subject to some special error. Using the *Q*-test for rejection, errors of the first kind are highly unlikely. However, when applied to small sets of data (say, three to five results), the *Q*-test allows rejection only of results that deviate widely, and hence leads frequently to errors of the second kind (retention of erroneous results). Thus, the *Q*-test provides excellent justification for the rejection of grossly erroneous

[5] W. J. Blaedel, V. W. Meloche, and J. A. Ramsey, *J. Chem. Ed.*, **28,** 643 (1951).

[6] H. A. Laitinen, *Chemical Analysis*, McGraw-Hill Book Co., Inc., New York, 1960, p. 574.

[7] E. B. Wilson, Jr., *An Introduction to Scientific Research*, McGraw-Hill Book Co., Inc., New York, 1952, p. 256.

[8] R. B. Dean and W. J. Dixon, *Anal. Chem.*, **23,** 636 (1951).

values, but it does not eliminate the dilemma with suspicious but less deviant values. The reason for this, of course, is that with small samples only crude guesses of the real population distribution are possible and thus sound statistics lends assurance only to the rejection of widely divergent results.

The *Q-test* is applied as follows:

1. Calculate the range of the results.

2. Find the difference between the suspected result and its nearest neighbor.

3. Divide the difference obtained in step 2 by the range from step 1 to obtain the rejection quotient, Q.

4. Consult a table of Q values. If the computed value of Q is greater than the value in the table, the result can be discarded with 90% confidence that it was indeed subject to some factor which did not operate on the other results.

Some Q values are given in Table 3.8.

VALUES OF REJECTION QUOTIENT, Q   **Table 3.8**

Number of observations	$Q_{0.90}$
3	0.90
4	0.76
5	0.64
6	0.56
7	0.51
8	0.47
9	0.44
10	0.41

The following example illustrates the application of the above tests.

PROBLEM. Four results obtained for the normality of a solution are 0.1014, 0.1012, 0.1019, and 0.1016. Apply the above tests to see if the 0.1019 result can be discarded.

(a) Compute the mean and average deviation of the three "good" results:

Results	Deviations (*ppt*)
0.1014	0.0
0.1012	2.0
0.1016	2.0
Average: 0.1014	Average: 1.3

(b) Compute the deviation of the suspected result from the mean of the three "good" results:

$$0.1019 - 0.1014 = 0.0005 \text{ or } 5.0 \text{ ppt}$$

Using the 2.5 rule,

$$2.5 \times 1.3 = 3.3 < 5.0 \text{ (discard)}$$

Using the 4.0 rule,

$$4.0 \times 1.3 = 5.2 > 5.0 \text{ (do not discard)}$$

Using the Q-test,

$$Q = \frac{0.1019 - 0.1016}{0.1019 - 0.1012}$$

$$Q = \frac{0.0003}{0.0007}$$

$$Q = 0.43$$

Since $Q < 0.76$ (Table 3.8), do not discard.

As noted above, the Q-test affirms the rejection of a value at a confidence level of 90%. Willingness to reject a result with less confidence would make possible a Q-test which allowed retention of fewer deviant values (errors of the second kind). While this appears superficially attractive, there are valid reasons for conservatism in rejecting measurements. Actually, low confidence levels (say 50%) are scarcely meaningful when only a small number of observations is involved. Further, although to many students in introductory courses laboratory measurements are only exercises, it must be remembered that the collection of data is a scientific enterprise with a purpose, and the matter must be discussed as though it were important. The worker who has carefully conceived his measurement and executed it painstakingly, and who has reason to hope that the outcome will be significant, will not quickly throw his work away. He will be more likely to repeat the measurement until the dilemma of the discordant result has evaporated through the operation of two factors: Dilution of any one result by all of the others will lessen its significance, and, as the number of observations increases, statistical evaluation of the suspected result will become more meaningful.

A sort of compromise between outright rejection and the retention of a suspected value is sometimes recommended, viz., reporting the median of all the results rather than a mean either with or without the deviant value. The median is influenced by the *existence* of one discordant result, but it is not affected by the *extent* to which the result differs from the others. For a sample containing three to five values, Blaedel *et al.*[5] recommend testing the suspected value with the Q-test and rejecting it if the test allows this; if not, the median is reported rather than the mean. Some writers, e.g., Wilson, recommend that the highest and the lowest value both be rejected and the mean of the others reported: "The best procedure to use depends on what is known about the frequency of occurrence of wild values, on the cost of additional observations, and on the penalties for the various types of error. In the absence of special arguments, the use of the interior average . . .

would appear to be good practice." [9] It may be noted that this interior average and the median are necessarily identical in the special case where there are just three results.

CONTROL CHARTS

The control chart method was originally developed as a system for keeping track of quality during large-scale manufacturing operations. Often a production run is too large to permit individual inspection of each item (say, razor blades or ball bearings), and in some cases the quality test is destructive (as in measuring the stress required to break an object) and hence cannot be applied to each specimen produced by a company. In such cases, some sort of "spot-checking" of a few of the samples coming off the production line is necessary, and judgment is required in order to decide whether the manufacturing process is under control or whether a costly shutdown is justified in order to seek the cause of a deviation from the specifications in the tested results. The control chart method has also proved useful in keeping track of the performance of analytical methods in busy laboratories where the same types of samples are repeatedly analyzed day after day over long periods of time. The method tends to distinguish with a high degree of efficiency definite trends or periodically recurring anomalies from random fluctuations. The control chart method can be discussed only briefly here; the interested reader is referred to books on the subject[10,11] and several briefer discussions.[12-15]

Let us suppose that a company manufactures some chemical material, and that as part of the quality control program the analytical laboratory performs each day a certain analysis on samples bled from the plant output, perhaps for per cent water in the product. Let us further suppose that the laboratory checks its water determination each day by running a standard sample of known water content through the analytical procedure. We are interested here in how the control chart for the laboratory analysis is set up and used; the plant could also use a control chart method, based upon the laboratory reports, for monitoring the quality of the product, but here we are concerned with the laboratory's checking its own analytical method.

[9] E. B. Wilson, Jr., *loc. cit.*, p. 257.

[10] E. L. Grant, *Statistical Quality Control*, 2nd Ed., McGraw-Hill Book Co., Inc., New York, 1952.

[11] W. A. Shewhart, *Economic Control of Quality of Manufactured Product*, D. Van Nostrand Co., New York, 1931.

[12] H. A. Laitinen, *loc. cit.*, p. 560.

[13] E. B. Wilson, Jr., *loc. cit.*, p. 263.

[14] G. Wernimont, *Ind. Eng. Chem.*, Anal. Ed., **18**, 587 (1946).

[15] J. A. Mitchell, *Ibid.*, **19**, 961 (1947).

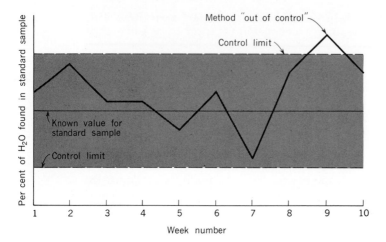

Fig. 3.4. Control chart.

The control chart for the analysis is set up as follows (see Figure 3.4). The per cent water in the standard sample is indicated on the chart by a horizontal line. The standard sample is analyzed every day, and the average of five weekly results is plotted, week after week, on the chart. Also placed on the chart are the *control limits*. Analytical results falling outside these limits are considered to result from the operation of some definite factor which is worth investigating and correcting. When results fall within the limits, the method is "under control" and fluctuations are only random and indeterminate. (The analogous conclusion with a production control chart is that when samples test outside the control limits there is justification for shutting down the process and looking for the trouble.) Clearly, the control limits must be set in an arbitrary manner; one must decide how large must be the probability of an assignable cause for a deviant result before he is willing to say that something is wrong with the analysis. It seems usual in practice to set the control limits at the expected value $\pm 3s$; there is no fundamental aspect of probability theory demanding this, but apparently experience has shown that these are sound limits economically as a basis for action. Sometimes two sets of control limits are placed on the chart, "inner limits" at about $\pm 2s$ to warn of possible trouble, and "outer limits" of $\pm 3s$ demanding a corrective. (Actually, the chances are 1 in 20 that an observation subject only to random scatter will lie outside limits of $\pm 1.96\sigma$; 99.7% of a group of results should fall within the $\pm 3\sigma$ limits unless a definite cause is operating on the analysis.) If the analysis is one that has been performed many times, the laboratory may have a value for s which is a good estimate of σ. Otherwise, the control limits can be established temporarily on the basis of an s value obtained from a few results, and then adjusted later as more data become available. Parallel control charts for ranges, standard deviations, etc., may be employed to help the laboratory personnel keep track of the precision of an analytical method.

PROPAGATION OF ERRORS

Usually the numerical result of a measurement is not of interest in its own right, but rather is used, sometimes in conjunction with several other measurements, to calculate the quantity which is actually desired. Attention is naturally focused upon the precision and accuracy of the final, computed quantity, but it is instructive to see how errors in the individual measurements are propagated into this result. A rigorous treatment of this problem requires more space than is available and mathematics beyond that presupposed for this book. An interesting elementary approach has been given by Waser,[16] and the interested student may find the elements of a more sophisticated treatment discussed briefly by Wilson[17] and by Shoemaker and Garland.[18] A discussion with particular emphasis on analytical chemistry has been given by Benedetti-Pichler.[19]

Determinate errors

Consider a computed result, R, based upon the measured quantities A, B, and C. Let α, β, and γ represent the absolute determinate errors in A, B, and C, respectively, and let ρ represent the maximum resulting error in R. To see how the errors are transmitted through addition and subtraction, suppose that $R = A + B - C$. Changing each quantity by the amount of its error, we may write

$$R + \rho = (A + \alpha) + (B + \beta) - (C - \gamma)$$

or

$$R + \rho = (A + B - C) + (\alpha + \beta + \gamma)$$

Subtracting $R = A + B - C$ gives

$$\rho = \alpha + \beta + \gamma$$

Now suppose, on the other hand, that multiplication and division are involved, i.e., let $R = AB/C$. Again insert the appropriate errors:

$$R + \rho = \frac{(A + \alpha)(B + \beta)}{C - \gamma} = \frac{AB + \alpha B + \beta A + \alpha\beta}{C - \gamma}$$

[16] J. Waser, *Quantitative Chemistry*, Rev. Ed., W. A. Benjamin, Inc., New York, 1964, p. 371.
[17] E. B. Wilson, Jr., *loc. cit.*, p. 272.
[18] D. P. Shoemaker and C. W. Garland, *Experiments in Physical Chemistry*, McGraw-Hill Book Co., Inc., New York, 1962, p. 30.
[19] A. A. Benedetti-Pichler, *Ind. Eng. Chem.*, Anal. Ed., **8**, 373 (1936).

Let us neglect $\alpha\beta$, since it may be supposed that the errors are very small compared with the measured values. Then subtracting $R = AB/C$ gives

$$\rho = \frac{AB + \alpha B + \beta A}{C - \gamma} - \frac{AB}{C}$$

Placing the right-hand terms over a common denominator gives

$$\rho = \frac{\alpha BC + \beta AC + \gamma AB}{C(C - \gamma)}$$

It is now convenient to consider the relative error, ρ/R, by dividing by $R = AB/C$, which leads, after appropriate cancellation, to

$$\frac{\rho}{R} = \frac{\alpha BC + \beta AC + \gamma AB}{AB(C - \gamma)}$$

Since γ is very small compared with C, this reduces to:

$$\frac{\rho}{R} = \frac{\alpha}{A} + \frac{\beta}{B} + \frac{\gamma}{C}$$

Thus it is found that determinate errors are propagated as follows:

1. Where addition or subtraction is involved, the *absolute* determinate errors are transmitted directly into the result.

2. Where multiplication or division is involved, the *relative* determinate errors are transmitted directly into the result.

Indeterminate errors

In the case of determinate errors, it was reasonable to assume, at least for the purpose of illustration, that each measurement of some quantity A was attended by a definite error α; we were able to work with the errors of individual measurements. Indeterminate errors, on the other hand, are manifested by scatter in the data when a measurement is performed more than once. In considering the propagation of indeterminate errors, then, we must inquire how scatter in measurements of quantities A, B, C, etc., is translated into random variation in the final result R.

Suppose again that $R = A + B - C$ on the one hand, and that $R = AB/C$ on the other. The result of statistical theory is:

1. In addition or subtraction, the variances (squares of the standard deviations) of the measured values are additive in determining the variance of the result, i.e., for $R = A + B - C$, $s_R^2 = s_A^2 + s_B^2 + s_C^2$.

2. With multiplication or division, the squares of the relative standard deviations are transmitted, i.e., for $R = AB/C$,

$$\left(\frac{s_R}{R}\right)^2 = \left(\frac{s_A}{A}\right)^2 + \left(\frac{s_B}{B}\right)^2 + \left(\frac{s_C}{C}\right)^2$$

Consideration of error propagation leads to a conclusion of prime importance. This conclusion, although intuitively obvious to experienced workers, should be pointed out for beginners: Thought should be given to the attainable precisions and accuracies of the various measurements in a multistep operation; once the weakest link in the operation is found, then the care taken in the other steps should be adjusted so that the result will not be impaired while at the same time valuable labor and time will not be uselessly expended.

For example, suppose that an error of 10 parts per thousand is expected in a certain analysis for the percentage of some constituent in a sample because of the known limitations of a certain instrument. Then for this analysis, it would be a waste of time to weigh out a starting sample of 10 g to the nearest 0.0001 g, even though the balance might be capable of this. A weighing to the nearest 0.1 g would represent 10 parts per thousand and would then be adequate, although admittedly a cautious person might well prefer to weigh to the nearest 0.01 g just to be on the safe side. In this example, it is supposed that multiplication and division are involved in calculating the result, e.g., a formula of this sort might be used:

$$\% \text{ of constituent} = \frac{\text{instrument reading} \times \text{some factor}}{\text{weight of sample}}$$

Where addition or subtraction is used, the *absolute* rather than the relative errors must be considered. For example, suppose that a 50-g vessel is weighed; then a sample of 0.1 g is added to it, and the weighing is repeated. If the weight of the sample is desired to a part in a thousand, then weighing to the nearest 0.0001 g is required, even though this represents precision of 1 part in 500,000 so far as the weight of the container is concerned.

SIGNIFICANT FIGURES AND COMPUTATION RULES

Significant figures

When a computation is made from experimental data, the error, or uncertainty, in the final result can be calculated by the procedures just described. A widely used procedure for making a crude estimate of this uncertainty involves the use of *significant figures*. The principal advantage of this procedure is that it is less laborious than the calculations of actual uncertainties, particularly those based on indeterminate errors. The principal disadvantage is that only a rough estimate of uncertainty is obtained. In most situations encountered in analyses, an estimate is all that is needed and hence significant figures are widely used.

Most scientists define significant figures as follows: All digits that are certain plus one which contains some uncertainty are said to be significant figures.[20] For example, in weighing an object on an analytical balance, the figures 10.746 can be recorded with certainty. The fourth decimal is estimated by reading a pointer scale or a vernier, and the final weight recorded as 10.7463. The last digit is uncertain, probably to ± 1 in a single reading, or ± 2 if a difference of two readings is involved. The six digits in this weight are all significant figures.

It is important to use only significant figures in expressing analytical data. The use of too many or too few figures may mislead another person with respect to the precision of the experimental data. If a volume is recorded as 1.234 ml, for example, it would be understood that the graduations on the buret were in 0.01-ml intervals and that the third decimal was estimated by reading between the graduations. The same volume read on an ordinary 50-ml buret could be estimated only to the second decimal, since the graduations are in 0.1-ml intervals. Hence the reading should have no more than three figures, say, 1.23 ml.

The digit zero may or may not be a significant figure, depending upon its function in the number. In a buret reading of, say, 10.06 ml, both zeros are measured and are therefore significant figures; the number contains four significant figures. Suppose the foregoing volume is expressed in liters, that is, .01006 l. We do not increase the number of significant figures by changing the unit of volume. The function of the initial zero is to locate the decimal point; hence, initial zeros are not significant. Usually a zero is also placed before the decimal, as 0.01006, and this also is not significant. Terminal zeros are significant. For example, a weight of 10.2050 g has six significant figures. When it is necessary to use terminal zeros merely to locate the decimal properly, powers of ten may be used to avoid confusion with regard to the number of significant figures. For example, a weight of 24.0 mg expressed as micrograms should not be written as 24,000. The last two zeros are not significant, and this is indicated by writing the number as 24.0×10^3 or 2.40×10^4.

Computation rules

1. In expressing the numerical value of a measured quantity retain only one uncertain figure. The uncertainty in this last figure is generally considered to be ± 1 unless a more precise statement of the actual uncertainty is appended.

2. In rounding off numbers, increase the last retained figure by 1 if the following discarded figure is 5 or greater. If the discarded figure is less than

---

[20] Note that in terms of this definition it is improper to say, as do many authors, that "one should use the appropriate number of significant figures." Rather one should say that only significant figures should be recorded. One can record too many digits, but not too many significant figures.

5, do not change the last figure retained. For example, 4.38 becomes 4.4, and 4.33 becomes 4.3 when rounded off to two significant figures.

3. In addition and subtraction, keep only as many decimal places as occur in that one of the numbers which has the fewest decimals. This is illustrated below:

$$
\begin{array}{cc}
50.1 & 50.1 \\
1.36 & 1.4 \\
\underline{0.518} & \underline{0.5} \\
& \text{Sum} = 52.0
\end{array}
$$

Alternatively, the rounding off may be done after the addition or subtraction, as below, but this involves unnecessary work:

$$
\begin{array}{l}
50.1 \\
1.36 \\
\underline{0.518} \\
51.978 \text{ which rounds off to } 52.0
\end{array}
$$

Occasionally a difference in the last retained digit may be seen, depending upon whether the rounding off was done before or after the addition or subtraction, but this difference will generally not be significant in terms of the uncertainty in the last digit.

4. In multiplication and division, retain in each term (and in the answer) a number of significant figures that will indicate a *relative* uncertainty no greater than that of the term with the greatest relative uncertainty. Note that it is the precision of the data, rather than the number of significant figures in the various terms, that dictates the proper number of significant figures in the computed result. Consider the following example, where the percentage of chromium in an unknown chromate sample is calculated from several experimental measurements (weight of sample, volume of titrant, concentration of titrant) and the atomic weight of chromium (the factor 3 comes from the stoichiometry of the titration reaction):

$$
\% \text{ Cr} = \frac{40.64 \text{ ml} \times 0.1027 \text{ mmol/ml} \times (51.996 \text{ mg/mmol}/3)}{346.4 \text{ mg}} \times 100
$$

$$
= 20.883096
$$

Assuming, in accord with Rule 1, an uncertainty of 1 in the last digit of each figure, we have relative uncertainties of 1 part in 4064 (about 1 part in 4000), 1 part in 1027 (about 1 part per thousand), about 1 part in 50,000, and 1 part in, roughly, 3000. There is no uncertainty in the numbers 3 and 100; sometimes these are called "counting numbers." The term with the greatest relative uncertainty is the concentration term, 0.1027, known to about 1 part per thousand. Thus, prior to the multiplication and division, the other terms may be rounded off, but only in such a manner that none of them comes out with an uncertainty greater than about 1 part per thousand. This means that 40.64 should be left as it is, because rounding to 40.6 would imply an uncertainty of about 1 part in 400, which is too great. Similarly,

346.4 should be left as it is, but 51.996 may be rounded off to 52.00. Thus, we may set up the operation as:

$$\% \text{ Cr} = \frac{40.64 \times 0.1027 \times 52.00}{3 \times 346.4} \times 100 = 20.884703 \ldots$$

To indicate a relative uncertainty in the answer no greater than 1 part per thousand, it must be rounded off to 20.88. There is nothing wrong with leaving all terms as they are and rounding off the answer at the end of the computation, but this entails carrying unneeded digits through the multiplication and division; this represents extra work for which there is no corresponding compensation.

It will be noted that in addition and subtraction *absolute* uncertainties are transmitted directly into the result (page 64). Hence, the number with the fewest digits to the right of the decimal contains the largest uncertainty and it makes no sense to carry further decimals in the other numbers. In multiplication and division *relative* uncertainties are transmitted directly into the result. This is the reason that the final result must be expressed so as to designate as nearly as possible the same relative uncertainty as that portion of the data with the largest relative uncertainty. It should also be noted that the ultimate criterion in rounding off an answer in multiplication or division is the relative uncertainty, not the number of significant figures in the data. For example, the results 9.99% and 10.01% each imply a relative uncertainty of about 1 part per thousand, but the first result contains three significant figures, the second contains four.

By now the alert student will have noticed certain seeming inconsistencies or at least what appear to be failures to use, in one section of this chapter, recommendations made in another. Thus, it seems worthwhile to explain briefly how some of the ideas discussed here are treated in practice. In many real analyses, the precision of the final result is determined largely by factors such as sample inhomogeneity and losses or contaminations when the sample is carried through complex separation steps. In view of the operation of such factors, which are essentially indeterminate, it may not be sensible to push certain of the measurements themselves to the point where indeterminate errors are seen. Thus, if experience has shown that errors from other causes amount to several parts per thousand, there is no point in weighing a sample to better than a part per thousand or so. In such a case, it may often turn out that the last recorded digit in the sample weight will not show random scatter at all, but rather will assume one of only two or three possible values. For example, in weighing a sample to the nearest 0.1 mg, the operator will ordinarily make no effort to estimate Vernier readings to any better than 0.05 mg, regardless of the capability of his particular balance; thus, in rounding these to the nearest 0.1 mg, he would expect to be in error by no more than 0.1 mg unless some special accident occurred. If he records a weight of, let us say, 0.1036 g, the operator is reasonably certain that the correct value, to four decimal places, is 0.1035, 0.1036, or 0.1037. These, of course, are not randomly distributed numbers. Rather, the maximum error, once decided upon, is treated as a determinate error with regard to its propagation through a series of computations. In treating this propagation, it is usual not to count upon even partial cancellation of the errors in the various measured quantities, but rather to predict the error in the result on the most pessimistic grounds. Actually, of course, the final computed results will tend to show random scatter because of unpredictable cancellations of errors in the various measurements and the operation of unknown factors. Thus, we often find, in practice, that the errors in individual measurements are treated as though they were determinate, while at the same time the final calculated results are subjected to a statistical analysis of random errors.

REFERENCES

1. C. A. Bennett and N. S. Franklin, *Statistical Analysis in Chemistry and the Chemical Industry*, John Wiley and Sons, Inc., New York, 1954.
2. E. B. Wilson, Jr., *An Introduction to Scientific Research*, McGraw-Hill Book Co., Inc., New York, 1952.
3. W. J. Youden, *Statistical Methods for Chemists*, John Wiley & Sons, Inc., New York, 1951.
4. W. L. Gore, *Statistical Methods for Chemical Experimentation*, Interscience Publishers, Inc., New York, 1952.
5. W. J. Dixon and F. J. Massey, Jr., *Introduction to Statistical Analysis*, 2nd Ed., McGraw-Hill Book Co., Inc., New York, 1957.

QUESTIONS

1. Student A reported three values for the normality of a solution as 0.12, 0.12, and 0.12, with a precision of 0.0 ppt. Student B reported 0.1243, 0.1237, and 0.1240 with a precision of 5.0 ppt. Comment on the merit of the two reports.

2. Explain whether the following errors are determinate or indeterminate and whether they affect the accuracy or the precision of the measurement. If the error is determinate, tell whether it is methodic, operative, or instrumental, and how it could be eliminated.

   (a) The analytical weights are corroded.
   (b) The analyst unknowingly spatters some solution from his flask during a titration.
   (c) A sample picks up moisture during a weighing.
   (d) A reagent is used which contains some of the substance being determined.
   (e) The buret is misread once.
   (f) A student uses the wrong equivalent weight in his calculations.

3. Explain clearly the meaning of the following terms: mean, median, standard deviation, range, central tendency, average deviation, variability, variance, coefficient of variation, relative average deviation, degrees of freedom, null hypothesis, and Student's *t*.

4. Two students determined the volume ratio of an acid and base solution. Student A reported his precision as 0.0 ppt and Student B obtained 1.0 ppt. How should their work be compared? What can be said about the accuracy of each student's results?

5. Explain clearly the meaning of a confidence interval of 95%.

6. Explain clearly how to test two sets of results to determine if they differ significantly.

7. Why can no definite answer be given regarding the rejection of a discordant result? Why aren't confidence levels of 50% used in applying the Q-test?

8. Explain how errors are propagated in the operations of addition-subtraction and of multiplication-division. What is the difference in the cases of determinate and indeterminate errors?

9. Show that the conclusions regarding propagation of errors are consistent with the rules for rounding off numbers so that only significant figures are recorded.

10. Criticize this statement from a text: "Remind the student if he gives too many significant figures, he is making an erroneous scientific statement."

11. Explain briefly the nature of the statistical problem involved in deciding whether to retain or reject a suspicious value in a small series of replicate measurements. What may be wrong with using the so-called *2.5 d rule* in this connection? With the Q-test?

12. Explain what are meant by *additive* and *proportional* determinate errors. Suppose a certified sample whose "true" composition is known is used to check out a new analytical method. How could you tell whether an observed determinate error is proportional or additive?

13. You are in charge of the clinical laboratory in a large hospital. Explain briefly how you would set up a control chart for blood calcium analyses so you could tell at a glance how well your technicians were doing on this determination.

PROBLEMS

(Unless otherwise indicated it is to be understood that any weight or volume involves the difference of two readings.)

1. Refer to the Table of Atomic Weights.
  (a) Noting the uncertainties in the last digits as given in the footnotes, the weight of which element is known with the greatest precision? The least precision?
  (b) Express these precisions in parts per thousand.

2. Analysts A and B reported the following percentages of iron in the same sample: A: 30.18, 30.25, 30.28, 30.30, 30.23, and 30.20. B: 30.14, 30.34, 30.26, 30.40, 30.08, and 30.22. For each set of results calculate the mean, median, range, average deviation, relative average deviation (ppt), standard deviation, and coefficient of variation. Also calculate the confidence intervals, first from the standard deviations, and second from the ranges. What can you say about the work of the two analysts?

3. The Bureau of Standards' value for the percentage of iron in the sample in the previous problem was 30.15. Calculate the absolute and relative errors of Analysts A and B.

4. Two sets of results for the percentage of manganese in an ore are obtained using two methods of analysis:

Method 1	Method 2
$\bar{x} = 9.64\%$	$\bar{x} = 9.56\%$
$s = 0.10$	$s = 0.12$
$n = 11$	$n = 11$

(a) Are the standard deviations significantly different?

(b) Are the two means significantly different?

5. A student obtained the following results for the normality of a solution: 0.1121, 0.1123, 0.1130, and 0.1122. Can the third result be rejected according to the Q-test? What value should be used for the normality and what is the 99% confidence interval?

6. A student obtained the following three results for the normality of a solution: 0.1223, 0.1221, and 0.1225. What is (a) the highest, and (b) the lowest value a fourth result could be without being discarded by the Q-test?

7. A student obtained the following values for the normality of a sodium hydroxide solution: 0.1061, 0.1060, 0.1068, and 0.1062. Can the third result be rejected by the Q-test? A fifth result was run and a value of 0.1061 obtained. Can the third result now be discarded? Explain.

8. An analyst reported the following percentages of manganese in a compound: 30.44, 30.36, 30.50, 30.40, 30.34. Suppose another determination is made and it is higher than any of these. How high would it have to be (that is, the minimum value) before you could justifiably discard it by the Q-test?

9. An analyst obtained the following results in an analysis for tin: 10.50, 10.40, 10.30, 10.36, 10.39, 10.45, 10.54, 10.48, 10.52. The Bureau of Standards' value for this sample was 10.34%. Test the result to see if it is significantly different from that reported by the Bureau.

10. How should the percentage of (a) chlorine in $AgCl$ and (b) iron in Fe_2O_3 be properly expressed according to the precision with which the atomic weights of the elements are known?

11. How many significant figures does each of the following numbers contain?

(a) 0.02040

(b) 6.023×10^{23}

(c) 4.80×10^{-10}

(d) 200,000

(e) 99

12. What is the precision in ppt expressed in each of the numbers in the preceding problem if the uncertainty in the last digit of each number is ± 1?

13. How should the number fifty be properly expressed to indicate that the uncertainty is no more than (a) 1% (b) 0.2% (c) 0.1% (d) 5%.

14. An analyst wishes to weigh a sample of 2 mg to within 1 ppt. How precisely does his balance need to weigh? What if the sample weighs 0.2 g?

15. If one uses only 10 ml in a titration, how precisely will one need to make each buret reading in order to insure an uncertainty of only 1 ppt?

16. The readings on a rough balance can be made to within ± 1 g. How large a sample should be taken for analysis to insure an uncertainty of no more than 5% in the weight?

17. Answer the following:

    (a) An error of 0.4% is how many parts per 500?

    (b) An error of 0.5% is how many parts per 250?

    (c) An error of 0.02% is how many parts per 2000?

18. If the uncertainty in reading a semimicro balance is 0.01 mg, what size sample should be weighed to insure an uncertainty of no more than 1 ppt in the weight?

19. The average of a series of sixteen results is how many more times reliable than the average of four results?

20. If a drinking water contains 1.5 parts per million of NaF, how many liters of water can be fluoridated with 1 lb of NaF? 1.0 parts per million is how many milligrams per liter of water?

21. If the uncertainty in reading a microburet is 0.002 ml, how large a volume should be taken to insure an uncertainty of at least 1.0 ppt?

22. Calculate the following properly, giving the maximum uncertainties:

    (a) $(10.12 \pm 0.04) + (15.34 \pm 0.02) - (9.28 \pm 0.03)$.

    (b) $\dfrac{(10.18 \pm 0.02) \times (5.04 \pm 0.02)}{2.50 \pm 0.01}$.

23. Express the results of the following calculations properly using the correct number of digits:

    (a) $\dfrac{15.02 \times 2.51 \times 4.12}{6.14 \times 10^4}$.

    (b) $\dfrac{31.0 \times 211.4 \times 0.510}{0.01120}$.

    (c) $\dfrac{4.13 \times 10^{-3} \times 50.8}{0.02512 \times 0.002034}$.

    (d) $\dfrac{3.24 \times 8.1 \times 21.2}{0.0615}$.

    (e) $112.73 + 1.3 + 0.424$.

24. The error in a certain analysis is known to be at least 1%. A 0.4-g sample is to be analyzed. To within how many grams does the weight of the sample need to be determined?

25. A sample contains about 10% of the ion $B^=$. $B^=$ is determined by precipitating the compound A_2B. A has an atomic weight about twice that of B. If the uncertainty in determining the weight of the precipitate is not to exceed 1 ppt on a balance sensitive to 0.1 mg, what size sample should be taken for analysis?

26. A student analyzed a sample of soda ash weighing 0.4240 g, which actually contained 50.00% Na_2CO_3. He used 40.10 ml of 0.1000-N acid for titration. (Equivalent weight of Na_2CO_3 is 53.00.) Calculate (a) the absolute error, (b) the relative error in ppt.

27. A student analyzed a sample for chloride by precipitating and weighing AgCl. A 1.000-g sample gave him 0.6000 g of AgCl.

(a) Calculate the percentage chloride in the sample.

(b) If the student, by mistake, used the atomic weight of Cl as 35.345 instead of the correct value of 35.453, what was his relative error in ppt?

28. Given three measured results: $A = 15.00$, $B = 4.00$, $C = 20.00$ in which the uncertainties are 0.03, 0.04, and 0.04 respectively. If the uncertainties are determinate errors, calculate the maximum error in a derived result involving (a) addition of A, B, and C; (b) multiplication and/or division of A, B, and C.

29. Repeat the previous problem except that the uncertainties are the standard deviations in the measured results, that is, a measure of indeterminate errors.

chapter 4

Acid-Base Equilibria

INTRODUCTION

Acid-base equilibrium is an extremely important topic throughout chemistry and in other fields, like agriculture, biology, and medicine, which utilize chemistry. Titrations involving acids and bases are widely employed in the analytical control of many products of commerce, and the ionization of acids and bases exerts an important influence upon metabolic processes in the living cell. Acid-base equilibrium, as it is taught in analytical chemistry courses, offers the inexperienced student opportunity to broaden his understanding of chemical equilibrium and to gain the confidence to apply this understanding to a wide variety of problems.

In the evaluation of a reaction which is to serve as the basis for a titration, one of the most important aspects is the extent to which the reaction proceeds toward completion near the equivalence point. Stoichiometric calculations, which have been considered previously, do not take into account the position of equilibrium toward which a chemical reaction tends. In stoichiometry, one calculates maximal yields of products (or consumption of reactants) with the implicit assumption that the reaction proceeds to completion, whereas in actuality the realization of completeness may require that one of the reactants be present in large excess or that a reaction product be removed from the mixture. Titrimetry by its very nature generally precludes forcing a reaction to completion by a large excess of reactant, and we shall see that the feasibility of a titration depends, at least in part, upon the position of equilibrium established when equivalent quantities of reactants have been mixed. Although our main goal in this chapter will be the understanding of acid-base titrations, other important aspects of acid-base chemistry will be discussed at appropriate points.

BRØNSTED TREATMENT OF ACIDS AND BASES

Although substances with acidic and basic properties had been known for hundreds of years, the quantitative treatment of acid-base equilibria became possible after 1887, when Arrhenius presented his theory of electrolytic dissociation. In water solution, according to Arrhenius, acids dissociate into hydrogen ions and anions, and bases dissociate into hydroxyl ions and cations:

$$\text{Acid:} \quad HX \rightleftharpoons H^+ + X^-$$

$$\text{Base:} \quad BOH \rightleftharpoons OH^- + B^+$$

By applying to these dissociations the principles of chemical equilibrium which had been well systematized before the turn of the century, the behavior of acids and bases in aqueous solution could be quantitatively described, at least approximately. The Debye-Hückel theory (1923) permitted a refined treatment that was even better.

In 1923, Brønsted presented a new view of acid-base behavior which retained the soundness of the Arrhenius equilibrium treatment but which was conceptually broader and facilitated the correlation of a much larger body of information.[1] In Brønsted terms, an acid is any substance that can give up a proton and a base is a substance that can accept a proton. The hydroxyl ion, to be sure, is such a proton acceptor and hence a Brønsted base, but it is not unique; it is one of many species that can exhibit basic behavior. When an acid yields a proton, the deficient species must have some proton affinity and hence it is a base. Thus in the Brønsted treatment we encounter "conjugate" acid-base pairs:

$$\underset{\text{acid}}{HB} \rightleftharpoons H^+ + \underset{\text{base}}{B}$$

---

[1] The same ideas were proposed independently by Lowry in 1924; some writers speak of the Brønsted-Lowry theory.

The acid HB may be electrically neutral, anionic, or cationic (e.g., HCl, HSO_4^-, NH_4^+), and thus we have not specified the charges on either HB or B.

As the elemental unit of positive charge, the proton possesses a charge density which makes its independent existence in a solution extremely unlikely. Thus, in order to transform HB into B, a proton acceptor (i.e., another base) must be present. Often, as in the dissociation of acetic acid in water, this base may be the solvent itself:

$$
\begin{aligned}
\text{HOAc} &\rightleftarrows \text{H}^+ + \text{OAc}^- \\
\text{H}_2\text{O} + \text{H}^+ &\rightleftarrows \text{H}_3\text{O}^+ \\
\hline
\text{HOAc} + \text{H}_2\text{O} &\rightleftarrows \text{H}_3\text{O}^+ + \text{OAc}^-
\end{aligned}
$$

$$\text{acid}_1 \qquad \text{base}_2 \qquad \text{acid}_2 \qquad \text{base}_1$$

The interaction of the two conjugate acid-base pairs (designated by subscripts 1 and 2) leads to an equilibrium in which some of the acetic acid molecules have transferred their protons to water. The protonated water molecule or hydrated proton, H_3O^+, may be called a "hydronium ion" but it is usually designated simply "hydrogen ion" and often written "H^+".[2]

Water is not the only solvent to which acids can transfer their protons, and we may write a general ionization equation, where S is any solvent capable of accepting a proton:

$$\text{HB} + \text{S} \rightleftarrows \text{HS}^+ + \text{B}$$

The species HS^+ is the solvated proton (H_3O^+ in water solution, H_2OAc^+ in glacial acetic acid, $H_3SO_4^+$ in sulfuric acid, $C_2H_5OH_2^+$ in ethanol, etc.). One of the important contributions of Brønsted theory is its emphasis on the role of the solvent in the ionization of acids and bases. We may suppose that an acid has a certain intrinsic "acidity" if we wish, but the Brønsted treatment makes clear that the extent to which such an acid is ionized in solution depends importantly upon the basicity of the solvent. Thus perchloric acid, $HClO_4$, is a strong acid, completely ionized, in water solution, but it is only slightly ionized in nonaqueous sulfuric acid.

The solvated proton is the strongest acid that may exist in a given solvent. If HB is inherently a stronger acid than HS^+, it will transfer its proton to the solvent; in other words, the position of equilibrium in the reaction HB + S $\rightleftarrows$ HS^+ + B will lie far toward the right. A series of different acids all of which are stronger than the solvated proton will ionize completely; such solutions will be brought to a level of acidity governed by the acid strength of HS^+. This is known as the *levelling effect*. Thus, in aqueous solution the acids perchloric, nitric, and hydrochloric are equally strong, whereas in the

---

[2] The proton in aqueous solution may actually be more heavily hydrated than H_3O^+. For example, a species $H_9O_4^+$ ($H_3O^+ \cdot 3H_2O$ or $H^+ \cdot 4H_2O$) has been postulated on the basis of the infrared spectra of strong acid solutions, studies of the extraction of strong acids from water into certain organic solvents, and other experimental evidence. For an interesting review, see H. L. Clever, *J. Chem. Educ.*, **40**, 637 (1963).

less basic solvent, glacial acetic acid, the three acids are not levelled, and perchloric is stronger than the other two.

In Brønsted terms, the dissociation of bases is treated in a similar fashion except that here the process is promoted by the *acidity* of the solvent. Again, the general case may be formulated as the interaction of two conjugate pairs:

$$\text{SH} \rightleftharpoons \text{S}^- + \text{H}^+$$
$$\underline{\text{B} + \text{H}^+ \rightleftharpoons \text{BH}^+}$$
$$\text{B} \quad + \quad \text{SH} \rightleftharpoons \text{BH}^+ + \quad \text{S}^-$$

$$\text{base}_1 \qquad \text{acid}_2 \qquad \text{acid}_1 \qquad \text{base}_2$$

An example is $\text{NH}_3 + \text{H}_2\text{O} \rightleftharpoons \text{NH}_4^+ + \text{OH}^-$. As with acids, bases may be of any charge type (neutral, cationic, or anionic); the charges have been placed in the above equations simply to show that the base and its conjugate acid differ by one. If the solvent is sufficiently acidic, we may again encounter a levelling effect in which a series of bases are brought to a level of basicity in solution determined by the species S^-. In water, for example, so-called basic anhydrides like CaO yield OH^- by a process which may be written:

$$\text{O}^= + \text{H}_2\text{O} \rightleftharpoons 2\text{OH}^-$$

The strongest base possible in anhydrous sulfuric acid is similarly the solvent anion, HSO_4^-; sulfates are then analogous to the basic anhydrides in the aqueous system:

$$\text{SO}_4^= + \text{H}_2\text{SO}_4 \rightleftharpoons 2\,\text{HSO}_4^-$$

Neutralization reactions involving strong acids and bases in the various solvents become, in Brønsted terms, simply reactions between the cation and the anion of the solvent because of the levelling effect. Water, for example, dissociates as follows:

$$2\,\text{H}_2\text{O} \rightleftharpoons \text{H}_3\text{O}^+ + \text{OH}^-$$

One of the two water molecules in the equation acts as an acid, the other as a base, which is to say that water is *amphoteric*. Neutralization of strong acids and bases is simply the reverse of this self-dissociation or autoprotolysis reaction:

$$\text{H}_3\text{O}^+ + \text{OH}^- \rightleftharpoons 2\,\text{H}_2\text{O}$$

Likewise, in liquid ammonia solution, strong acids and bases are levelled to NH_4^+ and NH_2^- respectively, and neutralization may be written

$$\text{NH}_4^+ + \text{NH}_2^- \rightleftharpoons 2\,\text{NH}_3$$

In sulfuric acid as a solvent, the reaction becomes

$$\text{H}_3\text{SO}_4^+ + \text{HSO}_4^- \rightleftharpoons 2\,\text{H}_2\text{SO}_4$$

The Brønsted treatment offers the conceptual advantage of unifying a number of acid-base processes which, in other terms, may appear different. Hydrolysis, for example, need no longer be distinguished as a special process.

The hydrolysis of a salt like sodium acetate is simply the dissociation reaction of the acetate ion as a base:

$$OAc^- + H_2O \rightleftharpoons HOAc + OH^-$$

It may be seen that it will be a property of a conjugate acid-base pair that a strong acid has a weak conjugate base and vice versa. Thus chloride ion, the conjugate base of the strong acid hydrochloric, is too weak a base to abstract protons from water, and hydrolysis of the chloride ion is negligible.

Using this introduction as a basis, we shall refer repeatedly to the Brønsted ideas throughout this chapter.

IONIZATION CONSTANTS

Chemical equilibrium

When reactive chemical substances are mixed together, the products of the reaction are formed at a rate which decreases with time until finally it becomes equal to the rate at which the products react to form the starting substances. Consider a reaction:

$$A + B \rightleftharpoons C + D$$

When A and B are mixed, they react to form C and D. The rate of this reaction progressively decreases, while the rate at which C and D react to form A and B increases, until, when the two rates become equal, there is no further net change in the quantities of A, B, C, and D in the system. It is then said that the system is in a state of equilibrium. The rate at which equilibrium is attained is of the order of a microsecond for the ionization that occurs when acetic acid is mixed with water; on the other hand, a mixture of hydrogen and oxygen, standing at room temperature, would change little in thousands of years unless the reaction were catalyzed, even though at equilibrium H_2O is greatly favored over H_2 and O_2. If a reaction is to be useful as part of an analytical method, obviously its rate must be reasonably fast under the conditions employed; this is often the case with the relatively simple reactions involving ions in solution, although not necessarily so. The best proof that a system is in equilibrium is a demonstration that a mixture of the same composition is obtainable by mixing reactants A and B as by mixing products C and D.

The equilibrium constant

The law of chemical equilibrium states that the activities of reactants and products for the general reaction

$$a\,A + b\,B \rightleftharpoons c\,C + d\,D$$

will attain values at equilibrium such that the quotient given below will be a constant at a given temperature:

$$\frac{a_C^c \times a_D^d}{a_A^a \times a_B^b} = K_{eq}$$

The constant, K_{eq}, is called the equilibrium constant. We may accept the equilibrium law as an experimental fact at this time, although it is derivable from thermodynamic principles which the student encounters in physical chemistry courses. The terms a_C^c, a_D^d, etc., represent the activities of the species C, D, etc., raised to the powers indicated by the coefficients in the balanced chemical equation.

We should hasten to warn the unwary that this discussion of chemical equilibrium has been greatly simplified. Many chemical reactions under laboratory conditions are not reversible in the sense suggested above. In many organic reactions and a number of inorganic ones as well, a true equilibrium involving reactants and products is never attained. Ideally, if A, B, C, and D were in equilibrium, addition to the mixture of a tiny amount of, say, D would cause the reaction to proceed to a slight extent to the left, forming a tiny quantity of A and B and consuming a slight amount of C. But it often happens in practice that while C and D are obtainable from A and B, a mixture of C and D will not produce A and B at an appreciable rate; they may even react to form entirely different products. Reactions in which covalent bonds are broken and formed are especially likely to proceed via various paths and at varying rates to mixtures of products which are ill-suited for illustrating the law of chemical equilibrium under practical conditions. On the other hand, acid-base reactions of simple ions are particularly favorable in this regard.

Activity

The concept of activity may be explained to the student in a rigorous fashion only after he has encountered partial molal free energy or chemical potential in thermodynamics. However, he is probably acquainted with the concept of free energy, the measure of the driving force of a chemical reaction and the maximum work that can be obtained at constant temperature and pressure from the reaction as it proceeds to equilibrium. This change in free energy for the transfer of one mole of a given substance from a state of activity a_1 to activity a_2 is given by:

$$\Delta G = 2.3 RT \log \frac{a_2}{a_1}$$

In the case of solutions, the volumes must be so large that the transfer does not change the concentrations.

It is evident that the change in free energy is determined by the *ratio* of the two activities. Hence, to define an individual activity it is customary to adopt an *arbitrary* reference or *standard state* and to assign to it an activity of unity at any given temperature and pressure. The customary choices are as follows:

1. For a perfect gas the standard state is one atmosphere, and the activity is then the same as the pressure of the gas. For a real gas the standard state is that in which the so-called fugacity is unity.[3] Since at low pressures the real gas approaches ideal behavior, making fugacity and pressure approximately equal, we will take the pressure of a gas as its activity. Thus,

$$\frac{a}{P} = 1 \quad \text{when} \quad P \longrightarrow 0$$

2. The activity of a pure liquid or solid (in its most stable crystalline state) acting as a solvent for other substances is unity. That is, the standard state is a mole fraction of unity, where X is the mole fraction of the solvent.

$$\frac{a}{X} = 1 \quad \text{when} \quad X \longrightarrow 1$$

If the activity of the liquid or solid is changed by dissolving in it a solute, the activity of the solvent is still given by the mole fraction. In most examples that we shall encounter it will still be acceptable to take a value of unity as the activity of the solvent. For example, a liter of a 0.1-M aqueous solution of a solute contains 0.1 mole of that solute and about 55.3 moles of water. The mole fraction of water is thus about $55.3/55.4 \cong 1$. The possible effect of the solute upon the activity of water will be ignored in our calculations.

3. The activity of a solute is the same as its molality in very dilute solution, where ideal behavior may be assumed. That is,

$$\frac{a}{m} = 1 \quad \text{when} \quad m \longrightarrow 0$$

where m is the molality.[4] Here, as for a real gas, the standard state is a hypothetical one in which the solute is at 1 molal concentration (1 atmosphere pressure), but the environment about the solute would be the same as that of an ideal solution. In dilute solutions the behavior of the solute does approach ideal and we use molality for activity for such solutions.

Activity coefficient

In solutions where the activity of a solute is expressed as concentration, deviations from ideal solution behavior are generally expressed in terms of the *activity coefficient*, γ defined as

$$a = \gamma m$$

---

[3] The fugacity is the same as the vapor pressure when the vapor is a perfect gas, and may be regarded as an "ideal" or "corrected" vapor pressure.

[4] This is also defined in terms of mole fraction, i.e., $a/X = 1$ when $X \to 0$, where X is the mole fraction solute. Since in very dilute solution molality becomes proportional to mole fraction, either definition can be used.

The more nearly ideal a solute behaves, the closer to unity is γ and hence the closer activity is to concentration. According to our chosen standard state, as $m \to 0$, $\gamma \to 1$ and $a \to m$. For solutions of electrolytes the activity coefficient is a measure of the deviation from ideality because of ion-ion interactions. Such interactions are general, not just between the specific ions undergoing chemical reaction. For instance, the activities of ions such as Ag^+ and Cl^- in the formation of a precipitate of AgCl are lowered by the addition of a nonreacting electrolyte such as potassium nitrate. Debye and Hückel interpreted this diminished activity in terms of electrostatic interactions of the ions: Clustering of NO_3^- about the Ag^+ and of K^+ around the Cl^- tends to shield the Ag^+ and Cl^- from each other and thus hampers the effectiveness of these ions in forming AgCl.

Either the activity or the activity coefficient could be made dimensionless, but generally it is the activity coefficient which is so treated. Since our limiting definition is $a/m = 1$, it seems logical to make the units of activity the same as those of molality, thereby making the activity coefficient dimensionless. It should also be noted that in analytical chemistry most concentrations are expressed in the molarity system rather than molality. Since these two systems are very nearly the same in dilute aqueous solution, we shall use molarity in place of molality.

Equations arising from the theoretical treatment of Debye and Hückel permit the calculation of activity coefficients in solutions which are not too concentrated, and various physicochemical techniques may be employed to measure them. Some values of activity coefficients of typical electrolytes are given in Table 4.1 to give the student an idea of the magnitude of the

		ACTIVITY COEFFICIENTS OF TYPICAL ELECTROLYTES AT 25°				Table 4.1
Concentration..........	0.005	0.01	0.05	0.10	0.50	
HCl...................	0.93	0.90	0.83	0.79	0.76	
HCl (0.01-M in NaCl)....	...	0.87	0.82	0.78	0.73	
NaCl.................	0.93	0.90	0.82	0.79	0.68	
KOH.................	0.93	0.90	0.81	0.76	0.67	
BaCl$_2$.................	0.78	0.72	0.56	0.50	0.44	
K$_2$SO$_4$.................	0.78	0.71	0.53	0.44	0.26	
MgSO$_4$.................	0.57	0.47	0.26	0.19	0.09	
CuSO$_4$.................	0.56	0.44	0.23	0.16	0.04	

error involved in using molar concentration in place of activity. It may be seen in the table that the activity of an electrolyte such as HCl depends not only on the concentration of this solute itself but also upon the presence of other ions such as those of NaCl. It may also be noted that activity coefficients are lowered when the electrical charges of the ions are increased; compare, for example, the values for comparable concentrations of NaCl and MgSO$_4$.

In general, the presence of ions will have a lesser effect upon the activity of a neutral molecule than upon that of another electrolyte. However, ions do influence molecules to some degree by interacting with existing dipoles or even inducing them.

Throughout this text we shall use molar concentrations as though they were activities in most of the calculations we make. It is rare that activity coefficients are known in the complex, concentrated solutions encountered in analytical chemistry. Furthermore, many of the answers we seek regarding, for example, the feasibility of a titration, can be obtained by approximate calculations. We shall make a practice, however, of reminding the student that activities should be used in equilibrium calculations, and shall point out instances where activity effects may appreciably affect the answer we are seeking.

Ionization constants of acids and bases

Autoprotolysis constant of water. Equilibrium constants for ionization reactions like those discussed earlier are often given distinctive names. The equilibrium constant for the self-ionization of a solvent is often called the *autoprotolysis constant.* In the case of water, this constant is designated K_w:

$$2\ H_2O \rightleftharpoons H_3O^+ + OH^-$$

$$K_w = [H_3O^+][OH^-]$$

We have simply written the equilibrium constant for the ionization reaction, using molar concentrations for the activities of H_3O^+ and OH^- and unity for the activity of water, H_2O. K_w is sometimes called the *ion product* or the *ion product constant* of water. At room temperature (25°C), the value of K_w is 1.01×10^{-14}. In pure water, $[H_3O^+] = [OH^-] = 1.0 \times 10^{-7}$-$M$. In acidic solutions, $[H_3O^+] > 1.0 \times 10^{-7}$ and, correspondingly, $[OH^-] < 1.0 \times 10^{-7}$. In basic solution, the situation is reversed, and $[OH^-] > [H_3O^+]$.

Ionization constants of acids and bases. With strong acids that are essentially completely ionized, such as HCl, the concentration of unionized molecules, [HCl], is negligible, and $[H_3O^+]$ is readily calculated from the quantity of HCl introduced into the solution. On the other hand, with weak acids, which are only partially ionized, we must work with appropriate equilibrium constants in order to calculate $[H_3O^+]$.

For the ionization of a weak acid HB, we may write:

$$HB + H_2O \rightleftharpoons H_3O^+ + B$$

where HB and B are a conjugate acid-base pair with their charges unspecified for generality. Then, again using molar concentrations to approximate activities and taking $a_{H_2O} = 1$, we obtain for the equilibrium expression:

$$K_a = \frac{[H_3O^+][B]}{[HB]}$$

K_a is called the *ionization constant* (or sometimes the *acidity constant*) of the acid HB.

Similarly, for the ionization of a weak base B,

$$B + H_2O \rightleftharpoons HB + OH^-$$

we may obtain an ionization constant K_b,

$$K_b = \frac{[HB][OH^-]}{[B]}$$

There is a simple relation between K_a and K_b for a conjugate pair. From the autoprotolysis constant of water, we obtain by rearrangement

$$[OH^-] = \frac{K_w}{[H_3O^+]}$$

Substitution of this for $[OH^-]$ in the above K_b expression yields

$$K_b = \frac{[HB]K_w}{[B][H_3O^+]}$$

But note that $[HB]/[B][H_3O^+] = 1/K_a$, where K_a is the ionization constant of the conjugate acid of the base in question. Thus, in general for an acid-base pair,

$$K_b = \frac{K_w}{K_a}$$

or

$$K_a \times K_b = K_w$$

Hence it is really unnecessary to tabulate ionization constants for both acids and bases; one can always be obtained from the other. For convenience, however, both K_a and K_b values are given in Table I, Appendix I, with conjugate acid-base pairs shown side by side.

Hydrolysis reactions of salts of weak acids or bases, which are treated as a distinct topic in many books, are viewed in Brønsted terms as ordinary ionization reactions, and there is no need to designate a special "hydrolysis constant." Thus the equilibrium constant for the hydrolysis of, say, sodium acetate,

$$OAc^- + H_2O \rightleftharpoons HOAc + OH^-$$

which some writers designate K_h, is found in Table I, Appendix I, simply as K_b for acetate ion, the conjugate base of acetic acid. Similarly, the hydrolysis of ammonium chloride,

$$NH_4^+ + H_2O \rightleftharpoons H_3O^+ + NH_3$$

is viewed as the ionization of the acid NH_4^+, and the equilibrium constant is K_a for this species, the conjugate acid of the base ammonia. In the hydrolysis of sodium acetate and of ammonium chloride, Na^+ and Cl^- ions, respectively, do not participate in any acid-base equilibrium, and hence are not included in the equation above for the hydrolysis reactions.

CALCULATIONS OF pH VALUES OF AQUEOUS SOLUTIONS

pH and other p-functions

The concentrations of H_3O^+ and OH^- ions as encountered in typical analytical situations such as titrations vary over many orders of magnitude. Thus, in 0.1-M HCl, the concentration of H_3O^+ is 10^{-1}-M (0.1-M), and the hydroxyl concentration is 10^{-13}-M (0.0000000000001-M). In 0.1-M NaOH solution, $[H_3O^+] = 10^{-13}$-M. Cumbersome decimals of this sort are avoided, and numbers are obtained which are much more manageable graphically, by defining a logarithmic function of the hydrogen ion concentration. In order to obtain in usual aqueous solutions, numbers on a positive scale, the function pH is defined as a negative logarithm:

$$pH = -\log [H_3O^+] = \log \frac{1}{[H_3O^+]}$$

Thus a hydrogen ion concentration of 1.0×10^{-1}-M corresponds to a pH value of 1.00, and a hydrogen ion concentration of 1.0×10^{-13} becomes pH = 13.00. Such numbers, ranging from, say, 0 or 1 up to perhaps 13 or 14 are conveniently plotted on titration curves as seen later in this chapter. In a later chapter, it is seen that the electromotive force developed by certain galvanic cells is more directly related to the logarithmic function than to the hydrogen ion concentration itself.

The student should note that the digit before the decimal point in a pH value is not really a significant figure in the usual sense, but is merely obtained from the position of the decimal point in the original hydrogen ion concentration. For example, a hydrogen ion concentration expressed as 1.00×10^{-5}-M implies a precision of measurement of 1 part in 100; the 10^{-5} term merely fixes the decimal point, and in the corresponding pH value of 5.00 . . . , the digit 5 is related only to the position of the decimal point in the original number. The student may, as an exercise, show the manner in which an error in y is transformed into an error in x, given a function like $x = 10^y$ ($y = \log x$). For our purposes, pH values will ordinarily be given to two decimal places.

It is often convenient to define other p-functions analogous to pH, for example, $pOH = -\log [OH^-]$, $pK_a = -\log K_a$, or $pAg = -\log [Ag^+]$. Note that since $[H_3O^+][OH^-] = K_w = 1.0 \times 10^{-14}$, then $pH + pOH = pK_w = 14$.

Strong acid-strong base titration

Let us now consider the calculations involved in obtaining the pH of a solution of a strong acid titrated with a strong base. We are interested in whether such a reaction goes to completion, as it must to fulfill one of the requirements for volumetric analysis (page 17). It is convenient and instructive to construct a *titration curve*, a plot of pH against the milliliters of titrant. We shall do this in the next section (page 88) after completing the calculations.

Strong acids and strong bases are completely ionized in water solutions. Hence the hydrogen or hydroxyl ion concentration can be calculated directly from the stoichiometric concentration of acid or base that has been added. At the equivalence point the pH is determined by the extent to which water ionizes; that is, the pH is 7.00 at 25°C. All calculations made in this section are approximate. See page 96 for a complete treatment of the nature of these approximations. Consider the following problem:

PROBLEM. 50.0 ml of 0.100-M HCl is titrated with 0.100-M NaOH. Calculate the pH at the start of the titration and after the addition of 5.00, 50.0, and 55.0 ml of titrant.

Initial pH. HCl is a strong electrolyte and is completely ionized. Hence,

$$[H_3O^+] = 0.100$$

and

$$pH = 1.00$$

pH after addition of 5.00 ml of base. This is less than an equivalent quantity of base; the pH is calculated on the basis of the concentration of HCl remaining in the solution:

$$\text{original mmols HCl} = 50.0 \text{ ml} \times 0.100 \text{ mmol/ml} = 5.00$$
$$\text{mmols NaOH added} = 5.00 \text{ ml} \times 0.100 \text{ mmol/ml} = 0.50$$
$$\text{mmols HCl remaining} = 5.00 - 0.50 = 4.50$$
$$[H_3O^+] = \frac{4.50 \text{ mmol}}{55.0 \text{ ml}} = 8.18 \times 10^{-2}\text{-}M$$
$$pH = 2 - \log 8.18 = 1.09$$

Notice that the pH changed very little despite the fact that strong base was added to the solution. The pH values for other volumes of added titrant would be calculated in a similar fashion.

pH at the equivalence point. The equivalence point occurs at 50.0 ml of NaOH solution. Because the salt formed in the titration reaction (NaCl) is neither acidic nor basic in water solution (not hydrolyzed), the solution is neutral and its pH is 7.00, as in pure water.

pH after addition of 55.0 ml of base. This is 5.00 ml past the equivalence point. The pH is calculated on the basis of the excess NaOH in the solution:

$$\text{mmols NaOH added} = 55.0 \text{ ml} \times 0.100 \text{ mmol/ml} = 5.50$$
$$\text{original mmols HCl} = 5.00$$
$$\text{mmol NaOH remaining} = 5.50 - 5.00 = 0.50$$
$$OH^- = \frac{0.50 \text{ mmol}}{105 \text{ ml}} = 4.76 \times 10^{-3}\text{-}M$$
$$pOH = 3 - \log 4.76 = 2.32$$
$$pH = 14.00 - pOH = 11.68$$

Weak acid-strong base titration

In the titration of a weak acid or weak base, the hydrogen or hydroxyl ion concentration is calculated from the ionization constant of the weak electrolyte. The following situations are encountered in the titration of acetic acid with sodium hydroxide:

(a) *Weak acid alone.* This is the situation before any titrant is added.

(b) *Weak acid plus salt.* After the titrant is added and up to the equivalence point the solution contains acetic acid plus acetate ion.

(c) *Salt alone.* At the equivalence point the solution contains sodium acetate.

(d) *Beyond the equivalence point.* The solution contains excess strong base and the calculation is the same as in the previous section.

The following problem illustrates these situations. Again approximate calculations are made. See page 96 for a complete treatment of the nature of these approximations.

PROBLEM. 50.0 ml of a 0.100-M solution of a weak acid, HB, whose ionization constant is 1.0×10^{-5} is titrated with 0.100-M NaOH. Calculate the pH at the start of the titration and after the addition of 5.00, 50.0, and 55.0 ml of titrant.

(a) *Initial pH.* The weak acid ionizes as follows:

$$HB + H_2O = H_3O^+ + B^-$$

We assume that

$$[H_3O^+] = [B^-] \text{ and}$$

$$[HB] = 0.100 - [H_3O^+] \cong 0.100$$

Substituting in the ionization constant expression,

$$\frac{[H_3O^+][B^-]}{[HB]} = 1.0 \times 10^{-5}$$

gives

$$\frac{[H_3O^+]^2}{0.10} = 1.0 \times 10^{-5}$$

$$[H_3O^+] = 1.0 \times 10^{-3}$$

$$pH = 3.00 - \log 1.0 = 3.00$$

(b) *pH after addition of 5.00 ml of base.* The reaction of the titrant with acid is

$$HB + OH^- = B^- + H_2O$$

The concentration of B^- is no longer the same as that of H_3O^+ but is obtained from the amount of base added:

$$\text{original mmols HB} = 50.0 \text{ ml} \times 0.100 \text{ mmol/ml} = 5.00$$

$$\text{mmols NaOH added} = 5.00 \text{ ml} \times 0.100 \text{ mmol/ml} = 0.50$$

$$\text{mmols HB remaining} = 5.00 - 0.50 = 4.50$$

$$\text{mmol } B^- \text{ formed} = \text{mmol NaOH added} = 0.50$$

Then

$$[HB] = \frac{4.50}{55.0} - [H_3O^+] \cong \frac{4.50}{55.0}$$

and

$$[B^-] = \frac{0.50}{55.0} + [H_3O^+] \cong \frac{0.50}{55.0}$$

Substituting in the ionization constant expression,

$$\frac{[H_3O^+](0.50/55.0)}{4.50/55.0} = 1.0 \times 10^{-5}$$

Note that the volume of the solution cancels out of the numerator and denominator. Then

$$[H_3O^+] = 9.0 \times 10^{-5}$$
$$pH = 5 - \log 9.0 = 4.05$$

The above calculation is sometimes set up in a manner that seems different at first glance but which really amounts to the same thing. Rearrange the K_a expression so that it is explicit in $[H_3O^+]$, take logarithms of both sides of the equation, and multiply by -1:

$$\frac{[H_3O^+][B^-]}{HB} = K_a$$

$$[H_3O^+] = K_a \times \frac{[HB]}{[B^-]}$$

$$-\log [H_3O^+] = -\log K_a - \log \frac{[HB]}{[B^-]}$$

$$pH = pK_a - \log \frac{[HB]}{[B^-]}$$

This equation explicitly shows that the pH is a function of pK_a and the ratio of acid concentration to that of the salt, or conjugate base. Since HB and B^- are present in the same volume of solution, the volume cancels and the ratio of mmols is the same as the ratio of molar concentrations. This logarithmic form of the ionization expression frequently appears in biochemistry and physiology textbooks under the designation *Henderson-Hasselbalch equation*. For a weak base B and its conjugate acid HB^+ the corresponding expression is

$$pOH = pK_b - \log \frac{[B]}{[BH^+]}$$

(c) *pH at the equivalence point.* 50.0 ml of NaOH has been added and 5.00 mmol of B^- has been formed. The situation is the same as would be obtained by dissolving 5.00 mmol of the salt NaB in 100 ml of water. The B^- ion is a base and it is convenient to consider the equilibrium (hydrolysis):

$$B^- + H_2O = HB + OH^-$$

$$[B^-] = \frac{5.00 \text{ mmol}}{100 \text{ ml}} = 0.0500\text{-}M$$

and

$$\frac{[HB][OH^-]}{[B^-]} = \frac{K_w}{K_a}$$

Approximately,

$$[HB] \cong [OH^-]$$

Hence

$$\frac{[OH^-]^2}{0.050} = \frac{1.0 \times 10^{-14}}{1.0 \times 10^{-5}}$$

$$[OH^-]^2 = 5.0 \times 10^{-11}$$

$$2pOH = 11 - \log 5 = 10.30$$

$$pOH = 5.15$$

$$pH = 8.85$$

(d) *pH after addition of 55.0 ml of base.* This is 5.00 ml past the equivalence point. The *pH* can be calculated from the excess strong base, neglecting the contribution of the base B⁻ (hydrolysis is suppressed by excess OH⁻):

$$\text{mmol excess NaOH} = 5.00 \text{ ml} \times 0.100 \text{ mmol/ml} = 0.50$$

$$OH^- = \frac{0.50 \text{ mmol}}{105 \text{ ml}} = 4.8 \times 10^{-3}\text{-}M$$

$$pOH = 2.32$$

$$pH = 11.68$$

ACID-BASE TITRATION CURVES

As previously mentioned it is convenient and instructive to construct titration curves in considering the equilibrium aspects of acid-base reactions. The *pH* values calculated in the previous section, plus a number of additional ones, are shown in Table 4.2, and are plotted against milliliters of NaOH in Figure 4.1. The most striking features of these graphs are the very gradual *pH* changes both before and after the equivalence point and the large "break" with the addition of a very small volume of titrant close to the equivalence point. It will be noted that the magnitude of the change in *pH* at the equivalence point is less for a weak acid than for a strong acid. Titration curves for several weak acids are also shown in Figure 4.1, where it can be seen that the weaker the acid the smaller is the change in *pH* at the equivalence point. This is brought about by the fact that the neutralization reaction is not as complete at the equivalence point for a weak acid as for a stronger acid. We shall see that the sharpness of this break relates to the sharpness of an indicator color change and hence to the precision with which the titration end point can be located.

ACID-BASE INDICATORS

The analyst takes advantage of the large change in *pH* that occurs in titrations in order to determine when the equivalence point is reached. There

TITRATION OF HCl WITH NaOH AND
OF A WEAK ACID WITH NaOH

(50.0 ml of 0.100-*M* acid titrated with 0.100-*M* NaOH)

Table 4.2

ml NaOH	Volume of solution	pH, HCl	pH, weak acid‡
0.00	50.0	1.00	3.00
5.00	55.0	1.09	4.05
10.00	60.0	1.18	4.40
15.00	65.0	1.27	4.63
20.00	70.0	1.37	4.82
25.00	75.0	1.48	5.00
30.00	80.0	1.60	5.18
40.00	90.0	1.95	5.60
45.00	95.0	2.28	5.95
49.00	99.0	3.00	6.69
49.50	99.5	3.30	7.00
49.90	99.9	4.00	7.70
† 49.95	99.95	4.30	8.00
50.00	100.0	7.00	8.85
† 50.05	100.05	9.70	9.70
50.10	100.10	10.00	10.00
50.50	100.50	10.70	10.70
51.00	101.0	11.00	11.00
55.00	105.0	11.68	11.68
60.00	110.0	11.96	11.96
70.00	120.0	12.23	12.23

† Assuming 20 drops per milliliter, these are one drop before and one drop after the equivalence point.
‡ $K_a = 1.0 \times 10^{-5}$.

are many weak organic acids and bases in which the undissociated and ionic forms show different colors. Such molecules may be used to determine when sufficient titrant has been added and are termed *visual indicators*. A simple example is *para*-nitrophenol, which is a weak acid, ionizing as follows:

Colorless   **Yellow**

The undissociated form is colorless, but the anion, which has a system of alternating single and double bonds (a conjugated system), is yellow. Molecules or ions having such conjugated systems absorb light of longer wavelengths than comparable molecules in which no conjugated system exists. The light absorbed is often in the visible portion of the spectrum, and hence the molecule or ion is colored (see Chapter 12).

The well-known indicator phenolphthalein (below) is a dibasic acid and

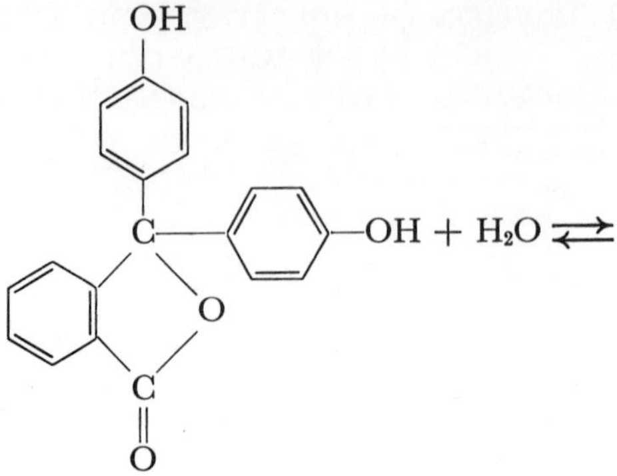

H$_2$In, colorless
Phenolphthalein

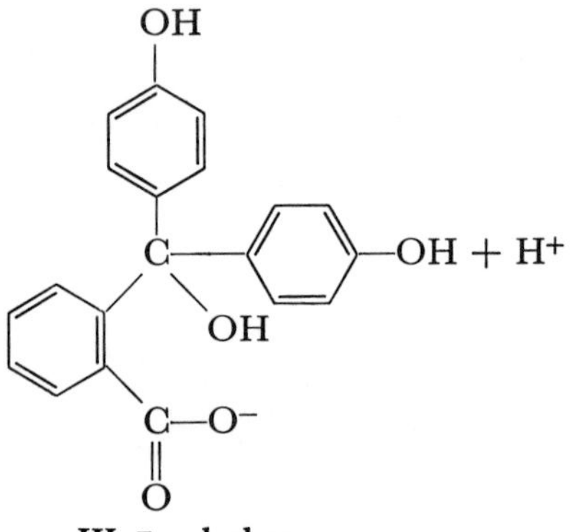

+ H$_2$O $\rightleftharpoons$

HIn$^-$, colorless

$\updownarrow$

=O + H$^+$ + H$_2$O

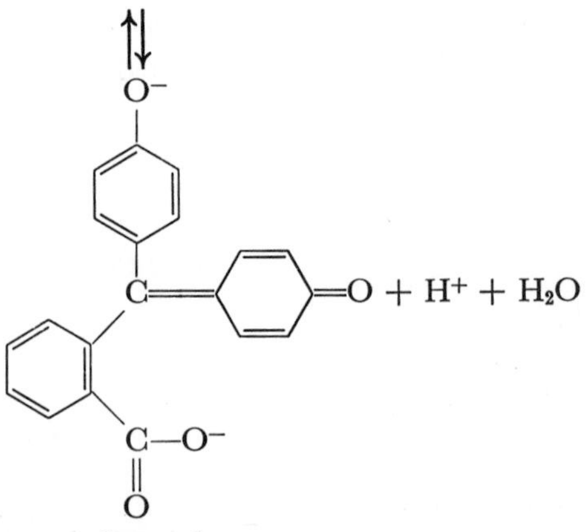

In$^-$, red

is colorless. It ionizes first to a colorless form and then on losing the second hydrogen to an ion with a conjugated system, red color results. Methyl orange, another widely used indicator, is a base and is yellow in the molecular form. Addition of a hydrogen ion gives a cation which is pink in color.

$$Na^+ \; {}^-O_3S\!\!-\!\!\left\langle \bigcirc \right\rangle\!\!-\!\!N\!\!=\!\!N\!\!-\!\!\left\langle \bigcirc \right\rangle\!\!-\!\!N(CH_3)_2 + H^+ \rightleftharpoons$$

In, yellow

$$Na^+ \; {}^-O_3S\!\!-\!\!\left\langle \bigcirc \right\rangle\!\!-\!\!\overset{\overset{\displaystyle H}{|}}{N}\!\!-\!\!N\!\!=\!\!\left\langle \bigcirc \right\rangle\!\!=\!\!\overset{+}{N}(CH_3)_2$$

In⁺, pink

For simplicity, let us designate an acid indicator as HIn, a basic indicator as InOH. The ionization expressions are

$$HIn + H_2O \rightleftharpoons H_3O^+ + In^-$$

$$InOH \rightleftharpoons In^+ + OH^-$$

The ionization constant of the acid is

$$K_a = \frac{[H_3O^+][In^-]}{[HIn]}$$

In the logarithmic form, this becomes

$$pH = pK_a - \log \frac{[HIn]}{[In^-]}$$

Fig. 4.1. Typical acid-base titration curves: 50.00 ml of 0.1000-M monobasic acid titrated with 0.1000-M NaOH; pK_a values of the **acids are** shown on the curves.

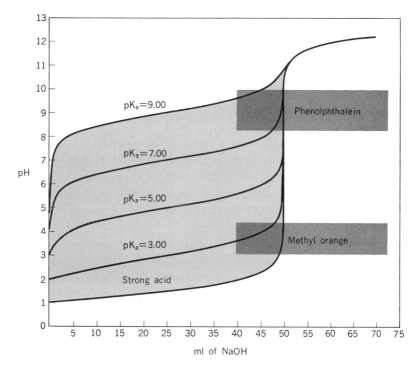

Let us for illustration assume that the molecule HIn is red in color and the ion In$^-$ is yellow. Both forms are present, of course, in a solution of the indicator, their relative concentrations depending upon the *p*H. The color that the human eye detects depends upon the relative amounts of the two forms. Obviously, in solutions of low *p*H, the acid HIn predominates and we would expect to see only a red color. In solutions of high *p*H, In$^-$ should predominate and the color should be yellow. At intermediate *p*H values, where the two forms are in about equal concentrations, the color might be orange.

Suppose that the *p*K_a of HIn is 5.00 and that a few drops of HIn are added to a solution of a strong acid which is being titrated with a strong base. The quantity of HIn added is so small that the amount of titrant used by HIn can be considered negligible. Now let us follow the ratio of the two colored forms as the *p*H changes during the titration. This is shown in Table 4.3. Let us also assume that the solution appears red to the eye when

Table 4.3 RATIO OF COLORED FORMS OF INDICATOR AT VARIOUS *p*H VALUES

*p*H solution	Ratio: [HIn]/[In$^-$]	Color	
1	10,000:1	Red	
2	1000:1	Red	
3	100:1	Red	
4	10:1	Red	⎫
5	1:1	Orange	⎬ Range
6	1:10	Yellow	⎭
7	1:100	Yellow	
8	1:1000	Yellow	

the ratio of [HIn]/[In$^-$] is as large as 10:1, and yellow when this ratio is 1:10 or less. In such a case, the minimum change in *p*H, designated ΔpH, required to cause a color change from red to yellow is two units:

$$\text{Red:} \quad p\text{H}_r = pK_a - \log 10/1 = 5 - 1$$
$$\underline{\text{Yellow:} \quad p\text{H}_y = pK_a - \log 1/10 = 5 + 1}$$
$$\Delta p\text{H} = p\text{H}_r - p\text{H}_y = (5-1) - (5+1) = -2$$

This minimum change in *p*H required for a color change is referred to as the "indicator range." In our example, the range is 4 to 6. At intermediate *p*H values, the color shown by the indicator is not red or yellow but some shade of orange. At *p*H 5, the *p*K_a of HIn, the two colored forms are in equal concentration; that is, HIn is half-neutralized. Frequently one hears terminology such as "An indicator which changed color at *p*H 5 was employed." By this is meant that the *p*K of the indicator is 5, and the range is approximately from *p*H 4 to 6.

Table 4.4

SOME ACID-BASE INDICATORS

Indicator	Color change with increasing *p*H	*p*H range
Picric acid	Colorless to yellow	0.1–0.8
Thymol blue	Red to yellow	1.2–2.8
2,6-Dinitrophenol	Colorless to yellow	2.0–4.0
Methyl yellow	Red to yellow	2.9–4.0
Bromphenol blue	Yellow to blue	3.0–4.6
Methyl orange	Red to yellow	3.1–4.4
Bromcresol green	Yellow to blue	3.8–5.4
Methyl red	Red to yellow	4.2–6.2
Litmus	Red to blue	4.5–8.3
Methyl purple	Purple to green	4.8–5.4
Para-nitrophenol	Colorless to yellow	5.0–7.0
Bromcresol purple	Yellow to purple	5.2–6.8
Bromthymol blue	Yellow to blue	6.0–7.6
Neutral red	Red to yellow	6.8–8.0
Phenol red	Yellow to red	6.8–8.4
para-α-Naphtholphthalein	Yellow to blue	7.0–9.0
Phenolphthalein	Colorless to red	8.3–10.0
Thymolphthalein	Colorless to blue	9.3–10.6
Alizarin yellow R	Yellow to violet	10.1–12.0
1,3,5-Trinitrobenzene	Colorless to orange	12.0–14.0

Table 4.4 lists some acid-base indicators together with their approximate ranges. It will be noted that the ranges are roughly one to two *p*H units, in general agreement with the assumption we made above. Actually the range may not be symmetrical about the *pK* of the indicator, since a higher ratio may be required for the observer to see one form than is required to see the other. It should also be noted that various indicators change color at widely different *p*H values. It is necessary for the analyst to select the proper indicator for his titration.

Selection of proper indicator

In Figure 4.1 the shaded areas are the indicator ranges of methyl orange (3.1 to 4.4) and phenolphthalein (8.2 to 10). It is apparent that as a strong acid is titrated, the large break in the curve at the equivalence point is sufficient to span the ranges of both these indicators. Hence either indicator would change color within one or two drops of the equivalence point, as would any other indicator changing color between *p*H 4 to 10.

In the titration of weaker acids, the choice of indicators is much more limited. For an acid of pK_a 5, approximately that of acetic acid, the *p*H is higher than 7 at the equivalence point and the change in *p*H is relatively small. Phenolphthalein changes color at approximately the equivalence point and is a suitable indicator.

In the case of a very weak acid, for example, $pK_a = 9$, no large change in pH occurs in the vicinity of the equivalence point. Hence a large volume of base would be required to change the color of an indicator and the equivalence point could not be detected with the usually desired precision.

As a general rule, then, one should select an indicator which changes color at approximately the pH at the equivalence point of the titration. For weak acids, the pH at the equivalence point is above 7 and phenolphthalein is the usual choice. For weak bases, where the pH is below 7, methyl red (4.2 to 6.2) or methyl orange is widely used. For strong acids and strong bases, methyl red, bromthymol blue, and phenolphthalein are suitable.

Indicator errors

There are at least two sources of errors in the determination of the end point of a titration using visual indicators. One occurs when the indicator employed does not change color at the proper pH. This is a determinate error and can be corrected by the determination of an *indicator blank*. The latter is simply the volume of acid or base required to change the pH from that at the equivalence point to the pH at which the indicator changes color. The indicator blank is usually determined experimentally.

A second error occurs in the case of very weak acids (or bases) where the slope of the titration curve is not great and hence the color change at the end point is not sharp. Even if the proper indicator is employed, an indeterminate error occurs and is reflected in a lack of precision in deciding exactly when the color change occurs. The use of a nonaqueous solvent (page 115) may improve the sharpness of the end point in such cases.

In order to sharpen the color change shown by some indicators, mixtures of two indicators, or of an indicator and an indifferent dye, are sometimes used. The familiar "modified methyl orange" for carbonate titrations is a mixture of methyl orange and the dye xylene cyanole FF. The dye absorbs some of the wavelengths of light that are transmitted by both colored forms, thus cutting down on the overlapping of the two colors. At an intermediate pH, the methyl orange assumes a color which is almost complementary to that of xylene cyanole FF, and the solution thus appears gray. This color change is more easily detected than the gradual change of methyl orange from yellow to red through a number of shades of orange. Many mixtures of two indicators have been recommended for improved color changes.

FEASIBILITY OF ACID-BASE TITRATIONS

An acid-base titration is said to be feasible if the change in pH at the equivalence point for the addition of a few drops of titrant is one to two pH units. If this condition is satisfied, a visual indicator will change color upon the addition of a few drops of titrant, and the volume of titrant can be determined with a precision of a few parts per thousand. If less precision will satisfy the analyst, say one part per hundred, the rate of change in pH need not be so large.

The magnitude of the change in pH near the equivalence point (ΔpH) depends upon three factors. One is the strength of the acid or base being titrated. The others are the two concentrations, that of the substance titrated and that of the titrant. The effect of concentration upon the change in pH for the strong acid-strong base titration is shown in Figure 4.2. The ΔpH decreases as the concentrations of substance titrated and titrant decrease. A ΔpH of about two units for the addition of 0.20 ml of titrant is obtained even with concentrations as low as 0.001-M.

For weak acids, the effect of the magnitude of K_a and of the concentrations on ΔpH is shown in Table 4.5. The following conclusions can be drawn:

1. The smaller the value of K_a, the higher the pH at the equivalence point and the smaller ΔpH.

2. Increasing the concentration of HA decreases ΔpH. However, this increases the volume of titrant required, rendering a given error in determining the end point a smaller percentage error.

3. Increasing the concentration of titrant increases ΔpH. This decreases the volume of titrant required, however, thus making a given error a larger percentage error.

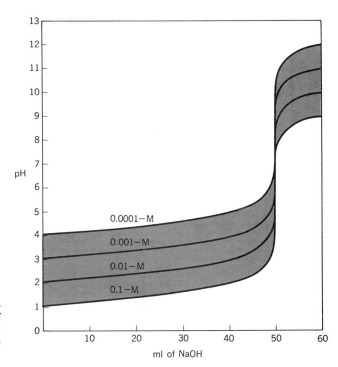

Fig. 4.2. Effect of concentration on titration curves of strong acids with strong bases. 50 ml acid titrated with base of same molarity.

**Table
4.5**

ΔpH FOR TITRATION OF WEAK ACID, HA,
WITH 0.1-*M* STRONG BASE
(100 ml volume at equivalence point)

K_a of HA	mmol HA titrated	pH, 0.05 ml before eq. pt.	pH at eq. pt.	pH, 0.05 ml after eq. pt.	ΔpH for 0.10 ml
1×10^{-5}	2.5	7.70	8.70	9.70	2.00
1×10^{-5}	5.0	8.00	8.85	9.70	1.70
1×10^{-5}	10.0	8.30	9.00	9.70	1.40
5×10^{-6}	2.5	8.00	8.85	9.70	1.70
1×10^{-6}	2.5	8.70	9.20	9.70	1.00
5×10^{-7}	2.5	9.00	9.35	9.70	0.70
1×10^{-7}†	2.5	9.70	9.70	9.70	0.00

† Usual approximate calculations.

As a general rule it can be said that a precision of a few parts per thousand can be obtained in the titration of a 0.025-*M* solution of a weak acid or base of ionization constant as low as 1×10^{-6}, using 0.1-*M* titrant. Still weaker acids or bases may be titrated with considerable sacrifice of precision in determining the end point.

A salt of a weak acid, that is, a Brønsted base, can be titrated feasibly with a strong acid if the acid itself is too weak for feasible titration. For example, an acid HA, with $K_a = 1 \times 10^{-9}$, is too weak for feasible titration. The ionization constant of the conjugate base A⁻ is 1×10^{-5}, since (page 83)

$$K_a \times K_b = 1 \times 10^{-14}$$

Hence, A⁻ can be titrated feasibly with a strong acid. Similar conclusions can be drawn for the titration of salts of weak bases.

APPROXIMATIONS IN ACID-BASE CALCULATIONS

In our calculations of the *p*H of aqueous solutions of acids and bases we made frequent assumptions and approximations to simplify the problem at hand. Most of these assumptions are valid and the approximate answers we obtained are accurate enough for our purposes in determining the feasibility of titrations. Nevertheless, it is worthwhile to examine more critically the short cuts we have taken. A much better understanding of all aspects of acid-base equilibria should be gained by such a study.

The general approach normally used is to find a set of equations sufficient in principle to permit the calculation of the concentration of each chemical species in a solution. This means we need as many equations as unknowns. But when we obtain in a particular case more equations than can be solved simultaneously with convenience, we shall invoke our chemical knowledge to simplify the mathematical problem. Frequently, for example, we shall be able to drop certain terms because, as chemists, we know that they are negligible. Once we have obtained approximate answers, we can substitute them in our original equations and see the actual magnitude of the error introduced by the approximations.

We shall consider the same types of solutions we encountered in the titrations of strong and weak acids.

Solutions of strong acids or bases

Consider the following problem:

PROBLEM. Calculate the concentrations of all species in a 0.10-M solution of HCl. This strong acid is completely ionized, i.e., [HCl] = 0. There are three species which will be present in the solution: H_3O^+, OH^-, and Cl^-. Thus we need three equations in order to determine the concentrations of these ions. We always have available the autoprotolysis constant of water,

$$[H_3O^+][OH^-] = K_w \tag{1}$$

Secondly, it is always required that there be an equal number of positive and negative charges in any solution (beakers of aqueous solutions might jump across the room if this were not the case), so we may write the *electroneutrality condition:*

$$[H_3O^+] = [OH^-] + [Cl^-] \tag{2}$$

Since HCl is completely ionized, our third equation (which we may call a *mass balance* on chloride) is simply

$$[Cl^-] = 0.10 \tag{3}$$

Substituting (3) into (2), we obtain

$$[H_3O^+] = [OH^-] + 0.10$$

But we recognize that water is a very weak acid compared with HCl (also, of course, a very weak base, if you wish), and thus [OH$^-$] is very small, smaller, indeed, than the 10^{-7}-M found in pure water, because the ionization of water is repressed by the H_3O^+ from the strong acid HCl. Thus we neglect [OH$^-$] as compared with [Cl$^-$] = 0.10-M, and obtain

$$[H_3O^+] = [OH^-] + 0.10 \cong 0.10$$

From equation (1) it is now readily obtained that

$$[OH^-] = \frac{K_w}{[H_3O^+]} = \frac{1.0 \times 10^{-14}}{1.0 \times 10^{-1}} = 1.0 \times 10^{-13}$$

Thus the pH of the solution is 1.00 and its pOH is 13.00.

The approximation made above, that $[H_3O^+] = [Cl^-]$, is obviously all right in reasonably concentrated HCl solutions. Consider, however, a 10^{-10}-M solution of HCl. This same approximation would lead to $[H_3O^+] = [Cl^-] = 10^{-10}$-$M$. That is, we would have added HCl (albeit a tiny amount) to neutral water of pH 7 and made it alkaline (pH 10)! A correct solution in this situation would be developed as follows:

$$[H_3O^+] = [OH^-] + [Cl^-]$$

Since from equation (1), $[OH^-] = K_w/[H_3O^+]$,

$$[H_3O^+] = \frac{K_w}{[H_3O^+]} + [Cl^-]$$

Substituting 1.0×10^{-14} for K_w and 10^{-10} for $[Cl^-]$, we could solve the equation for $[H_3O^+]$. This is a quadratic equation, which we obviously would avoid except in situations where $[OH^-]$ and $[Cl^-]$ were of comparable magnitude and neither could be neglected. This would clearly be the case if the HCl concentration were not far from 10^{-7}-M. Roughly, if it is greater than 10^{-6}-M, the quadratic need not be solved; if it is less than 10^{-8}-M, the pH can safely be based upon the ionization of water alone, and will be very close to 7.0.

With solutions of strong bases such as NaOH or KOH, the pH is calculated in essentially the same manner. Here we directly obtain $[OH^-]$ rather than $[H_3O^+]$, but one is readily converted to the other via K_w.

Weak acids or bases

Consider the following problem:

PROBLEM. Calculate the concentrations of all species in a 0.10-M solution of the weakly ionized acetic acid. The species in the solution are: H_3O^+, OH^-, HOAc, and OAc^-. With four unknown concentrations, the problem requires four equations. Three are already familiar: The autoprotolysis constant of water, the electroneutrality condition, and the ionization constant of the weak acid.

$$[H_3O^+][OH^-] = K_w \tag{1}$$

$$[H_3O^+] = [OH^-] + [OAc^-] \tag{2}$$

$$\frac{[H_3O^+][OAc^-]}{[HOAc]} = K_a \tag{3}$$

The fourth equation is obtained by writing what is termed a *mass balance* on acetate; that is, all of the acetic acid introduced into the solution ends up as HOAc and OAc^-:

$$[HOAc] + [OAc^-] = 0.10 \tag{4}$$

In seeking a simple solution for these equations, we may first, recognizing that acetic acid, although weak, is appreciably acidic, decide to neglect $[OH^-]$ as compared with $[OAc^-]$. Thus equation (2) becomes

$$[H_3O^+] = [OH^-] + [OAc^-] \cong [OAc^-]$$

Also, since acetic acid is weak, $[OAc^-]$ is small compared with $[HOAc]$. Thus equation (4) becomes

$$[HOAc] + [OAc^-] \cong [HOAc] = 0.10$$

Substitution of the modified (2) and (4) into (3) gives

$$\frac{[H_3O^+]^2}{0.10} = K_a = 1.8 \times 10^{-5}$$

Whence

$$[H_3O^+]^2 = 1.8 \times 10^{-6}$$

$$[H_3O^+] = 1.34 \times 10^{-3}\text{-}M$$

We may then obtain from (1),

$$[OH^-] = 7.5 \times 10^{-12}\text{-}M$$

and from (2),

$$[OAc^-] = 1.34 \times 10^{-3}\text{-}M$$

Now we may check the assumptions of neglecting $[OH^-]$ in equation (2) and $[OAc^-]$ in equation (4). Equation (2) becomes

$$[H_3O^+] = [OH^-] + [OAc^-]$$

$$1.34 \times 10^{-3} \cong 7.5 \times 10^{-12} + 1.34 \times 10^{-3}$$

This is obviously a good approximation. Equation (4) becomes

$$[HOAc] + [OAc^-] = 0.10$$

$$0.10 + 0.00134 \cong 0.10$$

The relative error incurred here (which is so small that we cannot calculate it without disregarding significant figures) is

$$\frac{0.00134}{0.10} \times 100 = 1.3\%$$

Weak acid plus salt

Let us next consider the situation in which a strong base is added to a weak acid solution in less than equivalent amount. This is illustrated by the following problem:

PROBLEM. 50 ml of 0.20-M NaOH is added to 50 ml of 0.40-M HOAc. Calculate the concentrations of all the species in the solution. In the presence of the excess acetic acid, we may assume that the neutralization reaction goes practically to completion, so that we end up with $50 \times 0.20 = 10$ mmol of NaOAc and $(50 \times 0.40) - (50 \times 0.20) = 10$ mmol of HOAc in a final volume of 100 ml. The solution contains the five species: H_3O^+, OH^-, HOAc, OAc^-, and Na^+. The required five equations are:

$$\frac{[H_3O^+][OAc^-]}{[HOAc]} = K_a \tag{1}$$

$$[H_3O^+][OH^-] = K_w \tag{2}$$

$$[Na^+] + [H_3O^+] = [OAc^-] + [OH^-] \tag{3}$$

$$[HOAc] + [OAc^-] = \frac{50 \times 0.40}{100} = 0.20 \tag{4}$$

$$[Na^+] = \frac{50 \times 0.20}{100} = 0.10 \tag{5}$$

The following approximations are appropriate. In the charge balance equation (3), since the solution is acidic we may consider that $[OH^-]$ is negligible. Thus $[Na^+] + [H_3O^+] = [OAc^-]$. Substituting $[Na^+] = 0.10$ into this, we obtain $0.10 + [H_3O^+] = [OAc^-]$. But HOAc is a weak acid, and we may assume that $[H_3O^+]$ is small as compared with 0.10. Thus $[OAc^-] \cong 0.10$. Now substitute this into the acetate mass balance (4), to obtain $[HOAc] + 0.10 = 0.20$ and $[HOAc] = 0.10$. Substitution into (1) yields

$$\frac{[H_3O^+] \times 0.10}{0.10} = K_a = 1.8 \times 10^{-5}$$

$$[H_3O^+] = 1.8 \times 10^{-5}\text{-}M$$

Also,

$$[OH^-] = 5.5 \times 10^{-10}$$

The assumptions may be checked. Equation (3) gives

$$0.10 + 1.8 \times 10^{-5} \cong 0.10 + 5.5 \times 10^{-10}$$

The left-hand term differs from the right by only 0.0185%. Equation (4) gives simply $0.10 + 0.10 = 0.20$.

Salt of a weak acid

Finally, let us consider the case of a salt of a weak acid (it could just as well be the salt of a weak base), such as sodium acetate. This situation results at the equivalence point of a titration, or from dissolving the salt in water.

PROBLEM. Calculate the concentrations of all species in a 0.10-M solution of sodium acetate, NaOAc.

As pointed out earlier, the acetate ion is the base, but Na^+ cannot be ignored because it will appear in the charge balance (electroneutrality condition). Thus there are five species to be considered: H_3O^+, OH^-, HOAc, OAc^-, and Na^+. The five equations are the K_a expression for acetic acid, the ion product expression for water, the charge balance, a mass balance on acetate, and a mass balance on sodium:[5]

$$\frac{[H_3O^+][OAc^-]}{[HOAc]} = K_a \tag{1}$$

$$[H_3O^+][OH^-] = K_w \tag{2}$$

$$[Na^+] + [H_3O^+] = [OH^-] + [OAc^-] \tag{3}$$

$$[HOAc] + [OAc^-] = 0.10 \tag{4}$$

$$[Na^+] = 0.10 \tag{5}$$

Because OAc^- is a weak base, $[OH^-]$ will be small, and since this is a basic solution, $[H_3O^+]$ will likewise be small. Thus equation (3) simplifies to $[Na^+] =$

---

[5] One of our equations could be the K_b expression for acetate ion, but we could not elect to use for three of our equations this K_b and both the K_a of acetic acid and K_w. The equations must be independent, and it is recalled that $K_a \times K_b = K_w$. Thus only two of these three expressions can be used.

[OAc$^-$]. In equation (4) we assume, again because OAc$^-$ is a weak base, that [HOAc] is small, and obtain [OAc$^-$] = 0.10. We wish now to go to equation (1) and solve for [H$_3$O$^+$], but notice that we do not have as yet a number to substitute into (1) for [HOAc]. Generally, this situation arises when the charge balance equation includes ions present in major concentration (compare with the charge balance equation of the previous problem). The term we wish is low and is negligible compared with the large concentration of salt ions. However, a useful expression can be obtained as follows: Add equations (3) and (4),

$$[Na^+] + [H_3O^+] + [HOAc] = [OH^-] + 0.10$$

Since [Na$^+$] = 0.10, this becomes

$$[H_3O^+] + [HOAc] = [OH^-] \qquad (6)$$

Some writers refer to this equation as the *proton condition*. It may also be arrived at by considering the major species H$_2$O and OAc$^-$ and noting that other species with excess protons (H$_3$O$^+$ and HOAc) must have formed at the expense of the proton deficient species, OH$^-$. Now, since the solution is basic and [H$_3$O$^+$] is small, we may write:

$$[HOAc] = [OH^-]$$

Substitution into equation (1) then yields

$$\frac{[H_3O^+] \times 0.10}{[OH^-]} = K_a$$

But

$$[OH^-] = \frac{K_w}{[H_3O^+]}$$

Thus

$$\frac{[H_3O^+]^2 \times 0.10}{K_w} = K_a$$

$$[H_3O^+]^2 = \frac{K_w \times K_a}{0.10} = \frac{1.0 \times 10^{-14} \times 1.8 \times 10^{-5}}{1.0 \times 10^{-1}}$$

$$= 1.8 \times 10^{-18}$$

$$[H_3O^+] = 1.34 \times 10^{-9}\text{-}M$$

Also, [OH$^-$] = 7.5 $\times$ 10^{-6}-M. To check our approximations, equation (6) becomes

$$1.34 \times 10^{-9} + 7.5 \times 10^{-6} = 7.5013 \times 10^{-6}$$

Thus, neglecting 1.34 $\times$ 10^{-9} as compared with 7.5 $\times$ 10^{-6} introduced an error of only about 0.017%.

POLYPROTIC ACIDS

A solution of the dibasic acid H$_2$B contains two acids, H$_2$B and HB$^-$, ionizing as follows:

$$H_2B + H_2O = H_3O^+ + HB^- \qquad K_{a_1} = \frac{[H_3O^+][HB^-]}{[H_2B]}$$

$$HB^- + H_2O = H_3O^+ + B^= \qquad K_{a_2} = \frac{[H_3O^+][B^=]}{[HB^-]}$$

With a tribasic acid (e.g., phosphoric, H_3PO_4), there are three stages of ionization; occasionally, even a tetrabasic acid is encountered, the best-known example being the chelon ethylenediaminetetraacetic acid (EDTA) which is discussed in detail in Chapter 7. A complete treatment of all of the equilibria involved in solutions of polyprotic acids and their several salts is complicated and beyond the scope of this text. However, for many purposes fairly valid approximations may be made which greatly simplify the treatment.

Usually the successive K_a values for a polyprotic acid differ by several orders of magnitude, as may be seen in Table I, Appendix I. As a result, the pH of a solution of an acid H_2B can usually be calculated accurately enough by considering only K_{a_1} and ignoring the further stages of ionization. The problem thus reduces to one that we have already considered. Similarly, the K_b values of the conjugate bases usually differ sufficiently to permit a fairly good calculation of the pH of a $B^=$ solution on the basis of K_{b_1} alone. (Recalling the relationship for a conjugate pair, $K_a \times K_b = K_w$, the student should note that K_{b_1} for the species $B^=$ is K_w/K_{a_2} and that K_{b_2} is K_w/K_{a_1}, where K_{a_1} and K_{a_2} are the successive constants for the acid H_2B.) The student may acquire a better "feeling" for this matter after reading the next section of this chapter on distribution of species as a function of pH.

Let us next consider the pH of a solution in which the intermediate species HB^- predominates. This might have been obtained simply by dissolving the salt $NaHB$ in water, or by mixing equimolar quantities of H_2B and $NaOH$. Suppose we calculate the pH of a 0.10-M solution of $NaHB$ for the case where K_{a_1} and K_{a_2} are 1.0×10^{-3} and 1.0×10^{-7}, respectively. There are three equilibria that may be considered, the ionizations of the two acids H_2B and HB^- as written above, and the ionization of water. The equilibrium expressions for these processes may be combined in various ways, but it is most convenient to focus attention upon the fate of the principal species HB^-. This ion can react in three ways, all of which are of course acid-base reactions in the Brønsted sense.

Disproportionation:

$$HB^- + HB^- \rightleftarrows H_2B + B^= \qquad K = \frac{K_{a_2}}{K_{a_1}} = 1.0 \times 10^{-4}$$

Ionization as a base:

$$HB^- + H_2O \rightleftarrows H_2B + OH^- \qquad K_{b_2} = \frac{K_w}{K_{a_1}} = 1.0 \times 10^{-11}$$

Ionization as an acid:

$$HB^- + H_2O \rightleftarrows H_3O^+ + B^= \qquad K_{a_2} = 1.0 \times 10^{-7}$$

From the magnitudes of the constants of the three reactions, it is evident that the first reaction (disproportionation) proceeds farthest to the right. This suggests that we might neglect the amounts of H_2B and $B^=$ formed by the second and third reactions as compared with the quantities formed by the first one. Thus, at least approximately, we may write[6]

$$[H_2B] \cong [B^=]$$

Note that the product of the two ionization constants contains these two terms:

$$K_{a_1} \times K_{a_2} = \frac{[H_3O^+]^2[B^=]}{[H_2B]}$$

Thus

$$[H_3O^+]^2 = K_{a_1} \times K_{a_2}$$

$$[H_3O^+] = \sqrt{K_{a_1} \times K_{a_2}}$$

or

$$pH = \tfrac{1}{2}(pK_{a_1} + pK_{a_2})$$

In our example, this gives a pH value of 5.00 for the solution of NaHB.

Titration curves of polyprotic acids

As previously mentioned, the pH of a solution of an acid, H_2B, can be calculated accurately enough by considering only K_{a_1}, provided K_{a_1} is several orders of magnitude larger than K_{a_2}. Let us calculate the titration curve of an acid for which this is true. Then we shall consider an example where the two constants are closer in value.

PROBLEM. 50.0 ml of 0.100-M H_2B is titrated with 0.100-M NaOH. The ionization constants are: $K_{a_1} = 1 \times 10^{-3}$, $K_{a_2} = 1 \times 10^{-7}$. Calculate the pH at various stages of the titration, using the usual approximation methods, and plot the titration curve.

(a) *Initial pH.* Consider only the first ionization,

$$H_2B = H^+ + HB^-$$

---

[6] The magnitude of the error involved in this approximation can be obtained readily as follows. Write the charge balance and the mass balance for the species obtainable from H_2B. Adding the two equations will give

$$[H_2B] + [H_3O^+] = [B^=] + [OH^-] \tag{a}$$

Since the solution is acidic, $[H_3O^+] > [OH^-]$, and we may assume that

$$[H_2B] + [H_3O^+] = [B^=] \tag{b}$$

Noting that $[HB^-]$ is about 0.10-M and substituting this into the expression for K_{a_1} we get

$$[H_3O^+] = 0.01 \, [H_2B] \tag{c}$$

Substitution of (c) into (b) gives

$$1.01 \, [H_2B] = [B^=]$$

Hence, in our particular problem, the error in this approximation is 1%.

$$\frac{[H_3O^+]^2}{0.10} = 1 \times 10^{-3}$$

$$[H_3O^+] = 1 \times 10^{-2}$$

and

$$pH = 2.00$$

(b) *pH after addition of 10.0 ml of base.*

$$\text{mmol } H_2B = 50.0 \times 0.100 - 10.0 \times 0.100 = 4.00$$
$$\text{mmol } HB^- \text{ formed} = 10.0 \times 0.100 = 1.00$$

$$pH = pK_{a_1} - \log \frac{[H_2B]}{[HB^-]}$$

$$pH = 3.00 - \log \frac{4.00}{1.00}$$

$$pH = 2.40$$

The *p*H at other points up to the first equivalence point is calculated in the same manner.

(c) *pH at first equivalence point.* 50.0 ml of base has been added and the species HB$^-$ is the predominant one. The *p*H is readily approximated (see page 103) by the expression

$$pH = \tfrac{1}{2}(pK_{a_1} + pK_{a_2})$$

Hence

$$pH = \tfrac{1}{2}(3.00 + 7.00)$$

$$pH = 5.00$$

(d) *pH during titration of HB$^-$: 60.0 ml of base added.* The second acid, HB$^-$, is now being neutralized,

$$HB^- + OH^- \rightleftarrows H_2O + B^=$$

and the *p*H is calculated from the ionization constant for HB$^-$,

$$HB^- + H_2O \rightleftarrows H_3O^+ + B^= \qquad K_{a_2} = 1 \times 10^{-7}$$

$$pH = pK_{a_2} - \log \frac{[HB^-]}{[B^=]}$$

Here

$$\text{mmol } HB^- = 50.0 \times 0.100 - 10 \times 0.100 = 4.00$$
$$\text{mmol } B^= = 10.0 \times 0.100 = 1.00$$

$$pH = 7.00 - \log \frac{4.00}{1.00}$$

$$pH = 6.40$$

The *p*H at other points up to the second equivalence point is calculated in the same manner.

(e) *pH at second equivalence point.* 100 ml of base has been added. The *p*H can be approximated by considering the first step in the hydrolysis of B$^=$,

$$B^= + H_2O \rightleftarrows HB^- + OH^-$$

$$[B^=] = \frac{50.0 \times 0.100}{150} = 0.0333\text{-}M$$

$$\frac{[HB^-][OH^-]}{[B^=]} = \frac{K_w}{K_{a_2}}$$

Since

$$[HB^-] \cong [OH^-]$$

$$\frac{[OH^-]^2}{0.0333} = \frac{1 \times 10^{-14}}{1 \times 10^{-7}}$$

$$[OH^-] = 5.8 \times 10^{-5}$$

$$pOH = 4.24$$

$$pH = 9.76$$

Values beyond the second equivalence point are calculated from the amount of excess base.

The titration curve is shown in Figure 4.3, curve A, where two distinct breaks are evident. In the same figure (curve B) is shown the curve for a dibasic acid in which the ratio of K_{a_1} to K_{a_2} is 10^2. In this case only a slight tendency toward a break at the first equivalence point can be seen. In curve C for H_2SO_4, where both the H_2SO_4 and HSO_4^- ionize extensively ($K_{a_2} = 0.012$), the shape is essentially the same as that for a monoprotic strong acid.

In general, one can conclude that the successive constants of a polyprotic acid must differ by a factor of about 10^4, or the pK_a values must differ by 4, in order for a reasonably good break to occur between the two stages of the titration. Maleic and phosphoric acids have pK_a values differing by 4.3 and 5.1 units, respectively, and hence give two breaks. In the case of sulfurous

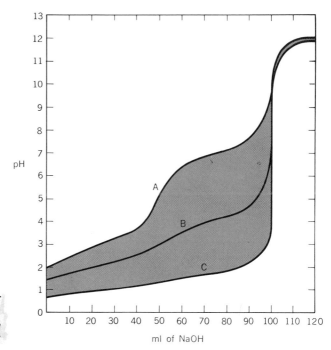

Fig. 4.3. Titration curves for diprotic acids. A, $Ka_1/Ka_2 = 10^4$; B, $Ka_1/Ka_2 = 10^2$; C, H_2SO_4, Ka large, $Ka_2 = 0.012$.

pH

ml of NaOH

acid, the two pK_a values differ by 3.4 units and the break is not extremely sharp.

Titration of carbonates

The first pK_a of carbonic acid is 6.5 and the second 10.2, making the difference 3.7 units. We might expect a fair break between the two curves in this case, but K_{a_1} is so small that the break at the first equivalence point is poor. Usually the carbonate ion is titrated as a base with a strong acid titrant, in which case two fair breaks are obtained, as shown in Figure 4.4, corresponding to the reactions

$$CO_3^= + H_3O^+ = HCO_3^- + H_2O$$

$$HCO_3^- + H_3O^+ = H_2CO_3 + H_2O$$

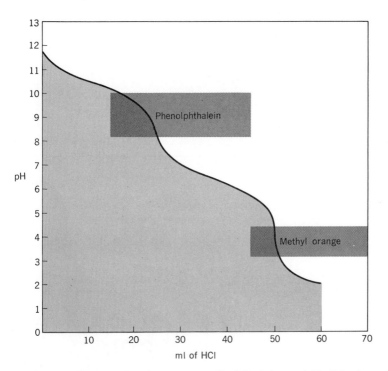

Fig. 4.4. Titration curve of Na_2CO_3 2.5 mmol Na_2CO_3 titrated with 0.10-M HCl.

Phenolphthalein is a suitable indicator for the first end point and methyl orange for the second. Usually samples containing only sodium carbonate (soda ash) are neutralized to the methyl orange end point and excess acid is added. Carbon dioxide is then removed by boiling, and the excess acid is titrated with standard base. The end point is not sharp unless carbon dioxide is removed.

Mixtures of carbonate and bicarbonate, or of carbonate and hydroxide, can be titrated with acid to the two end points mentioned above. From the volumes used to each end point it is possible to identify the components of such mixtures and to determine fairly accurately the amount of each constituent. In Table 4.6 are listed the relations between the volumes of acid used

VOLUME RELATIONS IN CARBONATE TITRATIONS   Table 4.6

Substance	Relation for qualitative identification	Millimoles of substance present	
NaOH	$v_2 = 0$		$N \times v_1$
Na$_2$CO$_3$	$v_1 = v_2$		$N \times v_1$
NaHCO$_3$	$v_1 = 0$		$N \times v_2$
NaOH + Na$_2$CO$_3$	$v_1 > v_2$	NaOH:	$N(v_1 - v_2)$
		Na$_2$CO$_3$:	$N \times v_2$
NaHCO$_3$ + Na$_2$CO$_3$	$v_1 < v_2$	NaHCO$_3$:	$N(v_2 - v_1)$
		Na$_2$CO$_3$:	$N \times v_1$

to the two end points for single components and mixtures. Here v_1 is the volume of acid used from the start of the titration to the phenolphthalein end point, and v_2 is the volume from the phenolphthalein to methyl orange end point, corrected for indicator blank. The normality of the acid is designated by N. The student should be able to verify these relationships, recalling that sodium hydroxide is completely neutralized at either the phenolphthalein or methyl orange end points. The mixture of sodium hydroxide and sodium bicarbonate is not considered since in solution these two compounds react to form either a mixture of carbonate and hydroxide, bicarbonate and carbonate, or carbonate alone, depending upon the relative amounts of the two compounds in the sample.

DISTRIBUTION OF ACID-BASE SPECIES AS A FUNCTION OF pH

It is convenient for various purposes to be able to see at a glance the status of the ionization of common acid-base species as a function of pH. Graphs which show this enable us to determine which of several possible species predominate at a given pH, and they aid in selecting the regions of buffer effectiveness for mixtures of acids or bases and their salts. For example, the pH of blood plasma is held at about 7; it might be of interest to know whether plasma phosphate exists as H_3PO_4, $H_2PO_4^-$, $HPO_4^=$, PO_4^{3-}, or as some mixture of these species at physiological pH. The type of graph we discuss below can provide answers to such questions almost instantly. This is illustrated in the following problem:

PROBLEM. In a solution of acetic acid, calculate the fraction present as HOAc molecules and as OAc⁻ ions at various pH values. Draw an appropriate graph.

Let c_a represent the *total* concentration of all species arising from acetic acid, ionized or not (this is sometimes called the *analytical concentration*, and it is simply a mass balance as used above):

$$c_a = [\text{HOAc}] + [\text{OAc}^-]$$

From the ionization constant expression for HOAc, we obtain

$$[\text{OAc}^-] = \frac{[\text{HOAc}]K_a}{[\text{H}_3\text{O}^+]}$$

Substitution into the expression for c_a gives

$$c_a = [\text{HOAc}] + \frac{[\text{HOAc}]K_a}{[\text{H}_3\text{O}^+]}$$

$$c_a = [\text{HOAc}]\left\{1 + \frac{K_a}{[\text{H}_3\text{O}^+]}\right\}$$

$$\frac{[\text{HOAc}]}{c_a} = \frac{1}{1 + (K_a/[\text{H}_3\text{O}^+])} = \frac{[\text{H}_3\text{O}^+]}{[\text{H}_3\text{O}^+] + K_a}$$

$[\text{HOAc}]/c_a$ is the fraction of total acetate present in the undissociated form. By a similar approach, it may be shown that the fraction of the acetic acid in the ionized form is given by

$$\frac{[\text{OAc}^-]}{c_a} = \frac{K_a}{[\text{H}_3\text{O}^+] + K_a}$$

Graphs of these fractions vs. pH are shown in Figure 4.5. Notice that at a pH roughly two units below pK_a, practically all of the acetate (about 99%) is in the undissociated form, HOAc, and that the acid is almost completely ionized at a pH of $(pK_a + 2)$. At the intersection of the two curves, $[\text{OAc}^-]/c_a = [\text{HOAc}]/c_a = 0.5$ and $pH = pK_a$ or $[\text{H}_3\text{O}^+] = K_a$.

PROBLEM. In a solution of the dibasic acid, oxalic, (H_2Ox), calculate the fractions present as H_2Ox molecules and as HOx⁻ and Ox⁼ ions as a function of pH. Draw appropriate graph.

Here the analytical concentration is given by

$$c_a = [\text{H}_2\text{Ox}] + [\text{HOx}^-] + [\text{Ox}^=]$$

We also have the two ionization expressions

$$K_{a_1} = \frac{[\text{H}_3\text{O}^+][\text{HOx}^-]}{[\text{H}_2\text{Ox}]}$$

$$K_{a_2} = \frac{[\text{H}_3\text{O}^+][\text{Ox}^=]}{[\text{HOx}^-]}$$

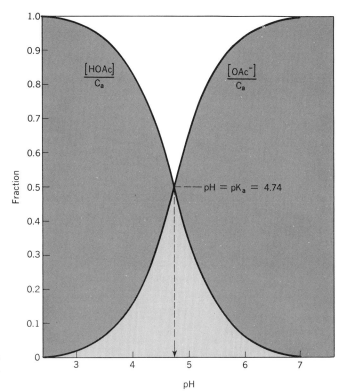

Fig. 4.5. Distribution of acetate species as a function of pH.

Rearrangement of the two K_a expressions gives

$$[HOx^-] = \frac{[H_2Ox]K_{a_1}}{[H_3O^+]}$$

$$[Ox^=] = \frac{[HOx^-]K_{a_2}}{[H_3O^+]} = \frac{[H_2Ox]K_{a_1}K_{a_2}}{[H_3O^+]^2}$$

Substitution into the expression for the analytical concentration yields

$$c_a = [H_2Ox] + \frac{[H_2Ox]K_{a_1}}{[H_3O^+]} + \frac{[H_2Ox]K_{a_1}K_{a_2}}{[H_3O^+]^2}$$

Whence

$$c_a = [H_2Ox]\left\{1 + \frac{K_{a_1}}{[H_3O^+]} + \frac{K_{a_1}K_{a_2}}{[H_3O^+]^2}\right\}$$

$$\frac{[H_2Ox]}{c_a} = \frac{1}{1 + \dfrac{K_{a_1}}{[H_3O^+]} + \dfrac{K_{a_1}K_{a_2}}{[H_3O^+]^2}}$$

$$\frac{[H_2Ox]}{c_a} = \frac{[H_3O^+]^2}{[H_3O^+]^2 + [H_3O^+]K_{a_1} + K_{a_1}K_{a_2}}$$

With no more difficulty, the expressions for the fractions present as HOx^- and $Ox^=$ can be derived,

$$\frac{[HOx^-]}{c_a} = \frac{[H_3O^+]K_{a_1}}{[H_3O^+]^2 + [H_3O^+]K_{a_1} + K_{a_1}K_{a_2}}$$

$$\frac{[\text{Ox}^=]}{c_a} = \frac{K_{a_1}K_{a_2}}{[\text{H}_3\text{O}^+]^2 + [\text{H}_3\text{O}^+]K_{a_1} + K_{a_1}K_{a_2}}$$

Fractions of total oxalate present as H_2Ox, HOx^-, and $\text{Ox}^=$ are shown as functions of $p\text{H}$ in Figure 4.6.

Derivation of similar equations for tri- or even tetra-basic acids, H_3B or H_4B, is more tedious but no more difficult than the above. Figure 4.7 shows the distribution of phosphoric acid species as a function of $p\text{H}$. It may be seen that below $p\text{H}$ 5 or so, the only species present in significant concentration are H_3PO_4 and its first ionization product, H_2PO_4^-. Thus the $p\text{H}$ of an H_3PO_4 solution could safely be calculated on the basis of the first ionization alone, as though the acid were only monobasic. As a matter of fact, at no $p\text{H}$ are more than two species present in appreciable amount. In the case of oxalic acid, the two K_a values are closer than are any pair of H_3PO_4 values; however, only in the $p\text{H}$ region 2.5 to 3.0 are all three species discernible in Figure 4.6, and even here one of the three is predominant.

BUFFER SOLUTIONS

A solution which resists large changes in $p\text{H}$ when an acid or base is added or when the solution is diluted is called a *buffer solution*. A solution containing a conjugate acid-base pair is an example of a buffer. The acid reacts with any hydroxyl ions added to the solution, and the conjugate base combines with hydrogen ions. Consider, for example, a solution of acetic acid and sodium acetate. Hydrogen and hydroxyl ions are removed by the reactions:

$$\text{HOAc} + \text{OH}^- = \text{OAc}^- + \text{H}_2\text{O}$$

$$\text{OAc}^- + \text{H}_3\text{O}^+ = \text{HOAc} + \text{H}_2\text{O}$$

The $p\text{H}$ is dependent upon the logarithm of the ratio of acid to salt (base),

$$p\text{H} = pK_a - \log\frac{[\text{HOAc}]}{[\text{OAc}^-]}$$

and it is necessary to change this ratio by a factor of 10 to change the $p\text{H}$ by one unit. The flat portion of the titration curve (Figure 4.1) for weak acids results from the buffering action just described. It should also be noted in the above equation for $p\text{H}$ that dilution should have no effect on $p\text{H}$, at least theoretically, since the volume term cancels out.

The effectiveness of a buffer solution in resisting change in $p\text{H}$ per unit of strong acid or base added is greatest when the ratio of buffer acid to salt is unity. In the titration of a weak acid this point of maximum effectiveness is reached when the acid is half-neutralized, or the $p\text{H} = pK_a$. This can be seen from the following calculation:

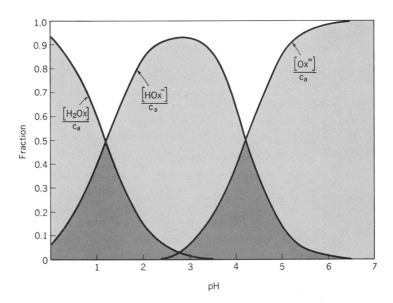

Fig. 4.6. Distribution of oxalate species as a function of pH.

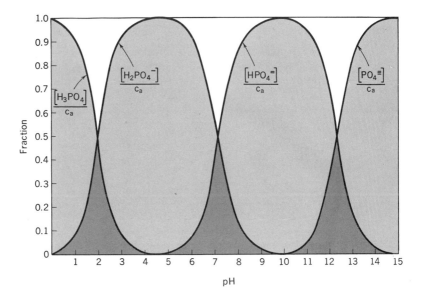

Fig. 4.7. Distribution of phosphate species as a function of pH.

PROBLEM. Calculate the slope of the titration curve of the weak acid, HA, titrated with OH^-, and find its minimum value. Let a = original mmol of HA and b = mmol of OH^- added. Then

$$[HA] = \frac{(a - b)}{v}$$

$$[A^-] = \frac{b}{v}$$

where v is the volume of solution.

$$pH = pK_a - \log \frac{a - b}{b} = pK_a - \log (a - b) + \log b$$

Differentiating, the slope is

$$\frac{dpH}{db} = \frac{0.43}{a - b} + \frac{0.43}{b} = \frac{0.43\,a}{b(a - b)}$$

To find the minimum value of the slope, differentiate the above expression and equate to zero,

$$\frac{d^2pH}{db^2} = -\frac{0.43\,a(a - 2b)}{b^2(a - b)} = 0$$

$$b = \frac{a}{2}$$

That is, $[HA] = [A^-]$ and at this point $pH = pK_a$.

It may be instructive to examine Table 4.7 which shows the change in pH produced during the titration of two different amounts of acetic acid at intervals of 1 mmol of added base. It is apparent that at the start of the titration the solution is not well buffered, and the pH rises rapidly as base is added. This explains the initial rapid rise in the titration curves of weak acids shown in Figure 4.1. The rate of rise in pH decreases, passes through a minimum at $pH = pK_a$, and then slowly increases again. At the equiva-

Table 4.7   CHANGE IN pH DURING TITRATION OF ACETIC ACID

mmol OH^- added to 10 mmol HOAc	pH†	ΔpH	mmol OH^- added to 20 mmol HOAc	pH†	ΔpH
0	2.87	. . .	0	2.72	. . .
1	3.79	0.92	1	3.46	0.74
2	4.14	0.35	2	3.79	0.33
3	4.37	0.23	3	3.99	0.20
4	4.56	0.19	9	4.65	. . .
5	4.74	0.18	10	4.74	0.09
6	4.92	0.18	11	4.83	0.09
7	5.11	0.19	12	4.92	0.09
8	5.34	0.23	18	5.69	. . .
9	5.69	0.35	19	6.02	0.33
10	8.87	3.18	20	9.02	3.00

† Calculated for 100 ml volume, assuming no change in volume as base added.

lence point a large change occurs since the acid is exhausted and the solution is no longer buffered.

The flat portion of a titration curve corresponds to the steep portion of curves such as are shown in Figures 4.5, 4.6 and 4.7. In such a region, any base (or acid) which is added causes a large change in the fraction of the species in solution. This indicates, of course, that the base (or acid) is being consumed by some species in the solution.

Concentrated solutions of strong acids and bases resist large changes in pH and the titration curves are flat over a wide range of pH (Figure 4.1). However, such solutions are sometimes not regarded as buffers in the strictest sense, since the pH is markedly changed by dilution.

The capacity of a buffer is the tendency of the solution to resist changes in pH upon the addition of acid or base. It is defined as the number of moles of strong base required to change the pH of one liter of solution by one pH unit. The reciprocal of the slope of a titration curve[7] is also used to express the effectiveness of buffering action. It is usually desirable to have a high buffer capacity, and this can be achieved by using high reagent concentrations. Note that the greater the initial concentration of acid, the greater is the capacity. This is evident from Table 4.7 in that twice as much base is required to increase the pH of the more concentrated solution from 3.79 to 4.74 than is needed for the more dilute solution. The term "range" of a buffer is ill-defined, but it is evident from Table 4.7 that little buffering action is obtained if the acid-salt ratio is greater than 9 to 1 or less than 1 to 9.

In preparing a buffer of a desired pH, the analyst should select an acid-salt (or base-salt) system in which the pK_a of the acid is as close as possible to the desired pH. By this selection the ratio of acid to salt is near unity and maximal effectiveness against increase or decrease in pH is obtained. The actual concentrations of acid and salt employed depend upon the desired resistance to change in pH. These points are illustrated in the following problem:

PROBLEM. (a) It is desired to prepare 100 ml of a buffer of pH 5.00. Acetic, benzoic, and formic acids and their salts are available for use. Which acid should be used for maximum effectiveness against increase or decrease in pH? What acid-salt ratio should be used?

The pK_a values of these acids are: acetic, 4.74; benzoic, 4.18; and formic, 3.68. The pK_a of acetic is closest to the desired pH and this acid and its salt should be used. Then

$$pH = pK_a - \log \frac{[HOAc]}{[OAc^-]}$$

$$5.00 = 4.74 - \log \frac{[HOAc]}{[OAc^-]}$$

[7] This is also referred to as van Slyke's *Buffer Index* symbolized β. See T. B. Smith, *Analytical Processes*, Edward Arnold and Co., London, 2nd Ed., 1940, p. 197.

Taking antilogs $[HOAc]/[OAc^-] = 1/1.8$, or the salt to acid ratio should be 1.8 to 1. This is the molar ratio, not the ratio of grams.

(b) If it is desired that the change in pH of the buffer be no more than 0.10 unit for the addition of 1 mmol of either acid or base, what minimum concentrations of the acid and salt should be used?

Since there is less acid present than salt, a greater change in pH will result if base is added. Hence if we calculate on the basis that base is added, the condition will be more than satisfied for the addition of acid. Then if

$$x = \text{mmol acid originally present}$$

$$1.8x = \text{mmol salt originally present}$$

If 1 mmol OH^- is added, then

$$x - 1 = \text{mmol acid remaining}$$

$$1.8x + 1 = \text{mmol salt}$$

Then

$$5.10 = 4.74 - \log \frac{x-1}{1.8x+1}$$

Solving gives $x = 6.6$ mmol, and $1.8x = 11.9$ mmol. The molar concentrations are then, $[HOAc] = 0.066$ mmol/ml, and $[OAc^-] = 0.119$ mmol/ml.

PHYSIOLOGICAL BUFFERS

It is of interest to point out that the principles of acid-base chemistry discussed in this chapter are of direct significance in such fields as biochemistry and physiology. The great physiologist Claude Bernard was the first to emphasize that the fluids of the body provide an "internal environment" in which the body cells live and perform their many functions protected from the inconstancy of the external environment. Living tissues are extremely sensitive to changes in the composition of the fluids that bathe them, and the regulatory mechanisms within the body which maintain the constancy of the internal environment comprise one of the most important phases in the study of the biological sciences.

A very important aspect of this regulation is the maintenance of a nearly constant pH in the blood and other fluids of the body. Substances that are acidic or alkaline in character are ingested in the diet and are formed continually by metabolic reactions, but the pH of the blood normally remains constant within about 0.1 pH unit (7.35 to 7.45). For our present purpose, which is not to examine the subject in detail, the rough statement will suffice that the general scheme by which the body manages acid or base is to buffer it until it can be excreted. The pH of the urine is quite variable (normally between about 4.8 and 7.8), reflecting the elimination of acids or bases, and much acid is eliminated through the lungs as carbon dioxide. Pending excretion, these substances are handled by the buffers present in significant quantity in the blood, and buffering action under these circumstances is no different in principle from that in the chemistry laboratory.

The principal buffers in the blood are the plasma proteins (albumins and globulins), bicarbonates, phosphates, and hemoglobin and oxyhemoglobin. The bicarbonate, albumins, and globulins are important plasma buffers, while the hemoglobin and most of the phosphate are found in the red cells. Let us consider the phosphate system as an example of these. The reaction with which we are concerned is

$$H_2PO_4^- + H_2O \rightleftharpoons HPO_4^= + H_3O^+$$

The K_a value is 6.2×10^{-8}, and pK_a is 7.2. Thus, at pH 7.2, $[H_2PO_4^-] = [HPO_4^=]$ and the system exhibits maximal effectiveness for buffering either acid or alkali. Reasonable buffer effectiveness extends over the range of roughly pH 6 to 8, which includes the physiological value[8] of about 7.4. Thus the phosphate system is well-suited to operate in the region of physiological pH.

The system $H_2CO_3 - HCO_3^-$ is an important buffer in the blood plasma. The pK_a value is well below physiological pH, but the system is valuable at pH 7.4 and becomes very important in any condition which lowers the plasma pH (acidosis). Proteins contain carboxyl, amino, and other weakly acid and basic groups, and hence they and their salts constitute buffer systems.

Disturbances in the pH of the blood are seen clinically in certain diseases. For example, untreated diabetes sometimes gives rise to an acidosis which may be fatal. Acidic metabolic products are produced, ordinarily, in greater quantities than are alkaline substances, and the capacity of the blood to buffer acids is correspondingly greater than is the capacity toward alkali.

NONAQUEOUS TITRATIONS

Consider an acid, HB, which we wish to titrate with base, say NaOH. We have discussed the feasibility of this titration in terms of the "strength" of HB, using its ionization constant, K_a, as a measure. But, as pointed out earlier, in terms of the Brønsted theory, K_a is really a measure of the tendency of HB to transfer a proton to the solvent, water:

$$HB + H_2O \rightleftharpoons H_3O^+ + B$$

That is, K_a is not a measure of an "intrinsic" acid strength of HB, because the basicity of water is also involved in this reaction. The same acid might

---

[8] This discussion is only approximate. The K_a value cited is valid at 25°, but body temperature is 37°. (At 37°, $pK_w = 13.6$ and the pH of a neutral solution is 6.8 instead of 7.0; thus the physiological pH of 7.4 is somewhat more alkaline than it appears to be.)

ionize to a much greater degree in a more basic solvent, say an organic amine:

$$HB + RNH_2 \rightleftharpoons RNH_3^+ + B$$

That is, there will be a greater concentration of solvated protons in the latter solvent. Thus it might appear that if HB were too weak an acid to be titrated feasibly in aqueous solution, we could enhance its "acidity" and hence its "titratibility" by choosing a solvent more basic than water.

Actually, in a practical sense, this is often the case, but the above discussion is misleading as it stands. In fact, ionization is not at all necessary for successful acid-base titrations. Excellent titrations have been performed in nonpolar solvents like benzene or chloroform which do not promote ionization to any appreciable extent. Indeed, it is *not* the greater basicity of the organic amine that makes it a better solvent than water for the titration of the very weak acid, HB. It is a better solvent for this titration because it is a *weaker acid* than water. In the aqueous system, water is actually a product of the titration reaction

$$HB + OH^- \rightleftharpoons H_2O + B$$

Further, it is present in a large excess. Thus, to the extent that water is acidic it competes against the acid we wish to titrate, and prevents the above reaction from going nearly to completion unless HB is itself sufficiently strong. We need, then, for a successful titration of a very weak acid a solvent that is a weaker acid than water. It is acceptable if this solvent, as often happens, is more basic than water, but it is not correct to fixate upon this latter aspect. This point has been confused by many writers.

In any case, we find that many titrations of weak acids and bases which are not feasible in water solution can be performed in other solvents. A variety of solvents have now been studied, and various methods of end point detection are available. Much of the work is empirical because we do not have acidity scales in all of these solvents as we have for water, but even on this basis, the field of nonaqueous titrations has become important in analytical chemistry.

Solvent systems

Several classifications of solvents have been proposed. Laitinen[9] considers four types: (1) amphiprotic, i.e., possessing both acidic and basic properties, as does water; (2) aprotic, i.e., neither appreciably acidic nor basic (termed *inert* by some writers), e.g., benzene, carbon tetrachloride, chloroform; (3) basic but not appreciably acidic, e.g., ether, pyridine, ketones; (4) acidic but not basic, no examples known. The amphiprotic

---

[9] H. A. Laitinen, *Chemical Analysis*, McGraw-Hill Book Co., Inc., New York, 1960, p. 60.

solvents undergo autoprotolysis, as noted earlier in this chapter. The inert solvents, which do not possess appreciable acidic or basic properties, exert no levelling effect, and hence may be most suitable for titrations of mixtures where compounds of varying acidity are to be differentiated. Essentially, the magnitude of the break in a titration curve in amphiprotic solvents is limited by the autoprotolysis reaction. Thus the inert solvents give the largest breaks. On the other hand, these solvents often will not dissolve the titrants or polar compounds which it may be desired to titrate. In such cases, solvent mixtures such as benzene-methanol may be used, diluting the acid-base properties of the methanol with as much benzene as is compatible with adequate solubility.

Kolthoff and Bruckenstein[10] subdivide the amphiprotic solvents into three classes: (1) those with acid-base properties comparable with water, e.g., alcohols; (2) protogenic solvents, which are much stronger acids and weaker bases than water, e.g., glacial acetic acid, sulfuric acid; (3) protophilic solvents, with much greater basicity and weaker acidity than water, e.g., liquid ammonia, ethylenediamine.

Titrants

Perchloric acid is by far the most widely used acid for the titration of weak bases, because it is a very strong acid which is readily available. It is normally obtained commercially as 72% $HClO_4$ by weight, the remainder being water; this is an azeotrope of $HClO_4$ and H_2O, and represents approximately the composition $HClO_4 \cdot H_2O$, which some writers formulate as hydronium perchlorate $H_3O^+ ClO_4^-$. Weak bases are titrated most often in glacial acetic acid solution. In such cases, the titrant is perchloric acid, say 0.1-M, in the same solvent. Because the presence of water may be deleterious (see above), the desired quantity of 72% $HClO_4$ is mixed with acetic acid, and then acetic anhydride is added in approximately the correct amount to react with the water estimated to be present. The product of this reaction is, of course, acetic acid.

A somewhat larger variety of strong bases are used, including alkali hydroxides, tetraalkylammonium hydroxides, and sodium or potassium methoxide or ethoxide. Common solvents for these bases are lower alcohols and mixtures of benzene with methanol or ethanol.

Normally the effect of temperature upon measured titrant volumes can be ignored with aqueous solutions under ordinary room temperature variations. Organic solvents such as acetic acid, benzene, or methanol, on the other hand, have fairly large coefficients of thermal expansion, and the

---

[10] I. M. Kolthoff and S. Bruckenstein, "Acid-Base Equilibria in Nonaqueous Solutions," Chapter 13 in I. M. Kolthoff and P. J. Elving, Eds., *Treatise on Analytical Chemistry*, Part I, Vol. 1, Interscience Publishers, Inc., New York, 1959, p. 476.

volume changes may not be negligible if the titrant is at a different temperature from that at which it was standardized. Correction for the effect of a temperature change upon the volume of titrant may be made by means of an equation of the type

$$V_t = V_0(1 + \alpha t + \beta t^2 + \gamma t^3)$$

where V_0 is the volume at 0°C and V_t the volume at t°C. Values of α, β, and γ for various liquids may be found in handbooks. Practically, β and γ are usually small enough so that βt^2 and γt^3 may be ignored. Suppose the titrant were at 30°C when an unknown was titrated, whereas it had been standardized at 25°C. Neglecting the higher order terms in the above equation and eliminating V_0 between the two temperatures involved gives

$$V_{25} = V_{30} \times \frac{1 + 25\alpha}{1 + 30\alpha}$$

Using a handbook value for α, the volume of titrant that would have been consumed had the titration been performed at 25°C can be readily calculated. For a mixed solvent such as benzene-methanol, a value for α will not be found in the usual tables; in such cases, a mean value of α may be used, weighted according to the volume fractions or the mole fractions of the two solvents in the mixture (if the mixture is nonideal, an exact, theoretically valid value of α cannot be calculated from the information that is normally available, but an adequate value can be obtained with weighted means).

End point detection

A number of visual indicators are available, generally under trivial names such as cresol red, methyl red, azo violet, and crystal violet. The rationale of indicator selection is not on a good theoretical base, and the choice is often best made on the basis of experience, trial-and-error, or reference to analogous cases which may be found in the literature.

Potentiometric end point methods (Chapter 8) are frequently employed, although, in general, electrode behavior in nonaqueous solvents is not well understood. Again, the safest approach is to see what other workers have used in similar situations. Other instrumental end points such as conductometric and photometric (Chapter 12) have been used successfully.

Applications

The number of compounds which have been titrated in nonaqueous media is much too large for listing here. Very weak acids such as phenols and very weak bases like aromatic amines and urea have been titrated with excellent results. Salts of carboxylic acids can be titrated in acetic acid solution with perchloric acid. For example, potassium acid phthalate, which is used as an acid in water, behaves as a base in acetic acid solution and serves as a good primary standard for perchloric acid titrants. Nonaqueous titrations have become important in the pharmaceutical industry; many drugs possess very weak acid or basic properties which do not permit titration in water but which lead to good nonaqueous titrations. For example, most of the well-known sulfa drug group can be determined by titration as acids (the acidity is conferred by the sulfonamide group, $-SO_2NH-$) with alkali methoxide in benzene-methanol or dimethyl-formamide solution.

REFERENCES

1. H. Freiser and Q. Fernando, *Ionic Equilibria in Analytical Chemistry*, John Wiley & Sons, Inc., New York, 1963.
2. H. A. Laitinen, *Chemical Analysis*, McGraw-Hill Book Co., Inc., New York, 1960.
3. T. B. Smith, *Analytical Processes*, 2nd Ed., Edward Arnold and Co., London, 1940.
4. L. G. Sillen, "Graphic Presentation of Equilibrium Data," I. M. Kolthoff, "Concepts of Acids and Bases," S. Bruckenstein and I. M. Kolthoff, "Acid-base Strength and Protolysis Curves in Water," and I. M. Kolthoff and S. Bruckenstein, "Acid-base Equilibria in Nonaqueous Solutions," Chapters 8, 11, 12, and 13, Part I, Vol. 1, of *Treatise on Analytical Chemistry*, I. M. Kolthoff and P. J. Elving, Eds., Interscience Publishers, Inc., New York, 1959.
5. J. N. Butler, *Ionic Equilibrium, A Mathematical Approach*, Addison-Wesley Publishing Co., Inc., Reading, Mass., 1964.

QUESTIONS

1. Sketch a graph of hydrogen ion concentration (ordinate) vs. volume of alkali (abscissa) for the neutralization of 50 ml of 0.10-M HCl with 0.10-M NaOH. How would the graph look if solid NaOH were used and the volume remained constant? Does the ordinate ever reach zero? What is its minimum value?

2. Plot the function $y = \log x$. Comment on any relation of the shape of this plot to the shape of a titration curve. Calculate the pH after the addition of 0.00, 0.01, 0.10, 1.00 and 10.0 ml of 0.10-M NaOH to 100 ml of water and plot the graph. Does this look like part of a titration curve?

3. Plot the pH vs. the logarithm of the ratio of the concentrations of acetic acid to acetate ion during the neutralization of 10 mmol of acetic acid with NaOH. What is the significance of the pH value when the logarithm of the ratio is zero?

4. Plot curves such as shown in Figure 4.2 for the following acids: (a) carbonic, (b) phthalic, (c) citric. Point out the best buffering range or ranges for each acid, and the principal components of the solution in these pH ranges.

5. Derive the error in y resulting from an error in x, where the function is $x = 10^y$, or $y = \log x$.

6. What color will be shown if to a 0.10-M solution of sodium acetate there are added a few drops of (a) methyl red, (b) bromthymol blue, (c) phenolphthalein, (d) thymolphthalein?

7. Given two indicators, A an acid, and B a base, both having ionization constants of 1×10^{-9}, which would you choose for the following titrations?
  (a) Formic acid with NaOH.
  (b) Aniline hydrochloride with NaOH.
  (c) H_2SO_4 with KOH.

8. If one calculates the pH of a 10^{-6}-M solution of a weak acid, $K_a = 1 \times 10^{-10}$, with the usual approximations, the result is a pH of 8. What is the fallacy in this calculation? What is the correct pH?

9. A student once asked if pH could be defined as the logarithm of the volume of solution required to furnish 1 mole of hydrogen ion. Is this correct? Explain.

10. What is the significance of a negative pH or pOH? of a pH or pOH greater than 14?

11. The ion product constant of water, K_w, is about 10^{-12} at 100°C. What is the pH of a neutral solution at 100°?

12. If the change in pH per change in volume of titrant is plotted against the volume of titrant (strong acid vs. strong base), what is the shape of the curve? Check your conclusion with Figure 8.4.

13. A student standardized a solution of sodium hydroxide against a standard solution of hydrochloric acid, using methyl orange as the indicator (no indicator blank). He then titrated a potassium acid phthalate unknown with the base, using phenolphthalein indicator. Were his results high, low, or correct? Explain.

14. Write all equations needed to calculate the concentrations of all the species in a 0.10-M solution of NaH_2PO_4. Write the proton condition expression.

15. Plot the buffer index of 0.10-M acetic acid as a function of pH. What does the maximum in the curve correspond to? Which has a greater buffer capacity, a solution containing only acetic acid, or one containing only sodium acetate? Explain.

16. Plot log C (ordinate, from -9 vertically to 0) vs. pH (0 to 12) for a 0.01-M solution of HOAc in water, letting C be the following: HOAc, OAc$^-$, H$^+$, and OH$^-$. Comment on the utility of such a plot.

PROBLEMS

1. Convert the following to pH:
  (a) $[H_3O^+] = 0.00040$ (e) $[OH^-] = 4.0 \times 10^{-6}$
  (b) $[H_3O^+] = 1.0$ (f) $[OH^-] = 10$
  (c) $[H_3O^+] = 5.0$ (g) $[OH^-] = 2.0 \times 10^{-15}$
  (d) $[H_3O^+] = 3.0 \times 10^{-8}$ (h) $[OH^-] = 0.80$

2. Convert the following to hydrogen ion concentration:
  (a) $pH = -1.30$ (e) $pOH = -0.70$
  (b) $pH = 0.70$ (f) $pOH = 14.40$
  (c) $pH = 6.74$ (g) $pOH = 8.36$
  (d) $pH = 13.18$ (h) $pOH = 1.04$

3. Calculate the pH of the following solutions:
 (a) 20 g of NaOH in 250 ml of solution
 (b) 0.365 g of HCl in 1.00 l of solution
 (c) 0.30 g of HOAc in 100 ml of solution
 (d) 2.00 g of NH_3 in 200 ml of solution
 (e) 0.50 g of NaOAc in 100 ml of solution
 (f) 0.50 g of NH_4Cl in 100 ml of solution
 (g) 200 ml of solution containing 0.50 g of HOAc and 0.50 g of NaOAc
 (h) 200 ml of solution containing 5.0 mmol of HOAc and 5.00 mmol of NaOAc
 (i) 10^{-10} moles of HCl in 1 l of solution
 (j) 12 g of $NaHSO_4$ in 1 l of solution

4. Calculate the pH of the following solutions:
 (a) 60 ml of 0.10-M NH_3 + 40 ml of 0.15-M HCl
 (b) 80 ml of 0.080-M HOAc + 20 ml of 0.16-M NaOH
 (c) 50 ml of 0.12-M H_3PO_4 + 30 ml of 0.20-M NaOH
 (d) 40 ml of 0.10-M H_3PO_4 + 20 ml of 0.40-M NaOH
 (e) 10 ml of NaOH, $pOH = -0.30$ + 90 ml of HCl, $pH = 0.70$
 (f) 50 ml of HCl, $pH = 1.00$ + 50 ml pure H_2O
 (g) 50 ml of HCl, $pH = 2.00$ + 50 ml of HCl, $pH = 4.00$
 (h) 50 ml of HCl, $pH = 6.00$ + 50 ml of NaOH, $pH = 12.00$
 (i) 3.00 mmol of Na_2CO_3 + 40 ml of H_2O + 60 ml of 0.10-M HCl
 (j) 60 ml of 0.10-M NaOAc + 40 ml of 0.15-M HCl

5. A chemist wishes to prepare 250 ml of a solution of pH 2.40. (a) Calculate the number of grams of HCl needed. (b) If he used formic acid, how many grams of it would be required? He also wished to prepare 250 ml of a solution of pOH 2.40. (c) Calculate the number of grams of NaOH needed. (d) If he used ammonia, calculate the number of grams of NH_3 needed.

6. Calculate the concentrations of the various species in the following solutions, writing all exact equations and making appropriate assumptions:
 (a) 0.01-M HOAc + an equal volume of 0.05-M NaOAc
 (b) 0.01-M NaCN
 (c) 0.01-M HCl plus an equal volume of 0.01-M NaOAc

7. Calculate the pH of the solutions resulting from mixing equal volumes of the following solutions of strong electrolytes:
 (a) pH 2 + pH 3   (d) pH 2 + pH 12
 (b) pH 2 + pH 4   (e) pH 5 + pH 12
 (c) pH 2 + pH 5   (f) pH 2.3 + pH 12

8. An analyst wishes to prepare 100 ml of a solution of pH 1.40 from solutions of HCl, $pH = 0.40$, and NaOH, $pH = 13.30$. How many milliliters of each solution should be mixed to give the desired solution? Assume volumes additive.

9. An analyst wishes to prepare 100 ml of a solution of pH 9.00 from 0.20-M ammonia and 0.050-M HCl. How many milliliters of each solution should be mixed to give the desired solution? Assume volumes additive.

10. An acid HX has a molecular weight of 80. A solution made by dissolving 1.60 g of HX in 250 ml of solution has a pH of 2.70. Calculate the ionization constant of HX.

11. A base BOH is 1.0% ionized in a 0.050-M solution.
 (a) Calculate the percentage ionization in a 0.10-M solution.
 (b) At what concentration is the ionization 0.50%?

12. Calculate the percentage hydrolysis of the following in 0.10-M solutions: (a) OAc^- (b) CN^- (c) $S^=$.

13. The pH of a solution of a 0.10-M solution of NaX (salt of the weak acid, HX) is 11.30. Calculate the percentage ionization of HX in a 0.10-M solution of the acid.

14. A base BOH has an ionization constant of 1×10^{-5}. It is desired to prepare a solution of the salt BCl such that the percentage hydrolysis of B^+ is the same as the percentage ionization of BOH in a 0.10-M solution of the base. What should be the concentration of the solution of BCl?

15. Derive the following expressions for calculating the pH of a solution under the specified conditions:

(a) Equivalence point in titration of weak acid HA with NaOH:

$$pH = \tfrac{1}{2}pK_w + \tfrac{1}{2}pK_a + \tfrac{1}{2} \log [A^-]$$

(b) Equivalence point in titration of weak base BOH with HCl:

$$pH = \tfrac{1}{2}pK_w - \tfrac{1}{2}pK_b - \tfrac{1}{2} \log [B^+]$$

(c) Solution of a weak acid, HA:

$$pH = \tfrac{1}{2}pK_a - \tfrac{1}{2} \log [HA]$$

(d) First equivalence point in titration of two weak acids; HA, the stronger, K_{a_1}, concentration C_1; HB, the weaker, K_{a_2}, concentration C_2:

$$pH = \tfrac{1}{2}(pK_{a_1} + pK_{a_2}) - \tfrac{1}{2} \log \frac{C_2}{C_1}$$

16. Calculate the pH of the following solutions in two ways: (1) Use the approximation as on page 86; i.e., $[OAc^-]$ was neglected, and (2) do not neglect $[OAc^-]$ and solve complete quadratic. Note the differences in the answers by the two procedures.

(a) 0.10-M dichloroacetic acid
(b) 0.10-M sodium bisulfate
(c) 0.10-M chloroacetic acid
(d) 0.10-M formic acid
(e) 0.10-M acetic acid

17. On page 85 the hydroxyl ion concentration was neglected in calculating the pH of 0.10-M HCl. Calculate the error in making this same approximation for the following HCl solutions: (a) 1.0×10^{-6}-M (b) 5.0×10^{-7}-M (c) 2.0×10^{-7}-M (d) 1.0×10^{-7}-M.

18. How many grams of NaOAc must be added to 100 ml of a 0.10-M solution of HOAc to make the $pH = 5.00$?

19. A solution is prepared by dissolving 3.4 g of NH_3 in 125 ml of solution. How many grams of NH_4Cl should be added to make the $pH = 9.56$?

20. A solution of benzoic acid is titrated with NaOH. Calculate the pH when the following percentages of the acid have been neutralized: (a) 25% (b) 33% (c) 50% (d) 75% (e) 99% (f) 99.9% (g) 99.99%.

21. A weak base, BOH, $K_b = 4.0 \times 10^{-5}$, is titrated with HCl. Calculate the percentage of base neutralized at the following pH values: (a) 10.55 (b) 9.60 (c) 9.30 (d) 8.60 (e) 7.60.

22. A student is to titrate a sample containing the weak acid, HA, $pK_a = 5.00$. By mistake he stops the titration at pH 7.00. If his sample actually contained 50.0% HA, what percentage would he find?

23. Calculate the volume of 0.10-M HCl required to change the pH of 100 ml of water from 7.00 to 4.00.

24. A 0.50-g sample containing 30% HOAc is titrated with 0.100-M NaOH. The volume of the solution at the equivalence point is 100 ml. The titration is stopped at a pH 0.50 units higher than the pH at the equivalence point. How much excess base was used?

25. 30.00 ml of 0.0900-M HCl is diluted to 100 ml and titrated with 0.1000-M NaOH. Calculate the pH after the addition of the following amounts of titrant: (a) 0.00 (b) 10.00 ml (c) 13.50 ml (d) 25.00 ml (e) 26.95 ml (f) 27.00 (g) 27.05 ml (h) 32.00 ml. Sketch the titration curve and select a suitable indicator.

26. Repeat problem 25 for the titration of 30.00 ml of 0.0900-M NH_4OH with 0.1000-M HCl.

27. 3.0 mmol of Na_2CO_3 are dissolved in 90 ml of water and titrated with 0.10-M HCl. The reaction is

$$CO_3^= + 2\,H^+ \rightleftharpoons H_2CO_3$$

Calculate the pH at the equivalence point and two drops (0.10 ml) beyond the equivalence point. Choose a suitable indicator. Would you expect the end point to be very sharp?

28. 25 ml of 0.20-M NaOAc is diluted to 50 ml and titrated with 0.10-M HCl. Calculate the pH at the equivalence point and two drops (0.10 ml) beyond. Is the titration feasible?

29. Calculate the pH (a) at the equivalence point, and (b) two drops (0.10 ml) beyond the equivalence point for the titration of 5.00 mmol of a weak acid, $pK_a = 6.00$, with (1) 0.10-M NaOH, (2) 0.50-M NaOH, and (3) 1.0-M NaOH. Assume the volume at the equivalence point is 100 ml in each case. Discuss the feasibility of the titration, and the effect of the concentration of titrant.

30. The pH range of an indicator, HIn, is 1.50 units. The ratio of $[HIn]/[In^-]$ to see only the acid color is the same as the ratio of $[In^-]/[HIn]$ to see only the basic color. What percentage of the indicator must be in the HIn form for the eye to detect only the acid color?

31. The pH of a solution of NH_4Cl is 5.28. What is the concentration of the salt?

32. A 2.000-g sample containing an acid HX (M.W. = 125) is dissolved in 60.00 ml of water and titrated with 0.1000-M NaOH. When half of the acid is neutralized, the pH is 6.00; at the equivalence point the pH is 9.30. Calculate the percentage of HX in the sample.

33. A buffer solution is prepared by dissolving 6.0 g of acetic acid and 16.4 g of sodium acetate in 1.0 l of solution.
   (a) Calculate the pH of the solution.
   (b) To 10 ml of the buffer is added 0.020 g of NaOH. Calculate the pH of the resulting solution.
   (c) To another 10 ml of the buffer is added 0.0365 g of HCl. What is the pH of the resulting solution?
   (d) Calculate the buffer capacity of the solution.

34. It is desired to prepare a buffer of pH 5.00. Three weak acids plus their salts are available: A, $K_a = 2 \times 10^{-5}$; B, $K_a = 5 \times 10^{-5}$; C, $K_a = 5 \times 10^{-6}$. Calculate the ratio of acid to salt required for each acid to prepare such a buffer.

35. The three buffers of pH 5.00 (previous problem) are prepared, with the component in larger concentration being 0.20-M in each solution. Calculate the change in pH which results if 5.00 mmol of (a) hydroxyl ion, and (b) hydrogen ion is added to 100 ml of each buffer.

36. It is desired to prepare 250 ml of a buffer solution of pH 9.56 using NH_3 and NH_4Cl such that the change in pH will not be greater than 0.14 pH units for the addition of 1.0 mmol of either acid or base. What weight of NH_4Cl and what volume of a 1.0-M solution of NH_3 should be used to prepare the buffer?

37. A sample that might be a sodium carbonate-bicarbonate or sodium carbonate-hydroxide mixture was titrated using the two indicator method. A 1.000-g sample required 31.64 ml of 0.2000-M HCl to reach the phenolphthalein end point and an additional 14.36 ml to reach the methyl orange end point. Identify the mixture and calculate the percentage of each component.

38. A 1.000-g sample of a carbonate mixture required 18.56 ml of 0.1500-M HCl to reach the phenolphthalein end point and an additional 29.74 ml to reach the methyl orange end point. Identify the mixture and calculate the percentage of each component.

39. Carbonate mixtures are sometimes analyzed by titrating two samples of the same size, one using phenolphthalein, the second using methyl orange as the indicator. If V_1 is the volume of acid used with phenolphthalein and V_2 that with methyl orange, answer the following:

(a) What is the relationship between V_1 and V_2 if the mixture is Na_2CO_3 and $NaHCO_3$, with an equal number of millimoles of the two?

(b) What is the relationship between V_1 and V_2 if the mixture is NaOH and Na_2CO_3, with twice as many millimoles of NaOH as Na_2CO_3?

40. A sample of $NaHCO_3$ weighing 0.840 g was dissolved in water, and 0.240 g of NaOH was added to the solution. The solution was then diluted to 250 ml in a volumetric flask. A 50-ml aliquot was titrated with 0.1200-M HCl using phenolphthalein indicator. How many milliliters were required? What volume would have been required had methyl orange been used?

41. A 1.000-g sample consisting of $NaHCO_3$, Na_2CO_3, and impurities was analyzed as follows: It was first titrated to the phenolphthalein end point, 25.00 ml of 0.1000-M HCl being required. To this solution was added a 50.00-ml portion of 0.1000-M NaOH. Then Ba^{++} ions were added to precipitate $BaCO_3$. The precipitate was separated by filtration and the filtrate titrated with 0.1000-M HCl using phenolphthalein indicator. 10.00 ml of acid was required. Calculate the percentages of Na_2CO_3 and $NaHCO_3$ in the sample.

42. A sample consists of only NaOH and Na_2CO_3. A portion weighing 0.2660 g required 50.00 ml of 0.1000-M HCl for titration to the phenolphthalein end point. What additional volume would be required to reach the methyl orange end point?

43. A 0.4110-g sample consisting of only $NaHCO_3$ and Na_2CO_3 is dissolved in 50.0 ml of solution and titrated with standard HCl, using methyl orange as the indicator. The normality of the solution as a base is found to be 0.120. What normality would have been found had phenolphthalein been used as the indicator?

Oxidation-Reduction Equilibria

INTRODUCTION

Chemical reactions which involve oxidation-reduction are more widely used in volumetric analysis than acid-base, precipitation, or complex-formation reactions. The ions of a large number of elements can exist in different oxidation states, resulting in the possibility of a very large number of oxidation-reduction (redox) reactions. Many redox reactions may seem complex when compared to acid-base reactions. The overall reaction may involve the loss and gain of several electrons, and frequently many hydrogen ions are involved. Nevertheless, many of these reactions satisfy the requirements for use in volumetric analysis, and applications are quite numerous.

It should be recalled that *oxidation* is defined as the loss of electrons by an atom, molecule, or ion, and *reduction* is the gain of electrons by such particles. When an ion, such as Fe^{++} loses an electron to form Fe^{3+}, the

125

oxidation number increases.[1] Thus oxidation is often defined as an increase in oxidation number. Reduction, in turn, results in a decrease in oxidation number.

A redox reaction involves the exchange of electrons between two redox couples. For example, the two couples

$$Fe^{3+} + e \rightleftarrows Fe^{++}$$

$$Ce^{4+} + e \rightleftarrows Ce^{3+}$$

(or in general: oxidant $+ n$ e = reductant) can interact, resulting in the reaction

$$\underset{\text{reductant}_1}{Fe^{++}} + \underset{\text{oxidant}_2}{Ce^{4+}} \rightleftarrows \underset{\text{oxidant}_1}{Fe^{3+}} + \underset{\text{reductant}_2}{Ce^{3+}}$$

In this reaction (left to right) ferrous ion loses an electron, being oxidized to ferric. Ferrous ion is referred to as the *reducing agent* (or reductant), and ceric is called the *oxidizing agent* (or oxidant). Thus, in a redox reaction the reducing agent is oxidized and the oxidizing agent is reduced. The student may note that the electron transfer involving the interaction of two such redox systems is analogous to proton transfer in Brønsted terms, as discussed in Chapter 4.

The analogy between acid-base and redox behavior must not, however, be blindly extended without an appreciation of important differences that develop in practice. No acid is too strong to be used as a titrant in aqueous solution, because it is simply levelled by water, with the result that the hydrated proton is available for transfer to a base. On the other hand, a reducing agent strong enough to transfer an electron to water leads to the decomposition:

$$2\ H_2O + 2\ e \rightleftarrows 2\ OH^- + H_2$$

The gaseous hydrogen, while it might be viewed as available for reduction, tends to escape from the solution, and, in any case, reacts too slowly with most oxidants to serve in a titration. Thus in practice we avoid redox reagents that react with water at an appreciable rate, and we see no analog of the levelling effect; rather, each redox couple exerts its characteristic reactivity relative to the other redox couple with which it is allowed to react.

The reactivity of a redox couple is determined by its tendency to gain or lose electrons. The measure of this tendency is the *oxidation potential* and the difference in oxidation potentials of two couples can be related to the equilibrium constant of the redox reaction. Hence, the extent to which a

---

[1] Today oxidation numbers are often designated by a Roman numeral in parentheses following the symbol or name of the element. Iron, with a 3+ oxidation number, is written as iron (III) or Fe(III); ferrous iron is written Fe(II), etc. This system avoids occasional ambiguity in the classical "ic" and "ous" nomenclature, and also avoids any commitment as to the degree of hydration or complexation of an ion of a particular oxidation number. Just as with the hydrated proton (Chapter 4), we shall continue to write the simple charged ion, with the understanding that it may be hydrated or complexed to some degree.

reaction is complete at the equivalence point of a titration can be calculated from the oxidation potentials of the two redox couples. We wish to learn how to make such quantitative calculations in this chapter, and we shall also consider the selection of the proper indicator for a redox titration.

We should keep in mind that although equilibrium calculations may indicate that a redox reaction goes well to completion, such calculations tell us nothing about the rate at which the reaction proceeds to equilibrium. Many redox reactions that are otherwise suitable cannot be used in titrations because they are too slow.

SINGLE ELECTRODE POTENTIAL

Let us consider first the meaning of the "potential" of a redox couple, using as an example a couple consisting of the metal zinc in equilibrium with a water solution of its ions:

$$\underset{\text{oxidant}}{Zn^{++}} + 2\,e \rightleftarrows \underset{\text{reductant}}{Zn}$$

Suppose a strip of zinc is placed in a beaker containing a solution of zinc sulfate (Figure 5.1). Atoms of zinc tend to leave the metal strip and enter

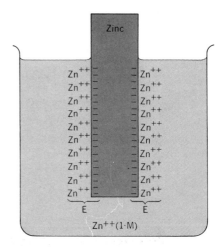

Fig. 5.1. Development of electrode potential.

the solution as ions. In this process, zinc is oxidized, since it loses electrons, and the electrons are left on the surface of the strip. Zinc ions tend to leave the solution and deposit as atoms on the metal strip, gaining electrons and hence undergoing reduction. Thus zinc atoms act as the reductant, and zinc ions as the oxidant, in this system. When the rates of the two processes are the same, the system is, of course, at equilibrium.

The reaction just described cannot occur to any great extent because the metal becomes negatively charged and the solution positively charged, as pictured in Figure 5.1. An electrostatic force, or difference in potential, is set up at the interface of the solid and liquid phases. However, unless some other redox couple is present to remove electrons from the metal strip and neutralize the positive charge in the solution, no chemical change is observed. The potential set up at the metal-solution interface is a measure of the tendency of the Zn-Zn^{++} system to lose electrons and is referred to as a "single electrode potential."

A single electrode potential has never been measured absolutely.[2] In order to measure the affinity of one redox couple for electrons, it is necessary to introduce another couple for comparison. The H_2-H^+ couple (hydrogen electrode) is the reference chosen, and its single electrode potential is arbitrarily assigned a value of exactly zero at all temperatures when the pressure of hydrogen gas is 1 atmosphere and the hydrogen ion concentration is 1-M (really unit activity). Now, the difference in potential between the hydrogen electrode and the zinc electrode described above (zinc ion concentration 1-M) is found to be 0.76 v. Since the hydrogen electrode potential is taken as zero volts, the electrode potential of the zinc-zinc ion couple is said to be 0.76 v. According to the recommendations of the International Union of Pure Applied Chemistry (IUPAC) meeting in Stockholm in 1953, a negative sign should be assigned to this value since zinc is negative with respect to hydrogen. The electrode potential of the zinc system is then -0.76 v and this is regarded as an *invariant* quantity. Further aspects of the IUPAC recommendations are discussed later.

Different redox couples have different electron affinities and hence different electrode potentials. The potential of any couple is dependent upon the temperature and upon the concentration (activity) of the reactants, as is expected of any equilibrium process. The effect of temperature will not be considered here. Analytical applications are based entirely on the concentration factor, and we shall center our attention upon this.

GALVANIC CELLS

A system consisting of two single electrodes (half-cells), such as that shown in Figure 5.2 is called a *cell*. Here a strip of zinc is placed in a 1-M solution of a zinc salt in beaker A, and a strip of copper is placed in a 1-M solution of a copper salt in beaker B. Wires from the metal strips lead to an ammeter. The circuit is completed by connecting the two solutions with a so-called

[2] I. Oppenheim, *J. Phys. Chem.*, **68**, 2959 (1964), has proposed a hypothetical experiment for measuring single electrode potentials, but this has not been accomplished as yet.

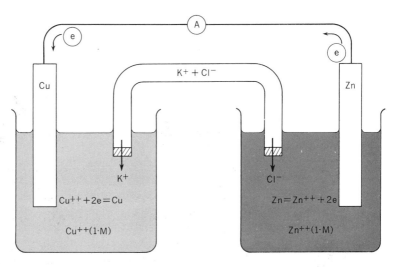

Fig. 5.2. A galvanic cell.

"salt bridge." This may be an inverted U-tube containing a solution of a salt, such as potassium chloride, with an agar plug at each end.

As mentioned above, zinc atoms tend to leave the strip and enter the solution as ions, leaving electrons on the metal surface. In the cell as pictured, the Cu-Cu^{++} redox couple can now remove these electrons and allow more zinc to enter the solution. Electrons flow through the wire from zinc to copper. Cupric ions deposit on the copper strip as copper atoms by taking up electrons. The flow of current is completed inside the cell by diffusion of chloride ions from the salt bridge into beaker A. Potassium ions diffuse into beaker B. The flow of electrons through the wire is, of course, an electric current that can be measured with the ammeter. A cell acting in the manner just described—that is, one in which chemical reactions occur spontaneously at each electrode and the resulting energy is converted into useful electrical energy—is called a galvanic cell in contrast to an electrolytic cell (Chapter 9).

At present we are not concerned with the action of a galvanic cell in furnishing electrical energy. Rather we are interested in the magnitude of the potential difference between the two electrodes, because this frequently relates to the concentration of the ions in solution. If, in the outer circuit of our cell, the ammeter is replaced by a potentiometer, then the potential, or voltage, of the cell can be measured. In using a potentiometer, an opposing voltage is applied to that of the cell, and the potential just required to prevent the electrode reactions from occurring is measured. If an appreciable current is allowed to flow through the cell, the concentrations will change, of course.

CONVENTIONS

A cell such as pictured in Figure 5.2 is represented as follows:

$$\text{Cu} \mid \text{Cu}^{++}(1\text{-}M) \parallel \text{Zn}^{++}(1\text{-}M) \mid \text{Zn}$$

E_1	E_3	E_2
Left-hand electrode		**Right-hand electrode**

Reading from left to right, the left-hand electrode is first specified, followed by the ion or ions in solution in equilibrium with the electrode, with their concentrations given in parentheses. Then the right-hand electrode is specified in the reverse manner, as indicated. The single vertical line (some books use a slant line, and some a semicolon) indicates a phase boundary across which a potential exists (E_1 and E_2, above). A double line indicates a junction of two liquid phases across which a potential exists but which is considered small enough to be disregarded in calculations.[3] This potential, indicated by E_3 above, usually cannot be evaluated accurately, but if the solutions in the two half-cells are similar, and if a salt bridge of potassium chloride is employed, its magnitude is made negligibly small. If no difference in potential exists between two phases, the two are separated by a comma. For example, the hydrogen electrode is written

$$\text{Pt, H}_2 \ (1 \text{ atm}) \mid \text{H}^+(1\text{-}M)$$

The pressure of a gas is specified in parentheses.

To represent the reaction that occurs in the cell when the electrodes are connected by a wire (short-circuited), the following procedure should be used.

1. Write down the reaction at the left-hand electrode with electrons on the left, and list the standard potential:

$$\text{Ox} + n \text{ e} \rightleftarrows \text{Red} \qquad E°$$

In the cell above this is

$$\text{Cu}^{++} + 2 \text{ e} \rightleftarrows \text{Cu} \qquad E_1° = + 0.34 \text{ v}$$

It should be noted that the IUPAC (Stockholm) agreement previously mentioned used the word potential only to describe the quantity associated with the half-reaction written as a reduction process and with the sign which corresponds to the charge of the metal with respect to a standard hydrogen electrode. The standard potentials listed in Table 4 of Appendix I are in accord with this agreement. Here the reaction at the copper electrode is written as reduction and +0.34 is the potential of the electrode, copper

---

[3] The diffusion of ions across the interface of two solutions leads to the development of a so-called "liquid junction" potential. This subject is treated in detail in courses in physical chemistry.

being positive with respect to hydrogen. Confusion has often arisen over the common practice of writing such a reaction as oxidation from left to right:

$$Cu \rightleftharpoons Cu^{++} + 2\ e$$

It is proper then to change the $+0.34$ to -0.34 v. However, the IUPAC agreement did not offer a name for this quantity of opposite sign to the electrode potential. Nevertheless, some writers use terms such as "electromotive force of a half-cell," or "potential of a half-reaction" as a quantity which can be plus or minus depending upon the direction in which the half-reaction is written. Others use the term "oxidation potential" when the reaction is written as oxidation from left to right, and "reduction potential" when the reaction is written as reduction from left to right.[4]

2. Repeat (1) for the right-hand electrode:

$$Zn^{++} + 2\ e \rightleftharpoons Zn \qquad E_2^\circ = -0.76\ v$$

3. Multiply, if necessary, one or both equations by the proper integer in order to balance the number of electrons. The standard potentials are not so multiplied.

4. Subtract the reaction at the right-hand electrode from the reaction at the left-hand electrode, and also the potentials, giving

$$Cu^{++} + Zn = Cu + Zn^{++} \qquad E_{1-2}^\circ = +1.10\ v$$

This is the reaction that tends to occur in the cell, and the calculated potential can be verified with a potentiometer. We shall designate at present the potential of a cell as E_{1-2} to emphasize that this is a difference between the potentials designated E_1 and E_2. Normally the symbol E is sufficient.

When the foregoing procedure is followed, two important conclusions can be drawn from the sign of the potential of the cell:

(a) When the sign is positive, the cell reaction takes place spontaneously from left to right, according to the last equation. That is, if the electrodes of the given cell are short-circuited, zinc dissolves at one electrode and copper plates out at the other. If the sign is negative, the cell reaction takes place spontaneously from right to left.

(b) The polarity of the left-hand electrode is the same as the sign of the cell potential. In our example, copper is the positive pole of the cell, zinc the negative pole.

Students sometimes ask what would happen if they had written the cell in the reverse manner, that is, with zinc as the left-hand electrode rather than the right-hand one:

$$Zn \mid Zn^{++}(1\text{-}M) \parallel Cu^{++}(1\text{-}M) \mid Cu$$

---

[4] For references to several discussions of the IUPAC agreement see P. Van Rysselberghe, *J. Chem. Ed.*, **41**, 487 (1964).

If the procedure outlined above is followed, the cell potential will be found to be −1.10 v, but the cell reaction is reversed:

$$Cu + Zn^{++} \rightleftharpoons Cu^{++} + Zn$$

Hence the conclusions regarding the direction of spontaneous reaction and the polarity of the electrodes are the same as before.

STANDARD POTENTIALS

The potential of a cell such as we have just considered is a measure of the chemical force tending to drive the cell reaction toward equilibrium. Hence the concentrations of the reacting species affect the magnitude of the potential. In the example just used, the cell reaction is

$$Cu^{++} + Zn \rightleftharpoons Cu + Zn^{++}$$

and the potential, 1.10 volt, is the value when each of the ions, cupric and zinc, is at a concentration of 1-M (really unit activity). Increasing the concentration of cupric ion favors the rightward reaction and increases the potential; increasing the zinc ion concentration decreases the potential. At equilibrium the potential is zero.

By definition the "standard potential" is the potential of a cell (or electrode) in which each reactant is at unit activity. Similarly, a substance having an activity of unity is said to be in its "standard state." On page 80 are listed the conventions which are generally used to define the activity of pure and impure liquids and solids, gases, and solutes. These conventions are employed here in specifying standard potentials. A list of standard potentials of electrodes, all referred to the standard hydrogen electrode, is given in Table 4 of Appendix I.

FREE ENERGY

One of the most important concepts in chemistry is the quantity called free energy. The change in free energy is a measure of the driving force of a chemical reaction and of the maximum work that can be obtained from the reaction at constant temperature and pressure. The change in free energy is related to the potential of a galvanic cell, as we shall see below.

There are two factors influencing the tendency of a chemical reaction to proceed spontaneously toward an equilibrium state: the energy factor and the probability factor (entropy). Equilibrium favors the state of lowest energy and highest probability and is a compromise between these two factors. Free energy is defined as the difference between these factors by the equation

$$G = H - TS$$

where H is the energy term (heat content or enthalpy), S (entropy) is related to the probability, and T the absolute temperature. The change in free energy at constant temperature (and constant pressure) is given by

$$\Delta G = \Delta H - T \Delta S$$

Conventionally, if both factors are favorable for spontaneous reaction, ΔH is negative and ΔS positive. Hence ΔG is negative. A decrease in free energy of the system is the characteristic criterion for spontaneous reaction. A process which can do useful work is accompanied by a decrease in free energy. If the system is at equilibrium, $\Delta G = 0$, and no useful work can be obtained from the system at this temperature and pressure.

In a chemical reaction such as

$$a\,A + b\,B \rightleftharpoons c\,C + d\,D$$

the free energy change is given by the equation

$$\Delta G = \Delta G^\circ + 2.3RT \log \frac{[C]^c[D]^d}{[A]^a[B]^b}$$

where ΔG°, the standard free energy change, is the free energy change when all the reactants and products are in their standard states (unit activity). The brackets, indicating concentrations, should be activities, of course. R is the gas constant, 8.314 joules/degree-mole, and T is the absolute temperature.

The free energy change, or work done, by driving Avogadro's number of electrons through a voltage E, is $(Ne)E$, where N is Avogadro's number, and e is the charge on the electron. The product Ne is 96,500 coulombs, called one faraday, or F. Hence,

$$\Delta G = -nFE$$

where n is the number of moles of electrons involved in the reaction. If all reactants and products are in their standard states, this becomes

$$\Delta G^\circ = -nFE^\circ$$

Hence

$$-nFE = -nFE^\circ + 2.3RT \log \frac{[C]^c[D]^d}{[A]^a[B]^b}$$

or

$$E = E^\circ - \frac{2.3RT}{nF} \log \frac{[C]^c[D]^d}{[A]^a[B]^b}$$

Finally

$$E = E^\circ - \frac{0.059}{n} \log \frac{[C]^c[D]^d}{[A]^a[B]^b} \quad \text{at} \quad 298°K$$

This general equation is usually referred to as the Nernst equation, after the physical chemist Nernst, who in 1889 first used such an equation to express the relationship between the potential of a metal-metal ion electrode and the concentration of the metal ion in solution.[5]

---

[5] W. Nernst, *Z. physik. Chem.*, **4**, 129 (1889).

At equilibrium, $E = 0$, $\Delta G = 0$, and the logarithmic quantity above is the equilibrium constant. Hence,

$$\Delta G° = -2.3RT \log K$$

and

$$E° = \frac{0.059}{n} \log K \quad \text{at} \quad 298°K$$

The following problem will illustrate the application of the Nernst equation, as well as other points covered thus far.

PROBLEM. A cell is set up as follows:

$$\text{Fe} \mid \text{Fe}^{++}(a = 0.1) \parallel \text{Cd}^{++}(a = 0.001) \mid \text{Cd}$$

(a) Write the cell reaction.

(b) Calculate the voltage of the cell, the polarity of the electrodes, and the direction of spontaneous reaction.

(c) What is the value of the equilibrium constant of the cell reaction?

(d) What is the value of the free energy change at the given activities and at standard conditions?

(a) The electrode reactions and standard potentials are

$$\text{Fe}^{++} + 2\,e \rightleftarrows \text{Fe} \qquad\qquad E_1° = -0.44$$
$$\text{Cd}^{++} + 2\,e \rightleftarrows \text{Cd} \qquad\qquad E_2° = -0.40$$

Subtracting, $\text{Fe}^{++} + \text{Cd} \rightleftarrows \text{Fe} + \text{Cd}^{++} \qquad E_{1\text{-}2}° = -0.04$

(b) The cell potential can be evaluated from the electrode potentials:

$$E_1 = -0.44 - \frac{0.059}{2} \log \frac{1}{0.1} = -0.47$$

$$E_2 = -0.40 - \frac{0.059}{2} \log \frac{1}{0.001} = -0.49$$

Thus

$$E_{1\text{-}2} = E_1 - E_2 = +0.02 \text{ v}$$

Alternatively,[6] the potential can be evaluated from the expression

$$E_{1\text{-}2} = E_{1\text{-}2}° - \frac{0.059}{2} \log \frac{a_{\text{Cd}^{++}}}{a_{\text{Fe}^{++}}}$$

$$E_{1\text{-}2} = -0.04 - \frac{0.059}{2} \log \frac{0.001}{0.1}$$

$$E_{1\text{-}2} = -0.04 + 0.06 = +0.02 \text{ v}$$

Therefore the cell reaction, as written above, tends to occur spontaneously from left to right at the given activities. The iron electrode is positive, the cadmium negative. Note that if both ions are at unit activity, $E_{1\text{-}2}° = -0.04$ v, and the direction of reaction is from right to left. The polarity of the electrodes is also reversed, of course.

---

[6] The equation for the overall potential should be used with caution. Sometimes the same ion is present in both half-cells, but at different concentrations. If the cell reaction is obtained by subtraction, as above, the student may overlook the effect of concentration on the potential by cancelling the two ions.

(c) The equilibrium constant is given by

$$E^\circ_{1\text{-}2} = \frac{0.059}{n} \log K_e$$

$$-0.04 = \frac{0.059}{2} \log K_e$$

$$\log K_e = -1.36 = 0.64 - 2$$

$$K_e = 0.044$$

(d) The free energy change for standard conditions is

$$\Delta G^\circ = -2 \times 96{,}500 \times -0.04$$

$$\Delta G^\circ = +7720 \text{ joules, or } +1852 \text{ calories}[7]$$

At the given activities, the free energy change is

$$\Delta G = -2 \times 96{,}500 \times 0.02$$

$$\Delta G = -3680 \text{ joules or } -923 \text{ calories}$$

Note the negative sign of ΔG when the reaction is spontaneous from left to right.

As a further illustration, consider the following problem:

PROBLEM. Calculate the potential of the following cell, giving the polarity of the electrodes and the direction of spontaneous reaction.

$$\text{Pt, } H_2(0.9 \text{ atm}) \mid H^+(0.1\text{-}M) \parallel KCl(0.1\text{-}M), AgCl \mid Ag$$

The electrode reactions are

$$2\,H^+ + 2\,e \rightleftarrows H_2 \qquad\qquad E^\circ_1 = 0.00$$

$$\underline{2\,AgCl + 2\,e \rightleftarrows 2\,Ag + 2\,Cl^- \qquad E^\circ_2 = 0.22}$$

Subtracting, $2\,H^+ + 2\,Ag + 2\,Cl^- \rightleftarrows 2\,AgCl + H_2 \qquad E^\circ_{1\text{-}2} = -0.22$

$$E_{1\text{-}2} = -0.22 - \frac{0.059}{2} \log \frac{(a_{AgCl})^2 \times a_{H_2}}{(a_{H^+})^2 \times (a_{Ag})^2 \times (a_{Cl^-})^2}$$

In accordance with our conventions regarding activities,

$a_{AgCl} = 1$, since AgCl is a pure solid (slightly soluble electrolyte).
$a_{H_2} = 0.9$, since this is the partial pressure of the gas in atmospheres.
$a_{H^+} = 0.1$, since this is a soluble electrolyte.
$a_{Ag} = 1$, since silver is a pure solid.
$a_{Cl^-} = 0.1$, since this is a soluble electrolyte.

Substituting these values and solving gives

$$E_{1\text{-}2} = -0.34 \text{ v}$$

Hence the hydrogen electrode is negative and the reaction moves spontaneously toward equilibrium from right to left.

---

[7] 1 calorie = 4.1840 joules.

OTHER ELECTRODES

Reference electrodes

Although electrode potentials are normally referred to the hydrogen electrode, other electrodes are often used as the reference when a potential is measured experimentally. The hydrogen electrode, pictured in Figure 5.3,

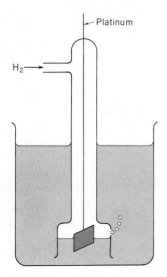

Fig. 5.3. Hydrogen electrode.

consists of a metal such as platinum immersed in an aqueous solution, with hydrogen gas bubbled around the metal surface. The platinum catalyzes the attainment of equilibrium between gaseous hydrogen and aqueous hydrogen ion:

$$2 \, H^+ + 2 \, e \rightleftharpoons H_2$$

In the standard hydrogen electrode the pressure of hydrogen gas is 1 atm, the concentration of hydrogen ions is 1-M, and the potential is assigned a value of 0.00 v.

Although any electrode whose potential is accurately known can be used as a reference, electrodes are normally chosen for their ease of preparation and reproducibility. They usually consist of a system made of a metal, a slightly soluble salt of the metal, and a solution containing an ion in common with the salt. The most commonly used reference electrode is the calomel electrode.

$$Hg \mid Hg_2Cl_2, \, KCl \, (x\text{-}M)$$

This electrode is essentially a mercury-mercurous ion electrode,

$$Hg_2^{++} + 2 \, e \rightleftharpoons 2 \, Hg$$

It has the advantage, however, that the concentration (activity) of mercurous ions, upon which the potential is dependent, is governed by the solubility of mercurous chloride. The latter, in turn, is dependent upon the concentration of potassium chloride. Thus, the concentration of the latter salt controls the potential of this electrode. The electrode reaction is usually written as

$$Hg_2Cl_2 + 2\ e \rightleftharpoons 2\ Hg + 2\ Cl^-$$

Since the activities of both mercury and mercurous chloride are unity, it is seen that the potential is dependent only upon the activity of chloride ion. If the solution is saturated with potassium chloride, the potential at 25°C is +0.2458 v. The standard calomel electrode (sometimes called "normal"), in which the potassium chloride concentration is 1-M, has potential of +0.2847 v at 25°C.

Let us consider the following problem illustrating the use of a reference electrode.

PROBLEM. (a) The potential of a cell made up of an electrode of unknown potential and a standard calomel electrode is 1.04 v. The calomel is the positive electrode. Calculate the potential of the unknown electrode referred to the hydrogen electrode.

If we consider our cell as having the unknown electrode on the left, calomel on the right, we must designate the potential as −1.04 v. If E_u is the unknown potential and E_r that of the reference electrode, then

$$E_{1\text{-}2} = E_u - E_r$$

$$-1.04 = E_u - 0.28$$

$$E_u = -0.76\ \text{v}$$

(b) In a second measurement with another unknown electrode, the potential of the cell is found to be 0.06 v, with the calomel electrode negative. Calculate the potential of the unknown referred to hydrogen.

In this case, if the calomel is the right-hand electrode as before, the potential is +0.06 v. Hence,

$$+0.06 = E_u - 0.28$$

$$E_u = +0.34\ \text{v}$$

The relation between these potentials is presented schematically in Figure 5.4.

Another reference electrode which is frequently used is the silver-silver chloride electrode,

$$Ag \mid AgCl,\ Cl^-(x\text{-}M)$$

The standard potential of this half-cell is +0.2221 v at 25°C. The potential is dependent only on the chloride concentration, as was that of the calomel, the electrode reaction being

$$AgCl + e \rightleftharpoons Ag + Cl^-$$

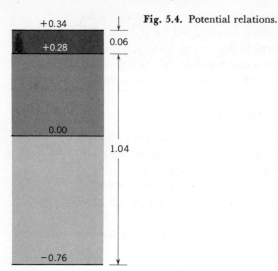

Fig. 5.4. Potential relations.

It might be noted that this electrode can be coupled with the hydrogen electrode without need of a salt bridge,

$$\text{Ag} \mid \text{AgCl, HCl (1-}M\text{)} \mid \text{H}_2 \text{ (1 atm), Pt}$$

Hydrochloric acid furnishes hydrogen ions for the hydrogen electrode as well as chloride ions for the silver-silver chloride electrode.

Inert electrodes

So far most of our examples of redox systems have consisted of metals in equilibrium with their ions. There are many important examples of redox systems involving only different oxidation states of ions in solution. A familiar example is the ferric-ferrous system,

$$\text{Fe}^{3+} + \text{e} \rightleftarrows \text{Fe}^{++}$$

A solution of ferric and ferrous ions is a possible source of electrons, but some metal must be inserted into the solution to act as a conductor. A metal such as platinum is normally used because it is not easily attacked by most solutions. The platinum is said to be an *inert* electrode, since it does not enter into the reaction.

A cell made up of the ferric-ferrous and ceric-cerous systems is written as

$$\text{Pt} \mid \text{Fe}^{3+}(x\text{-}M) + \text{Fe}^{++}(y\text{-}M) \mid\mid \text{Ce}^{4+}(a\text{-}M) + \text{Ce}^{3+}(b\text{-}M) \mid \text{Pt}$$

The student should confirm that the standard potential of this cell as written is -0.84 v, and that ceric ion oxidizes ferrous ion spontaneously if the concentration of each reactant is 1-M.

APPROXIMATIONS IN REDOX EQUILIBRIA CALCULATIONS

We have seen that the equilibrium constant of a redox reaction can be calculated from standard electrode potentials. From the equilibrium constant we can calculate the degree of completion of a redox reaction at the equivalence point, and thereby decide on the feasibility of the titration. We shall now consider this application of potential data to redox titrations, calculating the potential at different stages during the titration. It will be convenient to construct a titration curve as we did for acid-base titrations. Here we shall plot potential vs. milliliters of titrant.

Before considering the details of such calculations, it is important that we examine some of the limitations of the use of potential data in this regard. We have previously mentioned that it was necessary for us to make approximations for the activities of chemical species in redox titrations.

Complex redox reactions

The mechanism of many redox reactions is complex, and we do not know the exact nature of the reaction determining the potential at an electrode surface. For example, the reaction for the reduction of dichromate ion to chromic ion is

$$Cr_2O_7^= + 14\ H^+ + 6\ e \rightleftharpoons 2\ Cr^{3+} + 7\ H_2O$$

The standard potential, $+1.33$ v, is obtained indirectly, not from galvanic cell measurements. The reaction above simply represents the correct stoichiometry. It is thought that the reaction proceeds in steps through an unstable intermediate which is then converted into the products. The Nernst expression

$$E = 1.33 - \frac{0.059}{6} \log \frac{[Cr^{3+}]^2}{[Cr_2O_7^=][H^+]^{14}}$$

is not followed. Actually, the potential is practically independent of the concentration of chromic ions.

The same behavior is found with other complex redox systems, the permanganate-manganous system being one important example. With reactions which involve a large number of hydrogen ions, it is normally found that the potential is strongly dependent upon the hydrogen ion concentration, although the dependence cannot be predicted from the coefficients in the balanced equations. Hence, calculations of the potentials of such systems on the basis of these equations give incorrect results. In many cases, however, the error is small, and conclusions regarding the feasibility of a titration may not be invalidated.

Formal potentials

We have pointed out earlier that it is customary to substitute concentration (molarity) for activity of a soluble electrolyte, and that this assumption can lead to considerable error, particularly in solutions which contain high concentrations of highly charged ions. For example, we express the potential of the ceric-cerous redox couple using the Nernst equation as

$$E = E^\circ - 0.059 \log \frac{[Ce^{3+}]}{[Ce^{4+}]}$$

It would appear from the equation that the potential is independent of the nature and concentration of other electrolytes in the solution. Actually, the value found for E° varies from $+1.23$ v in 1-M HCl to $+1.70$ v in 1-M HClO$_4$, and varies with the concentration of a given acid. A similar effect is found with many other systems. The potential of the ferric-ferrous system is $+0.700$ v in 1-M HCl and $+0.732$ v in 1-M HClO$_4$.

There are two reasons for this behavior. First, the activity coefficients of the simple (uncomplexed) ions vary with the electrolyte concentration of the solution. Properly, one should write

$$E = E^\circ - 0.059 \log \frac{a_{Ce^{3+}}}{a_{Ce^{4+}}} = E^\circ - 0.059 \log \frac{\gamma_{Ce^{3+}}[Ce^{3+}]}{\gamma_{Ce^{4+}}[Ce^{4+}]}$$

or

$$E = E^\circ - 0.059 \log \frac{\gamma_{Ce^{3+}}}{\gamma_{Ce^{4+}}} - 0.059 \log \frac{[Ce^{3+}]}{[Ce^{4+}]}$$

and

$$E = E_f^\circ - 0.059 \log \frac{[Ce^{3+}]}{[Ce^{4+}]}$$

Here E_f° is the value of E at unit concentrations of the uncomplexed ions and is called the *formal potential* of the redox couple (see below). The formal potential varies with the ionic strength of the solution since the latter affects the activity coefficients. It also includes any liquid junction potential between the two half-cells.

Second, the occurrence of reactions such as complex formation and hydrolysis will affect the concentrations of the ions and thereby change the potential. Ceric and cerous ions undoubtedly form complexes with anions, as

$$Ce^{4+} + X^- \rightleftarrows CeX^{3+}$$

$$Ce^{3+} + X^- \rightleftarrows CeX^{2+}$$

where X$^-$ represents an anion. The extent of this complexing is normally not the same; that is, the formation constants of the ceric and cerous complexes are not equal. Hence, a solution prepared by dissolving an equal number of moles of a ceric salt and a cerous salt in hydrochloric acid does not have equal concentrations of simple ceric and cerous ions. The concentrations of the simple ions are also different from those obtained by dissolving the salts in sulfuric acid or nitric acid.

Another example of the effect of the medium upon a potential is the ferrocyanide-ferricyanide couple:

$$Fe(CN)_6^{3-} + e \rightleftharpoons Fe(CN)_6^{4-} \qquad E° = +0.356 \text{ v}$$

The potential of a system containing equal formal concentrations of the two ions varies with the concentration of HCl as follows: 1.0-M, $+0.71$ v; 0.1-M, $+0.56$ v; 0.01-M, $+0.48$ v. Both of these anions associate with hydrogen ions to form acids, but the hydroferrocyanic acids are weaker than the hydro-ferricyanic acids. Hence, as the hydrogen ion concentration is increased, the above equilibrium is shifted to the right and the potential increases.

It is obvious that even if a true standard potential is known, it is erroneous to use this value for a solution containing a high concentration of electrolytes. Hence many chemists prefer to use values called "formal potentials" rather than standard potentials. Swift[8] defines a formal potential as that potential shown by a redox couple in which the concentration of each reactant is one formal (molar) and the concentrations of any other constituents of the solution are specified. For example, the values quoted above for the ceric-cerous and ferrocyanide-ferricyanide couples are all formal potentials. Such potentials are subject, of course, to direct experimental measurement, and hence are normally of more practical value to the analytical chemist than are standard potentials. Titrations are frequently carried out in the presence of high electrolyte concentrations, and calculations based on formal potentials give in such cases much better agreement with experiment than those based on standard potentials.

It is often difficult to measure a standard potential, and many so-called "standard potentials" found in the literature are actually formal potentials. Table 4, Appendix I, in reality contains both types, but our calculations based upon these values will normally be sufficiently accurate for our purposes. In our examples, no false conclusions regarding feasibility of titrations will be drawn. We shall call attention to any case in which it is important to consider formal potentials. A short list of formal potentials is given in Table 5, Appendix I.

TITRATION CURVES

Titration of ferrous with ceric ion

Let us now consider the following problem:

PROBLEM. Five millimoles of a ferrous salt are dissolved in 100 ml of acid solution and are then titrated with 0.1-M ceric solution. Calculate the potential

---

[8] E. H. Swift, *Introductory Quantitative Analysis*, Prentice-Hall, Inc., Englewood Cliffs, N.J., 1950, p. 109.

of an inert electrode in the solution at various intervals during the titration and plot a titration curve.

(a) *Start of titration.* The potential is determined by the ferrous-ferric ion ratio; that is,

$$E = 0.77 - 0.059 \log \frac{[\text{Fe}^{++}]}{[\text{Fe}^{3+}]}$$

However, we do not know the ferric ion concentration, this being dependent upon how the ferrous salt was prepared, how much has been oxidized by air, etc. Let us assume that no more than 0.1% of the iron remains in the ferric state; that is, the ferrous to ferric ion ratio is 1000 to 1. For such a condition the potential can be calculated:

$$E = 0.77 - 0.059 \log 1000$$

$$E = 0.59 \text{ v}$$

(If the ferric ion concentration were actually zero, what would be the value of the potential?)

(b) *10 ml ceric solution added.* We now have mixed our two redox systems and allowed them to react and reach equilibrium,

$$\text{Fe}^{++} + \text{Ce}^{4+} \rightleftharpoons \text{Fe}^{3+} + \text{Ce}^{3+}$$

We can calculate the potential from the expression for either redox system; that is,

$$E = 0.77 - 0.059 \log \frac{[\text{Fe}^{++}]}{[\text{Fe}^{3+}]}$$

$$E = 1.61 - 0.059 \log \frac{[\text{Ce}^{3+}]}{[\text{Ce}^{4+}]}$$

The system is at equilibrium; that is, each redox couple has the same potential.[9] It is simpler at this stage of the titration to use the expression for the ferric-ferrous system since we can estimate the concentrations of these two ions more readily than that of the ceric ion as seen below:

$$[\text{Fe}^{++}] = \left\{ \frac{4}{110} + x \right\} \text{ mmol/ml}$$

$$[\text{Fe}^{3+}] = \left\{ \frac{1}{110} - x \right\} \text{ mmol/ml}$$

$$[\text{Ce}^{3+}] = \left\{ \frac{1}{110} - x \right\} \text{ mmol/ml}$$

$$[\text{Ce}^{4+}] = x \text{ mmol/ml}$$

[9] Some students ask why this is so. They have become accustomed to calculating the potential of a galvanic cell and think that the potentials of the two half-cells are different. They usually are, but at equilibrium the galvanic cell potential is zero, meaning that the two single electrodes have the same potential, here designated by E. In the titration we are placing the two reagents in the same container and allowing them to come to equilibrium. The solution has only one potential and it can be calculated from either redox system. This is the potential you would observe if you made your titration solution one-half of the galvanic cell, and the other electrode was the standard hydrogen electrode.

The value of x can be calculated, of course, from the equilibrium constant of the reaction. Assuming that the reaction goes well to completion, x is small and may be disregarded in estimating the ferric and ferrous ion concentrations. Hence

$$E = 0.77 - 0.059 \log \frac{4/110}{1/110}$$

or

$$E = 0.73 \text{ v}$$

(Note that the volume term cancels; that is, the potential is independent of volume.)

A more general treatment of the above problem would be to calculate the concentration of all four ionic species in the solution. For this we need four independent equations and these can be obtained as follows:

(1) The equilibrium constant for the reaction, which can be evaluated from the potential data:

$$\frac{[Ce^{3+}][Fe^{3+}]}{[Ce^{4+}][Fe^{++}]} = K = 1.7 \times 10^{14}$$

(2) Mass balance on iron: $[Fe^{++}] + [Fe^{3+}] = 0.045$
(3) Mass balance on cerium: $[Ce^{3+}] + [Ce^{4+}] = 0.009$
(4) Electron balance: $[Ce^{3+}] = [Fe^{3+}]$

Equation (4) is obtained from the principle that electrons lost by one ion must be gained by another. In this case for every cerous ion formed, one electron is gained. For every ferric ion formed, one electron is lost. The relation can also be obtained from the stoichiometry of the balanced equation for the reaction. The charge balance relationship, which we found useful in acid-base calculations, provides no useful equation in a system such as this.

The solution of the above equations is as follows: We first note that $[Ce^{4+}]$ is small and assume it to be negligible. From equation (3),

$$[Ce^{3+}] = 0.009$$

from (4),

$$[Fe^{3+}] = 0.009$$

from (2),

$$[Fe^{++}] = 0.036$$

from (1),

$$[Ce^{4+}] = 1.5 \times 10^{-17}$$

Our assumption that $[Ce^{4+}]$ is negligible is seen to be valid:

$$0.009 + 1.5 \times 10^{-17} \cong 0.009$$

Values of the potential of all other points before the equivalence point are calculated in the same manner. In Table 5.1 is a list of such values, and these are plotted in Figure 5.5. Note that the potential rises slowly in the earlier stages of the titration, and begins to increase more rapidly as the equivalence point is approached.

(c) *Equivalence point.* This point is reached when 50 ml of ceric solution are added. The concentrations of the reactants and products are then

$$[Fe^{++}] = [Ce^{4+}] = x$$

$$[Fe^{3+}] = [Ce^{3+}] = \frac{5}{150} - x$$

Table 5.1   REDOX POTENTIAL DURING TITRATION OF
5 mmol Fe^{++} WITH 0.1-M Ce^{4+}

ml Ce^{4+}	mmol Fe^{++} unoxidized	% Fe^{++} oxidized	E, volts
0.00	5.00	0	. . .
10.00	4.00	20	+0.73
20.00	3.00	40	0.76
25.00	2.50	50	0.77
30.00	2.00	60	0.78
40.00	1.00	80	0.81
45.00	0.50	90	0.83
49.00	0.10	98	0.87
49.50	0.05	99	0.89
49.95	0.005	99.9	0.95
50.00	. . .	100	1.19
	mmol excess Ce^{4+}		
50.05	0.005		+1.43
50.50	0.05		1.49
51.00	0.10		1.51
55.00	0.50		1.55
60.00	1.00		1.57
75.00	2.50		1.59

If either of the following expressions is employed, it is necessary to evaluate x, using the equilibrium constant in order to calculate the potential:

$$E = 0.77 - 0.059 \log \frac{[Fe^{++}]}{[Fe^{3+}]}$$

$$E = 1.61 - 0.059 \log \frac{[Ce^{3+}]}{[Ce^{4+}]}$$

Notice, however, that if the two equations are added, giving

$$2E = 2.38 - 0.059 \log \frac{[Fe^{++}][Ce^{3+}]}{[Fe^{3+}][Ce^{4+}]}$$

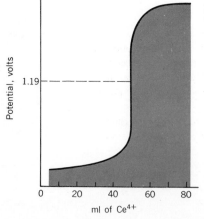

Fig. 5.5. Titration of ferrous with ceric ion.

the logarithmic term is zero, since at the equivalence point

$$[Fe^{++}] = [Ce^{4+}] \quad \text{and} \quad [Fe^{3+}] = [Ce^{3+}]$$

Hence

$$2E = 2.38 \quad \text{or} \quad E = 1.19 \text{ v}$$

For any reaction in which the number of electrons lost by the reductant is the same as the number gained by the oxidant, the potential at the equivalence point is simply the arithmetic mean of the two standard potentials:

$$E_{eq\ pt} = \frac{E_1^\circ + E_2^\circ}{2}$$

(d) *60 ml ceric solution added.* After the addition of 60 ml of titrant, the concentrations are

$$[Fe^{++}] = x$$

$$[Fe^{3+}] = \left\{ \frac{5}{160} - x \right\} \text{mmol/ml}$$

$$[Ce^{3+}] = \left\{ \frac{5}{160} - x \right\} \text{mmol/ml}$$

$$[Ce^{4+}] = \left\{ \frac{1}{160} + x \right\} \text{mmol/ml}$$

It is now the ferrous ion concentration that must be evaluated from the equilibrium constant. Hence, it is more convenient to employ the expression for the ceric-cerous system:

$$E = 1.61 - 0.059 \log \frac{[Ce^{3+}]}{[Ce^{4+}]}$$

Noting that x is small, we write

$$E = 1.61 - 0.059 \log \frac{5/160}{1/160} = 1.57 \text{ v}$$

Other values beyond the equivalence point are calculated in the same manner. The curve is plotted in Figure 5.5, where its similarity to a strong base titration curve may be seen. A large change in potential occurs in the vicinity of the equivalence point of the titration. The data are given in Table 5.1.

Titration of stannous with ceric ion

Let us consider now an example where the reductant loses two electrons while the oxidant gains one.

PROBLEM. Calculate the potential at the equivalence point in the titration of stannous ion with ceric ion:

$$Sn^{++} + 2\ Ce^{4+} \rightleftarrows Sn^{4+} + 2\ Ce^{3+}$$

The potential is given by either of the following expressions:

$$E = 0.15 - \frac{0.059}{2} \log \frac{[Sn^{++}]}{[Sn^{4+}]}$$

or

$$E = 1.61 - 0.059 \log \frac{[Ce^{3+}]}{[Ce^{4+}]}$$

Multiplying the first equation by two and adding it to the second gives

$$3E = 1.91 - 0.059 \log \frac{[Sn^{++}][Ce^{3+}]}{[Sn^{4+}][Ce^{4+}]}$$

The logarithmic term is zero since at the equivalence point[10]

$$[Ce^{4+}] = 2[Sn^{++}] \quad \text{and} \quad [Ce^{3+}] = 2[Sn^{4+}]$$

Hence

$$E = \frac{1.91}{3} = 0.64 \text{ v}$$

For the case in which one redox system gains or loses one electron and the other loses or gains two, the potential of the equivalence point is

$$E = \frac{E_1^\circ + 2E_2^\circ}{3}$$

where E_1° is the standard potential of the first system and E_2° that of the second. It should be noted that the titration curve is not symmetrical about the equivalence point in this case as it is in the titration of ferrous with ceric ion. This is always true when the two redox systems exchange a different number of electrons per molecule.

A completely general expression for the potential at the equivalence point can be derived in the same manner that we have employed here (see problem 6). Also see problems 20 and 21 for examples of the general treatment for a reaction of this type.

Titration of other redox couples

Figure 5.6 shows the variation of potential with fraction of reagent in the oxidized form for several redox couples. The curves for couples with oxidation potentials greater than 1 v have been plotted on a scale to the right of those couples with potentials less than 1 v. This is done to emphasize the fact that a single titration curve is the combination of two of the "branches" plotted here.

Several points should be noted:

1. The change in potential at the equivalence point in the titration of, say, ferrous ion, depends upon the oxidant used. The oxidants are not levelled by water and each couple exerts its characteristic potential. Hence, a much larger change in potential will occur at the equivalence point if ceric ion is used as the titrant than if bromine is used.

---

[10] Remember that the concentrations are molarities. Obviously, the number of equivalents of ceric ion is the same as that of stannous ion. But there are twice as many moles of ceric as of stannous ion.

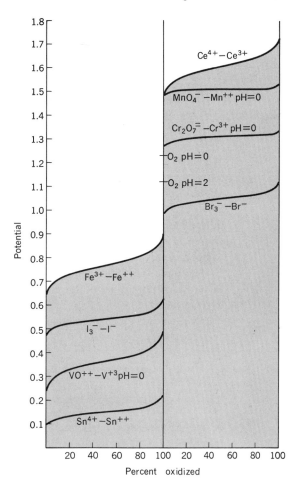

Fig. 5.6. Variation of potential with percent oxidized.

2. The shape of a curve depends upon the value of n, the number of electrons gained or lost by the oxidant or reductant. Note that the ferrous-ferric curve ($n = 1$) is steeper than the stannic-stannous curve ($n = 2$). Also note the flatness of the permanganate and dichromate curves, where n is 5 and 6, respectively. The shape of a titration curve will obviously be determined by that of the two halves which make up the curve.

3. The curves are asymptotic to the vertical axis at zero and 100% oxidation. The curves are flattest near the mid-points (50% oxidation), which corresponds to the standard potential for a couple such as Fe^{3+}-Fe^{++}. The stabilization of the potential in this region is analogous to buffering action of an acid-base pair about the pH region which corresponds to the pK_a. A redox couple is said to be *poised* in this region where the potential is stabilized.

4. In Figure 5.6 the potential of the reaction

$$O_2 + 4 H^+ + 4 e \rightleftharpoons 2 H_2O$$

is indicated at pH 0 and 2. Redox couples with standard potentials more positive than these values should not be stable in water at pH 0 and 2. Solutions of these couples are usually stable, however, since the reactions with water to liberate oxygen are generally slow.

FEASIBILITY OF REDOX TITRATIONS

We have previously noted that for a chemical reaction to be suitable for use in a titration, the reaction must be "complete" at the equivalence point. We do not mean absolute completion, of course, but it is generally understood that no more than 0.1 mg (or 0.1%, 1 ppt, etc.) of the substance being determined remains at the equivalence point. In order to calculate the degree of completeness, it is necessary to know the equilibrium constant of the reaction.

We have seen that the equilibrium constant is related to the difference in standard potentials of the two redox couples. For example, consider the two couples

$$Ox_1 + n\,e \rightleftharpoons Red_1 \qquad\qquad E_1^\circ$$

$$Ox_2 + n\,e \rightleftharpoons Red_2 \qquad\qquad E_2^\circ$$

$$\overline{Ox_1 + Red_2 \rightleftharpoons Red_1 + Ox_2 \qquad E_{1\text{-}2}^\circ = E_1^\circ - E_2^\circ}$$

$$E_{1\text{-}2}^\circ = \frac{0.059}{n} \log K$$

It should be readily obvious that the larger the difference in standard potentials, the larger is the value of K and the smaller is the amount of Ox_1 and Red_2 unreacted at the equivalence point.

Consider a specific case:

PROBLEM. (a) Calculate the difference in standard potentials of the two redox systems above ($n = 1$), if at the equivalence point in the titration of Red_2 with Ox_1 only 0.1% of Red_2 is left unoxidized. (b) Calculate the value of K.

(a) We see that

$$E_{1\text{-}2}^\circ = 0.059 \log K = 0.059 \log \frac{[Red_1][Ox_2]}{[Ox_1][Red_2]}$$

At the equivalence point $Ox_1 = Red_2$ and

$$\frac{[Red_1]}{[Ox_1]} = \frac{1000}{1} \qquad \frac{[Ox_2]}{[Red_2]} = \frac{1000}{1}$$

Hence,

$$E_{1\text{-}2}^\circ = 0.059 \log \frac{[1000][1000]}{[1] \quad [1]} = 0.35 \text{ v}$$

(b) The value of K is seen to be

$$K = \frac{[1000][1000]}{[1] \quad [1]} = 10^6$$

See problems 8 and 9 for calculations of K with other examples of redox systems.

The following is an example of a feasibility calculation involving a more complicated system. Two procedures are shown for handling the mathematical computations.

PROBLEM. Calculate the number of milligrams of ferrous iron remaining unoxidized when 4.0 mmol are titrated with 0.020-M permanganate, assuming the following conditions: two drops (0.10 ml) of permanganate in excess, final volume 100 ml, and hydrogen ion concentration 1-M.

The two half-reactions and the standard potentials are

$$MnO_4^- + 8\,H^+ + 5\,e \rightleftarrows Mn^{++} + 4\,H_2O \qquad E_1^\circ = +1.51$$

$$5\,Fe^{3+} + 5\,e \rightleftarrows 5\,Fe^{++} \qquad E_2^\circ = +0.77$$

The overall reaction is

$$5\,Fe^{++} + MnO_4^- + 8\,H^+ \rightleftarrows 5\,Fe^{3+} + Mn^{++} + 4\,H_2O$$

and the value of $E_{1\text{-}2}^\circ$ is +0.74 v.

(a) The equilibrium constant is given by

$$\frac{0.059}{5}\log K_e = 0.74$$

$$K_e = 10^{62.7}$$

The equations needed to specify all the concentrations are as follows:

(1) $\dfrac{[Fe^{3+}]^5[Mn^{++}][H_2O]^4}{[Fe^{++}]^5[MnO_4^-][H^+]^8} = 10^{62.7}$

(2) Mass balance on iron: $[Fe^{3+}] + [Fe^{++}] = 0.040$

(3) Mass balance on manganese: $[Mn^{++}] + [MnO_4^-] = 0.00802$ (40.10 ml of 0.020-M permanganate has been added).

(4) Electron balance: $[Fe^{3+}] = 5[Mn^{++}]$

(5) $[H^+] = 1$

(6) $[H_2O] = 1$

These can be solved by assuming that $[Fe^{++}]$ is negligible. Then from (2),

$$[Fe^{3+}] = 0.040$$

from (4),

$$[Mn^{++}] = 0.0080$$

from (3),

$$[MnO_4^-] = 0.00002$$

Substitution in equation (1) gives

$$[Fe^{++}] = 4 \times 10^{-14} \text{ mmol/ml}$$

$$mg\ Fe^{++} = 4 \times 10^{-14} \times 100 \times 55.85 = 2 \times 10^{-10}\ mg$$

(b) Alternatively, the potential of the permanganate-manganous ion system can be calculated as

$$E = 1.51 - \frac{0.059}{5}\log\frac{[Mn^{++}][H_2O]^4}{[MnO_4^-][H^+]^8}$$

Then

$$E = 1.51 - \frac{0.059}{5} \log \frac{(0.008)(1)^4}{(2 \times 10^{-5})(1)^4}$$

$$= 1.51 - 0.03 = 1.48 \text{ v}$$

The potential of the ferrous-ferric system must be the same. Hence

$$1.48 = 0.77 - 0.059 \log \frac{[\text{Fe}^{++}]}{[\text{Fe}^{3+}]}$$

$$1.48 = 0.77 - 0.059 \log \frac{[\text{Fe}^{++}]}{0.040}$$

$$x = 4 \times 10^{-14} \text{ mmol/ml}$$

as above.

REDOX INDICATORS

There are several types of indicators which may be used in redox titrations:

1. A colored substance may act as its own indicator. For example, potassium permanganate solutions are so deeply colored that a slight excess of this reagent in a titration can be easily detected.

2. A *specific* indicator is a substance which reacts in a specific manner with one of the reagents in a titration to produce a color. Examples are starch, which forms a deep-blue color with iodine, and thiocyanate ion, which forms a red color with ferric ion.

3. External, or *spot test*, indicators were once employed when no internal indicator was available. The ferricyanide ion was used to detect ferrous ion by formation of ferrous ferricyanide (Turnbull's blue) on a spot plate outside the titration vessel.

4. The redox potential can be followed during a titration and the equivalence point detected from the large break in the titration curve. Such a procedure is called potentiometric titration (see Chapter 8) and the titration curve may be plotted manually, or automatically recorded.

5. Finally, an indicator which itself undergoes oxidation-reduction may be employed. We shall refer to such a substance as a true redox indicator and it is with such a reagent that the rest of our discussion is concerned.

For simplicity, let us designate the redox couple as follows:

$$\text{In}^+ + e \rightleftharpoons \text{In}$$
$$\text{Color A} \qquad\qquad \text{Color B}$$

where one electron is gained by the oxidant and no hydrogen ions are involved in the reaction. Let us also say that the colors of the oxidized and reduced forms are different, as indicated above. The equation for the potential of this system is

$$E = E_1^\circ - 0.059 \log \frac{[\text{In}]}{[\text{In}^+]}$$

where E_1° is the standard potential of the indicator couple.

Let us now assume that if the ratio $[In]/[In^+]$ is 10 to 1 or greater, only color B can be seen by the eye. (See page 92 for similar treatment of acid-base indicators.) Also, if the ratio is 1 to 10 or smaller, only color A is observed. That is,

$$\text{Color B: } E = E_1^\circ - 0.059 \log 10/1 = E_1^\circ - 0.059$$

$$\underline{\text{Color A: } E = E_1^\circ - 0.059 \log 1/10 = E_1^\circ + 0.059}$$

Subtracting, $\qquad \Delta E = \pm 2 \times 0.059 = \pm 0.12 \text{ v}$

Thus a change in potential of about 0.12 v is required to bring about a change in color of the indicator, if our assumptions are reasonable.

Table 5.2 lists some true redox indicators with the colors observed and the "transition" potentials of the redox couple. The latter are the formal potentials of the systems in the media indicated and are usually of more practical value than the standard potentials. In many cases the oxidized and reduced forms of the indicator are weak acids or bases and their concentrations depend on the pH of the solution. In this case the equation given above is not strictly correct and the formal potentials, often called transition potentials in the case of indicators, are more properly employed.

TRANSITION POTENTIALS OF SOME   **Table**
REDOX INDICATORS   **5.2**

Indicator	Color of reductant	Color of oxidant	Transition potential, v	Conditions
Phenosafranine	Colorless	Red	+0.28	1-M acid
Indigo tetrasulfonate	Colorless	Blue	0.36	1-M acid
Methylene blue	Colorless	Blue	0.53	1-M acid
Diphenylamine	Colorless	Violet	0.76	1-M H_2SO_4
Diphenylbenzidine	Colorless	Violet	0.76	1-M H_2SO_4
Diphenylaminesulfonic acid	Colorless	Red-violet	0.85	Dilute acid
5,6-Dimethylferroin			0.97	1-M H_2SO_4
Erioglaucin A	Yellow-green	Bluish-red	0.98	0.5-M H_2SO_4
5-Methylferroin			1.02	1-M H_2SO_4
Ferroin	Red	Faint blue	1.11	1-M H_2SO_4
Nitroferroin	Red	Faint blue	1.25	1-M H_2SO_4

Selection of indicator

Obviously an indicator should change color at or near the equivalence potential. If the titration is feasible there will be a large change in potential at the equivalence point and this should be sufficient to bring about the change in color of the indicator. The following two examples illustrate more precisely the procedures that may be followed to select the proper indicator.

PROBLEM. (a) In the titration of iron with ceric sulfate, what indicator should be used?

We have already calculated the potential of the equivalence point as 1.19 v (page 145). We should consult a table of indicators and find one whose transition potential is near this value. Note in Table 5.2 that the transition potential of nitroferroin is appropriate. Actually, ferroin, with a transition potential of 1.11 v is normally used. The titration is often done in sulfuric acid medium and the potential of the system is more closely estimated by use of formal potentials (Table 5, Appendix I). Thus at the equivalence point

$$E = \frac{0.68 + 1.44}{2} = 1.06 \text{ v}$$

and the transition potential of ferroin is closer to this value than is that of nitro-ferroin. The standard potential of ferroin is 1.06 v but the color change occurs at 1.11 v since it is necessary to have more of the indicator in the oxidized form (light blue) than in the reduced form (dark red) (see problem 11). An indicator changes color over a range of potential, of course, not at a single value. Compare this with the action of acid-base indicators (page 92).

(b) What should be the transition potential of an indicator which is to change color when all but 0.1% of ferrous iron is oxidized to ferric?

This is easily calculated from the equation

$$E = 0.77 - 0.059 \log \frac{[\text{Fe}^{++}]}{[\text{Fe}^{3+}]}$$

$$\frac{[\text{Fe}^{++}]}{[\text{Fe}^{3+}]} = \frac{1}{1000}$$

$$E = 0.77 - 0.059 \log \frac{1}{1000}$$

$$E = 0.77 + 0.18 = 0.95 \text{ v}$$

Note from Table 5.1 and Figure 5.5 that this potential corresponds to the beginning of the steep rise near the equivalence point, where 99.9% of the iron has been oxidized. If ceric ion is the oxidizing agent, the end point shown by an indicator changing at 0.95 v would occur slightly before the equivalence point, but the error would be negligible.

The transition potential of diphenylaminesulfonic acid, the indicator frequently employed when iron is titrated with dichromate, is 0.85 v. A calculation based upon the standard potential of the ferric-ferrous couple indicates that 0.85 v is reached when only a little over 90% of the iron has been oxidized (Table 5.1). However, the formal potential of the ferric-ferrous system (Table 5, Appendix I) is 0.70 v in hydrochloric and 0.68 v in sulfuric acid. The iron titration with dichromate is usually carried out in the presence of one of these acids, and actually all but about 0.1% of the iron has reacted by the time a potential of 0.86 to 0.88 v has been reached. Further, phosphoric acid is often added to the titration medium lowering the potential of the iron system even more. (The formal potential of the iron system in 1-F sulfuric and 0.5-F phosphoric acids is 0.61 v.) It is customary to standardize a dichromate solution against pure iron before analyzing samples for iron. In this manner any end point error is compensated. An indicator blank is not usually determined since the reaction between dichromate and diphenylaminesulfonic acid is very slow in the absence of iron.

STRUCTURAL CHEMISTRY OF REDOX INDICATORS

The redox indicators to which we have referred in this chapter are organic molecules that undergo structural changes upon being oxidized or reduced. There are fewer such indicators than there are acid-base indicators, and their chemistry has not been as widely studied. Nevertheless, the structural changes which account for the different colors are known for a number of substances. We shall consider only two examples here, sodium diphenylaminesulfonate, and ferrous orthophenanthroline (ferroin).

Diphenylamine was one of the first redox indicators to be widely used in volumetric analysis. Since this compound is difficultly soluble in water, and since tungstate ion and mercuric chloride interfere with its action, the barium or sodium salt of diphenylaminesulfonic acid is more commonly used. The reduced form of this indicator is colorless, the oxidized form a deep violet. The mechanism of the color change has been shown to be as follows, using diphenylamine as the example:[11]

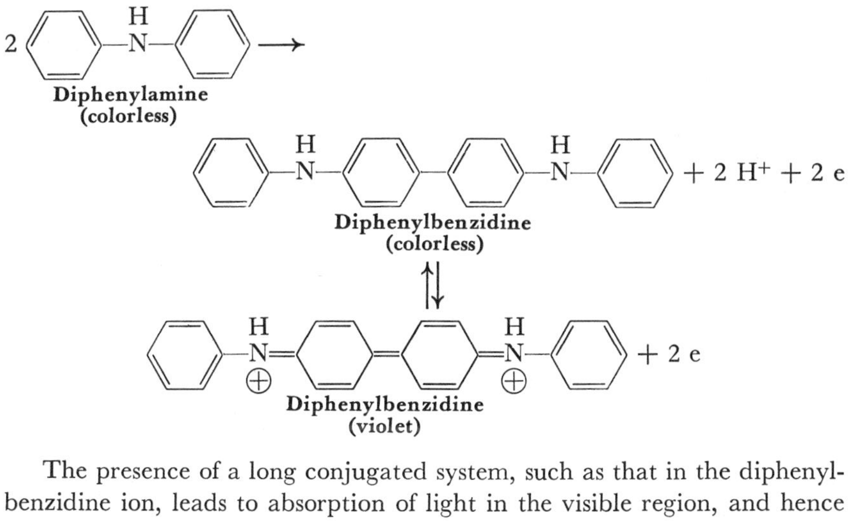

Diphenylamine
(colorless)

Diphenylbenzidine
(colorless)
$+ 2 H^+ + 2 e$

Diphenylbenzidine
(violet)
$+ 2 e$

The presence of a long conjugated system, such as that in the diphenylbenzidine ion, leads to absorption of light in the visible region, and hence the ion is colored.

The indicator ferroin is the ferrous complex of the organic compound 1,10-phenanthroline,

[11] I. M. Kolthoff and L. A. Sarver, *J. Am. Chem. Soc.*, **52**, 4179 (1930).

$$3 \quad + Fe^{++} \rightleftharpoons \quad Fe^{++}$$

1,10-phenanthroline   Ferrous 1,10-phenanthroline

Each of two nitrogen atoms in 1,10-phenanthroline has an unshared pair of electrons that can be shared with the ferrous ion. Three such molecules of the organic compound attach themselves to the metallic ion to form a blood-red complex ion. The ferrous ion can be oxidized to ferric, and the latter ion also forms a complex with three molecules of 1,10-phenanthroline. The color of the ferric complex is light blue, and hence a sharp color change occurs when ferrous is oxidized to ferric in the presence of 1,10-phenanthroline:

$$Ph_3Fe^{3+} + e \rightleftharpoons Ph_3Fe^{++} \qquad E^\circ = 1.06 \text{ v}$$
$$\text{light blue} \qquad\qquad \text{dark red}$$

The indicator is prepared by mixing equivalent quantities of ferrous sulfate and 1,10-phenanthroline. The complex salt is called *ferroin;* the complex salt of ferric ions is called *ferriin.* As previously mentioned, the color change occurs at about 1.11 v, since the color of ferroin is so much more intense than that of ferriin.

Substituted 1,10-phenanthrolines also form complexes with ferrous and ferric ions and act as redox indicators. The redox potentials are different from that of the ferroin-ferriin system. A few examples are included in Table 5.2, where a partial list of redox indicators is given.

REFERENCES

1. J. J. Lingane, *Electroanalytical Chemistry*, 2nd Ed., Interscience Publishers, Inc., New York, 1958.

2. H. A. Laitinen, *Chemical Analysis*, McGraw-Hill Book Co., Inc., New York, 1960.

3. H. F. Walton, *Principles and Methods of Chemical Analysis*, Prentice-Hall, Inc., Englewood Cliffs, N.J., 1964.

4. R. G. Bates, "Electrode Potentials," and F. R. Duke, "Oxidation-Reduction Equilibria and Titration Curves," Chapters 9 and 16, Part I, Vol. I, of *Treatise on Analytical Chemistry.* I. M. Kolthoff, P. J. Elving and E. B. Sandell, Eds., Interscience Publishers, Inc., New York, 1959.

QUESTIONS

1. Which is the strongest oxidant in Table 4, Appendix I? the weakest? Which is the strongest reductant? the weakest?

2. List the following in order of decreasing strength as reductants (all unit activity): Sn, Ag, Au, Cl^-, Fe^{++}, Cu^+, Zn, Ba.

3. Repeat question 2 for the following oxidants: Ca^{++}, Zn^{++}, Au^+, Ce^{4+}, Fe^{3+}, Pb^{++}, O_2.

4. Which is the better oxidant (unit activity), I_2 or H_3AsO_4? Explain how the titration of $HAsO_2$ with I_2 is carried out feasibly.

5. Explain the following statement: A redox indicator must gain electrons more readily than the reducing agent but less readily than the oxidizing agent. State this in terms of standard potentials.

6. Explain why the levelling effect is not observed with redox reagents as with acids and bases.

7. From inspection of Table 4, Appendix I, which of the following complex ions is more stable? Explain your reasoning on the basis of Le Chatelier's principle.

    (a) $PtBr_4^=$ or $PtCl_4^=$ (b) $AuBr_4^-$ or $AuCl_4^-$

Which of the following compounds is least soluble?

    (a) $PbCl_2$, $PbBr_2$, or $PbSO_4$ (b) CuCl, CuBr, or CuI

8. The standard potential of the ferrous-ferric couple is $+0.77$ v, and that of the ferroin-ferriin couple is $+1.06$ v. Which is the stronger complex, ferroin or ferriin? Explain.

9. Suppose redox reactions were written with electrons on the right-hand side of the equation, as

$$Zn \rightleftharpoons Zn^{++} + 2\,e$$

with $E° = +0.76$ v. If we followed the same procedures for subtracting equations, as on page 131, to obtain the cell reaction, what changes in the conclusions drawn from the sign of $E_{1-2}°$ would be necessary?

10. If the saturated calomel electrode were adopted as the primary reference electrode and assigned a potential of zero volts, what would be the standard potentials of the following couples?

$$2\,H^+ + 2\,e \rightleftharpoons H_2$$

$$Na^+ + e \rightleftharpoons Na$$

$$MnO_4^- + 8\,H^+ + 5\,e \rightleftharpoons Mn^{++} + 4\,H_2O$$

11. Draw a graph plotting the potential on the vertical axis, pH on the horizontal axis for the following redox couples:

$$2\,H^+ + 2\,e \rightleftharpoons H_2$$

$$O_2 + 4\,H^+ + 4\,e \rightleftharpoons 2\,H_2O$$

$$MnO_4^- + 8\,H^+ + 5\,e \rightleftharpoons Mn^{++} + 4\,H_2O \text{ (up to } pH \text{ 6)}$$

$$MnO_4^- + 4\,H^+ + 3\,e \rightleftharpoons MnO_2 + 2\,H_2O \text{ (above } pH \text{ 8)}$$

$$Ce^{4+} + e \rightleftharpoons Ce^{3+}$$

$$Cr^{3+} + e \rightleftharpoons Cr^{++}$$

$$Sn^{++} + 2\,e \rightleftharpoons Sn \text{ (up to } pH \text{ 4)}$$

12. Which of the ions in the previous question should not be stable in water solutions? How does pH affect the stabilities? Why are such solutions apparently stable in spite of this data?

13. Sketch a figure similar to 5.6 for a series of acids with pK_a values of 3, 4, 5, and 6 titrated with a series of strong bases, LiOH, NaOH, KOH, etc. Plot pH vs. fraction of acid neutralized. Explain similarities to and differences from Figure 5.6. Repeat using a series of weak bases as the titrants.

14. Suppose a redox indicator undergoes the following reaction:

$$In^{++} + 2\,e \rightleftharpoons In$$

What change in potential is required to bring about a color change?

15. The following relationship is given in some texts:

$$\log K = 16.9nE°$$

Show that this is the same as the relationship we derived in this chapter.

PROBLEMS

(For simplicity in arithmetical computations, round off 0.059 to 0.06 in all problems. The answers given in the back of the book have been obtained using 0.06.)

1. Calculate the potentials of the following cells. Write the cell reaction, indicate in which direction the reaction takes place at the specified conditions, and indicate the polarities of the electrodes.

(a) Fe | Fe^{++}(1-M) || Cd^{++}(0.001-M) | Cd

(b) Fe | Fe^{++}(0.001-M) || Cd^{++}(0.1-M) | Cd

(c) Zn | Zn^{++}(0.1-M) || Cr^{3+}(0.0001-M) | Cr

(d) Zn | Zn^{++}(0.001-M) || Cr^{3+}(0.1-M) | Cr

(e) Ag | AgCl, HCl(0.1-M) | H$_2$(1 atm), Pt

(f) Pt | Fe^{++}(0.1-M) + Fe^{3+}(10^{-5}-M) || Cr^{3+}(10^{-5}-M) + Cr$_2$O$_7^-$(0.1-M) + H$^+$(1-M) | Pt

(g) Ag | AgCl, HCl(0.01-M) || KCl(1-M), Hg$_2$Cl$_2$ | Hg

(h) Pt, H$_2$(0.64 atm) | HCl(0.1-M) | Cl$_2$(1 atm), Pt

2. Derive an equation relating the potential of the hydrogen electrode to the pH of the solution. Consider the hydrogen gas pressure as 1 atm. What is the potential at pH 7? in a 0.01-M solution of NaOH?

3. Calculate the equilibrium constant for the reduction of ferric ion by stannous to form ferrous and stannic ions. What is the concentration of ferric ion in a solution containing stannous, stannic, and ferrous ions each at a concentration of 0.1-M?

4. A platinum electrode is placed in the solution of the previous problem (3). This is made one electrode of a cell, the other half being a standard hydrogen electrode. What is the voltage of the cell? Calculate this from both redox couples, showing that both have the same potential.

5. Suppose one could lower the ferric ion concentration in a solution so that only one ferric ion remained per liter of solution.

(a) If the ferrous ion concentration is 0.1-M, what is the potential of the ferrous-ferric redox couple?

(b) How low would the ferric ion concentration need to be in order for the potential of the couple to be -3.00 v? The ferrous ion concentration is 0.1-M.

6. Show that the potential at the equivalence point in the titration of Red_1 with Ox_2 is

$$E = \frac{aE_1^\circ + bE_2^\circ}{a + b}$$

where

$$Ox_1 + ae \rightleftarrows Red_1 \qquad E_1^\circ$$

and

$$Ox_2 + be \rightleftarrows Red_2 \qquad E_2^\circ$$

7. Show that the potential at the equivalence point in the titration of ferrous ion with permanganate is

$$E = \frac{E_1^\circ + 5E_2^\circ}{6} - 0.08\, pH$$

where E_1° is the standard potential of the ferrous-ferric couple and E_2° is that of the permanganate-manganous couple.

8. Calculate the difference in standard potentials of the following two redox systems for a feasible titration of A^{++} with M^{3+}:

$$M^{3+} + e \rightleftarrows M^{++}$$

$$A^{4+} + 2\, e \rightleftarrows A^{++}$$

Assume that at the equivalence point only 0.1% of A^{++} is not oxidized. What is the value of the equilibrium constant?

9. Repeat problem 8 for the titration of A^{++} with N^{4+}, where

$$N^{4+} + 2\, e \rightleftarrows N^{++}$$

10. (a) Judging from the difference in standard potentials of the two redox couples, would the titration of Fe^{++} with B^{3+} be feasible, given that the standard potential of the couple

$$B^{3+} + e \rightleftarrows B^{++}$$

is $+1.07$ v? (b) Confirm your answer by calculating the number of milligrams of Fe^{++} remaining unoxidized when 5.0 mmol of Fe^{++} are titrated with 0.10-M B^{3+}, one drop (0.05 ml) of B^{3+} solution in excess, the final volume being 100 ml.

11. The indicator ferroin shows a color change at $+1.11$ v. The standard potential is $+1.06$ v. Calculate the percentage of the indicator in the oxidized form at the potential of the color change. A one-electron change is involved.

12. The following cell has a potential of -0.52 v.

$$Pt, H_2(1\ atm)\ |\ HB(0.1\text{-}M) + NaB(0.05\text{-}M)\ ||\ HCl(1\text{-}M), AgCl\ |\ Ag$$

The acid HB is a weak acid. Calculate its ionization constant.

13. Calculate the potential of the following cell, assuming that the acid HB is the same as in problem 12.

$$Pt, H_2(1\ atm)\ |\ NaB(0.2\text{-}M)\ ||\ KCl(sat), Hg_2Cl_2\ |\ Hg$$

14. Calculate the potential of the following cell. The acid HA is a weak acid with $K_a = 5 \times 10^{-4}$.

$$Pt, H_2(1\ atm)\ |\ HA(0.1\text{-}M)\ ||\ KCl(1\text{-}M), Hg_2Cl_2\ |\ Hg$$

15. Calculate the potential of the following cell.

$$Pt, H_2(1\ atm)\ |\ H^+(0.1\text{-}M)\ ||\ H^+(0.01\text{-}M)\ |\ H_2(1\ atm), Pt$$

16. It is desired to prepare a solution having a potential of $+0.09$ v using stannic and stannous ions. Calculate the ratio of stannic to stannous ion concentrations to give this potential.

17. When the A^{++} ion is 90% oxidized to A^{4+}, the potential of this couple is $+0.44$ v. Calculate the standard potential of the couple

$$A^{4+} + 2e \rightleftharpoons A^{++}$$

18. Calculate the potential at the equivalence point for the titration of 50 ml of 0.020-M Fe^{++} with 0.020-M Ce^{4+} in a solution which is originally 0.20-M in Fe^{3+}.

19. Five mmol of a ferrous salt is dissolved in 50 ml of acid solution and titrated with 0.10-M Ce^{4+}. Calculate the concentration of Fe^{3+}, Fe^{++}, Ce^{4+} and Ce^{3+} at the equivalence point. First write the four equations needed and then make the proper assumptions.

20. A sample containing 4.0 mmol of Sn^{++} is titrated with 0.10-M Ce^{4+}. Calculate the concentrations of Sn^{++}, Sn^{4+}, Ce^{3+}, and Ce^{4+} after 20.0 ml of titrant has been added. The volume is 100 ml. Write four independent equations, make the proper assumptions, and solve for the four concentrations. Check the validity of your assumptions.

21. Repeat the calculations of problem 20 except that the titration is now at the equivalence point. Assume the volume is 100 ml.

22. A 50-ml aliquot of 0.1-M Fe^{++} is titrated with 0.10-M Ce^{4+}. Let $V = $ ml of titrant and show that the potential before the equivalence point is given by

$$E = E_1^\circ - 0.06 \log \frac{50 - V}{V}$$

and after the equivalence point by

$$E = E_2^\circ - 0.06 \log \frac{50}{V - 50}$$

where E_1° and E_2° are the standard potentials of the ferrous-ferric and cerous-ceric redox couples, respectively.

23. (a) Refer to Table 4, Appendix I, and calculate the equilibrium constant for the reaction

$$2 H_2 + O_2 \rightleftharpoons 2 H_2O$$

at 25°C.

(b) Calculate the value of ΔG° at this temperature.

(c) How do you account for the fact that H_2 and O_2 can be mixed at 25°C and no reaction is noticeable?

24. An excess of pure copper turnings is added to a 0.12-M solution of Ag^+. Calculate the final concentration of Ag^+ after equilibrium is reached. Assume the equilibrium concentration of Cu^{++} is 0.06-M. Explain.

25. What concentration of cupric ions would be required to prevent copper from displacing silver in a solution which is 0.20-M in Ag^+? Is such a concentration possible?

26. Theoretically, what would the hydrogen ion concentration need to be in order for copper to displace hydrogen from an aqueous solution? Assume the Cu^{++} concentration to be 0.1-M and the hydrogen pressure to be 1 atm.

27. (a) Suppose a strip of pure copper is placed in 100 ml of 1-M HCl which contains no cupric ions. Assuming the following reaction reaches equilibrium,

$$Cu + 2 H^+ \rightleftarrows Cu^{++} + H_2$$

what is the concentration of cupric ions? How many copper atoms actually dissolve?

(b) Repeat the calculation, substituting silver for copper.

28. If 100 ml of a 0.10-M solution of ferric ion is shaken with metallic silver until equilibrium is reached,

$$Fe^{3+} + Ag \rightleftarrows Fe^{++} + Ag^+$$

calculate the volume of 0.020-M permanganate that would be required to titrate a 25-ml aliquot of the solution in acid media. Reactions:

$$Fe^{++} - Fe^{3+}; \qquad MnO_4^- - Mn^{++}$$

29. If 3.0 mmol of Fe^{++} is titrated with 0.025-M $Cr_2O_7^=$ solution, the final volume being 100 ml and the H^+ concentration 1-M, calculate the number of milligrams of Fe^{++} remaining when 0.10 ml of dichromate is in excess.

30. Theoretically, at what pH does tin cease to displace hydrogen from an aqueous solution which is 0.10-M in stannous ion?

31. The equilibrium constant for the following reaction

$$2 A^{4+} + B^{++} \rightleftarrows 2 A^{3+} + B^{4+}$$

is 100. Calculate the following points concerning this reaction:

(a) The difference in standard potentials of the two redox couples.

(b) The direction in which the reaction will tend to move to reach equilibrium if each reactant and product is at unit activity. What is the value of ΔG?

(c) The direction in which the reaction will tend to move to reach equilibrium if the activities are as follows: $A^{3+} = 1$, $B^{4+} = 1$, $A^{4+} = 0.01$, $B^{++} = 0.01$. What is the value of $E_{1\text{-}2}$? of $\Delta G°$?

32. (a) From the table of standard potentials determine whether or not the following disproportionation occurs spontaneously or not (all reactants at unit activity).

$$3 Br_2(aq) + 3 H_2O \rightleftarrows BrO_3^- + 5 Br^- + 6 H^+$$

(b) Calculate the equilibrium constant for the reaction as written.

33. The reaction in problem 32 can be written as follows (basic solution):

$$3 Br_2(aq) + 6 OH^- \rightleftarrows BrO_3^- + 5 Br^- + 3 H_2O$$

(a) Calculate the equilibrium constant for the reaction as written.

(b) At what pH does the disproportionation of bromine become spontaneous when the activities of Br_2, BrO_3^-, and Br^- are each unity?

34. (a) Refer to the table of standard potentials and calculate whether or not cuprous ion disproportionates spontaneously (unit activities) according to the equation

$$2 Cu^+ \rightleftarrows Cu^{++} + Cu$$

(b) What is the equilibrium constant of this reaction?

(c) How large a concentration of Cu^+ ions can exist in equilibrium with Cu^{++} ions at 1-M concentration?

35. Cuprous chloride is slightly soluble; hence addition of Cl^- to the equilibrium mixture (problem 34) shifts the equilibrium to the left. Given that the value of $E^{\circ}_{1\text{-}2}$ for the following reaction

$$2\ CuCl \rightleftarrows Cu + Cu^{++} + 2\ Cl^-$$

is -0.40 v, calculate the K_{sp} of CuCl.

36. Given that the K_{sp} of CuBr is 6×10^{-9}, calculate the standard potential of the redox couple

$$Cu^{++} + Br^- + e \rightleftarrows CuBr$$

37. Calculate the K_{sp} of AgCl using only data from the table of standard potentials (Table 4, Appendix I).

38. Excess hydrochloric acid is added to a silver nitrate solution, the final chloride concentration being $0.010\text{-}M$. The silver ion concentration in the solution is determined by inserting a silver electrode and measuring the potential of this electrode against a standard calomel electrode. The potential of the cell is found to be 0.050 v, with the silver electrode positive. Calculate the K_{sp} of AgCl.

39. (a) From the table of standard potentials calculate the solubility product constants of $PbSO_4$ and PbI_2.

(b) From the K_{sp} of AgI calculate the standard potential of the couple

$$AgI + e \rightleftarrows Ag + I^-$$

Compare this with the value in Table 4, Appendix I.

40. (a) Calculate the potential of the following cell:

$$Ag \mid Ag^+(0.010\text{-}M) \parallel H^+(1.0\text{-}M) \mid H_2(1.0\ atm),\ Pt$$

(b) Ammonia is added to the left-hand electrode until the final concentration of NH_3 is $1.0\text{-}M$. Calculate the potential of the cell. The constant for the reaction

$$Ag(NH_3)_2^+ \rightleftarrows Ag^+ + 2\ NH_3$$

is 7×10^{-8}.

41. (a) Calculate the value of the equilibrium constant for the following reaction:

$$HAsO_2 + I_3^- + 2\ H_2O \rightleftarrows H_3AsO_4 + 2\ H^+ + 3\ I^-$$

and compare it with the experimental value of 0.055 at $25°C$.

(b) If 2 mmol of arsenious acid are titrated with iodine at pH 5, how many mmol of acid remain unoxidized at the end point? Use the experimental value of K and assume the following: Final iodide concentration $= 0.1\text{-}M$, final volume $= 100$ ml, concentration of iodine $[I_3^-]$ required to develop a color with starch is $2 \times 10^{-5}\text{-}M$. Is the titration feasible? Why is the titration not carried out at pH 5?

42. Show that the slight excess of permanganate present at the end point of a titration with this reagent is sufficient to cause the following reaction to occur:

$$3\ Mn^{++} + 2\ MnO_4^- + 2\ H_2O \rightleftarrows 5\ MnO_2 + 4\ H^+$$

Assume $[Mn^{++}] = 0.10\text{-}M$, $[MnO_4^-] = 1 \times 10^{-5}\text{-}M$, and $[H^+] = 1\text{-}M$. Why in practice do we not observe this reaction?

43. "Preventive" solution, a mixture which minimizes the oxidation of Cl^- by MnO_4^- in the presence of iron, contains manganous ions. Show that this action is not caused by the effect of concentration on the potential of the MnO_4^--Mn^{++} couple by calculating the following:

(a) The change in potential caused by doubling the concentration of Mn^{++} ions.

(b) The factor by which the concentration of Mn^{++} ions would need to be increased to change the potential by 0.01 v. Assume the MnO_4^--Mn^{++} couple follows the Nernst equation.

chapter 6

Precipitation Titrations

Titrations involving precipitation reactions are not nearly so numerous in volumetric analysis as those involving redox or acid-base reactions. In fact, in a beginning course examples of such titrations are usually limited to those involving precipitation of silver ion with anions such as the halogens and thiocyanate. One of the reasons for the limited use of such reactions is the lack of suitable indicators. In some cases, particularly in the titration of dilute solutions, the rate of reaction is too slow for convenience of titration. As the equivalence point is approached and the titrant is added slowly, a high degree of supersaturation does not exist and the precipitation may be very slow. Another difficulty is that the composition of the precipitate is frequently not known because of coprecipitation effects (see Chapter 15). Although the latter can be minimized or partially corrected for by processes such as aging the precipitate, this is not possible in a direct titration involving the formation of a precipitate.

We shall limit our discussion here to precipitation titrations involving silver salts with particular emphasis on the indicators which have been successfully employed in such titrations.

PRECIPITATION EQUILIBRIA

The factor governing the completeness of a precipitation reaction is the solubility of the precipitate formed. The more insoluble a precipitate, the more complete is the reaction at the equivalence point and the larger is the change in concentration of the reacting ions.

The equilibrium constant expressing the solubility of a precipitate is the familiar *solubility product constant*. For a precipitate of silver chloride, the equilibrium constant of the reaction

$$AgCl_{(s)} \rightleftharpoons Ag^+_{(aq)} + Cl^-_{(aq)}$$

is

$$K = \frac{a_{Ag^+} a_{Cl^-}}{a_{AgCl_{(s)}}}$$

The activity of solid AgCl is constant and by convention we take it to be unity (page 80). The solid is only slightly soluble; hence the concentrations of Ag^+ and Cl^- ions are small and, unless large concentrations of other ions are present, activities can be approximated by molarities, giving

$$K_{sp} = [Ag^+][Cl^-]$$

The constant K_{sp} is called the solubility product constant.

Titration curves for precipitation titrations can be constructed and are entirely analogous to those for acid-base and redox titrations. The following example illustrates the calculations involved, using the titration of chloride ion with silver ion.

PROBLEM. 50.0 ml of 0.100-M NaCl solution are titrated with 0.100-M $AgNO_3$. Calculate the chloride ion concentration at intervals during the titration and plot pCl vs. ml of $AgNO_3$. $pCl = -\log [Cl^-]$, and K_{sp} of AgCl = 1×10^{-10}.

(a) *Start of titration.* Since

$$[Cl^-] = 0.100 \text{ mmol/ml}$$

$$pCl = 1.00$$

(b) *After addition of 10.0 ml $AgNO_3$.* Since the reaction goes well to completion,

$$[Cl^-] = \frac{[(50.0 \times 0.100) - (10.0 \times 0.100)] \text{ mmol}}{(50.0 + 10.0) \text{ ml}}$$

$$[Cl^-] = 0.067 \text{ mmol/ml}$$

$$pCl = 1.17$$

(c) *After addition of 49.9 ml AgNO₃.*

$$[Cl^-] = \frac{[(50.0 \times 0.100) - (49.9 \times 0.100)] \text{ mmol}}{(50.0 + 49.9) \text{ ml}}$$

$$[Cl^-] = 1.00 \times 10^{-4} \text{ mmol/ml}$$

$$p\text{Cl} = 4.00$$

In these calculations we have disregarded the contribution of chloride ions to the solution by the solubility of the precipitate. This approximation is valid except within one or two drops of the equivalence point. See next section for a more complete treatment of these calculations.

(d) *Equivalence point.* This point is reached when 50.0 ml of AgNO₃ have been added. There is neither excess chloride nor silver ion, and the concentration of each is given by the square root of K_{sp}.

$$[Ag^+] = [Cl^-]$$

$$[Cl^-]^2 = 1.0 \times 10^{-10}$$

$$[Cl^-] = 1.0 \times 10^{-5}$$

$$p\text{Cl} = 5.00$$

(e) *After addition of 60.0 ml of AgNO₃.* The concentration of excess silver ion is

$$[Ag^+] = \frac{[(60.0 \times 0.100) - (50.0 \times 0.100)] \text{ mmol}}{(50.0 + 60.0) \text{ ml}}$$

$$[Ag^+] = 9.1 \times 10^{-3}$$

$$p\text{Ag} = 2.04$$

Since

$$p\text{Cl} + p\text{Ag} = 10.00$$

$$p\text{Cl} = 7.96$$

The data for this titration are given in Table 6.1 and the titration curve is plotted in Figure 6.1. The curves for the titration of iodide and of bromide ions with silver are also plotted in this figure. The break in the curve at the

Table 6.1	TITRATION OF 50 Ml OF 0.10-M NaCl WITH 0.10-M AgNO₃		
ml AgNO₃	[Cl⁻]	% Cl⁻ pptd.	pCl
0.0	0.10	0.0	1.00
10.0	0.067	20.0	1.17
20.0	0.043	40.0	1.37
30.0	0.025	60.0	1.60
40.0	0.011	80.0	1.96
49.0	0.0010	98.0	3.00
49.9	1.0×10^{-4}	99.8	4.00
50.00	1.0×10^{-5}	100	5.00
50.10	1.0×10^{-6}	100	6.00
51.00	1.0×10^{-7}	100	7.00
60.00	1.1×10^{-8}	100	7.96

equivalence point is greatest for the titration of iodide, since silver iodide is the least soluble of the three salts. See problem 8 for calculations illustrating the dependence of the magnitude of the break in the titration curve upon the solubility of the precipitate.

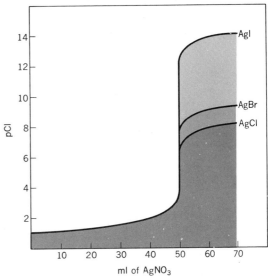

Fig. 6.1. Titration curves of NaCl, NaBr, and NaI. 50 ml of 0.1-M salt titrated with 0.1-M AgNO₃.

Approximations in solubility equilibria

A more complete treatment of the calculations made above can be made as follows. There are four ions whose concentrations may be considered: Cl^-, Ag^+, Na^+, and NO_3^-. A fifth variable is V, the volume of titrant, and the concentration of titrant will be taken as 0.100-M. We need five equations to specify these five quantities:

(1) $K_{sp} = [Ag^+][Cl^-]$

(2) Mass balance on chloride:

$$[Cl^-] + [AgCl]_s = \frac{50 \times 0.100}{V + 50}$$

(3) Mass balance on silver ion:

$$[Ag^+] + [AgCl]_s = \frac{V \times 0.100}{V + 50}$$

(4) Mass balance on sodium ion:

$$[Na^+] = \frac{50 \times 0.100}{V + 50}$$

(5) Mass balance on nitrate:

$$[NO_3^-] = \frac{V \times 0.100}{V + 50}$$

Here $[AgCl]_s$ is the number of moles of AgCl precipitated per liter of solution.

Equations (4) and (5) are not needed for constructing a titration curve and we will not consider them further. We may divide the problem of calculating pCl into three parts:

(1) *Before the equivalence point.* Assume that $[Ag^+]$ may be neglected in equation (3); substitute equation (3) into equation (2), giving

$$[Cl^-] + \frac{V \times 0.100}{V + 50} = \frac{50 \times 0.100}{V + 50}$$

$$[Cl^-] = \frac{(50 - V) \times 0.100}{50 + V}$$

Substituting in equation (1) gives

$$[Ag^+] = \frac{(50 + V) \times 1 \times 10^{-10}}{(50 - V) \times 0.100}$$

$$[Ag^+] = \frac{50 + V}{50 - V} \times 1 \times 10^{-9}$$

For $V = 10.0$ ml, $[Cl^-] = 0.067$, $[Ag^+] = 1.5 \times 10^{-9}$, and $pCl = 1.17$, $pAg = 8.83$. The assumption that $[Ag^+]$ can be neglected in equation (3) is seen to be valid. Near the equivalence point a larger error will result if the $[Ag^+]$ is neglected. The complete expression is obtained by subtracting equation (3) from equation (2), giving

$$[Cl^-] = [Ag^+] + \frac{(50 - V)}{(50 + V)} \times 0.100$$

Substituting in equation (1) gives

$$[Ag^+]^2 + \frac{50 - V}{50 + V} \times 0.10 \times [Ag^+] - 1.00 \times 10^{-10} = 0$$

The corresponding equation for chloride ion is

$$[Cl^-]^2 + \frac{V - 50}{V + 50} \times 0.10 \times [Cl^-] - 1.00 \times 10^{-10} = 0$$

Note that when $V = 49.9$ ml, the approximate equation gives

$$[Cl^-] = 1.00 \times 10^{-4}$$

The complete equation gives

$$[Cl^-] = 1.01 \times 10^{-4}$$

In each case pCl, rounded to two decimals, is 4.00. See problem 11 for another illustration of the error involved in such an approximation.

(2) *At the equivalence point.* Here $V = 50$ ml and the second term in the complete equation drops out, and

$$[Cl^-]^2 = 1.00 \times 10^{-10}$$

$$[Cl^-] = 1.00 \times 10^{-5}$$

$$pCl = 5.00$$

(3) *After the equivalence point.* Here the chloride ion concentration is small and we may neglect it in equation (2). Substitute equation (2) into equation (3), giving

$$[Ag^+] + \frac{50 \times 0.100}{V + 50} = \frac{V \times 0.100}{V + 50}$$

$$[Ag^+] = \frac{V - 50}{V + 50} \times 0.100$$

For $V = 60$ ml, $[Ag^+] = 9.1 \times 10^{-3}$ and $pAg = 2.04$. Since

$$pAg + pCl = 10.00$$

$$pCl = 7.96$$

INDICATORS FOR PRECIPITATION TITRATIONS INVOLVING SILVER

Formation of a colored precipitate: the Mohr method

Just as an acid-base system can be used as an indicator for an acid-base titration, and a redox system for redox titrations, the formation of another precipitate can be used to indicate the completion of a precipitation titration. The best known example of such a case is the so-called *Mohr* titration of chloride with silver ion, in which chromate ion is used as the indicator. The first permanent appearance of the reddish silver chromate precipitate is taken as the end point of the titration.

It is necessary, of course, that the precipitation of the indicator occur at or near the equivalence point of the titration. Silver chromate is more soluble (about 8.4×10^{-5} moles/liter) than silver chloride (about 1×10^{-5} mole/liter). If silver ions are added to a solution containing a large concentration of chloride ions and a small concentration of chromate ions, silver chloride will first precipitate; silver chromate will not form until the silver ion concentration increases to a large enough value to exceed the K_{sp} of silver chromate. One can readily calculate the concentration of chromate that will lead to precipitation of silver chromate at the equivalence point, where $pAg = pCl = 5.00$. Since the K_{sp} of Ag_2CrO_4 is 2×10^{-12}, and $[Ag^+] = 1 \times 10^{-5}$ at the equivalence point, then

$$[Ag^+]^2[CrO_4^=] = 2 \times 10^{-12}$$

$$[CrO_4^=] = \frac{2 \times 10^{-12}}{(1 \times 10^{-5})^2} = 0.02\text{-}M$$

Such a high concentration cannot be used in practice, however, since the yellow color of chromate ion makes it difficult to observe the formation of the colored precipitate. Normally a concentration of 0.005 to 0.01-M chromate is employed. The error caused by using such a concentration is quite small, as is shown in the following calculations.

PROBLEM. 5.00 mmol of NaCl are dissolved in 50.0 ml of a solution that is 0.0100-M in K_2CrO_4. This solution is titrated with 0.100-M $AgNO_3$ to the formation of a precipitate of Ag_2CrO_4. Calculate (a) the value of pCl at which precipitation of Ag_2CrO_4 begins, and (b) the error in the titration.

(a) The chromate ion concentration will be approximately 0.005-M at the end point, since about 50 ml of $AgNO_3$ will have been added. Thus

$$[Ag^+]^2(0.005) = 2 \times 10^{-12}$$

$$[Ag^+]^2 = 4 \times 10^{-10}$$

$$2\,pAg = 9.40$$

$$pAg = 4.70$$

$$pCl = 10.00 - 4.70 = 5.30$$

From Table 6.1 it can be seen that the end point occurs just beyond the equivalence point.

(b) At the end point,

$$pAg = 4.70$$

Hence

$$[Ag^+] = 2 \times 10^{-5} \text{ mmol/ml}$$

Then the mmol of Ag^+ in the solution is

$$100 \text{ ml} \times 2 \times 10^{-5} \text{ mmol/ml} = 0.002 \text{ mmol}$$

For no error in the titration,

$$\text{mmol } Ag^+ = \text{mmol } Cl^-$$

or

$$\text{mmol } Ag^+ - \text{mmol } Cl^- = 0$$

The chloride ion concentration is given by

$$(2 \times 10^{-5})[Cl^-] = 1.0 \times 10^{-10}$$

Hence

$$[Cl^-] = 5 \times 10^{-6}$$

and

$$\text{mmol } Cl^- = 100 \times 5 \times 10^{-6} = 0.0005$$

Thus

$$\text{mmol } Ag^+ - \text{mmol } Cl^- = 0.0015$$

Since 5.00 mmol of chloride were titrated, the error is

$$\frac{0.0015}{5.00} \times 100 = 0.03\%$$

It should be noted that we have not taken into account the millimoles of silver that are used to form the precipitate of Ag_2CrO_4, as well as additional AgCl precipitate. The millimoles of Ag^+ and Cl^- are equal, of course, in the

AgCl precipitate, and the quantity of Ag^+ in the chromate precipitate is fairly small under the conditions of the titration.[1]

In practice the error may be larger than this calculated value. It is best to correct for the end point error by determining an indicator blank, or by standardizing the silver nitrate against a pure chloride salt under conditions identical to those used in the analysis.

The Mohr titration is limited to solutions with *p*H values from about 6 to 10. In more alkaline solutions silver oxide precipitates. In acid solutions the chromate concentration is greatly decreased, since $HCrO_4^-$ is only slightly ionized. Furthermore, hydrogen chromate is in equilibrium with dichromate:

$$2\ H^+ + 2\ CrO_4^= \rightleftharpoons 2\ HCrO_4^- \rightleftharpoons Cr_2O_7^= + H_2O$$

A decrease in chromate ion concentration makes it necessary to add a large excess of silver ions to bring about precipitation of silver chromate, and thus leads to large errors (see problem 10). Dichromates are, in general, fairly soluble.

The Mohr method can also be applied to the titration of bromide ion with silver, and also cyanide ion in slightly alkaline solutions. Adsorption effects (page 172) make the titration of iodide with thiocyanate ions not feasible. Silver cannot be titrated directly with chloride, using chromate indicator. The silver chromate precipitate, present initially, redissolves only slowly near the equivalence point. However, one can add excess standard chloride solution, and then back-titrate, using the chromate indicator.

Formation of a colored complex: the Volhard method

The Volhard method is based on the precipitation of silver thiocyanate in nitric acid solution, with ferric ion employed to detect excess thiocyanate ion:

$$Ag^+ + SCN^- \rightleftharpoons AgSCN$$

$$Fe^{3+} + SCN^- \rightleftharpoons FeSCN^{++} \text{ (red)}$$

The method can be used for the direct titration of silver with standard thiocyanate solution, or for the indirect titration of chloride ion. In the latter case, an excess of standard silver nitrate is added, and the excess is titrated with standard thiocyanate. Other anions, such as bromide and iodide, can be determined by the same procedure. Anions of weak acids, such as oxalate, carbonate, and arsenate, the silver salts of which are soluble in acid, can be determined by precipitation at higher *p*H and filtration of

---

[1] See E. H. Swift, *Introductory Quantitative Analysis*, Prentice-Hall, Inc., Englewood Cliffs, N.J., 1950, p. 79.

silver salt. The precipitate is then dissolved in nitric acid and the silver titrated directly with thiocyanate.

The Volhard method is widely used for silver and chloride because of the fact that the titration can be done in acid solution. In fact, it is desirable to employ an acid medium to prevent hydrolysis of the ferric ion indicator. Other common methods for silver and chloride require a nearly neutral solution for successful titration. Many cations precipitate under such conditions, and hence interfere in these methods. Mercury is the only common cation that interferes with the Volhard method. In fact, mercury can be determined by titration with thiocyanate, since mercuric thiocyanate is a very slightly dissociated compound (see page 183). High concentrations of colored cations, such as cobaltous, nickelous, and cupric, cause difficulty in observation of the end point. Nitrous acid interferes in the titration, since it reacts with thiocyanate to produce a transitory red color.

In the direct titration of silver with thiocyanate there are two sources of error, both of which are minor. In the first place, the silver thiocyanate precipitate adsorbs silver ions on its surface (page 172), thereby causing the end point to occur prematurely. This difficulty can be largely overcome by vigorous stirring of the mixture near the end point. Secondly, the color change which marks the end point occurs at a concentration of thiocyanate slightly in excess of the concentration of the equivalence point. The magnitude of this error is calculated in the following problem.

PROBLEM. 2.5 mmol of $AgNO_3$ are dissolved in 75 ml of water and titrated with 0.10-M KSCN. The concentration of ferric ion indicator is about 0.015-M at the end point. At this concentration of indicator it is found that a thiocyanate concentration of about 1×10^{-5}-M is required to form a detectable color.[2] Calculate the volume of KSCN in excess of the equivalence point that is required to form a detectable color. K_{sp} of AgSCN $= 1 \times 10^{-12}$, $K_{\text{stab.}}$ of $FeSCN^{++} = 91$.

For no titration error,

$$\text{mmol SCN}^- - \text{mmol Ag}^+ = 0$$

However, at the end point the thiocyanate is present both as SCN^- and as $FeSCN^{++}$. The concentration of these species can be calculated from the stability constant. If

$$[FeSCN^{++}] = x$$

$$[Fe^{3+}] = 0.015 - x$$

$$[SCN^-] = 1 \times 10^{-5} - x$$

Hence

$$\frac{x}{(0.015 - x)(1 \times 10^{-5} - x)} = 91$$

Solving gives

$$x = [FeSCN^{++}] = 5.8 \times 10^{-6}$$

$$[SCN^-] = 4.2 \times 10^{-6}$$

---

[2] See E. H. Swift, *op. cit.*, p. 95.

From the K_{sp} of AgSCN,

$$[Ag^+] = 2 \times 10^{-7}$$

The difference in millimoles is

$$0.00058 + 0.00042 - 0.00002 = 0.00098$$

The error is

$$\frac{0.00098}{2.5} \times 100 = 0.04\%$$

It should be noted that it is not necessary to consider the millimoles of Ag^+ and SCN^- in the precipitate since these are equal.

In the indirect method a more serious error is encountered if the silver salt of the anion being determined is more soluble than silver thiocyanate. Silver chloride, for example, is more soluble than silver thiocyanate, and the chloride tends to redissolve according to the reaction

$$AgCl + SCN^- \rightleftarrows AgSCN + Cl^-$$

The equilibrium constant of this reaction is given by the ratio of the solubility product constant of silver chloride to that of silver thiocyanate. Since the former constant is larger than the latter, the foregoing reaction has a strong tendency to proceed from left to right. Thus thiocyanate can be consumed not only by excess silver ion, but also by the silver chloride precipitate itself. If this occurs, low results will be obtained in the chloride analysis. This reaction can be prevented, however, by filtering off the silver chloride or adding nitrobenzene before titration with thiocyanate.[3] The nitrobenzene apparently forms an oily coating on the silver chloride surface, preventing the reaction with thiocyanate. Another method of decreasing this error is to use a sufficiently high concentration of ferric ion (about $0.2\text{-}M$) so that the end point color is reached at a lower concentration of thiocyanate.[4] A smaller amount of silver chloride is then redissolved and there is still a sufficiently high concentration of the red $FeSCN^{++}$ complex to be visible. Swift *et al.*[4] found that the end point error was reduced to 0.1% by this procedure.

In the determination of bromide and iodide by the indirect Volhard method, the reaction with thiocyanate does not cause any trouble, because silver bromide has about the same solubility as silver thiocyanate and silver iodide is considerably less soluble.

Adsorption indicators

When a colored organic compound is adsorbed on the surface of a precipitate, modification of the organic structure may occur and the color

---

[3] J. R. Caldwell and H. V. Moyer, *Ind. Eng. Chem.*, Anal. Ed., **7**, 38 (1935).

[4] E. H. Swift, G. M. Arcand, R. Lutwack, and D. J. Meier, *Anal. Chem.*, **22**, 306 (1950).

may be greatly changed and may become more intense. This phenomenon can be used to detect the end point of precipitation titrations of silver salts. The organic compounds thus employed are referred to as "adsorption indicators."

The mechanism by which such indicators work is different from any we have discussed so far. Fajans,[5] who discovered the fact that fluorescein and some substituted fluoresceins could serve as indicators for silver titrations, explained the process as follows. When silver nitrate is added to a solution of sodium chloride, the finely divided particles of silver chloride tend to hold to their surface (adsorb) some of the excess chloride ions in the solution. These chloride ions are said to form the primarily adsorbed layer and thus cause the colloidal particles[6] of silver chloride to be negatively charged. These negative particles then tend to attract positive ions from the solution to form a more loosely held secondary adsorption layer:

$$(AgCl) \cdot Cl^- \ \vdots \ \ M^+$$

Primary layer	Secondary layer	Excess chloride

If one continues to add silver nitrate until silver ions are in excess, these ions will displace chloride ions in the primary layer.[7] The particles then become positively charged, and anions in the solution are attracted to form the secondary layer:

$$(AgCl) \cdot Ag^+ \ \vdots \ \ X^-$$

Primary layer	Secondary layer	Excess silver

Fluorescein is a weak organic acid, which we may represent as HFl. When fluorescein is added to the titration flask, the anion, Fl^-, is not adsorbed by colloidal silver chloride as long as chloride ions are in excess. However, when silver ions are in excess the Fl^- ion can be attracted to the surface of the positively charged particles, as

$$(AgCl) \cdot Ag^+ \ \vdots \ Fl^-$$

The resulting aggregate is pink, and the color is sufficiently intense to serve as a visual indicator.

A number of factors must be considered in choosing a proper adsorption indicator for a precipitation titration. These are summarized below.

1. Since the surface of the precipitate is the "active agent" in the operation of the indicator, the precipitate should not be allowed to coagulate

---

[5] K. Fajans and O. Hassel, *Z. Elektrochem.*, **29,** 495 (1923); see also I. M. Kolthoff, *Chem. Rev.*, **16,** 87 (1935), and K. Fajans, Chapter 7 of *Newer Methods of Volumetric Analysis*, W. Bottger, Ed., D. Van Nostrand and Co., N.Y., 1938.

[6] A more detailed discussion of colloids is given in Chapter 15.

[7] A precipitate tends to adsorb most readily those ions that form an insoluble compound with one of the ions in the lattice. Thus silver or chloride ions will be more readily adsorbed by a silver chloride precipitate than will, say, sodium or nitrate ions.

into large particles and settle to the bottom of the titration flask. Coagulation of a silver chloride precipitate will occur at the equivalence point, where neither chloride nor silver ions are in excess, unless a substance such as dextrin is present. Dextrin acts as a "protective colloid," keeping the precipitate highly dispersed. In the presence of dextrin the color change is reversible, and if the end point is overrun, one can back-titrate with a standard chloride solution.

2. The degree to which different indicator ions are adsorbed varies considerably, and an indicator must be chosen that is not too strongly or too weakly adsorbed. Ideally, adsorption should start just before the equivalence point is reached and increase rapidly at the equivalence point. Some indicators are so strongly adsorbed that they will actually displace the primarily adsorbed ion well before the equivalence point is reached. Eosin, for example, cannot be used for titration of chloride with silver because of this effect. On the other hand, eosin can be used for the titration of iodide or bromide with silver, since these two anions are so strongly adsorbed that eosin does not displace them. If the indicator is too weakly adsorbed, the end point will occur, of course, after the equivalence point is passed.

SOME ADSORPTION INDICATORS   Table 6.2

Indicator	Ion titrated	Titrant	Conditions
Dichlorofluorescein	Cl^-	Ag^+	pH 4
Fluorescein	Cl^-	Ag^+	pH 7–8
Eosin	Br^-, I^-, SCN^-	Ag^+	pH 2
Thorin	$SO_4^=$	Ba^{++}	pH 1.5–3.5
Bromcresol green	SCN^-	Ag^+	pH 4–5
Methyl violet	Ag^+	Cl^-	Acid solution
Rhodamine 6 G	Ag^+	Br^-	Sharp in presence of HNO_3 up to 0.3-M
Orthochrome T	Pb^{++}	$CrO_4^=$	Neutral 0.02-M solution
Bromphenol blue	Hg_2^{++}	Cl^-	0.1-M solution

3. Adsorption indicators are weak acids or bases, and thus the pH of the titration medium is of importance. The ionization constant of fluorescein, for example, is about 10^{-7}. In solutions more acidic than pH 7, the concentration of the Fl$^-$ anion is so small that no color change is observed. Fluorescein can be used only in the pH range of about 7 to 10. On the other hand, derivatives of fluorescein that are stronger acids can be used in solutions of lower pH. For example, dichlorofluorescein has an ionization constant of about 10^{-4} and can be used in the pH range 4 to 10. The anion of dichlorofluorescein also is more strongly adsorbed than the anion of

fluorescein. Eosin (tetrabromofluorescein) is a still stronger acid and can be used in bromide or iodide titrations even at a pH of 2.

4. It is preferable that the indicator ion be of opposite charge to the ion added as the titrant. Adsorption of the indicator will then not occur until excess titrant is present. For the titration of silver with chloride, methyl violet, the chloride salt of an organic base, can be employed. The cation is not adsorbed until excess chloride ions are present and the colloid is negatively charged. It is possible to use dichlorofluorescein in this case, but the indicator should not be added until just before the equivalence point.

A list of some adsorption indicators is given in Table 6.2.

REFERENCES

1. H. A. Laitinen, *Chemical Analysis*, McGraw-Hill Book Co., Inc., New York, 1960.
2. S. Lewin, *The Solubility Product Principle*, Interscience Publishers, Inc., New York, 1960.
3. J. N. Butler, *Ionic Equilibrium, A Mathematical Approach*, Addison-Wesley Publishing Co., Inc., Reading, Mass., 1964.
4. H. F. Walton, *Principles and Methods of Chemical Analysis*, 2nd Ed., Prentice-Hall, Inc., Englewood Cliffs, N.J., 1964.
5. D. L. Leussing, "Solubility," and J. F. Coetzee, "Equilibria in Precipitation Reactions and Precipitation Lines," Chapters 17 and 19, Part I, Vol. I, of *Treatise on Analytical Chemistry*, I. M. Kolthoff, P. J. Elving, and E. B. Sandell, Eds., Interscience Publishers, Inc., New York, 1959.

QUESTIONS

1. What effect do the concentrations of the reacting ions have upon the titration curve of a precipitation reaction, such as Cl^- with Ag^+? Show this by roughly sketching curves for 0.1-, 0.01-, and 0.001-M solutions, the titrant being the same concentration.

2. Compare the principles involved in calculating the titration curves in this chapter with those used in Chapter 4. Do these resemble the calculations of the strong-strong or weak-strong electrolyte type? Explain.

3. Why is the chance of error in the Volhard determination of chloride much greater than in the determination of bromide or iodide?

4. Explain clearly the mechanism by which adsorption indicators work. What is the function of dextrin? Why must the pH of the solution be controlled?

5. Explain how the following errors would affect the indicated determination, that is, make the result high, low, or have no effect:
   (a) Chloride (Mohr): solution at pH of 2.
   (b) Chloride (Volhard): failure to add nitrobenzene.
   (c) Chloride (Fajans): eosin used as indicator.
   (d) Bromide (Mohr): $AgNO_3$ standardized against $NaCl$, no indicator blank.

PROBLEMS

1. Calculate the following:
   (a) pCl of 0.05-M NaCl solution
   (b) pBr of 0.01-M NaBr solution
   (c) pI of 0.002-M NaI solution
   (d) pCl of 2.0-M NaCl solution

2. Calculate the following:
   (a) pCl of a solution made by mixing 75 ml of 0.10-M NaCl and 25 ml of 0.20-M AgNO$_3$.
   (b) pCl of a solution made by mixing 40 ml of 0.20-M NaCl and 60 ml of 0.25-M AgNO$_3$.
   (c) pCl and pAg of a solution made by mixing 60 ml of 0.10-M NaCl and 40 ml of 0.15-M AgNO$_3$.

3. Repeat problem 2, substituting NaBr for NaCl and calculating pBr instead of pCl.

4. Repeat problem 2, substituting NaI for NaCl and calculating pI instead of pCl.

5. How many grams of NaI must be dissolved in 200 ml of a solution to make the $pI = 2.40$?

6. 50 ml of HCl, pCl of 2.00 is mixed with 50 ml of HCl, pCl of 4.00. What is the pCl of the resulting solution?

7. A solution of AgNO$_3$ has a pAg of 1.70 and a solution of NaCl has a pCl of 2.00. If equal volumes of these solutions are mixed, what is the pAg of the resulting solution?

8. A 50 ml aliquot of 0.10-M NaBr is titrated with 0.10-M AgNO$_3$. Calculate the value of pBr at 49.9 and 50.1 ml of titrant. Repeat the calculations for the titration of NaI. Compare the change in pBr and pI with that of pCl (Table 6.1) and interpret the differences in terms of the solubilities of the salts.

9. (a) Calculate the end point error in the Mohr method for the titration of NaBr under the same conditions as in the problem on page 168. (b) Repeat the calculation for the titration of NaI. (c) Repeat for the titration of a salt NaX where the K_{sp} of AgX is 1×10^{-8}. (d) What should the value of K_{sp} be for there to be no error in this method? Make same assumption as was made on page 168.

10. Calculate the error in the Mohr titration of chloride for the same conditions as in the problem on page 168 except that the pH is such that the chromate ion concentration is reduced to (a) 0.001-M, and (b) 0.0001-M.

11. A 50 ml sample of a 0.10-M solution of the salt NaX is titrated with 0.10-M AgNO$_3$ forming the precipitate AgX. Calculate the value of pX after the addition of 49.9 ml of titrant, first by the complete equation (page 166) and then by the approximate expression which neglects the solubility of the salt. Use the following values for the K_{sp} of AgX: (a) 1×10^{-6}, (b) 1×10^{-8}, and (c) 1×10^{-10}.

12. (a) Calculate the value of pAg at the equivalence point for the titration of Ag$^+$ with CrO$_4^=$.
   (b) Calculate the value of $pCrO_4$ at the same point.

13. Calculate the error in the indirect Volhard procedure for the titration of 5.0 mmol of chloride, 100 ml volume at the end point. The same conditions apply for detecting the thiocyanate color as in the problem on page 170. *Hint:* For no error the meq of Ag^+ should equal the sum of the meq of SCN^- and Cl^- in the solution.

14. Repeat problem 13, substituting bromide for chloride ion. Is this error appreciable?

Complex Formation Titrations

INTRODUCTION

The origin of the term "complex" lies deep in the history of chemistry, and it is unlikely that it would be used today if a totally new nomenclature and classification scheme were developed on the basis of present concepts. However, as it stands, there are a host of chemical species which are called "complexes." One develops a feeling for what the term means, but it is not easily defined in such a way as to avoid confusion, particularly in borderline cases. Originally, it was considered that a complex resulted from the combination of chemical entities which themselves were capable of independent existence. Thus ammonia might combine with a cupric salt to form a complex, e.g.,

$$CuSO_4 + 4\,NH_3 \rightleftharpoons CuSO_4 \cdot 4\,NH_3$$

The dot was a symbol of ignorance as to the nature of the bonding between molecules which had hitherto been considered "saturated."

Later studies of solutions of complexes disclosed that complex ions such as $Cu(NH_3)_4^{++}$ existed as discrete species. The copper is referred to as the "central metal ion," and the four ammonia molecules which are grouped around the copper or "coordinated" with it are called "ligands." The geometry of the complex ion is definite: In the case of copper, the conformation is "square planar," which is to say that there is an ammonia nitrogen at each corner of a square with copper at the center. In other cases, tetrahedral, octahedral, and other arrangements of ligands around central ions are found. The nature of the bonding in complexes has been of much interest in recent years; it may be covalent, resulting from overlap of ligand and metal ion orbitals, but often coordination involves a largely ionic interaction.

Although the formation of $Cu(NH_3)_4^{++}$ is called "complex formation," it is now recognized that Cu^{++} does not exist as such in aqueous solution; rather, the copper is hydrated (cf. hydrated H^+ in Chapter 4), and we might better write it as a complex species, $Cu(H_2O)_4^{++}$. Thus the formation of $Cu(NH_3)_4^{++}$, at least in aqueous solution, represents a replacement reaction, and the hydrated ion is just as much a complex ion as is the ammonia derivative. Usually, though, the reaction is written simply

$$Cu^{++} + 4\,NH_3 \rightleftharpoons Cu(NH_3)_4^{++}$$

Largely as a result of studies by J. Bjerrum,[1] it is recognized that the species $Cu(NH_3)_4^{++}$ is not formed at once when ammonia is added to a cupric solution. Rather, a series of complexes is formed in a step-wise fashion:

$$Cu^{++} + NH_3 \rightleftharpoons Cu(NH_3)^{++} \qquad K_1 = \frac{[Cu(NH_3)^{++}]}{[Cu^{++}][NH_3]} = 10^{4.1}$$

$$Cu(NH_3)^{++} + NH_3 \rightleftharpoons Cu(NH_3)_2^{++} \qquad K_2 = \frac{[Cu(NH_3)_2^{++}]}{[Cu(NH_3)^{++}][NH_3]} = 10^{3.5}$$

$$Cu(NH_3)_2^{++} + NH_3 \rightleftharpoons Cu(NH_3)_3^{++} \qquad K_3 = \frac{[Cu(NH_3)_3^{++}]}{[Cu(NH_3)_2^{++}][NH_3]} = 10^{2.9}$$

$$Cu(NH_3)_3^{++} + NH_3 \rightleftharpoons Cu(NH_3)_4^{++} \qquad K_4 = \frac{[Cu(NH_3)_4^{++}]}{[Cu(NH_3)_3^{++}][NH_3]} = 10^{2.1}$$

This behavior explains why the titration of Cu^{++} with NH_3 is not feasible. Considering the overall reaction,

$$Cu^{++} + 4\,NH_3 \rightleftharpoons Cu(NH_3)_4^{++}$$

$$K = \frac{[Cu(NH_3)_4^{++}]}{[Cu^{++}][NH_3]^4} = K_1 K_2 K_3 K_4 = 10^{12.6}$$

the equilibrium constant seems to be large enough to provide a feasible titration. Compare, for example, $K = 10^{14}$ for the strong acid-strong base titration reaction, $H_3O^+ + OH^- \rightleftharpoons 2\,H_2O$, and $K = 10^{9.26}$ for the easily

---

[1] J. Bjerrum, *Metal Ammine Formation in Aqueous Solution*, P. Haase and Son, Copenhagen, 1941; reprinted 1957.

feasible titration of strong acid with ammonia, $H_3O^+ + NH_3 \rightleftharpoons NH_4^+ + H_2O$. But, as shown in Figure 7.1, the titration of strong acid with ammonia yields a good break around the equivalence point, whereas the titration of Cu^{++} with ammonia does not.

It may be seen in Figure 7.1 that the break in the copper titration would

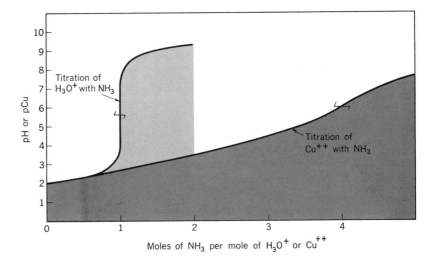

Fig. 7.1. Titration of strong acid and of cupric ion with ammonia calculated for $10^{-2}M$, H_3O^+, and Cu^{++}, assuming no volume change.

be better if the pCu ($pCu = -\log [Cu^{++}]$) remained lower in the early stages of the titration, as does the pH in the H_3O^+ titration. For example, 75% of the way to the equivalence point, if the ratio of $[Cu^{++}]$ to $[Cu(NH_3)_4^{++}]$ were close to 1:3, the pCu would be about 2.6, whereas in fact it is about 4.5 at this point. The reason that the pCu is too high lies in the fact that all of the added ammonia has not been used to form the complex $Cu(NH_3)_4^{++}$. Rather, lower complex species such as $Cu(NH_3)^{++}$ have formed, lowering the free $[Cu^{++}]$ below a desirable value for a feasible titration. Such behavior is predictable from the formation constants of the individual steps given above. It is seen, for example, that there is less tendency for $Cu(NH_3)^{++}$ to add a second ammonia than for free Cu^{++} to bind the first one. It is sometimes said, in a frivolous vein, that the titration would be feasible if one could titrate with little sacks, each containing four ammonia molecules; a cupric ion would then take four ammonia molecules or none, and the difficulty arising from the lower complexes would be averted.

The chemical equivalent of these little sacks can indeed be obtained. Consider, for example, the compound triethylenetetramine, often abbreviated "trien." Here, four nitrogen atoms are linked by ethylene bridges in a single molecule which can satisfy copper's normal coordination number of four in one step:

$$\left[\begin{array}{c} \text{CH}_2\text{CH}_2 \\ \text{H}_2\text{N} \qquad \text{NH--CH}_2 \\ \text{Cu} \\ \text{H}_2\text{N} \qquad \text{NH--CH}_2 \\ \text{CH}_2\text{CH}_2 \end{array}\right]^{++}$$

Heterocyclic rings formed by interaction of a metal ion with two or more functional groups in the same ligand molecule are called *chelate* rings; the organic molecule is a *chelating* agent, and the complexes are called *chelates* or *chelate compounds*. Ligands like ammonia which form only one bond with the metal are called *unidentate*. Chelating agents are bidentate, tridentate, etc. As shown in the above structural formula, trien is quadridentate.

It may be supposed that the formation of the first nitrogen-copper bond brings the other nitrogens of the trien molecule into such proximity that the formation of additional bonds involving these nitrogens is much more probable than the formation of bonds between the copper and other trien molecules. Similarly, it is unlikely that one trien molecule will coordinate with more than one copper. Thus, under ordinary conditions, the stoichiometry of complex formation in this system is 1 Cu^{++}:1 trien. The resulting 5-membered rings shown in the structural formula are relatively free of strain. The complex is very stable, as shown by its formation constant:

$$Cu^{++} + \text{trien} \rightleftarrows Cu(\text{trien})^{++} \qquad K = \frac{[Cu(\text{trien})^{++}]}{[Cu^{++}][\text{trien}]} = 10^{20.4}$$

Thus trien is a good titrant for copper: The ligand and the complex ion are both soluble in water, only a 1:1 complex is formed, the equilibrium constant for the titration reaction is large, and the reaction proceeds rapidly.

Only a few metal ions such as copper, cobalt, nickel, zinc, cadmium, and mercuric form stable complexes with nitrogen ligands such as ammonia and trien. Certain other metal ions, e.g., aluminum, lead, and bismuth, are better complexed with ligands containing oxygen atoms as electron donors. Certain chelating agents which contain both oxygen and nitrogen are particularly effective in forming stable complexes with a wide variety of metals. Of these, the best known is *ethylenediaminetetraacetic* acid, sometimes designated (ethylenedinitrilo)-tetraacetic acid, and often abbreviated EDTA:

$$\begin{array}{cc} \text{HOOCCH}_2 & \text{CH}_2\text{COOH} \\ \text{NCH}_2\text{CH}_2\text{N} \\ \text{HOOCCH}_2 & \text{CH}_2\text{COOH} \end{array}$$

We shall consider this reagent in detail later in this chapter.

The term *chelon* (pronounced "key-loan") has been proposed as a generic name for the entire class of reagents including polyamines such as trien, polyaminocarboxylic acids such as EDTA, and related compounds that form stable, water-soluble, 1:1 complexes with metal ions and which hence may be employed as titrants for metals. The complexes, a special class of chelate compounds, are called *metal chelonates,* and the titrations are termed *chelometric titrations.* Chelons have practically revolutionized the analytical chemistry of many of the metallic elements, and they are of great importance in many fields.

In Chapter 4 we defined acids and bases in terms of the tendency to release or accept protons (Brønsted). A broader definition, however, places complex-formation reactions within the acid-base category. G. N. Lewis pointed out that two reactions such as

$$H^+ + NH_3 \rightleftharpoons NH_4^+$$

$$Cu^{++} + NH_3 \rightleftharpoons Cu(NH_3)^{++}$$

are essentially similar. Both involve the interaction of a species which is seeking electrons (H^+ or Cu^{++}) with an electron donor (NH_3). Thus the proton, in Lewis' view, is only one of many possible acids, and basicity as manifested in proton acceptance is a special case of the general tendency of bases to donate electrons. In the Lewis sense, then, chelometric titrations are acid-base titrations in which the metal ion is a so-called Lewis acid and the chelon is a base.

TITRATIONS INVOLVING UNIDENTATE LIGANDS

Because of the step-wise formation of successive complexes as noted above, unidentate ligands are only rarely suitable for the titration of metal ions. However, there are a few examples of important titrations based upon such ligands, and we shall consider briefly the two best-known cases.

Titration of chloride with mercuric ion

The mercuric ion-chloride system is unusual in that the last two of the successive complexes in the formation of $HgCl_4^-$ are of much lesser stability than the first two, as shown by the successive formation constants given below:[2]

$$Hg^{++} + Cl^- \rightleftharpoons HgCl^+ \qquad K_1 = \frac{[HgCl^+]}{[Hg^{++}][Cl^-]} = 10^{6.74}$$

[2] A. Johnson, I. Quarfort, and L. G. Sillen, *Acta Chem. Scand.*, **1**, 461, 473 (1947).

$$HgCl^+ + Cl^- \rightleftarrows HgCl_2 \qquad K_2 = \frac{[HgCl_2]}{[HgCl^+][Cl^-]} = 10^{6.48}$$

$$HgCl_2 + Cl^- \rightleftarrows HgCl_3^- \qquad K_3 = \frac{[HgCl_3^-]}{[HgCl_2][Cl^-]} = 10^{0.85}$$

$$HgCl_3^- + Cl^- \rightleftarrows HgCl_4^= \qquad K_4 = \frac{[HgCl_4^=]}{[HgCl_3^-][Cl^-]} = 10^{1.0}$$

Thus in the titration of a chloride solution with an ionized mercuric salt such as mercuric nitrate or perchlorate, there is a sudden drop in pHg (pHg = $-\log [Hg^{++}]$) when the formation of $HgCl_2$ is essentially complete.

One of the common indicators for this titration is sodium nitroprusside, $Na_2Fe(CN)_5NO$. This compound forms a white precipitate of mercuric nitroprusside, and the end point is taken as the appearance of a white turbidity in the formerly homogeneous solution. The pHg at the equivalence point of the titration is not so low as might otherwise be expected because of the consumption of mercuric ion in the following reaction:

$$Hg^{++} + HgCl_2 \rightleftarrows 2\, HgCl^+ \qquad K = \frac{K_1}{K_2} \cong 1.8$$

Actually, the mercuric nitroprusside precipitate is first seen somewhat after the equivalence point, and a correction must be applied in order to obtain the best results. The correction is not really the same as an indicator blank run with distilled water, because the above reaction does not then take place appreciably. The correction depends upon the final concentration of mercuric chloride, and hence varies with the quantity of sample and the final volume. The acidity of the solution also affects the correction, and there is further variation which depends upon the rate at which the titration is performed and the manner in which the individual analyst views the turbid solution. Typical correction values are given by Kolthoff and Stenger;[3] for example, where the final solution is 100 ml of 0.025-M $HgCl_2$, the correction is roughly 0.2 ml. An advantage of this particular method lies in the fact that the titration may be performed in solutions which are quite acidic, and it works well even in fairly dilute solution, for example, at levels of chloride (e.g., 10 mg per liter) which frequently occur in natural waters.

Certain organic compounds which form colored complexes with mercuric ion have also been employed as indicators for the mercurimetric titration of chloride. The best known are diphenylcarbazide (colorless) and diphenylcarbazone (orange), which form intense violet mercuric complexes. With these indicators, it has been found important to control the pH of the solution being titrated. According to Roberts,[4] diphenylcarbazide performs

[3] I. M. Kolthoff and V. A. Stenger, *Volumetric Analysis*, 2nd Ed., Vol. II, Interscience Publishers, Inc., New York, 1947, p. 332.

[4] I. Roberts, *Ind. Eng. Chem.*, Anal. Ed., **8**, 365 (1936).

best at pH 1.5 to 2.0, while Clark[5] found that diphenylcarbazone is best employed at pH 3.2 to 3.3.

It should be pointed out that bromide, thiocyanate, and cyanide may be determined by mercurimetric titration, although there is no advantage over the usual titrations of these ions with silver nitrate. Nitroprusside cannot be used as the indicator in the thiocyanate titration, because the appearance of the mercuric nitroprusside precipitate is obscured by the slightly soluble mercuric thiocyanate. In this case, the usual indicator is ferric ion, which acts by the formation of red complexes with thiocyanate such as $FeSCN^{++}$. The titration of iodide with mercury is largely unsatisfactory. The complex $HgI_4^=$ forms during the titration; later, a red precipitate of HgI_2 appears through the reaction

$$Hg^{++} + HgI_4^= \rightleftarrows 2\,HgI_2$$

The appearance of this precipitate has been used as an end point, but actually it occurs much too early.

Titration of cyanide with silver ion

Another titration of some practical importance involving a unidentate ligand and a metal ion is the so-called Liebig titration of cyanide with silver nitrate. The basis of the method is the formation of the very stable complex ion, $Ag(CN)_2^-$:

$$2\,CN^- + Ag^+ \rightleftarrows Ag(CN)_2^-$$

The equilibrium constant for this reaction as written is about 10^{21}, and this is the only silver-cyanide complex of appreciable stability. Originally, the end point was based upon the appearance of turbidity due to the precipitation of silver cyanide, which may be written as

$$Ag^+ + Ag(CN)_2^- \rightleftarrows 2\,AgCN$$

or

$$Ag^+ + Ag(CN)_2^- \rightleftarrows Ag[Ag(CN)_2]$$

This precipitation occurs after $[CN^-]$ has dropped to a low value, although a calculation based upon the appropriate equilibria shows that it actually comes a little too early, corresponding to an end point error of the order of 0.2 parts per thousand. This error is small enough to be accepted, but there is an additional problem: Silver cyanide precipitated locally is slow to redissolve as the solution is stirred, and it is time consuming to perform the titration carefully. Also, there is some difficulty in seeing the silver cyanide precipitate.

In the Deniges modification of Liebig's method, iodide ion is added as

[5] F. E. Clark, *Anal. Chem.*, **22**, 553 (1950).

the indicator. Precipitated silver iodide is bulky and easy to see, and it is less soluble than silver cyanide and hence precipitates in place of the latter at the end point. This end point occurs, however, too early in the titration. For this reason, ammonia is added which, by forming the soluble species $Ag(NH_3)_2^+$, retards the precipitation of silver iodide until a more propitious time; ammonia does not prevent the formation of the much more stable $Ag(CN)_2^-$, and hence does not interfere with the titration reaction.

CHELOMETRIC TITRATIONS

The suitability of chelons such as EDTA as titrants for metal ions has been mentioned in the introduction to this chapter. We wish here to examine some of the equilibria involved in these titrations, consider end point techniques, and show some representative applications. Our discussion will be limited largely to EDTA.

EDTA is potentially a sexidentate ligand which may coordinate with a metal ion through its two nitrogens and four carboxyl groups. It is known from infrared spectra and other measurements that this is the case, for example, with the cobaltous ion, which forms an octahedral EDTA complex whose structure is somewhat as shown below:

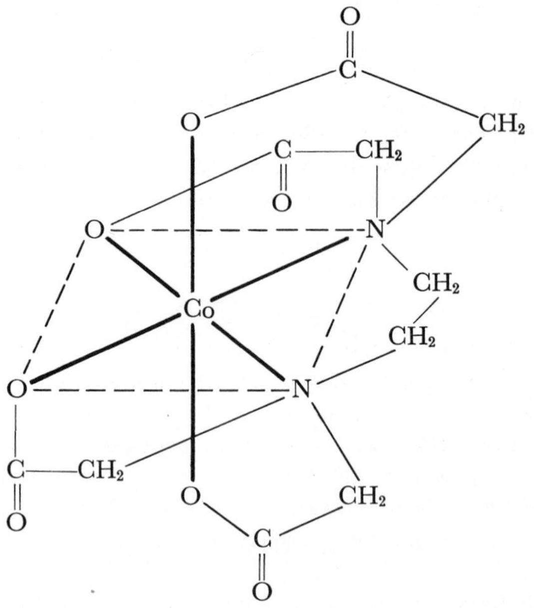

In other cases, EDTA may behave as a quinquedentate or quadridentate ligand having one or two of its carboxyl groups free of strong interaction with the metal.

For convenience, the free acid form of EDTA is often abbreviated H_4Y. The above cobalt complex is then written $CoY^=$, and other complexes become $CuY^=$, FeY^-, $CaY^=$, etc. In solutions which are fairly acidic, partial protonation of EDTA without complete rupture of the metal complex may occur, leading to species such as $CuHY^-$, but under the usual conditions all four hydrogens are lost when the ligand is coordinated with a metal ion. At very high pH values, hydroxyl ion may penetrate the coordination sphere of the metal and complexes such as $Cu(OH)Y^{3-}$ may exist.

Equilibria involved in EDTA titrations

We may consider a metal ion such as Cu^{++}, which is seeking electrons in its reactions, to be analogous to an acid like H_3O^+, and the EDTA anion Y^{4-}, which is an electron donor, to be a base. Then the reaction $Cu^{++} + Y^{4-} \rightleftarrows CuY^=$ is analogous to an ordinary neutralization reaction, and it should be a simple matter to calculate pCu values under various conditions, calculate titration curves, discuss feasibility, etc. As a matter of fact, however, the situation is more complicated than this because of the intrusion of other equilibria into the titration situation. We shall discuss some of these in the sections below.

The absolute stability or formation constant. It is customary to tabulate for various metal ions and various chelons such as EDTA, values of the equilibrium constants for reactions formulated as follows:

$$M^{n+} + Y^{4-} \rightleftarrows MY^{-(4-n)} \qquad K_{abs} = \frac{[MY^{-(4-n)}]}{[M^{n+}][Y^{4-}]}$$

K_{abs} is called the *absolute stability constant* or the *absolute formation constant*. Values of some of these constants may be found in Table 3, Appendix I.

The pH effect. The four ionization constants of the acid H_4Y are as follows:

$$H_4Y + H_2O \rightleftarrows H_3O^+ + H_3Y^-$$

$$K_{a_1} = \frac{[H_3O^+][H_3Y^-]}{[H_4Y]} = 1.02 \times 10^{-2} \qquad (pK_{a_1} = 1.99)$$

$$H_3Y^- + H_2O \rightleftarrows H_3O^+ + H_2Y^=$$

$$K_{a_2} = \frac{[H_3O^+][H_2Y^=]}{[H_3Y^-]} = 2.14 \times 10^{-3} \qquad (pK_{a_2} = 2.67)$$

$$H_2Y^= + H_2O \rightleftarrows H_3O^+ + HY^{3-}$$

$$K_{a_3} = \frac{[H_3O^+][HY^{3-}]}{[H_2Y^=]} = 6.92 \times 10^{-7} \qquad (pK_{a_3} = 6.16)$$

$$HY^{3-} + H_2O \rightleftarrows H_3O^+ + Y^{4-}$$

$$K_{a_4} = \frac{[H_3O^+][Y^{4-}]}{[HY^{3-}]} = 5.50 \times 10^{-11} \qquad (pK_{a_4} = 10.26)$$

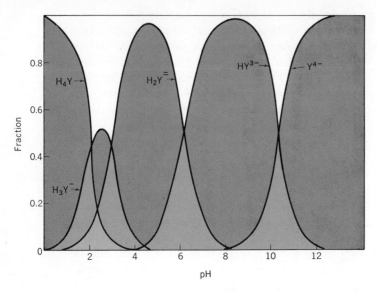

Fig. 7.2. Distribution of EDTA species as a function of pH.

The distributions of the five EDTA species as functions of pH are shown in Figure 7.2. It may be seen that only at pH values greater than about 12 does most of the EDTA exist as the tetra-anion Y^{4-}. At lower pH values, the protonated species HY^{3-}, etc., predominate. We may consider that H_3O^+, then, competes with a metal ion for EDTA, and it is clear that the real tendency to form the metal chelate at any particular pH value is not discernible directly from K_{abs}. For example, at pH 4 the predominant EDTA species is $H_2Y^=$, and the reaction with a metal such as copper may be written

$$Cu^{++} + H_2Y^= \rightleftarrows CuY^= + 2\,H^+$$

Obviously as the pH goes down, the equilibrium is shifted away from the formation of the chelate $CuY^=$, and we may expect that there will be a pH value below which the titration of copper with EDTA will not be feasible. We wish to be able to estimate what this value is. Clearly a calculation will involve K_{abs} and the appropriate K_a values of EDTA. Actually, as shown below, it is possible to estimate very easily the minimal pH for a feasible metal ion titration from the K_{abs} value and a simple graph.

In the expressions given above for the four K_a values of EDTA, let us begin with K_{a_4} and work up to K_{a_1}, solving for the term in the denominator of each expression and substituting one into the next so as to obtain terms in which Y^{4-} is the only EDTA species:

$$[HY^{3-}] = \frac{[H_3O^+][Y^{4-}]}{K_{a_4}}$$

$$[H_2Y^=] = \frac{[H_3O^+][HY^{3-}]}{K_{a_3}} = \frac{[H_3O^+]^2[Y^{4-}]}{K_{a_3} \times K_{a_4}}$$

$$[H_3Y^-] = \frac{[H_3O^+][H_2Y^=]}{K_{a_2}} = \frac{[H_3O^+]^3[Y^{4-}]}{K_{a_2} \times K_{a_3} \times K_{a_4}}$$

$$[H_4Y] = \frac{[H_3O^+][H_3Y^-]}{K_{a_1}} = \frac{[H_3O^+]^4[Y^{4-}]}{K_{a_1} \times K_{a_2} \times K_{a_3} \times K_{a_4}}$$

We now define a term $[Y]'$, which is the *total* concentration of free (i.e., uncomplexed with metal) EDTA, regardless of its state of ionization, i.e.,

$$[Y]' = [Y^{4-}] + [HY^{3-}] + [H_2Y^=] + [H_3Y^-] + [H_4Y]$$

Substituting into this equation the four expressions derived above and factoring out $[Y^{4-}]$ on the right-hand side gives

$$[Y]' = [Y^{4-}]\left\{ 1 + \frac{[H_3O^+]}{K_{a_4}} + \frac{[H_3O^+]^2}{K_{a_4} \times K_{a_3}} + \frac{[H_3O^+]^3}{K_{a_4} \times K_{a_3} \times K_{a_2}} \right.$$
$$\left. + \frac{[H_3O^+]^4}{K_{a_4} \times K_{a_3} \times K_{a_2} \times K_{a_1}} \right\}$$

The portion of the right-hand side of the equation which is enclosed within the braces is seen to be a function of only $[H_3O^+]$ (or pH), since the K_a values are constants for a given chelon. This function is given the symbol α, so we may write

$$[Y]' = [Y^{4-}]\alpha$$

or

$$[Y^{4-}] = \frac{[Y]'}{\alpha}$$

α may obviously be calculated at any desired pH value for any chelon whose ionization constants are known. Short cuts may be taken in the calculation of α; for example, it is obvious that at very high pH values, the term containing $[H_3O^+]^4$ will be negligible. In any case, the work has already been done, and graphs showing α values as functions of pH for a number of chelons may be found in the literature.[6] Because the values extend over a wide range of magnitudes, $\log \alpha$ is usually plotted vs. pH. Such a graph for EDTA is shown in Figure 7.3.

Substitution of $[Y]'/\alpha$ for $[Y^{4-}]$ in the absolute stability constant expression given above yields

$$K_{abs} = \frac{[MY^{-(4-n)}]\alpha}{[M^{n+}][Y]'}$$

or

$$\frac{K_{abs}}{\alpha} = \frac{[MY^{-(4-n)}]}{[M^{n+}][Y]'} = K_{eff}$$

K_{eff} is called the *effective* or *conditional stability constant*. Unlike K_{abs}, K_{eff} varies with pH because of the pH-dependence of α. In certain regards, K_{eff} is more immediately useful than K_{abs}, because it shows the actual tendency to form

[6] For example, C. N. Reilley, R. W. Schmid, and F. S. Sadek, *J. Chem. Educ.*, **36**, 555 (1959).

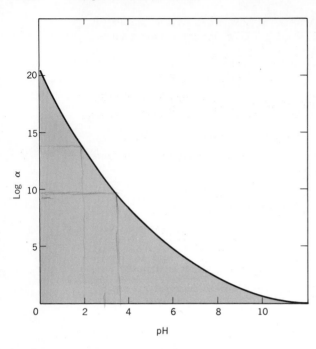

Fig. 7.3. Variation of log α with pH for EDTA.

the metal chelonate at the pH value in question. Although K_{eff} values are not customarily tabulated, it is apparent that they may be estimated readily from values of K_{abs}, which are found in tables of constants, and α values obtained from graphs such as Figure 7.3.

It may be noted that, as the pH goes down, α becomes larger, and hence K_{eff} becomes smaller. As a matter of fact, $1/\alpha$ represents the fraction of the uncomplexed EDTA which is present as the tetra-anion, Y^{4-}. Thus, at pH values above 12 or so, where EDTA is essentially ionized completely, α approaches unity (log α approaches zero), and K_{eff} approaches K_{abs}.

Normally the solutions of metal ions to be titrated with EDTA are buffered so that the pH will remain constant despite the release of H_3O^+ as the complexes are formed. Thus there is usually a definite basis for estimating K_{eff}, and with this value at hand, it is easy to calculate the titration curve, from which a judgment of feasibility may be made just as with acid-base titrations. The pH is often adjusted to as low a value as consistent with feasibility in order to gain selectivity in the titrations. At very low pH values, only metal ions which form very stable EDTA complexes are titrated. Furthermore, the hydrolysis of many metal ions leads to undesirable effects, sometimes even precipitation, if the pH is too high (see below).

PROBLEM. 50.0 ml of a solution which is 0.100-M Mg^{++} and buffered at pH 10.0 is titrated with a 0.100-M EDTA solution. Calculate values of pMg at various stages of the titration, and plot the titration curve.

K_{abs} for $MgY^=$ is 4.9×10^8. Referring to Figure 7.3, log α at pH 10.0 is about 0.5 (actually, 0.46). Then α is about 2.9. Thus for our circumstances, K_{eff} is about $4.9 \times 10^8/2.9 = 1.7 \times 10^8$.

(a) *Start of titration.*

$$[Mg^{++}] = 0.100\text{-}M$$

$$pMg = -\log [Mg^{++}] = 1.00$$

(b) *After addition of 10.0 ml of titrant.* There is a considerable excess of Mg^{++} at this point, and with a K value of the order of 10^8, we may assume that the reaction goes to completion. Thus

$$[Mg^{++}] = \frac{(5-1) \text{ mmols}}{60.0 \text{ ml}} = 0.067\text{-}M$$

$$pMg = 1.17$$

Similar calculations can be made at various intervals before the equivalence point. In the vicinity of the equivalence point, more accurate calculations could be made by not assuming complete reaction, i.e., by taking into account magnesium ions produced by dissociation of $MgY^=$, and solving the usual quadratic equation. The data in Table 7.1 were calculated by the approximate method.

TITRATION OF 50.00 ml OF 0.1000-M Mg^{++} **Table**
WITH 0.1000-M EDTA   **7.1**

ml EDTA	$[Mg^{++}]$	pMg	%Mg^{++} reacted
0.00	0.1000-M	1.00	0.00
10.00	0.067	1.17	20.00
20.00	0.043	1.37	40.00
30.00	0.025	1.60	60.00
40.00	0.011	1.96	80.00
49.00	0.001	3.00	98.00
49.90	1.00×10^{-4}	4.00	99.80
49.95	5.00×10^{-5}	4.30	99.90
50.00	1.71×10^{-5}	4.77	100.00
50.05	5.88×10^{-6}	5.23	100.00
50.10	2.94×10^{-6}	5.53	100.00
60.00	2.95×10^{-8}	7.53	100.00

(c) *Equivalence point.*

$$[Mg^{++}] = [Y]'$$

$$[MgY^=] \cong \frac{5.00 \text{ mmol}}{100 \text{ ml}} = 5 \times 10^{-2}\text{-}M$$

$$K_{eff} = \frac{5 \times 10^{-2}}{[Mg^{++}]^2} = 1.7 \times 10^8$$

$$[Mg^{++}] = 1.71 \times 10^{-5}\text{-}M$$

$$pMg = 4.77$$

(d) *After addition of 60.0 ml of titrant.*

$$\text{excess } [Y]' = \frac{1.00 \text{ mmol}}{110 \text{ ml}} = 9.09 \times 10^{-3}\text{-}M$$

$$[MgY^=] = \frac{5.00 \text{ mmol}}{110 \text{ ml}} = 4.55 \times 10^{-2}\text{-}M$$

$$\frac{4.55 \times 10^{-2}}{[Mg^{++}]\, 9.09 \times 10^{-3}} = 1.7 \times 10^8$$

$$[Mg^{++}] = 2.95 \times 10^{-8}\text{-}M$$

$$p\text{Mg} = 7.53$$

The data for this titration are given in Table 7.1, and the titration curve is plotted in Figure 7.4. The titration curve is of familiar shape, with a sharp

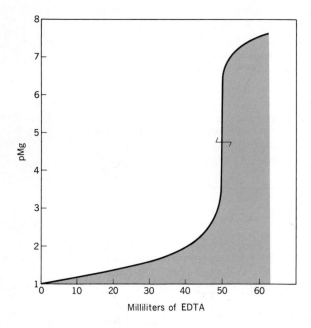

Fig. 7.4. Titration curve: 50 ml of 0.1-M Mg^{++} titrated with 0.1-M EDTA at pH 10.

break in the value of pMg in the vicinity of the equivalence point. Of course a method of detecting this break is required; this will be discussed later in the chapter.

Actually, based upon the experience of others, an estimate of feasibility can be made without calculating the titration curve. Reilley[6] has pointed out that the smallest value of K_{eff} that will permit a feasible titration can be represented by

$$\log K_{eff} = T - \log C$$

C is the initial concentration of the metal ion to be titrated, and T is a "titration factor" whose value depends upon the method used to locate the end point and upon the desired precision. Very roughly, T should be at least 5 for visual titrations, 4 for potentiometric titrations (Chapter 8), and

2 for titrations such as amperometric (Chapter 11) and photometric (Chapter 12) where the end point is located by a process of linear extrapolation. There is obviously a subjective factor in deciding just how small a T value one will settle for.

Substituting K_{abs}/α for K_{eff} in the above equation, we obtain

$$\log \frac{K_{abs}}{\alpha} = T - \log C$$

or

$$\log \alpha = \log K_{abs} - T + \log C$$

PROBLEM. It is desired to titrate a 0.01-M cupric solution with EDTA, employing a visual indicator. What is the lowest pH at which the titration could be performed?

Log K_{abs} for $CuY^=$ is 18.8. For a visual end point, we take $T = 5$. Log C is -2. Thus

$$\log \alpha = 18.8 - 5 - 2 = 11.8$$

Referring to the graph of $\log \alpha$ vs. pH (Figure 7.3), we find that the pH corresponding to $\log \alpha = 11.8$ is about 2.5.

On the other hand, if we were titrating a calcium solution rather than cupric, then $\log K_{abs} = 10.7$, and the minimal pH value would be about 6.7.

pH values obtained in this manner are only approximate, but they give at least a lower limit, much below which one would probably not find it profitable to attempt a titration.

The complex effect. Substances other than the chelon titrant which may be present in the metal ion solution may form complexes with the metal and thus compete against the desired titration reaction. Actually, such complexing is sometimes used deliberately to overcome interferences, in which case the effect of the complexer is called *masking*. For example, nickel forms a very stable complex ion with cyanide, $Ni(CN)_4^=$, whereas lead does not. Thus, in the presence of cyanide, lead can be titrated with EDTA without interference from nickel, despite the fact that the stability constants for $NiY^=$ and $PbY^=$ are nearly the same (log K_{abs} values are 18.6 and 18.3, respectively).

With certain metal ions that hydrolyze readily, it may be necessary to add complexing ligands in order to prevent precipitation of the metal hydroxide. As mentioned above, the solutions are frequently buffered, and buffer anions or neutral molecules such as acetate or ammonia may form complex ions with the metal. Just as the interaction of hydrogen ions with Y^{4-} lowers K_{eff}, so is it lowered by ligands which complex the metal ion. If the stability constants for all of the complexes involved were known, then the effect of the complexers upon the EDTA titration reaction could be calculated. We might, for example, introduce a correction term β to the stability constant, along with α, such that

$$K_{eff} = \frac{K_{abs}}{\alpha \times \beta}$$

Graphs showing values of β as a function of ammonia concentration for several metal ions are given by Schwarzenbach.[7]

Often the data needed to evaluate β are not available, and complexing effects may be estimated only in an empirical way. It may be noted that the addition of too much buffer is a common fault in EDTA titrations, the resulting complexing action often worsening the end point unnecessarily.

Hydrolysis effect. Hydrolysis of metal ions may compete with the chelometric titration process. Raising the pH makes this effect worse by shifting toward the right equilibria of the type

$$M^{++} + H_2O \rightleftarrows M(OH)^+ + H^+$$

Extensive hydrolysis may lead to the precipitation of hydroxides which react only slowly with EDTA even when equilibrium considerations favor the formation of the metal chelonate. Frequently, the appropriate hydrolysis constants for metal ions are not at hand, and hence these effects often cannot be calculated accurately, but of course there is much empirical information which serves experienced persons in deciding how high the pH may be for EDTA titrations of various metal ions. Solubility product constants may sometimes be used to predict where precipitation may occur, although often these constants are quite inaccurate in the case of metal hydroxides.

Sometimes precipitation is actually utilized as a sort of masking in order to circumvent a particular interference. For example, at pH 10, both calcium and magnesium are titrated together with EDTA, only the sum of the two being obtainable. But, if strong base is added to raise the pH above 12 or so, $Mg(OH)_2$ precipitates and calcium alone can be titrated.

Chelons other than EDTA. Many other chelons have been synthesized. A few of these offer advantages over EDTA in particular situations, although none is so frequently used. The all-nitrogen chelons such as triethylenetetramine, mentioned in the introduction of this chapter, are more selective than EDTA. For example, copper can be titrated with trien in the presence of nickel, zinc, and cadmium, whereas with EDTA these metals interfere.

Ethylene glycol-bis-(β-aminoethyl ether)-N,N'-tetraacetic acid (EGTA) (below) forms a much more stable chelonate with calcium than

$$\text{HOOCCH}_2 \diagdown \qquad\qquad \diagup \text{CH}_2\text{COOH}$$
$$\text{NCH}_2\text{CH}_2\text{—O—CH}_2\text{CH}_2\text{—O—CH}_2\text{CH}_2\text{N}$$
$$\text{HOOCCH}_2 \diagup \qquad\qquad \diagdown \text{CH}_2\text{COOH}$$

Ethylene glycol-bis-(β-aminoethyl ether)-N,N'-tetraacetic acid (EGTA)

with magnesium (log K_{abs} = 11.0 vs. 5.4), whereas with EDTA, as noted above, the stabilities are much more nearly the same (log K_{abs} = 10.7 vs. 8.7). Thus calcium can be titrated selectively with EGTA in the presence

[7] G. Schwarzenbach, *Complexometric Titrations*, translated by H. Irving, Interscience Publishers, Inc., New York, 1957. (A later version of the book, *Die komplexometrische Titration*, by G. Schwarzenbach and H. Flaschka, has appeared (1965), but has not yet been translated into English.)

of magnesium, whereas only the sum of the two can be obtained with EDTA unless the magnesium is precipitated as noted above.

Indicators for chelometric titrations. When EDTA was first introduced as a titrant, there was a dearth of good visual indicators, and various instrumental end point techniques were frequently employed. The latter are still valuable in certain situations, but a wide variety of good visual indicators is now available, and usually the visual titrations are the most convenient. We have seen above, using magnesium as an example, that there is a large and abrupt break in pM in the vicinity of the equivalence point in a feasible chelometric titration. We wish to convert this into a color change, just as acid-base indicators respond to pH changes by changing color. A variety of chemical substances, often called *metallochromic indicators*, is now available for this purpose. Whereas all pH indicators need respond only to hydrogen ion, for chelometric titrations we need a series of substances responsive to pMg, pCa, pCu, etc., although often one indicator may be useful with more than one metal ion.

Basically, the metallochromic indicators are colored organic compounds which themselves form chelates with metal ions; the chelate must have a different color from the free indicator, of course, and if large indicator blanks are to be avoided and sharp end points obtained, the indicator must release the metal ion to the EDTA titrant at a pM value very close to that of the equivalence point. This may be considered as analogous to the action of an indicator acid in releasing hydrogen ion to hydroxide ion in the titration of an acid. A complete treatment of the equilibria involved is somewhat more complicated than the analogous discussion of acid-base indicators, however, because of the circumstance that the common metallochromic indicators also have acid-base properties and respond as pH indicators as well as indicators for pM. Thus, in order to specify the color that a metallochromic indicator will assume in a certain solution, we generally must know both the pH value and the pM value for the particular metal ion which is present. A thorough discussion of the equilibria involved in the action of metallochromic indicators has been given by Reilley and Schmid.[8] We shall present here a somewhat simplified discussion of one indicator, Eriochrome Black T, and then simply note some of the others which are available.

The structure of Eriochrome Black T is shown below:

[8] C. N. Reilley and R. W. Schmid, *Anal. Chem.*, **31**, 887 (1959).

Metal chelates are formed with this molecule by loss of hydrogen ions from the phenolic —OH groups and the formation of bonds between the metal ions and the oxygen atoms as well as the azo group. The molecule is usually represented in abbreviated form as a tribasic acid, H_3In. The sulfonic acid group is shown in the figure above as ionized; this is a strong acid group which is dissociated in aqueous solution regardless of pH, and thus the structure shown is that of the ion H_2In^-. This form of the indicator is red. The pK_a value for the dissociation of H_2In^- to form $HIn^=$ is 6.3. The latter species is blue. The pK_a value for the ionization of $HIn^=$ to form In^{3-} is 11.6; the latter ion is a yellowish-orange color. The magnesium-indicator complex, $MgIn^-$, is wine-red.

Because both pH and pMg determine the color of Eriochrome Black T, it is instructive to examine a graph plotted in terms of these two variables as shown in Figure 7.5. The vertical line separating region (II) from region

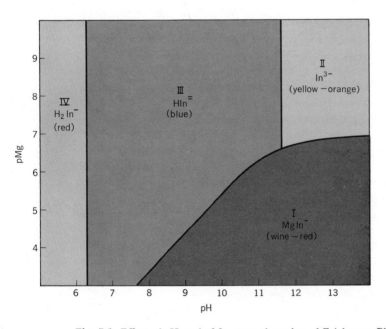

Fig. 7.5. Effect of pH and pMg upon the color of Erichrome Black T.

(III) is drawn at the pK_a value of the species HIn^-; in other words, at points along this line there will be equal concentrations of the two species $HIn^=$ and In^{3-}, with the former predominating to the left of the line and the latter predominating in the region to the right. Similarly, regions (III) and (IV) are separated by a vertical line drawn at the pK_a value of the species H_2In^-. The curved line separating regions (II) and (III) from region (I) represents values of pH and pMg where the indicator is half in the form $MgIn^-$. In other words as this line is crossed from region (I) into region (II), there will be a color change from wine-red to yellowish-orange; crossing from region (I) into region (III) gives a color change from wine-red to blue. Visually, the change from red to blue is much more easily seen than that from red to orange, and hence this indicator is more attractive to the analyst if the titration can be performed at a pH value below 11 or so.

We may now see why Eriochrome Black T is a useful visual indicator for the titration of magnesium with EDTA. We calculated previously that a good break was obtained at a pH value of 10, and the pMg at the equivalence point was about 4.8. Referring to Figure 7.5, we see that, at pH 10, the indicator will change from red to blue over a pMg interval not too far from 4.8.

In Table 7.2 are shown some other indicators which are used in chelometric titrations, along with some of the metal ions for which they are useful.

SOME COMMON INDICATORS FOR   **Table**
CHELOMETRIC TITRATIONS   **7.2**

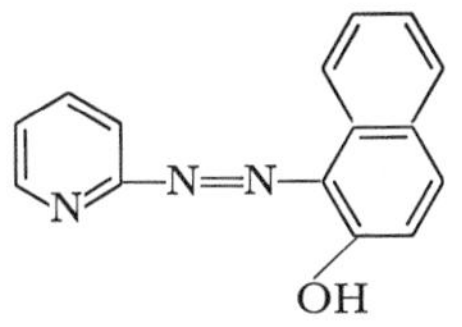

1-(2-pyridylazo)-2-naphthol (PAN)
Cu, Zn, Cd, Sc, In

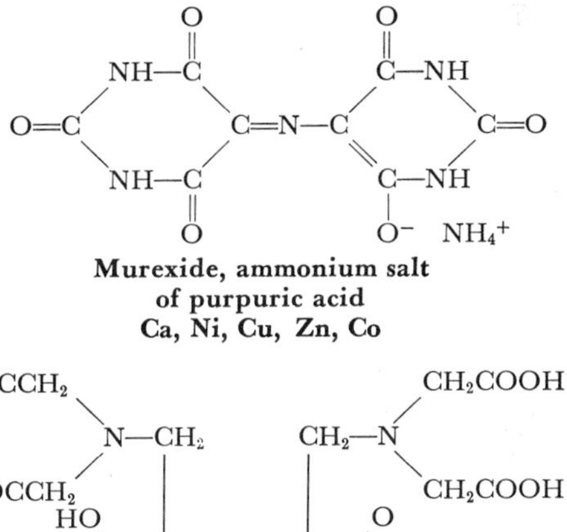

Murexide, ammonium salt
of purpuric acid
Ca, Ni, Cu, Zn, Co

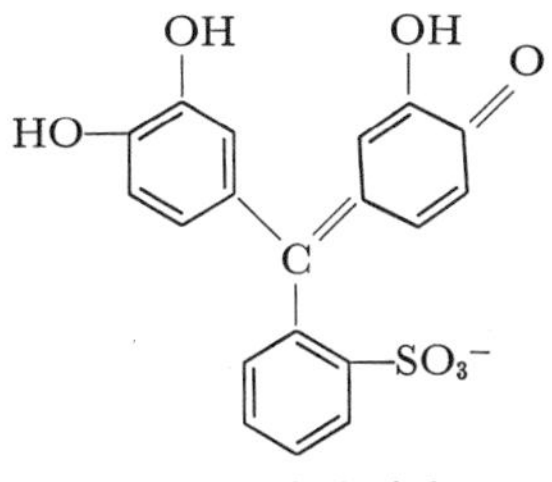

Pyrocatechol violet
Bi, Cu, Zn, Al

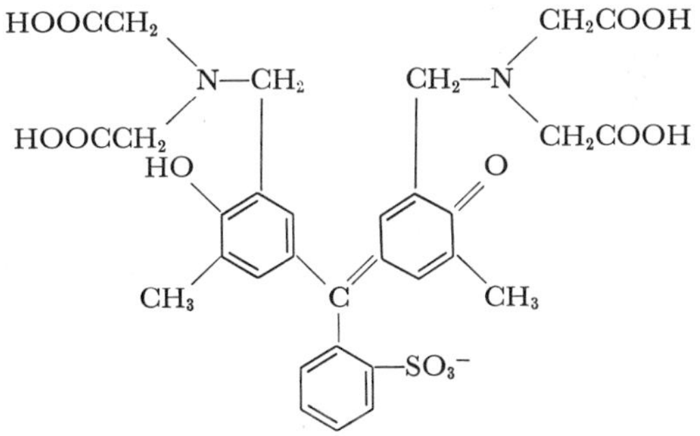

Xylenol orange
Bi, Th, Sc, Pb, Zn, La, Cd, Hg

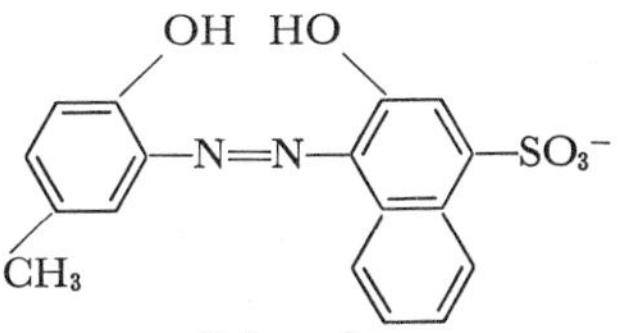

Calmagite
Ca, Mg

Applications of chelometric titrations

There is much detailed information about chelometric titrations that cannot be given in a chapter of this length but which should be looked into before undertaking a particular application. For example, certain indicators may be "blocked" by traces of heavy metals too small to interfere otherwise. Some metal ion-EDTA reactions as well as metal-indicator reactions are slow at room temperature. There is a wealth of information about masking interference for particular sorts of samples. The choice of indicator may not be obvious. Some indicator-metal complexes are quite insoluble. At least, however, a person who has studied this chapter should be able to read the available literature.

The EDTA titration has virtually replaced the former tedious gravimetric analyses for many metals in a variety of samples. One of the most important applications in terms of the number of analyses performed is the EDTA water hardness titration, which has replaced the crude titration of hardness with soap. The total hardness, roughly calcium plus magnesium for most waters, is determined by a single titration with EDTA using Eriochrome Black T or Calmagite, usually at pH 10 in an ammonia buffer. The EDTA is generally standardized against calcium carbonate as a primary standard.

Potentiometric EDTA titrations with a mercury indicator electrode are explained in Chapter 8, and photometric titrations of metal ions with EDTA are discussed briefly in Chapter 12.

METAL ION BUFFERS

We saw in Chapter 4 that certain systems containing Brønsted conjugate acid-base pairs resisted pH changes upon the addition of strong acids or bases. Such systems are said to be buffered. An analogous buffering action with respect to changes in pM is established in solutions containing a metal complex and excess complexing agent.

Consider the equilibrium involving a metal ion M, a ligand L, and a complex ML, where the charges are omitted for convenience:

$$M + L \rightleftharpoons ML$$

$$K_{eff} = \frac{[ML]}{[M][L]}$$

Solving for [M] and then taking logs, we obtain

$$[M] = \frac{1}{K_{eff}} \times \frac{[ML]}{[L]}$$

$$\log [M] = \log \frac{1}{K_{eff}} + \log \frac{[ML]}{[L]}$$

$$pM = \log K_{eff} - \log \frac{[ML]}{[L]}$$

Compare this with the Henderson-Hasselbalch equation (Chapter 4, page 87).

It is seen that the pM of such a solution is fixed by the value of K_{eff} and the molar ratio of metal complex to free ligand. Introduction of additional metal ion to the solution will lead to formation of more ML; in other words, the solution resists the lowering of pM that would otherwise occur if L were absent. Similarly, removal of metal ion will be resisted by the dissociation of ML, and metal ion can be drained by some other reaction without a large rise in pM so long as the capacity of ML to furnish metal ion is not exhausted.

Metal ion buffers have found application in biology and biochemistry in studies of enzyme systems whose catalytic activity exhibits a metal ion dependence. Just as pK_a must be considered in the analogous case of pH buffers, a metal ion buffer will be most efficient if $\log K_{eff}$ is nearly the same as the desired pM value.

REFERENCES

1. H. A. Laitinen, *Chemical Analysis*, McGraw-Hill Book Co., Inc., New York, 1960.
2. H. F. Walton, *Principles and Methods of Chemical Analysis*, 2nd Ed., Prentice-Hall, Inc., Englewood Cliffs, N.J., 1964.
3. J. N. Butler, *Ionic Equilibrium, A Mathematical Approach*, Addison-Wesley Publishing Co., Inc., Reading, Mass., 1964.
4. A. Ringbom, "Complexation Reactions," Chapter 14, Part I, Vol. I, of *Treatise on Analytical Chemistry*, I. M. Kolthoff, P. J. Elving, and E. B. Sandell, Eds., Interscience Publishers, Inc., New York, 1959.
5. J. Bjerrum, *Metal Ammine Formation in Aqueous Solutions*, P. Haase and Son, Copenhagen, 1941.

QUESTIONS

1. Explain the meaning of the following terms: complex, chelon, quadridentate chelating agent, trien, EDTA, metallochromic indicator, ligand.

2. Why is the titration of Cu^{++} with NH_3 not feasible? Why is the titration of I^- with Hg^{++} not satisfactory?

3. Explain why the concept of an effective stability constant is useful in chelometric titrations.

4. In selecting an indicator for a chelometric titration, the pH of the solution is an important factor. Explain.

5. Why cannot sodium nitroprusside be used as the indicator for the titration of SCN^- with Hg^{++}?

6. What effect does the concentration of the substance titrated have on a titration curve such as that shown in Figure 7.4? What is the effect of the titrant concentrations?

PROBLEMS

1. A sample of pure $CaCO_3$ weighing 0.4034 g was dissolved in 1:1 HCl, and the solution was diluted to 500 ml in a volumetric flask. A 50.0-ml aliquot required 39.70 ml of an EDTA solution for titration. Calculate the formality of the EDTA solution and the number of grams of $Na_2H_2Y \cdot 2 H_2O$ required to prepare a liter of the solution.

2. A 100-ml sample of water was titrated with the EDTA solution of the previous problem, and 35.60 ml were required. Calculate the degree of hardness of the water in parts per million of $CaCO_3$. Recall that 1 part per million is 1 mg per liter.

3. A sample weighing 0.7500 g and containing NaCN was dissolved in water and then concentrated ammonia and some KI solution were added. A volume of 30.32 ml of $0.0987\text{-}M$ $AgNO_3$ was required for titration. Calculate the percentage of CN^- in the sample.

4. A sample weighing 0.4600 g and containing only NaCN and KCN required 40.00 ml of $0.1000\text{-}M$ $AgNO_3$ for titration. Calculate the percentage of NaCN in the sample.

5. 50.0 ml of a solution which is $0.100\text{-}M$ in Ca^{++} and buffered at pH 10.0 is titrated with $0.100\text{-}M$ EDTA solution. Calculate the values of pCa when the following volumes of titrant are added: (a) 0.00 ml (b) 20.0 ml (c) 49.9 ml (d) 50.0 ml (e) 50.1 ml (f) 60.0 ml.

6. Repeat problem 5 for the titration at pH 8. Compare the feasibility of the titration at pH 10 and 8.

7. Calculate the following:
   (a) pMg of a $0.05\text{-}M$ $Mg(NO_3)_2$ solution
   (b) pCu of a $0.004\text{-}M$ $CuCl_2$ solution
   (c) pCa of a $1.0\text{-}M$ $CaCl_2$ solution
   (d) pZn of a $0.00025\text{-}M$ $ZnSO_4$ solution

8. Calculate the value of pM at the equivalence point for the titration of 2.00 mmol of each of the following metals with EDTA at pH 5.0. The final volume in each case is 100 ml.
   (a) Ni^{++} (b) Mn^{++} (c) Sr^{++}

9. It is desired to titrate a $0.020\text{-}M$ solution of Cd^{++} with EDTA employing a visual indicator. What is the lowest pH at which the titration could be performed? Take $T = 5$ for the visual end point.

10. Calculate the end point error in the Liebig titration with iodide ion indicator. Assume the following conditions: 50 ml of 0.2-M KCN titrated with 0.1-M AgNO$_3$; [NH$_3$] = 0.5 and [I$^-$] = 0.02-M at the end point. Assume that the end point occurs at the moment AgI starts to precipitate. In practice, of course, a small amount of AgI must be formed for the precipitate to be seen. How does this affect your calculation?

chapter 8

Potentiometric Titrations

The potential of a galvanic cell such as is described in Chapter 5 depends upon the concentration (activity) of some ion (or ions) in the cell solution, and this relationship between potential and concentration is expressed by the Nernst equation (page 133). The use of potential measurements to determine the concentrations of certain ions in solution is an obvious application. In some cases, conditions may be arranged so that the potential of the galvanic cell depends entirely upon the concentration of a single ionic species. One electrode is a reference, such as calomel, whose potential is known and remains constant, while the potential of the other electrode, sometimes called the *indicator electrode*, depends upon the concentration of the ion of interest. The potential of the entire cell is then a measure of the concentration of the latter ion.

There are two methods of performing the experimental measurement. First, a single measurement of the potential of the cell is made; this is sufficient to determine the concentration of the ion of interest. Second, the ion of interest may be titrated and the potential measured as a function of the volume of titrant. The first method is sometimes called *direct potentiometry* and is used principally in the determination of the pH of a solution. To give the degree of accuracy usually demanded by an analyst, such a measurement must be highly precise. The method also frequently lacks selectivity, the potential being affected by other ions in solution. More widely used by analytical chemists is the second method, termed *potentiometric titration*. Such titrations do not require as precise measurement of potential as does direct potentiometry. They are also less subject to influence by other substances in solution and usually do not require such careful control of experimental conditions.

In a potentiometric titration the end point is detected by determining the volume at which a relatively large change in potential occurs as the titrant is added. Figure 8.1 shows a schematic experimental setup for such a titration, using the glass electrode as an example of an indicator electrode. The method can be employed for all the common reactions used for volumetric purposes: acid-base, redox, precipitation, and complex formation. We have already discussed in some detail the equilibrium aspects of such reactions (Chapters 4, 5, 6, 7) in ordinary titrations. Our discussion in this chapter will be devoted primarily to the problem of selecting indicator electrodes, and to the techniques used to determine the end point. Since the measurement of pH is of such importance, we will discuss in some detail its determination by direct potentiometry.

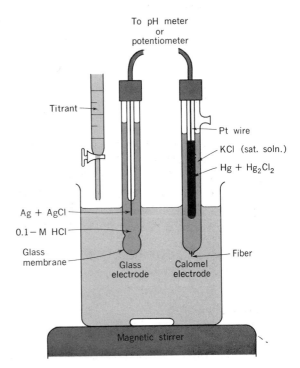

Fig. 8.1. Apparatus for potentiometric titration.

To pH meter or potentiometer

Titrant

Pt wire

KCl (sat. soln.)

Hg + Hg_2Cl_2

Ag + AgCl

0.1−M HCl

Glass membrane

Glass electrode

Calomel electrode

Fiber

Magnetic stirrer

ACID-BASE TITRATIONS

The hydrogen electrode

Of the several electrodes suitable for determining hydrogen ion concentration, the hydrogen electrode (page 136) is perhaps the most obvious. Let us assume that the glass electrode of the apparatus in Figure 8.1 is replaced by a hydrogen electrode, and that the reference electrode is the standard calomel. Consider the following problem.

PROBLEM. Derive an equation relating the pH of a solution to the potential of the following cell:

$$Hg \mid Hg_2Cl_2, KCl(1\text{-}M) \parallel H^+(x\text{-}M) \mid H_2(1 \text{ atm}), Pt$$

The electrode reactions are

$$
\begin{array}{lll}
Hg_2Cl_2 + 2 \text{ e} \rightleftarrows 2\,Hg + 2\,Cl^- & E_1^\circ & = +0.28 \\
2\,H^+ + 2\,e \rightleftarrows H_2 & E_2^\circ & = 0.00 \\
\hline
\text{Thus} \quad Hg_2Cl_2 + H_2 \rightleftarrows 2\,Hg + 2\,Cl^- + 2\,H^+ & E_{1-2}^\circ & = +0.28
\end{array}
$$

The potential of the cell is given by the equation

$$E_{1-2} = 0.28 - \frac{0.059}{2} \log \frac{a_{Hg}^2 \times a_{Cl^-}^2 \times a_{H^+}^2}{a_{Hg_2Cl_2} \times a_{H_2}}$$

But $a_{Hg} = 1$, $a_{Cl^-} = 1$, $a_{H_2} = 1$, and $a_{H^+} \cong [H^+]$. Thus

$$E_{1-2} = 0.28 - \frac{0.059}{2} \log [H^+]^2$$

Since $-\log [H^+] = pH$,

$$E_{1-2} = 0.28 + 0.059 \, pH$$

or

$$pH = \frac{E_{1-2} - 0.28}{0.059}$$

Thus the pH of a solution can be determined by measuring the potential of the foregoing cell. If the two electrodes are inserted in an acid solution and the acid titrated with base, the pH can be measured at different intervals during the titration, and the end point thereby detected.

The hydrogen electrode is not commonly employed for routine measurement of pH. A number of features, such as poisoning of the catalytic surface, and the possibility of hydrogen's reacting with substances in the solution that are easily hydrogenated have led to the use of experimentally simpler electrode systems.

The glass electrode

The most widely used indicator electrode for hydrogen ions is the glass electrode. This electrode consists of a glass bulb containing an internal reference electrode, usually silver-silver chloride. The bulb is immersed in the solution whose pH is being measured and the electrode is connected to a reference, such as calomel, via a salt bridge. A schematic diagram of the electrode is shown in Figure 8.1. The small hole in the bottom of the calomel electrode acts as the salt bridge by allowing KCl to flow through.

The cell can be represented as follows:

$$\underbrace{\text{Ag} \mid \text{AgCl, HCl } (0.1\text{-}M) \mid \text{Glass}}_{\textbf{Glass Electrode}} \mid \underbrace{\text{H}^+ \ (x\text{-}M)}_{\substack{\textbf{Test} \\ \textbf{Solution}}} \mid\mid \underbrace{\text{KCl (sat.), Hg}_2\text{Cl}_2 \mid \text{Hg}}_{\substack{\textbf{Reference} \\ \textbf{Electrode}}}$$

It is found experimentally that the potential of this cell obeys the relation

$$E = k + 0.0591 \ pH$$

at 25°C and over a pH range of 0 to 10–12, depending upon the composition of the glass and of the test solution.

A number of proposals have been made to explain the mechanism by which the glass electrode functions. The most plausible of these is that the glass acts as a semi-permeable membrane, permeable only to cations, principally hydrogen ions. Glass is known to consist of a negatively charged silicate network containing small cations, usually sodium ions. Other cations, such as hydrogen, can enter the glass by displacing sodium ions, but negative ions are repelled by the negatively charged silicate network.

In the glass electrode a potential is developed as is pictured in Figure 8.2,

Fig. 8.2. Potential at glass membrane.

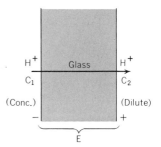

by the tendency of hydrogen ions to diffuse through the membrane from the more concentrated to the more dilute solution. In this process a positive charge builds up on one side of the membrane, a negative charge on the other, and a difference in potential results. The diffusion does not occur to a great extent, of course. It is possible to pass a current through a glass electrode and it has been found experimentally that the amount of hydrogen ions transferred through the glass is close to that predicted by Faraday's Law. It has also been found that the glass must contain water for such a transfer to occur; when the electrode is dried thoroughly by soaking it in concentrated H_2SO_4, the electrode is no longer sensitive to pH. The sensitivity can be restored by soaking the electrode in water for several hours.

The potential developed at the glass membrane is dependent upon the logarithm of the ratio of the hydrogen ion concentrations in the two solutions which are separated by the glass. This can be seen by considering the following cell (A):

$$\text{Reference} \mid H^+ (C_1) \mid \text{Glass} \mid H^+ (C_2) \mid \text{Reference} \qquad (A)$$

Let us consider also cell (B) in which the glass membrane is replaced by a "model"—two hydrogen electrodes connected in series.

$$\text{Reference} \mid H^+ (C_1) \mid H_2, \text{Pt} - \text{Pt}, H_2 \mid H^+ (C_2) \mid \text{Reference} \qquad (B)$$

In both cells the potential is a function of the driving force of hydrogen ion transfer from solution 1 to solution 2, but by different mechanisms. In cell (A), the transfer takes place by diffusion through the glass; in cell (B), hydrogen ion at C_1 is reduced to H_2 at the electrode in solution 1, and then H_2 is oxidized to hydrogen ion at C_2 at the electrode in solution 2.

Since the reference electrodes are the same, we may disregard them and consider in cell (B) the reactions

$$
\begin{array}{ll}
H^+ (C_1) + e \rightleftharpoons \tfrac{1}{2}H_2 & E_1^\circ = 0.00 \\
H^+ (C_2) + e \rightleftharpoons \tfrac{1}{2}H_2 & E_2^\circ = 0.00 \\
\hline
H^+ (C_1) \rightleftharpoons H^+ (C_2) & E_{1-2}^\circ = 0.00
\end{array}
$$

The potential is given by

$$E = 0.00 - 0.059 \log \frac{C_2}{C_1}$$

The cell represented by Figure 8.1 is the same as cell (A) except that the reference electrodes are not identical. Hence the potential of the cell will be given by

$$E = \Delta E_{\text{ref}} - 0.059 \log \frac{C_2}{C_1}$$

where ΔE_{ref} is the difference in potential of the two reference electrodes. Since the value of C_1 is fixed in the glass electrode (e.g., 0.1-M HCl) the term $0.059 \log C_1$ can be combined with ΔE_{ref} to give a single constant term, k. Hence the expression becomes

$$E = k - 0.059 \log C_2$$

or

$$E = k + 0.059 \, p\text{H}$$

Compared with other indicator electrodes for hydrogen ions, the glass electrode has several advantages. First, no foreign substance need be added to the solution whose pH is being measured. Second, substances that are easily oxidized or reduced can be present in the solution being measured without interfering. Such substances might react with hydrogen, for example, in the hydrogen electrode. Third, the electrode can be made quite small, so that very small volumes of solutions can be measured. Fourth, there is no catalytic surface susceptible to poisoning as in the hydrogen electrode.

Finally, sparingly buffered solutions can be measured accurately, and the electrode is well suited for continuous measurements.

The glass membrane is somewhat fragile, but this is not a serious disadvantage. One effect that can lead to a serious error, however, is the diffusion of ions other than hydrogen through the membrane in solutions of high pH. In a strongly basic solution, where the concentration of hydrogen ions is very low, the diffusion of other cations, such as sodium, becomes appreciable. If the membrane is made of soda-lime glass, this effect is sufficient to invalidate completely measurements in solutions of pH greater than about 10.0. It is possible to correct a pH reading for this effect. Manufacturers of glass electrodes furnish a chart of "sodium ion corrections" for use in solutions of pH greater than 10. In recent years other types of glass have been developed that do not show an appreciable error in solutions up to a pH of about 12.5.[1] These glasses contain a high percentage of lithium oxide in place of sodium oxide and are often referred to as "lithium glasses."

An error also occurs with the glass electrode in very acidic solutions (pH $<$ 0). This is thought to be caused by a change in activity of water in the glass membrane brought about by the transfer of H_3O^+ ions through the membrane.

The high resistance of the glass membrane makes it necessary to employ a "pH meter" in order to measure the potential. Many commercial models of pH meters are on the market today. These meters are used principally in connection with a glass electrode, but can be used, of course, with other electrodes. Such meters have a scale that reads directly in pH units. This scale is first "calibrated" by immersing the electrodes in a buffer solution of known pH and adjusting the scale to read this value. The same scale can be used for direct reading in millivolt units.

Two different glass electrodes are not likely to give exactly the same potential reading when immersed in the same solution. In fact a small potential may be developed at a glass membrane even if the same solution is on both sides of the membrane. It is thought that this effect results from "strains" in the glass, and it is often referred to as an "asymmetry potential." Because of this effect, it is necessary to calibrate the scale using a buffer, as described above, and it is necessary to repeat this calibration if one glass electrode is replaced by another.

The work of Eisenman and collaborators[2] on the relation between the ion exchange properties of a glass surface and the composition of the glass has led to the development of glass electrodes which can serve as indicator electrodes for cations other than hydrogen. Electrodes are now available for use in measuring the concentration of sodium and potassium ions and are finding use in the determination of these ions in biological systems.

---

[1] G. A. Perley, *Anal. Chem.*, **21**, 391, 394, 559 (1949).

[2] G. Eisenman, "The Electrochemistry of Cation-Sensitive Glass Electrodes," a chapter in *Advances in Analytical Chemistry and Instrumentation*, C. N. Reilley, Ed., Vol. 4, p. 213 (1965).

POTENTIOMETRIC DETERMINATION OF *p*H

As previously mentioned, one of the principal applications of direct potentiometry is the determination of the *p*H of aqueous solutions. We wish now to examine briefly the meaning of the term *p*H as it is measured experimentally by direct potentiometry. A complete discussion of this topic has been given by Bates.[3]

The term *p*H was defined by Sorensen in 1909 as the negative logarithm of the hydrogen ion *concentration*. It was later realized that the emf of galvanic cells used to measure *p*H was dependent upon the *activity* of hydrogen ions rather than the *concentration*. Hence the definition of *p*H was taken to be

$$pH = -\log a_{H^+}$$

This definition is satisfactory from a theoretical standpoint, but the quantity cannot be measured experimentally. There is no way to measure unambiguously the activity of a single ion species. (In thermodynamic terms it is said that *p*H is proportional to the work required to transfer hydrogen ions reversibly from the solution examined to one in which the activity of hydrogen ions is unity. No experiment can be performed in which hydrogen ions are transferred without at the same time transferring negative ions.)

The quantity measured potentiometrically is actually neither concentration nor activity of hydrogen ion. It is therefore preferable to define *p*H in terms of the emf of the cell employed for the measurement. For example, suppose that such a cell consisted of a suitable reference electrode connected by a salt bridge to the solution being treated, in which a hydrogen electrode was immersed:

$$\text{Reference} \parallel H^+ (x\text{-}M) \mid H_2, Pt$$

On page 202 we derived the equation relating the potential of such a cell to *p*H, where the reference was the standard calomel electrode:

$$E = 0.28 + 0.059 \, pH$$

Strictly speaking, this equation should also contain a term E_j, the liquid junction potential, which may be small with an appropriate salt bridge, but not zero. Hence the equation should read

$$E = E_{\text{ref}} + 0.059 \, pH + E_j$$

where E_{ref} is the potential of the reference electrode. Calling $E_{\text{ref}} + E_j$ a constant, k, this becomes

[3] R. G. Bates, *Determination of pH; Theory and Practice*, John Wiley & Sons, New York, 1964.

$$E = k + 0.059 \, p\text{H}$$

or

$$p\text{H} = \frac{E - k}{0.059}$$

The above equation contains two unknowns, pH and k, and hence cannot be used to evaluate both quantities. It is necessary to assign arbitrarily a pH value to some standard buffer in order to fix a practical scale of pH.

The Bureau of Standards determines the pH of certain buffers by careful measurements of selected cells, using reasonable assumptions regarding activity coefficients.[4] Table 8.1 contains a few examples of the buffers

pH VALUES OF NBS STANDARD BUFFERS † **Table 8.1**

Composition	pH		
	25°C	30°C	40°C
KH$_3$(C$_2$O$_4$)$_2$·2H$_2$O(0.05-M)‡	1.68	1.69	1.70
KHC$_4$O$_6$ (sat. at 25°C)	3.56	3.55	3.54
KHC$_8$H$_4$O$_4$(0.05-M)	4.01	4.01	4.03
KH$_2$PO$_4$(0.025-M) + Na$_2$HPO$_4$(0.025-M)	6.86	6.85	6.84
Na$_2$B$_4$O$_7$·10H$_2$O(0.01-M)	9.18	9.14	9.07
Ca(OH)$_2$ (sat. at 25°C)‡	12.45	12.30	11.99

† R. G. Bates in *Treatise on Analytical Chemistry*, Part I, Vol. I, I. M. Kolthoff and P. J. Elving, Editors, The Interscience Encyclopedia, Inc., New York, 1959, p. 375.
‡ Secondary standards; the other four are primary standards.

recommended by the Bureau. It would be possible, of course, to define a pH scale, according to the equation

$$E = k + 0.059 \, p\text{H}$$

using a single buffer. However, the term k is not strictly constant over a wide pH range largely because of changes in E_j with changes in composition of the solution. It is therefore recommended that a pH standard be chosen which is close to that of the unknown. Even better, two standards, one on either side of the unknown, are recommended.

It is possible to arrange experimental conditions so that the term k is constant to about ± 1 mv over the pH range 2 to 10. This leads to an uncertainty in the value of pH of about ± 0.01 to 0.02 units. Hence it is not possible to obtain significant pH numbers to any greater precision than this by potentiometric measurement.

[4] R. G. Bates, *op. cit.*; an excellent summary is given by H. F. Walton, *Principles and Methods of Chemical Analysis*, 2nd Ed., Prentice-Hall, Inc., Englewood Cliffs, N.J., 1964, pp. 246–248.

OTHER TITRATIONS

Redox titrations

Redox titrations normally involve different oxidation states of ions and the indicator electrode is an inert metal, such as platinum, whose function is simply to transfer electrons. The titration of ferrous with ceric ion (page 141) can be carried out potentiometrically, using platinum and calomel electrodes. The potential readings at various intervals in the titration can be obtained from Table 5.1, page 144. The values in this table are referred to the standard hydrogen electrode. To refer these to the standard calomel electrode it is necessary to subtract 0.28 v from the potentials given. For example, at the equivalence point the voltage of the cell made of the afore-mentioned two electrodes is 1.19 − 0.28, or 0.91 v. The platinum wire is the positive electrode.

Care must be taken in the use of platinum in the presence of strong oxidizing agents, especially in solutions that contain a high concentration of chloride ions. Platinum is more readily oxidized in the presence of chloride ions because of the formation of stable chloro-platinum complexes such as $PtCl_4^=$:

$$PtCl_4^= + 2\,e \rightleftarrows Pt + 4\,Cl^-$$

There is also danger in using platinum in the presence of very strong reducing agents such as chromous ion. The latter ion can reduce hydrogen ion in acid solution. This reaction is normally slow, but platinum acts as a catalyst for the reaction. For example, Lingane[5] found that mercury is a better electrode than platinum for the titration of the TiO^{++} ion with chromous ion in acid solution because of this effect.

Precipitation titrations

An indicator electrode for a precipitation titration is one whose potential depends upon the concentration of one of the ions involved in the precipitation. For example, a piece of silver wire acts as the indicator electrode for silver ions when silver is precipitated with anions such as chloride or bromide. The experimental cell can be

$$Ag \mid Ag^+ \,(x\text{-}M) \parallel KNO_3 \parallel KCl \,(\text{sat.}), Hg_2Cl_2 \mid Hg$$

A salt bridge of potassium nitrate is used to prevent the precipitation of silver by chloride ions from the calomel electrode. The relation between potential and silver ion concentration is shown in the following calculation.

[5] J. J. Lingane, *Anal. Chem.*, **20**, 797 (1948).

PROBLEM. Derive an equation relating the potential of the foregoing cell to the concentration of silver ion. Also express the relation between potential and pAg.

The electrode reactions are

$$\begin{array}{ll}
Ag^+ + e = Ag & E_1^\circ \ = +0.80 \\
\frac{1}{2} Hg_2Cl_2 + e = Hg + Cl^- & E_2 \ = +0.25 \\
\hline
Ag^+ + Hg + Cl^- = \frac{1}{2} Hg_2Cl_2 + Ag & E_{1-2}^\circ = +0.55
\end{array}$$

The potential is given by the expression

$$E_{1-2} = 0.55 - 0.059 \log \frac{1}{[Ag^+]}$$

because all other activities are unity. Since pAg $= \log \dfrac{1}{[Ag^+]}$,

$$E_{1-2} = 0.55 - 0.059 \, p\text{Ag}$$

The concentration of chloride ion throughout a titration with silver ion is calculated on page 163. The values of the silver ion concentration, or of pAg, can be readily obtained from the values of pCl in Table 6.1, page 164, since

$$p\text{Ag} + p\text{Cl} = pK_{sp} \quad \text{or} \quad p\text{Ag} + p\text{Cl} = 10$$

Hence the potential readings throughout the titration of silver with chloride, or of chloride with silver, can be calculated from the data in Table 6.1. For example, at the equivalence point, pCl $= 5.00$, pAg $= 5.00$, and thus

$$E_{1-2} = 0.55 - 0.059 \times 5.00 = 0.25 \text{ v}$$

A pH indicator electrode can be employed for a precipitation titration of a metal which forms an insoluble hydroxide. For example, magnesium can be titrated with sodium hydroxide using the glass electrode as the indicator electrode. There is a large increase in hydroxide ion concentration at the equivalence point and a corresponding decrease in hydrogen ion concentration. The response of the glass electrode to this large change signals the end point of the titration. Such titrations are frequently inaccurate because of the uncertain composition of the precipitate due to such factors as coprecipitation and formation of basic salts.

Complex formation titrations

A glass electrode can sometimes be employed as the indicator electrode in complex formation titrations involving chelating agents (page 180). For example, the last stage of ionization of EDTA is very slight; that is, the ion HY^{3-} is a weak acid, and hence Y^{4-} is a strong base. If a metal such as calcium is titrated with Y^{4-},

$$Ca^{++} + Y^{4-} \rightleftarrows CaY^=$$

the appearance of excess Y^{4-} is attended by a sudden increase in pH. In other words, the latter ion is strongly hydrolyzed:

$$Y^{4-} + H_2O \rightleftharpoons HY^{3-} + OH^-$$

Hence a pH indicator electrode can be used to detect the end point of the titration.

A silver wire serves as the indicator electrode for the titration of cyanide ion with silver,

$$Ag^+ + 2\ CN^- \rightleftharpoons Ag(CN)_2^-$$

The titration curve calculated for this reaction has been found to agree well with that obtained experimentally.[6]

The mercury electrode. Many cations can be titrated successfully with the complexing agent EDTA and it is of interest to follow the course of the reaction by measuring the metal ion concentration (or pM) by potentiometric methods. Most metal-metal ion systems, however, do not behave as reversible electrodes and thus cannot be used as indicator electrodes for their ions in solution. The observation of Reilley and Schmid[7] that the potential of a mercury electrode responds reversibly to other metal ions in solution in the presence of the Hg-EDTA complex has led to the use of mercury as the indicator electrode for the titration of many metals with EDTA. The electrode system (using M^{++} as the metal) is

$$M^{++} + MY^= + HgY^= + Hg^{++} \mid Hg$$

It is necessary that $MY^=$ be less stable than $HgY^=$. This is not a difficult requirement to fulfill since the $HgY^=$ complex is extremely stable ($\log K_{stab} = 22.1$). Many metals form weaker complexes and can be titrated using this indicator electrode.

To explain the response of the electrode to the concentration of M^{++} (or pM), let us consider the titration of M^{++} with titrant Y^{4-}. The reaction and the equilibrium constant are

$$M^{++} + Y^{4-} \rightleftharpoons MY^= \qquad K_{MY} = \frac{[MY^=]}{[M^{++}][Y^{4-}]} \qquad (1)$$

A small amount of $HgY^=$ is added to the solution. This complex dissociates very slightly; in other words, the mercury is practically all tied up in the complex and M^{++} does not remove any appreciable amount of Y^{4-} from the mercury since the $MY^=$ complex is less stable than $HgY^=$. The equations for mercury are

$$Hg^{++} + Y^{4-} \rightleftharpoons HgY^= \qquad K_{HgY} = \frac{[HgY^=]}{[Hg^{++}][Y^{4-}]} \qquad (2)$$

As the titrant Y^{4-} is added, both M^{++} and Hg^{++} react with it, but most of the mercury is already in the form $HgY^=$ and the latter concentration

[6] I. M. Kolthoff and N. H. Furman, *Potentiometric Titrations*, John Wiley & Sons, Inc., New York, 1931, pp. 40–41.

[7] C. N. Reilley and R. W. Schmid, *Anal. Chem.*, **30**, 947 (1958); R. W. Schmid and C. N. Reilley, *J. Am. Chem. Soc.*, **78**, 5513 (1956).

remains essentially constant. Thus, most of the titrant combines with M^{++}, but, of course, both $[Hg^{++}]$ and $[M^{++}]$ change[8] in accordance with the equilibrium expressions (1) and (2).

As the equivalence point of the titration is reached, the concentration of Y^{4-} changes abruptly, causing similar large changes in $[M^{++}]$ and $[Hg^{++}]$. This causes the potential of the mercury electrode to undergo a large change which is detected potentiometrically.

The electrode reaction is

$$Hg^{++} + 2\,e \rightleftarrows Hg \qquad E^\circ = 0.85 \text{ v}$$

The potential of this electrode is given by

$$E = E^\circ - \frac{0.059}{2} \log \frac{1}{[Hg^{++}]} \tag{3}$$

From equations (1) and (2) the concentration of Hg^{++} can be evaluated and substituted in equation (3), giving

$$E = E^\circ - \frac{0.059}{2} \log \frac{K_{HgY}[MY^=]}{K_{MY}[HgY^=][M^{++}]} \tag{4}$$

The terms K_{HgY} and K_{MY} are constant, of course. As explained above, $[HgY^=]$ is constant throughout the titration, and near the equivalence point the term $[MY^=]$ becomes essentially constant. Hence, near the equivalence point equation (4) becomes

$$E = K - \frac{0.059}{2} \log \frac{1}{[M^{++}]}$$

or

$$E = K - 0.03\,pM \tag{5}$$

The term K in equation (5) is a composite of all the constant terms.

It is thus evident that there is a linear relation between the potential of the mercury electrode and the pM of the metal ion solution. This electrode has proved applicable to the potentiometric titration of about thirty individual metal ions, either by direct or back-titration procedures.[9] Potentials are established fairly rapidly with the electrode since all the species except mercury itself are in solution. The absolute values of the potentials and the magnitude of the break in the titration curve depend upon the concentration and the stability constant of $MY^=$ [equation (4)]. It might also be noted that the fact that mercury is so noble ($E^\circ = +0.85$ v) keeps the equilibrium potential from being excessively negative despite the high stability of the $HgY^=$ complex.

---

[8] If it seems odd that $[Hg^{++}]$ can change appreciably whereas $[HgY^=]$ remains essentially constant, recall that $[Hg^{++}]$ is very small, $[HgY^=]$ relatively large. For example, $[Hg^{++}]$ could change from 10^{-8} to 10^{-4} without changing $[HgY^=]$ appreciably if the latter concentration is considerably greater than 10^{-4}.

[9] C. N. Reilley, R. W. Schmid, and D. W. Lamson, *Anal. Chem.*, **30**, 953 (1958).

TITRATION TECHNIQUES

In a potentiometric titration the experimental procedure may be very similar to that ordinarily employed with visual indicators except that potential readings instead of visual observations of color are made as the titration proceeds. However, the existence of an electrical voltage which varies in a distinctive fashion with the progress of the titration introduces the possibility of automating the procedure. We may consider the various techniques under three headings, recognizing that all variants cannot be discussed in a book of this sort: manual potentiometric titrations, automatic recording of the titration curve; automatic titrant shut-off at the end point.

Manual methods

In manual titrations the potential is measured after the addition of each successive increment of titrant, and the resulting readings are plotted on graph paper versus the volume of titrant to give a titration curve such as shown in Figure 8.3(a). In many cases, a simple potentiometer could be used. However, if the glass electrode is involved, as in most acid-base titrations, a measuring device with a high input impedance is required because of the high resistance of the glass; typically, a commercial "pH meter" is

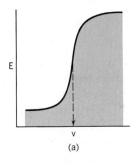
(a)

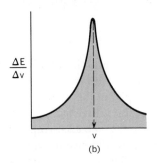
(b)

Fig. 8.3. Methods of plotting potential data.

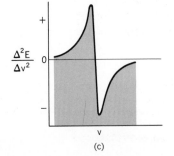
(c)

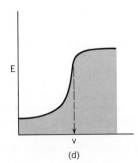
(d)

employed. Because these pH meters have become so common, they are widely utilized for all sorts of titrations, even where their use is not obligatory.

Once the titration curve is at hand, a subjective element enters the procedure. The analyst must determine where the curve is steepest, normally by some sort of inspection. He may draw a vertical line through the steep portion of the curve and find the intersection of this line with the volume axis. There must be some uncertainty in this procedure, and this will, of course, be reflected in the ultimate volume reading. For a reaction which goes well to completion, the titration curve is so steep near the equivalence point that the uncertainty is small; for a reaction with a smaller equilibrium constant, the precision with which an end point may be reproduced becomes poorer.

Figure 8.3(b) shows a plot of the slope of a titration curve, that is, the change in potential with change in volume ($\Delta E/\Delta V$) against volume of titrant. The resulting curve rises to a maximum at the equivalence point. The volume at the equivalence point is determined by dropping a vertical line from the peak to the volume axis. There is some uncertainty, of course, in locating exactly the peak in the curve. The more complete the reaction, the sharper the peak and hence the more accurate the location of the equivalence point.

Figure 8.3(c) shows a plot of the change in the slope of a titration curve ($\Delta^2 E/\Delta V^2$) against the volume of titrant. At the point where the slope $\Delta E/\Delta V$ is a maximum, the derivative of the slope is zero. The end point is located by drawing a vertical line from the point at which $\Delta^2 E/\Delta V^2$ is zero to the volume axis. The portion of the curve joining the maximum and minimum values of $\Delta^2 E/\Delta V^2$ is steeper the more complete the titration reaction.

The curves shown in Figures 8.3(a), (b), and (c) are for "symmetrical" reactions, that is, reactions in which 1 mole of titrant reacts with 1 mole of the substance titrated. Examples of acid-base, redox, and precipitation reactions that are symmetrical are

$$H_3O^+ + OH^- \rightleftarrows 2H_2O$$
$$Ag^+ + Cl^- \rightleftarrows AgCl \downarrow$$
$$Fe^{++} + Ce^{4+} \rightleftarrows Fe^{3+} + Ce^{3+}$$

For such reactions the mid-point of the steep portion of the curve in Figure 8.3(a) corresponds to the equivalence point (see page 145). Likewise, the peak in the curve of Figure 8.3(b) as well as the zero value of the second derivative in Figure 8.3(c) occur exactly at the equivalence point.

For nonsymmetrical reactions such as

$$2 Ag^+ + CrO_4^= \rightleftarrows Ag_2CrO_4 \downarrow$$

and

$$Sn^{++} + 2 Ce^{++} \rightleftarrows Sn^{4+} + 2 Ce^{3+}$$

the equivalence point does not occur at the mid-point of the curve of Figure 8.3(d). The potential at the equivalence point in the titration of stannous

Potentiometric Titrations

(E_1^0) with ceric ion (E_2^0) is $(2E_1^0 + E_2^0)/3$ (see page 146). Similarly, the maximal value of $\Delta E/\Delta V$ for a nonsymmetrical reaction does not coincide exactly with the equivalence point. Nevertheless, the maximum is usually taken as the end point of a titration. The error made by this procedure is quite small.[10]

It is possible to locate the end point by a simple systematic method based upon the actual data without resorting to a graph. Only potential readings near the equivalence point need be recorded. Some definite increment of volume, say 0.10 ml, is selected and a number of readings is taken, 0.10 ml apart, on either side of the equivalence point. An example is given in Table 8.2, where the values of the first and second derivatives are included. It can

Table 8.2   POTENTIAL READINGS NEAR THE EQUIVALENCE POINT

ml titrant	E(mv)	$\Delta E/\Delta V/0.1$ ml	$\Delta^2 E/\Delta V^2$
24.70	210		
		12	
24.80	222		+6
		18	
24.90	240		+102
		120	
25.00	360		+120
		240	
25.10	600		−224
		16	
25.20	616		−7
		9	
25.30	625		

be seen from the second derivative values that the slope changes sign, and hence goes through the value zero, between 25.00 and 25.10 ml of titrant. The volume at which the value of zero is reached is closer to 25.00 than to 25.10, since the reading of +120 is closer to zero than is −224. Since 0.10 ml caused a total change in the second derivative of 344[+120 − (−224)], the fraction (120/344) × 0.10 ml is the approximate number of milliliters in excess of 25.00 necessary to bring the second derivative to the value zero. Hence the calculated volume at the equivalence point is

$$V = 25.00 + 0.10 \left(\frac{120}{120 + 224} \right) = 25.035 \text{ ml}$$

By a very simple experimental modification, values of $\Delta E/\Delta V$, the change in potential with change in volume of titrant, may be obtained directly. These values can be plotted as shown in Figure 8.3(b), or the volume corresponding to the maximal value of $\Delta E/\Delta V$ may be obtained from inspection of the data.

No reference electrode is required for this method. Two indicator electrodes are employed, but one is kept separated from the main body of solution until a potential reading has been taken. A simple device that can be

---

[10] See Kolthoff and Furman, *op. cit.*

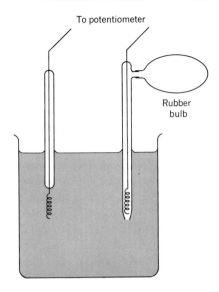

Fig. 8.4. Apparatus for differential titration.

used for performing such a titration is shown in Figure 8.4. One electrode is in the body of the solution, the other inside a small glass tube that dips into the same solution. When the solution inside and outside of the tube is uniform in composition, there is no difference in potential between the electrodes. When titrant is added to the main body of the solution, however, a difference in potential develops, since the solution inside the tube no longer has the same composition as that outside. The potential difference is noted, and then the solution is expelled from the tube by squeezing the rubber bulb so that the composition becomes uniform again. The potential difference falls to zero as bulk solution is sucked into the tube. The volume of solution in the tube must, of course, be kept small compared to the total volume of solution titrated. The method is rapid and the results can be accurate.

Automatic recording of titration curves

Recording potentiometers have become commonplace in chemistry laboratories. With typical "recorders," as they are called, voltages from many different origins can be plotted with pen and ink as a function of time. The voltage developed across a resistor in a circuit of inherently very high resistance, as encountered in glass electrode set-ups, cannot be fed· directly to a recorder for reasons that are beyond the scope of this book; suffice it here to say that it is necessary to "match" the input impedance of the recorder with the impedance of the voltage source. The circuitry of most modern pH meters does this. Thus the student who is not interested in instrumentation per se can simply note that with relatively inexpensive commercially available "black boxes," one may take the potential between the electrodes during a potentiometric titration and feed this to a recorder. Since the recorder plots voltage versus time, it is obvious that a potentiometric titration curve can be recorded provided the titrant is added at a constant rate. Thus, to record automatically a potentiometric titration curve, it is clear that one requires an electrode set-up, as in manual titrations, plus an impedance matching device, a recorder, and a constant-flow buret. Commercial pH meters serve for the impedance matching and many are fitted with terminals for wires connecting with the recorder. Constant-flow burets usually rely, not upon gravity feed as with ordinary burets, but upon the action of a motor-driven plunger in a syringe type of assembly. Such devices are available commercially. Rapid stirring, usually accomplished with a magnetic stirrer, is important in order to maintain a uniform concentration in the solution during the titration.

After the titration curve has been recorded, the analyst faces the same problem of selecting the end point as with graphs plotted manually. On the other hand, while the titration is in progress, he is free to perform other tasks, perhaps preparing the next sample for titration, and thus time may be saved. The continuous nature of the recording insures that features of the curve will be seen which might be missed in a manual titration unless points were taken at very close intervals. A real disadvantage of recording, at least with the typical titrant flow rates, lies in the fact that the titration reaction must be rapid. In a manual titration, if the reaction is slow, the operator can wait for a steady reading before adding the next increment of titrant, and although it may try his patience, the titration will work. With automatic recording, the potentials may never reach equilibrium values at any stage of the titration, the recorded curve may be distorted, and a large potential break may appear before the equivalence point is actually reached.

Automatic titrant shut-off

Finally, potentiometric titrations can be completely automated so that the buret is mechanically shut off at the end point. In some cases the buret is a conventional one and the meniscus is read in the usual manner. The drive mechanism of a syringe buret can be fitted with a revolution counter that provides direct digital read-out.

One type of automatic titrator titrates the sample to a pre-set potential. The difference between the indicator and reference electrodes at the equivalence point is determined ahead of time, and the instrument is then set to shut off the buret at this potential. Even with good stirring, mixing is not instantaneous, and it is necessary to provide for restarting the titrant flow if the buret shuts off too soon due to a high local concentration of titrant around the indicator electrode. End point "anticipation" is provided for by positioning the delivery tip of the buret very close to the indicator electrode.[11]

[11] J. J. Lingane, *Electroanalytical Chemistry*, Interscience Publishers, Inc., New York, 1958, p. 159.

Then the solution adjacent to the electrode is at a more advanced stage of titration than is the bulk of the solution. Thus the electrode reaches the equivalence potential somewhat early, and the delivery of titrant is stopped too soon. However, as the solution becomes uniform in concentration through further stirring, the potential drops back, and the buret is turned on again. This process is repeated until the entire solution reaches the equivalence potential. A human operator does the same sort of thing in a visual titration when he adds titrant rapidly in the early stages and then dropwise as fleeting color changes are seen near the equivalence point.

Another type of automatic titrator, developed by Malmstadt and Fett,[12] is based upon electronic differentiation. It is possible, by using a resistance-capacitance network with the right time constant, to construct an electronic circuit which produces a voltage that is proportional to the derivative (with respect to time) of a voltage which is fed into it. By combining two such circuits and including appropriate amplification, Malmstadt was able to trigger a relay system that shut off a buret when the second derivative of the voltage input from the electrodes changed sign. (Electronically, the second derivative is more suitable than the first derivative for actuating such a relay.) At constant titrant flow, differentiation with respect to time is equivalent to differentiation with respect to volume of titrant. Actually the commercial instrument based upon Malmstadt's ideas (E. H. Sargent Co.) employs an ordinary gravity-feed buret, but near the equivalence point (the only region of interest, really) the hydrostatic head is constant enough.

For a person with an occasional titration to perform, automatic titrators have little to offer. On the other hand, a laboratory with hundreds of samples to titrate each week, a repetitive and boring task, may find them nearly indispensable. The titrator cannot do anything that people cannot do, but it is cheaper than people and it does not complain about its work provided it is properly serviced.

REFERENCES

1. J. J. Lingane, *Electroanalytical Chemistry*, 2nd Ed., Interscience Publishers, Inc., New York, 1958.
2. R. G. Bates, "Concept and Determination of *p*H," Chapter 10, Part I, Vol. I, of *Treatise on Analytical Chemistry*, I. M. Kolthoff, P. J. Elving, and E. B. Sandell, Eds., Interscience Publishers, Inc., New York, 1959.
3. L. Meites and H. C. Thomas, *Advanced Analytical Chemistry*, McGraw-Hill Book Co., Inc., New York, 1958.
4. I. M. Kolthoff and N. H. Furman, *Potentiometric Titrations*, John Wiley & Sons, Inc., New York, 1926.

[12] H. V. Malmstadt and E. R. Fett, *Anal. Chem.*, **26**, 1348 (1954); **27**, 1757 (1955); **29**, 1901 (1957).

QUESTIONS

1. Explain clearly how the glass electrode functions as an indicator electrode for hydrogen ions.

2. What two assumptions are involved in the establishment of the conventional scale of pH? What is the uncertainty with which one can measure significant pH numbers?

3. Explain how the mercury electrode serves as an indicator electrode for various metal ions.

4. It was mentioned that the mercury electrode does not become excessively negative despite the stability of the $HgY^=$ complex. What would be the objection experimentally to the electrode's becoming very negative?

5. Would platinum be a suitable indicator electrode for the titration of Cr^{++} to Cr^{3+} with an oxidizing agent in strongly acid solution? Explain.

6. What are the advantages of potentiometric titration over direct potentiometry?

7. Would the pH reading of an ordinary glass electrode (soda-lime) in 0.1-M NaOH be too high or too low? Explain.

PROBLEMS

(For simplicity in arithmetical computations, round off 0.059 to 0.06 in all problems unless otherwise indicated.)

1. A 25.00-ml portion of 0.1000-M HCl is diluted to 100 ml and titrated with 0.1000-M NaOH. Calculate the pH of the solution after the following volumes of base are added: 0, 10, 12.5, 20, 24, 24.9, 25.0, 25.1, 25.5, 26.0, and 30 ml. From the pH values calculate the potential readings one would obtain in a potentiometric titration with a standard hydrogen-saturated calomel electrode pair. Plot the titration curve: potential vs. ml of titrant.

2. Repeat problem 1 except for the titration of acetic acid rather than hydrochloric acid.

3. Repeat the calculations of problem 1 for the titration of 0.10-M NH_4OH with 0.10-M HCl.

4. From the data of problems 1 and 2 plot also $\Delta E/\Delta V$ and $\Delta^2 E/\Delta V^2$ vs. volume of titrant.

5. Derive an equation relating the potential of the following cell to pH:

$$Ag \mid AgCl, HCl(0.1\text{-}M) \parallel H^+(x\text{-}M) \mid H_2(1 \text{ atm}), Pt$$

6. The so-called "quinhydrone" electrode is an indicator electrode for hydrogen ions. A platinum electrode is inserted in the test solution which is saturated with quinhydrone (a molecular compound of quinone and hydroquinone). The redox couple is

Derive an equation relating the pH of a solution to the potential of the following cell:

$$Hg \mid Hg_2Cl_2, KCl(1\text{-}M) \parallel H^+(x\text{-}M) + H_2Q + Q \mid Pt$$

H_2Q stands for hydroquinone, Q for quinone. You can assume the dissociation of quinhydrone produces an equal number of moles of quinone and hydroquinone.

7. Answer the following questions about the quinhydrone electrode (problem 6):
(a) What is the polarity of the calomel electrode at pH 5?
(b) At pH 9?
(c) At what pH is the potential of the cell zero?
(d) At high pH some H_2Q is neutralized and the ratio of Q to H_2Q is no longer unity. When this occurs, is the pH reading higher or lower than it should be?

8. The cell in problem 6 is used for the titration of 5.0 mmol of the weak acid, HA, with NaOH. The potential at the equivalence point is 0.06 v with the calomel electrode positive. The volume of solution at this point is 100 ml. What is the ionization constant of the acid, HA?

9. Show that the potential of the following cell

$$Hg \mid Hg_2Cl_2, KCl(1\text{-}M) \parallel M^{++} \mid M$$

is related to the pH of the solution in the right-hand electrode according to the equation

$$E = k + 0.06 \, pH$$

where k is a constant. Assume that M^{++} forms a slightly soluble hydroxide, $M(OH)_2$, and that the concentration of M^{++} depends on the hydroxyl ion concentration as expressed by the solubility product constant.

10. A sample of 4.0 mmol of M^{++} is titrated with X^- according to the reaction

$$M^{++} + X^- \rightleftharpoons MX^+ \qquad K = 1 \times 10^{12}$$

The potential of the cell

$$M \mid M^{++} \parallel KCl(1\text{-}M), Hg_2Cl_2 \mid Hg$$

is 0.00 v at the equivalence point. If the final volume is 100 ml, calculate $E°$ for $M^{++} + 2 e \rightleftharpoons M$.

11. How many grams of HCl should be dissolved in 1 liter of solution so that the potential reading obtained when a quinhydrone-standard calomel electrode pair (see problem 6) is inserted in the solution is 0.30 v? The polarity of the calomel electrode is negative.

12. What should be the ratio of acetic acid to sodium acetate in a buffer so that the potential reading obtained when a quinhydrone-standard Ag-AgCl electrode (see problem 6) is inserted in the solution is 0.28 v? The polarity of the quinhydrone electrode is positive.

13. A standard hydrogen electrode and a standard calomel electrode were inserted

in a solution of HCl and a potential of 0.322 v was measured. When these electrodes were inserted in a solution of NaOH, the reading was 1.096 v. The polarity of the hydrogen electrode is negative. How many milliliters of each solution should be mixed in order to prepare 100 ml of a solution that would give a reading of 0.346 v with the same electrodes?

14. A 2.00-g impure sample of an acid HA, M.W. of 100, is dissolved in 50.0 ml of water and titrated with 0.200-N NaOH using a standard hydrogen-standard calomel electrode pair. The potential reading is 0.58 v when half of the acid is neutralized and 0.82 v at the equivalence point. The polarity of the hydrogen electrode is negative. Calculate the percentage of HA in the sample.

15. A 50.0-ml portion of 0.100-M Fe^{++} is titrated potentiometrically with 0.100-M Ce^{4+}, using a platinum-standard calomel electrode pair. When the potential reading is 0.55 v, how many milliliters of the ceric solution have been added? The polarity of the platinum electrode is positive.

16. A 50.0-ml portion of 0.100-M Sn^{++} is titrated with 0.100-M Ce^{4+} using a platinum-standard calomel electrode pair. Calculate the potential reading after the addition of the following volumes of the ceric solution: 20.0, 50.0, 100, and 150 ml.

17. Calculate the potential for a few volumes on either side of the equivalence point in the previous problem, and plot $\Delta E/\Delta V$ and $\Delta^2 E/\Delta V^2$ for this titration. Note that these curves are not symmetrical.

18. Calculate the potential of the mercury indicator electrode at the equivalence point for the titration of 4.0 mmol of M^{++} with EDTA. Assume the following: volume at equivalence point = 100 ml; stability constants: HgY$^-$ = 10^{22}, MY$^-$ = 10^{12}; concentration of HgY$^-$ = 0.01-M.

19. A 50-ml portion of AgNO$_3$ is titrated with 0.10-M NaX in the cell described on page 208. Calculate the potential when 49.90, 50.00, and 50.10 ml of titrant are added. Consider X$^-$ as Cl$^-$, then as Br$^-$, and also as I$^-$. Note the dependence of the potential change on the solubility of the silver salt.

20. Consider the possibility of titrating a mixture of chloride, bromide, and iodide, each 0.10-M, with silver nitrate. Calculate the percentage of iodide unprecipitated when AgBr begins to precipitate, and the percentage of bromide unprecipitated when AgCl begins to precipitate. Sketch roughly a titration curve of potential (or pAg) vs. milliliters of titrant.

21. Three 50-ml portions of 0.10-M silver nitrate are titrated with 0.10-M solutions of the anions A$^-$, B$^-$, and C$^-$. The solubility products are: AgA, 1 × 10^{-6}; AgB, 1 × 10^{-8}; AgC, 1 × 10^{-10}. Calculate the potential of the single electrode system Ag$^+$ + e = Ag in each case for the addition of 49.90 ml of titrant. Do this in two ways: (a) by the usual approximation methods, and (b) including the contribution of solubility to the concentration of silver ions. What do you conclude as to the validity of the usual approximation?

Electrolysis

The cells described and used in previous chapters were termed *galvanic*. Such cells are sources of electric energy, but we have not considered their acting in such a fashion. Rather we have been interested in measuring their potentials in order to learn the concentrations of certain ions in solution. The measurement of voltage with a potentiometer is designed to draw as little current as possible from the cell. The electrode reactions that we write do not take place appreciably under such conditions. However, if we allow the cell to furnish electricity to some other system, or if we simply short-circuit the cell by joining the two electrodes with a wire, these reactions do occur spontaneously to an appreciable extent.

On the other hand, if the electrode reactions are forced to take place in the reverse manner to which they tend to occur spontaneously, the cell is termed *electrolytic* rather than galvanic. This reversal of the reactions is effected by application of an external voltage. The term *electrolysis* embraces all the phenomena occurring at the electrodes of an electrolytic cell as the reactions take place.

A given cell can function either as a galvanic or electrolytic cell depending upon the magnitude of the externally applied voltage. Consider the following example:

$$\overset{\oplus}{\text{Ag}} \mid \text{Ag}^+(1\text{-}M) \parallel \text{Cu}^{++}(1\text{-}M) \mid \overset{\ominus}{\text{Cu}}$$

The electrode and cell reactions are:

$2 \text{ Ag}^+ + 2 \text{ e} \rightleftarrows 2 \text{ Ag}$	$E_1^\circ = +0.80$
$\text{Cu}^{++} + 2 \text{ e} \rightleftarrows \text{Cu}$	$E_2^\circ = +0.34$
$2 \text{ Ag}^+ + \text{Cu} \rightleftarrows \text{Cu}^{++} + 2 \text{ Ag}$	$E_{12}^\circ = +0.46 \text{ v}$

The reaction tends to occur spontaneously from left to right, and the polarity of the silver electrode is positive. If an external voltage less than 0.46 v is applied in opposition to this cell, the reaction still occurs as indicated, and the cell is galvanic. However, if a battery with a voltage greater than 0.46 v is connected to the cell, with its negative pole connected to the copper and the positive to silver, the foregoing reaction will take place from right to left. That is, copper will deposit at the right-hand electrode, and silver will dissolve at the left-hand electrode. The electrode reactions are being forced to take place in the opposite direction to that indicated in the galvanic formulation above, and the cell is electrolytic. An ordinary storage battery, used to start an automobile, acts as a galvanic cell. A discharged battery that is being recharged by application of a higher voltage acts as an electrolytic cell.

Because of the opposite directions of electron flow in electrolytic and galvanic cells, confusion regarding signs may occur. The cathode is defined as the electrode at which reduction occurs, and the anode is the electrode at which oxidation occurs. Hence, in the galvanic cell above, copper is the anode and silver the cathode; when the cell acts as an electrolytic cell, copper is the cathode, silver the anode. The cathode, which is often thought of as the negative electrode of a cell, is actually negative only in the electrolytic cell. Its polarity is positive in the galvanic cell. The polarity of the electrodes in the two types of cells is summarized below:

	Cathode	*Anode*
Galvanic	+	−
Electrolytic	−	+

In the apparatus normally used to deposit a substance from a solution, the electrodes of the electrolytic cell are at first inert. For example, if it is desired to determine the amount of copper in a copper sulfate solution electrolytically, two platinum electrodes are inserted in the solution and an external voltage is applied (see Figure 9.1). Once the electrolysis is started, the products of the reactions at the electrodes form a galvanic cell. Copper is

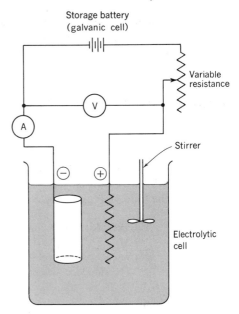

Fig. 9.1. Apparatus for electrolysis.

deposited on the cathode, and oxygen is liberated at the anode. The resulting galvanic cell is

$$Pt, O_2 \mid H^+ + H_2O + Cu^{++} \mid Cu$$

Copper has a tendency to go back into solution as cupric ions, and oxygen has a tendency to take up electrons and combine with hydrogen ions to form water. Thus the tendency of these reactions to occur spontaneously is reversed by the applied voltage.

Electrolysis is most commonly used in analytical chemistry as a method of separating substances from one another. Some substances may be deposited by an electric current, whereas others are not, and hence a separation may be effected. Often the final step in the determination of metals is made by electrolytic deposition and weighing of the deposit. In other cases separations are made electrolytically, but the final determinations are made by other methods. In all such applications the electric current may be regarded as the precipitating agent and the procedures are often called *electrogravimetric* methods of analysis.

Another application of electrolysis is called *coulometric analysis*. In this method the quantity of electricity required to oxidize or reduce a given substance is measured. From this quantity the concentration of the substance can be calculated using Faraday's laws. This method may be regarded as a volumetric method in which electrons act as the titrant.

Before discussing the applications to analysis, it will be helpful to consider the products obtained at the electrodes during electrolysis and also the potential requirements for electrolysis to occur. Current requirements were considered in Chapter 2 as a stoichiometric problem based on Faraday's laws.

PRODUCTS OF ELECTROLYSIS

It is easy to predict the products which should be formed at the cathode and anode during electrolysis. Reduction occurs at the cathode, and hence the substance that is most readily reduced will be the first liberated. Consider the following example.

> **PROBLEM.** A solution contains the following ions, each at a concentration of 1.0-M: Zn^{++}, H^+, Cu^{++}, and Ag^+. Which ion is reduced first when an electric current is passed through the solution?
> The standard potentials from Table 4, Appendix I, are

$$Ag^+ + e \rightleftharpoons Ag \qquad E° = +0.80$$
$$Cu^{++} + 2\,e \rightleftharpoons Cu \qquad E° = +0.34$$
$$2\,H^+ + 2\,e \rightleftharpoons H_2 \qquad E° = 0.00$$
$$Zn^{++} + 2\,e \rightleftharpoons Zn \qquad E° = -0.76$$

It is apparent that the silver ion is most readily reduced. In other words, silver ion has the greatest electron affinity of the ions in the solution. As a general rule the oxidant of the redox system having the most positive potential (reactions written with electrons on the left) is the first reduced at the cathode. It should be recalled that the effect of concentration on the potential of the electrode must be considered in making such predictions.

At the anode, where oxidation occurs, the reductant that loses electrons most readily is the first oxidized. Consider the following example.

> **PROBLEM.** A water solution is 1-M in chloride, bromide, iodide, and hydrogen ions. Two platinum electrodes are placed in the solution and an electric current passed. What substance is first liberated at the anode?
> The possible reactions at the anode are

$$I_2 + 2\,e \rightleftharpoons 2\,I^- \qquad E° = +0.54$$
$$Br_2 + 2\,e \rightleftharpoons 2\,Br^- \qquad E° = +1.09$$
$$2\,H^+ + \tfrac{1}{2}\,O_2 + 2\,e \rightleftharpoons H_2O \qquad E° = +1.23$$
$$Cl_2 + 2\,e \rightleftharpoons 2\,Cl^- \qquad E° = +1.35$$

The reactions as written take place at the anode from right to left. Iodide ion has the greatest tendency to lose electrons, and hence iodine is the first product at the anode. As a general rule the reductant of the system having the least positive potential is first oxidized at the anode, concentration effects being accounted for.

If an electrode is not inert, but can react with components of the solution, this reaction must also be considered in predicting the products of electrolysis. Consider the following example.

PROBLEM. What are the first products of electrolysis in the following cells?

	Cathode	Electrolyte	Anode
(A)	Pt	$NaI(1\text{-}M)$	Ag
(B)	Ag	$AgNO_3(1\text{-}M)$	Ag

The student should verify that the products are:

(A) Hydrogen at the cathode, silver iodide at the anode. The latter results from the reaction

$$AgI + e \rightleftharpoons Ag + I^- \qquad E^\circ = -0.15 \text{ v}$$

(B) Silver is deposited at the cathode and silver is oxidized to silver ions at the anode. The reaction at each electrode, but in opposite directions, is

$$Ag^+ + e \rightleftharpoons Ag \qquad E^\circ = +0.80 \text{ v}$$

POTENTIAL REQUIREMENTS

We have already seen that in order for electrolysis to occur in a cell, the applied voltage must be sufficient to reverse the normal tendency for electron flow in the galvanic cell. This voltage is called the *equilibrium decomposition voltage* of the cell, or sometimes the "back emf." The decomposition voltage for equilibrium conditions is readily calculated by the methods of Chapter 5. Consider the following example.

PROBLEM. Calculate the equilibrium decomposition voltage of a 0.1-M solution of copper sulfate; two platinum electrodes are employed and the solution is 1-M in hydrogen ion.

The products of electrolysis are copper at the cathode and oxygen at the anode. The products form a galvanic cell, which we represent as

$$\text{Pt, } O_2 \mid H_2O + H^+(1\text{-}M) + Cu^{++}(0.1\text{-}M) \mid Cu$$

The electrode reactions are

$$
\begin{array}{ll}
2\,H^+ + \tfrac{1}{2}\,O_2 + 2\,e \rightleftharpoons H_2O & E_a^\circ = +1.23 \\
\underline{Cu^{++} + 2\,e \rightleftharpoons Cu} & \underline{E_c^\circ = +0.34} \\
Cu + 2\,H^+ + \tfrac{1}{2}\,O_2 \rightleftharpoons Cu^{++} + H_2O & E_a^\circ - E_c^\circ = 0.89
\end{array}
$$

Here we have designated by E_a° and E_c° the standard potentials of the reactions that take place at the anode and cathode. Let us call the equilibrium decomposition potential E_d. Then

$$E_d = 0.89 - \frac{0.059}{2} \log \frac{a_{Cu^{++}}}{a_{O_2} \times a_{H^+}^2}$$

According to our usual assumptions,

$$a_{Cu^{++}} = 0.1$$

$$a_{H^+} = 1$$

$$a_{O_2} = p_{O_2} = 1^1$$

Therefore

$$E_d = 0.89 - \frac{0.059}{2} \log 0.1 = 0.92 \text{ v}$$

The decomposition voltage changes during the electrolysis, of course, since concentration changes occur. The voltage can be calculated by the last equation under any given conditions. It should be apparent that as the concentration of copper decreases, the concentration of hydrogen ion increases and the decomposition voltage increases; that is, a higher voltage is required to force the reactions to occur as the amount of copper in the solution decreases.

In addition to the equilibrium decomposition voltage, sufficient voltage must be applied in order to overcome the resistance of the cell, that is, to force the ions to migrate to the electrodes. This voltage is given by Ohm's law. If the resistance of the cell is 2 ohms, for example, and it is desired to pass a current of $\frac{1}{2}$ amp, the additional voltage requirement is

$$E = I \times R$$

$$E = 0.5 \times 2 = 1.0 \text{ v}$$

It is apparent that if a larger current is desired, a larger voltage must be applied.

If the voltage initially applied to the cell is merely the equilibrium value, no net current flows, of course, and the concentration of cupric ions remains 0.1-M. In order for a finite current to flow, the voltage must be greater than the equilibrium, or *reversible*, value and the difference, $E - E_d = \eta$, is commonly called the *overvoltage* or *activation overpotential*.[2] This overpotential is caused by some slow kinetic process in the electrode reactions. An electrode is said to be *polarized*, implying a deviation of the potential of the electrode from its reversible value.

As current flows, the concentration of cupric ions in the portion of solution in contact with the electrode becomes less than the value we used above, 0.1-M. This decrease in concentration at the electrode-solution interface occurs even though the solution is stirred vigorously. It is practically impossible to replenish the volume element adjacent to the electrode rapidly

---

[1] Oxygen is liberated on the platinum below the surface of the solution. Hence its pressure must be atmospheric, plus a slight hydrostatic pressure, in order for bubbles to be liberated.

[2] H. A. Laitinen, *Chemical Analysis*, McGraw-Hill Book Co., Inc., New York, 1960, uses the term *voltage* to refer to a cell, and *potential* to refer to a single electrode. We shall use the terms *overvoltage* and *overpotential* in this same context.

enough to keep the concentration uniform throughout the solution. The ions in the immediate vicinity of the electrode are, of course, the ones in equilibrium with the electrode. The concentration of these ions at the surface rather than the concentration in the bulk of the solution should be used in calculating the equilibrium decomposition potential. Since the former concentration is lower than the latter, the actual value of E_d is greater than that which we calculated above. This additional potential is often referred to as "concentration polarization," although this is really a misnomer since the electrode is presumably acting reversibly with respect to the activity of cupric ions at the surface. Many chemists refer to this term today as "concentration overpotential."

The magnitude of the concentration overpotential is normally small in solutions that are well-stirred and under conditions such that the applied voltage is not far above the equilibrium decomposition voltage. The activation overpotential can be quite large, especially in cases where a gas is liberated at an electrode. Hydrogen and oxygen are the two gases normally encountered in electrolyses with water solutions, and we shall limit our discussion here to them. The mechanism leading to the activation overpotential in the liberation of hydrogen can be pictured as follows. The steps in the process are thought to be:

$H^+ + e \rightleftarrows H$ (discharge of hydrogen ions at the electrode surface)

followed by

$H + H \rightleftarrows H_2$ (catalytic combination of hydrogen atoms on the electrode surface)

or

$H \text{ (surface)} + H^+ + e \rightleftarrows H_2$ (electrochemical desorption of the gas)

One of these steps is the slowest, and requires an additional potential to force it to occur at a reasonable rate. It is thought that any one of the steps above can be the slow one, depending upon conditions of electrolysis.

The magnitude of activation overpotential depends upon the nature of the electrode material, the physical state of the electrode surface, the temperature, and the current density (amperes per square centimeter of surface). Increasing the temperature decreases the overpotential, whereas increasing the current density increases overpotential. Some values for hydrogen and oxygen activation overpotentials are listed in Table 9.1.

The actual voltage required for electrolysis can be considered as the sum of three terms: (1) the reversible or equilibrium decomposition voltage, (2) the activation and concentration overpotentials, and (3) the IR drop through the solution. If we let ω_c and ω_a represent the overpotential terms at the cathode and anode respectively, then the voltage required for electrolysis, E_{app}, is given by

$$E_{app} = (E_a - E_c) + (\omega_c + \omega_a) + IR$$

The following problem illustrates the concepts we have described.

Table 9.1   OVERPOTENTIALS OF HYDROGEN AND OXYGEN ON DIFFERENT METALS†

Current density amp/cm²	Smooth Pt	Platinized Pt	Hg	Zn	Cu	Fe	Ni
			Hydrogen				
0.0001	. . .	0.0034	. . .	. . .	0.35	0.22	. .
0.001	0.024	0.015	0.9	0.72	0.48	0.40	0.56
0.01	0.068	0.030	1.04	0.75	0.58	0.56	0.75
0.1	0.29	0.041	1.07	1.06	0.80	0.82	1.05
1.0	0.68	0.048	1.11	1.23	1.25	1.29	1.24
			Oxygen				
0.001	0.72	0.40			0.42		0.35
0.01	0.85	0.52			0.58		0.52
0.1	1.28	0.64			0.66		0.64
1.0	1.49	0.77			0.79		0.85

† *International Critical Tables*, Volume VI, pp. 339–40.

PROBLEM. What voltage must be applied to a pair of smooth platinum electrodes immersed in a 0.1-M solution of copper sulfate in order that the initial current be 1.0 amp? The area of the anode is 100 cm², the cell resistance is 0.50 ohm, and the hydrogen ion concentration is 1-M. Assume that the term ω_c is 0.10 v.

The products of electrolysis are copper at the cathode and oxygen at the anode, setting up the galvanic cell shown on page 225. The reaction at the anode is

$$2\,H^+ + \tfrac{1}{2}\,O_2 + 2\,e \rightleftarrows H_2O$$

Since the hydrogen ion concentration is 1-M, and the pressure of oxygen 1 atm, the anode potential is

$$E_a = E_a^\circ = 1.23\ \text{v}$$

Since the current density is 0.01 amp/cm², the term ω_a is 0.85 v (Table 9.1).

The reaction at the cathode is

$$Cu^{++} + 2\,e \rightleftarrows Cu$$

Since the copper ion concentration is 0.1-M, the cathode potential is

$$E_c = +0.34 - \frac{0.059}{2} \log \frac{1}{0.1} = +0.31$$

We were given that the term ω_c is 0.10 v. Hence

$$
\begin{aligned}
E_{app} &= (E_a - E_c) + (\omega_c + \omega_a) + IR \\
&= (1.23 - 0.31) + (0.10 + 0.85) + 1.0 \times 0.50 \\
&= 2.37\ \text{v}
\end{aligned}
$$

CURRENT-VOLTAGE CURVES

It is instructive to consider the relationship between the voltage applied to an electrolytic cell and the current that flows through the cell. We shall find this especially useful in Chapter 11. Let us consider two cases of electrolytic cells: (1) one in which the electrodes are in equilibrium with ions in solution; (2) one in which the electrodes are inert at the start of the electrolysis. As an example of the first type we may take the cell described on page 222:

$$\text{Ag} \mid \text{Ag}^+(1\text{-}M) \parallel \text{Cu}^{++}(1\text{-}M) \mid \text{Cu}$$

If the cell acts as a galvanic cell, the reaction

$$2\,\text{Ag}^+ + \text{Cu} \rightleftharpoons \text{Cu}^{++} + 2\,\text{Ag}$$

tends to occur from left to right. The potential is 0.46 v. Now suppose that a variable external voltage is applied to this cell, with the applied voltage opposing that of the silver-copper cell. If the applied voltage is less than 0.46 v, the cell reaction occurs from left to right according to the equation above. The cell still acts as a galvanic cell. At applied voltages greater than 0.46 v, however, the cell is electrolytic, the reaction above being forced to take place from right to left. Thus copper is plated out at the cathode, and silver dissolves at the anode. At an applied voltage of exactly 0.46 v, no current flows through the cell; this point corresponds to the usual measurement of the cell voltage using a potentiometer. This relation is plotted in Figure 9.2. Below the voltage of 0.46 v, the current is given a negative sign,

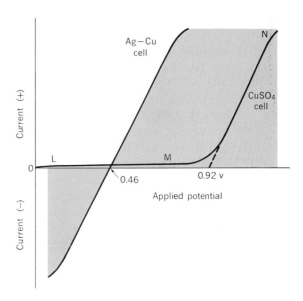

Fig. 9.2. Current-voltage curves (schematic).

and above 0.46 v, it is given a positive sign. The decomposition voltage has a discrete value in this case, 0.46 v. Above this voltage the cell reaction, that is, the reverse of the spontaneous reaction, starts to take place.

As an example of the second type of cell, let us take the cell studied on page 225, that is, a solution of copper sulfate with two platinum electrodes. The cell is

$$Pt, O_2 \mid H_2O + H^+(1\text{-}M) + Cu^{++}(0.1\text{-}M) \mid Cu$$

For the purpose of the present discussion we may disregard the effects of concentration and activation overpotentials, and focus our attention on the equilibrium decomposition potential. We calculated on page 226 that the equilibrium decomposition voltage of this cell is 0.92 v. If we now apply a voltage smaller than 0.92 v, the cell cannot operate as a galvanic cell since there are as yet no products of electrolysis. Hence we expect the current to be zero. Actually, a small "residual current" flows, as shown in Figure 9.2. This current gradually increases along LM as the value of 0.92 v is approached. The curve is rounded near the point M, and then the current increases rapidly along MN.[3] The current I is given by Ohm's law, $I = E/R$, where R is the cell resistance in ohms, and E is the "effective" voltage. The effective voltage is that voltage above the decomposition voltage. The decomposition voltage is taken as the point of intersection of the extrapolated portion of MN with the voltage axis. Note that there is no discrete voltage at which the cell reaction begins, as there was in the case of the silver-copper cell above. A slight reaction is apparently occurring at all voltages along the line LM. This behavior is characteristic of cells in which one or more of the electrodes is not in equilibrium with the solution as the voltage is first applied.

The residual current is sometimes attributed to the electrolysis of trace impurities in the solution. With a dropping mercury electrode (Chapter 11) the residual current is due chiefly to the charging of the mercury-solution interface; the mercury surface increases continuously as the drop grows, and the process is somewhat like charging a condenser of continuously increasing area. With solid electrodes of constant area, it is thought that the first small amounts of metal deposited are not sufficient to cover the electrode surface completely. In the example above, the activity of the copper metal is variable until the voltage nears the equilibrium decomposition value. Here sufficient copper is deposited to cover completely the electrode surface, the electrode becoming a copper electrode and the activity of copper becoming constant (unity). Extensive studies have been made on the deposition of metals from extremely dilute solutions, and evidence has been found to support this explanation.[4] However, a completely satisfactory theoretical treatment of the process has not been made.[5]

---

[3] Actually there is some nonlinearity in the rising portion of the curve, since the oxygen overpotential is a function of current density.

[4] L. B. Rogers, *et al., J. Electrochem. Soc.*, **98**, 447, 452, 457 (1951); *Trans. Electrochem. Soc.*, **95**, 25, 33, 129 (1949).

[5] See *Treatise on Analytical Chemistry*, Part I, Vol. 4, I. M. Kolthoff and P. J. Elving, Eds., Interscience Publishers, Inc., New York, 1963, pp. 2441–2443.

SEPARATIONS BY ELECTROLYSIS

Separation from hydrogen

Let us consider first the factors determining the ease with which a metal can be deposited from aqueous solutions. Usually, acidic solutions are employed and hence the deposition of the metal is, in a sense, a separation from hydrogen ion. Metals fall into two groups, those with greater electron affinities (more positive standard potentials) than hydrogen, and those with lesser affinities. Metals that are more readily reduced than hydrogen ion, such as copper and silver, are readily deposited from acid solution. Many metals that are less readily reduced than hydrogen ion can be deposited from aqueous solution by taking advantage of one or more of the following factors.

Effect of pH. The reduction of hydrogen ion is made more difficult (E made more negative) by lowering the hydrogen ion concentration. For example, the hydrogen-hydrogen ion potential in a solution of pH 7 is

$$E = 0.00 - \frac{0.059}{2} \log \frac{1}{(10^{-7})^2} = -0.413 \text{ v}$$

Many metals are precipitated as hydroxides at this pH. Zinc, however, can be deposited from ammoniacal sulfate or chloride solutions, or from solutions of sodium hydroxide. This is not widely used for determining zinc since the results are often poor.

Activation overpotential. As previously mentioned, the effect of activation overpotential is to require a higher potential to liberate hydrogen than is normally expected. If the overpotential is 1 v, for example, the potential required to liberate hydrogen from a solution that is 1-M in hydrogen ion is -1.00 v. Under these conditions, metals with more positive potentials than this value are reduced more readily than hydrogen ion. One of the reasons for the frequent use of mercury as a cathode material is the fact that hydrogen has a high overpotential on mercury.

Mercury cathode. A metal is more readily reduced, that is, the potential required is less negative, if a mercury cathode is employed and the metal dissolves in the mercury to form an amalgam. The activity of the metal in the mercury is less than the activity of the pure metal (see page 80), and hence the metal has less tendency to go back into solution. In other words, the reaction

$$M^{++} + Hg + 2 \text{ e} \rightleftarrows M(Hg)$$

is made to go further to completion by dilution of the product. The mercury cathode is particularly advantageous for the deposition of active metals from acid solutions, both because of amalgamation, and because of the high over-

potential of hydrogen on mercury. Approximately one-third of the elements
are deposited, either completely or partially, in the mercury cathode. An
excellent discussion of the mercury cathode and its applications is available
in the literature.[6]

Separation of metals by electrolysis

The separation of two metals from one another by depositing one
electrolytically while leaving the other in solution is sometimes a difficult
problem. The difficulty arises in the fact that as one substance is deposited,
the cathode potential[7] becomes more negative and may reach a sufficiently
negative value to deposit the second substance. This effect is illustrated in
the following calculation.

>   **PROBLEM.** On page 228 we calculated a value of 0.31 v for the E_c of a
>   0.1-M copper sulfate solution. Calculate the value of E_c after the concentration
>   of copper is reduced to 10^{-6}-M. (A concentration of 10^{-6}-M is sufficiently small
>   so that under usual experimental conditions, less than 0.1 mg of metal remains
>   in solution.)
>   Since
>
> $$E_c = +0.34 - \frac{0.059}{2} \log \frac{1}{[Cu^{++}]}$$
>
> $$E_c = +0.34 - \frac{0.059}{2} \log \frac{1}{10^{-6}} = +0.16 \text{ v}$$

Thus the cathode potential is 0.15 v more negative than at the start of
the electrolysis, and 0.18 v more negative than the standard potential. If a
second metal whose standard potential is about +0.20 v is also in the
solution, this metal will begin to deposit before the deposition of copper is
complete. It is usually said that the standard potentials of two divalent
metals must differ by at least 0.2 v before the metals can be separated feasibly
by electrolysis. In the case of a univalent cation, the potential becomes 0.36 v
more negative as the concentration of the cation is reduced from unity to
10^{-6}-M.

The separation of two metals, one of which has a greater and the other a
smaller affinity for electrons than hydrogen ion, is experimentally simple.

---

[6] J. A. Maxwell and R. P. Graham, *Chem. Rev.*, **46**, 471 (1950).

[7] It should be noted that the cathode is always negative with respect to the anode
in an electrolytic cell. Since we are following the IUPAC conventions, we write electrons
on the left:

$$Cu^{++} + 2e \; \rightleftarrows \; Cu \qquad E° = +0.34 \text{ v}$$

As electrolysis proceeds, the electrode potential becomes more negative because of the
decrease in the concentration of Cu^{++} ions.

The separation of copper and nickel is a familiar example of this. In acid solution, copper is deposited while nickel remains in solution. The cathode potential becomes more negative as the copper concentration decreases (Figure 9.3), and finally hydrogen is evolved at the cathode. Since the

Fig. 9.3. Change of cathode potential during electrolysis. (After J. J. Lingane, *Electroanalytical Chemistry*, 2nd ed., Interscience Publishers, Inc., New York, 1958.)

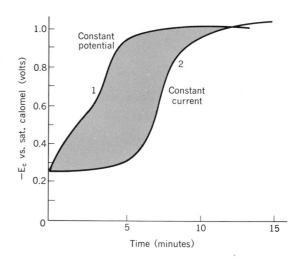

hydrogen ion concentration is quite large and since hydrogen ion is formed at the anode, the potential does not become appreciably more negative. The electrolysis is stopped, and the cathode is weighed to determine the amount of copper. The solution containing nickel is then neutralized with ammonia and the electrolysis continued. The pH is now sufficiently high that nickel is reduced more readily than hydrogen ion. In this manner the two metals are separated and also determined by electrolysis.

In order to separate two metals, both of which have greater (or smaller) electron affinities than hydrogen ion, it is necessary to control the cathode potential to prevent this electrode from becoming sufficiently negative to reduce the second metal before the deposition of the first is complete. The apparatus shown in Figure 9.1 cannot be used. A more elaborate apparatus, described in the next section, is necessary to maintain a good control over the cathode potential.

The action of the hydrogen ion-hydrogen redox system in preventing the cathode potential from becoming very negative is often referred to as "potential buffering." Other redox systems act in the same way and have been employed as "potential buffers." For example, the ferric-ferrous system,

$$Fe^{3+} + e = Fe^{++}$$

limits the cathode potential to a value no more negative than $+0.77$ v if the concentrations of the two ions are equal. If no substance is present that is more readily oxidized than ferrous ion, the latter is oxidized at the anode, and since ferric ion is reduced at the cathode, a fairly constant ratio of the two ions is maintained. Furman and Bricker[8] used the U(IV)-U(III) system as a potential buffer to limit a mercury cathode to about -0.6 v. They separated metals such as cobalt and cadmium from chromium, manganese, and molybdenum.

Complexing agents are sometimes employed to aid in effecting the separation of two metals. The technique of internal electrolysis can also be used. These methods are discussed later.

Controlled potential electrolysis

In carrying out an electrolysis using the apparatus shown in Figure 9.1, there are two techniques that are commonly used. In the *constant potential* method the applied voltage is set at the desired value and left there during the electrolysis. The current is allowed to decrease during the run. In the *constant current* method the applied voltage is increased during the electrolysis in order to maintain the current at the selected value. With both of these techniques the cathode potential rapidly becomes more negative and a second metal may be deposited also. This is illustrated in the following problems.

PROBLEMS. (a) A solution is 0.10-M in silver ion, 0.10-M in cupric ion, and 1.0-M in hydrogen ion. Smooth platinum electrodes are inserted in the solution, the area of the anode being 100 cm^2. Calculate the voltage that must be applied to the electrodes in order for the initial current to be 1.00 amp, if the cell resistance is 0.50 ohm. The solution is stirred, and $\omega_c = 0.10$ v.

The initial products are silver at the cathode, and oxygen at the anode. Then

$$E_c = 0.80 - 0.059 \log \frac{1}{0.10} = 0.74 \text{ v}$$

Since $[H^+] = 1\text{-}M$, $E_a = 1.23$ v (see page 228), $\omega_a = 0.85$ v (Table 9.1) because the current density is 0.01 amp/cm^2. Therefore

$$E_{app} = (1.23 - 0.74) + (0.85 + 0.10) + 1.00 \times 0.50 = 1.94 \text{ v}$$

(b) The voltage is held constant at 1.94 v and the current allowed to decrease to a very low value. Calculate the value of the total cathode potential $(E_c - \omega_c)$, assuming that the IR term is so small that it can be disregarded, and that ω_a is 0.72 v.

The hydrogen ion concentration increases, of course, as the electrolysis proceeds. For example, as the silver is deposited from a 0.1-M solution, the hydrogen ion concentration increases from 1.0-M to 1.1-M

$$2 \text{ Ag}^+ + \text{H}_2\text{O} \rightleftarrows 2 \text{ Ag} + 2 \text{ H}^+ + \tfrac{1}{2} \text{O}_2$$

[8] N. H. Furman and C. E. Bricker, *Analytical Chemistry of the Manhattan Project*, C. J. Rodden, Ed., McGraw-Hill Book Co., Inc., New York, 1950, p. 520.

However, the value of E_a is not changed appreciably by this increase. Therefore

$$1.94 = (1.23 - E_c) + (0.72 + \omega_c)$$
$$E_c - \omega_c = 0.01 \text{ v}$$

This is a hypothetical calculation.[9] The cathode potential never actually reaches this value because copper begins to plate out on the silver when E_c reaches a value of $+0.31$ v (see page 228). The example shows, however, that the constant potential method is not useful for separations of the type we are considering.

If the applied voltage is increased sufficiently to keep the current at a constant value, the potential at the cathode is made more negative through a decrease in the concentration of silver ions and an increase in concentration overpotential. This is illustrated in the following example.

PROBLEM. If the applied voltage in the foregoing problem is increased to 2.44 v in order to maintain the current at 1.00 amp, calculate the value of $(E_c - \omega_c)$. Assume that R is still 0.50 ohm, $E_a = 1.23$ v, and $\omega_a = 0.85$ v.

Then

$$2.44 = (1.23 - E_c) + (0.85 + \omega_c) + 1.00 \times 0.50$$
$$(E_c - \omega_c) = +0.14 \text{ v}$$

Again the cathode potential is sufficiently negative to bring about the reduction of copper, and hence the constant current method is not suitable for effecting the separation.

In Figure 9.3 is shown a plot of the cathode potential against time during an electrolysis of copper from a tartrate solution.[10] Curve 1 was obtained when the applied voltage was held constant at 2.00 v. Curve 2 was obtained when the current was held constant at 1.00 amp. In both cases the cathode potential becomes more negative by about 0.75 v in a short interval of time. The negative drift of the cathode potential is stopped at about -1.00 v by evolution of hydrogen.

It is evident from these examples that the cathode potential must be prevented from becoming so negative if the desired separation is to be achieved. It is necessary to measure the cathode potential with reference to an external electrode throughout the electrolysis. Then the applied voltage can be decreased as the electrolysis proceeds, thereby "controlling" the cathode and preventing its becoming any more negative than is necessary to deposit the desired metal. The apparatus shown in Figure 9.4 can be used for this purpose. The electrolysis circuit is the same as that in Figure 9.1,

---

[9] For a discussion of the practical problems of separating silver and copper electrolytically, see H. Diehl, *Electro-Chemical Analyses with Graded Cathode Potential Control*, G. Frederick Smith Chemical Co., Columbus, Ohio, p. 32.

[10] J. J. Lingane, *Electroanalytical Chemistry*, Interscience Publishers, Inc., New York, 2nd Ed., 1958, p. 217.

but a reference electrode (in this case a saturated calomel) is inserted in the solution and the difference in potential between the reference and cathode is measured with a potentiometer. The tip of the salt bridge from the calomel electrode is placed very close to the cathode and on the side away from the

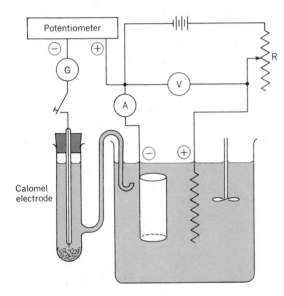

Fig. 9.4. Apparatus for measuring cathode potential.

anode. In this manner the calomel-cathode voltage is affected least by the flow of current between the cathode and anode (*IR* drop).

In using this apparatus, one first selects a "limiting" value of the cathode potential, this value being sufficiently negative to deposit quantitatively one metal without depositing any of the second. The difference between this value and that of the reference electrode is then calculated and this voltage is set on the potentiometer. Then whenever the cathode is at the desired potential the galvanometer does not deflect when the key is tapped. If the cathode is more positive or negative than the desired value, the galvanometer shows a deflection, and the applied voltage can be adjusted accordingly. At the start of the electrolysis the applied voltage is adjusted by the rheostat *R* to give the desired current. The potential of the cathode is much more positive than the limiting value at this time, but it becomes more negative rapidly, as was shown in the example in Figure 9.3. As the limiting potential is approached, careful control is required to prevent the cathode from becoming too negative. This requires the constant attention of the operator if the control is manual. The key is tapped and *R* is adjusted to make the galvanometer deflection zero. A few moments later the key is tapped again and the applied voltage is again decreased to keep the deflection zero.

Electronic instruments, called *potentiostats*, are now available which automatically adjust the applied voltage and the constant attention of the operator is not necessary.[11] Figure 9.5 shows the change of the total applied voltage during the electrolysis of copper from a tartrate solution (see reference 10 and Figure 9.3). A potentiostat was used and the cathode potential was limited to -0.36 v versus a saturated calomel electrode. The potentiostat

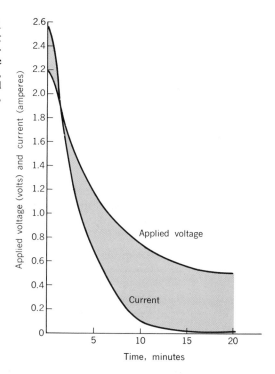

Fig. 9.5. Change in applied voltage and current during controlled potential electrolysis of copper from a tartrate solution. (After J. J. Lingane, *Electroanalytical Chemistry*, 2nd ed., Interscience Publishers, Inc., New York, 1958.)

continuously decreased the applied voltage from 2.2 v to 0.48 v. The current decreased continuously from an initial value of 2.6 amp to 0.03 amp after 17 minutes and finally to less than 0.01 amp after 30 minutes.[12] Under appropriate conditions, the current-time curve obeys the relation[13]

$$i_t = i_0 10^{-kt}$$

where i_0 is the initial current, i_t the current at time t, and k is a constant. On the other hand, the current may remain nearly constant in the early stages of the electrolysis if the cathode potential is only slightly more negative than the equilibrium value. However, if the potential is more negative by at least 0.10 v than the equilibrium value, then the above equation is generally followed from the start of the electrolysis.

[11] See page 8 of reference 9, and page 308 of reference 10.
[12] See page 223 of reference 10.
[13] See page 224 of reference 10.

The following problem illustrates the above procedure.

PROBLEM. The electrolysis described in the problem on page 234 is to be carried out.

(a) Select a reasonable value for the limiting cathode potential so that silver will be quantitatively deposited and copper will not begin to deposit. Calculate the voltage that should be set on the potentiometer (Figure 9.4), a saturated calomel electrode being used as the reference.

(b) Calculate the final value of the applied voltage after the current drops to a sufficiently small value so that the IR term is negligible. Assume that ω_a is about 0.50 v at this time.

(a) When $[Ag^+]$ is reduced to 10^{-6}-M,

$$E_c = +0.80 - 0.059 \log \frac{1}{10^{-6}} = +0.45 \text{ v}$$

There will be a small concentration overpotential even when the current is small. Diehl[9] has measured this and found it to be about 0.07 v. Then

$$E_c - \omega_c = +0.38 \text{ v}$$

Note that the value of E_c for the deposition of copper is $+0.31$ v.

The galvanic cell made up of the cathode-calomel electrodes is

$$\overset{\oplus}{Ag} \,\Big|\, Ag^+ \,\Big\|\, KNO_3 \,\Big\|\, KCl(sat.),\ Hg_2Cl_2 \,\Big|\, \overset{\ominus}{Hg}$$

A potassium nitrate salt bridge is used to prevent chloride ions from entering the solution. Since the potential of the saturated calomel electrode is about $+0.25$ v, the silver electrode is to be 0.13 v more positive than the calomel. Hence the potentiometer is set at 0.13 v, with the positive terminal connected to the cathode, the negative to the calomel electrode.

(b) We know that

$$E_{app} = (E_a - E_c) + (\omega_a + \omega_c) + IR$$

Since $IR = 0$, $E_a = 1.23$, $\omega_a = 0.50$, $E_c = +0.45$, and $\omega_c = 0.07$,

$$E_{app} = 1.35 \text{ v}$$

The initial voltage calculated for this electrolysis was 1.94 v (page 234). In practice, this initial value might be much higher in order to increase the starting current and decrease the time required for electrolysis. The decrease in the applied voltage during the electrolysis would then be much larger than in the example.

Diehl,[9] in his work on the separation of copper and silver, concluded that a simple calculation of E_c using the Nernst equation was insufficient for estimation of the optimum value of the limiting potential. There are two reasons for this. First, the concentration overpotential term must be known and this varies with such factors as the rate of stirring, current, and nature of the surface of the electrode. Second, activities rather than concentrations should be used in the calculations and these are usually not known for the particular experimental conditions. The most reliable procedure is to determine the current-electrode potential curve under the same experimental conditions as will be used in the separation. Lingane[14] discusses this topic in detail.

Complex formation

If a cation forms a complex with an anion or neutral molecule, the concentration of the cation is reduced by addition of complexing agent, and hence the potential required for reduction is made more negative. If one cation forms a much more stable complex than another cation, the potentials required for electrolytic deposition of the two may be made sufficiently different in the presence of the complexing agent for a separation to be feasible. Copper, for example, can be deposited in the presence of antimony by the addition of tartaric acid. The antimony is complexed to a greater extent than is copper. Copper forms very stable cuprous cyanide complexes, and bismuth or cadmium can be deposited from cyanide solutions without the deposition of copper. In Table 9.2 there are listed the standard potentials

EFFECT OF COMPLEX ION FORMATION ON STANDARD POTENTIALS OF SOME CATIONS†		Table 9.2

Reaction	$E°$, v
$Cu^{++} + 2e \rightleftharpoons Cu$	$+0.34$
$Cu(NH_3)_4^{++} + 2e \rightleftharpoons Cu + 4NH_3$	-0.06
$Cd^{++} + 2e \rightleftharpoons Cd$	-0.40
$Cd(NH_3)_4^{++} + 2e \rightleftharpoons Cd + 4NH_3$	-0.61
$Cd(CN)_4^{=} + 2e \rightleftharpoons Cd + 4CN^{-}$	-1.03
$Zn^{++} + 2e \rightleftharpoons Zn$	-0.76
$Zn(NH_3)_4^{++} + 2e \rightleftharpoons Zn + 4NH_3$	-1.03
$Zn(CN)_4^{=} + 2e \rightleftharpoons Zn + 4CN^{-}$	-1.26

† From W. M. Latimer, *Oxidation Potentials*, 2nd Ed., Prentice-Hall, Inc., Englewood Cliffs, N.J., 1952.

of several redox systems, along with the potentials in the presence of complexing agents.

Internal electrolysis

An electrolysis carried out by short-circuiting a galvanic cell is called an *internal electrolysis* or *spontaneous electrogravimetric analysis*. No external potential is needed. A galvanic cell is arranged, using as the anode a metal that is more active (better reducing agent) than the substance to be deposited. Active metals such as magnesium and aluminum are often used as anode

[14] See pages 229–233 of reference 10.

materials. The cathode and anode are usually in separate compartments, separated by a membrane of parchment or collodion.

The process is a simple displacement of the less active by the more active metal. The cell is allowed to discharge until the current falls to zero. The anode and cathode are then at the same potential and hence the cathode potential cannot become any more negative than the anode potential. By choice of the anode material some control of the cathode potential is achieved. This is illustrated by the following example.

PROBLEM. A galvanic cell is set up as follows:

$$Cu \mid Cu^{++}(0.1\text{-}M) \parallel Pb^{++}(0.1\text{-}M) \mid Pb$$

The cell is short-circuited and allowed to run down. Calculate the potential of the copper electrode at the end of the electrolysis. What is the final concentration of copper ions?

The electrode reactions are

$$Cu^{++} + 2\,e \rightleftharpoons Cu \qquad E_1^\circ = +0.34$$
$$Pb^{++} + 2\,e \rightleftharpoons Pb \qquad E_2^\circ = -0.12$$

Thus
$$Cu^{++} + Pb \rightleftharpoons Cu + Pb^{++} \qquad E_{1\text{-}2}^\circ = +0.46\text{ v}$$

The spontaneous reaction is from left to right and, assuming that the reaction is essentially complete, the final concentration of lead ions is 0.2-M. The final potential of the lead electrode is then

$$E_2 = -0.12 - \frac{0.059}{2}\log\frac{1}{0.2} = -0.14\text{ v}$$

Since equilibrium is reached, $E_1 = E_2$, and hence $E_1 = -0.14$ v. The final concentration of copper is given by

$$-0.14 = +0.34 - \frac{0.059}{2}\log\frac{1}{[Cu^{++}]}$$

$$[Cu^{++}] = 4 \times 10^{-17}\text{-}M$$

The deposition of copper is thus complete. No metal that is more active than lead can be precipitated, of course, and so the separation of copper from such metals is easily effected.

The principal disadvantage of the technique of internal electrolysis is that the driving voltage is usually small and hence the rate of deposition is slow. For this reason the resistance of the cell must be low, and the quantity of a metal deposited must be small if the time required for completion of the electrolysis is to be reasonable. The experimental details of cell construction and methodology are discussed in the literature.[15]

[15] H. J. S. Sand, *Analyst*, **55**, 1930; B. L. Clarke, L. A. Wooten, and C. L. Luke, *Ind. Eng. Chem.*, Anal. Ed., **8**, 411 (1936). See also J. J. Lingane, *Electroanalytical Chemistry*, Interscience Publishers, Inc., New York, 2nd Ed., 1958, Chapter XVII.

NATURE OF THE DEPOSIT

When electrolysis is used to determine a cation by deposition of the metal on the cathode, conditions must prevail which assure a fine-grained, adherent deposit. If the deposit is not adherent, some of it will be lost when the electrode is rinsed. Also, flaky or spongy deposits are more likely to contain impurities than a coherent, dense deposit. Many factors influence the nature of the deposit.[16] Some of the more important ones are discussed below.

Evolution of hydrogen. The simultaneous evolution of hydrogen along with the deposition of a metal may lead to the formation of a brittle deposit. This can be avoided by careful control of the cathode potential instrumentally, or by addition of nitric acid. The nitrate ion is reduced to ammonium ion more readily than hydrogen ion is reduced to hydrogen:

$$NO_3^- + 10\ H^+ + 8\ e \rightleftharpoons NH_4^+ + 3\ H_2O$$

Conditions which produce a large decrease in the concentration of the cation at the electrode interface, that is, concentration overpotential, should be avoided. The cathode is then prevented from becoming sufficiently negative for hydrogen to be evolved. Good stirring, either with a rotating cathode or anode, or with an independent stirrer, is used to decrease concentration overpotential.

Current density. Deposition of a metal at a very rapid rate may result in an irregular, spongy deposit. As a general rule, low current densities of the order of 0.01 to 0.1 amp/cm² lead to smooth adherent deposits. Excessively high current densities lead to a depletion of ions in the vicinity of the electrode, that is, concentration overpotential, with the results mentioned above.

Temperature. An increase in temperature decreases the resistance of an electrolytic cell by decreasing the viscosity of the solution and increasing the mobility of the ions. Concentration overpotential is decreased by thermal diffusion and the effectiveness of stirring is increased. On the other hand, activation overpotential is decreased by increased temperature and hence hydrogen may be liberated more readily and lead to brittle deposits.

Concentration of ions. The concentration of the ion being deposited should not be very high since this leads to the formation of a coarsely crystalline deposit. Generally, more satisfactory deposits are obtained from solutions in which the cation concentration is reduced by formation of a complex. Silver, for example, is best deposited from a cyanide solution in which the silver ion concentration is reduced by formation of the $Ag(CN)_2^-$ complex.

[16] See S. Glasstone, *Introduction to Electrochemistry*, D. Van Nostrand Co., Inc., New York, 1942, Chapter 14.

Nature of metal and electrode. Finally, the properties of the metal itself affect the nature of the deposit. Some metals such as copper readily form adherent deposits; others, such as silver, are likely to form spongy deposits. The material on which the metal is deposited has some effect. For example, many metals adhere better to copper than to platinum.

DEPOSITIONS ON THE ANODE

The principal applications of electrolysis in gravimetric analysis involve the reduction of a cation at the cathode of an electrolytic cell. However, there are some examples in which metals are deposited on the anode and weighed. In order for a cation to be deposited on the anode, it must first be oxidized to a higher valence state and then be precipitated by formation of an insoluble compound. The deposition of lead dioxide on the anode is a well-known example of such a reaction. Divalent lead is oxidized to tetravalent lead,

$$Pb^{++} \rightleftarrows Pb^{4+} + 2\ e$$

Then lead dioxide precipitates,

$$Pb^{4+} + 2\ H_2O \rightleftarrows PbO_2 + 4\ H^+$$

The overall reaction, written with electrons on the left, is

$$PbO_2 + 4\ H^+ + 2\ e \rightleftarrows Pb^{++} + 2\ H_2O \qquad E^\circ = +1.46\ v$$

Note that this reaction, in 1-M acid, does not occur as readily as the liberation of oxygen from water ($E^\circ = +1.23$ v). However, the high overpotential normally required for the liberation of oxygen enables the deposition of lead dioxide to occur. Nitric acid is used rather than hydrochloric when it is desired to deposit lead dioxide. Chloride ion acts as an anodic depolarizer; it is more readily oxidized than is lead. If hydrochloric acid is used, lead is deposited on the cathode as the metal rather than on the anode as the dioxide.

COULOMETRIC ANALYSIS

As previously mentioned, the quantity of a substance in solution may sometimes be determined by measuring the number of coulombs required to react with it completely. According to Faraday's second law, one equivalent of any substance requires 96,500 coulombs of electricity for complete reaction. By measuring the number of coulombs required for reaction, the analyst can calculate the number of equivalents of the substance undergoing the reaction. A fundamental requirement for accurate results is a current efficiency of

100%; that is, only a single reaction must occur, with no "side reactions." Two experimental approaches are commonly used in coulometric analysis: The potential of the working electrode is controlled, or a constant current is employed. Further discussion is based on these two approaches.

Controlled potential coulometry

The technique of controlled potential electrolysis has been previously described. As applied here to a cathodic process, a potentiostat is set to give the desired limiting potential, thereby allowing only the desired reaction to take place. The electrolysis is then run until the current falls to zero. No indicator is necessary, the electrolysis ceasing when the current reaches zero.

Hickling[17] introduced this method and it was further developed by Lingane.[18] Lingane used a mercury cathode rather than platinum, since 100% current efficiencies are more easily obtained with this metal. The current actually never reaches a value of zero, but decreases according to the equation (see page 237)

$$i_t = i_0 10^{-kt}$$

The electrolysis is stopped when the ratio of i_t/i_0 is sufficiently small to correspond to essentially complete reaction. In many cases an appreciable current is observed to flow in a solution containing only the supporting electrolyte. This is called the "background current" and when it is observed, the current is allowed to decay until it reaches this value rather than zero.

Coulometers. A number of types of coulometers have been employed in controlled potential coulometry. The silver coulometer is one of the oldest. Silver is deposited on a platinum electrode from a silver nitrate solution and the electrode is then weighed. The oxidation of iodide ion to iodine electrolytically is also a classical example. In this case the iodine is determined by titration. Such methods are usually slow and inconvenient for routine analytical work.

The hydrogen-oxygen coulometer has been widely used because of its simplicity and the fact that it is direct reading. The current is passed through a sodium sulfate solution and the evolved hydrogen and oxygen are collected in a single bulb. The volume is read directly on a buret and the coulombs calculated. The device designed by Lingane[19] can be adapted for measurements from a large number down to about 10 coulombs with an accuracy of ±0.1%.

Other chemical coulometers which have been investigated include the following:

[17] A. Hickling, *Trans. Faraday Soc.*, **38**, 27 (1942).
[18] J. J. Lingane, *J. Am. Chem. Soc.*, **67**, 1916 (1945).
[19] See page 453 of reference 10.

1. The hydrogen-nitrogen coulometer in which hydrazine sulfate is electrolyzed rather than sodium sulfate. Nitrogen rather than oxygen is evolved at the anode, the net coulometer reaction being

$$N_2H_5^+ \rightleftharpoons N_2 + 2\ H_2 + H^+$$

2. A "titration coulometer" in which hydroxide ion is produced by the reaction

$$2\ Ag + 2\ Br^- + 2\ H_2O \rightleftharpoons 2\ AgBr + H_2 + 2\ OH^-$$

The base is titrated with standard acid.

3. A "colorimetric coulometer" in which the color change produced by an electrode reaction is followed using some type of colorimeter. The reduction of permanganate ion is an example.

4. A "coulometric" coulometer in which a metal, such as copper, is plated on a platinum cathode during the electrolysis, and then the amount deposited is determined by an electrolytic "stripping" process. The deposit is oxidized at constant current and the time required is a measure of the number of coulombs used.[20] The stripping process can be made completely automatic.

A number of mechanical and electronic devices which perform the function of integrating the current-time curve have been developed and are described in some detail by Lingane.[21] A very convenient integrator has been described by Wise[22] and by Bard and Solon.[23] This instrument integrates the current-time function by feeding the *IR* drop across a standard resistor into a voltage-to-frequency converter whose pulsed output is counted electronically by a scaling circuit with digital readout. The device is capable of a high degree of accuracy and can be used over a wide range of coulomb values.

Applications. Controlled potential coulometry has been shown by research workers to be applicable to the determination of a wide variety of substances. However, the technique has not been widely applied to practical analyses. The principal reason for this is the availability of techniques such as polarography and voltammetry which can usually be used for the same determination. The latter techniques are generally faster and require simpler apparatus.

Metal ions which have been studied by the controlled potential technique include copper, cadmium, lead, nickel, cobalt, and silver. Successive determinations of several metal ions in a single sample have been carried out. The mercury cathode has been most widely employed in these determinations.

Halide ions have been determined by the reaction

$$Ag + X^- \rightleftharpoons AgX + e$$

[20] V. B. Ehlers and J. W. Sease, *Anal. Chem.*, **26,** 613 (1954).
[21] See pages 340–350 of reference 10, also pages 2500–2503 of reference 5.
[22] E. N. Wise, *Anal. Chem.*, **34,** 1181 (1962).
[23] A. J. Bard and E. Solon, *Anal. Chem.*, **34,** 1181 (1962).

The salts are deposited on a silver anode. The following oxidations at a platinum anode have been shown to be quantitative:

$$Fe^{++} \rightleftarrows Fe^{3+} + e$$

$$H_3AsO_3 + H_2O \rightleftarrows H_3AsO_4 + 2\ H^+ + 2\ e$$

$$2\ Tl^+ + 3\ H_2O \rightleftarrows Tl_2O_3 + 6\ H^+ + 4\ e$$

Quantitative procedures for the determination of a few organic compounds have also been reported.[24]

Constant current coulometry—coulometric titrations

In contrast to controlled potential coulometry, coulometric titrations have been widely applied to practical analyses. The technique employs constant current rather than controlled potential. The number of coulombs used in the reaction is calculated from the value of the current and the time required for complete reaction. Some type of indicator is required to tell when the reaction is complete. The substance determined can react directly at the electrode, or with a reagent which is generated at an electrode.

Direct process. In a *direct* or *primary* process, the substance being determined reacts directly at the cathode or anode of the electrolytic cell. Only a relatively few substances have been determined by a primary coulometric titration. The reason is evident from our previous discussion of the constant current technique. If the unknown substance reacts directly at one of the electrodes, the potential of that electrode changes fairly quickly as the reaction proceeds, and very soon reaches a value where a second reaction begins. The current efficiency is no longer 100% and the analysis is invalidated.

Indirect process. In an *indirect*, or *secondary*, method the substance to be determined reacts with a reagent which is generated by the electrolytic cell. This is a much more practical technique because it is relatively easy to obtain 100% current efficiency. This method is used in practically all coulometric titrations.

The potential of the working electrode is kept fairly constant by maintaining a high concentration of the substance which is undergoing the electrode reaction to generate the titrant. For example, in the coulometric titration of ferrous ion, electrolytically generated ceric ion can be used.[25] Cerous ion, from which ceric ion is generated by anodic oxidation, is present in large concentration, and hence the anode potential is kept from becoming sufficiently positive for oxygen to be evolved. At the start of the electrolysis, ferrous ion is directly oxidized at the anode; then the potential becomes more positive, reaching a value sufficiently positive to oxidize cerous to ceric ion.

---

[24] See page 465 of reference 10, and page 2515 of reference 5.

[25] N. H. Furman, W. D. Cooke and C. N. Reilley, *Anal. Chem.*, **23**, 945 (1951).

The ceric ion in turn oxidizes any remaining ferrous ion in the body of the solution. The quantity of electricity used is the same, of course, as if the ferrous ion alone were directly oxidized at the anode. If the direct oxidation of ferrous ion were attempted, however, oxygen would be liberated before the oxidation of ferrous ion were complete, and the analysis would not be valid.

Experimental techniques. (a) *Detection of the end point.* Since a coulometric titration is no different in principle from any ordinary titration, the same methods for detecting the end point can be employed. Methods which have been used include: (1) visual, (2) potentiometric, (3) amperometric, (4) conductometric, and (5) photometric techniques. We shall not discuss these techniques further except to point out that when the end point method employs electrodes, there are then two pairs of electrodes in the solution. The electrolysis circuit itself contains a *generator* (working) and an *auxiliary* electrode; if the potentiometric technique is used, the other two are the indicator and reference electrodes.

(b) *Cells.* A typical cell[26] in which the generator electrode is a solid metal, such as platinum, is shown in Figure 9.6. The platinum generator electrode

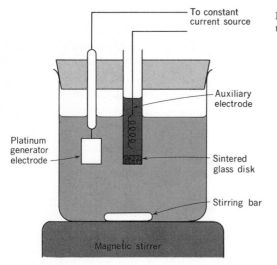

Fig. 9.6. Cell for coulometric titration.

is placed directly in the test solution, but the auxiliary electrode is in a separate tube, the bottom of which is a sintered glass disk. This isolation of the auxiliary electrode prevents products formed here from interfering with the analysis.

(c) *Constant-current sources.* A constant-current source is often referred to as a *galvanostat.* One of the simplest types is a high-voltage battery connected

[26] J. J. Lingane and A. M. Hartley, *Anal. Chim. Acta,* **11**, 475 (1954).

to the electrolysis cell through a large series resistance. More convenient and precise are automatically regulated constant-current supplies. Many of these have been described in the literature and several are available commercially.[27] These are generally electromechanical or electronic regulators. They are capable of maintaining constant currents of 1 to 100 milliamp or more with a precision of ± 0.01 to $\pm 0.1\%$. Several of these are described in detail by Lingane.[28]

(d) *Measurement of time.* It is necessary to measure the time required for a coulometric titration to within $\pm 0.1\%$. The timer should be turned off and on by the same switch that is used to close the electrolysis circuit. If several off-on cycles are employed in detecting the end point, the error in the time measurement accumulates and can become large. Ordinary stopclocks are generally not satisfactory because there is a lag in the starting and stopping of the motor. Clocks with solenoid-operated brakes are precise to ± 0.01 second per operation, but are somewhat higher priced than ordinary laboratory timers.

The accuracy of a timer also depends upon the variation in the frequency of the line voltage. Generally such variations lead to errors of less than 0.2% but the error can be appreciable.[29]

(e) *External generation of titrant.* Occasionally difficulties are encountered in coulometric titrations because of undesired electrode reactions with certain substances in the test solution. For example, the titration of acids with electrolytically generated base involves the formation of hydroxyl ion at the cathode by the reaction

$$2\ H_2O + 2\ e \rightleftharpoons H_2 + 2\ OH^-$$

This cannot be carried out in the presence of substances which reduce more readily at the cathode than hydrogen ion. However, the titrant can be generated outside the titration vessel and allowed to flow into the vessel where it reacts with the substance being determined. A simplified version of the apparatus suggested by DeFord, Johns, and Pitts[30] is shown in Figure 9.7. This illustrates the generation of hydroxide ion at the cathode of the generator cell by electrolysis of a solution such as sodium sulfate. Many other titrants have been generated in a similar fashion.

Applications. As previously mentioned, coulometric titrations have found widespread applications to practical analytical problems. A large number of titrants have been generated[31] for the purpose of carrying out

[27] See page 2497 of reference 5.

[28] See pages 499–511 of reference 10.

[29] See page 511 of reference 10.

[30] D. D. DeFord, J. N. Pitts, and C. J. Johns, *Anal. Chem.*, **23**, 938, 941 (1951); see also N. Bett, W. Cook, and G. Morris, *Analyst*, **79**, 607 (1954).

[31] See page 2516 of reference 5 for an extensive table and pages 536–616 of reference 10 for a detailed discussion of various applications.

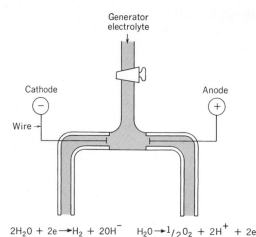

Generator
electrolyte

Fig. 9.7. Cell for external generation of titrant.

Cathode

Anode

Wire

$2H_2O + 2e \rightarrow H_2 + 2OH^-$ $H_2O \rightarrow \frac{1}{2}O_2 + 2H^+ + 2e$

acid-base, redox, precipitation, and complex formation reactions. In principle, any titration that can be carried out by classical volumetric techniques can also be done coulometrically provided the titrant can be generated with 100% current efficiency. Some common reagents such as permanganate and thiosulfate cannot be generated electrolytically, but other reagents, such as bromine, silver(II), and copper(I), which are unstable and difficult to employ as standard solutions can be generated and employed as needed by the coulometric technique.

Coulometric titrations are comparable in precision and accuracy to classical volumetric titrations and are more easily automated. With simple instrumentation the precision in measuring the number of coulombs is of the order of ±0.1% and this can be improved considerably if more sophisticated apparatus is employed. Sample sizes from 100 mg down to a few hundredths of a microgram in volumes of 10 to 50 ml have been employed. Excellent results have even been reported with solution volumes as small as 10 μl.[32]

The reason that the method can be employed for such small samples can be seen as follows:

96,500 coulombs = 1 equivalent

1 coulomb = 0.00001036 equivalent or 10.36 microequivalents

Since a quantity of electricity as small as 0.1 coul can be determined with a precision of about 1 ppt, 1.036 microequivalents can be determined with equal precision. For a substance of equivalent weight 100, this means a precision of about 0.1 μg.

The fact that coulometric titrations are so widely applicable, involve only the fundamental quantities current and time, and are capable of such high precision and accuracy, has led one worker to suggest that the coulomb be

[32] R. Schreiber and W. D. Cooke, *Anal. Chem.*, **27**, 1475 (1955).

adopted as the ultimate primary standard for all titrimetry.[33] Actually the coulomb is based on the atomic weight of silver, and silver, not the coulomb, would be the primary standard. This proposal has not been adopted at this time.

REFERENCES

1. J. J. Lingane, *Electroanalytical Chemistry*, 2nd Ed., Interscience Publishers, Inc., New York, 1958.

2. H. A. Laitinen, *Chemical Analysis*, McGraw-Hill Book Co., Inc., New York, 1960.

3. C. N. Reilley, "Fundamentals of Electrode Processes"; C. N. Reilley and R. W. Murray, "Introduction to Electrochemical Techniques"; N. Tanaka, "Electrodeposition"; D. D. DeFord and J. W. Miller, "Coulometric Analysis"; I. Shain, "Stripping Analysis"; Chapters 42, 43, 48, 49, 50, Part I, Vol. IV, of *Treatise on Analytical Chemistry*, I. M. Kolthoff, P. J. Elving, and E. B. Sandell, Eds., Interscience Publishers, Inc., New York, 1963.

4. L. Meites and H. C. Thomas, *Advanced Analytical Chemistry*, McGraw-Hill Book Co., Inc., New York, 1958.

QUESTIONS

1. Compare the conditions used to obtain pure and filterable precipitates by chemical precipitation (Chapter 15) with conditions used to obtain a good deposit on an electrode by electrolysis.

2. Predict the first products of electrolysis in the following cells. Each electrolyte is $0.1\text{-}M$, and the solution is $0.1\text{-}M$ in H^+.

Cathode	Electrolyte	Anode
Pt	KCl	Pt
Pt	KI	Cu
Cu	CuSO$_4$	Cu
Pt	FeCl$_3$	Hg
Pt	H$_2$C$_2$O$_4$	Pt

3. Is the flow of current through a cell the result or the cause of the electrode reactions? Criticize the statement: "The current was increased until the electrode reactions began."

4. In the lead storage battery one electrode is made of lead, the other of lead dioxide, and the electrolyte is sulfuric acid. Write the reactions which occur at each electrode when the battery acts as a galvanic cell. Which electrode is negative?

[33] P. S. Tutundzic, *Anal. Chim. Acta*, **8**, 182 (1953); P. S. Tutundzic and S. Mladenovic, *Anal. Chim. Acta*, **8**, 184 (1953).

5. The Edison cell has electrodes of iron and nickel oxide, sodium hydroxide being the electrolyte. The cell reaction during discharge is

$$Fe + Ni_2O_3 + 3 H_2O \rightleftarrows Fe(OH)_2 + 2 Ni(OH)_2$$

Which electrode is the cathode? Which is the negative electrode?

6. Distinguish between activation and concentration overpotential. Under what conditions are these terms negligible?

7. Explain clearly the reason for the two different types of current-voltage curves shown in Figure 9.2.

8. Explain how some metals which are more active than hydrogen can be quantitatively removed by electrolysis even from acidic solutions.

9. Constant potential electrolysis can be used to separate copper and nickel in an acidic solution of the two metals, but it cannot be used to separate silver and copper. Explain the difference.

10. Compare the problem of separating two metals (same side of hydrogen) by electrolysis with that of separating two metals which form insoluble hydroxides by fractional precipitation.

11. Explain what is meant by a potential buffer.

12. Explain why an indirect coulometric titration is more practical than a direct one.

13. Suppose some H_2O_2 is formed at the anode of a hydrogen-oxygen coulometer and is then reduced at the cathode. Does the coulometer give high, low, or correct results? Explain.

14. The potentiometric titration curve obtained for the oxidation of ferrous ion with electrolytically generated ceric ion (as described in this chapter) is asymmetrical in contrast to the symmetrical curve ordinarily obtained (Chapter 5). Explain.

PROBLEMS

(0.059 may be rounded off to 0.06 for convenience.)

1. Calculate the equilibrium decomposition voltages of the following electrolytes (all with platinum electrodes): (a) 1.0-M $HClO_4$ (b) 0.10-M $HClO_4$ (c) 0.010-M $HClO_4$

2. What potential must be applied to the electrodes in part (a) of the previous problem to obtain an initial current of 0.10 amp if the cell resistance is 0.20 ohm, and the cathode and anode are each 100 cm² and are platinized platinum?

3. Calculate the equilibrium decomposition voltages of the following cells:

(a) $\overset{\ominus}{Pt} \mid Cu^{++}(1\text{-}M) + H^+(0.1\text{-}M) + H_2O \mid \overset{\oplus}{Pt}$

(b) $\overset{\ominus}{Pt} \mid Na^+(0.1\text{-}M) + H^+(0.1\text{-}M) + Cl^-(0.2\text{-}M), AgCl \mid \overset{\oplus}{Ag}$

(c) $\overset{\ominus}{Pt} \mid Ag^+(0.2\text{-}M) + H^+(0.1\text{-}M) \mid \overset{\oplus}{Ag}$

(d) $\overset{\ominus}{Pt} \mid Ag^+(0.1\text{-}M) + H^+(0.01\text{-}M) \mid \overset{\oplus}{Pt}$

4. What is the value of the equilibrium decomposition voltage of the cell in 3(d) after the electrolysis has proceeded until the concentration of Ag^+ has been reduced to 0.00010-M? Note increase in H^+ concentration.

5. (a) What voltage must be applied to a pair of smooth platinum electrodes (each 50 cm²) immersed in a 0.010-M solution of $AgNO_3$ in order for the initial current to be 0.50 amp? The hydrogen ion concentration is 1-M, the cell resistance 0.30 ohm, and the overpotential term at the cathode can be assumed to be 0.10 v.
(b) Repeat the calculation if the initial current is to be 5.0 amp.

6. What is the minimum concentration to which zinc can be reduced by electrolysis from a solution of pH 4.30, if the activation overpotential term for hydrogen is 0.74 v?

7. A 0.10-M solution of $CuSO_4$ is electrolyzed between platinum electrodes.
(a) Assuming that the overpotential term for hydrogen is negligible, what is the concentration of cupric ions when hydrogen begins to be liberated at the cathode? The original hydrogen ion concentration is 0.10-M.
(b) Repeat the calculation for the electrodeposition of silver.

8. (a) Theoretically, what must be the pH of a solution so that the concentration of nickel can be reduced by electrolysis to 10^{-6}-M before evolution of hydrogen (no overpotential)?
(b) Repeat the calculation for zinc.
(c) Repeat for aluminum.

9. (a) Repeat the previous problem for a case where the overpotential of hydrogen is 0.30 v.
(b) What overpotential would be required for the above electrolysis of aluminum from a solution of pH 10?

10. The standard potential for the reduction of a metal ion M^{++} to M is -1.50 v. Calculate the pH of a solution so that the concentration of M^{++} can be reduced to 10^{-6}-M before evolution of hydrogen for the following conditions:
(a) no overpotential,
(b) 1.0-v overpotential,
(c) mercury cathode, 1.0-v overpotential and activity of the metal in the amalgam $= 10^{-6}$.

11. If a cathode having a potential of $+0.52$ v is actually in equilibrium with a 0.10-M solution of Cu^{++}, what is the activity of the metallic copper on the surface of the electrode?

12. In a controlled potential electrolysis of a silver solution the cathode potential reaches a value of $+0.10$ v when the silver ion concentration in the body of the solution is still 10^{-3}-M.
(a) What is the overpotential term at the cathode?
(b) What is the concentration of silver ions actually in equilibrium with the electrode surface?

13. What should be the ratio of the concentrations of ferric to ferrous ions in a potential buffer in order to limit the cathode potential to $+0.71$ v?

14. If an internal electrolysis is run using an anode of magnesium, to what concentration can cupric ion be reduced theoretically if the final magnesium concentration is 0.10-M? What would prevent the copper from reaching such a low value?

15. The concentration of a hydrochloric acid solution is determined by coulometric titration using a platinum cathode and a silver anode. What are the products at the two electrodes? If 10.00 ml of acid solution is electrolyzed and a weight of 0.2158 g of silver is deposited in a silver coulometer, what is the molarity of the acid?

16. If the titration in problem 15 is performed at constant current, what must the current be in order for the reaction to be complete in 10 min?

17. The hydroxide ion produced by a titration coulometer (page 244) is titrated with standard acid. What must the molarity of the acid be if 1.000 ml corresponds to 1.000 coul?

18. Calculate the volume of hydrogen plus oxygen (STP) that should be produced per coulomb in a hydrogen-oxygen coulometer. What volume would this be if saturated with water vapor at 25°C and 740 mm pressure?

19. It is desired to reduce the concentration of lead ions in a solution to 10^{-6}-M by plating out PbO_2 on the anode from a solution which is 2.0-M in hydrogen ion. What must be the overpotential of oxygen in order for this to be possible?

20. Calculate the equilibrium decomposition voltage of a solution containing $Cu(NH_3)_4^{++}$, NH_4^+, and NH_3, each at a concentration of 0.10-M. Oxygen is liberated at the anode.

21. (a) Theoretically, to what concentration can Cu^{++} be reduced by electrolysis before starting the deposition of cadmium from a 0.10-M solution of Cd^{++}? (Assume no evolution of H_2.)

(b) Repeat the calculation for $Cu(NH_3)_4^{++}$ in the presence of 0.10-M $Cd(NH_3)_4^{++}$, assuming the final concentration of NH_3 to be 1-M. Why is this value larger than that of part (a)?

10 *chapter*

Other Electrical Methods
of Analysis

In previous chapters we have discussed potentiometry and electrolysis as these methods are applied to quantitative analysis. Both of these techniques are in a sense "classical," having been employed in analytical chemistry for many years.

Today the field of electrochemistry is a vast one, with a wide variety of techniques and applications employing complicated and sophisticated instrumentation. Some of the techniques have analytical applications, while others are of interest primarily in providing fundamental information on the nature of electrode processes. A detailed study of the entire field is obviously beyond the scope of an introductory text. Excellent treatments can be found in the book of Delahay[1] and in the chapters by Reilley and by Reilley and Murray[2]

---

[1] P. Delahay, *New Instrumental Methods in Electrochemistry*, Interscience Publishers, New York-London, 1954.

[2] I. M. Kolthoff and P. J. Elving, Eds., *Treatise on Analytical Chemistry*, Part I, Vol. 4, Interscience Publishers, Inc., New York, 1963, Chapters 42 and 43.

in a recent treatise. It is of interest, however, to examine here the entire field very briefly in order to gain some appreciation of the areas of current research. This summary could have been considered, perhaps more logically, at the outset of our discussion of electrochemistry. It is placed here, however, because of its complexity. It is hoped that the student will be better able to comprehend some of the newer electrochemical techniques after his introduction to the more classical topics of potentiometry and electrolysis. Following this chapter, we shall examine in some detail only a few topics which have widespread application to analysis and which are not beyond the level and purpose of this text.

CLASSIFICATION OF ELECTROCHEMICAL METHODS

The following discussion is based on the classification scheme of Reilley and Murray[2] with appropriate simplifications. Let us consider a schematic diagram (Figure 10.1) of the usual apparatus for electrochemical measurements.

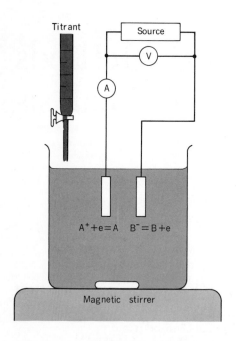

Fig. 10.1. Schematic apparatus for electrochemical measurements.

Some device for applying a potential across a pair of electrodes is provided, with current and potential measuring devices. A titrant may be supplied from a buret, and some provision is made for stirring the solution. Now consider the wide variety of operations that the experimenter can employ:

He can stir the solution or not, make a single measurement or add titrant and make successive measurements, use alternating or direct current, control the potential and measure the current, control the current and measure the potential, use various voltage-time functions (e.g., linear or sinusoidal), employ sweep techniques, exhaustively electrolyze the solution, employ various types of electrodes (e.g., solid metals or dropping mercury). The potential or current excitations (i.e., actions which disturb the electrochemical system from its initial state) applied to a working electrode may have a wide variety of shapes as a function of time.[2] The nature of the solvent and composition of the solution can be varied; the electroactive species in solution can be molecular or ionic. It is thus no wonder that many techniques have been developed and that the nomenclature is frequently confusing.

There are two fundamental processes which occur in electrochemical systems: electron-transfer reactions, and mass transfer (or mass transport). An electron-transfer reaction is one in which oxidation or reduction occurs at the electrode-solution interface; for example, in the solution of Figure 10.1 it could be

$$A^+ + e \rightleftarrows A$$

and

$$B^- \rightleftarrows B + e$$

By mass transfer is meant the process by which the reacting species is brought up to the electrode surface where electron transfer can take place. There are three methods for accomplishing mass transport: *migration, diffusion,* and *convection.* In migration, the driving force causing the species to approach (or leave) the electrode surface is a *potential gradient*, with a positively charged species being attracted to the negative electrode, and negatively charged species to the positive electrode. In diffusion, the driving force is a *concentration gradient;* such a gradient is set up during electrolysis between the bulk of the solution and the electrode surface (see page 227). In convection, the driving force is the stirring of the solution which brings the species up to the surface of the electrode.

Using the above processes, plus the experimental conditions of potential or current control, we can classify[2] electrochemical methods in a fairly meaningful manner as outlined in Table 10.1.

I. Electron transfer not important

This situation is encountered in *conductometric* and *dielectric constant* measurements. In conductance measurements the electrodes are placed in contact with the solution and alternating potential is applied. The use of alternating currents of fairly high frequencies prevents polarization at the electrode surfaces. The limiting factor in the current-voltage relationship is attributed to the rate of migration of ions and the displacement of charge in the bulk of the solution. Since the conductance of a solution varies with concentration

Table   CLASSIFICATION OF ELECTROCHEMICAL
10.1   METHODS

I. Electron Transfer Not Important
  A. Conductometric Titrations
  B. High Frequency Titrations
  C. Dielectric Constant Measurements
II. Electron Transfer Involved
  A. Zero Faradaic Current
    1. Direct Potentiometry
    2. Potentiometric Titrations
  B. Net Faradaic Current
    1. Mass Transport by Convection-Diffusion (Stirring)
      a. Voltammetry
      b. Potentiometric Titrations with Polarized Electrodes
      c. Amperometric Titrations
      d. Electrolysis
        i. Electrogravimetry
        ii. Coulometry
        iii. Stripping Analysis
    2. Mass Transport by Diffusion (No Stirring)
      a. Potential Held Constant
        i. Chronoamperometry
          1. Polarography
      b. Potential Varied Linearly with Time
        i. Chronoamperometry
        ii. Oscillographic Polarography
      c. Potential Varied Periodically with Time
        i. a-c Polarography
        ii. Square Wave Polarography

of a particular electrolyte, the property has obvious analytical applications. In so-called *high-frequency* techniques, the electrodes are not in intimate contact with the solution but are separated by the walls of the containing vessel. Measurements based upon dielectric polarization may be used for analytical purposes, although the property, like conductance, is not specific for a given molecule in the presence of others.[3]

II. Electron transfer involved

At electrode-solution interfaces the processes important in current flow are electron-transfer reactions and the charging of the electrical double layer.[4] The former is referred to as *Faradaic* current, the latter *non-Faradaic*

---

[3] See reference 2, Chapter 52.

[4] A potential difference always occurs at the interface of two phases containing ions, polar molecules, or electrons; we encountered an example of this on page 127 for a strip of zinc immersed in a solution containing zinc ions. Phase boundary potentials are complicated by the fact that they are dependent upon the state of the surfaces of the two phases, and the relation between surface properties and the potential difference has been studied extensively.

A positively charged mercury surface immersed in a solution of sodium chloride current. By control of the current flowing in the cell, the net Faradaic current can be made zero. In the ideal case, equilibrium exists and it may be said that principles of thermodynamics govern the potential of the cell. [For example, the Nernst equation is obeyed (see page 133).] Since the net current is zero, the method of mass transport is not important. In cells with net Faradaic current flow, the behavior of the system is governed by kinetics, i.e., the rate factors of the various steps in the process. The overall rate may be governed by the rate of mass transport and/or the rate of the electron transfer process itself. Hence we can further subdivide possible processes as follows:

A. Zero Faradaic current. This is the technique known as *potentiometry* which we have discussed in detail in Chapter 8. As we saw in that discussion, this technique is further subdivided into (1) *direct potentiometry*, which utilizes single measurements of a cell potential to determine concentration, and (2) *potentiometric titrations*, which employ several measurements of potential during a titration of the species whose concentration is of interest. In such measurements we have seen that the potential of the cell is related to the concentration of some species through the Nernst equation.

B. Net Faradaic current. As mentioned above, when a net Faradaic current flows through a cell the method of mass transport is important. It is convenient to divide processes further into two classes depending upon the method: (1) convection-diffusion, which prevails when the solution is stirred, and (2) diffusion, which prevails when the solution is not stirred.

1. *Mass transport by convection-diffusion.*

(a) *Voltammetry.* The experimenter can now control the potential of his cell and measure the current, or vice versa. A study of the current-potential relationships of electrode reactions in stirred solutions is referred to as *voltammetry.* The current obtained as the potential is increased approaches a maximum or *limiting* value and it is possible to relate this current to concentration. In the experimental determination of unknown concentrations, the relationship between concentration and the limiting current is determined using standard solutions and identical experimental conditions.

(b) *Potentiometric titrations with polarized electrodes.* Another type of experiment that can be performed with net Faradaic current while the solution is stirred is as follows: A small constant current can be imposed on the electrodes and the potential difference measured as the concentration of one of the species in solution is lowered by titration. The potential changes abruptly at the equivalence point, rising to a maximum value.[5] The technique is referred to as a potentiometric titration with polarized electrodes, and can be

---

attracts negatively charged chloride ions to form a double layer. If the positive charge on the mercury is decreased, some chloride ions leave the surface and this redistribution of ions leads to a net flow of current. The process is similar to charging or discharging a capacitor. See page 2127 of reference 2 for a complete discussion.

[5] C. N. Reilley, W. D. Cooke, and N. H. Furman, *Anal. Chem.*, **23**, 1223, 1226 (1951).

employed with either one or both of the electrodes polarized. The procedure is not widely used, but it does have an advantage in cases of slow irreversible reactions. The use of polarized electrodes causes a steady potential to be reached much faster than is the case when the titration is performed at zero current (II,A above).

(c) *Amperometric titrations.* Instead of measuring potential, as in the preceding case, the experimenter can apply a constant potential across the electrodes and measure the current as the concentration of one of the species in solution is lowered by titration. Such titrations are called amperometric titrations and can be performed with one or both of the electrodes polarized.[6] The current measured may be the limiting current of the species being titrated, the titrant, and/or the product produced in the reaction. The so-called *dead-stop* titration, first studied many years ago,[7] is such an amperometric titration with two polarized electrodes. The name apparently arose from the fact that the titration was carried out until the current dropped to zero.

(d) *Electrolysis.* Analytical techniques normally falling under this heading are performed with net Faradaic current and with stirring to yield mass transport by convection-diffusion. They are characterized normally by nearly complete exhaustion of the electroactive species. We have discussed this topic in detail in Chapter 9, where it was pointed out that two techniques are commonly employed: *electrogravimetry* and *coulometry*. We shall not discuss these topics further, but it should be pointed out that a third technique, called *stripping analysis*, is usually included under this same heading. This technique consists of two separate and distinct operations: exhaustive electrolysis to deposit the desired material on the working electrode, followed by dissolution or stripping of the deposit from the electrode. A coulometric measurement is made during the stripping step. The advantages of the method are primarily in the area of trace analysis.[8]

2. *Mass transport by diffusion.*

When the solution is not stirred, a concentration gradient develops between the electrode interface and the bulk of the solution and mass transport occurs via diffusion. It is easier to treat diffusion than convection-diffusion, and diffusion processes have a more solid theoretical foundation. As in case (1) above, either the current or potential can be controlled. Since the response in an unstirred solution is *transient* in nature, it is customary to apply a constant potential or current and measure the other as a function of time. Sweep techniques can be employed and are therefore considered under this heading.

---

[6] This is really an example of "concentration polarization," or better, "concentration overpotential." See page 227.

[7] C. W. Foulk and A. T. Bawden, *J. Am. Chem. Soc.*, **48**, 2045 (1926); see also R. G. Van Name and F. Fenwick, *J. Am. Chem. Soc.*, **47**, 19 (1925).

[8] See reference 2, Chapter 50.

(a) *Potential held constant.* If the potential is held constant at a value sufficient to cause an electrode reaction to occur, and the current is measured as a function of time, the technique is referred to as *chronoamperometry.* The current may be governed by the rate of the electron-transfer reaction, the rate of diffusion, or some combination of the two. The technique is rarely used for analysis but is useful in studies of electrode kinetics. On the other hand, the technique known as *polarography* has been widely used in analysis. It is a special case of chronoamperometry using the *dropping mercury electrode.* The current decays with time regardless of the type of electrode because of the progressive depletion of the electroactive species at the electrode-solution interface. With a dropping mercury electrode, however, the increase in surface area and the movement of the surface toward the bulk of the solution causes a continuous increase in the current as the drop grows. Fall of the drop stirs the solution sufficiently to destroy any concentration gradient. As a result current-time curves remain about the same for successive drops and the *average* current appears steady. Hence current-potential curves are usually recorded and the limiting, or diffusion, current is related to the concentration of the electroactive species in the solution. The polarographic technique is discussed in some detail in the next chapter.

(b) *Potential varied linearly with time.* This technique is still *chronoamperometry* but with *potential sweep.* The current rises to a peak value and as the depletion of the electroactive species occurs at the electrode surface the current slowly decreases. The peak current is related to the concentration and is more sensitive than the polarographic technique. *Oscillographic polarography* falls under the present heading. A potential sweep is performed at the dropping mercury electrode at such a rate that the area of the electrode does not change appreciably. An oscilloscope is not necessary to record the current-potential curve, but it was used in early work and the name has remained.

(c) *Potential varied periodically with time. Alternating current* and *square-wave* polarography fall in this category. An a-c or a square-wave signal is superimposed on the applied d-c potential and the a-c current is recorded as a function of the applied d-c potential. A peak current is obtained in a-c polarography and it is proportional to the bulk concentration of the electroactive species.

(d) *Current held constant.* If a constant current is suddenly caused to flow in an unstirred solution and the potential of the working electrode is measured as a function of time, the technique is called *chronopotentiometry.* At the electrode surface the concentration of the most readily reduced (or oxidized) species decreases with time and eventually drops to zero. Some other electrode reaction must occur to support the imposed current, and the electrode potential shifts to that of the new reaction. The time at which the potential shifts is called the *transition time,* τ. The Sand equation[9] states that

---

[9] See reference 2, page 2210.

the square root of the transition time is proportional to the concentration of the substance undergoing electrolysis. The shape of the potential-time curve (*chronopotentiogram*) is similar to that of an ordinary potentiometric titration curve. This is not surprising when it is noted that in chronopotentiometry, one is essentially titrating with electrons the electroactive species in the volume element adjacent to the electrode. When the concentration in this volume element drops to zero, the potential shifts to that of the new reaction, just as in a potentiometric titration.

REFERENCES

1. C. N. Reilley, "Fundamentals of Electrode Processes," and C. N. Reilley and R. W. Murray, "Introduction to Electrochemical Techniques," Chapters 42 and 43, Part I, Vol. IV, of *Treatise on Analytical Chemistry*, I. M. Kolthoff, P. J. Elving, and E. B. Sandell, Eds., Interscience Publishers, Inc., New York, 1963.
2. P. Delahay, *New Instrumental Methods in Electrochemistry*, Interscience Publishers, Inc., New York-London, 1954.

11 *chapter*

Polarography and Amperometric Titrations

POLAROGRAPHY

In the previous chapter it was pointed out that *polarography* is a special case of *chronoamperometry* in which the dropping mercury electrode is employed. The technique is one in which mass transport takes place by diffusion. The process is classified among those in which the voltage is held constant, although a current-voltage curve, called a *polarogram*, is frequently recorded in practice. A limiting (diffusion) current is obtained which is proportional to the concentration of the electroactive species in the bulk of the solution. Analytical applications are widespread and the technique is considered to be of major importance in quantitative analysis. The originator of the technique, Jaroslav Heyrovsky, received the Nobel Prize for this work.

Potential requirements

A typical experimental set-up for determining a polarogram is shown in Figure 11.1. The cathode is a dropping mercury electrode, a narrow glass capillary from which very small drops of mercury grow and fall. This is a *micro*electrode, in contrast to the anode, which is a calomel electrode of

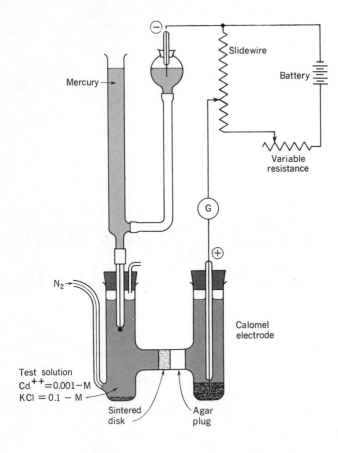

Mercury →

Slidewire

Battery

Variable resistance

G

(+)

N$_2$ →

Calomel electrode

Test solution
Cd^{++}=0.001-M
KCl = 0.1 − M

Sintered disk

Agar plug

Fig. 11.1. Apparatus for polarography using *H*-cell with dropping mercury electrode.

normal, or *macro*, size. The test solution contains a cadmium salt at low concentration (0.001-*M*) and potassium chloride at a concentration of 0.1-*M*. The solution is not stirred. The voltage applied to the cell is varied by use of a calibrated slide wire, and the current is read on a galvanometer. These conditions should be contrasted with those used in ordinary electrogravimetric methods discussed in Chapter 9.

We have seen that the voltage applied to an electrolytic cell is given by

$$E_{app} = (E_a - E_c) + (\omega_a + \omega_c) + IR$$

Let us consider the magnitude of these terms when the voltage applied is sufficiently large to cause cadmium to be reduced at the cathode. Because the cathode is very small, the current is correspondingly small, normally only a few microamperes. Thus, unless the cell resistance is very large, the IR term is negligible. For example, if the value of I is 5 μamp and R is as large as 100 ohms, the IR term is only 0.5 mv.

As cadmium is reduced at the cathode, mercury reacts with chloride ions at the anode to produce mercurous chloride. The reaction, written with electrons on the left, is

$$Hg_2Cl_2 + 2\ e \rightleftarrows 2\ Hg + 2\ Cl^- \qquad E_a = +0.25\ v\ (sat.)$$

Since such a small current flows, the concentration of chloride ions is not changed appreciably and hence the term E_a remains constant. The overpotential term at the anode, ω_a, is negligibly small since the current is small and the electrode is large. Hence the total anode potential, $E_a + \omega_a$, is constant at +0.25 v.

It is apparent that any change in the applied voltage must be reflected in a corresponding change in the total cathode potential, $E_c - \omega_c$. In our present example,

$$E_{app} = 0.25 - (E_c - \omega_c) + 0$$

if the applied voltage is increased by, say, 0.20 v, the term $E_c - \omega_c$ becomes 0.20 v more negative. In other words the applied voltage is a direct measure of the cathode potential. In polarography, voltages are commonly referred to the saturated calomel electrode rather than to the hydrogen electrode. Thus an applied voltage of 1.00 v usually means that the cathode is -1.00 v with respect to the saturated calomel electrode.

The polarogram

The current-voltage curve, or polarogram, for the electrolysis being considered is shown in Figure 11.2. Along LM a small residual current flows. Near M the decomposition voltage of the cell is reached and the current increases rapidly with further increase in voltage. The cell reaction that is occurring is

$$Cd^{++} + 2\ Hg + 2\ Cl^- \rightleftarrows Cd + Hg_2Cl_2$$

The cadmium is dissolved in the mercury as an amalgam. Along the portion of the curve MN the concentration of cadmium ions at the electrode interface drops to a smaller value than the concentration in the body of the solution, since the solution is not stirred. This difference in concentration (concentration gradient) causes cadmium ions to move toward the cathode by the process of diffusion. The rate of diffusion is proportional to the concentration gradient,

$$\text{Rate of diffusion} \propto [Cd^{++}]_{bulk} - [Cd^{++}]_{interface}$$

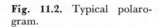

Fig. 11.2. Typical polaro-gram.

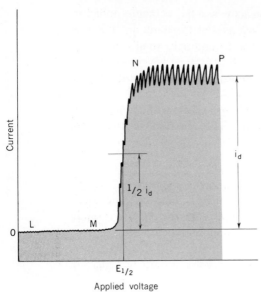

As point N is approached, the concentration of cadmium ions at the interface falls to a very low value, and between N and P the concentration is so small it can be considered negligible. Hence, the rate of diffusion becomes constant and is given by

$$\text{Rate of diffusion } = k_1[\text{Cd}^{++}]_{\text{bulk}}$$

where k_1 is the proportionality constant. Since the current is proportional to the rate of diffusion,

$$i_d = k[\text{Cd}^{++}]$$

where i_d is the so-called *diffusion current* and $[\text{Cd}^{++}]$ represents the concentration in the body of the solution. The current, i_d, is sometimes referred to as a diffusion-controlled limiting current. The current oscillates from practically zero to a maximum value as the mercury drop grows and falls (Figure 11.2). The average current is readily determined by damping the galvanometer.

Since the concentration of cadmium ions can be determined from the value of the diffusion current, the method is of obvious interest to analytical chemists. Much of our later discussion will be devoted to the techniques used to convert current measurements into concentration.

The dropping mercury electrode

As previously mentioned, the microelectrode used in polarography is the dropping mercury electrode (abbreviated DME). Mercury is forced through a very fine capillary from which small drops grow and fall at regular intervals of about 3 to 5 sec. The drop time can be adjusted by varying the height of the mercury reservoir (Figure 11.1).

There are several advantages that the DME possesses over a solid micro-electrode, such as platinum. In the first place, the surface exposed to the solution is reproducible, smooth, and continually renewed. This makes it possible to obtain highly reproducible current-voltage curves, independent of the previous use of the electrode. Second, the DME furnishes ideal conditions for obtaining a completely diffusion-controlled limiting current. The diffusion layer remains quite thin because of the periodic dropping of the mercury which stirs the solution sufficiently to destroy the concentration gradient. The current does tend to decrease with time, of course, as the concentration of the electroactive species decreases at the mercury-solution interface. This is more than compensated, however, by the increase in surface area and the movement of the surface toward the bulk of the solution as the drop grows. The current falls when the drop falls and hence an oscillation is observed. This oscillation is so uniform, however, that the average current can be observed as readily as a steady current. The average current assumes a steady, reproducible value very quickly as the applied voltage is changed. With solid electrodes the current does not become steady until sufficient time has elapsed to establish a steady state of diffusion and convection.

The third advantage of the DME results from the high overpotential of hydrogen on mercury and the fact that many metals form amalgams with mercury, thereby decreasing the tendency of the metal to redissolve (see page 231). Hence, it is possible to reduce from aqueous solutions many metals which are more active than hydrogen. For example, polarograms have been obtained even for the alkali metals. Mercury is not equally useful as an anode material, since it is rather readily oxidized. An unlimited current increase, caused by the anodic dissolution of mercury, occurs about $+0.4$ v vs. SCE. A platinum anode can be used up to the potential at which water is oxidized (about $+1.4$ v vs. SCE).

The residual current

As seen in Figure 11.2 a small residual current flows along LM as the applied voltage is increased. This current may be regarded as the sum of two components: (1) a faradaic current resulting from the electrolysis of trace impurities in a solution, and (2) a "charging" or "capacity" current resulting from the charging of the mercury drop and the electrical double layer around its surface (Chapter 9). The faradaic current can be minimized by purification of the reagents employed in the test solution. The charging current cannot be eliminated. It can be either positive or negative, depending upon the potential at the mercury surface. At potentials more positive than about −0.5 v vs. SCE, the mercury surface is positively charged with respect to the solution. At potentials more negative than −0.5 v, the surface is negatively charged. At approximately −0.5 v (the exact value depends upon the nature and concentration of ions in the solution), the mercury surface is uncharged and this point is called the *electrocapillary zero* of mercury. The interfacial tension at the mercury-solution interface is a maximum at the electrocapillary zero (Figure 11.3), since less work is required to increase the area of the interface if the surface carries a charge.

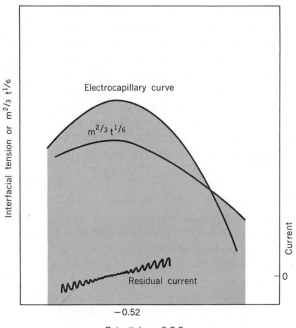

Fig. 11.3. Elctrocapillary curve for mercury.

Consider the situation at a potential more positive than −0.5 v. As the area of the drop grows, electrons flow from the mercury reservoir (Figure 11.1) toward the calomel electrode. This is conventionally called a negative, or anodic, current since electrons are flowing in the same direction as if an oxidation were occurring at the mercury drop. At a potential more negative than the electrocapillary zero, the growth of the drop leads to a flow of electrons into the mercury from the calomel electrode. A current in this direction is conventionally called a positive, or cathodic, current, since electrons are flowing in the same direction as if a reduction were occurring at the mercury drop.

In Figure 11.3 is plotted the variation of the charging current with the potential of the DME. It can be seen that on the positive side of the electrocapillary zero, the current is anodic during the growth of the drop. As the potential of the mercury is made more negative, this current decreases, passes through zero at the electrocapillary zero, and becomes cathodic at more negative potentials.

The migration current

It has been pointed out previously that there are three methods for accomplishing mass transport: migration, diffusion, and convection. In polarography, conditions are adjusted so that the limiting current is controlled principally by diffusion. Convection is minimized by not stirring the solution, and the migration current is minimized by the addition of a *supporting electrolyte*, the potassium chloride in Figure 11.1. The migration current results from the attraction of positive ions by the cathode and negative ions by the anode. All ions in the solution contribute to the migration current, the fraction of current carried depending upon the concentration and mobility of the particular ion. In the absence of KCl, cadmium ions reach the electrode by migration and diffusion and the limiting current is about twice as large as the diffusion current alone. Addition of KCl lowers the limiting current, which becomes constant when the concentration of this electrolyte is about 50 times that of the cadmium. Potassium ions are attracted to the cathode but do not contribute to the current because they are not reduced at the potential required to reduce cadmium ions. The latter ions contribute negligibly to the conduction through the solution and hence reach the cathode by the force of diffusion alone.

The supporting electrolyte also serves to lower the resistance of the cell, thereby decreasing the IR drop to a very low value. As a general rule, polarographic conditions call for the supporting electrolyte to be 50 to 100 times the concentration of the reducible ion.

In the reduction of anions, such as iodate or chromate, the limiting current in the absence of supporting electrolyte is smaller than the diffusion current obtained after excess supporting electrolyte is added. The reason for this is that the direction of the electrical field is such that anions are repelled from the electrode, thereby lowering the current. In oxidation processes of cations and anions, the effects just described are reversed.

The diffusion current

In spite of the complex geometry of the DME, theoretical treatment of the diffusion current has been very successful. Ilkovic, in 1934, derived the following equation for the average diffusion current at a DME:

$$i_d = 607nD^{1/2}Cm^{2/3}t^{1/6}$$

The term i_d is the average diffusion current in microamperes, n is the number of faradays per mole of reactant, D is the diffusion coefficient (cm^2/sec), C is the concentration (millimolar), m is the mass of mercury flowing per second (mg/sec), and t is the drop time (sec). The constant 607 is a combination of natural constants including the faraday; the value is slightly temperature dependent and the figure given here is for 25°C. The principal importance of the Ilkovic equation is that it shows in a quantitative manner the influence of many factors on the diffusion current.

It is convenient to divide the factors in the Ilkovic equation into two parts: (1) $nCD^{1/2}$, which is determined by the properties of the solution, and (2) $m^{2/3}t^{1/6}$, which is dependent upon the characteristics of the capillary. The first part contains the concentration of the electroactive species. We have previously mentioned that the diffusion current is proportional to concentration, and this is the factor of primary interest to the analytical chemist. The term n, of course, is a property of the solute, the number of faradays per mole of reactant. The diffusion coefficient D is also a property of the solute in a given solvent. For simple ions this factor is related to the equivalent conductance and charge of the ion as well as to the temperature. The diffusion current increases with increase in temperature, this being about 2% per degree for the DME. Hence, to insure an error no greater than ±1% in the diffusion current, the temperature should be controlled to within ±0.5°C.

The second part, $m^{2/3}t^{1/6}$, can be evaluated by measuring the mass of mercury flowing through the capillary per second and the drop time in the diffusion current region. Currents obtained with different capillaries can be compared when this factor is known. The proportionality between the diffusion current and $m^{2/3}t^{1/6}$ does not hold at very short drop times. It is usually recommended that this time be adjusted to three to five seconds per drop. The surface tension of mercury and hence the drop time varies with the potential of the microelectrode. In Figure 11.3 is a plot of the variation of the term $m^{2/3}t^{1/6}$ as a function of the potential of the DME. This term passes through a maximum at the electrocapillary zero, but for practical purposes it can be considered approximately constant from 0 to about −1.0 v. At more negative potentials this term decreases much more rapidly and this must be taken into account in calculating diffusion currents. All other factors being constant, the diffusion current is found to depend upon the effective pressure on the dropping mercury. The current should be proportional to the square root of the height of the mercury column if the process is diffusion controlled.

Kinetic and catalytic currents

There are many examples of chemical systems in which the limiting current is governed by the rate of production of an electroactive species rather than by the rate of diffusion to the electrode surface. In such a case the current does not follow the Ilkovic equation and is termed a *kinetic current*. Consider the following example in which the nonreducible substance A is transformed at the surface of the mercury drop into a reducible substance B:

$$A \overset{r_1}{\underset{}{\rightleftarrows}} B \overset{e}{\longrightarrow} \text{reduction product}$$

If the rate at which B is produced, r_1, is small compared to the rate at which B is reduced, the overall rate of reduction is determined by r_1, not by the rate of diffusion to the electrode.

In such a situation, the current is often described as a pure kinetic current and it has two distinguishing characteristics:

1. It is smaller than would be predicted for the direct conversion of A to the reduction product based on the concentration of A in the solution. It is larger than would be predicted from the equilibrium concentration of B.

2. It is independent of the values of the drop time and the mass of the mercury drop, and hence independent of the height of the mercury column above the drop.

As might be expected, there are situations in which the current is not purely kinetic or purely diffusion controlled. Such situations arise when the rate of conversion of A to B is large or if the equilibrium concentration of B is large compared to that of A. The situation can be further complicated if both A and B are reducible.

Many examples of systems which show kinetic currents have been reported in the literature.[1] One of the classic examples is that of aldose and ketose sugars which give waves which are dependent upon the rate of conversion of the nonreducible hemiacetal form to the reducible aldehyde or keto form. Such currents have not been found particularly useful in practical quantitative analyses.

A *catalytic current* is observed in a mixture of two substances, A and B, at a potential such that A is reduced but B is not. However, the reduction product of A is reoxidized by B at the surface of the mercury drop. If the quantity of A thus regenerated is large compared to the quantity of A reaching the electrode by diffusion, the current will be enhanced. An example is as follows, where A is Fe^{++} and B is H_2O_2:

$$Fe^{3+} + e \rightleftarrows Fe^{++} \tag{1}$$

$$2\ Fe^{++} + H_2O_2 \rightleftarrows 2\ Fe^{3+} + 2\ OH^- \tag{2}$$

The H_2O_2 is not reduced at the electrode at the potential required for reaction (1) because of an activation overpotential effect. The diffusion current originally obtained from reaction (1) is then greatly enhanced by the cyclic process in which more Fe^{3+} is produced by reaction (2) and again reduced by reaction (1).

[1] I. M. Kolthoff and J. J. Lingane, *Polarography*, Vol. I, Interscience Publishers, Inc., New York, 1952, p. 268.

Catalytic currents have been found very useful for the determination of trace concentrations of certain substances. For example, molybdate ion in hydrogen peroxide solutions has been detected in this manner at concentrations as low as 5 μg (of molybdenum) per liter.[2] Vanadates and tungstates have been determined in a similar manner.

Maxima

The current-voltage curves obtained with a dropping mercury electrode frequently have maxima, such as the one shown in Figure 11.4. The shapes

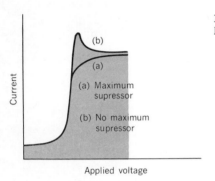

Fig. 11.4. Maximum on polarographic wave.

of maxima vary from sharp peaks to rounded humps. Both the height and shape depend upon the concentration of the reducible substance, the concentration and charge of the supporting electrolyte, and the drop time of the capillary. Maxima are not observed with a stationary platinum electrode if one waits for the current to become steady.

For a maximum to occur it is evident that the concentration of the reducible substance at the electrode interface must be increased by some process other than diffusion. There is some reason to believe that this added factor is an absorption on the growing drop.[3] At any rate, maxima must be eliminated to insure that the current is dependent strictly upon diffusion and is proportional to the concentration of the electroactive substance. Maxima can normally be eliminated by surface-active agents, such as gelatin or the ions of certain dyes. Gelatin, at a concentration of 0.002 to 0.01%, Triton X-100, a commercial surface-active agent, and methyl red are particularly useful as maxima suppressors.

[2] See page 287 of reference 1.
[3] See pages 156–188 of reference 1 for a discussion of theories concerning maxima.

The half-wave potential

The potential at which the current in a polarographic cell is one-half the diffusion current (that is, where $i = \frac{1}{2}i_d$) is called *the half-wave potential* and is given the symbol $E_{1/2}$ (see Figure 11.2). In other words, at the half-wave potential, one-half of the ions that reach the cathode during a given time are reduced. The relationship between the half-wave potential and the standard potential of the redox system involved in the electrode reaction can be found by deriving an equation for the polarographic wave.

Let us consider the simplest case in which a substance undergoes reversible reduction at the DME:

$$\text{Ox} + n\,\text{e} \rightleftarrows \text{Red} \qquad E^\circ$$

We shall consider that the reduction product is soluble either in the solution or in the mercury as an amalgam. Since the reaction proceeds reversibly, that is, without overpotential, the potential at any point on the polarographic wave is given by the Nernst equation.

$$E = E^\circ - \frac{0.059}{n} \log \frac{[\text{Red}]_i}{[\text{Ox}]_i}$$

where the subscripts i indicate the concentrations (activities) of the oxidized and reduced forms at the surface of the electrode. The potential E and the concentrations refer to the average value during the lifetime of a mercury drop.

The current at any point on the polarographic wave is proportional to the difference between the concentration of the oxidant in the body of the solution and the concentration at the interface:

$$i = k_1\{[\text{Ox}]_b - [\text{Ox}]_i\}$$

Here $[\text{Ox}]_b$ is the concentration in the body of the solution. When $[\text{Ox}]_i$ drops to zero,

$$i_d = k_1[\text{Ox}]_b$$

Hence

$$i_d - i = k_1[\text{Ox}]_i$$

or

$$[\text{Ox}]_i = \frac{i_d - i}{k_1}$$

Assuming that none of the reduced form is present at the start of the electrolysis, the concentration of the reductant formed at the interface is proportional to the current passing. That is,

$$[\text{Red}]_i = \frac{i}{k_2}$$

Substituting these values of concentrations at the interface into the Nernst expression gives

$$E = E° - \frac{0.059}{n} \log \frac{i/k_2}{(i_d - i)/k_1}$$

or

$$E = E° - \frac{0.059}{n} \log \frac{i}{i_d - i} - k_0$$

where

$$k_0 = \frac{0.059}{n} \log \frac{k_1}{k_2}$$

At the half-wave potential $E = E_{1/2}$ and $i = \frac{1}{2}i_d$. Hence the term $\log i/(i_d - i)$ is zero and

$$E_{1/2} = E° - k_0$$

The values of k_1 and k_2 are approximately the same since they differ only in the values of the diffusion coefficients of the oxidant and reductant. Hence the term k_0 is very small and the half-wave potential is approximately the same as the standard potential.[4] The final equation for the polarographic wave is

$$E = E_{1/2} - \frac{0.059}{n} \log \frac{i}{i_d - i}$$

A plot of E vs. $\log i/(i_d - i)$ gives a straight line with a slope of $-0.059/n$ if the reaction proceeds reversibly (see Figure 11.5). The value of n, the number of electrons gained by the reductant, can be determined from the slope. If the value of n thus determined corresponds to the theoretical value and if the plot is a straight line, the reaction is regarded as proceeding reversibly. Practically, any reaction proceeding at a finite rate is, of course, irreversible in the strict sense. If the activation overpotential is very small, however, the above equation may be obeyed to within a small experimental error, and this is taken to be "reversible" behavior.

The half-wave potential can be determined from a plot such as that in Figure 11.5. This is the potential at which the term $\log i/(i_d - i)$ is equal to zero; that is, the current is one-half the diffusion current. The half-wave potential, like the standard potential, is characteristic of the particular redox system. It is independent of the concentration of the electroactive species in the solution, and thus can be used for qualitative identification of an unknown substance. This is seldom used as a method of identification, however, unless the number of possible substances is quite limited. There are many substances that have almost the same values of half-wave potentials, and they could not be distinguished from one another by such a measurement.

---

[4] Note that if the diffusion coefficients of the oxidant and reductant are equal, the interface concentrations of these two species are equal at the half-wave potential. If this fact is substituted in the original Nernst expression, it is immediately apparent that $E_{1/2} = E°$.

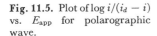

Fig. 11.5. Plot of $\log i/(i_d - i)$ vs. E_{app} for polarographic wave.

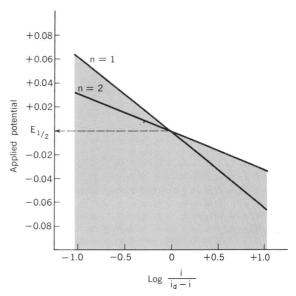

Applications

There are many substances that can be reduced or oxidized to yield well-defined polarographic waves. The concentrations of such substances in solution can be determined by the polarographic technique. We shall briefly summarize here the types of substances which give polarographic waves, as well as the types of waves formed, following the classification of Kolthoff and Laitinen.[5]

Cathodic waves. Many inorganic cations, anions, and neutral molecules, as well as a large number of organic molecules, undergo reduction at a dropping mercury electrode and yield *cathodic* waves.

1. *Inorganic cations.* A cation such as copper which is more easily reduced than hydrogen ion, readily yields a cathodic wave in water solution. Cations which are less readily reduced than hydrogen may also yield waves even at low pH values, since the activation overpotential of hydrogen on mercury is large and since the activity of the metal is reduced through amalgamation. Polarographic waves of very active metals, such as the alkali and alkaline earth metals, can be obtained under certain conditions. Very negative potentials are required, and hence the hydrogen ion concentration must be low and the cation of the supporting electrolyte must not be reduced more readily than the cation whose polarogram is desired. Salts of a tetraalkylammonium hydroxide, such as tetramethylammonium bromide, are used as

[5] I. M. Kolthoff and H. A. Laitinen, *pH and Electro Titrations*, John Wiley & Sons, Inc., New York, 1941, p. 148.

supporting electrolytes since they are not decomposed until about -2.6 v vs. SCE. The half-wave potential of sodium ion in 50% ethanol with 0.1-M tetraethylammonium hydroxide as the supporting electrolyte is -2.07 v.

2. *Inorganic anions.* Since diffusion is the process by which an ion reaches the microelectrode, the ion does not have to be of opposite charge to the electrode. Hence, anions may be reduced at the cathode and cations may be oxidized at the anode. The most important inorganic anions which give cathodic waves are the anions which contain oxygen, such as iodate, bromate, nitrate, tellurite, selenite, and permanganate. Hydrogen ions are involved in the reduction process, and hence the half-wave potentials are strongly dependent upon pH. In well-buffered solutions the waves are reproducible and the diffusion current is proportional to the concentration of the reducible anion.

3. *Neutral molecules.* Oxygen, sulfur dioxide, nitric oxide, cyanogen, carbon disulfide, and hydrogen peroxide are examples of uncharged inorganic substances which are reduced at the DME. The reduction of oxygen occurs at potentials more negative than about -0.2 v vs. SCE and the resulting waves may interfere with those of other substances. For this reason, dissolved oxygen is normally removed from a test solution by deaerating the solution with an inert gas such as nitrogen. The reduction of oxygen yields two waves of about equal height, corresponding to the following two reactions:

$$O_2 + 2\ H_2O + 2\ e \rightleftharpoons H_2O_2 + 2\ OH^-$$

$$H_2O_2 + 2\ e \rightleftharpoons 2\ OH^-$$

The polarographic method is an important one for the determination of oxygen.

Numerous organic molecules give cathodic waves, and the field of organic polarography is a large one. Organic groups which are reducible at the DME include the carbonyl (aldehydes, ketones, and quinones), nitro, nitroso, diazo, amine oxide, epoxide, peroxide, carbon-halogen, and carbon-carbon double bond in conjugated systems. The reductions are generally irreversible, but the current is usually proportional to concentration, enabling the analyst to use the method for quantitative determinations.

Since many organic compounds are practically insoluble in water, organic liquids, or mixtures of water and certain water-miscible organic liquids are usually employed as solvents. For example, mixtures of ethanol and water or dioxane and water have been widely employed as solvents. In such mixtures, buffering materials are reasonably soluble; buffers are often needed since many reductions consume hydrogen ions and the half-wave potential is dependent upon the pH of the solvent.

Chemists are interested in organic polarography not only because of its analytical applications but also to gain information about the mechanism of the reduction process itself. Many electrochemical techniques can be employed to gain information about the number of electrons involved in various steps of the reaction, the production of free radicals, the variation in mechanism and products produced at different pH values, etc. The technique of controlled potential electrolysis (Chapter 9) combined with polarography has been used to give a high degree of selectivity to electrolytic organic reductions and has led to the production of highly pure products.

Anodic waves. Some inorganic and organic substances may be directly oxidized at the DME to produce anodic waves. A few examples are ferrous and ferrocyanide ions, hydroquinone, mercaptans, and enediols. A second type of anodic wave is observed with substances which form either an insoluble salt or a stable complex with mercurous or mercuric ions. Mercury is oxidized according to the reaction (right to left)

$$Hg_2^{++} + 2 e \rightleftarrows 2 Hg \qquad E° = +0.80 \text{ v}$$

when the dropping mercury anode becomes about 0.45 v more positive than the SCE. If an anion which forms an insoluble salt or a stable complex with mercurous ion is in the solution, the foregoing oxidation is facilitated; that is, a less positive potential is required to dissolve the mercury. Chloride ion, for example, forms insoluble mercurous chloride at the anode according to the reaction

$$Hg_2Cl_2 + 2 e \rightleftarrows 2 Hg + 2 Cl^- \qquad E° = +0.28 \text{ v}$$

and the potential required for oxidation is considerably less positive than it is in the absence of chloride ions. As mercurous ions are produced at the anode, mercurous chloride precipitates, thereby lowering the chloride concentration at the electrode interface. Chloride ions then diffuse to the electrode and the current is dependent upon the concentration of chloride ions in the body of the solution. A linear relationship is found between the diffusion current and the concentration of chloride ions. Other halide ions, sulfate, thiosulfate, cyanide, and thiocyanate are a few examples of anions which can be determined by the use of such anodic waves.

Polarographic techniques

The polarographic method is commonly employed to determine concentrations in the range of 10^{-4}- to 10^{-2}-M. Under favorable conditions, concentrations as low as 10^{-6}-M can be detected. Errors of about $\pm 2\%$ are to be expected, although these may be reduced by a factor of ten in special circumstances. Since the concentration is proportional to the diffusion current, the main problem in polarographic analysis is to measure this current accurately.

Correction must be made, of course, for the residual current. This can be measured separately on a solution which contains the supporting electrolyte alone, and subtracted from the average current which is measured on the diffusion current plateau at the same voltage. When a recording polarograph is used, the portion of the residual current curve (LM in Figure 11.2) is extrapolated and a line parallel to it is drawn through the value of the limiting current (*NP* in Figure 11.2). This procedure is simpler than the first one, but is less exact, particularly when the plateau of the wave is not closely parallel to the residual current.

There are a number of procedures which can be used to obtain concentration values from diffusion currents. A brief discussion of these is given below; Taylor[6] gives a more detailed evaluation of these methods.

Absolute method. The concentration of a substance can be calculated from its diffusion current using the Ilkovic equation, provided the terms *n*, *D*, *m*, and *t* are known. The terms *m* and *t* can be readily determined for a particular capillary. Usually *n* is known but often *D*, the diffusion coefficient of the electroactive species, is not known. Lingane[7] suggested that the terms 607, *n*, and *D* be combined into a single constant *I*, termed the diffusion current constant. Thus

$$i_d = 607nD^{1/2}Cm^{2/3}t^{1/6}$$

$$I = 607nD^{1/2} = \frac{i_d}{Cm^{2/3}t^{1/6}}$$

The constant *I* can be evaluated for a particular substance, temperature, and supporting electrolyte by accurate measurement of the diffusion current at a known concentration. The terms *m* and *t* must also be measured for the capillary used. Once a value of *I* is reported in the literature, it can be used by other workers for determining the concentration of the same substance under the same solution conditions, provided they measure the values of *m* and *t* for their capillaries.

The principal advantage of the absolute method is that no extensive standardization experiments are required. If the required diffusion current constant is available, and if the value of $m^{2/3}t^{1/6}$ for his capillary is known, then the analyst need run only one polarogram in order to effect a determination. The accuracy of the method is normally less than that of the *comparative* methods discussed below. However, since the method is so rapid, it can be recommended for occasional analyses where a high degree of accuracy is not required.

The following is an illustration of the calculations involved in the use of the absolute method.

PROBLEM. The diffusion current constant of lead ion is 3.80 at 25°C in 0.1-*M* KCl solution containing 0.01% gelatin as a maximum suppressor.[7] The diffusion current obtained with an unknown lead solution under the same conditions as those above was 6.14 μamp. In a separate experiment, 20 drops of mercury were collected from the capillary in 100 sec and found to weigh 120 mg. Calculate the concentration of the unknown solution.

Since 100 sec were required for 20 drops to fall, the drop time is 5.00 sec. The value of *m* is 1.20 mg/sec. Hence,

[6] J. K. Taylor, *Ind. Eng. Chem.*, Anal. Ed., **19**, 368 (1947).
[7] J. J. Lingane, *Ind. Eng. Chem.*, Anal. Ed., **15**, 583 (1943).

$$m^{2/3}t^{1/6} = (1.20)^{2/3}(5.00)^{1/6} = 1.48$$

$$C = \frac{i_d}{Im^{2/3}t^{1/6}} = \frac{6.14}{3.80 \times 1.48}$$

$$C = 1.09 \text{ mmol/l or } 1.09 \times 10^{-3}\text{-}M$$

Wave height-concentration plots. In this method a calibration curve is prepared by measuring the diffusion currents in a series of standard solutions. Since the diffusion current is proportional to concentration, at least over a limited range of concentration, the graph is normally a straight line, as shown in Figure 11.6. The diffusion current of an unknown solution

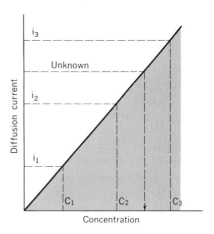

Fig. 11.6. Wave height-concentration plot.

is measured and the concentration of the solution can then be read from the graph.

This method is strictly empirical, but it is straightforward and simple to use and gives good results. A particular standardization graph can be used only with a given capillary, at a given temperature, and under essentially constant solution conditions. The method is particularly useful in situations where many determinations of the same substance must be made under identical conditions.

Pilot ion method. This method involves a comparison of the diffusion current produced by the substance of interest with the current produced in the same solution by a second substance referred to as the *pilot ion*. The unknown and pilot ions must have sufficiently different half-wave potentials so that two well-defined waves are obtained in a solution containing both ions (as in Figure 11.7). An example is cadmium, used as the pilot ion in the determination of lead. The diffusion currents of the two ions are given by the expressions

$$i_{Cd} = I_{Cd}C_{Cd}m^{2/3}t^{1/6}$$

$$i_{Pb} = I_{Pb}C_{Pb}m^{2/3}t^{1/6}$$

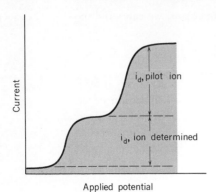

Fig. 11.7. Polarograms for pilot ion method.

The ratio of the diffusion currents is

$$\frac{i_{Cd}}{i_{Pb}} = \frac{I_{Cd} \times C_{Cd}}{I_{Pb} \times C_{Pb}}$$

The concentration of the lead solution is given by the expression

$$C_{Pb} = \frac{R \times C_{Cd} \times i_{Pb}}{i_{Cd}}$$

where R, the pilot ion ratio, is the value of I_{Cd}/I_{Pb}. The value of R is first determined using known concentrations of lead and cadmium. A solution of unknown lead can then be determined by adding a known concentration of cadmium to the unknown and measuring the two diffusion currents.

It will be noted that this method is independent of the characteristics of the capillary and hence is particularly useful in situations where different capillaries must be employed. If solution conditions are changed in any way, the pilot ion ratio should be redetermined. The method is of somewhat limited application, particularly in cases where the solution contains more than one reducible substance. It is sometimes difficult to find a pilot ion whose wave does not overlap with a wave of one of the substances in the test solution. The accuracy of the method is good, particularly if the pilot ion ratio is determined at several concentrations of the substance being determined.

Method of standard addition. In this method a known quantity of the substance being determined is added to a definite volume of the solution of unknown concentration. (See problem 9 for a variation in the procedure.) The diffusion current is recorded before and after addition of the standard solution, and from these data the concentration of the unknown can be calculated. This is shown in the following example.

PROBLEM. A lead solution of concentration c_1 is found to give a diffusion current of i_1 μamp. A volume v_2 of a lead solution of known concentration c_2 is added to v_1 ml of the unknown. The diffusion current of the new solution is i_2 μamp. Derive an equation for finding the concentration of the unknown.

Since the solution and capillary conditions are constant, we can write the Ilkovic equation as

$$i_1 = kc_1 \quad \text{and} \quad i_2 = k \frac{v_1c_1 + v_2c_2}{v_1 + v_2}$$

where k is the proportionality constant. Eliminating k and solving for c_1 gives

$$c_1 = \frac{i_1v_2c_2}{i_2(v_1 + v_2) - i_1v_1}$$

The method of standard addition is independent of the characteristics of the capillary and hence is useful where different capillaries must be employed. The method gives good results and is particularly advantageous for occasional determinations where time does not allow the preparation and examination of many standard solutions.

AMPEROMETRIC TITRATIONS

As pointed out in Chapter 10, amperometric titrations involve a measurement of current at constant voltage as the concentration of an electroactive species is changed by titration. The method was classified under the case where mass transport occurs by convection-diffusion, i.e., with stirring of the solution. In practice, stirring is sometimes employed, sometimes not. The polarographic technique, where the current is diffusion controlled, is widely employed for amperometric titrations. The applied voltage is set on the diffusion plateau where the current is proportional to concentration. The dropping mercury electrode is polarized[8] and the reference electrode, usually calomel, is not polarized. In the alternative technique, two identical electrodes are employed and a small constant voltage is impressed across the pair. Both electrodes are polarizable, although one normally functions as a reference electrode and the other as an indicator electrode. The two may exchange roles during the course of a titration, as will be seen below.

Our further discussion is divided according to whether one or two of the electrodes are polarizable.

---

[8] We have previously avoided using the term *polarization* in connection with the additional voltage required at an electrode because of concentration gradients (page 227). The term *concentration overpotential* was employed to avoid any implication of irreversibility of the electrode reaction. On the other hand, an electrode is said to be *polarized* when the potential of the electrode can be changed by a relatively large amount without appreciably changing the current which results from the reaction at the electrode. Hence, along the diffusion current plateau (*NP* in Figure 11.2) the DME is polarized. The electrode reaction may be reversible; the effect here is one of concentration overpotential. If the *activation overpotential* is large, the electrode reaction is irreversible. Even in this case the electrode can be polarized or depolarized depending upon the above criterion concerning the rate of change of current with change of potential. See J. J. Lingane, *Electroanalytical Chemistry*, 2nd Ed., Interscience Publishers, Inc., New York, 1958, p. 284.

One polarizable electrode

The polarizable electrode can be either a dropping mercury electrode or a platinum microelectrode. In order for the technique to be applicable, it is necessary for the substance titrated or the titrant to give a cathodic or anodic diffusion current. The titration reaction may be one of precipitation, complex formation, or oxidation-reduction. The applied voltage is set at a value which yields a diffusion current and is left there during the titration. The diffusion current is plotted against the volume of titrant (corrected for dilution) in order to determine the volume required to reach the equivalence point.

It is convenient to classify these titrations according to the types of titration curves that result from plotting the diffusion current against volume of titrant.[9] The type of curve depends upon whether the substance titrated or the titrant, or both, give diffusion currents at the voltage used during the titration. Let us consider as a general case the reaction

$$A + B \rightleftarrows AB$$

where A is the substance titrated and B is the titrant. We assume that the reaction goes well to completion, for example, by the formation of an insoluble compound AB. The following cases may result.

1. *A gives a diffusion current, B does not.* The polarograms of A and B are illustrated in Figure 11.8 and the titration curve which results when the

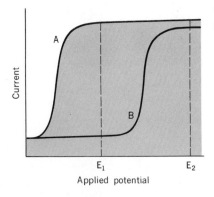

Fig. 11.8. Polarograms of substance titrated and of titrant.

applied potential is E_1 is shown in Figure 11.9. At the start of the titration a large diffusion current results, but as the concentration of A is lowered by reaction with B, the current decreases. If the reaction goes well to comple-

[9] See I. M. Kolthoff and H. A. Laitinen, *pH and Electro Titrations*, John Wiley & Sons, Inc., New York, 1941, p. 165.

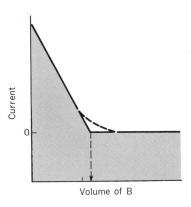

Fig. 11.9. Amperometric titration of *A* with *B* at E_1.

Volume of B

tion, the current drops to a very small value at the equivalence point and then levels off as excess B is added. If the reaction is somewhat incomplete, the concentration of A does not fall to a very low value at the equivalence point and hence the current does not reach its minimal value until an excess of B is added. This results in a rounded titration curve, as shown in Figure 11.9.

In amperometric titrations no attempt is made to obtain readings very close to the equivalence point. Rather, readings are taken on either side of the equivalence point and the two lines are extrapolated to find the point of intersection (Figure 11.9). If readings are taken near the equivalence point and plotted, they fall on a smooth curve connecting the two straight line portions of the graph (dotted portion in Figure 11.9).

Examples of titrations which fall in this class are lead titrated with oxalate or sulfate, and silver titrated with chloride.

2. *B gives a diffusion current, A does not.* The polarograms are illustrated in Figure 11.8 by simply interchanging the letters A and B, and the titration curve obtained when the applied potential in E_1 is shown in Figure 11.10. At the start of the titration and up to the equivalence point the current is

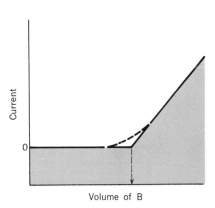

Fig. 11.10. Amperometric titration of *A* with *B*; *B* reducible and *A* not.

Volume of B

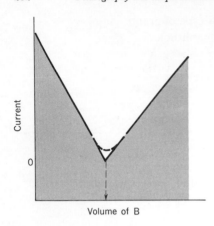

Fig. 11.11. Amperometric titration of *A* with *B* at E_2.

very small. As B is added, it reacts with A and hence does not contribute to the current until all of A is removed. Then excess B causes an increase in current and the end point is determined as before by the intersection of the two straight line portions of the graph.

Examples of reactions giving this type of graph are oxalate or sulfate titrated with lead, and lead titrated with dichromate in acid solution. In the latter case, the applied voltage is 0.0 v; lead is not reduced at this potential but dichromate is reduced to chromic ions. The titration of arsenite with bromate at a rotating platinum microelectrode is another example.

3. *Both A and B give diffusion current.* The polarograms are illustrated in Figure 11.8, and the titration curve, when the applied potential is E_2, is shown in Figure 11.11. At the start of the titration the current is large because A is reduced at the cathode. As B is added, the concentration of A (and hence the current) decreases. Beyond the equivalence point the current increases as excess B is reduced at the cathode. The titration of lead with

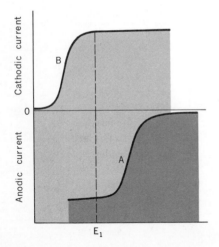

Fig. 11.12. Polarograms of *A* (anodic wave) and *B* (cathodic wave).

dichromate at -1.2 v is an example that gives this type of graph. Another example is the titration of copper with α-nitroso-β-naphthol.

4. *A gives anodic, B cathodic diffusion current.* The polarograms are shown in Figure 11.12 and the titration graph in Figure 11.13. At the start of the

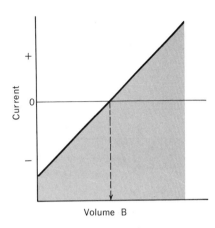

Fig. 11.13. Amperometric titration of *A* with *B* at E_1 (Fig. 11.12).

titration the current is anodic (indicated by negative values in Figure 11.13) and decreases as B is added. Beyond the equivalence point excess B is reduced at the cathode and the current increases (indicated by positive values in Figure 11.13). The two lines normally have slightly different slopes since A and B have different diffusion coefficients. The current passes through zero in the vicinity of the equivalence point. An example of a titration that gives such a curve is that of titanous ion with ferric ion at -0.3 v. At this potential titanous ion is oxidized to titanic, and ferric ion is reduced to ferrous.

Two polarizable electrodes

As previously mentioned this technique employs two identical electrodes across which a small constant voltage is applied. The only requirement for the method to be applicable is that a reversible redox couple be present either before or after the equivalence point.

Let us consider a case involving two reversible redox systems, the ferrous-ferric and cerous-ceric. Suppose we titrate 0.10-M Fe^{++} with 0.10-M Ce^{4+} in a 1.0-M perchloric acid solution. Two identical platinum electrodes are inserted in the solution and a constant voltage of 200 mv is applied. The following reactions might occur at the electrodes:

Anode:

$$\text{Fe}^{++} \rightleftarrows \text{Fe}^{3+} + \text{e} \tag{1}$$

$$\text{H}_2\text{O} \rightleftarrows \tfrac{1}{2}\,\text{O}_2 + 2\,\text{H}^+ + 2\,\text{e} \tag{2}$$

Cathode:

$$Fe^{3+} + e \rightleftarrows Fe^{++} \qquad (3)$$

$$H^+ + e \rightleftarrows \tfrac{1}{2} H_2 \qquad (4)$$

For reactions (1) and (3) to occur, the applied potential can be very small

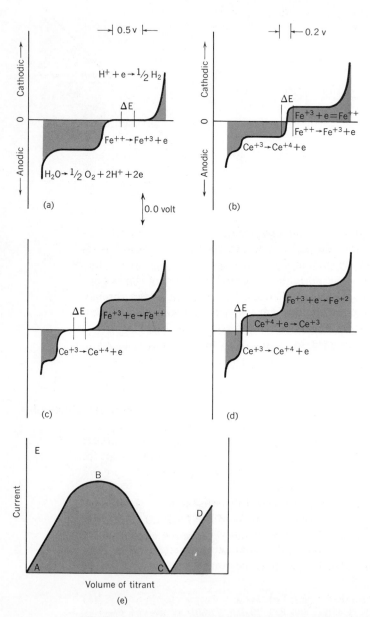

Fig. 11.14. Titration of Fe^{++} with Ce^{4+} using two polarizable electrodes.

since the decomposition potential is 0.00 v; on the other hand, reactions (1) and (4), (2) and (3), or (2) and (4) require a relatively large applied voltage, much larger than the 200 mv we have applied. Hence, we might expect reactions (1) and (3) to proceed, giving an appreciable current before any titrant is added. Such is not the case, however.

Let us refer to Figure 11.14, where schematic current-potential curves for the above reactions are shown at various stages of the titration.[10] At the start of the titration (11.14a) the concentration of ferric ion is zero (actually very small), and reaction (3) is not possible. Note that no cathodic current caused by the reduction of ferric ion is shown on the graph. Since the applied potential of 200 mv is insufficient to bring about reactions (1) and (4), no current flows (11.14e). One can say that the cathode is polarized.

Consider the situation as the titration is begun by the addition of ceric ions. Ferrous ions are oxidized to ferric, and the latter can now diffuse to the cathode and depolarize it. At the same time ferrous ions are oxidized at the anode, the applied potential of 200 mv now being sufficient to cause reactions (1) and (3) to occur since the concentration of ferric ions is appreciable. It should be kept in mind that the current at the two electrodes must be the same and cannot be any greater than that which results from the diffusion of the ion in smaller concentration. In the early stages of the titration the concentration of ferric ions is less than that of ferrous, and hence the rate of diffusion of ferric ions to the cathode limits the overall current flow. The cathode is said to function as the indicator electrode and the current rises steadily along the segment AB of Figure 11.14e as the concentration of ferric ions increases during the titration. In Figure 11.14 the applied voltage of 200 mv, designated ΔE, is indicated at various stages of the titration. The applied voltage causes as large a current flow as possible, of course, and the location of ΔE on the potential axis is determined by this fact plus the fact that the current at the anode and cathode must be the same.

When half of the ferrous ions are oxidized to ferric, the situation is represented by Figure 11.14b and the point B in 11.14e. Since the concentrations of the two ions are the same, the current is maximal. In 11.14b it will be noted that another anodic reaction is now possible,

$$Ce^{3+} \rightleftarrows Ce^{4+} + e \qquad (5)$$

since cerous ions have been produced during the titration. This oxidation occurs at a more positive potential than does the oxidation of ferrous ions.

Beyond the half-way point, the current begins to decrease (BC in 11.14e) and the concentration of ferrous ion is now the limiting factor in determining the magnitude of the current. Hence, the anode now functions as the indicator electrode. The current falls to zero at the equivalence point since the

[10] See J. J. Lingane, *Electroanalytical Chemistry*, 2nd Ed., Interscience Publishers, Inc., 1958, pp. 287–288, and I. M. Kolthoff and P. J. Elving, *Treatise on Analytical Chemistry*, Part 1, Vol. 4, Interscience Publishers, Inc., New York, 1963, p. 2189.

concentration of ferrous ion has dropped to such a low value. The situation is shown in 11.14c, where it should be noted that reactions (3) and (5) are now possibilities, but not with an applied voltage of only 200 mv.

Beyond the equivalence point, excess ceric ions are available for reduction,

$$Ce^{4+} + e \rightleftharpoons Ce^{3+} \tag{6}$$

and now reactions (5) and (6) can occur since the voltage required is very small. The current starts to rise again along *CD* in 11.14e, and at this stage the cathode is again the indicator electrode, since the ceric concentration is small and limits the current.

There are numerous other examples of amperometric titrations with two polarizable electrodes.[11] The titration curves may be different from the one we have just considered. For example, chloride ion can be titrated with silver ion, using two identical silver electrodes and a constant voltage of 100 mv. Very little current flows up to the equivalence point, but a sharp increase occurs when the cathode is depolarized by excess silver ions. The well-known titration of iodine with thiosulfate gives a titration curve of shape like that in Figure 11.9. The current is large at the start of the titration since both iodine and iodide are present in appreciable concentration and depolarize both electrodes. As thiosulfate is added, the iodine concentration decreases, as does the current, until it is approximately zero at the equivalence point. No current flows after the equivalence point since thiosulfate does not depolarize the anode.

Applications and techniques

The amperometric technique has been particularly useful for determining the end points of titrations involving precipitation and complex formation reactions. In many cases, suitable indicators are lacking and the amperometric method can be employed if either reactant gives a diffusion current. Substances which cannot be titrated potentiometrically may yield well-defined diffusion currents and hence be suitable for amperometric titration. The two-electrode technique has been employed with a number of redox systems and a very important use is the titration of water with the Karl Fischer reagent.[12]

As in ordinary polarography, the substance titrated is usually in the concentration range of 0.10- to 0.0001-M. The diffusion current should be

[11] See pages 280–295 of reference 10 (Lingane) for a detailed discussion.

[12] Many practical examples of amperometry are given in a chapter by J. Jordan and J. H. Clausen in *Handbook of Analytical Chemistry*, L. Meites, Ed., McGraw-Hill Book Co., New York, 1963, pp. 5–155.

corrected for the effect of dilution by multiplying the current reading by the factor $(v_1 + v_2)/v_1$, where v_1 is the original volume of the solution titrated and v_2 is the volume of titrant added. This correction can be minimized by making the titrant concentration at least ten times that of the substance titrated. A microburet is employed to keep the error small in determining the volume of titrant. The overall error in amperometric techniques is often as small as 0.1%, and is generally smaller than that which can be obtained with polarographic techniques. For best results, the indicator current is plotted and the end point determined by linear extrapolation.

The two-electrode technique is subject to greater errors than that employing a single polarized electrode. The indicator electrode in the two-electrode method is usually not completely polarized, and hence a slight change in the applied voltage can cause an appreciable change in the indicator current. On the other hand, the single-electrode technique employs a completely polarized electrode. The applied voltage is set at a value along the diffusion current plateau where a slight change in the voltage hardly affects the current. Lingane and Anson[13] have discussed in some detail the problems involved in precise measurements with the two-electrode technique in the bromine-cuprous system.

As compared with potentiometric, amperometric titrations share with photometric (Chapter 12, page 327) the advantage that the measured quantity is directly proportional to concentration; hence the end point may be found by a linear extrapolation from points far from the equivalence point, where the reaction goes essentially to completion.

REFERENCES

1. I. M. Kolthoff and J. J. Lingane, *Polarography*, Vols. I and II, Interscience Publishers, Inc., New York, 1952.

2. J. J. Lingane, *Electroanalytical Chemistry*, 2nd Ed., Interscience Publishers, Inc., New York, 1958.

3. I. M. Kolthoff and H. A. Laitinen, *pH and Electro Titrations*, John Wiley & Sons, Inc., New York, 1941.

4. L. Meites and H. C. Thomas, *Advanced Analytical Chemistry*, McGraw-Hill Book Co., Inc., New York, 1958.

5. L. Meites, "Voltammetry at the Dropping Mercury Electrode (Polarography)," Chapter 46, Part I, Vol. IV, of *Treatise on Analytical Chemistry*, I. M. Kolthoff, P. J. Elving, and E. B. Sandell, Eds., Interscience Publishers, Inc., New York, 1963.

[13] J. J. Lingane and F. C. Anson, *Anal. Chem.*, **28**, 1871 (1956).

QUESTIONS

1. Point out the differences between the experimental conditions used in ordinary electrogravimetry and in polarography.

2. Explain why the total cathode potential $(E_c - \omega_c)$ is the only term affected by a change in the applied voltage under polarographic conditions.

3. Explain what is meant by a "completely polarized" electrode. Can the reaction at such an electrode be reversible?

4. What are the advantages of the DME over a solid microelectrode? Compare the usefulness of the DME as a cathode and as an anode.

5. Explain the reason for the charging current.

6. What is the function of the supporting electrolyte? Explain how a limiting current can be larger or smaller than the diffusion current.

7. How can a kinetic current be experimentally confirmed?

8. Suppose the reaction of A with B to form AB is essentially complete before the reaction of C with B to form CB begins. A solution containing both A and C is titrated with B. Simply sketch the shapes of the amperometric titration curves (single electrode technique) obtained at a potential where: (a) A and B give diffusion currents, C does not; (b) C gives a diffusion current, A and B do not; (c) B and C give diffusion currents, A does not.

9. Suppose A, B, and C form redox couples of the type

$$A^{++} \rightleftharpoons A^{3+} + e$$

and the oxidation of A^{++} with B^{3+} is complete before the oxidation of C^{++} begins. A solution containing both A^{++} and C^{++} is titrated with B^{3+} using the two-electrode amperometric technique. Simply sketch the shapes of the titration curves obtained at an applied voltage such that: (a) all three systems depolarize the electrodes; (b) A and B depolarize the electrodes, C does not; (c) B and C depolarize the electrodes, A does not.

10. Sketch an amperometric titration curve, such as that in Figure 11.9, and with a series of dotted lines show the effect of a decrease in the value of the equilibrium constant for the formation of AB on the shape of the curve. Make a similar sketch for titrations where the concentration of A is determined by potentiometric titration with B. Compare qualitatively the two methods as to the ease of determining the equivalence point of a reaction which does not go well to completion.

PROBLEMS

1. Suppose a cadmium solution is electrolyzed in the cell shown in Figure 11.1 for 5.00 min, the diffusion current being 1.00 μamp. Calculate (a) the number of milligrams of cadmium deposited at the cathode, and (b) the number of milligrams of mercurous chloride formed at the anode.

2. Calculate the time in hours that would be required to reduce the concentration of cadmium in 10 ml of solution from 0.0010-M to 0.00050-M by electrolysis at a current of 1.0 μamp.

3. A metal ion is reduced polarographically, the diffusion current being 10 μamp. The following currents were obtained at the indicated potentials (all potentials negative): 0.444 v, 1.0 μamp; 0.465 v, 2.0 μamp; 0.489 v, 4.0 μamp; 0.511 v, 6.0 μamp; 0.535 v, 8.0 μamp; 0.556 v, 9.0 μamp. Calculate (a) the half-wave potential, and (b) the value of n.

4. The diffusion current constant of zinc in 0.1-M KCl is 3.42. What diffusion current in microamperes is obtained from a 0.00200-M solution of zinc using a capillary with a drop time of (a) 3.00 sec, (b) 4.00 sec, and (c) 5.00 sec? Assume for each drop time that one drop of mercury weighs 5.00 mg.

5. What is the value of the slope of the line obtained in a wave height-concentration plot of zinc (previous problem), the drop time being 3.00 sec? How does a change in drop time affect the slope?

6. The ratio of the diffusion current constants of cadmium to lead is 0.924. A polarogram is run on a solution of unknown lead concentration, the cadmium concentration being 0.0012-M. The diffusion currents are: lead 4.50 μamp, cadmium 6.30 μamp. What is the concentration of lead?

7. A lead solution of unknown concentration gives a diffusion current of 6.0 μamp. To 5.0 ml of this solution are added 10 ml of a 0.0020-M solution of lead, and the polarogram is run again giving a diffusion current of 18 μamp. Calculate the concentration of the unknown lead solution.

8. A 0.0012-M solution of lead gives a diffusion current of 4.00 μamp. What should be the concentration of another lead solution so that when equal volumes of the two are mixed, the diffusion current will be 10 μamp?

9. The method of standard addition is sometimes done as follows: v_1 ml of the unknown is mixed with v_2 ml of the standard of concentration c_2. After any necessary chemical treatment, the solution is diluted to V ml and the polarogram recorded, the wave height being i_2. A separate sample of v_1 ml of the unknown is treated in the same manner, diluted to V ml, the polarogram recorded, and the wave height is i_1. Set up an expression for calculating c_1, the concentration of the unknown, from these quantities.

10. A 5.00-ml portion of a lead solution of unknown concentration was diluted to 25.0 ml and a polarogram run, the diffusion current being 0.40 μamp. Another 5.00-ml portion of the same lead solution was mixed with 10.0 ml of a 0.00100-M solution of lead, the mixture diluted to 25.0 ml, the polarogram run, and the wave height was 2.00 μamp. What was the concentration of the unknown lead solution?

11. A sample containing 10.0% CdCl$_2$ is to be dissolved and the solution diluted to 500 ml in a volumetric flask. A polarogram is to be recorded using 25 ml of the solution. What is the largest sample that can be taken so that the diffusion current does not exceed 50 μamp, if the diffusion current constant of cadmium is 3.50 and the value of $m^{2/3}t^{1/6}$ for the capillary is 1.20?

12. A certain metal undergoes reduction from M^{3+} to M^+ and the average diffusion current of a 0.00300-M solution of M^{3+} is 18.0 μamp. The value of $m^{2/3}t^{1/6}$ for the capillary is 1.80. Calculate the diffusion coefficient of M^{3+}.

chapter **12**

Spectrophotometry

INTRODUCTION

Chemists have long used color as an aid in the identification of chemical substances. Spectrophotometry may be thought of as an extension of visual inspection in which a more detailed study of the absorption of radiant energy by chemical species permits greater precision in their characterization and quantitative measurement. Replacing the human eye with other detectors of radiation permits the study of absorption outside the visible region of the spectrum, and frequently spectrophotometric experiments can be performed automatically. In current usage, the term spectrophotometry suggests the measurement of the extent to which radiant energy is absorbed by a chemical system as a function of the wavelength of the radiation, as well as isolated absorption measurements at a given wavelength. In order to understand spectrophotometry, we need to review the terminology employed in characterizing radiant energy, consider in an elementary fashion the interaction of

290

radiation with chemical species, and see in a general way what the instruments do. The student should understand that this chapter is only an introduction to the broad subject of spectrophotometry, and that it is possible to go much more deeply into nearly every topic that is mentioned here.

THE ELECTROMAGNETIC SPECTRUM

Various experiments in the physics laboratory are best interpreted in terms of the idea that light is propagated in the form of transverse waves. By appropriate measurements, these waves may be characterized with regard to wavelength, velocity, and the other terms which may be used to describe any wave motion. In Figure 12.1, it is indicated that the *wavelength* refers to

Fig. 12.1. Transverse wave.

the distance between two adjacent crests (or troughs) of the wave. The reciprocal of the wavelength, which is the number of waves in a unit length, is referred to as the *wave number*. The wave front is moving with a certain *velocity*. The number of complete cycles or waves passing a fixed point in a unit time is termed the *frequency*. The relationship of these properties is as follows, using the symbols λ for wavelength, $\bar{\nu}$ for wave number, ν for frequency, and c for the velocity of light:

$$\frac{1}{\lambda} = \bar{\nu} = \frac{\nu}{c}$$

The velocity of light is about 3×10^{10} cm/sec. Various units are employed for wavelength, depending upon the region of the spectrum: For ultraviolet and visible radiation, the Angstrom unit and the millimicron are widely used, while the micron is the common unit for the infrared region. A micron, μ, is defined as 10^{-6} m (meters), and a millimicron, mμ, is 10^{-9} m or 10^{-7} cm. One Angstrom unit, A, is 10^{-10} m or 10^{-8} cm. Thus there are ten Angstrom units in one millimicron. Wave number is often used by chemists as a frequency unit because it has convenient numerical values ($\bar{\nu}$ and ν are related by a constant factor, c, the velocity of light); the common unit of wave number is the reciprocal centimeter, cm^{-1}.

Luminous bodies such as the sun or an electric light bulb emit a broad spectrum comprising many wavelengths. Those wavelengths associated with *visible light* are capable of affecting the retina of the human eye and hence give rise to the subjective impressions of vision. But much of the radiation emitted by hot bodies lies outside the region where the eye is sensitive, and we speak of the *ultraviolet* and *infrared* regions of the spectrum which lie on either side of the visible. The entire electromagnetic spectrum is classified approximately as shown in Figure 12.2.

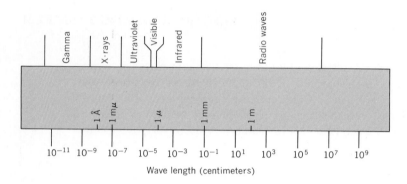

Fig. 12.2. Approximate classification of the electromagnetic spectrum.

Within the visible region of the spectrum, persons with normal color vision are able to correlate the wavelength of light striking the eye with the subjective sensation of color, and color is indeed sometimes used for convenience in designating certain portions of the spectrum, as shown in the rough classification in Table 12.1.

Table 12.1   VISIBLE SPECTRUM AND COMPLEMENTARY COLORS

Wavelength, mμ	Color	Complementary color
400–435	Violet	Yellow-green
435–480	Blue	Yellow
480–490	Green-blue	Orange
490–500	Blue-green	Red
500–560	Green	Purple
560–580	Yellow-green	Violet
580–595	Yellow	Blue
595–610	Orange	Green-blue
610–750	Red	Blue-green

We "see" objects by means of either transmitted or reflected light. When "white light," containing a whole spectrum of wavelengths, passes through a medium such as a colored glass or a chemical solution which is transparent to certain wavelengths but absorbs others, the medium appears colored to the observer. Since only the transmitted waves reach the eye, their wavelengths dictate the color of the medium. This color is said to be *complementary* to the color that would be perceived if the absorbed light could be inspected, because the transmitted and absorbed light together make up the original white light. Similarly, opaque colored objects absorb some wavelengths and reflect others when illuminated with white light.

THE INTERACTION OF RADIANT ENERGY WITH MOLECULES

The wave theory of light explains many optical phenomena such as reflection, refraction, and diffraction, but there are other experimental results, such as the photoelectric effect, that are best interpreted in terms of the idea that a beam of light is a stream of particulate energy packets called photons. Each of these particles possesses a characteristic energy which is related to the frequency of the light by the equation.

$$E = h\nu$$

where h is Planck's constant. Light of a certain frequency (or wavelength) is associated with photons, each of which possesses a definite quantity of energy. As explained below, it is the quantity of energy possessed by a photon which determines whether a certain molecular species will absorb or transmit light of the corresponding wavelength.

In addition to the ordinary energy of translational motion, which is not of concern here, a molecule possesses internal energy which may be subdivided into three classes. First, the molecule may be rotating about various axes, and possess a certain quantity of *rotational energy*. Second, atoms or groups of atoms within the molecule may be vibrating, that is, moving periodically with respect to each other about their equilibrium positions, conferring *vibrational energy* upon the molecule. Finally, a molecule possesses *electronic energy*, by which we mean the potential energy associated with the distribution of negative electric charges (electrons) about the positively charged nuclei of the atoms.

$$E_{int} = E_{elec} + E_{vib} + E_{rot}$$

One of the basic ideas of quantum theory is that a molecule may not possess any arbitrary quantity of internal energy, but rather can exist only in certain "permitted" energy states. If a molecule is to absorb energy and be raised to a higher energy level, it must absorb a quantity appropriate for the transition. It cannot absorb an arbitrary quantity of energy determined by the experimenter and linger in an energy state intermediate between its permitted levels. This quantization of molecular energy, coupled with the concept that photons possess definite quantities of energy, sets the stage for selectivity in the absorption of radiant energy by molecules. When molecules are irradiated with many wavelengths, they will abstract from the incident beam those wavelengths corresponding to photons of energy appropriate for permitted molecular energy transitions, and other wavelengths will simply be transmitted.

The rotational energy levels of a molecule are quite closely spaced, as indicated schematically in Figure 12.3. Thus pure rotational transitions

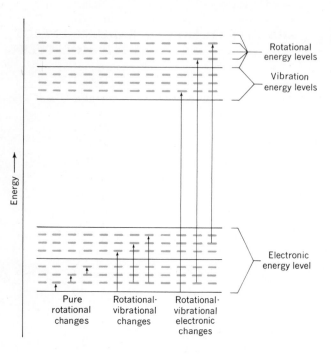

Fig. 12.3. Schematic energy level diagram.

require relatively little energy and are induced by radiation of very low frequency (long wavelength). It is in the far infrared and "microwave" regions of the spectrum (wavelengths of perhaps 100μ to 10 cm) that absorption of radiation is correlated with changes in rotational energy alone. Studies of absorption in this region have contributed fundamental information regarding molecular structure but have found relatively little application in analytical chemistry.[1]

Vibrational energy levels are farther apart (Figure 12.3), and more energetic photons are required if absorption is to increase the vibrational energy of a molecule. Absorption due to vibrational transitions is seen in the infrared region of the spectrum, roughly from 2 to 100μ. Pure vibrational changes are not observed, however, because rotational transitions are superimposed upon them. Thus a typical vibrational absorption spectrum is composed of complex bands rather than single lines. In practice, an in-

[1] J. H. Goldstein, "Microwave Spectrophotometry," Chapter 62, Part I, Vol. 5, of *Treatise on Analytical Chemistry*, I. M. Kolthoff and P. J. Elving, Eds., Interscience Publishers, Inc., New York, 1964.

frared absorption spectrum consists, not of discrete lines as might be supposed from Figure 12.3, but rather of a broad envelope extending over a wavelength span, because of distortion of molecular energy levels by neighboring molecules and because of the inability of the instrument to resolve closely spaced lines.

Infrared spectrophotometry is of tremendous importance in modern chemistry, especially to the organic chemist. It has become a routine tool for the identification of compounds, detection of particular functional groups, and the quantitative analysis of complex mixtures. Often the progress of a reaction may be followed by means of infrared spectra. The subject will not be treated further in this text because of space limitations and because it is often covered in organic chemistry courses.[2]

Absorption of visible light and ultraviolet radiation increases the electronic energy of a molecule. That is, the energy contributed by the photons enables electrons to overcome some of the restraint of the nuclei and move out to new orbitals of higher energy. Vibrational and rotational effects are superimposed upon the electronic change, but the region where the absorption is found is determined by the electronic energy levels of the molecule. The vibrational and rotational changes introduce "fine structure" into the spectrum, so that the absorption involves a band of wavelengths rather than a single line. The individual lines making up the band are usually not resolved under experimental conditions, and the observed visible or ultraviolet absorption spectrum generally consists of peaks exhibiting a smooth curvature.

Once the absorption has been recorded, the fate of the excited molecules is usually not of interest in ordinary spectrophotometry for analytical purposes, but we may briefly note, for the curious student, that the molecule tends not to remain in the excited state but rather to get rid of the excess energy. Commonly, the energy is degraded into heat by a step-wise process involving collisions with other molecules. (This heat is not noticeable in an ordinary spectrophotometric experiment.) Sometimes the energy is reemitted as radiation, usually of longer wavelength than was originally absorbed; this phenomenon is known as *fluorescence* (if there is a detectable time delay in reemission, the term *phosphorescence* is used). Fluorescence can lead to errors in absorption measurements if the reemitted radiation reaches the detector of the instrument. Finally, in some cases the absorbed energy may cause the molecule to dissociate into free radicals or ions, which may then proceed through a complicated series of reactions.

It may be expected that the spacing of the electronic energy levels of a particular type of molecule will reflect what we commonly call its electronic structure, and that the wavelengths of absorption bands will relate to molecular structure in a unique way. Absorption in a saturated hydrocarbon

[2] For an introduction, see, for example, J. R. Dyer, *Applications of Absorption Spectroscopy of Organic Compounds*, Chapter 3, Prentice-Hall, Inc., Englewood Cliffs, N.J., 1965, p. 22.

like ethane, CH_3—CH_3, occurs at very short wavelength (< 160 mμ) to the accompaniment of bond rupture. Compounds with π-bonds like ethylene, CH_2=CH_2, absorb at longer wavelengths ($\sim$195 mμ); it is easier to form the excited structure $\overset{\displaystyle \diagdown}{\underset{\displaystyle \diagup}{C}}\overset{+}{}\ \overset{-}{}\overset{\displaystyle \diagup}{\underset{\displaystyle \diagdown}{C}}$ from $\overset{\displaystyle \diagdown}{\underset{\displaystyle \diagup}{C}}$=$\overset{\displaystyle \diagup}{\underset{\displaystyle \diagdown}{C}}$ than to rupture the σ-bond

of ethane, —$\overset{|}{\underset{|}{C}}$—$\overset{|}{\underset{|}{C}}$—. Unsaturated groups have long been known to confer prominent absorptive power upon a molecule; such groups as $\overset{\displaystyle \diagdown}{\underset{\displaystyle \diagup}{C}}$=O,

—N=N—, —N=O, phenyl (C_6H_5—), and —NO_2 were designated *chromophores* (color-bearing groups) many years ago because molecules into which they were introduced shifted their absorption toward, or even into, the visible region.

The presence of a particular chromophore often leads to absorption in a certain region of the spectrum, but the exact position of the absorption maximum depends upon other substituent groups in the molecule. Ingenious, albeit empirical, rules have been developed by the organic chemists for deducing features of molecular structure from visible-ultraviolet absorption spectra.[2,3]

QUANTITATIVE ASPECTS OF ABSORPTION

Absorption spectra can be obtained using samples in various forms, e.g., gases, thin films of liquids, solutions in various solvents, and even solids. Most analytical work involves solutions, and we wish here to develop a quantitative description of the relationship between the concentration of a solution and its ability to absorb radiation. At the same time, we must realize that the extent to which absorption occurs will depend also upon the distance traversed by the radiation through the solution. As we have seen, absorption also depends upon the wavelength of the radiation and the nature of the molecular species in solution, but for the time being we may suppose that we can control these.

Bouguer's (Lambert's) law

The relationship between the absorption of radiation and the length of the path through the absorbing medium was first formulated by Bouguer

---

[3] A. E. Gillam and E. S. Stern, *An Introduction to Electronic Absorption Spectroscopy in Organic Chemistry*, Edward Arnold, Ltd., London, 1954.

(1729), although it is sometimes attributed to Lambert (1768). Let us subdivide a homogeneous absorbing medium such as a chemical solution into imaginary layers, each of the same thickness. If a beam of monochromatic radiation (i.e., radiation of a single wavelength) is directed through the medium, it is found that each layer absorbs an equal fraction of the radiation, or each layer diminishes the radiant power of the beam by an equal fraction. Suppose, for example, that the first layer absorbed half of the radiation incident upon it. Then the second layer would absorb half of the radiation incident upon *it*, and the radiant power emerging from this second layer would be one-fourth that of the original power; from the third layer, one-eighth, etc.

Bouguer's finding may be formulated mathematically as follows, where P_0 is the incident radiant power and P is the power emergent from a layer of medium b units thick:

$$-\frac{dP}{db} = k_1 P$$

The minus sign indicates that the power decreases with absorption. For the student who is unfamiliar with calculus, we may express this equation verbally as: The decrease in radiant power per unit thickness of absorbing medium is proportional to the radiant power. For the student who has studied calculus, let us rearrange the above equation to

$$-\frac{dP}{P} = k_1 \, db$$

and integrate between limits P_0 and P and 0 and b:

$$-\int_{P_0}^{P} \frac{dP}{P} = k_1 \int_{0}^{b} db$$

$$-(\ln P - \ln P_0) = k_1 b$$

$$\ln P_0 - \ln P = k_1 b$$

$$\ln \frac{P_0}{P} = k_1 b$$

Usually the equation is written with base 10 logarithms, which simply changes the constant:

$$\log \frac{P_0}{P} = k_2 b$$

A verbal statement of this equation might be: The power of the transmitted radiation decreases in an exponential fashion as the thickness of the absorbing medium increases arithmetically. Some writers consider this integration step to be a "derivation" of Bouguer's law, but actually the two formulations are equivalent representations of what we are here taking as an experimental finding.

Bouguer's law appears to describe correctly, without exception, the absorption of monochromatic radiation by various thicknesses of a homogeneous medium. The student can convince himself that the law applies strictly only with monochromatic radiation by considering an extreme case. Pass two wavelengths through a medium, one of which is absorbed appreciably and the other not at all. According to Bouguer's law, if we allow the thickness of the medium to increase indefinitely, then the transmitted radiant power should approach zero. But it cannot fall to zero if an appreciable fraction is not absorbed at all.

It may be noted that Bouguer's law takes the same form as other familiar functions such as the rate expression for first-order kinetics or radioactive decay, and the compound interest law.

Beer's law

The relationship between the concentration of an absorbing species and the extent of absorption was formulated by Beer in 1859. Beer's law is analogous to Bouguer's law in describing an exponential decrease in transmitted radiant power with an arithmetic increase in concentration. Thus,

$$-\frac{dP}{dc} = k_3 P$$

which upon integration and conversion to ordinary logarithms becomes

$$\log \frac{P_0}{P} = k_4 c$$

Beer's law is strictly applicable only for monochromatic radiation and where the nature of the absorbing species is fixed over the concentration range in question. We shall comment further on this point in connection with so-called "deviations" from Beer's law.

Combined Bouguer-Beer law

Bouguer's and Beer's laws are readily combined into a convenient expression. We note that in studying the effect of changing concentration upon absorption, the path length through the solution would be held constant but the measured results would depend upon the magnitude of the constant value. In other words, in Beer's law as written above, $k_4 = f(b)$. Similarly, in Bouguer's law, $k_2 = f(c)$. Substitution of these fundamental relationships into Bouguer's and Beer's laws gives

$$\log \frac{P_0}{P} = f(c)b \quad \text{and} \quad \log \frac{P_0}{P} = f(b)c$$

(Bouguer)   **(Beer)**

The two laws must apply simultaneously at any point, so that

$$f(c)b = f(b)c$$

or, separating the variables,

$$\frac{f(c)}{c} = \frac{f(b)}{b}$$

Now, the only condition under which two functions of independent variables can be equal is that they both equal a constant:

$$\frac{f(c)}{c} = \frac{f(b)}{b} = K$$

or

$$f(c) = Kc \quad \text{and} \quad f(b) = Kb$$

Substitution into either the Bouguer or the Beer expression yields the same result:

$$\log \frac{P_0}{P} = f(c)b = Kbc$$

$$\log \frac{P_0}{P} = f(b)c = Kbc$$

Nomenclature and units

Unfortunately, the development of the nomenclature regarding the Bouguer-Beer law has not been systematic, and a confusing array of terms appears in the literature. In analytical chemistry, the tendency in the United States has been to adopt recommendations of a Joint Committee on Nomenclature in Applied Spectroscopy, established by the Society for Applied Spectroscopy and the American Society for Testing Materials (ASTM).[4]

The symbols P_0 and P as used here are recommended for the incident and transmitted radiant powers, respectively.[5] The term $\log (P_0/P)$ is called the absorbance and given the symbol A. Other terms which have been used synonymously with absorbance and which the student may encounter in the literature are *extinction, optical density,* and *absorbancy.*

The symbol b is accepted for the length of the path through the absorbing medium; it is ordinarily expressed in centimeters. Other writers have used the letter l for the same quantity, and, more rarely, the letters d or t.

Two different units for c, the concentration of absorbing solute, are often used, grams per liter and moles per liter. It is apparent that the value of the constant (designated K above) in the Bouguer-Beer law will depend upon which concentration system is used. When c is in grams per liter, the

---

[4] For the report of this committee, see H. K. Hughes *et al., Anal. Chem.,* **24,** 1349 (1952).

[5] Many writers use I_0 and I for these terms, standing for *intensity* of the beam, but in ordinary spectrophotometers the quantity actually measured is the rate at which radiant energy is absorbed at the detector; this is best called "radiant power." Such units as watts or ergs per second might be employed, but in spectrophotometry we deal with a ratio (P/P_0) or the logarithm of a ratio $(\log P_0/P)$, and the units cancel.

constant is called the *absorptivity*, symbol *a*. When *c* is in moles per liter, the constant is the *molar absorptivity*, symbol ϵ. Thus, in the recommended system, the Bouguer-Beer law may take two forms:

$$A = abc_{g/l} \quad \text{or} \quad A = \epsilon bc_{moles/l}$$

It is apparent that $\epsilon = a \times$ M. W., where M. W. refers to the molecular weight of the absorbing substance in the solution. Other designations for *a* are *specific extinction, extinction coefficient, Bunsen coefficient,* and *specific absorption.* Similarly, some writers call ϵ the *molar extinction coefficient, molecular extinction,* and various other names.

The *transmittance*, $T = P/P_0$, is simply the fraction of the incident power which is transmitted by a sample. The *percent transmittance*, $\%T = P/P_0 \times 100$, is also encountered. If $A = \log(P_0/P)$ and $T = P/P_0$, then $A = \log(1/T)$. Since, from Beer's law, absorbance is directly proportional to concentration, it is clear that transmittance is not; $\log T$ must be plotted vs. *c* to obtain a linear graph. Figure 12.4 shows the situation. Analytical chemists prefer

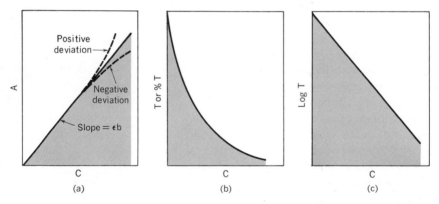

Fig. 12.4. Appearance of Beer's law plots.

absorbance plots, but the student should be familiar with transmittance because it is encountered frequently. The detectors of most instruments generate a signal which is linear in transmittance, because they respond linearly to radiant power. Thus, if an instrument is to be read in absorbance units, there must be a logarithmic scale on the readout device or the signal must be altered logarithmically by an electronic circuit or in some mechanical fashion.

Deviations from the Bouguer-Beer law

According to the Bouguer-Beer law (or, as many writers say, simply Beer's law), a plot of absorbance vs. molar concentration will be a straight line of slope ϵb. Frequently, however, measurements on real chemical systems yield Beer's law plots which are not linear over the entire concentration range of interest, as shown by the dashed lines in Figure 12.4a. Such curvature suggests that ϵ is not a constant, independent of concentration, for such systems, but closer consideration leads to a somewhat more sophisticated view. The value of ϵ is expected to depend upon the nature of the absorbing species in solution and upon the wavelength of the radiation. Most deviations from Beer's law encountered in analytical practice are attributable to failure or inability to control these two aspects, and hence may be called apparent deviations because they reflect experimental difficulties more than any inadequacy of Beer's law itself.[6]

Consider, for example, absorbance measurements on a series of solutions of a weak acid, HB. The degree of dissociation of HB (fraction ionized) varies with the quantity of HB introduced into each solution if the final volumes are the same. Under this circumstance, it is possible to encounter either positive or negative Beer's law deviations, depending upon the ϵ-values of the two species, HB and B^-, at the wavelength employed. Since the fraction of the material present as B^- decreases with increasing analytical concentration of HB, a negative deviation from Beer's law will be seen if $\epsilon_{B^-} > \epsilon_{HB}$. On the other hand, if $\epsilon_{HB} > \epsilon_{B^-}$, a positive deviation will result. The system should follow Beer's law at a wavelength[7] where $\epsilon_{HB} = \epsilon_{B^-}$. These deviations from Beer's law may be circumvented, not only by performing measurements at the isosbestic wavelength (which lowers the sensitivity because ϵ-values generally are not maximal here), but by adjusting all of the solutions to a very low pH by addition of strong acid so as to repress the ionization of HB, or by addition of sufficient strong alkali to transform all of the material into B^-.

Many examples of this sort of Beer's law deviation are known. The general viewpoint here is that there is nothing wrong with Beer's law, that ϵ-values for individual species are constant over a wide concentration range, and that the deviations are predictable from a knowledge of the equilibria in which these species participate. Equilibria involving ions are often sensi-

---

[6] There is another class of deviations which may be considered *real* rather than apparent, but they are not likely to be encountered in analytical chemistry. For example, it is shown in the theory of optics that ϵ for a substance in solution will change with changes in the refractive index of the solution. Since changes in refractive index attend concentration changes, Beer's law should not hold, even ideally. However, this effect is very small and is generally well within the experimental errors of spectrophotometry. Another real deviation from Beer's law sometimes occurs when relatively strong radiation passes through a medium containing only a few absorbing molecules. Under these conditions, all of the molecules may be elevated to higher energy states by only a fraction of the available photons, and hence there will be no opportunity for further absorption regardless of how many more photons may be available. This situation, known as *saturation*, is ordinarily not encountered in analytical practice.

[7] A wavelength where two or more species in equilibrium with one another have the same ϵ-value is called an *isosbestic point*.

tive to added electrolytes, and failure to control the ionic strength may create problems in spectrophotometry. Temperature and various other factors may further complicate the situation.

Even with systems that are "well-behaved" chemically, deviations from Beer's law may occur because of characteristics of the instruments used in measuring absorbance values. In days past, such deviations sometimes resulted from fatigue effects in detectors, nonlinearity in amplifiers and readout devices, and instability in the sources of radiant energy. These problems have largely been solved in modern spectrophotometric instruments.

We pointed out earlier that the Bouguer-Beer law demands monochromatic radiation. Because ε-values depend upon wavelength, measured absorbance values reflect the wavelength distribution in the radiation, which, in a practical spectrophotometer, is never strictly monochromatic. Think again of an absorbing solution as a series of imaginary layers of equal thickness. Now if heterochromatic radiation passes through the first layer, the more strongly absorbed wavelengths are abstracted from the beam to a greater extent than the others. Thus the radiation impinging upon the second layer will be richer in the less strongly absorbed wavelengths, and the second layer will not absorb the same fraction of the radiation incident upon it as did the first layer. Since the Bouguer-Beer law states that each layer will absorb an equal fraction, deviation from the law will clearly result.[8]

Although it must be pointed out that instrumental characteristics can lead to deviations from the Bouguer-Beer law, it is a practical fact that the better modern spectrophotometers are capable of performing well in this regard. This is not the case with the colorimeters or filter photometers which employ broad band pass filters to isolate the desired radiation and which are still widely used in clinical and control laboratories. Further, good spectrophotometers can be operated in such a way as to lose some of their fine characteristics. Thus the student should file away in the back of his mind the warning to check before assuming the Bouguer-Beer law to hold for a particular chemical system with a particular instrument.

INSTRUMENTATION FOR SPECTROPHOTOMETRY

A spectrophotometer is an instrument for measuring the transmittance or absorbance of a sample as a function of wavelength; measurements on a series of samples at a single wavelength may also be performed. Such instruments may be classified as manual or recording, or as single or double beam. In practice, single beam instruments are usually operated manually and

---

[8] A mathematical analysis of this type of deviation may be found in L. Meites and H. C. Thomas, *Advanced Analytical Chemistry*, McGraw-Hill Book Co., Inc., New York, 1958, p. 255.

double beam instruments generally feature automatic recording of absorption spectra, but it is possible to record a spectrum with a single beam instrument. An alternative classification is based upon the spectral region, and we speak of infrared or ultraviolet spectrophotometers, etc. A complete understanding of spectrophotometers requires a detailed knowledge of optics and electronics which is far beyond the scope of this book. It is possible, though, for the student at this stage to understand what the instruments do. By combining this general, fundamental understanding with detailed instructions furnished in the form of "manuals" by the manufacturers, the chemist can obtain good data with modern spectrophotometers. Manually operated, single beam spectrophotometers will be discussed first, because this provides the background for appreciating the capabilities of the more complex instruments.

Single beam spectrophotometers

The essential components of a spectrophotometer, which are shown schematically in Figure 12.5, are the following: (1) a continuous source of

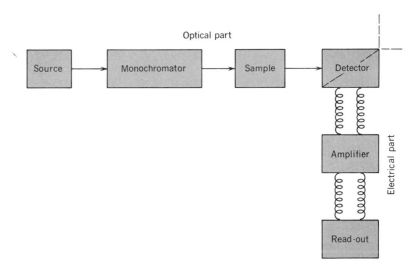

Fig. 12.5. Block diagram showing components of single beam spectrophotometer. Arrows represent radiant energy, coiled lines electrical connections. The optical part and the electrical part of the instrument meet at the detector, a transducer which converts radiant into electrical energy.

radiant energy covering the region of the spectrum in which the instrument is designed to operate; (2) a monochromator, which is a device for isolating a narrow band of wavelengths from the broad spectrum emitted by the source (of course, strict monochromaticity is not attained); (3) a container for the sample; (4) a detector, which is a *transducer* that converts radiant energy into an electrical signal; (5) an amplifier and associated circuitry which renders the electrical signal appropriate for readout; and (6) a read-out system on which is displayed the magnitude of the electrical signal. Both single and double beam spectrophotometers, and instruments which operate in various regions of the spectrum, all have these essential components, although the details are quite different in the several cases. In accord with the goal set forth above, we shall discuss these components briefly.

Source. The usual source of radiant energy for the visible region of the spectrum as well as the near infrared and near ultraviolet is an incandescent lamp with a tungsten filament. Under ordinary operating conditions, the output of this tungsten lamp is adequate from about 325 or 350 mμ to about 3μ. The energy emitted by the heated filament varies greatly with wavelength, as shown in Figure 12.6. The energy distribution is a function of the

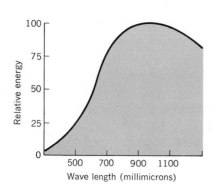

Fig. 12.6. Relative output of a typical tungsten lamp as a function of wavelength.

temperature of the filament, which depends in turn upon the voltage supplied to the lamp; an increase in operating temperature increases the total energy output and shifts the peak of Figure 12.6 to shorter wavelength. Thus the voltage to the lamp should be a stable one; a 6-v storage battery with a well-maintained charge is sometimes employed, whereas a regulated power supply is incorporated into some instruments. The heat from a tungsten lamp may be troublesome in an instrument; often the lamp housing is water-jacketed to prevent warming of the sample or of other instrument components.

Below about 325 to 350 mμ, the output of a tungsten lamp is inadequate for spectrophotometers, and a different source must be used. Most common is a hydrogen (or deuterium) discharge tube, which is used from about 185 to 375 or 400 mμ. When a discharge between two electrodes excites emission by a sample of a gas such as hydrogen, a discontinuous line spectrum characteristic of the gas is obtained provided the pressure is relatively low. As the hydrogen pressure is increased, the lines broaden and eventually overlap, until at relatively high pressures, a continuous spectrum is emitted. The pressure required in a hydrogen discharge tube is lower than that with certain other gases; also the tube runs cooler. Such tubes are conveniently small—about the size of common radio tubes. The envelope is usually glass, but a quartz window is provided to pass the ultraviolet radiation. A high voltage power supply is required for gaseous discharge tubes. In a number of spectrophotometers, provision is made for interchanging tungsten and hydrogen discharge sources in order to cover the visible and ultraviolet regions through which the instruments operate.

The source for infrared spectrophotometers, which commonly operate from about 2 to 15 μ, is usually the Nernst glower. This is a small rod of ceramic appearance fabricated from a special mixture of metal oxides, with platinum leads sealed into the ends. The rod is nonconducting at room temperature, but is brought into a conducting state when heated, after which a flow of current maintains a glow which is rich in infrared radiation.

Monochromator. This is an optical device for isolating from a continuous source a beam of radiation of high spectral purity of any desired wavelength. The essential components of a monochromator are a slit system and a dispersive element. Radiation from the source is focused upon the entrance slit, then collimated by a lens or mirror so that a parallel beam falls upon the dispersing element, which is either a prism or a diffraction grating. By mechanically turning the prism or grating, various portions of the spectrum produced by the dispersive element are focused on the exit slit, whence, by a further optical path, they encounter the sample.

The student may recall from elementary physics the action of a prism in dispersing white light into a spectrum. When a beam of light passes through the interface between two different media, such as air and glass, bending takes place which is called *refraction*. The extent of the bending depends upon

Fig. 12.7. Dispersion of white light by a prism.

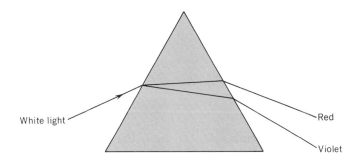

the index of refraction of the glass. This index of refraction varies with the wavelength of the light; the blues are bent more than the reds, as shown in Figure 12.7. As a result of the variation of refractive index with wavelength, the prism is able to disperse or spread out a beam of white light into a spectrum, in which the various colors making up the white light may be recognized separately. Infrared and ultraviolet radiation are dispersed in the same manner, but here the words *light* and *color* are not used and the prism material is not glass. The material of choice represents a compromise between dispersive power and transparency in the desired wavelength region, along with several other factors. Spectrophotometers covering mainly the visible region of the spectrum have glass prisms, whereas quartz is the prism material for instruments covering the ultraviolet and near infrared as well as the visible; infrared spectrophotometers commonly have prisms of rock salt.

The spectral purity of the emergent radiation from the monochromator depends upon the dispersive power of the prism and the width of the exit slit. At first thought, one might suppose that monochromaticity could be approached as closely as desired by merely decreasing the slit width sufficiently, but this is not the case. Eventually the slit becomes so narrow that diffractive effects at its edges only create a loss of radiant power with no increase in spectral purity (this is the so-called "Rayleigh diffraction limit"); actually, before this limit is approached in a typical spectrophotometer, the narrowed slit is passing insufficient energy to activate the detector.

With prism monochromators, a given slit width does not yield the same degree of monochromaticity throughout the spectrum. The wavelength dependence of the dispersion of a prism is such that the wavelengths in the spectrum are not spread out uniformly. The dispersion is greater for the shorter wavelengths, and hence wider slits may here achieve the same degree of spectral purity as would narrower slits at longer wavelengths.

Figure 12.8 is a schematic diagram of the optical system of a particular

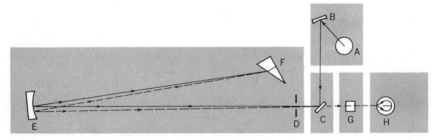

Fig. 12.8. Schematic diagram of optical system of Beckman model DU spectrophotometer. *A*, light source; *B*, *C*, mirrors; *D*, slit; *E*, collimating mirror; *F*, quartz prism with reflecting back surface; *G*, cell; *H*, phototube. (Courtesy of Beckman Instruments, Inc.)

single beam spectrophotometer with a quartz prism. The back of the prism is coated with a reflective metallized surface so that the radiation actually passes twice through the dispersive element. This not only enhances the dispersion but also is of great geometric convenience.

A diffraction grating is made by ruling, usually on a glass or polished metal surface, a large number of parallel lines or grooves (tens of thousands to the inch). When light is reflected from this surface, that which strikes the rulings themselves is dissipated by scattering, and the spaces between the rulings act as individual light sources. Overlapping of the waves from these sources establishes an interference pattern which results in the dispersion of the reflected light into a series of spectra. The student is referred to elementary physics texts for an explanation of this phenomenon.

The machines for ruling the lines on a grating must be constructed to very close tolerances, and original gratings are expensive. Much cheaper, and much more widely used, are *replica gratings*, large numbers of which can be prepared from a single master grating. The original is coated with a plastic material, which, after hardening, is stripped off to yield a replica. The plastic is made reflective by evaporating a film of metal, generally aluminum, onto the ruled face; the grating is mounted in the monochromator in such a way that rotation allows various portions of the spectrum to illuminate the exit slit.

Gratings differ from prisms in rendering a uniform dispersion throughout the entire spectrum; in other words, a single slit width yields the same degree of monochromaticity of the emergent radiation throughout the spectrum. Figure 12.9 shows the optical path through a widely used grating instrument.

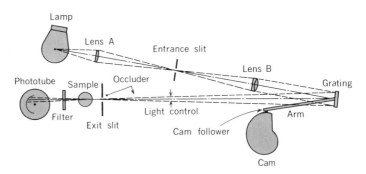

Fig. 12.9. Schematic diagram of optical system of Spectronic 20. (Courtesy of Bausch and Lomb, Inc.)

As mentioned earlier, the radiation emergent from a monochromator is not monochromatic, although it is much more nearly so than is the original source. The wavelength distribution is somewhat as shown in Figure 12.10. The terminology employed in describing the width of the band shown in the figure is not entirely standard, and advertisements for instruments often quote figures for "band width" without specifying what is meant. A particular terminology which is widely understood is shown in the figure.

A problem in monochromators is so-called "stray light," by which is meant radiation of unspecified wavelengths which is reflected about inside the monochromator and which may find its way to the exit slit. In good

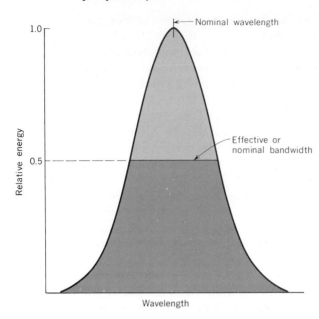

Fig. 12.10. Wavelength distribution of the energy emergent from a monochromator.

instruments, this is minimized by using dull black surfaces, and by inserting baffles in appropriate positions. It is cut to an extremely low level in the finer instruments which employ double monochromators, generally combining both prism and grating. With ordinary instruments, spurious absorbance readings due to stray light may be obtained in spectral regions where very little energy of the desired wavelengths is available.

Until quite recently, instruments without true monochromators were widely used for absorbance measurements, mainly in the visible region, in laboratories where a low initial investment, simplicity, and speed were more important than the quality of the results. These instruments, designated *filter photometers*, utilized colored glass filters to isolate fairly broad wavelength bands from the source. They served admirably for many routine analyses, but they are rapidly being displaced by inexpensive grating spectrophotometers.

Sample container. Most spectrophotometry involves solutions, and thus most sample containers are cells for placing liquids in the beam of the spectrophotometer. The cell must transmit radiant energy in the spectral region of interest; thus glass cells serve in the visible region, quartz or special high-silica glasses in the ultraviolet, and rock salt in the infrared. It must be remembered that the cell, which in a sense is merely a container for the sample, is actually more than this; when in position, it becomes part of the optical path through the spectrophotometer, and its optical properties are important. In less expensive instruments, cylindrical test tubes are sometimes used as sample containers. It is important that such tubes be positioned reproducibly by marking one side of the tube and facing the mark in the same direction whenever it is placed in the instrument. The better cells have flat optical surfaces. The cells must be filled so that the light beam goes through the solution, with the meniscus entirely above the beam. Cells are generally held in position by kinematic design of the holder or by spring clips which insure reproducible positioning in the cell compartment of the instrument.

Typical visible and ultraviolet cells have path lengths of 1 cm, but a wide variety is available, ranging from very short paths, fractions of a millimeter, up to 10 cm or even more. Special microcells may be obtained, by means of which minute volumes of solution yield an ordinary path length, and adjustable cells of variable path length are also available, particularly for infrared work. The variety of infrared cells currently on the market is beyond the scope of this discussion. Problems in the infrared are different from those in the ultraviolet and visible regions. Because solvents which are infrared-transparent are not available, the tendency is to run concentrated solutions at short path lengths (0.1 mm or even less) to minimize absorption by the solvent, and the cells are thus quite different from those employed at shorter wavelengths.

Detector. In a detector for a spectrophotometer, we desire high sensitivity in the spectral region of interest, linear response to radiant power, a fast response time, amenability to amplification, and high stability or low "noise" level, although in practice it is necessary to compromise among these factors. Higher sensitivity, for example, can be bought only at the expense of increased noise. The types of detection that have been most widely used are based upon (1) photochemical change (mainly photographic), (2) the photoelectric effect, and (3) thermal effects. Photography is no longer used in ordinary spectrophotometry; generally speaking, photoelectric detectors are employed in the visible and ultraviolet regions and detectors based upon thermal effects are used in the infrared.

The commonest photoelectric detector is the *phototube*. This is an evacuated envelope, with a transparent window, containing a pair of electrodes across which a potential is maintained. The surface of the negative electrode is photosensitive, i.e., electrons are ejected from this surface when it is irradiated with photons of sufficient energy. The electrons are accelerated across the potential difference to the positive electrode, and a current flows in the circuit. Whether or not electrons are emitted depends upon the nature of the cathode surface and the frequency of the radiation; the number of electrons emitted per unit time, and hence the current, depends upon the radiant power. A variety of phototubes are available which differ in the material of the cathode surface (also in the transparent window) and hence in their response to radiation of various frequencies. A number of spectrophotometers provide for interchanging detectors so as to maintain a good response over a broad wavelength range.

Photomultiplier tubes are more sensitive than ordinary phototubes because of high amplification accomplished within the tube itself. Such a tube has a series of electrodes, each at a progressively more positive potential than the cathode. The geometry of the tube is such that the primary photoelectrons are focused into a beam and accelerated to an electrode which is, say, 50 to 90 v more positive than the cathode. The bombardment of this electrode (or dynode, as it is called) releases many more secondary electron which are accelerated to a third, more positive, electrode, etc., for perhaps ten stages. A regulated high-voltage power supply, furnishing about 500 to 900 v, is required to operate the tube; a number of batteries in series can also be used. The output of the photomultiplier may be still further amplified with an external electronic amplifier. The enhanced sensitivity of this detector permits narrower slit widths in the monochromator and hence better resolution of spectral fine structure.

The common infrared detector is the thermocouple. The student may recall the thermoelectric effect: If two dissimilar metals are joined at two points, a potential is developed if the two junctions are at different temperatures. Heating of one of the junctions by the infrared radiation is thus the basis of detection. This junction is specially designed to have a low heat capacity so that it will be warmed appreciably by radiant energy of the power encountered in the instrument.

Amplification and readout. It is beyond the scope of this text to discuss the detailed electronics of amplification and readout as they are accomplished in various spectrophotometers. To give an idea of what may be involved, we may briefly consider one possibility. Let us place a large load resistor in series with a phototube, as shown schematically in Figure 12.11. Suppose

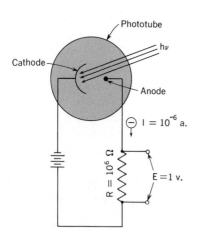

Fig. 12.11. Simple phototube circuit (see text).

the radiant power supplied to the cathode is such that a current of one microampere (10^{-6} amp) flows in the circuit. If the resistor has a value of one megohm (10^6 ohms) as shown in the figure, then according to Ohm's law the voltage across the resistor, $E = IR$, is $10^{-6} \times 10^6 = 1$ v. Although 1 v is a fair voltage, it cannot be measured by connecting an ordinary voltmeter across the resistor. As soon as such a connection is made, the meter becomes part of the circuit, establishing a parallel shunt around the resistor. Since the resistance of a typical voltmeter is very low as compared with 10^6 ohms, most of the current bypasses the large resistance and flows through the meter, and the voltage across the resistor, although measured correctly as it is, is no longer 1 v, but perhaps only a few millivolts.

The problem may be handled by applying the voltage across the load resistor to the control grid of a vacuum tube. The grid circuit of such a tube draws very little current, and thus the voltage holds up as it should. Small changes in grid potential are translated by the vacuum tube into large changes in plate current. The amplified output may be taken to a meter for direct reading, or it may be "bucked out" by another voltage under the control of the operator, with the meter used as a null device. The amplified signal may also be fed to a recording potentiometer.

Operation of a single beam spectrophotometer

We shall first describe the usual mode of operation of a typical manually operated single beam spectrophotometer, and then examine briefly some possible variations on the common procedure.

Ordinary operation. Typically, there is an opaque shutter, controlled by the operator, which may be placed in front of the phototube so that the tube is in darkness. With this shutter in position, a small current ("dark current") flows in the phototube circuit due to thermal emission of electrons by the cathode or perhaps a small leakage in the tube. By means of a knob on the instrument, the operator cancels out the dark current and sets the scale on the instrument to read infinite absorbance (zero transmittance). Next, with the wavelength set at the desired value and a cell containing a reference solution in the beam (the reference may be the pure solvent, a "blank" from an analytical procedure, etc.), the shutter is removed to expose the detector. Now, by adjusting the radiant power to the detector by means of the monochromator slit control, and/or by changing electronically the gain of the amplifier, the instrument scale is set to read zero absorbance (100% transmittance). With a scale thus established, the sample solution is placed in the beam and its absorbance or transmittance is read off. (The scale is generally linear in transmittance, but most instruments have an absorbance scale alongside the transmittance scale and either one can be read.)

The scale, set up as described above, must be reestablished whenever the wavelength is changed, in order to compensate for the variation of source output with wavelength and the wavelength-dependence of the detector response, as well as any absorption by the reference solution or the cell. It is good practice to check the dark current and reference solution settings frequently because of possible drift in the circuit and in the output of the source. Usually two cells are used, one for the reference solution and one for the samples to be measured; it is obvious that these cells should be matched with regard to path length and optical qualities.

Differential measurements. Ordinarily the reference solution in spectrophotometry is the pure solvent or a "blank" solution of some kind which contains little or none of the substance being determined. Using this reference and the dark current adjustment, a scale is set up as described above and shown in the upper part of Figure 12.12. Also shown along the scale

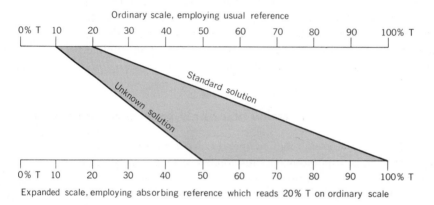

Fig. 12.12. Scale expansion in differential spectrophotometry.

are the transmittance values of two solutions, one an unknown which is to be measured and the other a standard solution containing a known quantity of the substance being determined.

Now we must recognize that the instrument does not know anything about the sort of solution that is in the beam. All it is capable of is to produce a reading of 100% T (or zero absorbance) when a certain radiant power falls upon the detector and the amplification of the electronic circuit is appropriate. Thus the instrument can be set to read 100% T with a strongly absorbing solution instead of the usual reference in the beam, by opening the slits of the monochromator and/or increasing the gain of the amplifier. Suppose, then, that we place the standard solution shown in Figure 12.12 in the beam and set the transmittance reading at 100%. As we have attempted to show in the figure by the lower scale and the lines tying it to the upper scale, we have now accomplished essentially a scale expansion. What was only a portion of the upper scale becomes full scale on the lower, and we may naturally expect that the unknown concentration can now be determined with enhanced accuracy and precision. Actually in some cases the error can be reduced to as little as a part per thousand, and the spectrophotometric measurement (normally not this good, see below) can compete with ordinary volumetric and gravimetric techniques, which are usually considered more precise. Several applications of differential spectrophotometry have been given by Bastian,[9] and a detailed mathematical analysis of the technique and its errors has been developed by Hiskey.[10]

To see more clearly how the error is reduced in differential spectrophotometry, let us consider an example. Suppose we wish to determine copper by measuring the absorbance of blue cupric solutions. Let us simply assume, to establish a specific basis for our discussion, that a solution with a copper concentration of 2 mg per ml (solution A) can be measured against a pure water reference with an error of 1%. Now consider the error if a solution containing 20 mg of copper per ml (solution B) were measured, using as a reference, not water, but another cupric solution containing 18 mg of copper per ml (solution C). The concentration difference between B and C is the same as the difference between solution A and water. Thus, if Beer's law is obeyed, the foregoing two measurements will give rise to the same absorbance value and the same error. In other words, supposing solution B were our unknown solution, we could determine how much it differed from solution C with a 1% error. But we know *accurately* the concentration of solution C, because it is a carefully prepared reference solution (by *accurately*, we mean that no spectrophotometric error is involved). Thus, so far as errors in spectrophotometry are concerned, the concentration of solution B can be determined with an error of only 0.1%. (In measuring solution A versus water, the error is $0.02/2 \times 100 = 1\%$; if B is measured against C, the error is still $0.02/2 \times 100 = 1\%$, but the error in the absolute concentration of B is only $0.02/20 \times 100 = 0.1\%$.)

The differential approach not only leads to lower errors, as explained above, but also permits the extension of spectrophotometry to the analysis of solutions which would be too highly absorbing for ordinary measurements.

It is possible to achieve even greater precision by setting both ends of the scale with standard solutions in the beam. In other words, the 100% T is set as described above using a standard solution more dilute than the unknown, but the 0% T is set, not with a shutter in the beam, but with a more concentrated standard solution. Reilley and Crawford, whose definitive paper[11] should be consulted for further details, refer to this as the "method of ultimate precision."

Double beam spectrophotometers

Recording spectrophotometers which automatically plot the absorbance of a sample as a function of wavelength are almost always double beam

[9] R. Bastian *et al.*, *Anal. Chem.*, **21**, 972 (1949); **22**, 160 (1950); **23**, 580 (1951).

[10] C. F. Hiskey *et al.*, *Anal. Chem.*, **21**, 1440 (1949); **22**, 1464 (1950); **23**, 506 (1951); **23**, 1196 (1951); **24**, 342 (1952).

[11] C. N. Reilley and C. M. Crawford, *Anal. Chem.*, **27**, 716 (1955).

instruments. It is far beyond the scope of this text to present a full discussion of these marvelous devices which have practically revolutionized the taking of absorption spectra for modern chemists, but it is obligatory at least to give an idea of what they do. The student should realize that, easy as they may be to operate, these instruments are extremely complicated. We shall discuss here one type of instrument, the optical null type, and that only briefly and in very general and schematic terms. Reference should be made to Figure 12.13 throughout this discussion. The figure is not intended to repre-

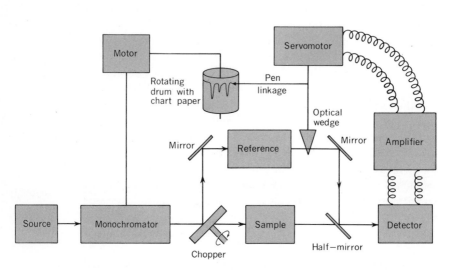

Fig. 12.13. Schematic diagram of a possible double beam optical null recording spectrophotometer.

sent any particular real instrument, but is presented only to give the student an idea of the sort of thing that the instrument makers have been able to do for chemists.

Radiation from the source passes through a monochromator as in a single beam instrument, and encounters a chopper. The chopper, driven by a synchronous motor (not shown in the figure), is a rotating mirror of such shape and such placement that it permits the beam to pass straight through during half of its period of rotation, while during the other half the beam encounters a reflective surface that turns it through a right angle, directing it upward in the figure. The direction may be changed again by other stationary mirrors as desired. Thus we now have two beams, from the same source, which are not steady but pulsate at a frequency determined by the chopper. One beam is passing while the other is blocked, and they alternate perhaps many times a second. One beam next passes through the sample while the other encounters a reference solution. The beams are then recombined so that they both fall upon a single detector.

Now as the chopper rotates, the detector "sees" first one beam, then the other. Suppose the monochromator is set at a wavelength where the sample does not absorb. Then the sample beam and the reference beam are of equal power, and the detector sees the same thing, regardless of the position of the chopper. A steady, constant power impinges upon the detector, and the electrical output of the detector circuit is a voltage which does not vary with time, in other words, a d-c voltage. Now the signal from the detector is fed to an amplifier, and the important characteristic of this amplifier is that it is an a-c amplifier which is tuned to the frequency of the chopper. The d-c voltage from the detector is not amplified, and the output of the amplifier is inadequate to do anything in the instrument.

Let us now change the wavelength so that the sample absorbs. Now the radiant power in the reference beam is greater than in the sample beam, and the detector, looking first at one and then the other, generates an electrical signal which reflects this pulsation in radiant power. This signal is an a-c voltage, a square wave, actually, superimposed upon the d-c signal mentioned above. The amplifier amplifies this a-c voltage, which is then fed to a motor (a so-called "servo").

The motor drives an "optical wedge" or "variable density wedge" into the reference beam. This wedge is a special device which blocks part of the beam and diminishes the radiant power in a smoothly progressive fashion as it moves. Now, when the wedge has moved so as to attenuate the reference beam to the same extent as the sample absorption has attenuated the sample beam, then once again the detector sees the same thing regardless of where the chopper is in its rotational period. Thus the electrical signal is again d-c, the amplifier output falls off, and the motor stops. This is an example of "feed-back"; the imbalance which set the servomotor in motion has "committed suicide." The position of the optical wedge at this point is reflected mechanically by the position of a pen which moves up and down on a piece of chart paper.

If we drive the monochromator with a motor which also moves the chart paper at right angles to the pen motion, we are then able to obtain a plot of wavelength vs. optical wedge position which becomes wavelength vs. transmittance or absorbance if the wedge is shaped properly and the chart paper is appropriately calibrated.

Real instruments are more complicated than we have suggested above and in the figure. For example, there may be a slit servomotor controlling the radiant power from the monochromator, and we have not indicated how an imbalance signal tells the motor which way to move the wedge. While some instruments operate on an optical null principle as discussed here, there are others which employ an electrical null that is quite different.

These instruments are extremely complicated, but they have been engineered so well that anyone can operate them by merely inserting samples and pushing buttons. Obtaining the top performance of which the instrument is capable, however, requires more knowledge than this. Most chemists must strike a compromise between the extremes of total ignorance and devoting a lifetime to the study of instrumentation. Unfortunately, the compromise in many cases falls so far toward the side of ignorance that data are obtained which are no better than a less expensive instrument could have furnished, and the instrument may even be needlessly damaged.

ERRORS IN SPECTROPHOTOMETRY

Errors in spectrophotometric measurements may arise from a host of causes, some of which have been anticipated in the discussion of instrumentation above. Many can be countered by care and common sense. Sample cells should be clean. Certain substances, e.g., proteins, sometimes adsorb very strongly on the cell and are washed out only with difficulty. Fingerprints may absorb ultraviolet radiation. The positioning of the cells in the beam must be reproducible. Gas bubbles must not be present in the optical path. The wavelength calibration of the instrument should be checked occasionally, and drift or instability in the circuit must be corrected. It must not be assumed that Beer's law holds for an untested chemical system. Sample instability may lead to errors if the measurements are not carefully timed.

The concentration of the absorbing species is of great importance in determining the error after all other controllable errors have been minimized. It is intuitively reasonable that the solution being measured should not absorb practically all of the radiation nor should it absorb hardly any. We might expect, then, that the error in a spectrophotometric determination of concentration would be minimal at some intermediate absorbance value away from the extreme ends of the scale. An expression can be derived from Beer's law which shows where this minimum error occurs.

Recall that

$$A = \log \frac{P_0}{P} = \frac{1}{2.3} \ln \frac{P_0}{P} = \epsilon bc$$

Let the relative error in concentration be $dc/c = dA/A$. We want to obtain an expression for dc/c and then inquire where this expression has a minimum. Differentiating Beer's law, $A = (1/2.3) \ln (P_0/P)$, we obtain

$$dA = \frac{1}{2.3} d \ln \frac{P_0}{P} = \frac{(-P_0/P^2) \, dP}{2.3(P_0/P)}$$

Dividing numerator and denominator by P_0/P yields

$$dA = -\frac{(1/P) \, dP}{2.3} = -\frac{dP}{2.3P}$$

Dividing both sides by A,

$$\frac{dA}{A} = -\frac{dP}{2.3PA}$$

From Beer's law, $P = P_0 \times 10^{-A}$; substitution into the above equation gives

$$-\frac{dA}{A} = -\frac{dP}{2.3AP_0 \times 10^{-A}} = \frac{dc}{c}$$

It is convenient to normalize the equation by setting $P_0 = 1$, corresponding to the customary actual operation of setting the instrument to 100% T or zero absorbance with a reference solution in the beam. This gives

$$\frac{dc}{c} = -\frac{dP}{2.3A \times 10^{-A}}$$

Now the minimum in dc/c occurs when the denominator, $2.3A \times 10^{-A}$, is at a maximum. To find this maximum, we differentiate and set the derivative equal to zero:

$$\frac{d(2.3A \times 10^{-A})}{dA} = 10^{-A} - 2.3A \times 10^{-A} = 0$$

or

$$10^{-A}(1 - 2.3A) = 0$$

If 10^{-A} is zero, A is infinite and the error is infinite. Setting the other term equal to zero,

$$1 - 2.3A = 0$$

$$2.3A = 1$$

$$A = \frac{1}{2.3} = 0.43$$

An absorbance value of 0.43 corresponds to 36.8% transmittance. (The student who is familiar with calculus may notice that the absorbance of 0.43 could, so far as we have actually shown above, represent either a maximum or a minimum error. Such a student will know that the first derivative may be tested for this; it turns out that we are dealing with a minimum error.)

The term dP in the equations above, following the usual practice in calculus, may be taken as an approximation of ΔP, the error in P. This is often called the *photometric error*, and for our purposes simply represents the uncertainty in reading the instrument scale. This uncertainty is considered constant in the present discussion, and is probably roughly so with many actual instruments. To find the relative error in concentration as a function of the photometric error at the optimal concentration, substitute 0.43 for A in the above equation for dc/c:

$$\frac{dc}{c} = -\frac{dP}{2.3 \times 0.43 \times 10^{-0.43}} = -2.72 \, dP$$

Thus, if a 1% error were made in reading the instrument, the relative error in c would be 2.72% at best; with absorbance values above and below 0.43, it would be even larger. Photometric errors may range from 0.1% to several per cent, depending upon the instrument employed.

The relative error in concentration resulting from a 1% photometric error is plotted against per cent transmittance in Figure 12.14. The curve approaches infinity at both 0 and 100% T, passes through a minimum at 36.8% T, but is actually not very far from minimal over a fair range, say 10 to 80% T (absorbance values of about 0.1 to 1.0).

The student who has difficulty in visualizing why there should be a minimum in the error curve, or in following the calculus treatment above, could think of the situation this way: Refer to Figure 12.4b. A given error in measuring % T gives a small error, Δc, in concentration at very low concen-

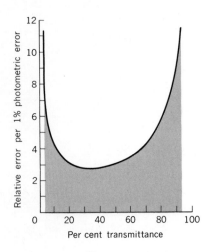

Fig. 12.14. Error curve.

trations, because the % T vs. c curve is very steep. But, where c is very low, a small error in c becomes a large relative error, $\Delta c/c$. At high concentrations, the same error in % T represents a much larger absolute error in c, because the % T vs. c curve is much flatter. Somewhere in between, there will be a point where these two effects meet to give a minimal relative error, $\Delta c/c$. This happens to fall at 36.8% T.

In the error treatment above, it was supposed that the error in measuring transmittance was constant, independent of the value of the transmittance; the error was considered to arise entirely from uncertainty in reading the instrument scale. In some of the best modern instruments, on the other hand, the limiting factor in the accuracy lies elsewhere, usually in the "noise" level of the detector circuit. In such cases, dP is not constant, and a different error function is obtained which is minimal, not at 36.8% T but at a lower T value. Actually, with a complex instrument it may be difficult to decide which of several factors limits the accuracy; thus the way in which dP varies with P may not be clear, and hence it may not be legitimate to calculate a % T value corresponding to minimal error.[12] With one of the well-known,

[12] R. P. Bauman, *Absorption Spectroscopy*, John Wiley & Sons, Inc., New York, 1962, p. 376.

high-quality, modern instruments, the Cary Model 14 recording spectro-photometer, the minimal error is said to occur at about 10% T $(A = 1)$.[13]

APPLICATIONS OF SPECTROPHOTOMETRY

Plotting spectrophotometric data

Absorption spectra are most frequently plotted as %T vs. wavelength (λ), A or ϵ vs. λ, and log A or log ϵ vs. λ. Comparison of these plots may be made clear by reference to Figures 12.15, 12.16, and 12.17. Analytical

Fig. 12.15. Transmittance-wavelength curves for solutions of potassium permanganate. (M. G. Mellon (editor), *Analytical Absorption Spectroscopy*, John Wiley & Sons, Inc., New York, 1950. Used by permission of the author and publisher.)

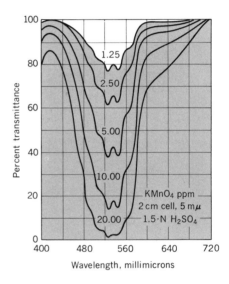

chemists generally prefer absorbance to %T for the ordinate. Note that a minimum in %T corresponds to a maximum in A; the two curves are not mirror images, however, because A and %T are related logarithmically $[A = \log(1/T)]$. Sometimes ϵ-values are calculated from absorption data and plotted against λ.

It may be seen from Figure 12.16 that the shape of the absorption spectrum depends upon the concentration of the solution if the ordinate is linear in absorbance. That is, the curves in Figure 12.16 are not superimposable by simple vertical displacement. This is clear from Beer's law, $A = \epsilon bc$, which shows that changing the concentration changes the absorbance at

---

[13] *Instructions for Cary Recording Spectrophotometer Model 14*, Applied Physics Corporation, Monrovia, Calif., p. 5.

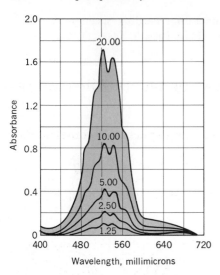

Fig. 12.16. Absorbance-wavelength curves for solutions of potassium permanganate. (M. G. Mellon (editor), *Analytical Absorption Spectroscopy*, John Wiley & Sons, Inc., New York, 1950. Used by permission of the author and publisher.)

each wavelength by a constant *multiple*. On the other hand, as seen in Figure 12.17, the shape of the curve is independent of concentration if the ordinate is log A. That this should be the case is seen by taking logarithms of both sides of the Beer's law equation:

$$\log A = \log (\epsilon b c) = \log \epsilon + \log b + \log c$$

Now the concentration term is *added* rather than multiplied, and hence increasing the concentration adds a constant increment to log A at each wavelength across the spectrum. The curve for the higher concentration is thus displaced upward, but could be superimposed upon the lower one by a

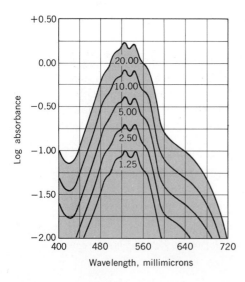

Fig. 12.17. Log absorbance-wavelength curves for solutions of potassium permanganate. (M. G. Mellon (editor), *Analytical Absorption Spectroscopy*, John Wiley & Sons, Inc., New York, 1950. Used by permission of the author and publisher.)

simple vertical movement. The same ϵ vs. λ plot should be obtained regardless of concentration provided the system follows Beer's law at all wavelengths. It is common practice, particularly among organic chemists, to plot log ϵ vs. λ.

Identification of chemical substances

The student is familiar with simple color tests which are used for identification purposes. The purple color of permanganate solutions, the blue of copper, the yellow of chromate, and many others might be mentioned. The absorption spectrum of a compound, determined with a spectrophotometer, may be considered as a more elegant, objective, and reliable indication of identity. The spectrum is another physical constant, so to speak, which along with melting point, refractive index, and other properties, may be used for characterization. Like the others, absorption spectra are not infallible proof of identity, but simply represent another tool available for intelligent application.

It must be remembered that an absorption spectrum depends upon not only the chemical nature of the compound in question but also other factors. Changing the solvent often results in shifts in absorption bands. The shape of a band and particularly the appearance of "fine structure" may well depend upon instrument characteristics such as the resolution of the monochromator, the amplifier gain, and the rate of scan as it relates to inertia in the recorder. Treating a recording spectrophotometer as a "black box" can lead to peculiar absorption spectra.

Spectra of many thousands of compounds and materials have been recorded, and locating the proper ones for comparison in connection with a particular problem may be extremely difficult. Several catalogues and compilations are available.[14] Increasingly, large laboratories are employing machine data handling techniques to store and retrieve spectra as well as other important information.

Multicomponent analysis

A spectrophotometer cannot *analyze* a sample. It becomes a useful tool only after the sample has been treated in such a way that the measurement is interpretable in unambiguous terms. In many cases, however, it is not necessary that each individual component of a complex sample be isolated from all others. In spectrophotometry, for example, it is sometimes possible

---

[14] For example, H. M. Hershenson, *Ultraviolet and Visible Absorption Spectra: Indexes for 1930–1954 and 1955–1959*, Academic Press, New York, 1956 and 1961; R. A. Friedel and M. Orchin, *Ultraviolet Spectra of Aromatic Compounds*, John Wiley & Sons, Inc., New York, 1951.

to measure more than one constituent in a single solution. Let us suppose a solution to contain two absorbing constituents, X and Y. The complexity of the situation depends upon the absorption spectra of X and Y.

Case 1. The spectra do not overlap, or at least it is possible to find a wavelength where X absorbs and Y does not and a similar wavelength for measuring Y. Figure 12.18 shows such a situation. The constituents X and Y are simply measured at the wavelengths λ_1 and λ_2, respectively.

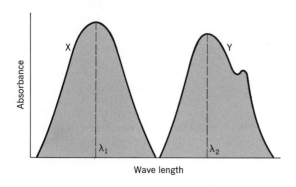

Fig. 12.18. Spectra of X and Y, no overlapping.

Case 2. One-way overlap of the spectra. As shown in Figure 12.19, X does not interfere with the measurement of Y at λ_2, but Y does absorb appreciably along with X at λ_1. The approach to this problem is simple in principle. The concentration of Y is determined directly from the absorb-

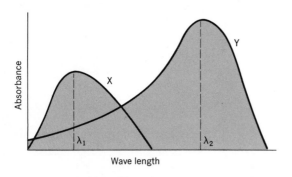

Fig. 12.19. One-way overlap of spectra.

ance of the solution at λ_2. Then the absorbance contributed at λ_1 by this concentration of Y is calculated from the previously known molar absorptivity of Y at λ_1. This contribution is subtracted from the measured absorbance of the solution at λ_1, yielding the absorbance due to X, whose concentration is then calculated in the usual manner.

Case 3. Two-way overlap of the spectra. When no wavelength can be

Fig. 12.20. Two-way overlap of spectra.

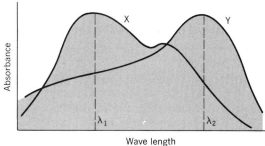

found where either X or Y absorbs exclusively, as suggested in Figure 12.20, it is necessary to solve two simultaneous equations in two unknowns. Let

A_1 = measured absorbance at λ_1

A_2 = measured absorbance at λ_2

ϵ_{X_1} = molar absorptivity of X at λ_1

ϵ_{X_2} = molar absorptivity of X at λ_2

ϵ_{Y_1} = molar absorptivity of Y at λ_1

ϵ_{Y_2} = molar absorptivity of Y at λ_2

C_X = molar concentration of X

C_Y = molar concentration of Y

b = path length

Since the total absorbance is the sum of the contributions of the individual absorbing constituents of the solution:

$$A_1 = \epsilon_{X_1}bC_X + \epsilon_{Y_1}bC_Y$$

$$A_2 = \epsilon_{X_2}bC_X + \epsilon_{Y_2}bC_Y$$

C_X and C_Y are the only unknowns in these equations and hence their values can be readily determined. The ϵ-values must be known, of course, from measurements on pure solutions of X and Y at the two wavelengths.

Equations can be set up in principle for any number of components provided absorbance values are measured at as many wavelengths. However, the importance of small errors in measurement is magnified as the number of components increases, and in practice this approach is generally limited to two- or possibly three-component systems. An exception to this is possible if a computer is available. Then, particularly if the spectrum is recorded, it becomes not too difficult to "over-determine" the system (i.e., take absorbance values at many more wavelengths than there are components) and by a rapid series of successive approximations obtain reliable values for a large number of components.

Preparation of samples for spectrophotometric analysis

So far we have said little about chemistry in this chapter. But seldom will the analyst receive a sample which is ready to be measured without some sort of pretreatment. Often separations of interfering substances are necessary; some of the available techniques are considered in later chapters.

Many organic compounds absorb in the ultraviolet region of the spectrum, and pretreatment then involves only separation of interferences. Some elements in the periodic table absorb strongly in the visible or ultraviolet, at least in certain oxidation states, and the preliminary steps may involve redox reactions as well as separations. Manganese, for example, is often determined spectrophotometrically after oxidation to Mn(VII) by means of persulfate or periodate:

$$2\,Mn^{++} + 5\,S_2O_8^= + 8\,H_2O \rightleftharpoons 2\,MnO_4^- + 10\,SO_4^= + 16\,H^+$$

The purple MnO_4^- solution is measured at about 525 mμ. Chromium is determined similarly after oxidation to Cr(VI).

Development of absorption by means of inorganic reagents is occasionally possible. For example, iron may be determined by means of the red color obtained by treating ferric solutions with thiocyanate:

$$Fe^{3+} + SCN^- \rightleftharpoons (FeSCN)^{++}$$

The system is complicated by the tendency to form higher complexes such as $[Fe(SCN)_2]^+$. Other examples of colored complexes formed with inorganic reagents are the blue tetraammine copper complex, $[Cu(NH_3)_4]^{++}$, and the several complex heteropoly acids such as phosphomolybdic, $H_3P(Mo_3O_{10})_4 \cdot 29\,H_2O$, which are used to determine elements such as phosphorus and silicon. Iodide ion forms yellowish complex ions which exhibit absorption maxima in the ultraviolet region with several metals, including bismuth, antimony, and palladium (e.g., $PdI_4^=$).

The colored complexes formed by metal ions with organic reagents offer the most impressive variety of spectrophotometric methods, and are especially useful in the field of trace analysis. Most of these complexes are of the *chelate* type where the metal becomes one of the members of a heterocyclic ring through bonding with two (or more) functional groups in the organic molecule. The formation and properties of the metal chelate compounds are discussed more fully elsewhere (Chapters 7, 14, and 17), and we mention here only a few points of special interest regarding their adaptation to spectrophotometric analysis.

In some regards, the low aqueous solubility of many of the metal chelate compounds is disadvantageous, but on the other hand, extraction of metals into nonaqueous solvents by means of chelating agents may lead to very powerful analytical methods. In favorable cases, it may be possible to concentrate the metal, separate it from interferences, and develop the absorbing system in a single step.

Table 12.2 shows some examples of chelating agents which are useful in the spectrophotometric determination of metals. The 8-quinolinolate chelates of aluminum, ferric iron, cadmium, gallium, lead, copper, and numerous other metals are soluble in chloroform, and extractions with this solvent generally precede the spectrophotometric determination. By controlling the pH of the aqueous phase and by adding complexing agents which "mask" certain metal ions, the extraction can be made quite selective. Reasonable absorbance values are generally obtained with chloroform solutions whose metal concentrations are of the order of a few micrograms per milliliter.

Dithizone has been used mainly for the determination of traces of lead, although it is a useful reagent for copper, zinc, cadmium, and other metals as well. Solutions of dithizone in chloroform or carbon tetrachloride are generally employed, with extraction of the metal preceding the measurement, as in the case of 8-quinolinol. A few tenths of a microgram of lead per milliliter of chloroform can be easily measured.

1,10-phenanthroline gives an intense red color with ferrous iron. The use of the ferrous-phenanthroline complex ("ferroin") as a redox indicator has been mentioned in Chapter 5, but the reagent also serves for the spectrophotometric determination of iron. The reduction to the ferrous form may be accomplished with hydroxylamine. For very small amounts of iron, bathophenanthroline and tripyridyltriazine are preferred because of their greater sensitivity; these reagents are useful, for example, in determining iron in such samples as sea water, municipal water supplies, wine, urine, and reagent chemicals. The ferrous complexes may be extracted into such solvents as isoamyl alcohol or nitrobenzene as ion pairs with certain anions; thus the iron in large samples may be concentrated into a small volume for measurement. Reagent solutions used in the analysis, which may themselves contain traces of iron, can be cleaned up by a similar prior extraction, thus lowering the "blank" value of the overall method. The sensitivities of methods based upon these reagents may be inferred from the following molar absorptivities:[15] ϵ for the ferrous bathophenanthroline complex in isoamyl alcohol at 533 mμ is 22,350; the corresponding value for the tripyridyl triazine complex in nitrobenzene is 24,100 at 595 mμ; for ferroin, as ordinarily used in aqueous solution, the value is only 11,100. The student may readily calculate that a 4-μM (4 micromolar, 4×10^{-6}-M) solution of the ferrous complex of tripyridyl triazine will give an absorbance reading of about 0.1 in a 1-cm cell.

[15] H. Diehl and G. F. Smith, *The Iron Reagents: Bathophenanthroline, 2,4,6-Tripyridyl-s-triazine, Phenyl-2-pyridyl ketoxime*, published by the G. Frederick Smith Chemical Co., Columbus, Ohio, 1960.

Table
12.2

SOME IMPORTANT ORGANIC
SPECTROPHOTOMETRIC REAGENTS

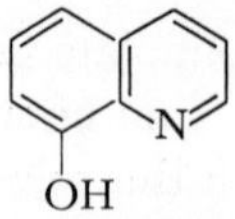

8-Quinolinol
(8-Hydroxyquinoline, oxine)

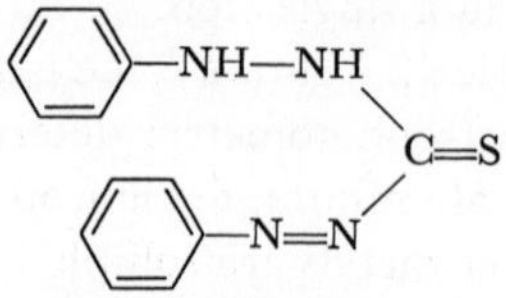

Diphenylthiocarbazone
(Dithizone)

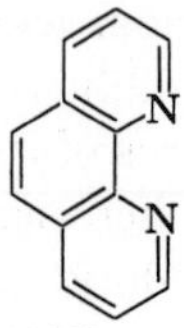

1,10-Phenanthroline

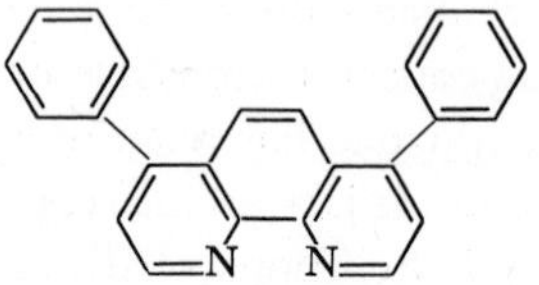

4,7-Diphenyl-1,10-phenanthroline
(Bathophenanthroline)

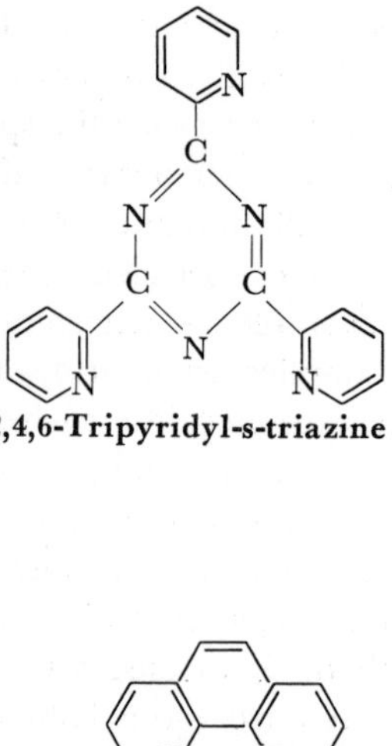

2,4,6-Tripyridyl-s-triazine

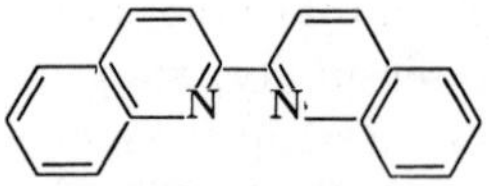

2,2′-Biquinoline
(Cuproine)

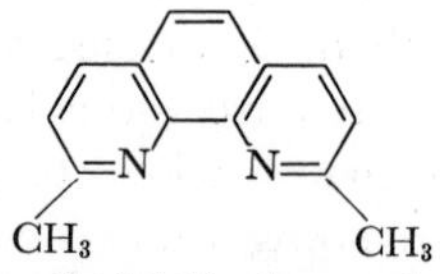

2,9-Dimethyl-1,10-phenanthroline
(Neocuproine)

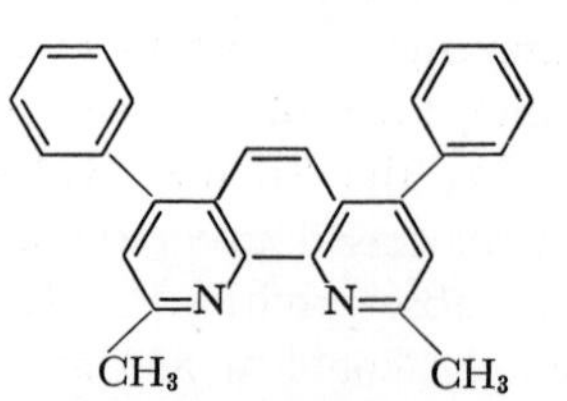

2,9-Dimethyl-4,7-diphenyl-1,10-
phenanthroline
(Bathocuproine)

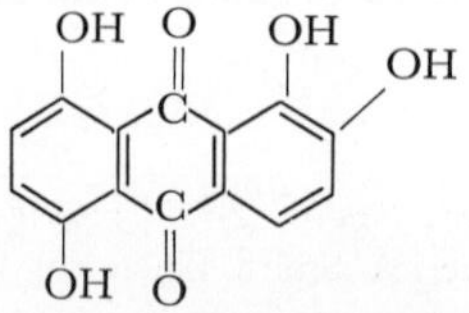

1,2,5,8-Tetrahydroxyanthraquinone
(Quinalizarin)

Cuproine, neocuproine, and bathocuproine form cuprous chelates which are extremely useful for determining low concentrations of copper.[16] These reagents are specific for copper, and as with the iron reagents above, extraction into organic solvents may be performed. It is said that 0.008 μg of copper per ml gives a visually detectable color with cuproine on a white spot plate. The ϵ-value for the cuprous cuproine complex is 6220 in isoamyl alcohol at 546 mμ; for neocuproine, the value is 7950; for bathocuproine, the value is 13,900.

Quinalizarin is placed in Table 12.2 as an example of a group of hydroxy-quinones which have been widely employed as spectrophotometric reagents for various metals, for example, beryllium, aluminum, thorium, zirconium, and the rare earths. Often the complexes are not very soluble, either in water or organic solvents; sometimes protective colloids such as gelatin, gum arabic, or polyvinyl alcohol are added to stabilize very fine suspensions upon which spectrophotometric measurements are performed. Such dispersions are often sensitive to time, temperature, electrolyte concentration, and other factors, and great care must be taken to obtain reproducible absorbance measurements.

PHOTOMETRIC TITRATIONS

Various properties of a solution may be measured in order to assess the progress of a titration toward the equivalence point. We have seen, for example, in Chapter 8 that the potential of an indicator electrode may be used for this purpose, and we have described another end point technique, amperometric, in Chapter 11. The absorbance of a solution may likewise be measured during the course of a titration; we have available, then, still another end point technique which may be useful in certain circumstances. Our discussion of photometric titrations will be brief; a more complete treatment may be found in two reviews which also provide a guide to the recent literature.[17,18]

As a matter of fact, visual titrations are really photometric in nature. "The color change reflects a change in the absorption of light by the solution, accompanying changes in the concentrations of absorptive species. In a visual titration, one actually employs all of the features of an automatic photometric titrator: Light passes through the solution to the eye, which is a photosensitive transducer responding with a signal to the brain; the brain is analogous to the circuitry of an instrument which amplifies the signal and

---

[16] H. Diehl and G. F. Smith, *The Copper Reagents: Cuproine, Neocuproine, Bathocuproine,* published by the G. Frederick Smith Chemical Co., Columbus, Ohio, 1958.

[17] J. B. Headridge, *Photometric Titrations,* Pergamon Press, New York, 1961.

[18] A. L. Underwood, "Photometric Titrations," a chapter in *Advances in Analytical Chemistry and Instrumentation,* Vol. 3, C. N. Reilley, Ed., Interscience Publishers, Inc., New York, 1964, p. 31.

otherwise renders it appropriate for transmission to an electromechanical shutoff system; traversing a motor neuron, the signal triggers a muscular response that closes the buret to terminate the titration. In visual titrations, the most complicated and expensive instruments of all—people—act as automatic photometric titrators." [18]

Photometric titrations often possess advantages of sensitivity of end point detection and circumvention of interferences over visual titrations. Further, they are not restricted to the wavelength region where the human eye responds, and they are fairly easily automated. In comparison with potentiometric titrations, the photometric approach is often advantageous for borderline cases of titrations which are approaching nonfeasibility. While the potential of an indicator electrode responds to the logarithm of a concentration (or a concentration ratio), the absorbance of a solution is directly proportional to concentration. If the equilibrium constant of a titration reaction is undesirably small, concentrations will not change as rapidly as one would like in the vicinity of the equivalence point, and the potential, because of the logarithmic compression, will change even less rapidly. The absorbance, on the other hand, will change just as rapidly as the concentration. This is not a unique advantage of photometric titrations, of course. The same consideration applies to amperometric and other end points which are obtained by linear extrapolation. (Compare values of T, the titration factor, for visual, potentiometric, and photometric or amperometric titrations in Chapter 7, page 190.)

Just as with amperometric titrations (Chapter 11, page 286), it is necessary to correct measured absorbance values for dilution if the volume of titrant is appreciable compared with the initial volume of the solution.

Titrations without indicators

Sometimes a substance directly involved in the titration reaction absorbs appreciably at an accessible wavelength, and the titration can be followed spectrophotometrically without adding an indicator. The shapes of the titration curve are predictable from the ϵ-values of the chemical species concerned. Some typical photometric titration curves of this type are shown in Figure 12.21. If the titration reaction is appreciably incomplete in the vicinity of the equivalence point, the curve will become rounded, as shown by the dotted portion of curve A in Figure 12.21. The end point is then located by the intersection of extrapolated straight lines drawn through points taken sufficiently before and after the rounded portion. Titration curves of this sort are easily calculated: One simply computes the concentrations of absorbing species at any point using the equilibrium constant of the reaction; then the contribution of each species to the absorbance of the solution is calculated from Beer's law, using known ϵ-values and path length.

Fig. 12.21. Typical photometric titration curves: (A) $\epsilon_t > \epsilon_s = \epsilon_p$ (usually $\epsilon_s = \epsilon_p = 0$); (B) $\epsilon_p = \epsilon_s$; $\epsilon_t = 0$; (C) $\epsilon_s > \epsilon_p$; $\epsilon_t = 0$; (D) $\epsilon_s > \epsilon_p < \epsilon_t$; (E) $\epsilon_p > \epsilon_s$; $\epsilon_t > \epsilon_p$; (F) $\epsilon_p > \epsilon_s$; $\epsilon_t < \epsilon_p$. ϵ_s, ϵ_p, and ϵ_t are the molar absorptivities of substance titrated, reaction product, and titrant, respectively.

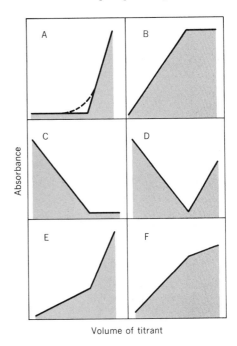

Volume of titrant

Titrations with indicators and the titration of mixtures

In cases where none of the species involved in the titration reaction absorbs sufficiently, an indicator may be added to the solution. Figure 12.22 shows an example of an indicator titration, a chelometric titration of cupric ion with EDTA using the metallochromic indicator pyrocatechol violet. In this titration, a wavelength was selected where the free indicator absorbs more strongly than the copper-indicator complex. We see in the figure, first the reaction of free cupric ion with EDTA, which does not affect the absorbance of the solution at this wavelength; then, as the end point is approached,

Fig. 12.22. Titration of copper with EDTA, using pyrocatechol violet indicator: 14.01 mg of Cu in 150 ml titrated with 10^{-1}-M EDTA at 440 mμ. (Data of T. M. Robertson.)

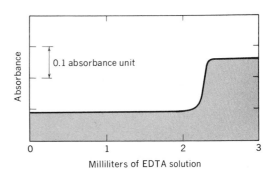

0.1 absorbance unit

Milliliters of EDTA solution

copper is pulled away from the indicator by the titrant, and the absorbance rises as free indicator accumulates, until finally all of the copper has been titrated and the absorbance becomes constant again.

Figure 12.23 shows a photometric titration of a mixture of bismuth and

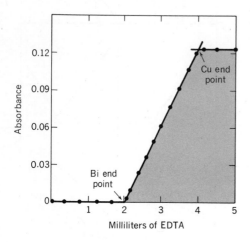

Fig. 12.23. Titration of bismuth-copper mixture with EDTA: 41.8 mg of Bi and 13.1 mg of Cu in 100 ml (each 2×10^{-3}-M) buffered at pH 2, titrated at 745 mμ with 10^{-1}-M EDTA.

copper with EDTA. At the wavelength selected, the cupric-EDTA chelate absorbs strongly, while the other species (Bi^{3+}, bismuth-EDTA chelate, and EDTA) have ϵ-values of zero. The bismuth chelate is much more stable than the cupric one. Thus, as EDTA is added to the Bi^{3+}-Cu^{++} mixture, the bismuth chelate is formed first. When $[Bi^{3+}]$ has been reduced to a very low value, the cupric-EDTA chelate begins to form, and, because this is the strongly absorbing species, the absorbance begins to rise. After the copper end point, the curve levels off as excess, nonabsorbing EDTA is added.

Instrumentation

The simplest approach to a photometric titration is to titrate in a flask or beaker on the laboratory bench, taking samples out of the titration vessel for absorbance measurements as the titration proceeds. Of course the samples must be returned each time, and this technique is inconvenient for more than an occasional single titration. On the other hand, any good spectrophotometer can be used without modification, and it is more obvious to a beginner exactly what is going on than might be the case if more elaborate instrumentation were employed.

Sometimes it is possible to fit a spectrophotometer with a modified cell compartment so that a titration vessel such as a beaker can be positioned in the light beam. It is convenient to stir by means of a magnetic stirrer underneath the compartment. The buret tip is introduced into the solution through a hole in the cover of the cell compartment; care must be taken that this arrangement be light-tight.

With a recording spectrophotometer, it is possible to record absorbance vs. time at a constant wavelength. If titrant is introduced into a titration vessel in the sample beam at a constant flow rate, if adequate stirring is provided, and also if the titration reaction is rapid, then the plot of absorbance vs. time readily becomes a photometric titration curve. With relatively simple on-the-spot modification, the output signal of a manual spectrophotometer can be recorded; thus an expensive double beam recording instrument is not really required for this application.

Finally, photometric titrators which terminate titrant flow at the end point are on the market. The operator merely sets up and starts the titration, and then later reads a buret. We described briefly in Chapter 8 an automatic potentiometric titrator based upon double electronic differentiation of the voltage from a pair of electrodes. Now the first derivatives of photometric titration curves like those in Figure 12.21 exhibit the sigmoid shape associated with a typical potentiometric titration. By differentiating electronically a signal arising from a photodetector and then feeding this into the circuit of the existing potentiometric titrator, an instrument was devised for automatic photometric titration. Of course it was necessary to add to the potentiometric titrator not only an additional differentiating circuit but also optical components, source, photodetector, etc.[19]

REFERENCES

1. J. R. Dyer, *Applications of Absorption Spectroscopy of Organic Compounds*, Prentice-Hall, Inc., Englewood Cliffs, N.J., 1965.

2. A. E. Gillam and E. S. Stern, *An Introduction to Electronic Absorption Spectroscopy in Organic Chemistry*, Edward Arnold, Ltd., London, 1954.

3. R. P. Bauman, *Absorption Spectroscopy*, John Wiley & Sons, Inc., New York, 1962.

4. H. M. Hershenson, *Ultraviolet and Visible Absorption Spectra: Indexes for 1930–1954 and 1955–1959,* Academic Press, New York, 1956 and 1961.

5. R. A. Friedel and M. Orchin, *Ultraviolet Spectra of Aromatic Compounds*, John Wiley & Sons, Inc., New York, 1951.

6. J. B. Headridge, *Photometric Titrations*, Pergamon Press, New York, 1961.

7. A. L. Underwood, "Photometric Titrations," a chapter in *Advances in Analytical Chemistry and Instrumentation*, Vol. 3, C. N. Reilley, Ed., Interscience Publishers, Inc., New York, 1964.

[19] H. V. Malmstadt and C. B. Roberts, *Anal. Chem.*, **28**, 1408 (1956).

QUESTIONS

1. Explain how a molecule absorbs radiant energy. Compare the absorption of light in the far infrared and microwave region with that in the ultraviolet portion of the spectrum.

2. Explain the following terms: wavelength, wave number, frequency, micron, Angstrom unit, millimicron, complementary color, fine structure, fluorescence, phosphorescence, chromophore.

3. Define the following: absorbance, absorptivity, transmittance, molar extinction coefficient, optical density, specific extinction, extinction, isosbestic point.

4. Distinguish between real and apparent deviations from Beer's law. Under what circumstances does one get positive deviations from Beer's law in the case of a weak acid, HB?

5. To what would you attribute nonadherence to Beer's law with the following systems: (a) picric acid solutions, (b) ferric chloride in water, (c) cobalt chloride in water?

6. What are the essential components of a spectrophotometer? What is the function of each?

7. Describe the sources of radiation used for the ultraviolet, visible, and infrared regions of the spectrum.

8. Describe the two types of monochromators used in spectrophotometers, giving the advantages and disadvantages of each.

9. Describe how phototubes, photomultiplier tubes, and thermocouples serve as detectors of radiation.

10. Explain how a differential measurement reduces the error in spectrophotometry.

11. Describe the operation of a double beam, optical null spectrophotometer.

12. What is the advantage of plotting the logarithm of the absorbance rather than the absorbance against wavelength?

13. In the so-called Ringbom plot, the per cent absorptance $(100 - \%T)$ is plotted against the log (base 10) of the concentration. Sketch such a curve for a colored compound.

14. Show that the following relation holds for a Ringbom plot (question 13)

$$\frac{dc/c}{dP} = \frac{230}{\text{slope}} = \frac{\% \text{ relative error}}{1\% \text{ photometric error}}$$

where the slope is that of the Ringbom curve.

15. A worker reported that a substance could be determined photometrically in the range of 0 to 15 ppm with an accuracy of ±0.08 ppm. Criticize this statement.

16. A plot of absorbance versus concentration at constant b gives a straight line if Beer's law is obeyed. What property of the line is represented by the absorptivity? Why are photometric measurements of concentration usually carried out at the maximum value of the absorptivity?

17. Describe the effect of stray light on a photometric titration curve. How would the error compare at high and low absorbances?

PROBLEMS

1. The scale on a spectrophotometer extends from 1 to 100% transmittance.
(a) What are the values of the absorbance at these two extremes?
(b) If the per cent transmittance is actually zero, what is the value of the absorbance?

2. If absorbance were defined in terms of natural, rather than common logarithms, what would be the extreme values of the absorbance in part (a) of the previous problem? What would be the absorbance of a solution which transmits 36.8%?

3. Convert the following values of per cent transmittance to absorbance: (a) 80, (b) 40, (c) 20, (d) 10.

4. Convert the following values of absorbance to per cent transmittance: (a) 0.03, (b) 0.30, (c) 0.70, (d) 1.00, (e) 1.70, (f) 2.00.

5. The per cent transmittance of a solution in a 2.0-cm cell is 40. What is the per cent transmittance of the solution in (a) a 4.0-cm cell, (b) a 1.0-cm cell, and (c) in a 0.10-cm cell.

6. A solution contains 3.0 mg of iron per liter. The iron is converted into the complex with 1,10-phenanthroline and the absorbance of the solution in a 2.0-cm cell is found to be 1.20. Calculate (a) the absorptivity, and (b) the molar absorptivity of the ferrous complex.

7. A compound of molecular weight 200 has a molar absorptivity of 4.0×10^5. How many grams of this compound should be dissolved in 1.0 l so that after a 250-fold dilution the resulting solution will give an absorbance reading of 0.80 in a 1.0-cm cell?

8. A sample of an amine of unknown molecular weight was converted into the amine picrate (a 1:1 addition compound) by treatment with picric acid (M.W. = 229). Most amine picrates have about the same molar absorptivities: $\log \epsilon = 4.13$ at 380 mμ in 95% ethanol. A solution of the amine picrate was prepared by dissolving 43.7 mg of the material in exactly 1 l of 95% ethanol. The absorbance of the solution in a 1.00-cm cell at 380 mμ was 1.40. Estimate the molecular weight of the unknown amine.

9. A 1.00-g sample of steel is dissolved in nitric acid and the manganese oxidized to permanganate with potassium periodate. The solution is then made up to 100 ml in a volumetric flask and found to have an absorbance which is 2.50 times as great as that of a 0.00200-M solution of $KMnO_4$. Calculate the percentage of manganese in the steel.

10. A 1.25-g sample of steel is dissolved in acid and the manganese oxidized to permanganate. The solution is made up to 500 ml in a volumetric flask and the absorbance at 520 mμ in a 2.0-cm cell is found to be 0.80. Calculate the percentage of manganese in the steel if the molar absorptivity of permanganate at this wave length is 2235.

11. The absorption spectra of two colored substances, A and B, are determined and the following data obtained in a 1.00-cm cell:

Solution	Concentration	A at 450 mμ	A at 700 mμ
A alone	0.00100-M	0.900	0.150
B alone	0.0100-M	0.200	0.600
A + B	Unknown	0.500	1.00

Calculate the concentrations of A and B in the unknown solution.

12. If the error in determining concentration is to be 0.40% in a solution which gives an absorbance reading of 0.80, what must be the photometric error?

13. The molar absorptivity of the compound A (M.W. = 100) at 500 mμ is 2000. What weight of a sample containing 2.00% of A should be taken for analysis to get maximum accuracy in the photometric determination of A? The solution is finally diluted to 100 ml and the cell used is 1.00 cm in length.

14. In a conventional spectrophotometric measurement, an unknown solution read A = 1.000 and a standard solution which was 0.0001-M read A = 0.699. Later, the standard solution was set to read A = 0.000, and the unknown was measured on this basis.

(a) What was then the measured absorbance of the unknown?
(b) What were the differences in %T of the two solutions in the two measurements?

15. Solution A, concentration c, gives an absorbance reading against a blank of 0.25.

(a) Calculate the absorbance readings of solutions B, C, and D, of concentrations $2c$, $3c$, and $4c$, respectively.
(b) Calculate the percentage transmittances of the four solutions and the differences between A and B, B and C, and C and D.
(c) If A is used as the reference and is set to give an absorbance of 0.000, repeat the calculations of parts (a) and (b).

16. Calculate the error in determining concentration per 1% photometric error for the following values of the per cent transmittance: (a) 1, (b) 25, (c) 75, (d) 99.

17. A solution of concentration c has an absorbance of 0.4343 when the reference is the pure solvent.

(a) What is the relative error in c if the photometric error is 0.5%?
(b) If a solution whose concentration is $3c$ is used as the reference, and one of $4c$ is measured, what is the relative error in the latter concentration, the photometric error being the same as in (a)?

18. A colored complex, MX_3^-, is formed when the colorless ions M^{++} and X^- are mixed in solution. A solution which was 0.0020-F in M^{++} was made 0.20-F in X^- and the absorbance was found to be 1.00 in a 1.00-cm cell. Another 0.0020-F solution of M^{++} was made 0.0086-F in X^- and the absorbance found to be 0.90 in the same cell. Assuming that all of M^{++} was converted to the complex in the first solution but not in the second, calculate the stability constant of the complex.

19. Lead forms a chelate $PbY^=$ with EDTA, the log of whose absolute stability constant (Chapter 7) is 18.3. This chelate has an absorption maximum at 240 mμ, with a molar absorptivity of 6.5×10^3. Suppose 100 ml of a 5.0×10^{-5}-M solution of a lead salt is titrated with a 1.0×10^{-3}-M EDTA solution. The lead solution is buffered at pH 3.0, where α for EDTA (Chapter 7) is 4.0×10^{10}. The length of the path through the titration cell is 3.0 cm. Calculate the absorbance of the solution at the following volumes of titrant, correcting for dilution: (a) 1.00, (b) 2.00, (c) 4.00, (d) 5.00, (e) 6.00, (f) 8.00 ml. Plot the titration curve.

20. Exactly 1.00 mmol portions each of a weak acid HA and its salt NaA are dissolved in 1.00-l volumes of various buffer solutions. The absorbances of the resulting solutions are measured at 650 mμ in 1.00-cm cells and found to be:

pH	Absorbance
12.00	0.960
11.00	0.960
10.00	0.960
7.00	0.576
2.00	0.000
1.00	0.000
0.00	0.000

Calculate the molar absorptivities of HA and A$^-$ at 650 mμ, and calculate the ionization constant of the weak acid.

Introduction to Phase Distribution Phenomena

INTRODUCTION

As pointed out in Chapter 1 there are four basic steps in an analysis. First is sampling, the selection of a small laboratory sample which will be representative of the material under investigation; with materials which are not homogeneous, sampling may be a difficult and critical part of the analysis. Second, the desired constituent must be converted into a form suitable for measurement, and potential interferences must be circumvented. The third step is the measurement itself. Fourth is a proper interpretation of the measurement, along with any calculations which must be performed to convert the measurement into useful information.

Although the improvement of measurements is always an important activity, the third step is often not the really critical one. Measurement is usually emphasized in elementary courses, and indeed must be thoroughly understood, but in practice there is usually some satisfactory way to measure any chemical species provided there is enough of it present and provided other substances which may affect the measured value are absent. Real analytical problems arise only when mixtures are encountered. It then becomes necessary to ask whether the measurement is related to the quantity of the desired constituent in an unequivocal way, or whether other substances are contributing to the measured value.

If such interference is the case, then steps to eliminate it become crucial to the analysis. The second step noted above represents the real challenge in most analytical situations because during this part of the analysis not only is the desired constituent converted into a form suitable for measurement but interferences are eliminated. If present initially at a concentration too low to measure, the desired constituent may also be concentrated during this stage of the analysis.

There are two general approaches to the elimination of interferences. First, the interfering substance may be converted into a species which is still present in the measured system but which does not interfere. "Masking," which was mentioned in Chapter 7, is an example of this approach. For instance, the interference of Fe^{3+} in the iodometric determination of copper is countered by fluoride, which forms complexes such as FeF_6^{3-}. Sometimes an interference can be eliminated by a change in oxidation state. For example, the interference of Fe^{3+} in certain analyses can be eliminated by reduction to Fe^{++} with some reagent that does not itself interfere, perhaps hydroxylamine.

The second general approach involves the actual physical segregation of the desired constituent from interfering substances. This is what is normally meant by the term *separation*, and it is the topic to which we direct our attention in this and the next three chapters. The theory and practice of analytical separation processes are perhaps of greatest interest to analytical chemists but are obviously extremely important to research workers in other fields. It makes no difference in principle, for example, whether a separation is performed as part of an analysis, or for the purpose of purifying a natural product or a newly-synthesized organic compound prior to proof-of-structure work, or by a physical chemist who wants to perform some highly sophisticated measurement on a pure compound. Modern researchers in fields which use chemistry should be familiar with some of the powerful separation techniques which are now available and be on the lookout for new ones which may appear.

PHASE TRANSFER OPERATIONS

All separation processes share a common principle, viz., a transfer of matter from one phase into another. By a *phase* we mean a physically discernible portion of matter separated by definite boundaries from other such portions;

a phase is a homogeneous region separated from other phases by surfaces of discontinuity. For example, ice, liquid water, and water vapor constitute a three-phase system. In usual thermodynamic discussion it is immaterial whether one piece of ice or many pieces are in contact with the other phases; we still consider the ice to be one phase.

Phase boundaries are not surfaces in a strict mathematical sense, because a mathematical surface has no thickness, whereas at a phase boundary there may be a region, very thin but still finite, across which various properties change. However, for certain purposes it is often assumed that a phase boundary has no thickness.

In most thermodynamic calculations, the area of the phase boundary is neglected as a factor. For example, the solubility of a solid in a liquid is often considered to be independent of the state of subdivision of the solid. In general this is satisfactory until the subdivision becomes extremely fine, when it may then be found that the surface area of the solid is very important. In this connection, it is important to distinguish equilibrium effects from kinetic (rate) effects. The area of a boundary will have a large effect upon the rate at which equilibrium is established between two phases, whereas the position of equilibrium will not be a function of area except in some cases when the area is relatively enormous.

In order to separate one substance from another, the phase transfer process obviously must be selective; if two substances distribute between the two phases in exactly the same degree, then clearly nothing was accomplished by introducing a second phase. After the substances have distributed themselves between two phases, the process generally culminates in a mechanical separation such as filtration, centrifugation, or a "cut" with a separatory funnel. Thus the process terminates with two physically distinct portions of matter in which the relative amounts of desired constituent and interfering substance are different from what they were in the original sample.

Sometimes a distinction is made between phase formation and phase competition processes.[1] In phase formation, the substance being separated is used to construct a new phase. This would be the case, for example, in precipitation and distillation. Phase competition refers to the partition of substances between two already-existent phases. Solvent extraction in which a solute is distributed between two immiscible liquids would come in this category.

In a very few cases, a quantitative separation is achieved in one stage of transfer of material from one phase into another. That is, all of the desired constituent ends up in one phase, while all interfering substances are in the other. However, such all-or-none transfer from one phase to another is rare, and we are much more likely to encounter mixtures of substances that differ only somewhat in their tendencies to pass from one phase into another. Thus one transfer does not lead to a clean separation. In such cases, we must

---

[1] P. J. Elving, *Anal. Chem.*, **23**, 1202 (1951).

consider how best to combine a number of successive partial separations until we eventually achieve the desired degree of purity.

In considering how two phases may be brought together repetitively, four levels of complexity may be distinguished.[2] First would be the simple, one-shot contact as mentioned above. Second, one phase could be brought repeatedly into contact with fresh portions of a second phase. This would be applicable where one substance remained quantitatively in one phase, while another substance was distributed between the two phases. An example might be repeated extraction of an aqueous solution with successive portions of an organic solvent. The Soxhlet extractor would fall in this category, as would the technique of reprecipitation in gravimetric analysis.

Third, one phase may move while in contact with a second phase which remains stationary. The moving phase may move continuously, as in the various chromatographic techniques, or in a series of equilibrium steps, as in the Craig apparatus. In Chapters 16 and 17 we shall examine several very important separation processes which fall into this category. Some techniques of this type have been designated "countercurrent," but this is not really the case, since only one phase moves. The term "pseudocountercurrent" is sometimes applied to such processes.

Fourth, we list true countercurrent methods, in which both phases move, continually in contact with each other, in opposite directions. Fractional distillation is an example of a true countercurrent process: Refluxing liquid runs continuously down the distilling column in contact with rising vapors. Countercurrent processes are extensively employed by chemical engineers in large-scale plant operations. Because of experimental difficulties as well as problems in the theoretical treatment, however, they are not nearly so common in the research laboratory as techniques in the third category.

THE PHASE RULE

Gibbs' phase rule is a general and useful expression from which predictions and correlations may be made in connection with phase distribution processes. The phase rule is discussed in physical chemistry texts, where it is presented as a logical expression. Here, we ask that it simply be accepted. Actually, with simple systems, the phase rule states what many students would have figured out anyway, and it is most useful in dealing with complicated cases. Our use of the phase rule here will be very limited, mainly to show that there should be mathematical relationships describing phase equilibria.

We must first define the terms that occur in the phase rule expression.

[2] H. A. Laitinen, *Chemical Analysis*, McGraw-Hill Book Co., Inc., New York, 1960, p. 472.

In the previous section of this chapter we have already indicated what is meant by a *phase*. The *components* of a system are the chemical substances required to make each of the phases in whatever quantity they may be present. Some examples may clarify this definition. Liquid water, ice, and water vapor are considered to originate from one substance (e.g., both liquid water and water vapor are obtainable from ice), and thus a three-phase system with these forms present would be considered a one-component system. A solution of, say, sugar in water would be a one-phase, two-component system; a two-phase system of ice in equilibrium with the sugar solution would still have two components. A pair of immiscible solvents like water and benzene with some solute dissolved in them, as in an extraction process, would be a two-phase, three-component system.

With certain systems it requires some thought to establish the number of components, which is really the smallest number of independently variable constituents which could be used to construct the system. This is not necessarily the same as the number of chemical substances present. For example, suppose ammonium chloride were heated in an evacuated chamber so that, at a certain temperature, the system consisted of solid NH_4Cl in equilibrium with a vapor phase obtained entirely from the decomposition of the solid:

$$NH_4Cl(s) \rightleftarrows NH_3(g) + HCl(g)$$

The system contains three chemical species, but since all are obtainable from NH_4Cl, it is a one-component system. Note, however, that if extra HCl were introduced into the vapor, so that HCl was present in excess over NH_3, we would now have a two-component system because the vapor phase could no longer be obtained from NH_4Cl alone.

The *degrees of freedom* or *variance* of a system is the number of factors such as temperature, pressure, and concentration that must be specified in order to define completely the condition of a system at equilibrium. Another definition which may seem different but which really amounts to the same thing may be stated: The degrees of freedom of a system are the number of properties which can be altered (at least within certain limits) without causing the disappearance of a phase or the appearance of a new one.

We may now state the phase rule and show its applicability to some simple systems. The rule may be written

$$F = C - P + 2$$

where F is the degrees of freedom, C the number of components, and P the number of phases in a system. It must be emphasized that this applies only to systems at equilibrium.

Consider, as a simple example, the system liquid water in equilibrium with water vapor. We have one component and two phases, so

$$F = 1 - 2 + 2 = 1$$

The system has one degree of freedom. This means, for example, that if we choose a certain temperature, we have used up the one degree of freedom, and we cannot then specify at our pleasure what some other property, say the vapor pressure, shall be. We must accept the value which is compatible with the temperature we chose. If we raised the pressure above this value, we could not be in equilibrium—vapor would condense; if we lowered the pressure, the liquid phase would disappear. This definite relationship between temperature and pressure is depicted on vapor pressure-temperature plots as seen in the phase diagram in Figure 13.1. Only at points on the line

Fig. 13.1. Typical phase diagram.

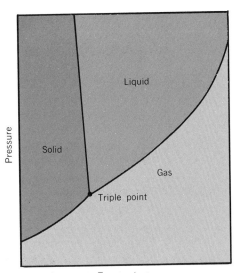

can the two phases coexist in equilibrium. Choosing T fixes P, and vice versa. Further, all other properties, refractive index for instance, are fixed.

Some students may remember from their beginning course the so-called "triple point" of water, where solid ice, liquid water, and water vapor are all in equilibrium (see Figure 13.1). Then $C = 1$ and $P = 3$.

$$F = 1 - 3 + 2 = 0$$

That is, with no degrees of freedom we have no choice of temperature, vapor pressure, or any other property. There is only one temperature, one vapor pressure, and one value of any other property of water at which we may have these three phases in equilibrium with each other.

Next, consider a solvent extraction situation, where a solute is distributed between two immiscible liquid phases, perhaps water and benzene. Here $C = 3$ and $P = 2$, whence

$$F = 3 - 2 + 2 = 3$$

Now let us decide to perform the extraction at a certain temperature, perhaps room temperature, and let the system be open so that the pressure upon it is one atmosphere. We have one degree of freedom left; suppose we specify the concentration of the solute in one of the liquid phases. We now have no choice regarding the concentration of solute in the other liquid phase; it will be whatever nature permits it to be.

This implies, of course, that under given conditions of temperature and pressure, there will be a definite, fixed relation between the solute concentrations in the solvent phases. Thus we would expect to find partition or distribution coefficients which were constant:

$$K = \frac{[\text{Solute}]_{\text{benzene}}}{[\text{Solute}]_{\text{water}}}$$

We shall discuss this further in Chapter 15.

REFERENCES

1. W. J. Moore, *Physical Chemistry*, 3rd Ed., Prentice-Hall, Inc., Englewood Cliffs, N. J., 1964, Chapter 4.

2. H. A. Laitinen, *Chemical Analysis*, McGraw-Hill Book Co., Inc., New York, 1960, Chapter 25.

3. J. E. Ricci, *The Phase Rule and Heterogeneous Equilibrium*, D. Van Nostrand Co., Inc., Princeton, N. J., 1951.

4. L. O. Case, "The Phase Rule in Analytical Chemistry," p. 957, Part I, Vol. 2, of *Treatise on Analytical Chemistry*, I. M. Kolthoff and P. J. Elving, Eds., Interscience Publishers, Inc., New York, 1961.

Separations by Precipitation

Precipitation is a very valuable method for separating a sample into its component parts, and until recent years it was the analyst's most widely used separation technique. As was pointed out in Chapter 13, the method is a phase formation process, in which a substance being separated is used to construct a new phase—the solid precipitate. The discussion of the present chapter will be devoted to a consideration of the equilibrium which exists between the solid and its saturated aqueous solution. We shall consider the factors that affect solubility, and hence the completeness of separation that can be effected by precipitation. In Chapter 15, we shall discuss the rate at which precipitation occurs, before equilibrium is established between the solid and solution.

SOLUBILITY EQUILIBRIUM

Solubility product constant

As pointed out in Chapter 6, the equilibrium constant expressing the solubility of a precipitate is the familiar *solubility product constant.* For a solid such as silver chloride in equilibrium with its ions, in solution,

$$AgCl(s) \rightleftharpoons Ag^+ + Cl^-$$

the equilibrium expression is

$$K = \frac{a_{Ag^+} \times a_{Cl^-}}{a_{AgCl}}$$

or

$$K_{sp} = [Ag^+][Cl^-]$$

Here we have taken the activity of solid AgCl as unity, and the activities of the ions have been approximated as the molarities.

It should be kept in mind, of course, that the value of an equilibrium constant changes with temperature. Values quoted here are for 25°C unless otherwise specified. It should also be noted that the expression is valid only for *slightly soluble electrolytes,* if concentrations rather than activities of the ions are employed. In such cases the solution is dilute and the approximation is reasonably valid. On the other hand, the solubility product expression in terms of concentrations does not hold true even for slightly soluble salts if the solution contains large quantities of other electrolytes. This deviation will be discussed later under the title of "Diverse Ion Effect."

The proper equilibrium expressions for a few other salts are given below:

Salt	K_{sp}
$BaSO_4$	$[Ba^{++}][SO_4^-]$
Ag_2CrO_4	$[Ag^+]^2[CrO_4^-]$
CaF_2	$[Ca^{++}][F^-]^2$
$Al(OH)_3$	$[Al^{3+}][OH^-]^3$

A general expression for the salt A_xB_y ionizing as follows:

$$A_xB_y = x\ A^{y+} + y\ B^{x-}$$

is

$$K_{sp} = [A^{y+}]^x[B^{x-}]^y$$

Calculation of K_{sp} from solubility

The numerical value of a solubility product constant can be readily calculated from the solubility of the compound. The calculation can be reversed, of course, and the solubility calculated from the K_{sp}. If the ions of the precipitate undergo reactions such as hydrolysis or complex formation, the calculations are more complicated. Such cases will be considered in a later section. Typical computations are illustrated in the following problems:

PROBLEM 1. The solubility of barium sulfate (M.W. = 233) at 25°C is 0.00023 g per 100 ml of solution. Calculate the value of K_{sp}.
   The solubility is 0.23 mg/100 ml or 0.0023 mg/ml. The molarity is

$$\frac{0.0023 \text{ mg/ml}}{233 \text{ mg/mmol}} = 1.0 \times 10^{-5} \text{ mmol/ml}$$

Since each mmol of $BaSO_4$ yields 1 mmol of Ba^{++} and 1 mmol of $SO_4^=$,

$$[Ba^{++}] = [SO_4^=] = 1.0 \times 10^{-5}$$

$$K_{sp} = [Ba^{++}][SO_4^=] = [1.0 \times 10^{-5}]^2 = 1.0 \times 10^{-10}$$

PROBLEM 2. The solubility of silver chromate (M.W. = 332) is 0.0279 g per l at 25°. Calculate K_{sp}, neglecting hydrolysis of the chromate ion.
   The molarity of Ag_2CrO_4 is

$$\frac{0.0279 \text{ g/l}}{332 \text{ g/mol}} = 8.4 \times 10^{-5} \text{ mol/l}$$

Since each Ag_2CrO_4 yields two Ag^+ ions and one $CrO_4^=$ ion,

$$[Ag^+] = 2 \times 8.4 \times 10^{-5} = 1.7 \times 10^{-4}$$

$$[CrO_4^=] = 8.4 \times 10^{-5}$$

Therefore

$$K_{sp} = [Ag^+]^2[CrO_4^=] = [1.7 \times 10^{-4}]^2[8.4 \times 10^{-5}]$$

$$K_{sp} = 2.4 \times 10^{-12}$$

PROBLEM 3. The K_{sp} of arsenious sulfide, As_2S_3, is 1.1×10^{-33}. Calculate the number of milligrams of As_2S_3 that will dissolve in 100 ml of water, neglecting hydrolysis of the sulfide ion.
   Let s = number of mmol/ml of As_2S_3 which dissolve. Since

$$As_2S_3 = 2 As^{3+} + 3 S^=$$

$$[As^{3+}] = 2s, \qquad [S^=] = 3s$$

Then

$$[2s]^2[3s]^3 = 1.1 \times 10^{-33}$$

$$108s^5 = 1.1 \times 10^{-33}$$

$$s^5 = 1.0 \times 10^{-35}$$

$$s = 1.0 \times 10^{-7}$$

Hence, 1.0×10^{-7} mmol/ml $\times$ 246 mg/mmol $\times$ 100 ml = 2.5×10^{-10} mg will dissolve in 100 ml water.

It should be noted that one can judge on inspection the relative molar solubilities of two compounds from their solubility product constants only if they are the same type of compounds, that is, both the type AB or AB_2, etc. The solubility product constants of both AgCl and $BaSO_4$ are about 1×10^{-10}, and hence both are soluble to the extent of 1×10^{-5} mole per l.

However, a compound of the type AB_2 with the same molar solubility would have a smaller solubility product constant, 4×10^{-15}.

FACTORS AFFECTING SOLUBILITY

The important factors that affect the solubility of crystalline solids are temperature, nature of the solvent, and the presence of other ions in the solution. In the latter category are included ions that may be common or not common to ions in the solid, and ions that form slightly ionized molecules or complex ions with ions of the solid.

Temperature

Most of the inorganic salts in which we are interested increase in solubility as the temperature is increased. The solubilities of a few analytically important salts at two temperatures are listed in Table 14.1.

Table 14.1   SOLUBILITY OF SOME SALTS AT TWO TEMPERATURES †

Salt	Solubility, g/l
AgCl	0.00070 (0°), 0.021 (100°)
BaSO$_4$	0.00115 (0°), 0.0024 (20°)
CaC$_2$O$_4$·H$_2$O	0.0056 (18°), 0.0140 (95°)
MgNH$_4$PO$_4$	0.23 (0°), 0.52 (20°)
PbCl$_2$	8.5 (15°), 31.0 (100°)
PbSO$_4$	0.041 (20°), 0.082 (100°)

† A. Seidell, *Solubilities of Inorganic and Metal Organic Compounds*, D. Van Nostrand Co., Inc., New York, 1953.

It is usually advantageous to carry out the operations of precipitation, filtration, and washing with hot solutions. Particles of larger size may result (Chapter 15), filtration is faster, and impurities are dissolved more readily. Therefore directions frequently call for employing hot solutions in those cases where the solubility of the precipitate is still negligible at the higher temperature. However, in the case of a fairly soluble compound, such as magnesium ammonium phosphate, the solution must be cooled in ice water before filtration. Quite an appreciable amount of this compound would be lost if the solution were filtered while hot.

The student may recall that lead chloride is separated from silver and mercurous chlorides in the qualitative analysis scheme by treatment with hot water (see Table 14.1). The lead salt dissolves at elevated temperature leaving the other two salts in the precipitate.

Solvent

Most inorganic salts are more soluble in water than in organic solvents. Water has a large dipole moment and is attracted to both cations and anions to form hydrated ions. We have already noted, for example, that the hydrogen ion in water is completely hydrated, forming the H_3O^+ ion. All ions are undoubtedly hydrated to some extent in water solutions, and the energy released by interaction of the ions and the solvent helps overcome the attractive forces tending to hold the ions in the solid lattice. The ions in a crystal do not have so large an attraction for organic solvents, and hence the solubilities are usually smaller than in water. The analyst can frequently utilize the decreased solubility in organic solvents to separate two substances which are quite soluble in water. For example, a dried mixture of calcium and strontium nitrates can be separated by treatment with a mixture of alcohol and ether. Calcium nitrate dissolves, leaving strontium nitrate. Potassium can be separated from sodium by precipitating K_2PtCl_6 from an alcohol-water mixed solvent.

Common-Ion effect

A precipitate is generally more soluble in pure water than in a solution which contains one of the ions of the precipitate. In a solution of silver chloride, for example, the product of the concentrations of silver and chloride ions cannot exceed the value of the solubility product constant, 1×10^{-10}. In pure water each ion has a concentration of 1×10^{-5}-M, but if sufficient silver nitrate is added to make the silver ion concentration 1×10^{-4}-M, the chloride ion concentration must decrease to a value of 1×10^{-6}-M. The reaction

$$Ag^+ + Cl^- \rightleftharpoons AgCl \downarrow$$

is forced to the right by excess silver ion, resulting in the precipitation of additional salt, and decreasing the quantity of chloride remaining in the solution.

The importance of the common-ion effect in bringing about complete precipitation in quantitative analyses is readily apparent. In carrying out precipitations, the analyst always adds some excess of the precipitating agent to insure complete precipitation. In washing a precipitate where solubility losses may be appreciable, a common ion may be used in the wash liquid to diminish solubility. The ion should be that of the precipitating agent, of course, not the ion sought. Likewise, the salt used in the wash water should be such that any excess is removed by volatilization when the precipitate is finally heated to constant weight.

In the presence of a large excess of common ion, the solubility of a precipitate may be considerably greater than the value predicted by the solubility product constant. This effect will be discussed later. In general, directions call for adding about 10% excess precipitating agent.

The effect of a common ion on the solubility of a precipitate is illustrated in the following calculations.

PROBLEM. Calculate the molar solubility of CaF_2 in (a) water, (b) 0.010-M $CaCl_2$, (c) 0.010-M NaF solution, given the K_{sp} as 4×10^{-11} and neglecting hydrolysis of the fluoride ion.

(a) The equilibrium is

$$CaF_2(s) \rightleftharpoons Ca^{++} + 2\,F^-$$

Let s = molar solubility of CaF_2. The mass balances are

$$[Ca^{++}] = s$$
$$[F^-] = 2s$$

Since

$$[Ca^{++}][F^-]^2 = K_{sp}$$
$$(s)(2s)^2 = 4 \times 10^{-11}$$

and

$$s = 2.1 \times 10^{-4}\ \text{mol/l}$$

(b) In 0.010-M $CaCl_2$ the mass balances are

$$[Ca^{++}] = 0.010 + s$$
$$[F^-] = 2s$$

Hence,

$$(0.01 + s)(2s)^2 = 4 \times 10^{-11}$$

Since $s \ll 0.01$, this becomes

$$4s^2 = 4 \times 10^{-9}$$
$$s = 3.2 \times 10^{-5}\ \text{mol/l}$$

(c) The mass balances are

$$[Ca^{++}] = s$$
$$[F^-] = 0.01 + 2s$$

Hence,

$$(s)(0.01 + 2s)^2 = 4 \times 10^{-11}$$

Since $2s \ll 0.01$, this becomes

$$s = 4 \times 10^{-7}\ \text{mol/l}$$

Note the extensive reduction in solubility brought about by the common ion. It should also be noted that excess F^- has a greater effect than excess Ca^{++}.

Diverse-Ion effect

It has been found that many precipitates show an increased solubility when salts that contain no ions in common with the precipitate are present in the solution. The effect is referred to by various names, such as *diverse-ion, neutral salt,* or *activity* effect. The data in Table 14.2 illustrate the magnitude of this increased solubility for silver chloride and barium sulfate in potassium nitrate solutions. It is seen that in 0.010-M KNO$_3$ the solubility of AgCl is increased from the value in water by about 12%, and that of BaSO$_4$ by about 70%.

SOLUBILITY OF AgCl AND BaSO$_4$ IN KNO$_3$ SOLUTIONS †   **Table 14.2**

Molarity KNO$_3$	Molarity AgCl $\times 10^5$	Molarity Ba SO$_4$ $\times 10^5$
0.000	1.00	1.00
0.001	1.04	1.21
0.005	1.08	1.48
0.010	1.12	1.70

† From data of S. Popoff and E. W. Neuman, *J. Phys. Chem.*, **34**, 1853 (1930); and E. W. Neuman, *J. Am. Chem. Soc.*, **55**, 879 (1933). The K_{sp} of each salt was taken as 1×10^{-10}.

It was pointed out earlier (page 81) that we were justified in substituting molarity for activity only in very dilute solutions, where activity coefficients are approximately unity. In more concentrated solutions of electrolytes, activity coefficients decrease rapidly because of greater attraction between oppositely charged ions. The effectiveness of the ions in maintaining equilibrium conditions is thus decreased and additional precipitate must dissolve to restore this activity. The solubility product expression for AgCl is

$$a_{Ag^+} \times a_{Cl^-} = K_{sp}^{\circ}$$

where K_{sp}° is the equilibrium constant in terms of activities. In terms of concentrations this becomes

$$\gamma_{Ag^+}[Ag^+] \times \gamma_{Cl^-}[Cl^-] = K_{sp}^{\circ}$$

or

$$[Ag^+][Cl^-] = \frac{K_{sp}^{\circ}}{\gamma_{Ag^+}\gamma_{Cl^-}} = K_{sp}$$

It is apparent that the smaller the activity coefficients of the two ions, the larger is the product of the molar concentrations of the ions (K_{sp}). This increase in solubility is greater for BaSO$_4$ than for AgCl, since activity coefficients of bivalent ions decrease more rapidly than those of univalent ions, as the electrolyte concentration is increased (page 81). In very dilute solutions the activity coefficients approach unity and K_{sp} is approximately the same as K_{sp}°.

The following problem illustrates a calculation that the chemist can make in estimating activity effects on solubilities.

PROBLEM. Calculate the K_{sp} of $BaSO_4$ in 0.010-M KNO_3 solution and compare with the experimental value from Table 14.2. Use the Debye-Hückel limiting law to estimate activity coefficients.[1]

The Debye-Hückel expression for the activity coefficient of an ion in water at 25° C is

$$-\log \gamma_i = 0.5 Z_i^2 \sqrt{\mu}$$

where μ, the ionic strength, is given by

$$\mu = \tfrac{1}{2} \sum C_i Z_i^2$$

Z_i is the charge on the ion and C_i is the concentration. The ionic strength in this case can be calculated on the basis of the KNO_3 alone, since the concentrations of Ba^{++} and $SO_4^{=}$ are so small. Hence

$$\mu = \tfrac{1}{2}[0.01(1)^2 + 0.01(-1)^2] = 0.01$$

The K_{sp} expression above in logarithmic form is

$$\log K_{sp} = \log K_{sp}^\circ - \log \gamma_{Ba^{++}} - \log \gamma_{SO_4^{=}}$$

or

$$\log K_{sp} = \log K_{sp}^\circ + 0.5(2)^2\sqrt{0.01} + 0.5(-2)^2\sqrt{0.01}$$

$$\log K_{sp} = -10.0 + 4\sqrt{0.01} = -10.0 + 0.4 = -9.6$$

and

$$K_{sp} = 2.5 \times 10^{-10}$$

From Table 14.2, $K_{sp} = 2.9 \times 10^{-10}$.

The diverse-ion effect does not cause serious problems for the analyst since conditions are normally chosen so as to make the loss from solubility negligibly small. It is rarely necessary to make a precipitation from a salt solution of very high concentration, and in such a case an estimate of the increased solubility can be made as illustrated above. Errors from other sources are normally more important.

Effect of pH

The solubility of the salt of a weak acid depends upon the pH of the solution. Some of the more important examples of such salts in analytical chemistry are oxalates, sulfides, hydroxides, carbonates, and phosphates. Hydrogen ion combines with the anion of the salt to form the weak acid, thereby enhancing the solubility of the salt. We shall limit our discussion in this section to solutions which are fairly acidic, so that the hydrogen ion concentration is not changed appreciably as the salt dissolves.

Let us consider first the simplest case, that of a salt MA of the weak acid HA. The equilibria to be considered are

$$MA(s) \rightleftharpoons M^+ + A^-$$

$$HA + H_2O \rightleftharpoons H_3O^+ + A^-$$

[1] P. Debye and E. Hückel, *Physik. Z.*, **24**, 185 (1923).

As we did previously (page 187), let us designate c_A as the total concentration of all species related to the acid HA. This is sometimes called the analytical concentration and it is given by the expression

$$c_A = [A^-] + [HA]$$

or

$$c_A = [A^-]\left\{1 + \frac{[H_3O^+]}{K_a}\right\}$$

$$c_A = [A^-]\left\{\frac{K_a + [H_3O^+]}{K_a}\right\}$$

If we designate the expression in brackets as α, as we did for an analogous expression on page 187, then

$$c_A = [A^-]\alpha$$

or

$$[A^-] = \frac{c_A}{\alpha}$$

The latter expression can be substituted in the K_{sp}, giving

$$K_{sp} = [M^+][A^-] = \frac{[M^+]c_A}{\alpha}$$

Rearranging,

$$\alpha K_{sp} = [M^+]c_A = K_{eff}$$

We have designated K_{eff} as the effective solubility product constant, in agreement with the terminology used on page 187 for the effective stability constant of complexes.[2] The value of K_{eff} varies with pH because of the pH dependence of α.

The student should be able to show that for a salt MA_2, the relation is

$$K_{eff} = [M^{++}]c_A^2 = K_{sp}\alpha^2$$

and that for a dibasic acid, H_2A, the concentration of $A^=$ is given by c_A/α_2, where

$$\alpha_2 = \left\{1 + \frac{[H_3O^+]}{K_{a_2}} + \frac{[H_3O^+]^2}{K_{a_2}K_{a_1}}\right\}$$

or

$$\alpha_2 = \left\{\frac{K_{a_1}K_{a_2} + K_{a_1}[H_3O^+] + [H_3O^+]^2}{K_{a_1}K_{a_2}}\right\}$$

and

$$K_{eff} = [M^{++}]c_A = K_{sp}\alpha_2$$

The following problems illustrate some calculations based on the concepts just described.

---

[2] See H. A. Laitinen, *Chemical Analysis*, McGraw-Hill Book Co., New York, 1960, p. 108. Laitinen uses the name *conditional* solubility product. Note also that his α is the reciprocal of the α we employ here.

PROBLEM. Calculate the molar solubility of CaF_2 in an HCl solution, $pH = 3.00$, given that K_{sp} of $CaF_2 = 4 \times 10^{-11}$, and K_a of HF $= 6 \times 10^{-4}$.

First evaluate α:

$$\alpha = \frac{6 \times 10^{-4} + 1 \times 10^{-3}}{6 \times 10^{-4}} = 2.7$$

$$\alpha^2 = 7.3$$

Hence

$$K_{eff} = 4 \times 10^{-11} \times 7.3 = 2.9 \times 10^{-10}$$

Let s = molar solubility of CaF_2. The mass balances are

$$[Ca^{++}] = s$$

$$c_F = [HF] + [F^-] = 2s$$

and

$$(s)(2s)^2 = 2.9 \times 10^{-10}$$

$$s = 4.2 \times 10^{-4} \text{ mol/l}$$

PROBLEM. Calculate the solubility of CaC_2O_4 in an HCl solution of pH 3.00 given $K_{sp} = 2 \times 10^{-9}$, $K_{a_1} = 6.5 \times 10^{-2}$, $K_{a_2} = 6.1 \times 10^{-5}$.

$$\alpha_2 = \frac{6.5 \times 10^{-2} \times 6.1 \times 10^{-5} + 6.5 \times 10^{-2} \times 10^{-3} + (10^{-3})^2}{6.5 \times 10^{-2} \times 6.1 \times 10^{-5}}$$

$$\alpha_2 = 17.5$$

Hence,

$$K_{eff} = 2 \times 10^{-9} \times 17.5 = 3.5 \times 10^{-8}$$

The mass balances are

$$[Ca^{++}] = s$$

$$c_{Ox} = s$$

Then

$$s^2 = 3.5 \times 10^{-8}$$

$$s = 1.9 \times 10^{-4} \text{ mol/l}$$

The separation of metal sulfides, based upon the control of pH, has been used for many years in the qualitative analysis scheme. The metals which form the less soluble sulfides (Group II) are precipitated by H_2S in about 0.10-M HCl. Then the pH is raised to precipitate the metals of Group III. Hydrogen sulfide is a dibasic acid, and the expression for α_2 (above) is applicable. However, since the two acid constants of H_2S are so small ($K_{a_1} = 9 \times 10^{-8}$, $K_{a_2} = 1 \times 10^{-15}$), the first two terms in the numerator of the expression are negligible compared to the last, giving approximately,

$$\alpha_2 \cong \frac{[H_3O^+]^2}{K_{a_1}K_{a_2}}$$

Also in strongly acidic solution, the analytical concentration of hydrogen sulfide becomes (approximately)

$$c_S = [H_2S] + [HS^-] + [S^=] \cong [H_2S]$$

Hence the sulfide ion concentration, c_S/α_2 becomes

$$[S^=] = \frac{[H_2S]K_{a_1}K_{a_2}}{[H_3O^+]^2}$$

Since a saturated solution of H_2S is about $0.10\text{-}M$, this gives

$$[S^=] = \frac{9 \times 10^{-24}}{[H_3O^+]^2}$$

This is the usual expression employed to show how the sulfide ion concentration can be varied by changing the hydrogen ion concentration. The following example illustrates the separation of two metals by employing this principle.

PROBLEM. 100 ml of a solution that is $0.10\text{-}M$ in both Cu^{++} and Mn^{++} and $0.20\text{-}M$ in H_3O^+ is saturated with H_2S.

(a) Show which metal sulfide precipitates. K_{sp} of CuS is 4×10^{-38}, of MnS 1×10^{-16}.

The sulfide concentration is given by

$$[S^=] = \frac{9 \times 10^{-24}}{(0.20)^2} = 2.3 \times 10^{-22}$$

The K_{sp} of CuS is greatly exceeded but that of MnS is not:

$$(0.10)(2.3 \times 10^{-22}) = 2.3 \times 10^{-23} \gg 4 \times 10^{-38}$$

$$2.3 \times 10^{-23} \ll 1 \times 10^{-16}$$

Hence CuS precipitates, but MnS does not.

(b) What must be the hydrogen ion concentration for MnS to start to precipitate?

The sulfide ion concentration needed in order for $[Mn^{++}][S^=]$ to equal the K_{sp} of MnS is

$$(0.10)[S^=] = 1 \times 10^{-16}$$

$$[S^=] = 1 \times 10^{-15}$$

Hence,

$$1 \times 10^{-15} = \frac{9 \times 10^{-24}}{[H_3O^+]^2}$$

$$[H_3O^+] = 9 \times 10^{-5}\text{-}M$$

The following example illustrates the separation of two metal hydroxides by control of pH.

PROBLEM. Calculate the pH at which the following hydroxides begin to precipitate if the solution is $0.1\text{-}M$ in each cation: $Fe(OH)_3$, $K_{sp} = 1 \times 10^{-36}$; and $Mg(OH)_2$, $K_{sp} = 1 \times 10^{-11}$.

Ferric hydroxide:

$$[Fe^{3+}][OH^-]^3 = 1 \times 10^{-36}$$

$$(0.1)[OH^-]^3 = 1 \times 10^{-36}$$

$$[OH^-]^3 = 1 \times 10^{-35}$$

$$3pOH = 35$$

$$pOH = 11.7$$

$$pH = 2.3$$

Magnesium hydroxide:

$$[Mg^{++}][OH^-]^2 = 1 \times 10^{-11}$$
$$(0.1)[OH^-]^2 = 1 \times 10^{-11}$$
$$[OH^-]^2 = 1 \times 10^{-10}$$
$$2pOH = 10.0$$
$$pOH = 5.0$$
$$pH = 9.0$$

Thus if an acidic solution containing these two ions is slowly neutralized with base, ferric hydroxide will precipitate first. This precipitate can be separated by filtration before the pH is sufficiently high to precipitate magnesium hydroxide. In actual practice, however, the ferric hydroxide precipitate is likely to be contaminated by magnesium hydroxide. This arises from the fact that in the region where the two solutions mix, the solubility product constant of magnesium hydroxide may be temporarily exceeded. The magnesium hydroxide may not redissolve as the solution is stirred, and the separation is then not a clean one. Usually a buffer solution of intermediate pH is employed to diminish the local increase in hydroxyl ion concentration. Better still, the pH can be gradually increased by the hydrolysis of a substance such as urea. (See discussion of precipitation from homogeneous solution, page 384.)

Effect of hydrolysis

In the previous section we limited our discussion to solutions of fairly high acidity, such that the anion of the weak acid did not change the pH appreciably. Let us now consider the case in which the salt of a weak acid is dissolved, not in strong acid, but in water. The problem is more complex than the previous one since the change in hydrogen ion concentration may be of considerable magnitude.

For simplification let us consider that whatever the amount of salt MA which dissolves, the anion is completely hydrolyzed:

$$A^- + H_2O \rightleftarrows HA + OH^-$$

This is a good approximation if HA is very weak and if MA is not very soluble, i.e., if both K_a and K_{sp} are small. It should be noted that the lower the concentration of A^-, the more complete the hydrolysis reaction.

Let us further consider two extremes, depending upon the magnitude of the K_{sp}:

1. The solubility is so low that the pH of water is not changed appreciably by the hydrolysis.

2. The solubility is sufficiently large so that hydroxyl ion contribution of water can be neglected.

These cases are illustrated in the following problem.

PROBLEM. Calculate the molar solubilities in water of (a) CuS, $K_{sp} = 4 \times 10^{-38}$, and (b) MnS, $K_{sp} = 1 \times 10^{-16}$. Consider the hydrolysis reaction

$$S^= + H_2O \rightleftarrows HS^- + OH^-$$

(a) Since the solubility of CuS is so low, we shall neglect the OH^- produced by hydrolysis, taking $[OH^-] = 1 \times 10^{-7}$. Hence

$$\alpha_2 = \frac{9 \times 10^{-23} + 9 \times 10^{-8} \times 1 \times 10^{-7} + (1 \times 10^{-7})^2}{9 \times 10^{-23}}$$

$$\alpha_2 = 2 \times 10^8$$

$$K_{eff} = 4 \times 10^{-38} \times 2 \times 10^8 = 8 \times 10^{-30}$$

Letting s = solubility, the mass balances are

$$[Cu^{++}] = s$$

$$c_S = s$$

Hence,

$$s^2 = 8 \times 10^{-30}$$

$$s = 3 \times 10^{-15}$$

(b) Since the hydrolysis is complete, we can write the reaction as

$$MnS(s) + H_2O \rightleftarrows Mn^{++} + HS^- + OH^-$$

the equilibrium constant for which is given by

$$K = \frac{K_{sp}K_w}{K_{a_2}} = \frac{1 \times 10^{-16} \times 1 \times 10^{-14}}{1 \times 10^{-15}}$$

$$K = 1 \times 10^{-15}$$

Letting s = solubility, then

$$[Mn^{++}] = s$$

$$[HS^-] = s$$

$$[OH^-] = s$$

Hence,

$$s^3 = 1 \times 10^{-15}$$

$$s = 1 \times 10^{-5}$$

The cation of a salt can undergo hydrolysis just as can the anion, and this will also increase the solubility. Typical hydrolytic reactions of ferric ion are

$$Fe^{3+} + HOH \rightleftarrows FeOH^{++} + H^+$$

$$FeOH^{++} + HOH \rightleftarrows Fe(OH)_2^+ + H^+$$

Many metals have been found to form ionic species containing more than one metal atom, as, for example

$$2\ Fe^{3+} + 2\ H_2O \rightleftarrows Fe_2(OH)_2^{4+} + 2\ H^+$$

In the case of aluminum, species such as $Al_6(OH)_{15}^{3+}$ have been postulated to explain certain experimental data.

Because of the complexity of these processes, we shall not consider the topic further here.

Effect of complexes

The solubility of a slightly soluble salt is also dependent upon the concentration of substances which form complexes with the cation of the salt. The effect of hydrolysis, mentioned above, is an example in which the complexing agent is hydroxyl ion. The complexing agents normally considered under a heading such as this are neutral molecules and anions, both foreign and common to the precipitate.

One of the best-known examples in analytical chemistry is the effect of ammonia on the solubility of the silver halides, especially silver chloride. Silver chloride can be dissolved in ammonia and this fact is utilized in separating silver from mercury in the first group of the traditional qualitative analysis scheme. Silver ion forms two complexes with ammonia,

$$Ag^+ + NH_3 \rightleftarrows Ag(NH_3)^+ \qquad K_1 = 2.3 \times 10^3$$

$$Ag(NH_3)^+ + NH_3 \rightleftarrows Ag(NH_3)_2^+ \qquad K_2 = 6.0 \times 10^3$$

The reaction is frequently written

$$Ag^+ + 2\,NH_3 \rightleftarrows Ag(NH_3)_2^+ \qquad K = K_1 \times K_2 = 1.4 \times 10^7$$

Many precipitates form soluble complexes with the ion of the precipitating agent itself. In such a case, the solubility first decreases because of the common-ion effect, passes through a minimum, and then increases as complex formation becomes appreciable. Silver chloride forms complexes with both silver and chloride ions, such as

$$AgCl + Cl^- \rightleftarrows AgCl_2^-$$

$$AgCl_2^- + Cl^- \rightleftarrows AgCl_3^=$$

and

$$AgCl + Ag^+ \rightleftarrows Ag_2Cl^+$$

In addition there is a certain amount of undissociated AgCl molecules in solution. Figure 14.1 shows the solubility of AgCl in NaCl and AgNO$_3$ solutions. It is interesting to note that AgCl is actually more soluble in 0.1-M AgNO$_3$ and in 1-M NaCl than it is in water. It is because of such effects that only a reasonable excess (usually about 10%) of precipitating agent is used in quantitative precipitations.

The following is an example of the calculations involved in finding the solubility of silver chloride in ammonia. This case can be treated by the same procedure we have previously used, calculating an effective solubility

Fig. 14.1. Solubility of AgCl in solutions of NaCl and AgNO₃. (From H. F. Walton, *Principles and Methods of Chemical Analysis*, 2nd ed., Prentice-Hall, Inc., Englewood Cliffs, N.J. Used by permission of the author and publisher.)

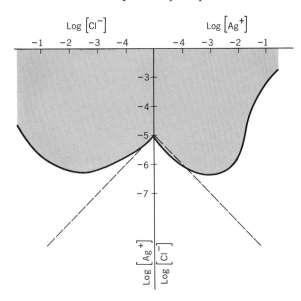

product constant. The quantitative treatment of other cases, which may become fairly complicated, can be found in more advanced texts.[3]

PROBLEM. Calculate the molar solubility of AgCl in 0.01-M NH₃. (Consider this the final concentration of NH₃.) Given K_{sp} of AgCl = 1.0×10^{-10} and stability constants: K_1 for Ag(NH₃)⁺ = 2.3×10^3, K_2 for Ag(NH₃)₂⁺ = 6.0×10^3.

Let us designate the total concentration of dissolved silver as c_{Ag}. Then

$$c_{Ag} = [Ag^+] + [Ag(NH_3)^+] + [Ag(NH_3)_2^+]$$

$$= [Ag^+]\left\{1 + \frac{[Ag(NH_3)^+]}{[Ag^+]} + \frac{[Ag(NH_3)_2^+]}{[Ag^+]}\right\}$$

$$= [Ag^+]\{1 + K_1[NH_3] + K_1K_2[NH_3]^2\}$$

Calling the quantity in brackets β, then

$$c_{Ag} = [Ag^+]\beta$$

Since

$$K_{sp} = [Ag^+][Cl^-] = \frac{c_{Ag}}{\beta}[Cl^-]$$

$$K_{sp}\cdot\beta = c_{Ag}[Cl^-] = K_{eff}$$

Evaluating β:

$$\beta = \{1 + 2.3 \times 10^3(10^{-2}) + 1.4 \times 10^7(10^{-2})^2\}$$

$$\beta = 1.4 \times 10^3$$

$$K_{eff} = 1.0 \times 10^{-10} \times 1.4 \times 10^3 = 1.4 \times 10^{-7}$$

[3] See reference 2, page 112, and J. N. Butler, *Ionic Equilibrium*, Addison-Wesley Publishing Co., Inc., Reading, Mass., 1964, Chapters 6 and 8.

Letting s = molar solubility,

$$s = c_{Ag} = [Cl^-]$$

Hence

$$s^2 = 1.4 \times 10^{-7}$$

$$s = 3.7 \times 10^{-4} \, mol/l$$

ORGANIC PRECIPITANTS

Recent years have seen dramatic development in the application of organic compounds as precipitants for inorganic ions. The vast number of such compounds and the possibilities for making systematic minor alterations in basic organic structures to increase selectivity have led to the development of a large number of very useful reagents of this type. Early work in the field was highly empirical, but in recent years chemists have taken advantage of increased knowledge of structural factors to prepare more selective reagents; increased knowledge of the equilibria involved has led to better separation methods. Many organic reagents are useful not only for separations by precipitation, but also by solvent extraction. This topic will be discussed in some detail in Chapter 16.

Most of the organic precipitants, about which our discussion will be centered, combine with cations to form *chelate* rings. We discussed such compounds in Chapter 7, where the emphasis was on reagents which form stable, 1:1 complex ions which remain in solution and which could be employed as titrants for metals. Here, we shall be concerned with neutral metal chelate compounds. There are a few examples of organic precipitants which form salt-like precipitates with metal ions and we shall consider them briefly also.

Reagents forming chelate compounds

Generally speaking most of the better known organic precipitants which form chelate compounds with cations contain both an acidic and a basic (electron-donating) functional group. The metal, interacting with both of these groups, becomes itself one member of a heterocyclic ring. From the strain theory of organic chemistry it is expected that rings of this type would be mainly 5- and 6-membered. Hence, the acidic and basic functional groups in the organic molecule must be situated in positions with respect to each other which permit the closure of such rings.

8-Hydroxyquinoline (often called 8-quinolinol, or "oxine") forms insoluble compounds with a number of metal ions, aluminum for one. The formation of this compound may be formulated as follows:

Aluminum replaces the acidic hydrogen of the hydroxyl group. At the same time, the previously unshared pair of electrons on the nitrogen is donated to the aluminum, thereby forming a 5-membered ring.

A neutral chelate compound of the type described is essentially organic in nature. The metal ion becomes simply one of the members of an organic ring structure and its usual properties and reactions are no longer readily demonstrable. With the reservation in mind that exceptions can be found, we may state generally that such chelate compounds are insoluble in water but soluble in less polar solvents such as chloroform or carbon tetrachloride. We shall see in Chapter 16 that this differential solubility may be utilized in effecting separations by extraction processes, and in Chapter 12 we mentioned briefly the use of chelates in colorimetric analysis. At this point, we wish to consider only the precipitation of metal ions by these organic reagents.

Let us consider first the advantages offered by organic precipitants.

1. Many of the chelate compounds are very insoluble in water, as noted above, so that metal ions may be quantitatively precipitated.

2. The organic precipitant often has a large molecular weight. Thus a small amount of metal may yield a large weight of precipitate.

3. Some of the organic reagents are fairly selective, yielding precipitates with only a limited number of cations. Certain people once thought that we should ultimately have available an absolutely specific reagent for each cation. Although there is little optimism in this regard today, modern research has demonstrated that a sound knowledge of the chemistry of ions in solution makes such specificity seem less necessary. By controlling such factors as *p*H and the concentration of masking reagents, the selectivity of an organic reagent can often be greatly enhanced.

4. The precipitates obtained with organic reagents are often coarse and bulky, and hence easily handled.

5. In some cases a metal can be precipitated with an organic reagent, the precipitate collected and dissolved, and the organic molecule titrated, furnishing an indirect volumetric method for the metal.

8-Hydroxyquinoline can be quantitatively brominated with a bromate-bromide mixture, and the stoichiometry of this reaction was described on

Table 14.3   SOME COMMON ORGANIC PRECIPITANTS

Compound	Chelate with metal of valence n	Comments
CH₃—C=N—OH CH₃—C=N—OH **Dimethyl glyoxime**		Principally used for determination of nickel
8-Hydroxyquinoline		Precipitates many elements but can be used for group separations by controlling pH
α-Nitroso-β-naphthol		Principally used for precipitation of cobalt in presence of large amounts of nickel
Cupferron		Mainly used for separations, such as iron and titanium from aluminum
α-Benzoin oxime		Good reagent for copper. Also precipitates bismuth and zinc
Thionalide		Used for precipitation and determination of elements of H₂S group
Quinaldic acid		Used for determination of cadmium, copper and zinc

page 11. Methods of this type are available for only a few organic precipitants because of the difficulty in finding organic oxidations which satisfy the general requirements for titrations. Since most organic precipitants are weak acids and bases (too weak to be titrated in water), it is sometimes possible to titrate the organic molecule in nonaqueous media.[4]

We must also consider certain disadvantages in the use of organic precipitants.

1. The low solubility of the metal chelate compounds was listed as an advantage. However, the very limited aqueous solubility of most organic reagents themselves is often troublesome. It is generally necessary to add at least a slight excess of the precipitant, and thus the danger of contaminating the precipitate with excess reagent is often a real one. Occasionally, but not always, the excess reagent can be washed out of the precipitate with a solvent such as hot water or alcohol.

2. Many of the organic precipitates do not have good weighing forms, largely because of uncertainty in the drying process. Some of the most attractive of the organic precipitants can be used only for separations, not for determinations, because of this difficulty in drying to a product of definite composition. Some of the metal chelates tend to volatilize at the temperatures required to remove water. In other cases, decomposition of the organic molecule sets in before drying to constant weight has been assured.

3. A minor disadvantage is the fact that the precipitates are not easily wet by water, and hence tend to float on the surface of the solution and to creep up the sides of glass vessels. This trouble can be alleviated by addition of a small amount of wetting agent to the solution before filtration.

A list of a few of the more widely used organic precipitants is given in Table 14.3.

Reagents forming saltlike precipitates

Some organic precipitants form salts rather than chelate complexes with inorganic ions. Oxalic acid is well known in analytical processes for its use in the precipitation of calcium; calcium oxalate is a typical insoluble salt. There are a number of such organic compounds which form precipitates with both cations and anions, and we shall describe here a few of the ones most widely used in quantitative analysis.

Sodium tetraphenyl boron. This compound has the formula

$$Na^+B(C_6H_5)_4^-$$

and has found widest use in precipitating potassium ion. If the precipitation

[4] C. H. Hill, Han Tai, A. L. Underwood, and R. A. Day, Jr., *Anal. Chem.*, **28**, 1688 (1956).

is carried out in a cold solution of about 0.1-M HCl, only NH_4^+, Hg^{++}, Rb^+, and Cs^+ interfere. At pH 6.5 in the presence of EDTA, the mercuric ion does not interfere. The precipitate can be dried and weighed, or dissolved in acetone and titrated with perchloric acid.

Bendizine. This compound is used primarily for the precipitation of sulfate ion. Its reaction with sulfuric acid is shown below:

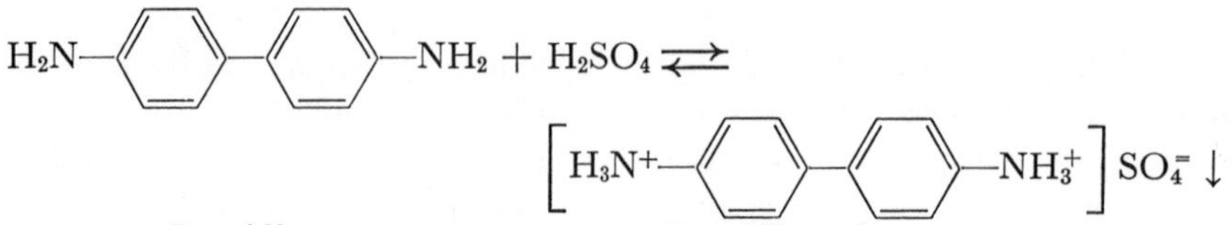

$$H_2N-\!\!\!\bigcirc\!\!-\!\!\bigcirc\!\!-\!\!NH_2 + H_2SO_4 \rightleftarrows$$

$$\left[H_3N^+-\!\!\bigcirc\!\!-\!\!\bigcirc\!\!-\!\!NH_3^+\right]SO_4^= \downarrow$$

Benzidine	**Benzidine sulfate**

The precipitate may be weighed as such or suspended in water and titrated with standard base using phenolphthalein indicator. It is the benzidinium ion, an acid, which reacts with base.

Tetraphenylarsonium chloride. This compound is used to precipitate a number of metals from sodium chloride solutions as the tetraphenylarsonium salt of the complex ion. An example is

$$(C_6H_5)_4As^+Cl^- + TlCl_4^- \rightleftarrows (C_6H_5)_4AsTlCl_4 \downarrow + Cl^-$$

Tetraphenylarsonium chloride

This precipitate with thallium can be weighed as such. Other metals which form precipitates include tin, gold, zinc, platinum, mercury, and cadmium.

Arsonic acids. Arsonic acids have the structure

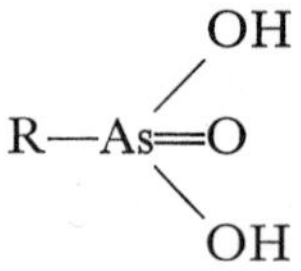

$$R-As{=}O \begin{cases} OH \\ \\ OH \end{cases}$$

where R is an organic group, especially phenyl, p-hydroxyphenyl, and n-propyl. These acids precipitate quadrivalent metal ions such as tin, thorium, and zirconium from acid media. The precipitates contain two moles of the acid per mole of quadrivalent cation, and are generally ignited to the oxides before weighing.

REFERENCES

1. H. A. Laitinen, *Chemical Analysis*, McGraw-Hill Book Co., Inc., New York, 1960.
2. J. N. Butler, *Solubility and pH Calculations*, Addison-Wesley Publishing Co., Inc., Reading, Mass., 1964.
3. D. L. Leussing, "Solubility," and J. F. Coetzee, "Equilibria in Precipitation Reactions and Precipitation Lines," Chapters 17 and 19, Part I, Vol. I, of *Treatise*

on Analytical Chemistry, I. M. Kolthoff, P. J. Elving, and E. B. Sandell, Eds., Interscience Publishers, Inc., New York, 1959.

QUESTIONS

1. Point out the various factors that affect the solubility of inorganic crystals and explain how each factor operates.

2. Explain why the following statements are true:
   (a) Silver chloride is more soluble in 1-*M* potassium nitrate than in water.
   (b) Silver chloride is more soluble in 1-*M* hydrochloric acid than in water.
   (c) Silver chloride is more soluble in 1-*M* ammonia than in water.
   (d) Silver chloride is less soluble in 0.001-*M* HCl than in water.
   (e) Ferrous hydroxide is less soluble in 0.1-*M* ammonia than in water.
   (f) Zinc hydroxide is more soluble in 0.1-*M* ammonia than in water.
   (g) Calcium fluoride is more soluble at *p*H 3 than at *p*H 4.
   (h) Silver chromate is less soluble in 0.001-*M* $AgNO_3$ than in 0.001-*M* K_2CrO_4 solution.

3. Which compound has the larger solubility product constant, AgCl or Ag_2CrO_4? Which has the larger molar solubility?

4. Compare the metal chelate precipitates with strictly inorganic precipitates with regard to their properties. What are some of the advantages and disadvantages of these organic precipitants?

5. Make plots of *p*Ag vs. *p*Cl and of *p*Ag vs. *p*CrO$_4$ for the precipitation of AgCl and Ag_2CrO_4. Note the difference in the two plots.

6. Make a plot of $\log [M^{++}]$ vs. $-\log [SO_4^=] = pSO_4$ for the following metal sulfates, MSO_4: $M^{++} = Ca^{++}$, Sr^{++}, and Ba^{++}. On the same diagram plot $\log [SO_4^=]$ vs. pSO_4. What are the values of the slopes of these lines? To what condition does the intersection of two lines correspond?

7. Examine the expression for α_2 on page 341. Can α_2 be less than 1? What happens to the value of α_2 as the *p*H increases? How large can α_2 become? What does this mean in an actual physical situation?

PROBLEMS

1. Calculate the solubility product constants of the following substances from the stated solubilities:
   (a) AgI: 0.00235 mg/l
   (b) $Mg(OH)_2$: 0.000793 g/100 ml
   (c) $Ag_2C_2O_4$: 3.28 mg/100 ml

2. From the solubility product constants listed in Appendix I, calculate the following solubilities in water. (You can neglect such effects as hydrolysis.)

    (a) $PbSO_4$ in mg/200 ml

    (b) CaF_2 in g/250 ml

    (c) $Cu(IO_3)_2$ in mg/ml

3. Calculate the molar solubilities of the following, neglecting complexing, hydrolysis, and diverse ion effects:

    (a) $SrSO_4$ in 0.01-M K_2SO_4 solution

    (b) MgF_2 in 0.10-M NaF solution

    (c) $Ag_2C_2O_4$ in 0.002-M $AgNO_3$ solution

4. Calculate the molar solubilities of the following:

    (a) $Mg(OH)_2$ at pH 12.00

    (b) CdS at pH 2.00, solution saturated with H_2S

    (c) ZnS at pH 1.00, solution saturated with H_2S

5. Calculate the molar solubilities of the following:

    (a) CaF_2 in HCl solution of pH 2.00

    (b) CaC_2O_4 in HCl solution of pH 2.70

    (c) MgF_2 in HCl solution of pH 3.30

6. Calculate the solubility in g/100 ml of the following:

    (a) AgCl in 1.0-M ammonia

    (b) AgBr in 5.0-M ammonia

    (c) AgI in 15-M ammonia

7. A certain hydroxide, $M(OH)_2$, has a molecular weight of 100 and is soluble to the extent of 0.2 mg per liter.

    (a) Calculate the K_{sp} of this hydroxide.

    (b) To 200 ml of a 0.020-M solution of M^{++}, solid NaOH is added (no volume change). At what pH does $M(OH)_2$ just start to precipitate?

    (c) What percentage of the metal is precipitated when the pH reaches 7.00?

8. Urea is added to 100 ml of a 0.10-M solution of $MgCl_2$, and the pH is gradually raised by boiling the solution. Calculate the pH values when 50, 90, 99.9, and 99.99% of the magnesium has been precipitated. Assume the solution is returned to 25°C and use the necessary data at this temperature.

9. (a) Calculate the pH required just to prevent the precipitation of CdS from a solution which is 0.010-M in Cd^{++}, and is saturated with H_2S.

    (b) What should the pH be if it is desired to lower the cadmium ion concentration to 10^{-6}-M by precipitating CdS?

10. Theoretically, what should the pH be to prevent the precipitation of Ag_2S from a solution which is 0.01-M in Ag^+? Is such a pH possible?

11. To a 0.050-M solution of a metal ion, A^{3+}, solid NaOH is added until the pH reaches a value of 4.70. At this point the hydroxide $A(OH)_3$ begins to precipitate. Calculate the K_{sp} of $A(OH)_3$.

12. To 60 ml of 0.10-M NaCl is added 40 ml of 0.16-M $AgNO_3$.

    (a) Calculate the number of milligrams of chloride not precipitated.

    (b) If the precipitate is washed with 75 ml of water at room temperature, what is the maximum number of milligrams of AgCl that could be lost by solubility in the wash water?

13. If 50 ml of 0.10-M $AgNO_3$ is mixed with 50 ml of 0.10-M KIO_3, how many milligrams of Ag^+ remain unprecipitated? What concentration of IO_3^- would be needed to reduce the Ag^+ concentration of 0.1 mg per 100 ml?

14. It is desired to separate two metals M^{++} and N^+ by precipitation of their sulfides from a solution which is 0.10-M in H^+ and saturated with H_2S. What is the minimum ratio of the K_{sp} of MS to that of N_2S in order that the concentration of N^+ be reduced to 10^{-6}-M without precipitating M^{++} at 0.10-M?

15. Calculate the molar solubilities in water of the following, taking into account hydrolysis of the anion:
  (a) Calcium carbonate
  (b) Barium chromate
  (c) Silver chromate
  (d) Zinc sulfide
  (e) Silver sulfide

16. The chloride ion in a solution is precipitated by addition of silver ion. Theoretically, what must be the final concentration of silver in order to precipitate all but 0.1 mg of chloride from 200 ml of solution?

17. What is the maximum amount of water that could be used to wash a precipitate of AgBr so that no more than 0.1 mg of Ag^+ is lost through solubility?

18. Magnesium hydroxide is precipitated by an NH_3-NH_4Cl buffer. What must be the concentration of NH_3 to precipitate all but 0.1 mg of magnesium from 100 ml of a solution which is 0.01-M in NH_4Cl?

19. 50 ml of 0.02-M RCl_2 is mixed with 50 ml of an NH_3-NH_4Cl buffer, precipitating the hydroxide, $R(OH)_2$. The buffer is 0.20-M in NH_4OH before the mixing. If it is found that a minimum of 0.945 g of NH_4Cl must be dissolved in the buffer before mixing just to prevent precipitation, what is the K_{sp} of $R(OH)_2$?

20. 4.00 mmol of Ag^+ is added to 100 ml of an ammoniacal solution which is 0.030-M in NaBr. Calculate the number of milligrams of Br^- unprecipitated if the final concentration of NH_3 in the solution is 0.10-M.

21. If exactly 1.00 liter of 2.0-M NH_3 (final concentration) is required to dissolve 5.75 mmol of the silver salt AgX what is the K_{sp} of the salt?

22. One mmol of AgCl is dissolved in 500 ml of ammonia, the final concentrations of NH_3 being 0.40-M. Calculate the concentration of uncomplexed Ag^+ ions in the solution.

23. 100 ml of a solution that is 0.10-M in Cd^{++} and 0.10-M in H^+ is saturated with H_2S. Calculate the milligrams of cadmium left in the solution, noting that the precipitation of CdS produces hydrogen ions.

24. The solubility product constant of M_2S is 1×10^{-14}. 100 ml of a solution contains 10 mmol of M^+ and 10 mmol of NaOAc. How many mmol of H^+ should be added to the solution to prevent precipitation of M_2S when the solution is saturated with H_2S?

25. A solution is 0.10-M in Sr^{++} and 0.05-M in Ca^{++}. Solid Na_2CO_3 is added to the solution, first precipitating $SrCO_3$. What percentage of the Sr^{++} is precipitated when $CaCO_3$ begins to precipitate?

26. Solid $AgNO_3$ is added to a solution which is 0.10-M in each Cl^-, Br^-, and I^-. Calculate the percentage of I^- unprecipitated when AgBr begins to precipitate, and the percentage of bromide unprecipitated when AgCl begins to precipitate.

27. The successive stepwise formation constants of $Cd(NH_3)_4^{++}$ are as follows: $k_1 = 550$, $k_2 = 162$, $k_3 = 23.5$, and $k_4 = 13.5$. Calculate the molar solubility of CdS in a 0.1-M solution of ammonia, calculating first α_2 for the anion, β for the cation, and then the solubility.

28. Calculate the K_{sp} of AgCl in 0.010-M KNO$_3$ solution using the Debye-Hückel limiting law. Compare your result with the value in Table 14.2.

29. (a) Show that the molar solubility of the salt MX, where

$$MX \rightleftarrows M^{++} + X^{=}$$

is given by

$$s = \sqrt{\frac{K_{sp} \times K_{a_1} \times K_{a_2} + K_{sp} \times K_{a_1}[H_3O^+] + K_{sp}[H_3O^+]^2}{K_{a_1} \times K_{a_2}}}$$

Here K_{a_1} and K_{a_2} are the two ionization constants of the acid, H$_2$X.

(b) Some texts give the following expression for the solubility of a metal sulfate, MSO$_4$, in acid media:

$$s = \sqrt{\frac{K_{sp} \times K_{a_2} + K_{sp}[H_3O^+]}{K_{a_2}}}$$

How do you rationalize this expression with that in part (a)?

30. (a) Calculate the molar solubility of BaSO$_4$ in 0.10-M HCl, using the expression in problem 29(b) above.

(b) Repeat part (a) using the expression in problem 29(a) above. Take K_{a_1} for H$_2$SO$_4$ to be (i) 10 (ii) 100.

Formation and Properties
of Precipitates

In our previous discussion of precipitation we have considered the process in terms of the equilibrium that exists between an ionic solid and a solution of the ions. We have examined several factors which influence solubility and which can be employed to effect separations. The present chapter will consider precipitation as a rate process, with particular emphasis on the mechanism by which solid particles are built up from ions in solution. This treatment should give us insight into the factors which influence the nature and size of the solid particles, as well as the purity of the precipitate. We shall learn how the analyst can exercise some control over the size and purity of the particles which separate from a solution. The substance finally weighed in a gravimetric analysis must be pure, or nearly so, for the analysis to be valid. Hence, this aspect of precipitation is of great importance in analytical chemistry.

PARTICLE SIZE[1]

Colloids

It has been known for many years that the solubility of certain crystalline solids is dependent upon the size of the particles in contact with the solution. Hulett[2] found, for example, that finely divided particles of calcium sulfate (gypsum) and barium sulfate were more soluble in water than coarse crystals. If, however, the finely divided particles are left in contact with the saturated solution long enough for equilibrium to be established, the continual interchange of ions between the solid and liquid phases leads to an increase in size of the solid particles. Eventually the particles become much larger (*macro* rather than *micro*), and the quantity of dissolved material becomes the ordinary equilibrium value. In other words, the solution is temporarily supersaturated with respect to the coarse crystals.

It has been found that crystals must be smaller than one to two microns (a micron is 10^{-4} cm) in diameter for this increased solubility to occur. When a solid phase of such small particles is dispersed in a liquid, a so-called *colloidal dispersion* results. It is important that we consider some of the properties of colloids here because in the process of building up a particle from the ions in solution, the particle reaches colloidal dimensions before it grows large enough to settle from the solution as a precipitate. We might picture the process as:

$$\text{Ions in true solution} \longrightarrow \text{colloidal particles} \longrightarrow \text{precipitate}$$
$$\text{(size } 10^{-8} \text{ cm)} \qquad \text{(size } 10^{-7}\text{--}10^{-4} \text{ cm)} \qquad \text{(size} > 10^{-4} \text{ cm)}$$

The ions in true solution are of the order of a few Angstrom units (10^{-8} cm) in diameter. Let us consider what happens when the two ions, A^+ and B^-, are made to precipitate as the compound AB. If we increase the concentration of one of these ions sufficiently to surpass the solubility product constant, precipitation must begin. The A^+ and B^- ions must start "clinging" together to build up a particle sufficiently large to settle from the solution. Imagine, for simplicity, that one thousand of these ions, five hundred of each sign, cling together to form a simple cube. There will then be ten ions on each edge of the cube, or one hundred on each face, and if the ions are about 10^{-8} cm in diameter, the cube will be about 10^{-7} cm on each edge. The particle is now of such size that it is entering the colloidal range. Subsequent growth of the particle by deposition of other ions on its surface will

---

[1] An excellent summary of this topic at a more advanced level is given by H. A. Laitinen, *Chemical Analysis*, McGraw-Hill Book Co., Inc., 1960, p. 117.

[2] G. A. Hulett, *Z. physik. Chem.*, **37**, 385 (1901); **47**, 357 (1909).

eventually lead to a size sufficiently large for the particle to settle as a visible crystal. However, the nature and purity of the final particles which settle are largely a consequence of the properties exhibited in the colloidal state. In order to appreciate fully the further discussion, we should recall some of the properties of colloids, as contrasted with properties of particles in true solution and with those "temporarily suspended" in a solution. Such a comparison is given in Table 15.1.

PROPERTIES OF COLLOIDS   **Table 15.1**

	True solution	Colloidal dispersion	Temporary suspension
Size............	10^{-8}	10^{-7}–10^4 cm	10^{-4} cm
Action of gravity...	None	None, but can cause to settle by centrifugation	Particles settle out
Filtration.........	Particles pass through finest filters	Particles pass through ordinary filters, but not through ultrafilters	Particles caught by ordinary filter paper
Electric charge....	Equal + and − (electrolytes)	All either + or all −	Uncharged
Tyndall effect.....	Not shown	Shown	Not shown

The most important characteristics of colloids, for our consideration in precipitation, are (1) the fact that the solubility of such small particles may be greater than that of larger particles, and (2) the fact that the particles carry an electric charge. Both of these characteristics result from the extremely large surface that is exposed to the solution by such small particles. Consider, for example, the aforementioned cube containing one thousand A^+ and B^- ions. If one counted the number of these ions that are on the faces of the cube, one would find there almost half of them (488). In contrast, consider a cube further built up to contain one million of the ions, one hundred on each edge, each edge being about 10^{-4} cm. There are now 59,164 ions on the surface, or only 5.9% of the total. Thus as the particle grows larger, a smaller and smaller fraction of the ions is on the surface.

Another way of illustrating the large surface area per unit mass exhibited by very small particles is as follows: Consider a cube 1 cm on edge. Each face has an area of 1 cm², or a total area of 6 cm². If this cube is divided into smaller cubes, 0.1 cm on edge, 1000 cubes result with a total area of 60 cm². The results of progressive subdivision in this manner are shown in Table 15.2. It is obvious that the surface area per unit mass is extremely large for particles which are of colloidal size.

Let us now consider the difference between an ion on the surface and one in the body of a crystal. In Figure 15.1 is pictured a simple cubic lattice,

Table 15.2   SURFACE AREA OF CUBE IN VARIOUS STATES OF SUBDIVISION

Length of edge of cube, cm	Number of cubes	Surface area, cm²
1	1	6
0.1	10^3	60
0.01	10^6	600
0.001	10^9	6,000
0.0001	10^{12}	60,000
0.00001	10^{15}	600,000
0.000001	10^{18}	6,000,000

with black circles representing A^+ ions and white circles B^- ions. In this case only one ion is not on one of the faces of the cube. This ion (A^+) is surrounded by six B^- ions, at equal distances from the central ion. In other words, an ion in the body of this crystal lattice has the capacity to attract and hold six ions of opposite charge. Each ion on the surface, however, has only five equidistant neighbors and thus will tend to attract oppositely charged ions from the solution, as well as the polar molecules of a solvent such as water.

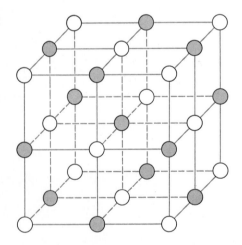

Fig. 15.1. Simple cubic lattice.

It is now apparent how a very small particle may be more soluble than a much larger one. The greater number of surface ions exert a much larger attractive force for the polar solvent, leading to a greater tendency for the ions to leave the solid and enter the solution. In the same manner it is easy to see how such particles acquire an electric charge. The surface ions attract oppositely charged ions from the solution and hold them quite strongly. The surface ions are said to *adsorb* other ions. Let us picture this process in greater detail, taking silver chloride as an example. Suppose a drop of silver nitrate is added to a sodium chloride solution. When the first particles grow to colloidal size, there are a large number of Ag^+ and Cl^- ions on the surfaces. In the solution are Na^+, Cl^-, and NO_3^- ions. The surface Ag^+ ions attract Cl^- and NO_3^- ions from the solution, and the surface Cl^- ions attract Na^+ ions. As a general rule (Paneth-Fajans-Hahn), the ion from the solution that is more strongly held is the one that is common to the lattice, in this case the chloride ion.[3] Thus the surface of the particle acquires a layer of chloride ions and the particle becomes negatively charged. The process is represented schematically in Figure 15.2. The chloride ions are said to form

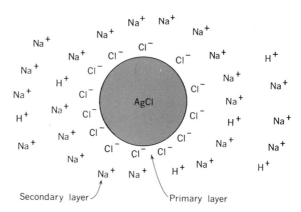

Fig. 15.2. Schematic picture of colloidal particle.

Secondary layer

Primary layer

the *primary layer;* they in turn attract sodium ions, forming a *secondary layer.* The secondary layer is held more loosely than is the primary layer.

Since colloidal particles all carry the same charge (negative in this case), they repel one another and resist combining to form larger particles that will settle from the solution. The particles move about in a zig-zag motion, because of the bombardment by molecules of the solvent. This motion is referred to as the Brownian movement, and it can be observed under an ultramicroscope. The particles can be made to *coagulate* (or *flocculate*), that is, to cohere and form larger clumps of material that will settle from the solution, by removal of the charge contributed by the primary layer. In the example of silver chloride, which was cited above, coagulation can be achieved by further addition of silver nitrate until equivalent amounts of silver and chloride ions are present. Since silver ions are more strongly attracted to the primary layer of chloride ions than are sodium ions, they replace sodium ions in the secondary layer and then "neutralize" the negative charge contributed by the primary layer. Stripped of their charge, the particles immediately cohere and form clumps of material which are sufficiently large to settle from the solution. Some colloids when coagulated,

---

[3] If no common ion is present, this rule says that the ion in solution that forms the least soluble compound with one of the lattice ions is the most strongly adsorbed.

carry down large quantities of water, giving a jelly-like precipitate. Such materials are termed *gels*, or *hydrogels* if water is the solvent. The solid material is also referred to as an *emulsoid*, or said to be *lyophilic*, meaning that it has a strong affinity for the solvent. (If water is the solvent, the term *hydrophilic* is used.) Ferric and aluminum hydroxides and silicic acid are familiar examples of emulsoids. A colloid that has only a small affinity for water is called a *suspensoid*, or said to be *lyophobic*, and when coagulation takes place very little solvent is retained. Silver chloride is this type of material, and the small amount of water that is retained upon coagulation of silver chloride is easily removed by drying above 110°C. The water retained by an emulsoid, such as ferric hydroxide, is much more strongly held, and high temperatures are required for complete dehydration.

Coagulation of colloidal dispersions can be brought about by ions other than those of the precipitate itself. For example, the negatively charged silver chloride colloid discussed above can be coagulated by adding a sufficiently large quantity of salts such as potassium nitrate, calcium chloride, or aluminum nitrate. A smaller concentration of aluminum nitrate is required to effect coagulation of a negative colloid than is required of the other two salts. The larger the charge on the cation, the more effective on a molar basis is the salt in effecting coagulation. If the colloid is positively charged, the charge on the anion of the salt determines the effectiveness of the coagulating salt. A few examples of the concentrations of different salts required to bring about coagulation are given in Table 15.3.

When coagulation of a colloid occurs, the coagulating ions may be dragged down with the precipitate. If these ions are dissolved when a pre-

Table 15.3 COAGULATING VALUES OF ELECTROLYTES FOR TYPICAL SOLS †

| As_2S_3 (negative) | | $Fe(OH)_3$ (positive) | |
Electrolyte	mmol/liter	Electrolyte	mmol/liter
LiCl	58.4	KI	16.2
NaCl	51.0	KBr	12.5
KNO_3	50.0	KNO_3	11.9
KCl	49.5	KCl	9.0
NH_4Cl	42.3		
HCl	30.8		
$MgSO_4$	0.81	$MgSO_4$	0.22
$MgCl_2$	0.72	Tl_2SO_4	0.22
$ZnCl_2$	0.69	K_2SO_4	0.20
$BaCl_2$	0.69	$K_2Cr_2O_7$	0.19
$CaCl_2$	0.65		
$Al(NO_3)_3$	0.095		
$AlCl_3$	0.093		
$Ce(NO_3)_3$	0.080		

† H. Freundlich, *Z. physik. Chem.*, **73**, 385 (1910).

cipitate is washed, the solid particles will go back into a colloidal dispersion and pass through the filter. Such a process of dispersing an insoluble material into a liquid as a colloid is termed *peptization*, and must be avoided in quantitative procedures. When peptization may occur, an electrolyte is dissolved in the wash water to replace the ions which are washed away. Dilute nitric acid is added for this reason to the water used to wash a silver chloride precipitate. When the precipitate is dried, any nitric acid retained by the silver chloride is volatilized and does not interfere in the analysis.

The precipitation process

When the solubility product constant of a compound is exceeded and precipitation begins, a number of small particles, called nuclei, are formed. Subsequent precipitation can take place on these initially formed particles, with the particles growing in size until large enough to settle from the solution. The particle size distribution of the precipitate is determined by the relative rates of the two processes, the formation of nuclei, called *nucleation*, and the growth of nuclei. It is apparent that if the rate of nucleation is small compared to the rate of growth of nuclei, fewer particles are finally produced and these particles are of relatively large particle size. Such a material is more easily filterable and frequently purer than is the case with small particles. Hence the analyst tries to adjust conditions during precipitation so that the rate of nucleation is relatively small in order that the particle size will be large.

According to Ostwald,[4] the relationship between solubility and temperature of a solid dissolved in a liquid can be expressed as in Figure 15.3. The normal solubility curve is represented by curve AA'. The region between AA' and LL' is a *metastable* one; a solution having conditions of temperature and concentration represented by this region is *supersaturated*. The system is not at equilibrium and precipitation will occur if a crystal of the solid is added to the solution (seeding). The concentration of solute will decrease to the equilibrium value given by the curve AA'. Ostwald proposed that beyond a certain degree of supersaturation, the solution becomes *labile*, that is, subject to spontaneous formation of nuclei and subsequent precipitation without the necessity of seeding. This limit is represented by the curve LL'.

At a certain temperature, say T_1, precipitation can be described as follows: As the concentration of solute increases, say by mixing two reagents, the solution becomes saturated at point S on curve AA'. If supersaturation occurs, the concentration continues to rise into the metastable region between S and Q. When the concentration reaches Q, nucleation begins spontaneously and precipitation begins. Note that the same point could be reached by lowering the temperature along the line EQ. The degree of

[4] W. Ostwald, *Z. physik. Chem.*, Leipzig, **22**, 289 (1897).

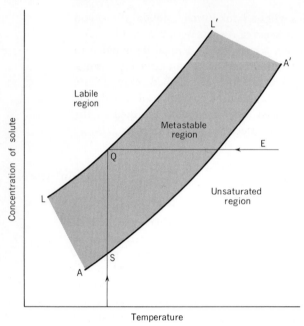

Fig. 15.3. Solubility curves.

supersaturation at point Q is given by $Q - S$; the relative supersaturation is given by the ratio $(Q - S)/S$.

Von Weimarn ratio

Von Weimarn[5] studied thoroughly the relationship between the size of particles of a precipitate and the rate of precipitation. He proposed that the initial rate of precipitation is proportional to the relative supersaturation,

$$\text{Initial rate of precipitation} = K\frac{Q - S}{S}$$

where Q is the total concentration of substance momentarily produced in solution by mixing the reactants, S is the solubility of the macro crystals, and K is a constant. The term $Q - S$ represents the degree of supersaturation at the moment precipitation begins, and the larger this term, the more rapid is the initial growth of particles, that is, the greater is the number of nuclei formed. The term S in the denominator represents the force resisting precipitation, or causing the precipitate to redissolve. The greater the value of S, the smaller will be the ratio, and the smaller will be the number of nuclei formed. Since the analyst is interested in obtaining large particles,

[5] P. P. von Weimarn, *Chem. Rev.*, **2**, 217 (1926).

he should try to adjust conditions to make the ratio $(Q - S)/S$ as small as possible.

Actually, the von Weimarn expression is only approximate, but it serves as an excellent guide to the selection of conditions of precipitation. Before discussing these conditions, let us examine the expression more closely. We have already seen that the solubility S may depend upon the size of the particles, and although we have indicated above that the solubility of macro crystals should be employed in the ratio, actually one should consider S as the solubility of the nuclei that are first formed as precipitation begins. In most cases such data are unavailable, but in the case of barium sulfate it has been found that particles as small as 0.04 μ or less are about one thousand times as soluble as large particles.[6] It has also been found that hard substances, of high surface tension, show a greater increase in solubility when the particles are of micro size than do soft substances, of low surface tension. While no data are available for silver chloride, this substance does form soft crystals, and it can be assumed that its solubility is fairly independent of particle size. With these facts in mind, let us consider the precipitation of barium sulfate and of silver chloride. The solubility product constants of the two salts are about the same, yet silver chloride precipitates as a coagulated colloid and barium sulfate as a crystalline substance.

PROBLEM. Calculate the value of $(Q - S)/S$ for $BaSO_4$ and for AgCl under the following conditions:
(a) 100 ml of 0.1-M Na_2SO_4 with 0.05 ml of 0.1-M $BaCl_2$ added.
(b) 100 ml of 0.1-M NaCl solution with 0.05 ml of 0.1-M $AgNO_3$ added (K_{sp} of each salt is 1×10^{-10}).
The momentary concentration of each salt is

$$Q = \frac{0.05 \text{ ml} \times 0.1 \text{ mmol/ml}}{100 \text{ ml}} = 5 \times 10^{-5} \text{ mmol/ml}$$

Since $[SO_4^=] = 0.1$, $[Ba^{++}] = S = 1 \times 10^{-9}$ (S is the same for AgCl).
Thus for AgCl, where S of micro particles is about the same as that for macro particles,

$$\frac{Q - S}{S} = \frac{5 \times 10^{-5} - 1 \times 10^{-9}}{1 \times 10^{-9}} = 50,000$$

However, for $BaSO_4$, S is about 1000 times 1×10^{-9}, or 1×10^{-6}. Thus

$$\frac{Q - S}{S} = \frac{5 \times 10^{-5} - 1 \times 10^{-6}}{1 \times 10^{-6}} = 49$$

Thus under the same conditions of precipitation, many more nuclei of silver chloride are formed than of barium sulfate. The silver chloride particles are extremely small, become electrically charged, and remain in the form of a colloidal dispersion. The barium sulfate particles are fewer in

[6] M. L. Dundon and E. Mack, *J. Am. Chem. Soc.*, **45**, 2479 (1923); M. L. Dundon, *J. Am. Chem. Soc.*, **45**, 2658 (1923).

number and of much larger size. Further precipitation results in a continued growth of these few particles until a well-formed crystalline solid separates from the solution.

Hydroxides of metals such as aluminum and iron are very insoluble and separate from solution as gelatinous precipitates. A calculation of $(Q - S)/S$ for ferric hydroxide (K_{sp} of 1×10^{-36}), under the same conditions as in the example above, gives a value of about 1×10^7. In other words, an extremely large number of nuclei are formed, with a subsequent aggregation of these tiny particles (carrying a large amount of water) into a gelatinous precipitate.

The three compounds discussed above, barium sulfate, silver chloride, and ferric hydroxide, are typical examples of the three types of precipitates encountered in gravimetric analysis: crystalline, curdy, and gelatinous. All three compounds are crystalline internally; that is, there is a regular arrangement of the ions inside the solid particles, as shown by X-ray examination.[7] However, only barium sulfate appears crystalline to an observer, since the particles are large and have well-defined crystal faces. Silver chloride and ferric hydroxide appear to be amorphous because they are made up of a large number of tiny crystals, clumped together in a curd or gel, with no apparent crystal faces.

Actually, barium sulfate can be made to precipitate as a gel or a curd by working under conditions which give a very large value of $(Q - S)/S$. In his classic experiments, von Weimarn mixed equal volumes of barium thiocyanate and manganese sulfate [each 3.5-M, $(Q - S)/S = 175,000$] and obtained such a stable gel that the beaker in which the solutions were mixed could be inverted without the contents running out. When equal volumes of 0.5-M solutions were mixed [$(Q - S)/S = 25,000$], a curdy precipitate of barium sulfate was obtained. With still lower concentrations of the reactants, definite crystals were obtained. When very dilute solutions were employed (about 0.0001-M), the precipitate did not appear until after about a month's time. At the end of six months some of the crystals were found to be as long as 0.003 cm and as broad as 0.00015 cm.

We can now summarize the conditions of precipitation which the analyst can employ to obtain particles as large as possible. It is necessary to decrease the value of $(Q - S)/S$, and this can be done by decreasing Q or increasing S. While it is possible to decrease Q sufficiently to bring about a large decrease in the ratio (using extremely dilute solutions as with barium sulfate above), an unduly long time may be required for precipitation. In practice, one routinely brings about a moderate decrease in Q by (1) using reasonably dilute solutions, and (2) adding the precipitating agent slowly. It is frequently possible to increase the value of S markedly and thus effect a large decrease in the ratio. This can be done by taking advantage of the factors that may increase solubility (Chapter 14): temperature, pH, or the use of

---

[7] A gel such as ferric hydroxide may be amorphous when first precipitated, but gradually becomes crystalline upon standing.

complexing agents. Precipitations are quite commonly carried out at elevated temperatures for this reason. Salts of weak acids, such as calcium oxalate and zinc sulfide, are better precipitated in weakly acidic, rather than in alkaline, solution.[8] Barium sulfate is better precipitated in 0.01 to 0.05-M hydrochloric acid solution since the solubility is increased by formation of the bisulfate ion. A compound such as ferric hydroxide is so insoluble that even in acidic solution the value of $(Q - S)/S$ is still so large that a gelatinous precipitate results. However, a dense precipitate of iron as the basic formate can be obtained by homogeneous precipitation (page 384).

In addition to controlling the conditions during the actual precipitation process, the analyst has one other recourse after the precipitate is formed. This is to *digest*, or *age*, the precipitate, that is, to allow the precipitate to stand in contact with the mother liquor, frequently at elevated temperature, for some time before filtration. The small particles of a crystalline substance, such as barium sulfate, being more soluble than the larger ones, dissolve more readily making the solution supersaturated with respect to the larger particles. In order to establish equilibrium with respect to the larger particles, additional material must leave the solution and enter the solid phase. The ions now deposit on the larger particles, causing these particles to grow even larger. Thus, the larger particles grow at the expense of the smaller ones. This process, sometimes called "Ostwald ripening," is useful for increasing the particle size of crystalline precipitates, but not for curdy or gelatinous precipitates. The latter are either so insoluble, or the small particles do not differ sufficiently in solubility from the larger ones, that no appreciable growth in size occurs.[9] Even with crystalline precipitates it is necessary to employ conditions which increase solubility if a beneficial effect is to be attained in a reasonable time. This is the reason for the frequent use of elevated temperatures during digestion.

Thus to obtain a precipitate of large particle size, precipitation is carried out by slow mixing of dilute solutions under conditions of increased solubility of the precipitate. Crystalline precipitates are normally digested at elevated temperature before filtration to further increase particle size.

PURITY OF PRECIPITATES

One of the most difficult problems that faces the analyst in employing precipitation as a means of separation and gravimetric determination is obtain-

---

[8] The solubility should not be increased to such an extent that precipitation is incomplete, of course. Frequently, precipitation is started under conditions of increased solubility. After most of the precipitate is formed, the solubility is lowered to insure complete precipitation.

[9] Some curdy precipitates do undergo "internal Ostwald ripening." See page 380 for discussion of the process.

ing the precipitate in a high degree of purity. We wish to look now at the ways in which a precipitate can become contaminated, and to see what conditions the analyst can employ to minimize contamination during the precipitation process. We shall also examine methods that can be employed to increase the purity of the precipitate after precipitation has been carried out.

Coprecipitation

The process by which a normally soluble substance is carried down during the precipitation of the desired precipitate is termed *coprecipitation*. For example, when sulfuric acid is added to a solution of barium chloride containing a small amount of nitrate ions, the precipitate of barium sulfate is found to contain some barium nitrate. The solution is not saturated with barium nitrate, and the precipitation of this salt is brought about by the precipitation of barium sulfate. Hence it is said that the nitrate is coprecipitated with the sulfate. Such a contamination of the barium sulfate may be entirely unsuspected by an analyst. Duplicate analyses carried out under identical conditions may lead to the coprecipitation of essentially the same amount of impurity in each sample. The precision of an analysis may be very good, but the accuracy so poor as to invalidate the results.

There are two ways by which coprecipitation may occur. One is by the formation of *mixed crystals*, or *solid solutions*, in which the impurity actually enters the crystal lattice, taking the place of normal lattice ions. Barium chromate and barium sulfate, for example, form mixed crystals over a certain range of concentrations. If there is any likelihood that such contamination may occur, the impurity should either be separated or converted to another form before precipitation is carried out. The chromate ion in this example could be reduced to chromic ion prior to precipitation of barium sulfate.

The second, and more common, way in which coprecipitation occurs is through adsorption of ions on the surface of small particles during the precipitation process. We have seen in our preceding discussion how small particles become electrically charged by adsorption of ions from solution. As these particles grow larger, or are coagulated, and settle from the solution, the adsorbed ions may be dragged down with the precipitate and remain as an impurity. Of course, an equivalent amount of ions of opposite charge must be carried along also, since the solid particles will have no net electric charge. A more detailed discussion of coprecipitation that results from adsorption can best be given in terms of the three types of precipitates previously described: crystalline, curdy, and gelatinous.

Crystalline precipitates. We have seen that in the process of precipitation, a crystalline substance, such as barium sulfate, forms a smaller number of nuclei, of larger size and smaller surface area, than does a curdy or gelatinous precipitate. Nevertheless, in the early stages of growth the particles have a large number of surface ions and will adsorb appreciable quantities of other ions on the surface. Barium nitrate, for example, is badly coprecipitated when sodium sulfate is added to a solution of barium chloride in the presence of nitrate ions. The nitrate ions are adsorbed while the barium sulfate particles are small and the crystal lattice is imperfectly formed. As the particles continue to grow in size, the impurity may become enclosed within the crystal; that is, the crystal grows around the impurity. This type of contamination, while resulting from adsorption, is usually referred to as *occlusion*, to distinguish it from the case where the solid has not grown around the impurity. The effect here is similar to that of a solid solution previously mentioned, in that the impurity cannot readily be washed out since it is inside the crystal. It is not a true solid solution, however, and the impurity can be removed by digestion (see below).

Some general rules can be formulated as a guide in predicting the tendency of ions to be coprecipitated.

1. Coprecipitation of foreign cations will predominate when the precipitation is carried out by adding the desired cation to a solution of the desired anion. The reverse is true for precipitation of anions. For example, if barium sulfate is precipitated by adding barium to sulfate, the initial particles are negatively charged by preferential adsorption of sulfate ions. Cations will then be attracted by the negatively charged particles (see Table 15.4).

COPRECIPITATION WITH BARIUM SULFATE † — **Table 15.4**

Ion coprecipitated	Moles contaminant/100 moles BaSO$_4$		Solubility of contaminating salt moles/1000 g H$_2$O (30°)
	Ba^{++} added to SO$_4^-$	SO$_4^-$ added to Ba^{++}	
I$^-$	0.005	0.033	5.64
Br$^-$	0.35	1.65	3.55
Cl$^-$	0.45	2.7	1.83
ClO$_3^-$	2.7	9.8	1.37
NO$_3^-$	5.4	19.6	0.46
Na$^+$	9.9	4.1	3.0
Ca^{++}	15.9	3.6	0.02

† Data, except Ca^{++}, of F. Schneider and W. Rieman, *J. Am. Chem. Soc.*, **59**, 354 (1937); Ca^{++} data from H. F. Walton, *Principles and Methods of Chemical Analysis*, Prentice-Hall, Inc., Englewood Cliffs, N.J., 2nd Ed., 1964.

2. The coprecipitation of a foreign ion is greater, the less soluble the compound formed with the oppositely charged ion in the lattice (Paneth-Fajans-Hahn rule). For example, barium nitrate is less soluble than barium

chloride, and the former salt is coprecipitated with barium sulfate to a greater extent than the latter.

The data given in Table 15.4 illustrate these rules.

There are several things, then, that the analyst can do to minimize such coprecipitation. If he is aware of the presence of an ion that readily coprecipitates, he can decrease (but not completely eliminate) the amount of coprecipitation by the method of addition of the two reagents. If it is known that either the sample or precipitant contains a contaminating ion, the solution containing this ion can be added to the other solution. In this way the concentration of the contaminant is kept at a minimum during the early stages of precipitation. If neither procedure gives a sufficiently pure precipitate, one can always resort to a separation or chemical conversion of the impurity before precipitation is made. For example, in the determination of sulfur in steel, the metal is dissolved in nitric acid, oxidizing sulfur to sulfate. Before precipitation of barium sulfate, the solution is evaporated to destroy nitrates, and the iron is reduced to the ferrous state. The divalent ion is adsorbed to a lesser extent than the trivalent ion.

After a crystalline precipitate is formed, the analyst can still increase the purity. If the substance can be readily redissolved (as salts of weak acids in stronger acids), it can be filtered, redissolved, and reprecipitated. The contaminating ion will be present in a lower concentration during the second precipitation, and consequently a smaller amount will be coprecipitated. This method is discussed in more detail in connection with gelatinous precipitates (below).

A substance such as barium sulfate is not readily redissolved, but its purity can be improved by the process of aging, or digestion. We have already seen that during aging the particle size is increased (Ostwald ripening). At the same time impurities held by these small particles are redissolved and are not readsorbed appreciably by the larger particles. In addition to Ostwald ripening, an internal perfection of the crystal may take place (sometimes called "internal Ostwald ripening"). Barium sulfate crystals, when first precipitated, are somewhat feathery, the crystal lattice being irregular and containing many imperfections. During aging the lattice becomes more compact, probably by ions dissolving at the corners and edges and redepositing in an orderly fashion. As the regular lattice is built up, the number of ions on the surface is decreased. During this perfection process, occluded impurities may be expelled, and since the number of surface ions has decreased, very little impurity is readsorbed. Figure 15.4 shows a schematic picture of the processes occurring during aging of a crystalline precipitate. It is apparent that the number of jagged edges in the original particle has decreased after aging and that the particle is more compact. As an example of the beneficial effect of aging, Kolthoff and Halverson[10] found that lead sulfate (crystalline) precipitated in the presence of nitrate

[10] I. M. Kolthoff and R. A. Halverson, *J. Phys. Chem.*, **43,** 605 (1939).

ion contained 0.64% coprecipitated nitrate. The precipitate was digested at 95° in contact with the mother liquor, and after one hour the amount of coprecipitated nitrate had decreased to 0.12%. At the end of twenty-four hours only 0.01% nitrate remained.

Fig. 15.4. Schematic picture of Ostwald ripening of crystalline precipitate.

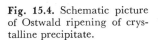

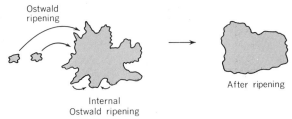

After ripening

Internal
Ostwald ripening

Curdy precipitates. Impurities are adsorbed by the primary particles of a substance such as silver chloride in the same manner as by particles of barium sulfate. However, silver chloride particles do not grow beyond colloidal dimensions, and finally precipitate as a coagulated colloid. The resulting curd is still made up of fine particles that have not grown together to form an extensive lattice structure. Thus curdy precipitates do not enclose, or occlude, foreign ions as do crystalline precipitates. The impurities on the surfaces of the tiny particles can normally be washed off, since the particles are not firmly bound to one another and the wash liquid can penetrate to all parts of the curd. As previously mentioned, peptization of the particles must be avoided, and hence the wash liquid must contain a volatile electrolyte.

The same rules regarding prediction of the ions coprecipitated with a crystalline precipitate hold also for curdy precipitates. Thus iodide ions are more strongly adsorbed than chloride ions by a silver halide precipitate, since silver iodide is less soluble than silver chloride. Digestion of a curdy precipitate is not normally needed for purification purposes, because there are no occluded impurities. However, a silver chloride precipitate is normally heated and allowed to stand for one or two hours in contact with the mother liquor containing nitric acid, in order to promote coagulation of the colloidal particles. In addition, some curdy precipitates show a rapid decrease in total surface area, even at room temperature, upon aging. It has been found, for example, that silver bromide contaminated with silver nitrate, which cannot be readily removed by washing, increases in purity during aging.[11] It is probable that the process taking place is an internal Ostwald ripening, with the tiny colloidal particles perfecting their surfaces and thus decreasing the amount of adsorbed impurity. The particles do not grow larger as a result of internal Ostwald ripening. However, they may

[11] I. M. Kolthoff and A. S. O'Brien, *J. Am. Chem. Soc.*, **61**, 3409, 3414 (1939).

form loose agglomerates by sharing their water jackets as pictured schematically in Figure 15.5. The agglomeration is considered reversible.[12]

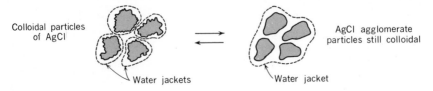

Colloidal particles
of AgCl

Water jackets

AgCl agglomerate
particles still colloidal

Water jacket

Fig. 15.5. Ripening of AgCl precipitate.

Gelatinous precipitates. We have seen in our previous discussion that the primary particles of a gelatinous precipitate are much larger in number and of much smaller dimensions than those of crystalline or curdy precipitates. The surface area exposed to the solution by such a precipitate is extremely large. A large quantity of water is adsorbed, of course, rendering the precipitate gelatinous, and also the adsorption of foreign ions can be quite extensive. Since the flocculated primary particles do not readily grow into larger crystals, the impurities are not occluded, as with barium sulfate, but are held by adsorption on the surface of the tiny particles.

The electric charge of the primary particles of substances such as ferric and aluminum hydroxides is primarily a function of the pH of the solution, since hydrogen and hydroxyl ions are readily adsorbed by such precipitates. Ferric hydroxide is positively charged at pH values less than about 8.5 and negatively charged at higher pH values. Thus anions tend to be coprecipitated by secondary adsorption at low pH, cations at high pH. This point is important in processes involving the separation of iron from other cations by precipitation of the hydrous oxide. In analyses of minerals such as limestone, where calcium and magnesium are present, iron is precipitated at as low a pH as possible to avoid coprecipitation of these cations.

Washing and reprecipitation can be employed to increase the purity of a gelatinous precipitate once it has been formed. Digestion is not beneficial, since the precipitate is so slightly soluble that the particles have little tendency to grow in size. Washing is normally employed, and, as with curdy precipitates, a volatile electrolyte must be present to avoid peptization. Ammonium nitrate, rather than ammonium chloride, is normally employed for aluminum and ferric hydroxides. The nitrate ion is more strongly adsorbed than chloride. Furthermore, iron and aluminum nitrates decompose to oxides on ignition, whereas it has been reported that the metallic chlorides

---

[12] I. M. Kolthoff, *Analyst*, **77**, 1000 (1952). It is also possible for the primary particles to become cemented together in the agglomerate by deposition of lattice ions between the particles. This process is not reversible, and in a sense there is an increase in size of the particles. The picture is not completely clear in regard to this idea.

may volatilize. Adsorbed divalent cations are very difficult to remove by washing. It is customary to employ reprecipitation as an additional means of purification. A precipitate such as ferric hydroxide is filtered, washed, and then redissolved in dilute hydrochloric acid. The concentration of impurities is lower in the new solution, and when the precipitate is reformed by raising the pH, a smaller degree of contamination results. The dissolving and reprecipitation, with intervening filtration, can be repeated several times, but usually one reprecipitation insures a sufficiently pure precipitate. This procedure, as previously mentioned, can also be employed for purification of crystalline precipitates that can be readily dissolved in acids. Calcium oxalate and magnesium ammonium phosphate are usually treated in this manner in the limestone analysis.

The amount of impurity adsorbed by a unit weight of solid at constant temperature is not directly proportional to the concentration of the impurity in solution. Rather it is given by the relation (Freundlich adsorption isotherm):

$$\text{Amount adsorbed per unit weight} = kC^{1/n}$$

where k is the proportionality constant, C is the concentration of impurity in solution, and n is a constant, usually having a value of about 2. A plot of the amount adsorbed against concentration of impurity results in a curve such as is shown in Figure 15.6. Here the value of k is taken as 0.1 and n as 2.

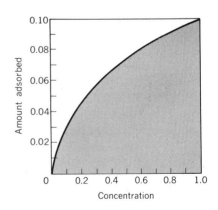

Fig. 15.6. Adsorption isotherm, $k = 0.1$, $n = 2$.

For unit concentration of impurity in solution, then, one-tenth, or 10%, is adsorbed in the first precipitation. When the precipitate is redissolved, the concentration of impurity in solution is one-tenth of the original amount, and in the second precipitation the amount adsorbed is the square root of one-tenth, or 3.2% of the original. Thus, the relative effectiveness of each succeeding reprecipitation is less than the preceding one, and normally only one reprecipitation is worthwhile.

Summary. We can now summarize the procedures that can be employed to minimize coprecipitation.

1. *Method of addition of the two reagents.* This can be used to control the concentration of impurity and the electric charge carried by the primary particles of precipitate. In the case of hydrous oxides the charge can be controlled by using the proper pH.

2. *Washing.* With curdy and gelatinous precipitates one must have an electrolyte in the wash solution to avoid peptization.

3. *Digestion.* This is of considerable benefit to crystalline precipitates, of some benefit to curdy precipitates, but not used for gelatinous precipitates.

4. *Reprecipitation.* This is used where the precipitate is readily redissolved, primarily for hydrous oxides and crystalline salts of weak acids.

5. *Separation.* The impurity may be separated or its chemical nature changed by some reaction before the precipitate is formed.

6. *Use of conditions that lead to large particle size* (page 376). This point needs further clarification. It would be expected that conditions which lead to large particles would result in a purer precipitate since the surface area of the particles is then relatively small. This is found to be true if the precipitation is sufficiently slow (next section), but not true under the usual conditions of precipitation. We have seen how crystalline precipitates, formed under conditions leading to large particles, can occlude impurities during their growth. Such impurities are not readily removed by washing, but digestion is beneficial. Therefore it is sometimes recommended that a crystalline substance be precipitated from reasonably concentrated solutions at room temperature, the solution then diluted and the precipitate digested under conditions of increased solubility. An electrolyte may be added and the digestion performed at elevated temperature for this purpose. The precipitate is then first formed in a finely divided state, with impurities held on the surfaces of the small particles, not occluded. Upon digestion, true Ostwald ripening occurs, leading finally to both large and pure particles. Kolthoff and Sandell[13] obtained large particles of calcium oxalate in this manner in the presence of iodate ions. Less iodate was coprecipitated using this procedure than when the compound was precipitated under conditions of increased solubility and then digested.

Precipitation from homogeneous solution

When a precipitant is added to a solution, even when the solution is dilute and well stirred, there will always be some local regions of high concentration. However, by using a procedure in which the precipitant is produced as the result of the reaction *taking place in the solution*, such local effects can be avoided. This technique is usually called *precipitation from homogeneous solution*, and it can lead to both large and pure particles of a precipitate. The best known example of this method is the use of the hydrolysis of urea to

[13] I. M. Kolthoff and E. B. Sandell, *J. Phys. Chem.*, **37**, 443, 459 (1933).

increase the pH and precipitate hydrous oxides, or salts of weak acids. Urea hydrolyzes according to the equation

$$CO(NH_2)_2 + H_2O \rightleftharpoons CO_2 + 2\ NH_3$$

The hydrolysis is slow at room temperature but is fairly rapid at 100°. Thus the pH can be well controlled in effecting separations by controlling the temperature and duration of heating. Also, the carbon dioxide liberated as bubbles prevents "bumping." Precipitation is usually complete in one to two hours. During this slow growth the particles have time to attain a large size without imperfections occurring in the lattice structure, and therefore the amount of occluded impurity is minimized.

The precipitation of a number of compounds used for gravimetric analysis has been carried out by this technique. Willard and Chan[14] recommend the precipitation of calcium oxalate solution by neutralizing an acid solution of calcium, containing excess oxalate, by hydrolysis of urea. The precipitate is not contaminated by magnesium or phosphate after only one precipitation. Barium sulfate can be precipitated in this manner by hydrolyzing dimethyl sulfate[15] or sulfamic acid to generate sulfate ions. The data in Table 15.5

COPRECIPITATION OF CALCIUM
WITH BARIUM SULFATE †
Table 15.5

Precipitant	Ca added, mg	Ca in precipitate, mg
Dilute H_2SO_4	5.4	3.4
Sulfamic acid	100	0.4
Ethyl sulfate	100	0.6

† Reprinted by permission from H. F. Walton, *Principles and Methods of Chemical Analysis*, Prentice-Hall, Inc., Englewood Cliffs, N.J., 2nd Ed., 1964.

show that much less calcium is coprecipitated with barium sulfate when the latter is precipitated homogeneously. Other ions that have been generated homogeneously include: chloride, from chlorohydrin; phosphate, from ethyl phosphate; and oxalate, from ethyl oxalate.

Hydrous oxides are gelatinous whether formed under ordinary analytical conditions or homogeneously. However Willard and his co-workers[16] have obtained dense precipitates of iron and aluminum by precipitation with urea in the presence of certain anions. The succinate ion is best for aluminum and formate is best for iron. The precipitates are of indefinite composition but contain basic salts of aluminum and succinate or of iron and formate. Coprecipitation of foreign ions is less than when the hydrous oxides are pre-

[14] H. H. Willard and F. L. Chan. See *Elementary Quantitative Analysis*, by H. H. Willard and N. F. Furman, D. Van Nostrand Co., New York, 1940, p. 344.

[15] P. J. Elving and R. E. Van Atta, *Anal. Chem.*, **22**, 1375 (1950).

[16] H. H. Willard, *Anal. Chem.*, **22**, 1372 (1950).

cipitated by addition of ammonia. The aluminum precipitate has been found to lose water more readily than the hydrous oxide.[17] Normally, a temperature of about 1100° is required for ignition of hydrous alumina, but the precipitate obtained using urea-succinate reaches constant weight at about 650°.

Postprecipitation

The process by which an impurity is deposited *after* the precipitation of the desired substance is termed *postprecipitation*. This process differs from coprecipitation principally in the fact that the amount of contamination increases, the longer the desired precipitate is left in contact with the mother liquor. When there is a possibility that postprecipitation may occur, directions call for filtration to be made shortly after the desired precipitate is formed.

Postprecipitation occurs when the solution is supersaturated with a foreign substance that precipitates very slowly. The phenomenon is quite common with metallic sulfides. For example, zinc sulfide does not readily precipitate from solutions that contain only a zinc salt and that are 0.1 to 0.2-M in hydrogen ion. Kolthoff and Pearson[18] found that only 0.1% of zinc was precipitated from a solution which was 0.025-M in zinc sulfate, 0.18-M in sulfuric acid, and saturated with hydrogen sulfide, even after shaking for thirty minutes. However, when mercuric sulfide was also precipitated under the same conditions, 91.3% of the zinc was found in the precipitate after only twenty minutes of shaking. Actually, from the solubility product constant of zinc sulfide, 1×10^{-24}, one would predict that the concentration of zinc remaining in a solution that is 0.2-M in hydrogen ion and is saturated with hydrogen sulfide would be only 0.005-M. It is apparent then that zinc sulfide forms very stable supersaturated solutions. This may be caused by the increased solubility of the first finely divided particles of precipitate. In the presence of mercuric sulfide, the supersaturation is broken and zinc sulfide precipitates. Other finely divided substances will aid in overcoming the supersaturation, but the effect of metallic sulfides is much more marked.[18] A metallic sulfide precipitate strongly adsorbs sulfide ions at the interface between the solid and solution. The solubility product constant of zinc sulfide is then exceeded to an even greater extent at the interface than in the bulk of solution, and the rate of precipitation is increased.

It is interesting to note that from the values of the solubility product constants, one would predict that nickel, cobalt, and zinc sulfides should precipitate in the acid hydrogen sulfide group in qualitative analysis. All

---

[17] T. Dupuis and C. Duval, *Anal. Chem. Acta*, **3**, 191 (1949).
[18] I. M. Kolthoff and E. Pearson, *J. Phys. Chem.*, **36**, 549 (1932).

three compounds, however, apparently form very stable supersaturated solutions, the first small particles of precipitate being more soluble than the larger ones. Cobalt and nickel sulfides, once formed, change rapidly into larger particles which are not readily redissolved in acid. This fact is utilized in separating cobalt and nickel from the remaining cations of the basic hydrogen sulfide group.

Magnesium oxalate forms stable, supersaturated solutions, and unless precautions are taken, postprecipitates on calcium oxalate when calcium and magnesium are separated by precipitation of the latter compound. Postprecipitation can be avoided by using as high acidity as possible and filtering off the calcium precipitate within one or two hours after precipitation.

IGNITION OF PRECIPITATES

In any gravimetric procedure involving precipitation, one must finally convert the separated substance into a form suitable for weighing. It is necessary that the substance weighed be pure, stable, and of definite composition for the results of the analysis to be accurate. Even if coprecipitation has been minimized, there still remains the problem of complete removal of water and of any electrolytes added to the wash water. Some precipitates are weighed in the same chemical form as that in which they precipitate. Others undergo chemical changes during ignition, and these reactions must go to completion for correct results. The procedure used in this final step depends both upon the chemical properties of the precipitate and upon the tenacity with which water is held by the solid.

Some precipitates can be dried sufficiently for analytical determination without resort to high temperature. For example, magnesium ammonium phosphate hexahydrate, $MgNH_4PO_4 \cdot 6 H_2O$, is sometimes dried by washing with a mixture of alcohol and ether and drawing air over the precipitate for a few minutes.[19] Generally, however, such a procedure is used only when considerable difficulty is encountered upon ignition of the precipitate. It is not usually recommended because of the danger of incomplete removal of water by washing. Water that merely *adheres* to the precipitate is removed, but water that is adsorbed or occluded (or water of hydration) is not removed by washing.

Some precipitates lose water readily in an oven at temperatures of 110° to 130°. Silver chloride does not adsorb water strongly and is normally dried in this manner for ordinary analytical work. In the determination of atomic weights, however, it has been found necessary to fuse silver chloride to remove the last traces of water.

---

[19] H. A. Fales, *Inorganic Quantitative Analysis*, Century Co., New York, 1925, p. 22; J. P. Mehlig, *J. Chem. Ed.*, **12**, 288 (1935).

Ignition at high temperature is required for complete removal of water that is occluded or very strongly adsorbed, and for complete conversion of some precipitates to the desired compound. Water can become enclosed within a particle during crystal growth and is then expelled only at high temperatures, probably by the crystal's bursting from the steam pressure generated. Gelatinous precipitates, such as the hydrous oxides, adsorb water quite strongly and must be heated to very high temperatures to remove water completely. Hydrous silica and alumina are well-known examples of precipitates that require very high ignition temperatures. The ignition of calcium oxalate to calcium oxide involves an example of a chemical change that requires a high temperature for complete reaction. At about 880° the dissociation pressure of calcium carbonate reaches one atmosphere, but the rate of decomposition is rather slow at this temperature. Therefore, it is usually recommended that temperatures in the range of 1100° be employed.

Errors other than incomplete removal of water or volatile electrolytes can occur during ignition. One of the most serious is reduction of the precipitate by carbon when filter paper is employed. Substances that are very easily reduced, such as silver chloride, are never filtered on paper; filtering crucibles are always employed. Students frequently encounter trouble with precipitates of barium sulfate and ferric oxide. Unless the paper is burned off with a plentiful supply of air, these precipitates will be reduced. Magnesium ammonium phosphate is also easily reduced when ignited to the pyrophosphate. This substance is frequently collected on a porcelain filter crucible to avoid using filter paper.

Precipitates can be over-ignited, leading to decomposition and to substances of indefinite composition. Errors can also result from an ignited precipitate's reabsorbing water or carbon dioxide upon cooling. Crucibles should be properly covered and kept in a desiccator while cooling.

The thermobalance

Until recent years very few careful studies had been made of the ignition temperatures required for different precipitates. In 1944 Chevenard[20] designed a balance, called a *thermobalance*, which allows a sample to be weighed while it is actually in a furnace. The balance is sensitive to 0.2 mg, and the temperature of the furnace can be measured to within about 1° between room temperature and 1100°. Duval[21] has used this balance to study the ignition of a large number of precipitates of analytical interest. The data

[20] P. Chevenard, X. Wache, and R. de la Tullaye, *Bull. Soc. chim.* (5), **11,** 41 (1944).

[21] C. Duval, *Inorganic Thermogravimetric Analysis*, 2nd Ed., Elsevier Publishing Co., New York, 1963.

are recorded in the form of a graph of weight of the precipitate against temperature. Such a graph is called a pyrolysis curve. It is evident that one should ignite a sample in a temperature range where the curve is flat, that is, where the weight is constant over a wide temperature range. The pyrolysis curves for a few substances are shown in Figure 15.7. The curves for calcium and magnesium oxalates are particularly interesting. The mono-

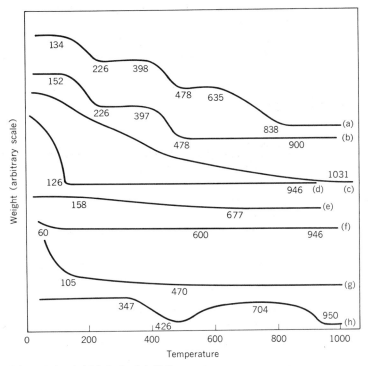

Fig. 15.7. Pyrolysis curves: (a) CaC_2O_4, (b) MgC_2O_4, (c) Al_2O_3, precipitated by aqueous NH_3, (d) Al_2O_3, precipitated by urea, (e) $BaSO_4$, (f) $AgCl$, (g) Fe_2O_3, (h) $CuSCN$. (Taken by permission from C. Duval, *Inorganic Thermogravimetric Analysis*, 2nd Ed., Elsevier Publishing Co., New York, 1963.)

hydrate $CaC_2O_4 \cdot H_2O$ is stable at $100°$, then loses water up to about $226°$. Up to $398°$ the form CaC_2O_4 is stable and then the oxalate loses carbon monoxide abruptly to form $CaCO_3$. The carbonate is stable in the range of about $420°$ to $600°$, and then the dissociation to calcium oxide commences. The weight finally becomes constant at about $850°$. Magnesium oxalate differs in its behavior in that it loses carbon monoxide and dioxide simultaneously, forming magnesium oxide directly with no intermediate carbonate.

REFERENCES

1. M. L. Salutsky, "Precipitates: Their Formation, Properties, and Purity," Chapter 18, Part I, Vol. I, of *Treatise on Analytical Chemistry*, I. M. Kolthoff, P. J. Elving, and E. B. Sandell, Eds., Interscience Publishers, Inc., New York, 1959.

2. L. Gordon, M. L. Salutsky, and H. H. Willard, *Precipitation from Homogeneous Solution*, John Wiley & Sons, Inc., New York, 1959.

3. H. F. Walton, *Principles and Methods of Chemical Analysis*, 2nd Ed., Prentice-Hall, Inc., Englewood Cliffs, N.J., 1964.

4. H. A. Laitinen, *Chemical Analysis*, McGraw-Hill Book Co., Inc., New York, 1960.

QUESTIONS

1. Suggest experimental methods by which you could determine whether a substance is temporarily suspended, a colloid, or in true solution.

2. Explain why small particles of some substances are more soluble than large particles. How does the analyst make use of this property to improve analytical methods?

3. Which of the following precipitates retains water more strongly: $Al(OH)_3$ or $AgBr$? Explain.

4. Verify the values of $(Q - S)/S$ (page 376) for mixing 3.5-M and 0.5-M solutions of barium thiocyanate and manganese sulfate. If 0.0001-M solutions are mixed, what is the value of this ratio?

5. Barium sulfate is washed with water, whereas the wash water for silver chloride contains a little nitric acid. Explain.

6. Barium sulfate is digested following precipitation, but this procedure is not used for silver chloride or ferric hydroxide. Explain.

7. A precipitate of ferric hydroxide is contaminated with magnesium hydroxide. What is the best way to get rid of the impurity? Explain.

8. The sulfate ion in a solution is to be precipitated by the addition of lead. The sulfate solution also contains small amounts of nitrate, chloride, and perchlorate ions. Which of these ions is most likely to be coprecipitated? Explain. How could you minimize the coprecipitation?

9. Freshly precipitated barium sulfate turns pink when shaken with a solution of potassium permanganate, and the color is not removed by washing. A precipitate which has stood for several days does not acquire the color. Explain.

10. The oxalate ion in a solution which contains a small amount of sulfate is to be precipitated as calcium oxalate. What conditions of precipitation would you use to minimize coprecipitation?

11. What conditions should be chosen to precipitate a sulfide, such as ZnS, in order to obtain as large particles as possible?

12. Ferric hydroxide is gelatinous even when precipitated from homogeneous solution. Explain.

13. Distinguish between Ostwald ripening and internal Ostwald ripening.

14. Why are not several reprecipitations of a precipitate such as ferric hydroxide normally required?

15. When is postprecipitation likely to occur? Will zinc sulfide be more likely to postprecipitate on mercuric sulfide or on barium sulfate? Explain.

16. Explain how precipitation from homogeneous solution leads to both a coarser and purer precipitate.

17. Under what conditions is it preferable to precipitate a crystalline substance so that the particles are in a finely divided state? Explain.

18. Point out possible errors in the final step of igniting and weighing a precipitate.

chapter **16**

Solvent Extraction

INTRODUCTION

The partition of solutes between two immiscible liquids offers many attractive possibilities for analytical separations. Even where the primary goal is not analytical but rather preparative, solvent extraction may be an important step in the sequence that leads to a pure product in the organic, inorganic, or biochemical laboratory. Although complicated apparatus is sometimes employed, frequently only a separatory funnel is required. Often a solvent extraction separation can be accomplished in a few minutes. The technique is applicable over a wide concentration range, and has been used extensively for the isolation of extremely minute quantities of carrier-free isotopes obtained by nuclear transmutation as well as industrial materials produced by the ton. Solvent extraction separations are usually "clean" in the sense that there is no analog of coprecipitation with such systems. Aside from its intrinsic interest, there is an important reason for discussing solvent

392

extraction in this text: We shall use a particular approach to solvent extraction, the Craig pseudocountercurrent technique, as a model to aid our understanding of chromatographic processes in Chapter 17.

DISTRIBUTION LAW

It was pointed out in Chapter 13 that a definite relationship between solute concentrations in two liquid phases at equilibrium is predicted from the phase rule. Nernst gave the first clear statement of the distribution law when he pointed out in 1891 that a solute will distribute itself between two immiscible liquids in such a way that the ratio of concentrations at equilibrium is constant at a particular temperature:

$$\frac{[A]_1}{[A]_2} = \text{constant}$$

$[A]_1$ represents the concentration of a solute A in the liquid phase 1.

Although this relationship holds fairly well in certain cases, in reality it is inexact. Strictly, in thermodynamic terms, it is the activity ratio rather than the concentration ratio that should be constant. The activity of a chemical species in one phase maintains a constant ratio to the activity of the same species in the other liquid phase:

$$\frac{a_{A_1}}{a_{A_2}} = K_{D_A}$$

Here a_{A_1} represents the activity of solute A in phase 1. The true constant K_{D_A} is called the *distribution coefficient* of species A.

Sometimes it is necessary or desirable to take into account chemical complications in extraction equilibria. For example, consider the distribution of benzoic acid between the two liquid phases benzene and water. In the aqueous phase, benzoic acid is partly ionized,

$$HBz + H_2O \rightleftharpoons H_3O^+ + Bz^-$$

In the benzene phase, benzoic acid is partially dimerized by hydrogen bonding in the carboxyl groups,

$$2\,HBz \rightleftharpoons (HBz)_2$$

Each particular species, HBz, Bz^-, $(HBz)_2$, will have its own particular K_D value. The system water, benzene, and benzoic acid may then be described by three distribution coefficients:

$$K_{D_{\text{HBz}}} = \frac{a_{\text{HBz}_{\text{org}}}}{a_{\text{HBz}_{\text{aq}}}}$$

$$K_{D_{\text{Bz}^-}} = \frac{a_{\text{Bz}^-_{\text{org}}}}{a_{\text{Bz}^-_{\text{aq}}}}$$

$$K_{D_{(\text{HBz})_2}} = \frac{a_{(\text{HBz})_2\,\text{org}}}{a_{(\text{HBz})_2\,\text{aq}}}$$

Now it happens that the benzoate ion in fact remains almost totally in the aqueous phase, and the benzoic acid dimer exists only in the organic phase. Further, in a practical experiment, the chemist will usually want to know where the "benzoic acid" *is*, not whether part of it is ionized or dimerized. Also, he will be more interested in how much is there than in its thermodynamic activity. He would be better served, then, by an expression combining the concentrations of all the species in the two phases:

$$D = \frac{\text{total benzoic in organic phase}}{\text{total benzoic in aqueous phase}}$$

$$= \frac{[\text{HBz}]_{\text{org}} + [(\text{HBz})_2]_{\text{org}}}{[\text{HBz}]_{\text{aq}} + [\text{Bz}^-]_{\text{aq}}}$$

The ratio D is called the *distribution ratio*.

It is clear that D will not remain constant over a range of experimental conditions. For example, raising the $p\text{H}$ of the aqueous phase will lower D by converting benzoic acid into benzoate ion, which does not extract into benzene. The addition of any electrolyte may affect D by changing activity coefficients. However, the distribution ratio is useful when its value is known for a particular set of conditions.

EXAMPLES OF SOLVENT EXTRACTION EQUILIBRIA

In this section we shall consider examples illustrating the manner in which equilibrium expressions may be manipulated to obtain equations which show the factors upon which D values depend.

Partition of a weak acid

Consider a weak acid, HB. Assume for simplicity that the acid is monomeric in both solvent phases, and that the anion of the acid does not penetrate the organic phase. The pertinent equilibrium expressions then are:

$$D = \frac{[\text{HB}]_{\text{org}}}{[\text{HB}]_{\text{aq}} + [\text{B}^-]_{\text{aq}}} \tag{1}$$

$$K_{D_{\text{HB}}} = \frac{[\text{HB}]_{\text{org}}}{[\text{HB}]_{\text{aq}}} \tag{2}$$

$$K_a = \frac{[\text{H}_3\text{O}^+]_{\text{aq}}[\text{B}^-]_{\text{aq}}}{[\text{HB}]_{\text{aq}}} \tag{3}$$

Rearranging (3) gives

$$[B^-]_{aq} = K_a \frac{[HB]_{aq}}{[H_3O^+]_{aq}}$$

and substitution into (1) yields

$$D = \frac{[HB]_{org}}{[HB]_{aq} + (K_a[HB]_{aq}/[H_3O^+]_{aq})}$$

or

$$D = \frac{[HB]_{org}}{[HB]_{aq}\{1 + (K_a/[H_3O^+]_{aq})\}}$$

Referring to (2), we see that

$$D = \frac{K_{D_{HB}}}{1 + (K_a/[H_3O^+]_{aq})}$$

Thus we have derived an expression showing explicitly the dependence of the distribution ratio upon the distribution coefficient of the weak acid, its ionization constant, and the pH of the aqueous phase. It might well be that we could capitalize upon inherent differences in the values of the appropriate constants to effect the separation of a mixture of acids by regulating the pH of the aqueous phase.

Extraction of a metal as a chelate compound

Many important separations of metal ions have been developed around the formation of chelate compounds with a variety of organic reagents. As an example, consider the reagent 8-quinolinol (8-hydroxyquinoline), often referred to by the trivial name "oxine,"

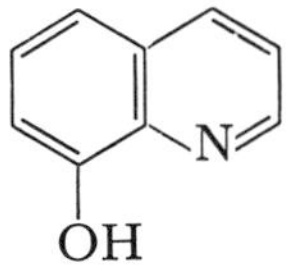

This reagent forms neutral, water-insoluble, chloroform- or carbon tetrachloride-soluble molecules with metal ions; the cupric oxinate chelate may be depicted as follows:

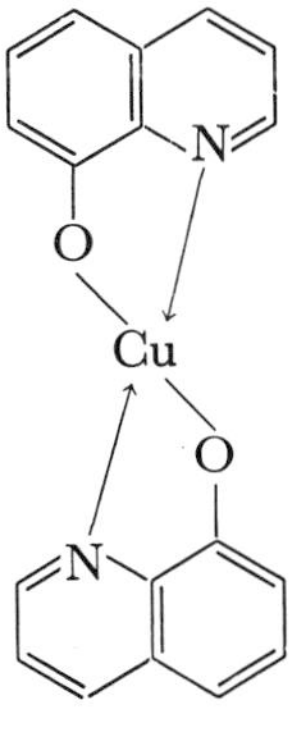

If we abbreviate oxine as HOx, we may write the chelation reaction as

$$Cu^{++} + 2\ HOx \rightleftharpoons Cu(Ox)_2 + 2\ H^+$$

Another very important chelating agent for the solvent extraction of metal ions is diphenylthiocarbazone or "dithizone,"

$$
\begin{array}{c}
C_6H_5 \\
| \\
NH{-}NH \\
\diagup \\
S{=}C \\
\diagdown \\
N{=\!=}N \\
| \\
C_6H_5
\end{array}
$$

The chelation reaction may be written as

$$M^{n+} + n\ HDz \rightleftharpoons M(Dz)_n + n\ H^+$$

Consider the extraction of an aqueous solution of the metal ion M^{n+} with an organic solvent containing a chelating agent HX. A distribution ratio may be written for the metal:

$$D = \frac{C_{M_{org}}}{C_{M_{aq}}}$$

where C_M is the total metal concentration regardless of what form it is in. Let us assume for simplicity (but not a bad assumption in many actual cases) that the only metal in the organic phase is present as the chelate, MX_n, i.e., $C_{M_{org}} = [MX_n]_{org}$. Also, let us ignore possible lower complexes such as MX or MX_{n-1} which may exist in the aqueous phase. (A large excess of HX would perhaps insure the validity of this assumption.) Thus

$$C_{M_{aq}} = [M^{n+}]_{aq} + [MX_n]_{aq}$$

If the partition of the chelate greatly favors the organic phase, which is frequently the case, we may neglect $[MX_n]_{aq}$ as compared with $[M^{n+}]_{aq}$, and thus we may write

$$D = \frac{[MX_n]_{org}}{[M^{n+}]_{aq}}$$

Rearranging the distribution coefficient expression for the chelate gives

$$[MX_n]_{org} = K_{D_{MX_n}}[MX_n]_{aq}$$

and substitution into the expression for D yields

$$D = \frac{K_{D_{MX_n}}[MX_n]_{aq}}{[M^{n+}]_{aq}} = \frac{K_{D_{MX_n}}}{[M^{n+}]_{aq}/[MX_n]_{aq}}$$

Next, consider the formation constant of the chelate in the aqueous phase:

$$M^{n+} + n\ X^- = MX_n$$

$$K_f = \frac{[MX_n]_{aq}}{[M^{n+}]_{aq}[X^-]_{aq}^n} \quad \text{or} \quad [M^{n+}]_{aq} = \frac{[MX_n]_{aq}}{K_f[X^-]_{aq}^n}$$

and the acid dissociation of the chelating agent:

$$HX + H_2O \rightleftarrows H_3O^+ + X^-$$

$$K_a = \frac{[H_3O^+]_{aq}[X^-]_{aq}}{[HX]_{aq}} \quad \text{or} \quad [X^-]_{aq} = \frac{K_a[HX]_{aq}}{[H_3O^+]_{aq}}$$

Thus,

$$[M^{n+}]_{aq} = \frac{[MX_n]_{aq}[H_3O^+]_{aq}^n}{K_f K_a^n [HX]_{aq}^n}$$

and

$$\frac{[M^{n+}]_{aq}}{[MX_n]_{aq}} = \frac{[H_3O^+]_{aq}^n}{K_f K_a^n [HX]_{aq}^n}$$

Returning to the expression for D, we obtain

$$D = \frac{K_{D_{MX_n}} K_f K_a^n [HX]_{aq}^n}{[H_3O^+]_{aq}^n}$$

Next consider the distribution coefficient for the chelating agent:

$$K_{D_{HX}} = \frac{[HX]_{org}}{[HX]_{aq}} \quad \text{or} \quad [HX]_{aq} = \frac{[HX]_{org}}{K_{D_{HX}}}$$

Then

$$D = \frac{K_{D_{MX_n}} K_f K_a^n [HX]_{org}^n}{K_{D_{HX}}^n [H_3O^+]_{aq}^n}$$

This equation gives the distribution ratio for the metal in terms of (a) constants $K_{D_{MX_n}}$, $K_{D_{HX}}$, K_f, and K_a which are properties of the particular compounds involved in the selected system, and (b) variables $[H_3O^+]_{aq}$ and $[HX]_{org}$ which are subject to experimental manipulation for a particular system. Let us lump together the constants into an *extraction constant*, K_{ex}:

$$\frac{K_{D_{MX_n}} K_f K_a^n}{K_{D_{HX}}^n} = K_{ex}$$

Then

$$D = \frac{K_{ex}[HX]_{org}^n}{[H_3O^+]_{aq}^n}$$

Taking logarithms,

$$\log D = \log K_{ex} + n \log [HX]_{org} - n \log [H_3O^+]_{aq}$$

or

$$\log D = \log K_{ex} + n \log [HX]_{org} + n\, pH$$

Thus a plot of $\log D$ vs. pH should be a straight line with a slope of n and an intercept on the $\log D$ axis of $\log K_{ex} + n \log [HX]_{org}$. The higher the charge on the metal ion, the steeper the slope of the line. Varying the concentration of the chelating agent shifts the curves along the pH axis.

Note that no term involving metal concentration appears in the final equation. One of the attractive aspects of solvent extraction (unlike, say, precipitation) is the fact that it works all the way from tracer levels up to macro quantities.

Of course, the constants K_f and $K_{D_{MX_n}}$ vary from one metal ion to another.

This is the basis for separations by extraction of aqueous solutions with organic solvents containing chelating agents.

EXTRACTION SYSTEMS INVOLVING ION PAIRS AND SOLVATES

Generally, simple metal salts tend to be more soluble in a highly polar solvent like water than in organic solvents of much lower dielectric constant. Many ions are solvated by water, and the energy of solvation contributes to the disruption of the crystal lattice of the solid salt. Furthermore, less work is required to separate ions of opposite charge in a high dielectric solvent. Usually, then, the formation of an uncharged species is necessary if an ion is to be extracted from water into an organic solvent. We have seen an example of this in the extraction of metals converted into neutral chelates of 8-quinolinol. The metal ion is bound in the chelate by definite chemical bonds, often largely covalent in character.

Sometimes, on the other hand, an uncharged species extractable into an organic solvent is obtained through the association of ions of opposite charge. In point of fact, it must be admitted that it is difficult to draw a line between an ion pair and a neutral molecule. Probably if the components stay together in water, it will be called a molecule; if the components are separated in water sufficiently that an entity cannot be detected, this entity will be called an ion pair if it does show up in a nonpolar solvent.

A common example of an extraction system involving ion pair formation in the organic phase is found in the use of tetraphenylarsonium chloride to extract permanganate, perrhenate, and pertechnetate from water into chloroform. The species which passes into the organic phase is an ion pair, $[(C_6H_5)_4As^+, ReO_4^-]$. Similarly, the extraction of uranyl ion, UO_2^{++}, from aqueous nitrate solutions into solvents such as ether (an important process in uranium chemistry) involves an association of the type $[UO_2^{++}, 2\ NO_3^-]$. It is believed that the uranyl ion is solvated by ether as well as by water, a fact which doubtless facilitates penetration of the organic phase by an ion pair which then takes on more of the character of the solvent.

It has been known for many years that ferric iron can be extracted into ether from strong hydrochloric acid solution. This process is useful for the separation of bulk quantities of iron prior to the determination of other elements in ferrous alloys. Despite extensive study, the system water-ether-HCl-Fe^{3+} is still not completely understood. There is evidence that the extractable species is an ion pair of the type $[H_3O^+, Fe(H_2O)_2Cl_4^-]$; other equilibria may intrude, such as solvation of both proton and ferric ion by ether:

$$H_3O^+ + C_4H_{10}O \rightleftarrows C_4H_{10}OH^+ + H_2O$$

$$Fe(H_2O)_2Cl_4^- + 2\ C_4H_{10}O \rightleftarrows Fe(C_4H_{10}O)_2Cl_4^- + 2\ H_2O$$

Thus under certain conditions the species in the ether phase may be $[C_4H_{10}OH^+, Fe(C_4H_{10}O)_2Cl_4^-]$. The system is undoubtedly complicated, and mixtures of various solvated ion pairs probably participate under the usual conditions of the extraction.

CRAIG PSEUDOCOUNTERCURRENT EXTRACTION

In Chapter 13 we distinguished among four levels of complexity by which two phases may be contacted in order to effect a transfer of matter from one to the other. These four approaches may all be employed in solvent extraction. In the brief treatment of this chapter, we shall be restricted to a thorough discussion of only one type—the Craig pseudocountercurrent extraction process. Actually, simple batch extractions of the first two types noted in Chapter 13 require little comment from the standpoint of technique. The usual apparatus is the separatory funnel; the student normally encounters such extractions in the organic laboratory.

Basic idea of the Craig experiment

Consider an aqueous solution containing 1000 mg of some solute in a separatory funnel. Let it be a simple solute whose partition is uncomplicated by ionization, dimerization, etc. Add to the funnel an equal (for convenience) volume of an immiscible organic solvent. Also, for simplicity, suppose that the distribution coefficient of the solute is unity. Now, after equilibration, there will be 500 mg of the solute in the aqueous phase and 500 mg in the organic phase.

Next, take a second funnel and drain the heavier liquid (say the aqueous phase) from the first funnel into it. Then add fresh organic solvent to this aqueous phase in the second funnel, and add fresh aqueous phase to the first funnel. Now shake both funnels until equilibration is achieved. There will then be 250 mg of the solute in each layer in each funnel.

As the student probably suspects by now, we next secure a third funnel, and drain the aqueous solution from the second funnel into the third and also introduce a fresh portion of the organic solvent. We replace the aqueous layer in the second funnel using the aqueous phase from the first one, and add fresh aqueous phase to the latter. Then all three funnels are shaken to secure equilibrium.

After two or three transfers, it becomes easier to keep track of what is going on by introducing a simple schematic representation. Portions of aqueous and organic solvent are represented by boxes, and where an aqueous box adjoins an organic box we have the equilibration of the phases. Within the box, we give the weight of solute present in that phase. Thus the first step above is depicted as follows:

funnel 0

	fresh org	fresh org	org 500 mg		
		aq 500 mg	fresh aq	fresh aq	

It is customary to count the number of *transfers* rather than the number of funnels; hence the first funnel is labelled number 0.

In the second step noted above, we have performed one transfer ($n = 1$), and the resulting situation may be represented by:

funnel 1   funnel 0

	fresh org	org 250 mg	org 250 mg		
		aq 250 mg	aq 250 mg	fresh aq	fresh aq

In effect, we are pushing the bottom row of boxes toward the left with each transfer.

For the third step, where n, the number of transfers, is 2, the resulting diagram is:

funnel 2   funnel 1   funnel 0

	fresh org	org 125 mg	org 250 mg	org 125 mg		
		aq 125 mg	aq 250 mg	aq 125 mg	fresh aq	fresh aq

Let us write the diagrams for two more steps: fourth step, $n = 3$

funnel 3   funnel 2   funnel 1   funnel 0

	fresh org	org 62.5 mg	org 187.5 mg	org 187.5 mg	org 62.5 mg	
		aq 62.5 mg	aq 187.5 mg	aq 187.5 mg	aq 62.5 mg	fresh aq

fifth step, $n = 4$

	4	3	2	1	0	
	31.25	125	187.5	125	31.25	
	31.25	125	187.5	125	31.25	

Perhaps we have carried this far enough to see what is happening: As the number of transfers is increased, the solute spreads out through more and more funnels, but it is "bunching up" toward the center (because $K_D = 1$) and the fraction of the solute in the extreme funnels is decreasing. It may also be surmised that for a different solute with a distribution coefficient, not 1, but favoring the aqueous phase, the peak concentration would not appear in the middle funnel but rather toward the left in our diagram. Likewise, a solute relatively more soluble in the organic layer would peak toward the right of the center.

Binomial distribution in the Craig extraction

Let us now formulate a more general mathematical treatment of the Craig countercurrent distribution. Actually, the mathematics is not difficult. In the first step of the treatment above, we distributed the solute between the two phases according to the distribution coefficient:

$$K_D = \frac{[\text{solute}]_{\text{org}}}{[\text{solute}]_{\text{aq}}}$$

If we started with weight W of solute, and weight w went over into the organic layer, then

$$K_D = \frac{w/V_{\text{org}}}{(W - w)/V_{\text{aq}}}$$

where V is the volume of the phase. To simplify, let the volumes be the same, so that

$$K_D = \frac{w}{W - w}$$

Rearranging and solving for W,

$$K_D W - K_D w = w$$

$$K_D W = K_D w + w$$

$$W = \frac{w + K_D w}{K_D} = \frac{w(1 + K_D)}{K_D}$$

Now the fraction of the solute in the organic phase, f_{org}, is given by

$$f_{\text{org}} = \frac{w}{W} = \frac{w}{w(1 + K_D)/K_D} = \frac{K_D}{1 + K_D}$$

Similarly, f_{aq} is

$$f_{\text{aq}} = \frac{W - w}{W} = \frac{\{w(1 + K_D)/K_D\} - w}{w(1 + K_D)/K_D} = 1 - \left\{\frac{wK_D}{w(1 + K_D)}\right\} = \frac{1}{1 + K_D}$$

In the apparatus that Craig developed, and in the formulations encountered in the literature, the lighter phase (here, organic) is transferred from vessel 0 to vessel number 1. Fresh organic phase is then introduced into 0, and fresh aqueous phase into 1. After equilibration of the two vessels,

$$f_{\text{org}_0} = \left(\frac{1}{1 + K_D}\right)\left(\frac{K_D}{1 + K_D}\right)$$

(The fraction $1/1 + K_D$ was present in the aqueous layer in the vessel after the first equilibration, as shown above, and the fraction $K_D/1 + K_D$ passed over into the fresh organic solvent upon equilibration. Thus the product of the two fractions gives the fraction of the original W now present in the organic layer of vessel 0.) Likewise,

$$f_{\text{aq}_0} = \left(\frac{1}{1 + K_D}\right)\left(\frac{1}{1 + K_D}\right)$$

(At the beginning of this step, the fraction $1/1 + K_D$ was present in the aqueous layer, as shown above, and the fraction $1/1 + K_D$ *of that* is what remains after equilibration with fresh organic phase.) Also,

$$f_{\text{org}_1} = \left(\frac{K_D}{1 + K_D}\right)\left(\frac{K_D}{1 + K_D}\right)$$

and

$$f_{\text{aq}_1} = \left(\frac{K_D}{1 + K_D}\right)\left(\frac{1}{1 + K_D}\right)$$

We have gone through the above steps to make certain that the student understands what is happening. Actually, it is easier finally to consider the total solute in each vessel instead of focusing upon the two phases separately, although we may add what is in the two phases to get the total. Let us work this out for vessels 0, 1, and 2 where $n = 2$, including for practice all stages up to $n = 2$.

$n = 0$

$$f_0 = \underbrace{\left(\frac{K_D}{1 + K_D}\right)}_{\substack{\text{Organic} \\ \text{phase}}} + \underbrace{\left(\frac{1}{1 + K_D}\right)}_{\substack{\text{Aqueous} \\ \text{phase}}} = \frac{1 + K_D}{1 + K_D} = 1$$

Since, where $n = 0$, all of the solute is in this vessel, the fraction contributed by the organic phase and the fraction in the aqueous phase must add up to 1.

$n = 1$

$$f_0 = \left(\frac{1}{1 + K_D}\right)\left(\frac{K_D}{1 + K_D}\right) + \left(\frac{1}{1 + K_D}\right)\left(\frac{1}{1 + K_D}\right) = \frac{1}{1 + K_D}$$

$$f_1 = \left(\frac{K_D}{1 + K_D}\right)\left(\frac{K_D}{1 + K_D}\right) + \left(\frac{K_D}{1 + K_D}\right)\left(\frac{1}{1 + K_D}\right) = \frac{K_D}{1 + K_D}$$

Here, $f_0 + f_1 = 1$, and we may confirm our result:

$$\frac{1}{1 + K_D} + \frac{K_D}{1 + K_D} = \frac{1 + K_D}{1 + K_D} = 1$$

$n = 2$

$$f_0 = \left(\frac{1}{1 + K_D}\right)\left(\frac{1}{1 + K_D}\right) = \left(\frac{1}{1 + K_D}\right)^2$$

$$f_1 = \left(\frac{1}{1 + K_D}\right)\left(\frac{K_D}{1 + K_D}\right) + \left(\frac{K_D}{1 + K_D}\right)\left(\frac{1}{1 + K_D}\right)$$

$$= 2\left(\frac{1}{1 + K_D}\right)\left(\frac{K_D}{1 + K_D}\right)$$

$$f_2 = \left(\frac{K_D}{1 + K_D}\right)\left(\frac{K_D}{1 + K_D}\right) = \left(\frac{K_D}{1 + K_D}\right)^2$$

Now, examine the above fractions:

$$f_0 = \left(\frac{1}{1 + K_D}\right)^2$$

$$f_1 = 2\left(\frac{1}{1 + K_D}\right)\left(\frac{K_D}{1 + K_D}\right)$$

$$f_2 = \left(\frac{K_D}{1 + K_D}\right)^2$$

The alert student will note that these three terms are the terms in the expansion of the binomial

$$\left(\frac{1}{1 + K_D} + \frac{K_D}{1 + K_D}\right)^2$$

In general, for any number of transfers, n, it may be shown that the fractions of the total solute to be found in the various vessels 0, 1, 2, . . . , n are given by the terms in the expression of the binomial

$$\left(\frac{1}{1 + K_D} + \frac{K_D}{1 + K_D}\right)^n$$

In working with the formulas above, we assumed equal volumes of the two phases. In general, where the volumes are not necessarily equal (but the same in all vessels), it may be shown that the fractions of solute in the various vessels are given by the terms in the expansion of the binomial

$$\left(\frac{1}{1 + E} + \frac{E}{1 + E}\right)^n$$

where

$$E = K_D \times \frac{V_{\text{upper}}}{V_{\text{lower}}}$$

and V_{upper} and V_{lower} are the volumes of upper and lower phases, respectively.

If n is not small, expansion of the binomial becomes tedious. Fortunately, mathematical tables are available where it is worked out. Any single term in the binomial expansion can be obtained directly, using the formula

$$f_{n\,r} = \left(\frac{n!}{r!\,(n - r)!}\right)\left(\frac{1}{1 + K_D}\right)^n K_D^r$$

where $f_{n,r}$ is the fraction of solute in the rth tube after n transfers. Some writers use the form

$$f_{n,r} = \frac{n!\, K_D^r}{r!\,(n-r)!\,(1+K_D)^n}$$

During a series of successive transfers, a solute moves through the vessels of a Craig apparatus as a sort of wave of diminishing amplitude. The solute spreads through more and more vessels as n increases, but at the same time the fraction of the vessels which contain the solute decreases. Figure 16.1

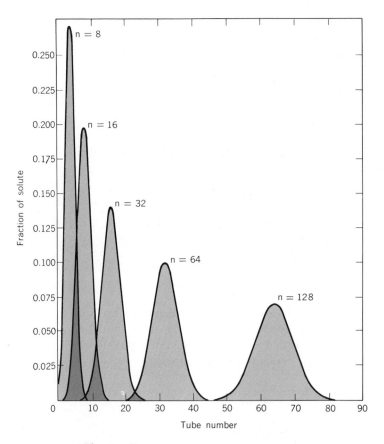

Fig. 16.1. Theoretical distributions for a solute with distribution coefficient $K_D = 1$ after various numbers of transfers (n) in a Craig experiment.

shows theoretical distributions of solute for various numbers of transfers, n, for the case where $K_D = 1$ and $V_{\text{org}} = V_{\text{aq}}$.

For a given number of transfers, substances with different distribution coefficients are distributed differently. Figure 16.2 shows theoretical distributions after 16 transfers for various values of the distribution coefficient. We

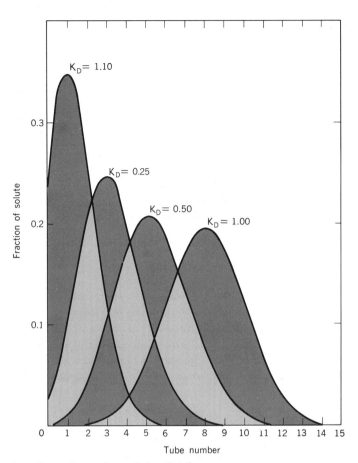

Fig. 16.2. Theoretical distributions for various values of the distribution coefficient, K_D, in a 16-transfer Craig experiment.

see in the figure that solutes with different K_D values are beginning to separate after the particular number of transfers indicated, but that separation is not complete in any case. This means that for these solutes more stages would be required in order to obtain pure components in quantitative yield.

It may be seen from the mathematical treatment given above why it is said that a Craig distribution is a *binomial* one. (Other types commonly encountered are *Gaussian*, as we saw in Chapter 3 for the distribution of random errors, and Poisson distributions.) However, as the number of transfers increases, the binomial distribution approximates more and more closely the Gaussian. (Poisson distributions also tend to Gaussian as n increases.) When n becomes large, say 50, although there is no definite demarcation, a Gaussian treatment is sufficiently accurate for describing a Craig distribution, and it is more convenient than the more cumbersome binomial theorem for such cases. The appropriate equations then are:

$$r_{max} = \frac{nK_D}{K_D + 1}$$

$$f_{max} = \frac{1}{\sqrt{2\pi nK_D/(1 + K_D)^2}}$$

$$f_x = f_{max} \times e^{-\left[\frac{x^2}{2nK_D/(1+K_D)^2}\right]}$$

where r_{max} is the number of the tube containing the maximal quantity of the solute, f_{max} is the fraction of solute in this tube, f_x is the fraction of solute in a tube x tubes distant from r_{max}, and e is the base of natural logarithms. To use these equations for the case of unequal volumes of the two phases, simply replace K_D by E as defined earlier in the chapter.

Apparatus for Craig extraction

For a large number of transfers, say 100 or 1000, manual operation with separatory funnels would be impossible in a practical sense. Craig, who expounded both the theory and practice of this type of extraction process, developed apparatus to take much of the labor out of the procedure. The typical Craig apparatus is based upon glass units shaped as shown in Figure 16.3. Although most people think in terms of vigorous shaking to equilibrate

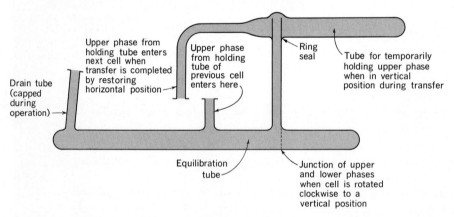

Drain tube (capped during operation) →

Upper phase from holding tube enters next cell when transfer is completed by restoring horizontal position →

Upper phase from holding tube of previous cell enters here

Ring seal

Tube for temporarily holding upper phase when in vertical position during transfer

Equilibration tube

Junction of upper and lower phases when cell is rotated clockwise to a vertical position

Fig. 16.3. Typical glass cell for Craig apparatus.

two liquid phases, Craig showed that a gentle sloshing of one liquid over another was actually more effective; further, troublesome emulsions were often avoided by the less vigorous technique. Thus it was unnecessary to

adhere to the usual separatory funnel shape when designing a more automated apparatus. In the unit shown in Figure 16.3, the two liquids are
equilibrated by gently rocking the apparatus about 20 times, and the phases
are allowed to separate. The apparatus is then rotated as indicated in the
figure so that the cell is in a vertical position, whereupon the upper phase
runs out of the equilibration tube and into a temporary holding tube.
Obviously the volume of the lower phase must be such that the solvent
interface occurs at the level of the run-off side arm. When the cell is returned
to a horizontal position, the lighter phase runs out of the holding tube and
into the equilibration tube of the next cell in line. (The liquid is prevented
from returning to the equilibration tube whence it came by the design of the
cell in the area labelled "ring seal" in the figure.)

A battery of cells is clamped firmly to a metal frame so that all may be
rocked and tilted together. The liquid-tight joints between adjacent cells are
held together by spring clamps. In practice, the lower phase is introduced
into all of the cells at the beginning of the experiment. The solute mixture
to be separated is placed in the first cell (number 0) in either phase. A solvent
reservoir and metering device introduces the appropriate volume of the

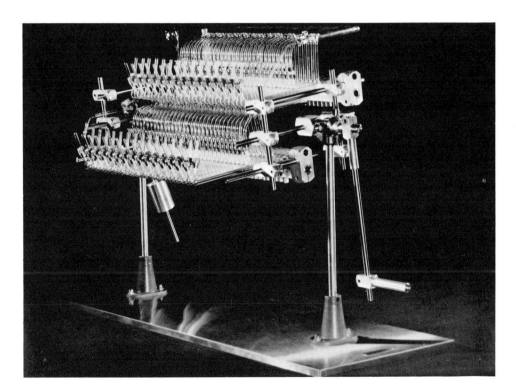

Fig. 16.4. Manually operated 60-cell Craig Countercurrent Distribution
Apparatus. The cells are arranged in 2 banks of 30 each. (Courtesy of
H. O. Post Scientific Instrument Co., Inc.)

lighter phase into the first cell after each transfer. In the simpler instruments, the rocking and tilting are done manually by the operator. Larger outfits with as many as 1000 cells are operated by a motorized robot so that the entire distribution experiment requires no attention once it is set in motion. Two commercial Craig machines are shown in Figures 16.4 and 16.5.

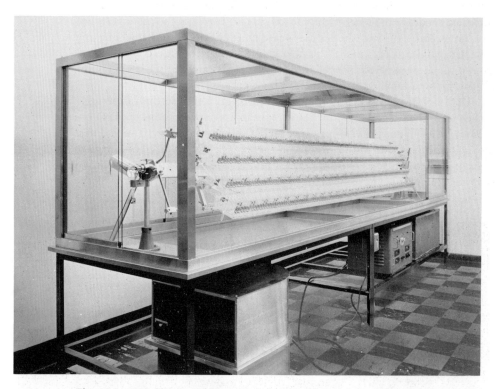

Fig. 16.5. 1000-Cell Craig Countercurrent Distribution Instrument for automatic operation. The instrument can also be operated as two 500-cell units running concurrently. Driving mechanism is on the right-hand side under the table, with a driving shaft extending through the table top to the instrument. The unit is enclosed in a fume hood with glass doors and removable sides and top to afford access. (Courtesy of H. O. Post Scientific Instrument Co., Inc.)

After the distribution has been completed, the bank of cells is tilted so that the liquids in the cells may be collected from the drain tubes shown in Figure 16.3. If the experiment is a preparative one, the pooled solvents from tubes containing the desired solute may be evaporated to obtain the desired material. In an analytical run, the solutions from the individual cells may be analyzed by appropriate means, for example, by spectrophotometry, titrimetry, or measurement of refractive index.

Applications of Craig extraction

Many of the applications of the Craig extraction process are found in the biochemical area. It has proved particularly useful for separating peptides in the molecular weight range of about 500 to 5000. Some antibiotics and certain hormones are polypeptides, and several examples of successful purification by the Craig method may be found. Crude tyrocidin from a bacterial source was separated after 673 transfers into three major components (A, B, and C) and several minor ones; 1600 transfers on component A led to a crystallizable material, and 2140 more transfers eliminated the last trace of a particularly troublesome impurity. Peptide hormones from the posterior lobe of the pituitary gland have been fractionated by Craig extraction; distribution between 2-butanol and 0.1-M aqueous acetic acid was employed in the final purification of synthetic oxytocin and in comparing this product with the naturally-occurring hormone, and similar work was done on vasopressin. Craig distribution has been employed for isolating and characterizing ACTH (adrenocorticotrophic hormone) from the anterior pituitary. Although proteins present many difficulties, some have been successfully handled by the Craig technique, notably insulin, ribonuclease, lysozyme, and the serum albumins. The technique is used for purification of many pharmaceutical preparations. Chemists other than biochemists have been slow to adopt the technique. Only a few inorganic applications appear in the literature.

Craig extraction as a model for continuous separation processes

In the Craig extraction experiment, the heavier liquid phase remains stationary, while the lighter phase is transported down the series of cells, carrying solutes with it to various extents in accord with their partition properties. In chromatography, which we shall consider in Chapter 17, there is likewise a stationary and a moving phase (not necessarily both liquid). But here the moving phase flows continuously, and equilibrium is not actually attained at any time during the experiment. This leads to great difficulty in formulating the separation process mathematically, and the difficulty appears in the form of complicated equations with many correction factors and adjustable parameters. It is easy for the student to lose sight of what is going on in such processes. In the Craig experiment, on the other hand, the intermittent flow of the moving phase permits equilibration in each step of the overall process, and as we have seen above, the theoretical treatment is not unusually difficult. The Craig extraction process then, while it is by no means real chromatography, is useful as a teaching tool in explaining chromatography to beginners. We shall try to show the similarities and differences in more detail in the next chapter.

REFERENCES

1. H. Irving and R. J. P. Williams, "Liquid-Liquid Extraction," Chapter 31, Part I, Vol. 3, p. 1309, of *Treatise on Analytical Chemistry*. I. M. Kolthoff and P. J. Elving, Eds., Interscience Publishers, Inc., New York, 1961.
2. H. A. Laitinen, *Chemical Analysis*, McGraw-Hill Book Co., Inc., New York, 1960, p. 483.
3. G. H. Morrison and H. Frieser, *Solvent Extraction in Analytical Chemistry*, John Wiley & Sons, Inc., New York, 1957.
4. C. J. O. R. Morris and P. Morris, *Separation Methods in Biochemistry*, Interscience Publishers, Inc., New York, 1963, p. 559.

QUESTIONS

1. Consider a substance which does not behave in a simple fashion, but rather participates in equilibria such as ionization or dimerization, so that its distribution between two liquid phases is not adequately described by a K_D value. We might then employ a distribution ratio, D, in describing its behavior in a Craig experiment. If D were not independent of the analytical concentration of the substance (why might it not be?), what would be the effect upon the shape of the Craig distribution curve?

2. Consider a solute, A, distributed between an organic solvent and water, with distribution coefficient (organic/aqueous), K_D. Show that the fraction of A left unextracted from a volume V_w of water by n extractions with V_o portions of organic solvent is given by

$$F_n = \left(\frac{V_w}{K_D V_o + V_w} \right)^n$$

3. Show that if the volume V_o of extracting solvent (question 2) is divided into n portions, the fraction of A left unextracted is given by

$$F_n = \left(\frac{n V_w}{K_D V_o + n V_w} \right)^n$$

4. The formation constants of complex ions can be determined by a solvent extraction method. A chelating agent is employed and the distribution ratio D is determined as a function of the concentration of the complexing agent in the aqueous phase. Consider a metal, M^{++}, forming a chelate, MT_2, with HT, and a complex ion, MX^+, with X^-. Derive an expression relating the distribution ratio to the concentration of X^-, involving the formation constant, K_f, for the reaction

$$M^{++} + X^- \rightleftarrows MX^+$$

You can assume that MT_2 is the only metal-containing species in the organic phase and that it exists predominantly in that phase. Also assume that no appreciable complexing occurs between M^{++} and HT in the aqueous phase.

5. Repeat question 4, except that the complexing agent is HX, rather than X^-. That is, the constant desired is for the reaction

$$M^{++} + HX \rightleftarrows MX^+ + H^+$$

PROBLEMS

1. The distribution coefficient for the extraction of solute A from water into ether (organic concentration/aqueous concentration) is 10.

(a) If 100 ml of water containing 1 g of A is shaken with 100 ml of ether, what percentage of A is extracted into ether?

(b) If the extraction is continued with fresh 100 ml portions of ether, how many separate extractions are required to remove all but 1 part per million of A from the aqueous phase? Round off answer to an even number.

2. Repeat problem 1(a) except that the extraction is carried out with two separate 50-ml portions of ether.

(a) What percentage of A is extracted?

(b) Suppose the extraction is carried out with five 20-ml portions of ether. What percentage of A is extracted?

3. When an aqueous solution of ferric chloride in HCl is shaken with twice its volume of ether (also containing HCl), 99% of the iron is extracted. What is the distribution ratio of the compound (organic to aqueous)?

4. Two extractions with 20-ml portions of an organic solvent removed 89% of a solute from 100 ml of an aqueous solution. What is the distribution ratio of the solute (organic to aqueous)?

5. The distribution coefficient for the extraction of solute A from water into an organic solvent is 10 (organic/aqueous). 1.00 g of A is dissolved in water and placed in tube 0 of a Craig extraction apparatus and extracted with the organic solvent. The organic phase is transferred from tube 0 to tube 1, and so on.

(a) Calculate the fraction of A remaining in tube 0 after five extractions and transfers.

(b) Calculate the fraction of A in tubes 1, 2, 3, 4, and 5.

6. A chelating agent, HT, dissolved in an organic solvent extracts a metal, M^{++}, from an aqueous solution according to the reaction

$$M_{aq}^{++} + 2\,HT_{org} \rightleftarrows MT2_{org} + 2\,H_{aq}^+$$

The equilibrium constant for this reaction as written is 1×10^{-2}.

(a) Identify this equilibrium constant in terms of other constants (page 396).

(b) Calculate the pH values at which 1, 25, 50, 75, and 99.9% of the metal is extracted into the organic phase. 10 ml of the aqueous solution is shaken with 10 ml of a 0.010-M solution of HT. Assume the concentration of the metal is so small that the concentration of HT in the organic phase is unchanged.

(c) Plot the results, per cent extracted vs. pH.

7. Repeat problem 6 for a metal, N^{++}, where the K of the extraction reaction is

1×10^{-6}. Suggest a pH at which these two metals could be separated quantitatively by this method.

8. A certain metal ion is extracted by a chelating agent as in the two previous problems. The concentration of chelating agent in the organic phase is 0.01-M. The following data are obtained:

pH	1	2	3	4	5
D	10^{-8}	10^{-4}	1	10^4	10^8

Make a plot of $\log D$ vs. pH (page 397) and evaluate n and K.

9. Given two acids, HA and HB, with the following distribution coefficients and ionization constants:

	K_D	K_a
HA	10	1×10^{-5}
HB	1000	1×10^{-10}

Calculate the distribution ratios (D) of the two acids at pH values 4, 5, 6, 7, 8, 9, and 10. Assuming that the ratio of the two distribution ratios needs to be 10^6 to 1 for a quantitative extraction of HB without extracting HA appreciably, what is the lowest pH (roughly) at which such a separation can be accomplished?

10. An acid, HX, has a distribution coefficient of 10 between an organic solvent and water. At pH 5.0, half the acid is extracted into the organic solvent. Calculate the ionization constant of HX. Equal volumes of liquids are employed.

17 *chapter*

Chromatography

INTRODUCTION

Separations of chemical substances are of the greatest importance throughout chemistry and the other fields which use chemistry for their own purposes. We have emphasized earlier that a separation step often precedes the measurement in chemical analysis. It is no less true that separations are an integral part of an organic synthesis, the isolation of a natural product, or the purification of a substance prior to physical measurements which may have theoretical significance. The impact of a powerful and versatile separation technique will be felt throughout much of modern science. In this connection, the significance of chromatography can scarcely be overstated. By means of chromatographic methods, separations are accomplished much more rapidly and effectively than before, and indeed many separations are routinely successful which would never have been attempted by other techniques. Unparalleled breakthroughs in biochemistry—for example, in our understanding of the structure of protein molecules or of hormone action —have stemmed directly from the application of chromatography to biological systems.

Chromatography was apparently first described in recognizable terms by the botanist Tswett in 1906 in connection with studies of plant pigments. His own description of the process was as follows:

"If a petroleum ether solution of chlorophyll is filtered through a column of an adsorbent (I use mainly calcium carbonate which is stamped firmly into a narrow glass tube), then the pigments, according to the adsorption sequence, are resolved from top to bottom into various colored zones, since the stronger adsorbed pigments displace the weaker adsorbed ones and force them farther downwards. This separation becomes practically complete if, after the pigment solution has flowed through, one passes a stream of pure solvent through the adsorbent column. Like light rays in the spectrum, so the different components of the pigment mixture are resolved on the calcium carbonate column according to a law and can be estimated on it qualitatively and also quantitatively. Such a preparation I term a chromatogram and the corresponding method, the chromatographic method."

Tswett's work was largely overlooked until 1931, when the prominent organic chemist Kuhn used chromatography in his work on plant carotene pigments. This research attracted more attention, and adsorption chromatography became widely used in the field of natural product chemistry. More recently, there have been three major developments: ion exchange chromatography in the late 1930's; partition chromatography in 1941, and its offshoot, paper chromatography, in 1944; and gas chromatography in 1952. Ion exchange became extremely important during World War II in the atomic energy programs. The development of inorganic chemistry as a field has been accelerated by ion exchange; for example, the preparation of significant quantities of pure rare earth metals was made possible by ion exchange, and many of the studies on the chemistry of the transuranic elements depended upon this technique. The major significance of paper chromatography was felt in biochemistry, where it proved very quickly to be the solution to a really difficult analytical problem—determination of the amino acids in samples such as protein hydrolyzates. This led directly to the first elucidation of the amino acid sequence in a protein (insulin) by Sanger, for which a Nobel Prize was awarded in 1958. Paper chromatography was also applied early to the separation of steroid hormones present in minute quantities. Gas chromatography has brought undreamed-of speed and simplicity to the analysis of the most complicated organic mixtures, and is now a preparative tool as well. The Nobel Prize is not generally awarded for the development of methods per se, but the impact of partition, and particularly paper, chromatography upon research in many different fields of science was recognized by the award to Martin and Synge in 1952. It is generally believed that if they had missed the Prize at that time, they would have received it later, for the same workers first described gas-liquid chromatography.

DEFINITION AND CLASSIFICATION OF CHROMATOGRAPHY

Although the meaning of the term is largely understood by chemists, a good definition of chromatography is difficult to formulate. It is a collective term applied to methods which are diverse in some regards but share certain common features. It should be emphasized that components of the sample are distributed between two phases, but this alone is not a suitable definition, because we do not wish the term to embrace all separation processes. We like Keulemans' definition as well as any:

"Chromatography is a physical method of separation, in which the components to be separated are distributed between two phases, one of these phases constituting a stationary bed of large surface area, the other being a fluid that percolates through or along the stationary bed." [1]

The stationary phase may be either a solid or a liquid, and the moving phase may be either a liquid or a gas. Thus all the known types of chromatography fall into the four categories that are seen in Table 17.1, viz., liquid-solid, gas-solid, liquid-liquid, and gas-liquid.

In all of the chromatographic techniques, the solutes to be separated migrate along a column (or, as in paper or thin layer chromatography, the physical equivalent of a column), and of course the basis of the separation lies in different rates of migration for the different solutes. We may think of the rate of migration of a solute as the result of two factors, one tending to move the solute and the other to retard it. In Tswett's original process, the tendency of solutes to adsorb on the solid phase retarded their movement, while their solubility in the moving liquid phase tended to move them along. A slight difference between two solutes in the firmness of their adsorption and in their interaction with the moving solvent becomes the basis of a significant separation when the solute molecules repeatedly distribute between the two phases over and over again throughout the length of the column.

Space will not permit a thorough discussion in this chapter of all the types of chromatography. We shall discuss gas-liquid and ion exchange chromatography fairly thoroughly, and thin layer chromatography briefly.

---

[1] A. I. M. Keulemans, *Gas Chromatography*, 2nd Ed., Reinhold Publishing Corp., New York, 1959, p. 2.

Table 17.1   SUMMARY OF TYPES OF CHROMATOGRAPHY

Stationary phase	Solid		Liquid	
Moving phase	Liquid	Gas	Liquid	Gas
Examples	Tswett's original chromatography with petroleum ether solutions and $CaCO_3$ columns; ion exchange chromatography; thin layer chromatography or TLC	Gas-solid chromatography or GSC	Partition chromatography on silica gel columns; paper chromatography	Gas-liquid chromatography or GLC

GAS-LIQUID CHROMATOGRAPHY

We shall first discuss briefly the apparatus and technique of GLC in a general way to obtain an idea of the basic nature of the process, then consider the theory, and finally indicate more fully the functions of components of the apparatus and give some illustrative applications which show the power and versatility of the method.

Basic apparatus for GLC

Figure 17.1 is a schematic diagram of the basic GLC apparatus. Additional components may be added for various purposes, but the fundamental aspects are shown in the figure. It may be seen that the equipment is really rather simple as instruments come these days. We shall see later in more detail what some of the components do.

The moving phase in GLC is a gas, and, in the United States at least, this is usually helium, for reasons we shall mention later. The user buys a cylinder of the compressed gas and attaches his own reducing valve to it. Commerical gas chromatographs usually provide an additional regulating valve for good control of the helium pressure at the inlet of the column. The pure helium then passes through one side of the detector and enters the column. Near the column inlet is a device whereby samples may be introduced into the carrier gas stream. The samples may be gases or volatile liquids. The injection port is heated so that liquid samples are quickly vaporized. Samples of a few microliters of liquid or a few milliliters of gas

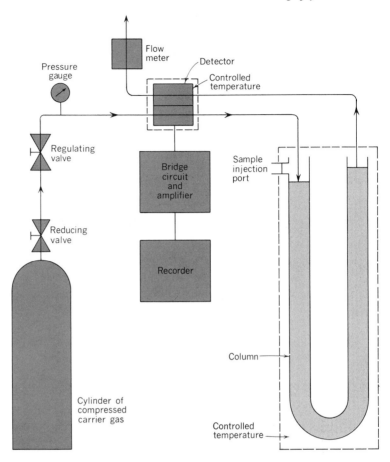

Fig. 17.1. Schematic diagram of a gas chromatograph. Large arrows indicate direction of gas flow.

are commonly introduced through a rubber septum by means of a hypodermic syringe.

The gas stream next encounters the column, which is mounted in a constant temperature oven. This is the heart of the instrument, the place where the basic chromatographic process takes place. Columns vary widely in size and packing material; a common size is 6 ft long and $\frac{1}{4}$ in. in diameter, made of copper or stainless steel tubing. To save space, it may be U-shaped or coiled into a spiral. The tubing is packed with a relatively inert, pulverized solid material of large surface area, frequently diatomaceous earth or firebrick. The solid, however, is actually only a mechanical support for a liquid; before it is packed into the column, it is impregnated with the desired liquid which serves as the real stationary phase. This liquid must be stable and nonvolatile at the temperature of the column, and it must be appropriate for the particular separation.

After emerging from the column, the gas stream passes through the other side of the detector. Elution of a solute from the column sets up an imbalance in the detector which is recorded electrically. The carrier gas flow rate is important, as we shall see, and usually a flow-meter of some sort is provided. There may be another regulating valve at the outlet end of the system, although normally the emerging gases are vented at atmospheric pressure. If noxious or toxic vapors are involved, the outlet should be vented into a hood. Provision can be made to trap separated solutes as they emerge from the column.

Theory of GLC

Although it is never done in practice, we may, for instructional purposes, imagine a gas-liquid partition experiment which is performed in a series of stages like the Craig countercurrent distribution experiment in liquid-liquid partition. Suppose we have a little chamber in which a vapor phase containing some compound of interest is brought into contact with a liquid. Some of the vapor will dissolve in the liquid, some will remain in the space above the liquid. The partition of the compound between the liquid and vapor phases may be described, at least to a first approximation, by Henry's law,

$$p = KC$$

where p is the partial pressure of the compound in the vapor phase and C its concentration in the liquid. Some other compound with a different Henry's law constant, K, will distribute itself differently, either more or less of it dissolving in the liquid as the case may be. Thus, after equilibration with the liquid, the vapor phase of a mixture will be richer in one compound than another as compared with vapor that had not contacted the liquid. But the enrichment is often slight with the K values usually encountered in actual practice.

Imagine, however, a whole series of little equilibrium chambers, and suppose that we could, by means of magic trap doors and a carrier gas stream, blow the vapor phase from one chamber into the next all down the line, allowing equilibration before each transfer. This is exactly like the Craig experiment discussed in Chapter 16, except that the moving phase is a vapor. It is apparent, then, that the vapor moving along through the chambers in a series of successive equilibrium steps would become progressively enriched in one compound at the expense of another, and that we could separate two compounds to any desired degree of purity if we employed enough chambers. In the parlance of the separation game, the little equilibrium chambers are called *theoretical plates*. Each cell in the Craig apparatus is a plate in this sense.

Now a chromatographic column operates under conditions of continuous flow of the moving phase, and equilibrium is not attained at any point in the column. However, after traversing a certain length of column, a mixture will have been subjected to the same degree of fractionation as would have been achieved in one equilibrium step. That length of column which accomplishes this is called the *height equivalent to a theoretical plate* or HETP. The total length of a column divided by HETP is the number, n, of theoretical plates in the column, and it is customary to describe column performance in terms of numbers of plates. The great efficiency of GLC for performing difficult separations lies in the fact that large numbers of plates are fairly easily obtained with columns of reasonable length. Columns with a few thousand plates may be only eight or ten feet long; the best packed columns described so far have perhaps 100,000 plates. (To give an idea of the power of the chromatographic technique, it may be noted that columns for fractional distillation are likewise rated in terms of theoretical plates; a fairly good six-foot conventional distilling column may have something like twenty plates.)

In gas chromatography, samples are injected as rapidly as possible, so that a substance is placed on the column as a narrow "plug." However, just as in the Craig extraction technique, when the substance moves along it spreads out through more and more plates but occupies progressively a smaller fraction of the total number of plates which it has encountered. In other words, as we increase the number of plates, the absolute width of the elution band increases, but there is a decrease in width relative to the total base of the operation. In this perspective, elution bands look narrow as they emerge from a good column, broad from a poor column.

A simple expression for column efficiency widely used in GLC is the following, based upon a theoretical treatment by Glueckauf:[2]

$$n = 16 \left(\frac{d}{w}\right)^2$$

n is the number of theoretical plates, and distance d and width w are measured on the chromatogram as shown in Figure 17.2. The values of d and w must of course be in the same units.

The performance of a GLC column is affected by several variables. The size of the column and the nature and uniformity of the packing material are obviously first considerations, but once a given column is in place, further control over performance is governed by operating parameters. The most important of these are sample size, temperature, and carrier gas flow rate.

The number of plates in a given column is found to vary with sample size in a fairly regular way. Overloading of any column leads to a deterioration of performance and poor separations. To obtain a value for n, sometimes extrapolation to zero sample size is performed on a graph of measured n-values vs. sample size.

[2] E. Glueckauf, *Trans. Faraday Soc.*, **51**, 34, 1540 (1955).

Changes in temperature influence column performance. Sample components generally pass through the column faster the higher the temperature, and thus an analysis is accomplished most rapidly at the highest temperature compatible with the desired separation and sample stability. On the other hand, improved resolution of components may often be obtained by lowering the temperature. Put rather crudely, the higher the temperature, the more similar the behavior of two compounds in a GLC column. *Programmed temperature GLC* is often applied to sample mixtures whose components boil over a wide range. The analysis is begun at a low temperature to get the best separation of lower-boiling components, but the temperature is con-

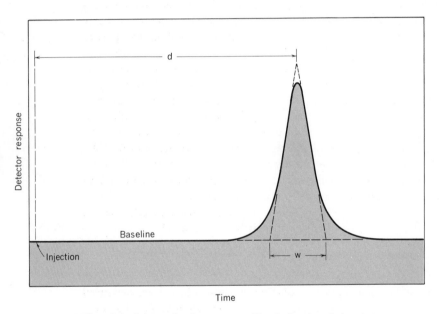

Fig. 17.2. Schematic chromatographic elution band showing measurement of *d* and *w* for estimating *n*, the number of theoretical plates.

tinually raised so that the less volatile components are eluted from the column in a reasonable time.

The plate theory of GLC, emphasizing the analogy to the Craig distribution and reaching its height in Glueckauf's theoretical work, provides, as noted above, a simple evaluation of column performance. However, a different theoretical approach has led to a better understanding of the experimental factors that influence performance. As we pointed out, the plate theory predicts that a solute band will broaden as it traverses the column; the so-called *rate theory* attempts to evaluate on a kinetic basis the factors that lead to broadening under realistic conditions of continuous flow of the moving phase. The name of van Deemter, the senior author of the first papers in the field, is associated with this treatment. Van Deemter *et al.*[3] considered three major factors that caused band broadening as a plug of solute moved down a column in a GLC experiment.

First is the fact that gas molecules follow a variety of paths as they wind their way among the particles of packing material; some molecules make faster progress than others which follow longer paths. This effect is referred to as *eddy diffusion*, a term which is perhaps unfortunate in that ordinary English usage does not connote the intended meaning. In any case, the magnitude of the contribution of this term to band broadening depends upon the particle size of the packing material, and upon the shape and uniformness of the particles.

The second factor contributing to band broadening is referred to as *longitudinal molecular diffusion*. Solute molecules tend to diffuse along concentration gradients. The student may visualize what this means by imagining that a solute be injected into a column which is then plugged up and allowed to await equilibrium with no flow of carrier gas. Eventually the solute would be spread uniformly throughout the length of the column as the molecules wandered about. With a flow of carrier gas, solutes are eluted before this unhappy event, but the tendency of diffusion to broaden the solute band is obvious. Solute molecules spend part of their time in the gas phase and part in the liquid phase; diffusion is much faster in the former, and diffusion in the liquid phase is generally considered negligible.

The third factor that causes bands to broaden relates to the fact that equilibration between the vapor and liquid phases is not instantaneous. A finite time would be required for the establishment of equilibrium. In the Craig-type of experiment, we would wait for this, but the moving phase in chromatography moves continually. Thus, for example, a solute molecule which at equilibrium might be in the vapor phase at a particular point in the column is perhaps still wandering around in the liquid, taking so long to escape that once it gets out, the vapor where it "belongs" is already further down the column. It is clear that this effect becomes more appreciable as the carrier gas flow rate is increased. The thickness of the liquid film applied to the solid column packing would also be expected to exert an effect.

Consideration of the three factors outlined above led to the so-called van Deemter equation:

$$\text{HETP} = 2\lambda d_p + 2\frac{\gamma D_{\text{gas}}}{\mu} + \frac{8kd_f^2}{\pi^2(1+k)^2 D_{\text{liq}}}\mu$$

where:

λ is a dimensionless parameter measuring the irregularity of the column packing.

d_p is the diameter of the packing particles.

[3] J. J. van Deemter, E. J. Zuiderwig, and A. Klinkenberg, *Chem. Eng. Sci.*, **5**, 258, 271 (1957).

γ is a correction factor accounting for the irregularity of diffusion pathways through the packing material.

D_{gas} is the diffusion coefficient of the solute in the gas phase.

μ is the carrier gas flow rate.

k is a constant for a particular solute and a particular column.

d_f is the "effective film thickness," a measure of the liquid loading of the solid packing material.

D_{liq} is the diffusion coefficient of the solute in the liquid phase.

Further refinements have led to an extended form of the van Deemter equation. Some of the terms in the equation are empirical, and the assignment of numerical values has been the subject of some dispute. However, this does not detract from a great accomplishment: Out of a terribly complicated situation, attention was focused upon factors important for the user of GLC, and there is now a rational basis for further work on the factors that determine column performance.

The van Deemter equation is often seen in the abbreviated form

$$\text{HETP} = A + \frac{B}{\mu} + C\mu$$

where:

A represents the eddy diffusion term.

B/μ represents the longitudinal diffusion term.

$C\mu$ represents the nonequilibrium in mass transfer term.

A typical plot of HETP vs. μ, the carrier gas flow rate, is shown in Figure 17.3. The dotted construction on the graph depicts the contributions of the A, B/μ, and $C\mu$ terms to HETP at various flow rates. The A term remains constant, independent of flow rate. At very slow flow rates, most of the band spreading is due to longitudinal diffusion, while at fast flow rates, the increasing departure from equilibrium becomes most important. There is an optimal flow rate where the best balance of these factors is obtained; here, HETP is a minimum (or the number of plates is a maximum).

Experimental aspects of GLC

Having seen what gas-liquid chromatography is, and after briefly considering the theory, we may now discuss, again briefly, some of the more practical aspects which will make the gas chromatograph less of a mysterious "black box."

Carrier gas. Various gases have been used in GLC, for example, hydrogen, nitrogen, carbon dioxide, argon, and helium. The lighter gases, hydrogen and helium, permit more longitudinal diffusion of solutes, which tends to lower column efficiency, particularly at lower flow rates. Thus nitrogen might be a better choice of carrier gas in order to accomplish a really difficult separation. However, there is another consideration, viz., the char-

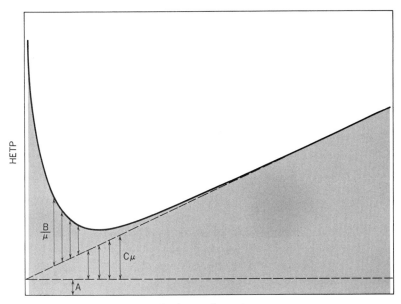

Carrier gas flow rate, μ

Fig. 17.3. Schematic depiction of the van Deemter equation, HETP = $A + B/\mu + C\mu$. Note that the contribution of the A term to HETP is independent of flow rate, that B/μ increases as flow rate decreases, and that $C\mu$ predominates at high flow rates.

acteristics of the detector. It is obviously desirable that the response of the detector to the components of the sample differ greatly from its response to the everpresent carrier gas. In the case of the most widely used detector, the thermal conductivity cell, this requirement is much better met by the lighter gases, hydrogen and helium, as we shall see below. Thus helium is by far the commonest carrier gas in the United States, while in Europe, where helium is very expensive, hydrogen is more widely used.

Sampling system. Liquid samples of perhaps 1 to 25 μl are usually injected through a rubber diaphragm or septum by means of a hypodermic syringe. Special syringes delivering various volumes in the microliter range are on the market. Gaseous samples may also be injected, or they may be introduced by means of various gas sampling devices designed for commercial chromatographs. The injection technique is important: The sample should be introduced as a sharp "plug" rather than being slowly bled into the carrier gas stream. Slow injection leads to much more band spreading than is necessary; actually HETP calculated from the elution peak as described above is a function of the injection rate. Good injection technique requires practice.

It is important that the size of the sample not be too large for the apparatus. Overloading has an extremely deleterious effect upon column efficiency. Preparative-scale gas chromatographs are on the market which will take milliliter samples, and GLC on an industrial scale is under development, but the usual analytical instruments perform best when the sample is as small as may be consistent with good detector response.

The temperature at the injection port is important. If a liquid sample evaporates slowly, the result is similar to that caused by injecting too slowly. The injection port is usually heated independently of the heating unit for the oven surrounding the column, and generally it should be held at a temperature above the boiling point of the injected liquid sample. On the other hand, the components of the sample should not decompose at the temperature of the injection port.

Column. The stationary phase in GLC is a liquid, but it cannot be allowed simply to slosh around inside a tube. The liquid must be immobilized, preferably in the form of a thin layer of large surface area. This is accomplished by impregnating a ground-up solid material with the liquid phase. The solid should be chemically inert toward the substances which will be put through the column, stable at the operating temperature, and of large surface area per unit volume. The pressure drop required for desired gas flow rates should not be excessive. Mechanical strength is desirable so that the particles will not break and alter the particle size distribution with handling. Most of the solids employed as supports in GLC are highly porous, but the characteristics of the pores are very important. For example, the pores in silica gel tend to be very narrow; they fill up with the liquid and hence do not furnish sufficient area of gas-liquid interface. The so-called active adsorbants such as activated charcoal and silica gel are poor solid supports: Even when covered with the liquid film, these solids adsorb sample components, which causes "tailing" of the elution bands. The commonest solid support materials are diatomaceous earth and firebrick.

The stationary liquid phase must be selected with the particular separation problem in mind. The liquid should have a very low vapor pressure at the column temperature; a rule-of-thumb suggests a boiling point at least 200°C above the temperature to which the liquid will be subjected. The two important reasons for desiring low volatility of the liquid are first, loss of liquid will cause deterioration of column performance, and second, the detector will respond to the vapor of the stationary phase with resulting drift of the recorder baseline and lowered sensitivity toward the components of the analytical sample. Some commercial gas chromatographs have dual columns to compensate for the effect of liquid bleed on the detector, but even here, excessive volatility is undesirable.

Obviously the liquid phase should be thermally stable at the column temperature, and, except in special cases, it should not react chemically with the sample components. The liquid must have an appreciable solvent power for the sample; as a general rule, it may be said rather crudely that there should be some chemical resemblance between the liquid substrate and the solutes to be separated. For example, a high molecular weight paraffin might be a good liquid for the separation of low molecular weight paraffinic hydrocarbons, while benzyldiphenyl might be a good substrate for separating aromatic hydrocarbons. A polyglycol column might be used to separate a mixture of alcohols. Lists of liquid phases and the types of compounds for whose separation they are recommended may be found in monographs on gas chromatography.

The quantity of liquid substrate applied to the solid support is important. If too much liquid is present, solutes spend relatively too much time in diffusing through the liquid phase, and the separation efficiency is lowered. Too little liquid may allow solutes to interact with the solid itself, in which case adsorption may cause "tailing" and overlapping of elution bands. The technique of preparing liquid-impregnated column packing materials used to be an important research asset. More recently, it has become common practice to buy columns which are ready to attach to the chromatograph, except for very special applications. Typical research laboratories have on hand a variety of columns from which a selection may be made for a particular type of sample.

Detector. The separation process occurs in the column, and this has to be considered the heart of the instrument. On the other hand, the separation would be of little value without some way to detect and measure the separated components present in the carrier gas as they emerge from the column. Among the characteristics of an ideal detector, we would list the following.

1. *Sensitivity.* The sensitivity of the detector rather than the column characteristics determines the size of the sample required for the analysis. Column efficiency not only remains good, but if anything, is better, as the sample size decreases. Various measures of detector sensitivity are found in the literature; basically, for our purposes, we may consider the sensitivity as the slope of a graph of detector response vs. the quantity measured, as shown in Figure 17.4. A general expression of the sensitivity, then, is

$$S = \frac{\Delta R}{\Delta Q}$$

as shown in the figure. Related to the sensitivity of the detector is the "limit of detection," the minimum quantity of a compound that can be detected with a specified degree of certainty. The baseline in a chromatogram is always subject to fluctuations of a short-term nature ("noise") or of a longer variety ("drift"). The smallest elution peak that can be distinguished from random fluctuation or noise corresponds to the limit of detection. This becomes essentially a statistical problem: How much larger than most of the random baseline fluctuations must a peak be in order to be identified properly as a peak? This involves an estimate of the level beyond which a recorder deflection is probably not noise but rather due to a definite cause, viz., the sample, a problem not entirely unlike some of those encountered in Chapter 3. The literature of gas chromatography contains various analyses of this problem based upon a Gaussian noise distribution and involved statistical

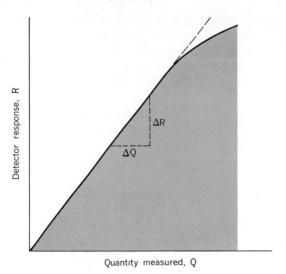

Fig. 17.4. Detector response curve.

Detector response, R

ΔR

ΔQ

Quantity measured, Q

considerations. In most cases, the individual researcher will have to decide for himself how small a sample he thinks he can detect.

2. *Linearity.* The ideal detector response would be linear with respect to the concentration of eluted solute in the carrier gas stream. This is the case with commonly used detectors within certain concentration limits; eventually, as shown in Figure 17.4, the response tends to fall off.

3. *Stability.* Freedom from noise and drift are important. As noted above, the noise level determines the limit of detection; drift affects the baseline, which in turn affects the accuracy of peak height or area measurements for quantitative purposes.

4. *Versatility.* Analysts prefer, with good reason, not to change detectors from one experiment to another. The ideal detector would respond to a wide variety of chemical compounds, and it should perform properly under all conditions which are likely to be encountered.

5. *Response time.* The detector should respond rapidly to changes in the composition of the gas passing through it, or there should be, as it is said, a small "time constant." The total response time of a GLC instrument is a function not only of the detector itself but also of inertia in other components, for example, the recorder.

6. *Signal adaptability.* The signal from the detector should be easily adapted to the input of a suitable recorder.

7. *Chemical activity.* The detector must not react chemically with the substances being chromatographed.

There are additional desiderata which may be classed as nonfunctional, such as low cost, simplicity, safety, and ability to withstand abuse.

The most widely used detector for general-purpose GLC is the thermal conductivity cell; we shall confine our discussion to this device. The thermal conductivity cell contains either a heated metal filament or a thermistor (a material of fused metal oxides which has a very large temperature coefficient of electrical resistance). The heated element, under steady-state conditions, adopts a certain temperature determined by the heat supplied to it and the rate at which it loses heat to the walls of the chamber which surrounds it. Ignoring a small amount of radiation heat transfer, the element adopts a temperature which depends upon the thermal conductivity of the gas in the space between the element and the walls. When the composition of the gas changes, because different gases have different thermal conductivities, the temperature of the wire or thermistor changes. This temperature change is reflected in a change in the electrical resistance of the sensing element.

As shown schematically in Figure 17.1, the detector actually has two sides, each with its own element. One side of the detector is encountered by the pure carrier gas ahead of the sample injection port, while the column effluent flows through the other side. This is seen in more detail in Figure 17.5, where one type of detector employing thermistors is illustrated sche-

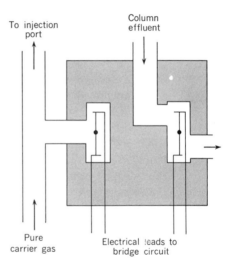

Fig. 17.5. Schematic diagram of a thermal conductivity cell. The black dots are thermistor beads.

matically. The geometry of the detector is important: The volume should be small, no stagnant pockets of gas should be formed, and the dead volume between the outlet of the column and the detector inlet should be as small as possible.

The detector elements are simply electrical resistances selected for their unusually high temperature coefficients of resistance. The two resistances in the two sides of the detector are two arms of a Wheatstone bridge circuit, as shown in Figure 17.6. Before the sample is injected into the chromatograph, pure carrier gas is flowing through both sides of the detector; the adjustable resistors are set so that the bridge is balanced, which establishes

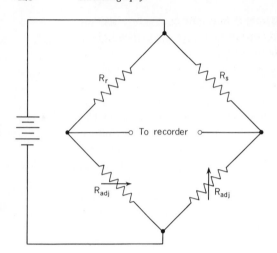

Fig. 17.6. Wheatstone bridge circuit for thermal conductivity detector. R_r and R_s are the resistive elements in the reference and sample sides of the detector, R_{adj} is adjustable by the operator in order to balance the bridge.

the baseline on the recorder chart. Now, after injection, when a solute emerges from the column, the value of R_s in Figure 17.6 changes, while the other resistances remain the same. The bridge goes out of balance, and a voltage appears across the leads labelled "to recorder" in the figure. After the solute has passed through the detector, the bridge returns to its original balance. Thus a record of the voltage across the bridge vs. time will exhibit a peak as shown in Figure 17.2 for the elution of each separated component of the sample.

Helium is an attractive carrier gas in conjunction with the thermal conductivity cell because its thermal conductivity, like that of hydrogen, is much greater than that of most organic compounds, while it does not represent an explosion hazard. Thus the appearance of an eluted solute at the detector causes a much greater change in the temperature of the resistive element than would be the case, say, with nitrogen. This implies, of course, greater sensitivity in detection, or a lower limit of detection. A few thermal conductivity values are given in Table 17.2.

Table 17.2   THERMAL CONDUCTIVITIES OF SOME GASES AND ORGANIC VAPORS †

Hydrogen	5.34	Benzene	0.44
Helium	4.16	Acetone	0.42
Methane	1.09	Ethyl acetate	0.41
Nitrogen	0.75	Chloroform	0.25
Ethane	0.73	Carbon tetrachloride	0.22
n-Butane	0.56		
Ethanol	0.53		

† Values are calories per second conducted through a 1-cm layer of the gas 1 m^2 in area at 100°C, with a temperature gradient of 1°C per cm.

There are now available detectors which are more sensitive than the thermal conductivity cell, such as the flame ionization and the β-ray ionization detectors. The demand for more sensitive methods of trace analysis, for example, in the determination of pesticide residues on fruits and vegetables, has brought continued effort to improve the sensitivity of detectors for GLC.

Applications of GLC

The GLC column is only a separation tool, but the gas chromatograph as a whole, because of the detection and recording of elution bands, is an analytical instrument which embraces the measurement step of the analysis as well. With a particular column and with all of the variables controlled, such as flow rate and temperature, the position of an elution band on the time axis of the recorder frequently serves to identify the eluted solute, provided its behavior is known from previous experiments. The time between injection of the sample and the appearance of the peak of the elution band is called the *retention time*, T_R, of the solute; retention times serve, then, for qualitative analysis. The product of retention time and flow rate, termed the *retention volume*, V_R, is frequently quoted instead of T_R. Retention volumes can be reproduced within perhaps 3 to 5% in careful work.

Within a homologous series, say a series of normal alkanes, log V_R is a linear function of the number of carbon atoms if the experiment is very carefully performed with all variables rigorously controlled. Such a plot is shown in (A) of Figure 17.7. Graphs of the sort shown in (B) of Figure 17.7, obtained for several homologous series on two different columns, may be useful in establishing the particular series in which an unknown compound belongs.

If two substances, perhaps a known compound and an unknown one, yield only one peak when run on several different columns, excellent evidence is provided that the two are identical. When known compounds are not available for comparison, it is often possible to collect a separated solute after it emerges from the column, for example, by means of a cold trap, so that the pure solute may be studied by other techniques such as infrared or mass spectroscopy.

Quantitative analysis by GLC depends upon the relationship between the quantity of an injected sample component and the size of the resulting elution band. Samples with low retention times yield sharp, narrow peaks, in which case it may only be necessary to measure the peak height on the chart paper. For solutes with longer retention times, band spreading leads to lower and broader bands. In such cases, the area under the peak may be a much better measure of the quantity of solute. Various integrative methods may be applied to the measurement of the area, including the use of a planimeter, cutting out the peak and weighing the paper, treating the area as approxi-

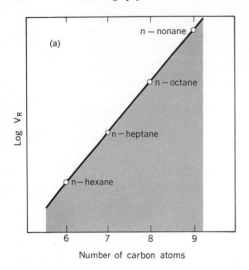

(a)

n — nonane

n — octane

n — heptane

n — hexane

Log V_R

6   7   8   9

Number of carbon atoms

Fig. 17.7. Identification of organic compounds by retention volume measurements.

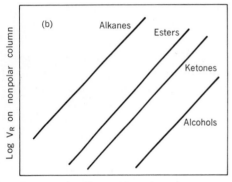

(b)

Alkanes

Esters

Ketones

Alcohols

Log V_R on nonpolar column

Log V_R on polar column

mately that of a triangle and multiplying the peak height by the width at half-height, and the use of various mechanical or electronic integrators which may be fitted to the recorder.

The difficulty in controlling experimental parameters adequately for the desired reproducibility of peak areas has led to the use of internal standards in quantitative GLC. A known quantity of an additional compound is added to the unknown sample, and the ratios of sample peak areas (or heights) to that of the internal standard are determined. Calibration plots of percentages of components vs. such ratios are then referred to. The idea is that uncontrolled variables that influence sample peaks will affect the internal standard in the same way. The compound selected as the standard must be resolved from the sample components by the column, but it is desirable that its retention not be greatly different from those of the unknown solutes.

The detector sensitivity is different for various compounds, as may be inferred from Table 17.2. Thus there is no simple way to relate peak areas with percentages of components in the sample in an absolute sense. Calibration based upon areas obtained with known quantities of the components is usually required if more than semiquantitative results are desired.

The applications of GLC are too ubiquitous to permit more than listing a few examples here. In the first papers on the subject, Martin and his colleagues reported the separation of a long series of fatty acids ranging from formic (C_1) up to those containing C_{12}, and a series of amines. The petroleum companies followed shortly with analyses of hydrocarbon mixtures that were practically impossible by classical techniques such as distillation. Since the early 1950's, the field has expanded at an exponential rate. Many compounds are sufficiently volatile to submit directly to GLC, and many others are readily converted into volatile derivatives. Amino acids, for example, can be determined by GLC following a simple chemical step in which the methyl esters are formed using reagents such as diazomethane. Steroids have recently yielded to GLC. The determination of pesticide residues on foods and pollutants in the atmosphere are among other examples. Various drugs in body fluid samples are determined by GLC following extraction into suitable organic solvents. Another important medical application is the analysis of respiratory gases, for example, during anesthesia or during the recovery period. Concentrations of oxygen, carbon dioxide, and anesthetic gases such as ether or nitrous oxide are obtained very rapidly, while they are still of critical interest to the operating team.

Most inorganic samples are not sufficiently volatile to permit direct application of GLC, although some work has been done at very high temperatures using molten salts or eutectic mixtures as the stationary liquid phase. Halides of some elements such as tin, titanium, arsenic, and antimony are fairly volatile and have been separated by GLC. The determination of boron by formation of volatile esters such as methyl or ethyl borate is an obvious application that no one seems to have reported yet. A number of metals such as beryllium, aluminum, copper, iron, chromium, and cobalt have been subjected to GLC in the form of fairly volatile chelate compounds with acetylacetone and its fluorinated derivatives.[4] For example, aluminum, iron, and copper have been determined in alloys by dissolution of the sample followed by extraction of the metals into a chloroform solution of trifluoro-acetylacetone which is then chromatographed.[5] Relative errors of the order of 0.2 to 3% were reported.

[4] R. W. Moshier and R. E. Sievers, *Gas Chromatography of Metal Chelates*, Pergamon Press, Oxford, 1965.
[5] R. W. Moshier and J. E. Schwarberg, *Talanta*, **13**, 445 (1966).

ION EXCHANGE CHROMATOGRAPHY

Ion exchange resins

A wide variety of materials, both natural and synthetic, organic and inorganic, exhibit ion exchange behavior, but in the research laboratory, where uniformity from one batch to another is important, the preferred ion exchangers are usually synthetic materials known as ion exchange resins. The resins are prepared by introducing ionizable groups into an organic polymer matrix.

The polymerization of styrene yields a linear polymer:

$$CH=CH_2 \qquad \cdots\cdots-CH-CH_2-CH-CH_2-CH-CH_2-CH-\cdots\cdots$$

Styrene   **Polystyrene**

The addition of a bifunctional monomer such as divinylbenzene to the polymerization mix, on the other hand, links together the styrene chains and yields a material with a 3-dimensional network structure:

$$CH=CH_2 \qquad CH=CH_2$$

$$+$$

$$CH=CH_2$$

$$\cdots\cdots-CH-CH_2-CH-CH_2-CH$$

$$\cdots\cdots-CH-CH_2-CH-CH_2-CH-CH_2-CH-\cdots\cdots$$

$$\cdots\cdots-CH-CH_2-CH-CH_2-CH-CH_2-CH-CH_2-\cdots\cdots$$

By varying the divinylbenzene content, the degree of cross-linking can be controlled quite reproducibly. General-purpose resins usually contain 8 to 12% divinylbenzene, and are commonly referred to as 8 to 12% "cross-linked." The resins are made in the form of spherical beads by the process of emulsion or pearl polymerization. The bead diameter is controlled; it is usually in the range of 0.1 to 0.5 mm, although other sizes can be made for special purposes.

To prepare a typical cation exchange resin, the polymer is sulfonated to introduce $-SO_3H$ groups into the aromatic rings. Because these sulfonic acid groups are highly polar, the polymer thus acquires a high affinity for water. When the resin particles are suspended in water, they actually increase in size because of the water uptake. This swelling is limited, however, by the cross-linking; the resin cannot swell indefinitely until it disperses as some linear polyelectrolytes do.

The arylsulfonic acids are strong acids. Thus these groups are ionized when water penetrates the resin beads:

$$R-SO_3H + H_2O \rightleftarrows R-SO_3^- + H_3O^+$$

But, unlike ordinary electrolytes, here the anion is permanently attached to the immovable polymer matrix and it cannot migrate through the aqueous phase within the pores of the resin. This fixation of the anion in turn restricts the mobility of the cation, H_3O^+. Electrical neutrality is maintained within the resin, and H_3O^+ will not leave the resin particle unless it is replaced by some other cation.

The introduction of basic groups into the polymer yields anion exchange materials. One of the common strong base anion exchangers may be represented as

$$R-\underset{}{\bigcirc}-CH_2-\overset{\overset{\displaystyle CH_3}{|}}{\underset{\underset{\displaystyle CH_3}{|}}{N^+}}-CH_3 \qquad X^-$$

where X^- is an anion such as OH^-, Cl^-, or NO_3^-. The ion which is not fixed to the polymer matrix is often called the "counter ion."

Ion exchange equilibrium

Selectivity coefficient. Suppose a resin containing the exchangeable counter ion B is placed in a solution containing ion A of the same charge. The exchange reaction takes place,

$$\underset{\text{Solution}}{A} + \underset{\substack{\text{Resin} \\ \text{phase}}}{RB} = \underset{\substack{\text{Resin} \\ \text{phase}}}{RA} + \underset{\text{Solution}}{B}$$

and equilibrium will be attained with some of each ion in the resin phase and some in solution, for which we may write an equilibrium constant,

$$K = \frac{a_{A_r} \times a_{B_s}}{a_{B_r} \times a_{A_s}}$$

where a_{A_r} represents the activity of ion A in the resin phase and a_{A_s} its activity in the solution outside the resin pores. This expression can be written

$$K = \frac{X_{A_r} \times (B)_s}{X_{B_r} \times (A)_s} \times \frac{\gamma_{A_r} \times \gamma_{B_s}}{\gamma_{B_r} \times \gamma_{A_s}}$$

or

$$K = Q \times \frac{\gamma_{A_r}\gamma_{B_s}}{\gamma_{B_r}\gamma_{A_s}}$$

where X_{A_r} and X_{B_r} are the concentrations in mole fraction in the resin phase, parentheses mean molal concentrations in the external solution, and γ is the activity coefficient. The term Q is called the concentration quotient, or "practical selectivity coefficient." Some workers use the term "selectivity coefficient" to refer to the product of Q and the activity coefficient ratio of the ions in solution:

$$Q_\gamma = Q \frac{\gamma_{B_s}}{\gamma_{A_s}} = K \frac{\gamma_{B_r}}{\gamma_{A_r}}$$

At low concentrations of the ions in solution, $Q_\gamma \cong Q$ since the activity coefficients approach unity.

If the Donnan theory is applied to the ion exchange equilibrium, the value of K should be unity. Hence the variation in Q_γ can be interpreted as depending upon the ratio of the activity coefficients of the ions in the resin phase.

It is clear why Q_γ values are called selectivity coefficients: If Q_γ is large, the resin is showing a preference for ion A; if Q_γ is small, the selectivity of the resin favors ion B. We may never speak of the tendency of a resin to pick up a certain ion without noting that there is already another ion in the resin; that is, we should consider, not the tendency for the resin to pick up ion A in an absolute sense, but rather the tendency to pick up A at the expense of ion B. The tendency to pick up ion A will be different if the resin phase contains some other ion C instead of B as the counter ion.

Distribution ratio. However, we can put a certain ion on a resin and then compare a series of other ions using this as a reference. For the ions in this series we may simply write distribution ratios:

$$D = \frac{\text{Concentration of an ion in the resin}}{\text{Concentration of the same ion in solution}}$$

The conventional units of D are

$$\frac{\text{Amount/kg of dry resin}}{\text{Amount/l of solution}}$$

The "amount" term may be in mg, mols, or whatever, since its units cancel in the D ratio.

A distribution ratio with different units is sometimes used, with the symbol D_V.

$$D_V = \frac{\text{Amount/l of resin bed}}{\text{Amount/l of solution}}$$

The conversion factor for D to D_V is the so-called bed density, ρ,

$$D_V = D \times \rho$$

where ρ is in kg of dry resin per liter of resin bed.

The significant aspect of ion exchangers is, of course, their selectivity; i.e., D values are different for various ions and hence separations may be accomplished by ion exchange.

Factors in selectivity

Ionic charge. Neutral molecules can find their way into the pores of an ion exchange resin, but they are not subject to forces so strong as those acting on ions, and in general they can be washed out by water or some other solvent. Solutes in the resin which are not so strongly held as ions are said to be "sorbed"; the pick-up of such solutes by the resin is called "sorption." Sorption can sometimes be used to effect separations, but in this discussion we are concerned only with legitimate ion exchange. Of course the sign of the charge on an ion is important in selectivity, but this is so obvious as to be trivial. A cation cannot participate in exchange on an anion exchange resin; it might find its way into the resin pores by some sort of general electrolyte sorption, but it would not be strongly held and could be washed out with water.

In a series of ions which have the proper sign to act as true counter ions, the magnitude of the charge is important. Normally, the resin prefers the ion of higher charge. Thus the extent of exchange with, say, H_3O^+, would decrease in the order

$$Th^{4+} > Al^{3+} > Ca^{++} > Na^+$$

provided proper allowance was made for other factors such as concentration. There are exceptions to this, but it is a good rule-of-thumb under ordinary conditions.

Ionic radius. With a series of ions of the same charge, the resin still shows selectivity. For example, with the alkali metals, the following order is generally found with cation exchange resins:

$$Cs^+ > Rb^+ > K^+ > Na^+ > Li^+$$

The important factor here is probably the radius of the ion; the smaller an ion of given charge, the more strongly it will be held by the resin. At first glance, the above order may not appear consistent with this statement, which would imply that Cs^+ is a smaller ion than Li^+. The usual values of ionic radii, however, are obtained by X-ray diffraction studies of solid crystals, and these "crystallographic" or "naked" radii are not the right ones to use here. The ions in solution are hydrated, and it is the radius of the hydrated ion that determines the ion exchange behavior. Such hydrated radii are much more difficult to measure, but estimates are available. While the naked radius of Li^+ is 0.68 A, the hydrated radius is about 10 A; the naked and hydrated radii for Cs^+ are 1.65 A and 5.05 A, respectively.

Column behavior

Ion exchange experiments can be carried out on a batch basis or by continuous flow through a column. Since one equilibrium step seldom accomplishes the desired separation, the column technique is by far the more efficient. The general approach involves introducing the sample at the top of the ion exchange column followed by elution of the sample components with a continual flow of moving liquid phase which is called the eluent. If the flow rate is constant and not too fast, and if the value of D for a particular solute is constant, independent of its concentration, the elution curve approximates the Gaussian shape, as shown in Figure 17.8. Such a curve

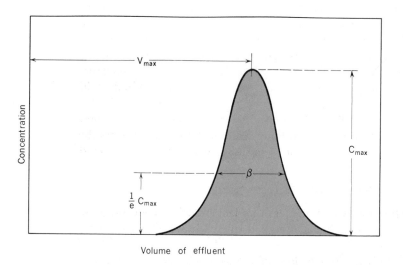

Fig. 17.8. Elution curve of an ion in ion exchange chromatography.

might be obtained by allowing the effluent solution from the column to flow continuously through an appropriate detector, or by collecting effluent fractions in a series of vessels for analysis by some appropriate technique. The abscissa in Figure 17.8 may be time or volume of effluent. The latter is often given in column volume units rather than ml. One column volume is simply the volume of the resin bed in the column, i.e., the product of the cross-sectional area and the length of the column.

As shown in Figure 17.8, V_{max} is the volume at which maximum concentration, C_{max}, is reached in the effluent solution. The band width, β, is the width at a particular height, $(1/e)C_{max}$, where e is the base of natural logarithms. It has been shown as a result of theoretical work by Glueckauf that the number of theoretical plates, n, may be estimated using the equation

$$n = 8 \left(\frac{V_{max}}{\beta} \right)^2$$

(Notice the similarity to the equation for estimating n in GLC; the different constant, 8 instead of 16, arises from the different place where the width of the band is measured.)

The theoretical plate idea is the same here as described previously: HETP is that length of column in which is accomplished the same degree of separation of two solutes as would have been achieved in one equilibrium step. The number of plates in a column is not constant, but varies with flow rate and even depends to some extent upon the nature of the ions being studied. However, it is, as in GLC, a convenient measure of column efficiency. In typical ion exchange columns, HETP is roughly of the same order as the diameter of the resin beads, perhaps $\sim$0.1 mm. This means that a large number of plates is obtained with a fairly short column.

Some writers refer to the elution constant, E, defined as follows:

$$E = \frac{d \times A}{V}$$

where A is the cross-sectional area of the column in cm^2 and d is the distance in cm down the column that a solute band has travelled after the passage of V ml of effluent. When the ion band has travelled all the way through the column and just emerged from the end, then $d \times A = 1$ column volume and $V = V_{max}$, whence

$$E = \frac{1}{V_{max}}$$

The larger the elution constant, the smaller the volume of eluent required to elute the ion. Now, the more easily an ion is eluted from the column, the less its affinity must be for the resin. Thus we might expect some sort of inverse relation between E and D. Actually, it has been shown that

$$\frac{1}{E} = V_{max} = D\rho + i = D_v + i$$

where i is the fractional interstitial volume of the column, that is, the fraction of the column volume that is not physically occupied by the resin particles. It is difficult to measure i accurately; it is usually about 0.4. If we had an ion that was not held by the resin at all, i.e., $D = 0$, then V_{max} would equal i. However, all materials penetrate the resin to some degree, and D is rarely zero for any substance. Where D is large, the uncertainty in i is not very important from a practical viewpoint.

We may next inquire how many plates are required for a given separation. For two ions A and B that we wish to separate, we define the separation factor, S, as the ratio of the two distribution ratios,

$$S = \frac{D_A}{D_B}$$

It is customary to place the larger D in the numerator so that S is always greater than 1. Of course where $S = 1$, no separation would be possible. The extent to which two elution bands overlap will obviously depend upon S and upon n, the number of plates in the column. The smaller S is, the more plates are needed to maintain a given degree of separation. Consider two overlapping elution bands as shown in Figure 17.9. Glueckauf has shown

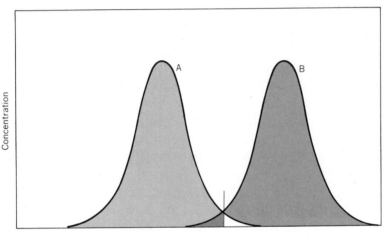

Fig. 17.9. Separation of ions A and B by ion exchange chromatography. Shaded area indicates contamination of A with B when cut is taken at the vertical line.

that for 0.01% overlap, i.e., 0.01% cross-contamination when a "cut" is made as shown in the figure, 20 plates are required when $S = 5$, 100 plates for $S = 2$, 1000 plates for $S = 1.2$, and 100,000 plates for $S = 1.02$.

Applications of ion exchange

Deionization of water. If a water sample containing dissolved electrolytes is passed through a column of a strong acid cation exchanger in the hydrogen form, the resin will pick up the cations from the water and release H_3O^+ to the effluent. If the water is then passed through a column of strong base anion exchanger in the hydroxyl form, the resin will pick up anions and release OH^- to the water. The H_3O^+ and the OH^- combine, of course, and thus a water sample very low in ions emerges from the process. It is more efficient to pass the water through a single column containing a mixture of cation and anion exchange resins; this is called "monobed deionization." In this process, OH^- from the anion exchanger lowers the H_3O^+ from the cation exchanger while the water is still encountering the resin, and similarly H_3O^+ lowers OH^-. In other words, the two exchange processes tend to drive each other:

$$\left.\begin{array}{l} RH + M^+ \rightleftharpoons RM + H^+ \\ ROH + A^- \rightleftharpoons RA + OH^- \end{array}\right\} \longrightarrow H_2O$$

The exchange equilibria are displaced toward the right, and deionization is more complete than would be the case if the two resins were in separate columns. Deionized water prepared by ion exchange is generally considerably lower in electrolytes than the best distilled water. Such deionized water is not necessarily extremely pure, however, since nonelectrolytes and colloidal matter may pass through the resin bed. Traces of unpolymerized organic matter may slowly bleed out of the resins. Replaceable cartridges for monobed deionization are on the market, ready to attach to the laboratory water supply.

Purification of other reagents. Aqueous solutions of nonelectrolytes, e.g., sucrose or ethanol, can be freed of ionic impurities by means of ion exchange columns. Small ions can sometimes be removed from polyelectrolytes such as proteins by means of resins which are cross-linked sufficiently to prevent the large molecules from penetrating the pores. Many other examples can be found in the literature.

Concentration of traces. Sometimes analyses are required on sample solutions that are so dilute that the usual measurements are not sufficiently sensitive. An example might be the determination of certain trace metals in sea water. It is often possible to pass a large volume of the sample through an ion exchange column which picks up, say, all of the metal ions. These metals are then eluted from the resin in a small volume of an effective eluent, perhaps strong acid. The process may well be cleaner and entail less loss of material than concentrating the metals by boiling off the solvent, by coprecipitation, or other techniques.

Separation of interfering ions. By means of ion exchange, it is often relatively simple to replace an ion that interferes in a subsequent part of an analysis with one which is innocuous. For example, phosphate interferes in certain methods for determining iron. By passing the solution through an anion exchanger in the chloride form, phosphate may be exchanged for chloride and its interference eliminated.

Separations by ion exchange chromatography. Ion exchange columns have provided separations, for both analytical and preparative purposes, that were extremely difficult or even impossible by older techniques. The separation of the chemically very similar rare earth elements is one of the most familiar examples. The amino acids are routinely separated on ion exchange columns; this is the basis of the highly-automated "amino acid analyzers" which are a fixture in many biochemical laboratories.

In many cases, solution chemistry can be combined with ion exchange to yield interesting separations. Elution of metals from cation exchangers by solutions containing complexing agents is an example of this. The rare earth separation was first accomplished in this way: Elution with a citrate buffer led to improved separation by combining slight differences in exchange behavior of the rare earth metals with slight differences in the stabilities of their citrate complexes. Kraus and his co-workers have shown that many interesting separations of metals are possible using anion exchangers and HCl solutions, where some of the metals form anionic chloro complexes. Many more applications of ion exchange chromatography may be found in the references at the end of this chapter.

THIN LAYER CHROMATOGRAPHY

GLC and ion exchange have been discussed in some detail as two examples of chromatographic processes. Space does not permit a thorough treatment of the topic, but we may mention thin layer chromatography or TLC as a different sort of chromatographic process which may help to round out the student's appreciation of the subject. TLC appears to be deceptively simple; it is easy to do, and the theory is relatively unsophisticated. Yet it has rapidly become one of the really powerful tools available to the chemist for solving difficult problems.

The separation medium is a layer perhaps 0.1 to 0.3 mm thick of an adsorbent solid on a glass plate. A typical plate is 8 × 2 inches. Typical solids are silica gel and alumina. The glass plates are coated with an aqueous suspension of the solid, which may contain a binder such as plaster of paris, and then dried in an oven. The sample, generally a mixture of organic compounds, is applied at one end of the plate as a small volume of a solution, usually a few microliters, containing a few micrograms of the compounds. A hypodermic syringe or a special applicator pipet may be employed. The sample spot is dried, and then the end of the plate is dipped into a suitable moving phase. The solvent moves up the thin layer of solid on the plate, and as it moves, sample solutes are carried along at rates depending upon their solubilities in the moving phase and their interactions with the solid.

After the liquid has migrated perhaps 10 cm, it is often found that solutes have become separated by their differential migration. The process may require less than half an hour. There must be some way of locating the separated solutes on the thin layer plate. If they are highly-colored compounds, they may be seen visually. Sometimes examination of the plate under an ultraviolet lamp will disclose spots which fluoresce; and sometimes the plate may be sprayed with a reagent that reacts with the solutes to form colored spots.

In cases where development of the chromatogram with one moving phase fails to yield a complete separation, a two-dimensional approach is possible. The sample is spotted at one corner of a square plate, and the solutes are moved up along one edge of the plate by means of one moving phase. The plate is then turned at right angles and dipped into a second moving phase, whereby solute spots are moved to various positions in what is sometimes called loosely a "fingerprint" of the sample.

Various solutes are characterized in TLC by their R_f values. The R_f value of a solute is defined as the ratio of the distance a solute moves to the distance moved by the moving phase in the same length of time. If two samples, say a known compound and an unknown, have identical R_f values on several different solids in several moving solvent phases, the probability is great that the two are identical.

TLC has achieved great popularity in a short period of time as all sorts of chemists have realized its power. Apparatus for coating the glass plates is commercially available, and ready-made plates can be purchased. Sheets of coated material, on plastic rather than glass, can be purchased and cut to size by the user. New developments appear at frequent intervals. Larger quantities of mixtures can be separated on plates with thicker coatings, although with some loss of efficiency. One of the most attractive aspects of TLC is its speed; development of a plate often requires only half an hour or even less. Quantitative TLC is rapidly developing. A spot may be scraped from a plate, the solute eluted from the solid material, and an analysis, perhaps spectrophotometric, accomplished in a few minutes.

REFERENCES

1. I. Rosenthal, A. R. Weiss, and V. R. Usdin, "Chromatography: General Principles"; B. J. Mair, "Chromatography: Columnar Liquid-Solid Adsorption Processes"; W. Reiman III and A. C. Breyer, "Chromatography: Columnar Liquid-Solid Ion Exchange Processes"; H. J. Pazdera and W. H. McMullen, "Chromatography: Paper"; C. E. Bennett, S. Dal Nogare and L. W. Safranski, "Chromatography: Gas," Chapters 33, 34, 35, 36, and 37, Part I, Vol. III of *Treatise on Analytical Chemistry*, I. M. Kolthoff, P. J. Elving, and E. B. Sandell, Eds., Interscience Publishers, Inc., New York, 1961.

2. E. Lederer and M. Lederer, *Chromatography*, Elsevier Publishing Co., Amsterdam, 1955.

3. R. J. Block, E. L. Durrum and G. Zweig, *A Manual of Paper Chromatography and Paper Electrophoresis*, Academic Press, Inc., New York, 1955.

4. S. Dal Nogare and R. S. Juvet, Jr., *Gas-Liquid Chromatography*, Interscience Publishers, Inc., New York, 1962.

5. A. I. M. Keulemans, *Gas Chromatography*, C. G. Verver, Ed., 2nd Ed., Reinhold Publishing Corp., New York, 1959.

6. E. Stahl, Ed., *Thin-Layer Chromatography; A Laboratory Handbook*, Springer-Verlag, New York, Berlin, 1965.

7. O. Samuelson, *Ion Exchange Separations in Analytical Chemistry*, John Wiley & Sons, Inc., New York, 1963.

8. F. Helfferich, *Ion Exchange*, McGraw-Hill Book Co., Inc., New York, 1962.

9. K. Kraus, in *Trace Analysis*, J. H. Yoe and H. J. Koch, Jr., Eds., John Wiley & Sons, Inc., 1957, pp. 34–101.

10. R. Kunin, *Ion Exchange Resins*, 2nd Ed., New York, 1958.

QUESTIONS

1. Suppose that a particular solution-solid adsorption process is correctly described by an equation of the Freundlich type and that a particular gas-liquid interaction follows Henry's law. Compare the shapes of the elution curves obtained in chromatographic experiments based upon these two processes and explain your comments.

2. Explain the difference between the selectivity coefficient, K_{AB}, of an ion exchange resin with regard to two ions, A and B, and the distribution coefficient, D, for an individual ion.

3. Explain clearly what is meant by height equivalent to a theoretical plate in connection with a continuous-flow separation process, such as ion exchange chromatography.

4. By discussing the factors causing band spreading in GLC, show qualitatively that it is reasonable to expect that there will be an optimal carrier gas flow rate. Would you predict a change in the optimal flow rate if the temperature of the column were raised? Explain.

5. Helium is much more expensive than nitrogen. In GLC, separations are as good (often better) with nitrogen carrier as with helium. Why then is helium the commonest carrier gas in GLC?

6. If a small sample is skillfully introduced onto a GLC column as a so-called "plug," it is generally supposed to be distributed uniformly through the first few plates of the column. When the sample emerges from the column, the detector shows us that it has spread out. Describe the factors that cause spreading or broadening of the sample band as it travels down the column; discuss the relative importance of these factors under various operating conditions, and explain how an operator who is knowledgeable can exercise some control over the spreading.

7. State and briefly explain the consequences of each of the following "goofs" upon the performance of the indicated separation technique:

(a) A sample containing a mixture of hydrocarbons is *slowly* injected into a gas chromatograph.

(b) An appreciable amount of ground-up firebrick which had not been loaded with liquid substrate is accidentally used along with some good material in packing a GLC column.

(c) After some previous work, an alumina column had been allowed to dry out; an organic chemist then uses the column without any preliminary treatment to separate some compounds by chromatography.

(d) A nitrogen cylinder is accidentally hooked up to a gas chromatograph rather than a helium cylinder.

8. Explain briefly the effect of a nonlinear isotherm upon the distribution coefficient for a two-phase partition process. How does a nonlinear isotherm affect the appearance of a chromatographic elution curve?

9. Kraus and Nelson (see reference 9) found that many cations are adsorbed on *anion* exchange resins from concentrated hydrochloric acid solutions. Suggest an explanation.

10. From the data in reference 9 suggest a scheme for separating potassium, silver (trace concentration), zinc, and cobalt, using an anion exchange resin and only hydrochloric acid solutions.

11. The different oxidation states of some elements can be separated by anion exchange. From the data in reference 9 suggest a method for separating (a) Sb(III) and Sb(V), and (b) Fe(III) and Fe(II).

12. It was learned in Chapter 15 that hydrous oxides are positively charged at low *p*H and negatively charged at high *p*H. Such substances can show anion and cation exchange properties at low and high *p*H values, respectively. How can you explain this behavior? [See K. A. Kraus and H. O. Phillips, *J. Am. Chem. Soc.*, **78**, 249 (1956).]

PROBLEMS

1. A 1.016-g sample of an anion exchange resin in the chloride form lost 0.3012 g of moisture when heated overnight at 60°C under vacuum. A sample of the undried resin weighing 0.6630 g was washed with nitric acid to remove the chloride. If 15.25 ml of 0.1000-M AgNO$_3$ was required to titrate the chloride, calculate the capacity of the dry resin in milliequivalents per gram.

2. A 5.00-ml solution containing a radioactive element is shaken with 100 mg of a cation resin. The original activity of the solution is 80,000 counts per ml, and after equilibration with the resin, the activity is 35,000 counts per ml. Calculate the distribution coefficient (weight) for this element.

3. The weight distribution coefficient of a certain metal ion on an anion exchange resin in 0.10-M HCl solution is 30. Given that 1.0 g of resin (dry) occupies a volume of 2.3 ml in a column and that the interstitial volume fraction is 0.40, calculate the volume of solution (cc) required to move a small amount of the cation from the top to the bottom of the column. The volume of the column is 5.0 ml.

4. A chromatogram obtained with a certain organic compound in a GLC experiment is shown below. Estimate the HETP in centimeters if the column was two meters long.

Fig. 17.10.

Detector response

0   2   4   6   8   10   12
Time after injection (arbitrary units)

5. A certain water sample contains the following ions at the listed concentrations:

Ion	mmol/l
Sulfate	0.020
Chloride	0.406
Nitrate	0.274
Calcium	0.140
Magnesium	0.080
Sodium	0.240
Potassium	0.040

500 ml of the water is passed through a column of a strong acid cation exchanger in the hydrogen form. Assuming complete exchange occurs, how many milliliters of 0.020-M NaOH will be required to titrate the column effluent?

6. The equilibrium constant for the reaction

$$Na^+ + HRes = NaRes + H^+$$

is 1.56 on a certain cation exchange resin. The resin is in the hydrogen form and has a capacity of 2.2 meq/ml. A thin layer of sodium ions is placed on top of a column whose volume is 6.0 ml. How many ml of 0.10-M HCl is required to elute the solute to its maximum concentration? The interstitial volume fraction is 0.4.

7. Given that an adsorption band of an element travels 10 cm down an ion exchange column of cross-sectional area 0.75 cm² upon passage of 75 ml of effluent. Calculate the volume distribution coefficient of the element if the interstitial volume fraction is 0.4.

Tables of Equilibrium Constants and Oxidation Potentials

Table 1   IONIZATION CONSTANTS OF WEAK ACIDS AND BASES (25°C)

Acid	Formula	K_a	pK_a	Conjugate base	K_b	pK_b
Acetic	CH_3COOH	1.8×10^{-5}	4.74	Acetate ion	5.6×10^{-10}	9.26
Ammonium ion	NH_4^+	5.6×10^{-10}	9.26	Ammonia	1.8×10^{-5}	4.74
Anilinium ion	$C_6H_5NH_3^+$	2.2×10^{-5}	4.66	Aniline	4.6×10^{-10}	9.34
Arsenic	H_3AsO_4	5.6×10^{-3}	2.26	Dihydrogen arsenate ion	1.8×10^{-12}	11.74
Dihydrogen arsenate ion	$H_2AsO_4^-$	1.7×10^{-7}	6.77	Monohydrogen arsenate ion	5.9×10^{-8}	7.23
Monohydrogen arsenate ion	$HAsO_4^=$	3×10^{-12}	11.5	Arsenate ion	3×10^{-3}	2.5
Arsenious	H_3AsO_3	6×10^{-10}	9.2	Dihydrogen arsenite ion	1.7×10^{-5}	4.8
Dihydrogen arsenite ion	$H_2AsO_3^-$	3×10^{-14}	13.5	Monohydrogen arsenite ion	3×10^{-1}	0.5
Benzoic	$HC_7H_5O_2$	6.6×10^{-5}	4.18	Benzoate ion	1.5×10^{-10}	9.82
Boric	H_3BO_3	5.8×10^{-10}	9.24	Dihydrogen borate ion	1.7×10^{-5}	4.76
Carbonic	H_2CO_3	4.6×10^{-7}	6.34	Bicarbonate ion	2.2×10^{-8}	7.66
Bicarbonate ion	HCO_3^-	4.4×10^{-11}	10.36	Carbonate ion	2.3×10^{-4}	3.64
Chloroacetic, mono	$CH_2ClCOOH$	1.5×10^{-3}	2.82	Monochloroacetate ion	7×10^{-12}	11.18
Chloroacetic, di	$CHCl_2COOH$	5×10^{-2}	1.3	Dichloroacetate ion	2×10^{-13}	12.7
Chloroacetic, tri	CCl_3COOH	2×10^{-1}	0.7	Trichloroacetate ion	5×10^{-14}	13.3
Chromic	H_2CrO_4	1.8×10^{-1}	0.74	Bichromate ion	5.6×10^{-14}	13.26
Bichromate ion	$HCrO_4^-$	3.2×10^{-7}	6.49	Chromate ion	3.1×10^{-8}	7.51
Citric	$H_3C_6H_5O_7$	8.4×10^{-4}	3.08	Dihydrogen citrate ion	1.2×10^{-11}	10.92
Dihydrogen citrate ion	$H_2C_6H_5O_7^-$	1.8×10^{-5}	4.74	Monohydrogen citrate ion	5.6×10^{-10}	9.26
Monohydrogen citrate ion	$HC_6H_5O_7^=$	4.0×10^{-6}	5.40	Citrate ion	2.5×10^{-9}	8.60
Cyanic	$HOCN$	2×10^{-4}	3.7	Cyanate ion	5×10^{-11}	10.3
Diethylammonium ion	$C_4H_{10}NH_2^+$	7.7×10^{-12}	11.11	Diethylamine	1.3×10^{-3}	2.89
Dimethylammonium ion	$C_2H_6NH_2^+$	1.9×10^{-11}	10.72	Dimethylamine	5.2×10^{-4}	3.28
Ethylammonium ion	$C_2H_5NH_3^+$	1.8×10^{-11}	10.75	Ethylamine	5.6×10^{-4}	3.25
Formic	$HCOOH$	1.8×10^{-4}	3.74	Formate ion	5.6×10^{-11}	10.26
Hydrazinium ion	$N_2H_5^+$	3.3×10^{-9}	8.48	Hydrazine	3.0×10^{-6}	5.52
Hydrocyanic	HCN	7.2×10^{-10}	9.14	Cyanide ion	1.4×10^{-5}	4.86
Hydrofluoric	HF	6×10^{-4}	3.22	Fluoride ion	1.7×10^{-11}	10.78

Acid	Formula	K_a	pK_a	Conjugate base	K_b	pK_b
Hydrogen sulfide	H_2S	9×10^{-8}	7.0	Bisulfide ion	1.1×10^{-7}	7.0
Bisulfide ion	HS^-	1×10^{-15}	15.0	Sulfide ion	10	-1.0
Hypochlorous	$HOCl$	3×10^{-8}	7.5	Hypochlorite ion	3×10^{-7}	6.5
Methylammonium ion	$CH_3NH_3^+$	2×10^{-11}	10.7	Methylamine	5×10^{-4}	3.3
Nitrous	HNO_2	4.5×10^{-4}	3.35	Nitrite ion	2.2×10^{-11}	10.65
Oxalic	$H_2C_2O_4$	6.5×10^{-2}	1.19	Bioxalate ion	1.5×10^{-13}	12.81
Bioxalate ion	$HC_2O_4^-$	6.1×10^{-5}	4.21	Oxalate ion	1.6×10^{-10}	9.79
Phenol	C_6H_5OH	1.3×10^{-10}	9.89	Phenolate ion	7.7×10^{-5}	4.11
Phosphoric	H_3PO_4	7.5×10^{-3}	2.12	Dihydrogen phosphate ion	1.3×10^{-12}	11.88
Dihydrogen phosphate ion	$H_2PO_4^-$	6.2×10^{-8}	7.21	Monohydrogen phosphate ion	1.6×10^{-7}	6.79
Monohydrogen phosphate ion	$HPO_4^=$	4.8×10^{-13}	12.32	Phosphate ion	2.1×10^{-2}	1.68
Phthalic	$C_6H_4(COOH)_2$	1.3×10^{-3}	2.89	Biphthalate ion	7.7×10^{-12}	11.11
Biphthalate ion	$C_6H_4C_2O_2H^-$	3.9×10^{-6}	5.41	Phthalate ion	2.6×10^{-9}	8.59
Pyridinium ion	$C_5H_5NH^+$	7.1×10^{-6}	5.15	Pyridine	1.4×10^{-9}	8.85
Sulfuric	H_2SO_4	Strong	—	Bisulfate ion	Weak	—
Bisulfate ion	HSO_4^-	1.2×10^{-2}	1.92	Sulfate ion	8.3×10^{-13}	12.08
Sulfurous	H_2SO_3	1.7×10^{-2}	1.77	Bisulfite ion	5.9×10^{-13}	12.23
Bisulfite ion	HSO_3^-	6.2×10^{-8}	7.21	Sulfite ion	1.6×10^{-7}	6.79
Tartaric	$H_2C_4H_4O_6$	9.4×10^{-4}	3.03	Bitartrate ion	1.1×10^{-11}	10.97
Bitartrate ion	$HC_4H_4O_6^-$	2.9×10^{-5}	4.54	Tartrate ion	3.4×10^{-10}	9.46

Table
2

STEP-WISE FORMATION CONSTANTS
OF COMPLEX IONS †

Ligand	Cation	Ionic strength	Temp. °C	Logarithm of equilibrium constant			
				K_1	K_2	K_3	K_4
Ammonia	Ag^+	1.0	25	3.37	3.78		
	Cd^{++}	2.1	25	2.74	2.21	1.37	1.13
	Cu^{++}	1.0	25	4.27	3.55	2.90	2.18
	Ni^{++}	1.0	25	2.36	1.90	1.55	1.23
	Zn^{++}	2.0	30	2.37	2.44	2.50	2.15
Chloride	Ag^+	0.2	25	2.85	1.87	0.32	0.86
	Fe^{3+}	1.0	25	0.62	0.11	−1.40	−1.92
	Hg^{++}	0.5	25	6.74	6.48	0.85	1.00
	Pb^{++}	1.0	25	0.88	0.61	−0.40	−0.15
Cyanide	Cd^{++}	3.0	25	5.48	5.14	4.56	3.58
	Hg^{++}	0.1	20	18.00	16.70	3.83	2.98
EDTA	Ag^+	0.1	20	7.32			
	Al^{3+}	0.1	20	16.13			
	Ba^{++}	0.1	20	7.76			
	Ca^{++}	0.1	20	10.70			
	Cd^{++}	0.1	20	16.59			
	Co^{++}	0.1	20	16.21			
	Cu^{++}	0.1	20	18.79			
	Fe^{++}	0.1	20	14.33			
	Fe^{3+}	0.1	20	25.1			
	Hg^{++}	0.1	20	21.80			
	Mg^{++}	0.1	20	8.69			
	Mn^{++}	0.1	20	13.58			
	Ni^{++}	0.1	20	18.56			
	Pb^{++}	0.1	20	18.3			
	Sr^{++}	0.1	20	8.63			
	Th^{4+}	0.1	20	23.2			
	TiO^{++}	0.1	—	17.3			
	VO^{++}	0.1	20	18.77			
	Zn^{++}	0.1	20	16.26			
Thiocyanate	Ag^+	4.0	25	4.59	3.70	1.77	1.20
	Fe^{3+}	1.8	18	1.96	2.02	< −0.41	> −0.14
	Ni^{++}	1.0	20	1.18	0.46	0.17	
Thiosulfate	Ag^+	0.2	20	10.00	3.36		

† Step-wise constants are defined as follows:

$$M^{4+} + X^- \rightleftarrows MX^{3+} \qquad K_1 = \frac{[MX^{3+}]}{[M^{4+}][X^-]}$$

$$MX^{3+} + X^- \rightleftarrows MX_2^{2+} \qquad K_2 = \frac{[MX_2^{2+}]}{[MX^{3+}][X^-]}$$

etc.

Compound	Formula	Solubility product constant, K_{sp}
Aluminum hydroxide	$Al(OH)_3$	5×10^{-33}
Barium carbonate	$BaCO_3$	7×10^{-9}
Barium chromate	$BaCrO_4$	2×10^{-10}
Barium fluoride	BaF_2	3×10^{-6}
Barium iodate	$Ba(IO_3)_2$	6×10^{-10}
Barium oxalate	BaC_2O_4	2×10^{-7}
Barium sulfate	$BaSO_4$	1×10^{-10}
Cadmium carbonate	$CdCO_3$	3×10^{-14}
Cadmium oxalate	CdC_2O_4	1×10^{-8}
Cadmium sulfide	CdS	5×10^{-27}
Calcium carbonate	$CaCO_3$	5×10^{-9}
Calcium fluoride	CaF_2	4×10^{-11}
Calcium oxalate	CaC_2O_4	2×10^{-9}
Calcium sulfate	$CaSO_4$	6×10^{-5}
Cupric hydroxide	$Cu(OH)_2$	2×10^{-19}
Cupric iodate	$Cu(IO_3)_2$	1×10^{-7}
Cupric oxalate	CuC_2O_4	3×10^{-8}
Cupric sulfide	CuS	4×10^{-38}
Cuprous bromide	$CuBr$	6×10^{-9}
Cuprous chloride	$CuCl$	3×10^{-7}
Cuprous iodide	CuI	1×10^{-12}
Cuprous thiocyanate	$CuSCN$	4×10^{-14}
Ferric hydroxide	$Fe(OH)_3$	1×10^{-36}
Ferrous hydroxide	$Fe(OH)_2$	2×10^{-14}
Ferrous oxalate	FeC_2O_4	2×10^{-7}
Ferrous sulfide	FeS	4×10^{-19}
Lead carbonate	$PbCO_3$	2×10^{-13}
Lead chloride	$PbCl_2$	1×10^{-4}
Lead chromate	$PbCrO_4$	2×10^{-14}
Lead fluoride	PbF_2	5×10^{-8}
Lead hydroxide	$Pb(OH)_2$	3×10^{-16}
Lead iodate	$Pb(IO_3)_2$	3×10^{-13}
Lead sulfate	$PbSO_4$	2×10^{-8}
Lead sulfide	PbS	3×10^{-28}
Magnesium ammonium phosphate	$MgNH_4PO_4$	3×10^{-13}
Magnesium carbonate	$MgCO_3$	3×10^{-5}
Magnesium fluoride	MgF_2	7×10^{-9}
Magnesium hydroxide	$Mg(OH)_2$	1×10^{-11}
Magnesium oxalate	$Mg(C_2O_4)_2$	9×10^{-5}
Manganous hydroxide	$Mn(OH)_2$	4×10^{-14}
Manganous sulfide	MnS	1×10^{-16}
Mercuric sulfide	HgS	3×10^{-52}
Mercurous bromide	Hg_2Br_2	3×10^{-23}
Mercurous chloride	Hg_2Cl_2	6×10^{-19}
Mercurous iodide	Hg_2I_2	7×10^{-29}

Compound	Formula	Solubility product constant, K_{sp}
Nickel sulfide	NiS	1×10^{-25}
Silver arsenate	Ag_3AsO_4	1×10^{-22}
Silver bromate	$AgBrO_3$	6×10^{-5}
Silver bromide	AgBr	4×10^{-13}
Silver carbonate	Ag_2CO_3	8×10^{-12}
Silver chloride	AgCl	1×10^{-10}
Silver chromate	Ag_2CrO_4	2×10^{-12}
Silver cyanide	$Ag[Ag(CN)_2]$	2×10^{-12}
Silver hydroxide	AgOH	2×10^{-8}
Silver iodate	$AgIO_3$	3×10^{-8}
Silver iodide	AgI	1×10^{-16}
Silver oxalate	$Ag_2C_2O_4$	5×10^{-12}
Silver sulfide	Ag_2S	1×10^{-48}
Silver thiocyanate	AgSCN	1×10^{-12}
Strontium carbonate	$SrCO_3$	2×10^{-9}
Strontium fluoride	SrF_2	3×10^{-9}
Strontium oxalate	SrC_2O_4	6×10^{-8}
Strontium sulfate	$SrSO_4$	3×10^{-7}
Thallous chloride	TlCl	2×10^{-4}
Thallous sulfide	Tl_2S	1×10^{-22}
Zinc carbonate	$ZnCO_3$	3×10^{-8}
Zinc hydroxide	$Zn(OH)_2$	2×10^{-14}
Zinc oxalate	ZnC_2O_4	3×10^{-9}
Zinc sulfide	ZnS	1×10^{-24}

Redox couple	$E°$
$F_2 + 2\,H^+ + 2\,e = 2\,HF(aq)$	3.06
$F_2 + 2\,e = 2\,F^-$	2.65
$O_3 + 2\,H^+ + 2\,e = O_2 + H_2O$	2.07
$S_2O_8^= + 2\,e = 2\,SO_4^=$	2.01
$Co^{3+} + e = Co^{++}$	1.82
$H_2O_2 + 2\,H^+ + 2\,e = 2\,H_2O$	1.77
$MnO_4^- + 4\,H^+ + 3\,e = MnO_2 + 2\,H_2O$	1.70
$PbO_2 + SO_4^= + 4\,H^+ + 2\,e = PbSO_4 + 2\,H_2O$	1.69
$Au^+ + e = Au$	1.68
$HClO_2 + 2\,H^+ + 2\,e = HClO + H_2O$	1.64
$HClO + H^+ + e = \frac{1}{2}\,Cl_2 + H_2O$	1.63
$Ce^{4+} + e = Ce^{3+}$	1.61
$Bi_2O_4 + 4\,H^+ + 2\,e = 2\,BiO^+ + 2\,H_2O$	1.59
$BrO_3^- + 6\,H^+ + 5\,e = \frac{1}{2}\,Br_2 + 3\,H_2O$	1.52
$MnO_4^- + 8\,H^+ + 5\,e = Mn^{++} + 4\,H_2O$	1.51
$PbO_2 + 4\,H^+ + 2\,e = Pb^{++} + 2\,H_2O$	1.46
$Cl_2 + 2\,e = 2\,Cl^-$	1.36
$Cr_2O_7^= + 14\,H^+ + 6\,e = 2\,Cr^{3+} + 7\,H_2O$	1.33
$MnO_2 + 4\,H^+ + 2\,e = Mn^{++} + 2\,H_2O$	1.23
$O_2 + 4\,H^+ + 4\,e = 2\,H_2O$	1.23
$IO_3^- + 6\,H^+ + 5\,e = \frac{1}{2}\,I_2 + 3\,H_2O$	1.20
$ClO_4^- + 2\,H^+ + 2\,e = ClO_3^- + H_2O$	1.19
$Br_2(aq) + 2\,e = 2\,Br^-$	1.09
$Br_2(liq) + 2\,e = 2\,Br^-$	1.07
$Br_3^- + 2\,e = 3\,Br^-$	1.05
$VO_2^+ + 2\,H^+ + e = VO^{++} + H_2O$	1.00
$AuCl_4^- + 3\,e = Au + 4\,Cl^-$	1.00
$NO_3^- + 4\,H^+ + 3\,e = NO + 2\,H_2O$	0.96
$NO_3^- + 3\,H^+ + 2\,e = HNO_2 + H_2O$	0.94
$2\,Hg^{++} + 2\,e = Hg_2^{++}$	0.92
$AuBr_4^- + 3\,e = Au + 4\,Br^-$	0.87
$Cu^{++} + I^- + e = CuI$	0.86
$NO_3^- + 2\,H^+ + e = NO_2 + H_2O$	0.80
$Ag^+ + e = Ag$	0.80
$Hg_2^{++} + 2\,e = 2\,Hg$	0.79
$Fe^{3+} + e = Fe^{++}$	0.77
$PtCl_4^= + 2\,e = Pt + 4\,Cl^-$	0.73
$Q + 2\,H^+ + 2\,e = H_2Q$	0.70
$PtBr_4^= + 2\,e = Pt + 4\,Br^-$	0.58
$MnO_4^- + e = MnO_4^=$	0.56
$I_3^- + 2\,e = 3\,I^-$	0.54
$I_2(s) + 2\,e = 2\,I^-$	0.54
$Cu^+ + e = Cu$	0.52
$4\,H_2SO_3 + 4\,H^+ + 6\,e = S_4O_6^= + 6\,H_2O$	0.51
$2\,H_2SO_3 + 2\,H^+ + 4\,e = S_2O_3^= + 3\,H_2O$	0.40
$Fe(CN)_6^{3-} + e = Fe(CN)_6^{4-}$	0.36
$VO^{++} + 2\,H^+ + e = V^{3+} + H_2O$	0.36
$Cu^{++} + 2\,e = Cu$	0.34
$Hg_2Cl_2 + 2\,e = 2\,Hg + 2\,Cl^-$	0.28
$IO_3^- + 3\,H_2O + 6\,e = I^- + 6\,OH^-$	0.26
$AgCl + e = Ag + Cl^-$	0.22
$HgBr_4^= + 2\,e = Hg + 4\,Br^-$	0.21
$SO_4^= + 4\,H^+ + 2\,e = H_2SO_3 + H_2O$	0.17
$Cu^{++} + e = Cu^+$	0.15
$Sn^{4+} + 2\,e = Sn^{++}$	0.15
$S + 2\,H^+ + 2\,e = H_2S$	0.14

Redox couple	$E°$
$CuCl + e = Cu + Cl^-$	0.14
$AgBr + e = Ag + Br^-$	0.10
$S_4O_6^= + 2\ e = 2\ S_2O_3^=$	0.08
$CuBr + e = Cu + Br^-$	0.03
$2\ H^+ + 2\ e = H_2$	0.00
$HgI_4^= + 2\ e = Hg + 4\ I^-$	-0.04
$Pb^{++} + 2\ e = Pb$	-0.13
$CrO_4^= + 4\ H_2O + 3\ e = Cr(OH)_3 + 5\ OH^-$	-0.13
$Sn^{++} + 2\ e = Sn$	-0.14
$AgI + e = Ag + I^-$	-0.15
$CuI + e = Cu + I^-$	-0.19
$Ni^{++} + 2\ e = Ni$	-0.25
$V^{3+} + e = V^{++}$	-0.26
$PbCl_2 + 2\ e = Pb + 2\ Cl^-$	-0.27
$Co^{++} + 2\ e = Co$	-0.28
$PbBr_2 + 2\ e = Pb + 2\ Br^-$	-0.28
$PbSO_4 + 2\ e = Pb + SO_4^=$	-0.36
$PbI_2 + 2\ e = Pb + 2\ I^-$	-0.37
$Cd^{++} + 2\ e = Cd$	-0.40
$Cr^{3+} + e = Cr^{++}$	-0.41
$Fe^{++} + 2\ e = Fe$	-0.44
$2\ CO_2(gas) + 2\ H^+ + 2\ e = H_2C_2O_4(aq)$	-0.49
$Cr^{3+} + 3\ e = Cr$	-0.74
$Zn^{++} + 2\ e = Zn$	-0.76
$Mn^{++} + 2\ e = Mn$	-1.18
$Al^{3+} + 3\ e = Al$	-1.66
$Mg^{++} + 2\ e = Mg$	-2.37
$Na^+ + e = Na$	-2.71
$Ca^{++} + 2\ e = Ca$	-2.87
$Sr^{++} + 2\ e = Sr$	-2.89
$Ba^{++} + 2\ e = Ba$	-2.90
$K^+ + e = K$	-2.93
$Li^+ + e = Li$	-3.05

† From W. M. Latimer's *Oxidation Potentials*, 2nd Ed., Prentice-Hall, Inc., Englewood Cliffs, N.J., 1952.

Redox systems	Standard potential	Formal potential	Solution
$Ce^{4+} + e = Ce^{3+}$	—	1.23	1-M HCl
		1.44	1-M H$_2$SO$_4$
		1.61	1-M HNO$_3$
		1.7	1-M HClO$_4$
$Fe^{3+} + e = Fe^{++}$	+0.771	0.68	1-M H$_2$SO$_4$
		0.700	1-M HCl
		0.732	1-M HClO$_4$
$Cr_2O_7^= + 14\ H^+ + 6\ e = 2\ Cr^{3+} + 7\ H_2O$	+1.33	1.00	1-M HCl
		1.05	2-M HCl
		1.08	3-M HCl
		1.08	0.5-M H$_2$SO$_4$
		1.15	4-M H$_2$SO$_4$
		1.03	1-M HClO$_4$
$Fe(CN)_6^{3-} + e = Fe(CN)_6^{4-}$	+0.356	0.48	0.01-M HCl
		0.56	0.1-M HCl
		0.71	1-M HCl
		0.72	1-M H$_2$SO$_4$
		0.72	1-M HClO$_4$
$H_3AsO_4 + 2\ H^+ + 2\ e = H_3AsO_3 + H_2O$	+0.559	0.557	1-M HCl
		0.557	1-M HClO$_4$
$TiO^{++} + 2\ H^+ + e = Ti^{3+} + H_2O$	+0.1	0.04	1-M H$_2$SO$_4$
$Pb^{2+} + 2\ e = Pb$	−0.126	−0.14	1-M HClO$_4$
$Sn^{2+} + 2\ e = Sn$	−0.136	−0.16	1-M HClO$_4$
$V^{3+} + e = V^{2+}$	−0.255	−0.21	1-M HClO$_4$

II *appendix*

INTERNATIONAL ATOMIC WEIGHTS, 1961
BASED ON THE ATOMIC MASS OF $^{12}C = 12$

Element	Symbol	Atomic number	Atomic weight‡
Actinium	Ac	89	(227)
Aluminum	Al	13	26.9815
Americium	Am	95	(243)
Antimony	Sb	51	121.75
Argon	Ar	18	39.948
Arsenic	As	33	74.9216
Astatine	At	85	(210)
Barium	Ba	56	137.34
Berkelium	Bk	97	(247)
Beryllium	Be	4	9.0122
Bismuth	Bi	83	208.980
Boron	B	5	10.811*
Bromine	Br	35	79.909†
Cadmium	Cd	48	112.40
Calcium	Ca	20	40.08
Californium	Cf	98	(249)
Carbon	C	6	12.01115*
Cerium	Ce	58	140.12
Cesium	Cs	55	132.905
Chlorine	Cl	17	35.453†
Chromium	Cr	24	51.996†
Cobalt	Co	27	58.9332
Copper	Cu	29	63.54
Curium	Cm	96	(247)
Dysprosium	Dy	66	162.50
Einsteinium	Es	99	(254)
Erbium	Er	68	167.26
Europium	Eu	63	151.96
Fermium	Fm	100	(253)
Fluorine	F	9	18.9984
Francium	Fr	87	(223)
Gadolinium	Gd	64	157.25
Gallium	Ga	31	69.72
Germanium	Ge	32	72.59
Gold	Au	79	196.967
Hafnium	Hf	72	178.49
Helium	He	2	4.0026
Holmium	Ho	67	164.930
Hydrogen	H	1	1.00797*
Indium	In	49	114.82
Iodine	I	53	126.9044
Iridium	Ir	77	192.2
Iron	Fe	26	55.847†
Krypton	Kr	36	83.80
Lanthanum	La	57	138.91
Lawrencium	Lw	103	(257)
Lead	Pb	82	207.19
Lithium	Li	3	6.939
Lutetium	Lu	71	174.97
Magnesium	Mg	12	24.312
Manganese	Mn	25	54.9380
Mendelevium	Md	101	(256)
Mercury	Hg	80	200.59
Molybdenum	Mo	42	95.94
Neodymium	Nd	60	144.24

Element	Symbol	Atomic number	Atomic weight‡
Neon	Ne	10	20.183
Neptunium	Np	93	(237)
Nickel	Ni	28	58.71
Niobium	Nb	41	92.906
Nitrogen	N	7	14.0067
Nobelium	No	102	(254)
Osmium	Os	76	190.2
Oxygen	O	8	15.9994*
Palladium	Pd	46	106.4
Phosphorus	P	15	30.9738
Platinum	Pt	78	195.09
Plutonium	Pu	94	(242)
Polonium	Po	84	(210)
Potassium	K	19	39.102
Praseodymium	Pr	59	140.907
Promethium	Pm	61	(147)
Protoactinium	Pa	91	(231)
Radium	Ra	88	(226)
Radon	Rn	86	(222)
Rhenium	Re	75	186.2
Rhodium	Rh	45	102.905
Rubidium	Rb	37	85.47
Ruthenium	Ru	44	101.07
Samarium	Sm	62	150.35
Scandium	Sc	21	44.956
Selenium	Se	34	78.96
Silicon	Si	14	28.086*
Silver	Ag	47	107.870†
Sodium	Na	11	22.9898
Strontium	Sr	38	87.62
Sulfur	S	16	32.064*
Tantalum	Ta	73	180.948
Technetium	Tc	43	(99)
Tellurium	Te	52	127.60
Terbium	Tb	65	158.924
Thallium	Tl	81	204.37
Thorium	Th	90	232.038
Thulium	Tm	69	168.934
Tin	Sn	50	118.69
Titanium	Ti	22	47.90
Tungsten	W	74	183.85
Uranium	U	92	238.03
Vanadium	V	23	50.942
Xenon	Xe	54	131.30
Ytterbium	Yb	70	173.04
Yttrium	Y	39	88.905
Zinc	Zn	30	65.37
Zirconium	Zr	40	91.22

* The atomic weight varies because of natural variations in the isotopic composition of the element. The observed ranges are boron, ±0.003; carbon, ±0.00005; hydrogen, ±0.00001; oxygen, ±0.0001; silicon, ±0.001; sulfur, ±0.003.
† The atomic weight is believed to have an experimental uncertainty of the following magnitude: bromine, ±0.002; chlorine, ±0.001; chromium, ±0.001; iron, ±0.003; silver, ±0.003. For other elements, the last digit given is believed to be reliable to ±0.5.
‡ Numbers in parentheses are atomic mass numbers of either the most stable or the best known isotopes.

III appendix

TABLE OF FORMULA WEIGHTS †

$AgBr$	187.779	KCN	65.120
$AgCl$	143.323	K_2CrO_4	194.196
$AgCN$	133.888	$K_2Cr_2O_7$	294.189
Ag_2CrO_4	331.732	$KHC_8H_4O_4(KHP)$	204.229
AgI	234.774	$KHC_2O_4 \cdot H_2C_2O_4$	218.166
$AgNO_3$	169.874	KI	166.006
$AgSCN$	165.952	KIO_3	214.003
Al_2O_3	101.961	$KIO_3 \cdot HIO_3$	390.003
As_2O_3	197.841	$KMnO_4$	158.036
$BaCl_2$	208.24	K_2O	94.203
$BaCO_3$	197.35	KOH	56.109
BaO	153.34	K_2PtCl_6	485.99
$Ba(OH)_2$	171.36	$KSCN$	97.184
$BaSO_4$	233.40	K_2SO_4	174.264
$CaCO_3$	100.09	$MgCl_2$	95.218
CaC_2O_4	128.10	$MgCO_3$	84.320
$CaCl_2$	110.98	MgO	40.310
CaF_2	78.08	$Mg_2P_2O_7$	222.465
CaO	56.08	MnO_2	86.937
$Ca(OH)_2$	74.10	MoO_3	143.94
$CaSO_4$	136.14	$NaBr$	102.899
$Ce(SO_4)_2$	332.24	$NaC_2H_3O_2$	82.035
CO_2	44.010	Na_2CO_3	105.989
Cr_2O_3	151.991	$Na_2C_2O_4$	134.000
$Cu(IO_3)_2$	413.35	$NaCl$	58.443
CuO	79.54	$NaCN$	49.008
$CuSCN$	121.62	$NaHCO_3$	84.007
$FeCO_3$	115.855	NaI	149.894
FeO	71.846	Na_2O	61.979
Fe_2O_3	159.691	$NaOH$	39.997
Fe_3O_4	231.537	Na_2SO_4	142.040
$FeSO_4$	151.907	$Na_2S_2O_3 \cdot 5\ H_2O$	248.180
$FeSO_4(NH_4)_2SO_4 \cdot 6\ H_2O$	392.135	NH_3	17.031
$FeSO_4C_2H_4(NH_3)_2SO_4 \cdot 4\ H_2O$	382.153	NH_4Cl	53.492
$HCOOH$	46.026	$(NH_4)_2C_2O_4$	124.096
$HC_2H_3O_2$	60.053	$(NH_4)_2Ce(NO_3)_6$	548.28
$H_2C_2O_4$	90.036	$(NH_4)_2HPO_4$	132.057
HCl	36.461	$(NH_4)_2SO_4$	132.138
$HClO_4$	100.457	$Ni(C_4H_7O_2N_2)_2$	288.97
HNO_2	47.014	P_2O_5	141.945
HNO_3	63.013	PbO	223.19
H_2O	18.015	PbO_2	239.19
H_3PO_4	97.995	Pb_3O_4	685.57
H_2S	34.080	$PbSO_4$	303.28
H_2SO_3	82.077	SO_2	64.062
H_2SO_4	98.076	SO_3	80.061
$HgCl_2$	271.50	SiO_2	60.084
Hg_2Cl_2	472.09	SnO_2	150.69
KBr	119.011	V_2O_5	181.879
$KBrO_3$	167.008	WO_3	231.85
KCl	74.555	ZnO	81.37
$KClO_3$	122.552	$Zn_2P_2O_7$	304.68
$KClO_4$	138.551		

† No more than three decimals are carried, although in some instances four could be retained according to rules of significant figures.

IV

The Literature of
Analytical Chemistry

People have referred to an "information explosion" which threatens to inundate the scientist in a sea of paper. The volume of published research in chemistry is possibly more than doubling every ten years, and wags are saying that it is easier to repeat work in the laboratory than to find it in the literature. Experts are considering various automated schemes for retrieving information, but it is impossible now to predict what library services may ultimately become available. Meanwhile, the chemist has to get along somehow, and there are ways of finding information in the literature that are more efficient than others. The student should certainly become familiar with the library during his undergraduate years.

The *primary* literature sources are published research papers in a host of journals, American and foreign. Some of these journals of a more general nature publish papers of broad interest, while others attract primarily a narrower readership, say, organic, physical, or analytical chemists. *Secondary* sources include brief abstracts of published papers, articles which review the literature in restricted areas, monographs in which experts describe at length the status of certain fields, treatises and other reference works, and textbooks. The beginning student will normally use mainly secondary sources, but as he pushes closer to the present boundary of knowledge, he should increasingly consult original research papers.

We can present here only a bare introduction to the literature of analytical chemistry. Further, it must be remembered that the research analytical chemist often confronts problems which have never been investigated before; it would be impossible to define ahead of time the fields in which he might read in order to find approaches to such problems, but it is not unusual to find organic reaction mechanisms, spectroscopy, electronics, and other such "nonanalytical" information brought to bear in analytical problems.

ANALYTICAL JOURNALS

Analyst, dating from 1877, is a publication of the Society for Analytical Chemistry in Great Britain.

Analytical Chemistry (Anal. Chem.), published monthly by the American Chemical Society. Prior to 1947, this was called the Analytical Edition of *Industrial and Engineering Chemistry (Ind. Eng. Chem.*, Anal. Ed.), but the yearly volumes are numbered consecutively, without break, dating from 1929.

Analytica Chimica Acta (Anal. Chim. Acta), published by Elsevier Publishing Co. in The Netherlands since 1947. Papers are written in English, French, or German; each has a summary in all three languages.

Chimie Analytique (Chim. Anal.), since 1896, the major French journal in the field.

Journal of Chromatography (J. Chromatog.), published since 1958 by Elsevier Publishing Co. in The Netherlands, deals with all aspects of chromatography and electrophoresis.

Journal of Electroanalytical Chemistry (J. Electroanal. Chem.), since 1962, an Elsevier publication dealing with all aspects of theory and practice of electrical methods of analysis.

Talanta, published since 1958 by the Pergamon Press, contains research papers in English, French, and German, with summaries in all three languages.

Zeitschrift für analytische Chemie (Z. anal. Chem.), dating from 1862, is the principal German analytical journal.

Zhurnal Analitischeskoi Khimii (Zh. Anal. Khim.) is the Russian analytical journal, available in English translation in many libraries.

ABSTRACTS

Chemical Abstracts (Chem. Abstr. or C.A.), published since 1907 by the American Chemical Society, is the outstanding source of information for all fields of chemistry, and certain related areas as well. Chemical Abstracts publishes brief abstracts of papers from nearly 10,000 periodicals, and covers the patent literature as well. It appears biweekly. The abstracts are grouped into 74 sections, such as section 2, analytical chemistry, section 3, general physical chemistry, section 4, surface chemistry and colloids, and section 60, biochemical methods. Annual indexes provide access by subject, authors' names, and chemical formula. Decennial indexes covering 10-year periods, e.g., 1907–16, 1917–26, appeared through 1956; the last collective index covered a 5-year period, 1957–61. The nomenclature and list of abbreviations used by C.A. are practically official for writers of American books and journal articles. A thorough search through C.A. is a tedious job, and workers frequently employ short cuts based upon their experience or upon information obtained from other sources such as reference books, review articles, and monographs. But C.A. is the ultimate source, and information which cannot be found there can probably be best obtained by original work in the laboratory.

Chemisches Zentralblatt, the German abstract journal, dates back to 1830 and hence covers literature published before C.A. began. It is particularly valuable for this period, but has no advantage over C.A. for more recent information.

Analytical Abstracts, published by the Society for Analytical Chemistry, was formerly a section of the now-discontinued *British Abstracts*, appearing now in its own right. This is a short periodical, and a routine scan each month doesn't take much time.

Chemical Titles, published by the American Chemical Society, lists the titles of most papers in the world's chemical literature very promptly. Indexes are prepared on the basis of key words in the titles.

In addition to these more or less general abstract journals, abstracts sometimes appear catering to a particular special field. An example of these is *Gas Chromatography Abstracts* published by the Institute of Petroleum in London. It appears annually, with subject and author indexes.

REVIEWS

Each April, *Analytical Chemistry* publishes along with its regular issue a separate Annual Review issue. In even years, e.g., 1964, 1966, fundamental topics are reviewed, while applied topics are covered in the alternate years. Typical fundamental reviews are gas chromatography, nucleonics, polarographic theory, emission spectrometry, nuclear magnetic resonance, and X-ray diffraction, while titles of applied reviews include clinical analysis, ferrous alloys, and paints and finishes. Each review will normally give hundreds of journal references, organized in some convenient fashion. These are the most comprehensive reviews of the analytical literature, but others are also published; for example, the *Annual Reports* on the progress of chemistry to the Chemical Society of London has an analytical section.

REFERENCE BOOKS AND ADVANCED TEXTS

Probably, at least for a few years, the best single reference work will be *Treatise on Analytical Chemistry*, edited by I. M. Kolthoff, P. J. Elving, and E. B. Sandell and published by Interscience Publishers, a Division of John Wiley & Sons, Inc., New York. Publication began in 1959, and volumes are still appearing. The goal is "to present a concise, critical, comprehensive, and systematic, but not exhaustive, treatment of all aspects of classical and modern analytical chemistry." Publication is in three parts: Part I, Theory and Practice; Part II, Analytical Chemistry of the Elements; Part III, Analysis of Industrial Products.

A second general reference work with a similar goal, *Comprehensive Analytical Chemistry*, edited by C. L. Wilson and D. W. Wilson and published by Elsevier Publishing Co., Amsterdam, began to appear in 1959. Chapters written by experts are well referenced with regard to the original literature.

There is much information of analytical interest in the multivolume series *Technique of Organic Chemistry*, edited by A. Weissberger (John Wiley & Sons, Inc., New York). Volumes have been appearing since 1959.

The following are textbooks of a more or less general nature which are more advanced than the present one.

G. H. Brown and E. M. Sallee, *Quantitative Chemistry*, Prentice-Hall, Inc., Englewood Cliffs, N.J., 1963.

H. A. Laitinen, *Chemical Analysis*, McGraw-Hill Book Co., New York, 1960.

L. Meites and H. C. Thomas, *Advanced Analytical Chemistry*, McGraw-Hill Book Co., New York, 1958.

T. B. Smith, *Analytical Processes: A Physico-Chemical Interpretation*, 2nd Ed., Arnold, Ltd., London, 1952.

C. R. N. Strouts, J. H. Gilfillan, and H. N. Wilson, *Analytical Chemistry*, Oxford University Press, Inc., New York, 1955.

H. F. Walton, *Principles and Methods of Chemical Analysis*, 2nd Ed., Prentice-Hall, Inc., Englewood Cliffs, N.J., 1964.

In addition, the elementary text *Textbook of Quantitative Inorganic Analysis*,

3rd Ed., by I. M. Kolthoff and E. B. Sandell (The Macmillan Co., New York, 1952) contains an unusual wealth of information for an elementary book.

SOME REPRESENTATIVE BOOKS ON SPECIAL TOPICS

M. R. F. Ashworth, *Titrimetric Organic Analysis*, Interscience-Wiley, New York, 1964–65.

R. G. Bates, *Determination of pH: Theory and Practice*, John Wiley & Sons, Inc., New York, 1964.

R. P. Bauman, *Absorption Spectroscopy*, John Wiley & Sons, Inc., New York, 1962.

E. W. Berg, *Physical and Chemical Methods of Separation*, McGraw-Hill Book Co., New York, 1963.

R. J. Block and G. Zweig, *A Practical Manual of Paper Chromatography and Electrophoresis*, Academic Press, New York, 1962.

D. F. Boltz, Ed., *Colorimetric Determination of Nonmetals*, John Wiley & Sons, Inc., New York, 1958.

S. J. Clark, *Quantitative Methods of Organic Microanalysis*, Butterworth & Co., Ltd., London, 1956.

W. M. Clark, *Oxidation-Reduction Potentials of Organic Systems*, The Williams and Wilkins Co., Baltimore, 1960.

F. E. Critchfield, *Organic Functional Group Analysis*, Pergamon Press, New York, 1962.

C. Duval, *Inorganic Thermogravimetric Analysis*, 2nd Ed., Elsevier Publishing Co., Inc., Amsterdam, 1963.

H. Flaschka, *EDTA Titrations*, Pergamon Press, New York, 1959.

J. S. Fritz and G. S. Hammond, *Quantitative Organic Analysis*, John Wiley & Sons, Inc., New York, 1957.

D. Glick, Ed., *Methods of Biochemical Analysis*, John Wiley & Sons, Inc., New York, 1954– (a continuing series).

E. Heftmann, *Chromatography*, Reinhold Publishing Corp., New York, 1961.

F. Helfferich, *Ion Exchange*, McGraw-Hill Book Co., New York, 1962.

W. F. Hillebrand, G. E. F. Lundell, H. A. Bright, and J. I. Hoffmann, *Applied Inorganic Analysis*, 2nd Ed., John Wiley & Sons, Inc., New York, 1953.

Kirk, P. L., *Quantitative Ultramicroanalysis*, John Wiley & Sons, Inc., New York, 1950.

I. M. Kolthoff and J. J. Lingane, *Polarography*, 2nd Ed., Interscience Publishers, Inc., New York, 1952.

I. M. Kolthoff and V. A. Stenger, *Volumetric Analysis*, 2nd Ed., John Wiley & Sons, Inc., New York, 1942–57.

W. M. Latimer, *The Oxidation States of the Elements and Their Potentials in*

Aqueous Solutions, 2nd Ed., Prentice-Hall, Inc., Englewood Cliffs, N.J., 1952.

J. J. Lingane, *Electroanalytical Chemistry*, 2nd Ed., Interscience-Wiley, New York, 1958.

L. Meites, *Polarographic Techniques*, 2nd Ed., Interscience-Wiley, New York, 1965.

M. G. Mellon, Ed., *Analytical Absorption Spectroscopy*, John Wiley & Sons, Inc., New York, 1950.

J. Mitchell, Jr., I. M. Kolthoff, E. S. Proskauer, and A. Weissberger, Eds., *Organic Analysis*, John Wiley & Sons, Inc., New York, 1953– (a continuing series).

G. H. Morrison and H. Freiser, *Solvent Extraction in Analytical Chemistry*, John Wiley & Sons, Inc., New York, 1957.

J. P. Phillips, *Automatic Titrators*, Academic Press, New York, 1959.

C. N. Reilley, Ed., *Advances in Analytical Chemistry and Instrumentation*, Interscience-Wiley, New ,York 1960– (a continuing series).

O. Samuelson, *Ion Exchangers in Analytical Chemistry*, 2nd Ed., John Wiley & Sons, Inc., New York, 1962.

E. B. Sandell, *Colorimetric Determination of Traces of Metals*, 3rd Ed., Interscience-Wiley, New York, 1959.

S. Siggia and H. J. Stolten, *An Introduction to Modern Organic Analysis*, John Wiley & Sons, Inc., New York, 1956.

H. A. Strobel, *Chemical Instrumentation: A Systematic Approach to Instrumental Analysis*, Addison-Wesley, Reading, Mass., 1960.

appendix V

FOUR-PLACE TABLE OF LOGARITHMS

No.	0	1	2	3	4	5	6	7	8	9
10	0000	0043	0086	0128	0170	0212	0253	0294	0334	0374
11	0414	0453	0492	0531	0569	0607	0645	0682	0719	0755
12	0792	0828	0864	0899	0934	0969	1004	1038	1072	1106
13	1139	1173	1206	1239	1271	1303	1335	1367	1399	1430
14	1461	1492	1523	1553	1584	1614	1644	1673	1703	1732
15	1761	1790	1818	1847	1875	1903	1931	1959	1987	2014
16	2041	2068	2095	2122	2148	2175	2201	2227	2253	2279
17	2304	2330	2355	2380	2405	2430	2455	2480	2504	2529
18	2553	2577	2601	2625	2648	2672	2695	2718	2742	2765
19	2788	2810	2833	2856	2878	2900	2923	2945	2967	2989
20	3010	3032	3054	3075	3096	3118	3139	3160	3181	3201
21	3222	3243	3263	3284	3304	3324	3345	3365	3385	3404
22	3424	3444	3464	3483	3502	3522	3541	3560	3579	3598
23	3617	3636	3655	3674	3692	3711	3729	3747	3766	3784
24	3802	3820	3838	3856	3874	3892	3909	3927	3945	3962
25	3979	3997	4014	4031	4048	4065	4082	4099	4116	4133
26	4150	4166	4183	4200	4216	4232	4249	4265	4281	4298
27	4314	4330	4346	4362	4378	4393	4409	4425	4440	4456
28	4472	4487	4502	4518	4533	4548	4564	4579	4594	4609
29	4624	4639	4654	4669	4683	4698	4713	4728	4742	4757
30	4771	4786	4800	4814	4829	4843	4857	4871	4886	4900
31	4914	4928	4942	4955	4969	4983	4997	5011	5024	5038
32	5051	5065	5079	5092	5105	5119	5132	5145	5159	5172
33	5185	5198	5211	5224	5237	5250	5263	5276	5289	5302
34	5315	5328	5340	5353	5366	5378	5391	5403	5416	5428
35	5441	5453	5465	5478	5490	5502	5514	5527	5539	5551
36	5563	5575	5587	5599	5611	5623	5635	5647	5658	5670
37	5682	5694	5705	5717	5729	5740	5752	5763	5775	5786
38	5798	5809	5821	5832	5843	5855	5866	5877	5888	5899
39	5911	5922	5933	5944	5955	5966	5977	5988	5999	6010
40	6021	6031	6042	6053	6064	6075	6085	6096	6107	6117
41	6128	6138	6149	6160	6170	6180	6191	6201	6212	6222
42	6232	6243	6253	6263	6274	6284	6294	6304	6314	6325
43	6335	6345	6355	6365	6375	6386	6395	6405	6415	6425
44	6435	6444	6454	6464	6474	6484	6493	6503	6513	6522
45	6532	6542	6551	6561	6571	6580	6590	6599	6609	6618
46	6628	6637	6646	6656	6665	6675	6684	6693	6702	6712
47	6721	6730	6739	6749	6758	6767	6776	6785	6794	6803
48	6812	6821	6830	6839	6848	6857	6866	6875	6884	6893
49	6902	6911	6920	6928	6937	6946	6955	6964	6972	6981
50	6990	6998	7007	7016	7024	7033	7042	7050	7059	7067
51	7076	7084	7093	7101	7110	7118	7126	7135	7143	7152
52	7160	7168	7177	7185	7193	7202	7210	7218	7226	7235
53	7243	7251	7259	7267	7275	7284	7292	7300	7308	7316
54	7324	7332	7340	7348	7356	7364	7372	7380	7388	7396
	0	1	2	3	4	5	6	7	8	9

No.	0	1	2	3	4	5	6	7	8	9
55	7404	7412	7419	7427	7435	7443	7451	7459	7466	7474
56	7482	7490	7497	7505	7513	7520	7528	7536	7543	7551
57	7559	7566	7574	7582	7589	7597	7604	7612	7619	7627
58	7634	7642	7649	7657	7664	7672	7679	7686	7694	7701
59	7709	7716	7723	7731	7738	7745	7752	7760	7767	7774
60	7782	7789	7796	7803	7810	7818	7825	7832	7839	7846
61	7853	7860	7868	7875	7882	7889	7896	7903	7910	7917
62	7924	7931	7938	7945	7952	7959	7966	7973	7980	7987
63	7992	8000	8007	8014	8021	8028	8035	8041	8048	8055
64	8062	8069	8075	8082	8089	8096	8102	8109	8116	8122
65	8129	8136	8142	8149	8156	8162	8169	8176	8182	8189
66	8195	8202	8209	8215	8222	8228	8235	8241	8248	8254
67	8261	8267	8274	8280	8287	8293	8299	8306	8312	8319
68	8325	8331	8338	8344	8351	8357	8363	8370	8376	8382
69	8388	8395	8401	8407	8414	8420	8426	8432	8439	8445
70	8451	8457	8463	8470	8476	8482	8488	8494	8500	8506
71	8513	8519	8525	8531	8537	8543	8549	8555	8561	8567
72	8573	8579	8585	8591	8597	8603	8609	8615	8621	8627
73	8633	8639	8645	8651	8657	8663	8669	8675	8681	8686
74	8692	8698	8704	8710	8716	8722	8727	8733	8739	8745
75	8751	8756	8762	8768	8774	8779	8785	8791	8797	8802
76	8808	8814	8820	8825	8831	8837	8842	8848	8854	8859
77	8865	8871	8876	8882	8887	8893	8899	8904	8910	8915
78	8921	8927	8932	8938	8943	8949	8954	8960	8965	8971
79	8976	8982	8987	8993	8998	9004	9009	9015	9020	9025
80	9031	9036	9042	9047	9053	9058	9063	9069	9074	9079
81	9085	9090	9096	9101	9106	9112	9117	9122	9128	9133
82	9138	9143	9149	9154	9159	9165	9170	9175	9180	9186
83	9191	9196	9201	9206	9212	9217	9222	9227	9232	9238
84	9243	9248	9253	9258	9263	9269	9274	9279	9284	9289
85	9294	9299	9304	9309	9315	9320	9325	9330	9335	9340
86	9345	9350	9355	9360	9365	9370	9375	9380	9385	9390
87	9395	9400	9405	9410	9415	9420	9425	9430	9435	9440
88	9445	9450	9455	9460	9465	9469	9474	9479	9484	9489
89	9494	9499	9504	9509	9513	9518	9523	9528	9533	9538
90	9542	9547	9552	9557	9562	9566	9571	9576	9581	9586
91	9590	9595	9600	9605	9609	9614	9619	9624	9628	9633
92	9638	9643	9647	9652	9657	9661	9666	9671	9675	9680
93	9685	9689	9694	9699	9703	9708	9713	9717	9722	9727
94	9731	9736	9741	9745	9750	9754	9759	9763	9768	9773
95	9777	9782	9786	9791	9795	9800	9805	9809	9814	9818
96	9823	9827	9832	9836	9841	9845	9850	9854	9859	9863
97	9868	9872	9877	9881	9886	9890	9894	9899	9903	9908
98	9912	9917	9921	9926	9930	9934	9939	9943	9948	9952
99	9956	9961	9965	9969	9974	9978	9983	9987	9991	9996
	0	1	2	3	4	5	6	7	8	9

Answers to Odd-Numbered Problems

Chapter 2 (review of stoichiometry)

1. (a) (1) 1.60 (2) 0.0125 (3) 0.125
      (4) 0.0125 (5) 4.00
   (b) (1) 1.60 (2) 0.0250 (3) 0.250
      (4) 0.0250 (5) 4.00

3. (a) 6.02 (b) 6.78 (c) 11.9 (d) 4.83

5. (a) 17.57 mg/ml (b) 0.5319 g

7. Base 0.0911-N; Acid 0.0876-N

9. 0.0800-M

11. 25.96 ml

13. 5.78%

15. (a) 0.82 g (b) 0.21 g (c) 3.3 g
    (d) 0.67 g (e) 0.79 g

17. 16.6 g

19. (a) 40.0 (b) 40.0 (c) 402 (d) 12.0

21. 27.80

23. 8.4 ml

25. 5.90

27. 59.9 ml

29. (a) 25.84% MnO_2 (b) 33.30 ml

31. 74.16

33. $V = (2NX/5B)$

35. 34.34% $Na_2C_2O_4$; 65.66% KHC_2O_4

37. 50.0

39. (a) 70.37 ml (b) 30.36

41. 33.22

43. 2.254 g

45. $\dfrac{VT}{100T} 100 = \%$

47. 22.88

49. (a) 32.93 (b) 42.36 (c) 47.08 (d) 45.51

51. 315.1 mg

53. 26.64% $CaCO_3$; 73.36% $MgCO_3$

55. 85.70

57. (a) 28.90% KCl; 24.96% KBr (b) 28.04% KCl; 26.38% KBr

59. (a) 48 (b) 48 (c) 77

61. (a) 5.6×10^{18} (b) 5.3×10^{19}

Chapter 3 (errors and the treatment of analytical data)

1. (a) Iodine, palladium
(b) 0.004 ppt, 2.7 ppt

3. (a) 0.09%, 3.0 ppt (b) 0.09%, 3.0 ppt

5. (a) Yes (b) 0.1122
(c) 0.1122 ± 0.0006

7. (a) No (b) Yes

9. Yes

11. (a) 4 (b) 4 (c) 3 (d) 6 (e) 2

13. (a) 50.0 (b) 50.0 (c) 50.00% (d) 50

15. 0.005 ml

17. (a) 2.0 (b) 1.3 (c) 0.4

19. Twice

21. 4 ml

23. (a) 0.00253 (b) 2.99×10^5
(c) 4.11×10^3 (d) 9.0×10^3
(e) 114.4

25. 0.40 g

27. (a) 14.84% (b) 2.0 ppt

29. (a) 0.064 (b) 10.3 ppt

Chapter 4 (acid-base equilibria)

1. (a) 3.40 (b) 0.00 (c) −0.70 (d) 7.52
(e) 8.60 (f) 15.00 (g) −0.70
(h) 13.90

3. (a) 14.30 (b) 2.00 (c) 3.02 (d) 11.52
(e) 8.76 (f) 5.15 (g) 4.60 (h) 4.74
(i) 7.00 (j) 1.52

5. (a) 0.0365 (b) 1.02 (c) 0.040 (d) 3.77 g

7. (a) 2.26 (b) 2.30 (c) 2.30 (d) 7.00
(e) 11.70 (f) 11.40

9. 28 ml NH_3, 72 ml HCl

11. (a) 0.7% (b) 0.20-M

13. 0.005

15. Derivation

17. (a) 1.0% (b) 3.8% (c) 17% (d) 38%

19. 5.4

21. (a) 10 (b) 50 (c) 67 (d) 91 (e) 99

23. 0.10 ml

25. (a) 1.57 (b) 1.81 (c) 1.92 (d) 2.80
(e) 4.40 (f) 7.00 (g) 9.60 (h) 11.58

27. 4.02; 3.85; no

29. (a) 9.35 (b) 10.00, 10.70, 11.00

31. 0.05-M

33. (a) 5.04 (b) 5.44 (c) 4.44 (d) 0.086 mol/l

35. (a) A, 5.40; B, 12.00; C, 5.30 (b) A, 4.70; B, 4.52; C, 4.60

37. 13.82% NaOH, 30.44% Na_2CO_3

39. (a) $3V_1 = V_2$ (b) $4V_1 = 3V_2$

41. 12.6% $NaHCO_3$, 26.5% Na_2CO_3

43. 0.0300

Chapter 5 (oxidation-reduction equilibria)

1. (a) $+0.05$, right, Fe positive
(b) -0.10, left, Fe negative
(c) $+0.03$, right, Zn positive
(d) -0.09, left, Zn negative
(e) $+0.34$, right, Ag positive
(f) -0.89, left, Pt(Fe) negative
(g) $+0.06$, right, Ag positive
(h) -1.47, left, Pt(H_2) negative

3. $K = 4.7 \times 10^{20}$; 4.1×10^{-12}-M

5. (a) -0.60 (b) 1.5×10^{-64}-M

7. Derivation

9. (a) 0.18 v (b) 1×10^6

11. 87%

13. -0.81 v

15. $+0.06$ v

17. $+0.41$ v

19. $[Fe^{++}] = 3.8 \times 10^{-9}$;
$[Fe^{3+}] = 0.05$;
$[Ce^{4+}] = 3.8 \times 10^{-9}$;
$[Ce^{3+}] = 0.05$

21. $[Sn^{++}] = 2.4 \times 10^{-18}$;
$[Sn^{4+}] = 0.04$;
$[Ce^{4+}] = 4.8 \times 10^{-18}$;
$[Ce^{3+}] = 0.08$

23. 1×10^{82}; 113 kcal

25. 8.4×10^{13}-M; No

27. (a) 4.7×10^{-12}-M; 2.8×10^{11}
atoms
(b) 4.7×10^{-14}-M; 2.8×10^9 atoms

29. 1.0×10^{-7}

31. (a) 0.06 v (b) right; -2.8 kcal (c)
left; -0.12 v, 5.5 kcal

33. (a) 1.5×10^{48}; 5.97

35. 3.2×10^{-7}

37. 2.1×10^{-10}

39. (a) 2×10^{-8}; 1×10^{-8} (b) -0.16 v

41. (a) 0.21 (b) 1.8×10^{-7}; yes; rate
slow

43. (a) 0.004 v; about seven-fold

Chapter 6 (precipitation titrations)

1. (a) 1.30 (b) 2.00 (c) 2.70 (d) -0.30

3. (a) 1.60 (b) 11.25
(c) $pBr = pAg = 6.20$

5. 0.120

7. 2.30

9. (a) 0.04% (b) 0.04% (c) -1.0%
(d) 4×10^{-10}

11. (a) 4.00, 2.98 (b) 4.00, 3.79 (c) 4.00,
4.00

13. -1.0%

Chapter 7 (complex-formation titrations)

1. 0.01015, 3.778

3. 20.77

5. (a) 1.00 (b) 1.37 (c) 4.00 (d) 5.77
(e) 7.53 (f) 9.53

7. (a) 1.30 (b) 2.40 (c) 0.00 (d) 3.60

9. 3.3

Chapter 8 (potentiometric titrations)

1.

Volume	pH	E
0	1.60	0.35
10	1.87	0.36
12.5	1.95	0.37
20.0	2.38	0.39
24.0	3.09	0.44
24.9	4.10	0.50
25.0	7.00	0.67
25.1	9.90	0.84
25.5	10.60	0.89
26.0	10.90	0.90
30.0	11.59	0.95

3.

Volume	pH	E
0	10.83	0.90
10	9.43	0.82
12.5	9.26	0.81
20	8.65	0.77
24	7.88	0.72
24.9	6.86	0.66
25.0	5.48	0.58
25.1	4.10	0.50
25.5	3.40	0.45
26.0	3.10	0.44
30.0	2.41	0.39

5. pH $= (E - 0.28)/0.06$

7. (a) Negative (b) Positive (c) 7 (d) High

9. Derivation

11. 0.365 g

13. 80 ml HCl, 20 ml NaOH

15. 45.5 ml

17. Graph

19. Cl^-: 0.28, 0.22, 0.16
Br^-: 0.28, 0.15, 0.02
I^-: 0.28, 0.04, -0.20

21. AgA: 0.56, 0.62
AgB: 0.56, 0.57
AgC: 0.56, 0.56

Chapter 9 (electrolysis)

1. (a) 1.23 v (b) 1.23 v (c) 1.23 v

3. (a) 0.83 v (b) 0.32 v (c) 0.00 v (d) 0.37 v

5. (a) 1.65 v (b) 3.43 v

7. (a) 4.2×10^{-13} (b) 9.3×10^{-15}

9. (a) 2.2, 10.7, 24.7 (b) 1.18 v

11. 1×10^{-7}

13. 0.10

15. H_2, AgCl; 0.2000

17. 0.01036

19. 0.43 v

21. (a) 2×10^{-26}-M (b) 5×10^{-20}-M

Chapter 11 (polarography and amperometric titrations)

1. (a) 1.74×10^{-4} (b) 7.4×10^{-4}

3. (a) -0.500 v (b) 1.0

5. 5.8

7. 0.00050-M

9. $c_1 = v_2 c_2 i_1 / [v_1 (i_2 - i_1)]$

11. 10.9 g

Chapter 12 (spectrophotometry)

1. (a) 2 to 0 (b) infinite
3. (a) 0.097 (b) 0.398 (c) 0.699 (d) 1.00
5. (a) 15.9 (b) 63.1 (c) 95.5
7. 0.10
9. 2.75
11. A = 0.000196; B = 0.0162
13. 0.109 g

15. (a) 0.50, 0.75, 1.00 (b) A: 56.4, B: 31.6, C: 17.8, D: 10.0; A − B = 24.8, B − C = 13.8, C − D = 7.8 (c) 0.25, 0.50, 0.75; A: 100, B: 56.4, C: 31.6, D: 17.8; A − B = 43.6, B − C = 24.8, C − D = 13.8.
17. (a) 1.36% (b) 0.34%
19. (a) 0.195 (b) 0.390 (c) 0.780 (d) 0.956 (e) 0.973 (f) 0.975

Chapter 14 (separations by precipitation)

1. (a) 1×10^{-16} (b) 1×10^{-11} (c) 5×10^{-12}
3. (a) 3×10^{-5} (b) 7×10^{-7} (c) 1×10^{-6}
5. (a) 1.5×10^{-3} (b) 2.6×10^{-4} (c) 1.8×10^{-3}
7. (a) 3.2×10^{-17} (b) 6.60 (c) 84
9. (a) −0.63 (b) 1.37
11. 6.3×10^{-30}
13. (a) 1.9 (b) 3×10^{-3}

15. (a) 1×10^{-4} (b) 1.8×10^{-6} (c) 1.1×10^{-5} (d) 1.4×10^{-8} (e) 3.7×10^{-14}
17. 1.5 l
19. 1×10^{-12}
21. 5.9×10^{-13}
23. 0.56
25. 80
27. 4.8×10^{-10}
29. Derivation

Chapter 16 (solvent extraction)

1. (a) 90.9% (b) 6
3. 50
5. (a) 6.2×10^{-6} (b) 3.1×10^{-4}; 0.0062; 0.062; 0.31; 0.62
7. 4.00; 4.76; 5.00; 5.24; 6.00; 6.50

9. (a) HA: 9.1, 5.0, 0.91, 0.10, 0.01, 0.001, 0.0001
HB: 10^3, 10^3, 10^3, 10^3, 990, 909, 500
(b) About 9

Chapter 17 (chromatography)

1. 3.29
3. 67.5

5. 18.0
7. 9.6

Index